Queens, Eunuchs and Concubines in Islamic History, 661–1257

Edinburgh Studies in Classical Islamic History and Culture
Series Editor: Carole Hillenbrand

A particular feature of medieval Islamic civilisation was its wide horizons. In this respect it differed profoundly from medieval Europe, which from the point of view of geography, ethnicity and population was much smaller and narrower in its scope and in its mindset. The Muslims fell heir not only to the Graeco-Roman world of the Mediterranean, but also to that of the ancient Near East, to the empires of Assyria, Babylon and the Persians – and beyond that, they were in frequent contact with India and China to the east and with black Africa to the south. This intellectual openness can be sensed in many interrelated fields of Muslim thought: philosophy and theology, medicine and pharmacology, algebra and geometry, astronomy and astrology, geography and the literature of marvels, ethnology and sociology. It also impacted powerfully on trade and on the networks that made it possible. Books in this series reflect this openness and cover a wide range of topics, periods and geographical areas.

Titles in the series include:

Arabian Drugs in Early Medieval Mediterranean Medicine
Zohar Amar and Efraim Lev

The Abbasid Caliphate of Cairo, 1261–1517
Mustafa Banister

The Medieval Western Maghrib
Amira K. Bennison

Keeping the Peace in Premodern Islam
Malika Dekkiche

Queens, Eunuchs and Concubines in Islamic History, 661–1257
Taef El-Azhari

Medieval Damascus: Plurality and Diversity in an Arabic Library
Konrad Hirschler

A Monument to Medieval Syrian Book Culture
Konrad Hirschler

The Popularisation of Sufism in Ayyubid and Mamluk Egypt, 1173–1325
Nathan Hofer

Defining Anthropomorphism
Livnat Holtzman

Making Mongol History
Stefan Kamola

Lyrics of Life: Saʻdi on Love, Cosmopolitanism and Care of the Self
Fatemeh Keshavarz

A History of the True Balsam of Matarea
Marcus Milwright

Ruling from a Red Canopy
Colin P. Mitchell

Islam, Christianity and the Realms of the Miraculous
Ian Richard Netton

Conquered Populations in Early Islam
Elizabeth Urban

edinburghuniversitypress.com/series/escihc

Queens, Eunuchs and Concubines in Islamic History, 661–1257

Taef El-Azhari

EDINBURGH
University Press

Edinburgh University Press is one of the leading university presses in the UK. We publish academic books and journals in our selected subject areas across the humanities and social sciences, combining cutting-edge scholarship with high editorial and production values to produce academic works of lasting importance. For more information visit our website: edinburghuniversitypress.com

© Taef El-Azhari, 2019, 2021

Edinburgh University Press Ltd
The Tun – Holyrood Road
12 (2f) Jackson's Entry
Edinburgh EH8 8PJ

First published in hardback by Edinburgh University Press 2019

Typeset in 11/15 Adobe Garamond by
Servis Filmsetting Ltd, Stockport, Cheshire

A CIP record for this book is available from the British Library

ISBN 978 1 4744 2318 2 (hardback)
ISBN 978 1 4744 8386 5 (paperback)
ISBN 978 1 4744 2319 9 (webready PDF)
ISBN 978 1 4744 2320 5 (epub)

The right of Taef El-Azhari to be identified as author of this work has been asserted in accordance with the Copyright, Designs and Patents Act 1988 and the Copyright and Related Rights Regulations 2003 (SI No. 2498).

Contents

List of Illustrations vii
Acknowledgements viii
Chronology ix
Map of the Muslim Middle East xiii
Figures xiv

Introduction 1

1 The Umayyad Empire and the Establishment of a Royal Court, 661–750 57

2 Princesses, Concubines and *Qahramanat* under the 'Abbasids: Gender and Politics, 749–1055 75

3 The Kingdom of Eunuchs under the 'Abbasids 142

4 Fatimid Royal Women and Royal Concubines in Politics: The Rise of the First Queens of Islam 196

5 The Fatimid Eunuchs and their Sphere 253

6 The Seljuqs from Syria to Iran: The Age of *Khatuns* and *Atabegs* 285

7 The Ayyubids: Their Two Queens and their Powerful Castrated *Atabegs* 349

Appendix 1:	*The 'Abbasid Caliphs from 749 to the Coming of the Seljuqs in 1055*	411
Appendix 2:	*The Fatimid Caliphs, North Africa and Egypt*	412
Appendix 3:	*Dynasties*	413

Glossary	418
Bibliography	422
Index	437

Illustrations

Figures

Between pages xiv and xix; all photos taken by the author

1. Statue of Kahina, queen of the Berbers (Kinshala, Algeria)
2. Naked woman in an Umayyad palace (Qusayr ʿAmra, Jordan)
3. Naked concubine (Qusayr ʿAmra, Jordan)
4. Queen Arwa's mosque (Dhu Jibla, Yemen)
5. Person with a cup, depicted on a Fatimid bowl (Museum of Islamic Arts, Cairo, Egypt)
6. Zengid dirham
7. Dirham of Queen Tamar of Georgia, 1200 CE
8. Gold dinar of Queen Abish, thirteenth century CE
9. Coin of Kay Khusraw II
10. Copper dirham showing four women mourning the death of Saladin
11. Dirham of Queen Radiyya of Delhi
12. Aleppo Citadel, palace of Queen Dayfa (Aleppo, Syria)
13. Queen Dayfa's madrasa (Aleppo, Syria)
14. Al-Salih Ayyub Dome (Cairo, Egypt)
15. Mausoleum of Queen Shajar al-Durr (Cairo, Egypt)

Table

On page 274

5.1 List of eunuchs holding the office of *wali* under the Fatimids

Acknowledgements

I am very grateful to a large number of dear colleagues and friends for their kind advice and stimulating discussions on various issues relating to the field and topic. I sincerely thank my friend and colleague Professor Carole Hillenbrand for her good faith in me, and her enthusiasm for this project as part of her prestigious series.

I am also very grateful to my senior colleague and mentor, Professor Robert Hillenbrand, the world's leading authority on Islamic art and architecture for bringing my attention to useful studies on Turkmen coins, which this book has certainly benefited from. I thank my friend Professor Mazhar al-Zoby for his encouragement while unravelling materials and documents for this work, and my friend Professor Sabry Hafiz, for his sincere and kind advice.

I wholeheartedly thank Mrs Lel Gillingwater for her impeccable and excellent copy-editing of the long and complex text of this book.

I also thank the pioneers of this field who have illuminated the way for others, and from whose works I have learned greatly: the late Professors Nabia Abbott, David Ayalon and Umar Kahala, as well as Professors Remke Kruk, Ruth Roded, Leila Ahmed, Amira Sonbol, Nadia El Cheikh, Hugh Kennedy, Gavin Hambly, Nikki Keddie, Delia Cortese, Leslie Pierce, Judith Tucker, George Land and James Lindsay.

Finally, my thanks go to my family, who were always very supportive while I was working hard on this book. They sacrificed their time and holidays in order to allow me to focus on this project.

Taef El-Azhari
October 2018

Chronology

632	Death of the Prophet Muhammad
632	Arab Queen Sajah declares war on Abu Bakr
632–61	Era of the Rashidun (Four Rightly Guided Caliphs)
640–1	Conquests of Iran and Egypt
656	Battle of the Camel between 'Aisha and 'Ali
661–750	Era of the Umayyad Caliphate
704	Death of Dihya, queen of the Berbers
711	Conquests of Spain and the Sind Valley
750–1258	Era of the 'Abbasid Caliphate
762	Foundation of Baghdad
786–809	Reign of Caliph Harun al-Rashid
789	Death of powerful royal mother Khayzuran
797	Irene becomes first woman to rule Byzantium as explicitly sole empress
800	Coronation of Charlemagne, foundation of the Holy Roman Empire
908	Concubine and royal mother Shaghab dominates the 'Abbasid caliphate with the help of the eunuch Mu'nis
909	Fatimid Shi'i caliphate is founded in North Africa
966	Kafur becomes the first eunuch in Islamic history to govern as a sovereign ruler, in Egypt and southern Syria
969	Fatimids seize Egypt and build Cairo
1021	Princess Sitt al-Mulk kills her brother caliph al-Hakim, and becomes de facto ruler of Egypt
1036	Concubine and queen mother Rasad becomes regent for her boy caliph al-Mustansir, and dominates politics

1066	Norman Conquest of England
1071	Battle of Manzikert and the start of the Turkification of the Middle East
1085	Alfonso VI, king of Leon and Castile, recaptures Toledo
1092–4	Queen mother Turkan Khatun leads a civil war in Iran and installs her son Mahmud as sultan
1097–8	Arwa becomes first sovereign queen and religious leader in Islamic history in Yemen, ruling until 1138
1099	The First Crusade leads to the capture of Jerusalem
1115	First recognised Seljuqid atabegate dynasty in the Muslim world of Tughtekin, in Damascus
1117	Turkish princess Amina fills the vacuum of power in Aleppo, and appoints the *atabeg* and army commander
1130	Almohads Berber dynasty founded in North Africa and Spain, ousting the Almoravids Berber dynasty
1135	Royal mother Zumurrud Khatun kills her son King Isma'il and appoints her son Mahmud; she dominates power
1139	*Atabeg* Unur of Damascus installs Muhammad as the new king, rules in his name and marries his mother
1143	Melisende becomes queen-regent of Crusader Jerusalem
1171	Saladin ends the Fatimid rule in Egypt and establishes his Kurdish dynasty, which extends gradually over Zengid dominions in Syria, northern Iraq, the Hijaz and Yemen
1184–1213	Queen Tamar rules the kingdom of Georgia
1187	Saladin defeats the Crusaders of Jerusalem at Hittin
1204	Fourth Crusade captures Constantinople
1216–31	Eunuch *atabeg* Tughril is the de facto ruler of Ayyubid Aleppo
1236–42	Dayfa Khatun is queen-regent of Ayyubid Aleppo
1237	Mongol Invasion of Rus
1237	*Atabeg* Eldiguz in Azerbaijan marries the widow of the Seljuqid Sultan Tughril II, and establishes his dynastic atabegate
1249	King Louis IX of France invades Ayyubid Egypt, is captured, then released by Queen Shajar al-Durr

1250	Shajar al-Durr becomes sovereign queen for all Muslims in Egypt for only eighty days; the caliphal rejects her
1250–1517	Mamluk dynasty rules Egypt, following the marriage of Queen Shajar al-Durr to Aybak and his elevation to the sultanate
1258	Mongols sack Baghdad, bringing an end to the 'Abbasid caliphate there

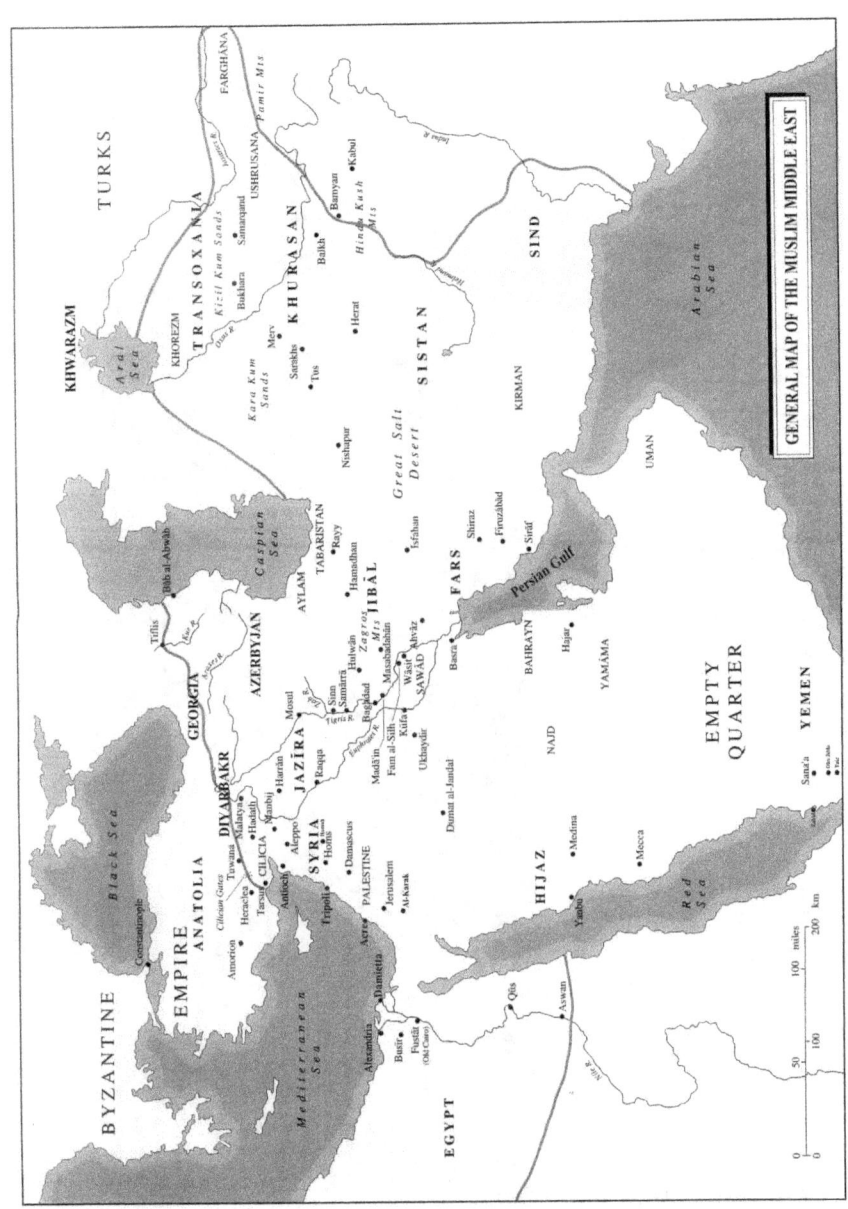

Map of the Muslim Middle East, eighth–twelve centuries CE.

Figure 1 Statue of Kahina, queen of the Berbers (Kinshala, Algeria).

Figure 2 Naked woman in an Umayyad palace (Qusayr 'Amra, Jordan).

FIGURES | XV

Figure 3 Naked concubine (Qusayr ʿAmra, Jordan).

Figure 4 Queen Arwa's mosque (Dhu Jibla, Yemen).

Figure 5 Person (presumably a eunuch) with a cup, depicted on a Fatimid bowl (Museum of Islamic Arts, Cairo, Egypt).

Figure 6 Zengid dirham, showing title of *atabeg*.

Figure 7 Dirham of Queen Tamar of Georgia, 1200 CE.

FIGURES | xvii

Figure 8 Gold dinar of Queen Abish, thirteenth century CE.

Figure 9 Coin of Kay Khusraw II.

Figure 10 Copper dirham showing four women mourning the death of Saladin.

Figure 11 Dirham of Queen Radiyya of Delhi.

Figure 12 Aleppo Citadel, palace of Queen Dayfa (Aleppo, Syria).

Figure 13 Queen Dayfa's madrasa (Aleppo, Syria).

Figure 14 Al-Salih Ayyub Dome, commissioned by Queen Shajar al-Durr (Cairo, Egypt).

Figure 15 Mausoleum of Queen Shajar al-Durr (Cairo, Egypt)

To Umm Kulthum
The voice of Egypt, and queen of Egyptian singing in the twentieth century. Her persona and legendary performance shaped the feelings of millions across the Middle East, and will continue to do so for a long time to come.

Introduction

Sajah bint al-Harith of the Banu Taghlib in the Jazira declared herself a prophetess (*tanabbat*) as soon as she learned of Muhammad's death in 632. Many leaders served under her command and she led an army to fight Abu Bakr. She commanded her forces to subdue Banu Tamim, and she dispatched her envoys to Banu Malik to conclude peace. Sajah marched with her forces until she reached al-Nabaj. After a number of confrontations, the tribal Arab leaders of the Jazira attended her camp and said to her: 'What do you order us to do?' She said: 'We march to invade al-Yamamah.' Musaylamah knew about her, and feared her power. She had a deep knowledge of Christianity. Musaylamah negotiated with her to divide the land of Quraysh between the two of them once they had achieved victory over Abu Bakr.[1]

This story, mentioned by al-Tabari, is about an Arab woman commander of the Banu Taghlib tribe in the Jazira in Iraq, who marched out with large forces to subdue Eastern Arabia, managed to form pacts with regional chiefs and planned to march as generalissimo to fight the first caliph, Abu Bakr, in Medina, although she never made it there. In addition, she declared herself a prophetess, a religious authority that did not exist in any of the Abrahamic faiths.[2]

The topic of women, eunuchs, *atabeg*s and politics and power in medieval Islamic history is a relatively new field of study. The pioneers of the field, from Nabia Abbott in 1941 to Nikki Keddie in 1990, Remke Kruk in 2014 and Nadia El Cheikh in 2015, are among the very few who have engaged in the critical examination of the history and historiography of women and the vital political role they played in Islamic dynastic formation. The majority of studies during the last twenty years, despite bearing titles such as, 'Women and gender in Islam', have in fact focused primarily on the religious (shari'a and Qur'an) dimensions of Islamic law, such as the veil, divorce, inheritance, equality, patriarchal readings and exegesis of the Qur'an. The majority of such studies contain a limited chapter on women in early Islamic history, and then they move to feminist movements in the so-called Arab or Islamic world.

Missing from these studies are the many rich sources and historical documents that discuss the sociopolitical, and even military, role of women and their entourages and advisers in the area extending from Iran and Central Asia to North Africa and Spain. To address the wider and more complex context and to redress this gap in the literature, further studies are required to understand why and how women and their entourages, including eunuchs, *atabegs*, concubines and *qahramanas*, influenced the movement of Islamic history.

How did diverse Muslim societies through the centuries view women, free or enslaved, within the diverse sociopolitical levels? Why we do not have one single book written by a woman from early Islam in the seventh century up to the thirteenth? This is in contrast to Byzantium, for example, where we have *The Alexiad*, written by Princess Anna Comnena in the eleventh century.[3] Although we have a number of women, including Muhammad's wives, as transmitters of Hadith, and in later centuries as teachers, none took up the pen to write about her opinions or teaching. Why did Islamic dynasties not produce ruling queens until the late eleventh century on the Shi'i side (Queen Arwa of Yemen)[4] and the thirteenth century on the Sunni side (Queen Dayfa of Aleppo)?[5] How did sexual and gender politics develop in medieval Islam? Did their contemporaries accept these women? How were they portrayed in medieval sources? Why were women who built madrasas not allowed to be educated in them? How and why did eunuchs govern as de facto rulers under several dynasties in medieval Islamic history, such as Kafur of the Ikhshidids (966–8), or Qaraqush, deputy of Egypt under Saladin and his successor al-'Aziz in the twelfth century. The military and political influence of eunuchs also existed under the Fatimids. We see cases in modern Islamic history, such as the Turkmen dynasty of the Qajars (1779–1924), that had the same tradition and was indeed founded by a eunuch, Agha Muhammad.[6]

This book will attempt to answer these questions, among others. It will examine and analyse the diverse political and socio-historical context from the Umayyads in 661 to the Ayyubid Turkicised Kurds in the thirteenth-century Middle East. (Due to the period covered here, as well as the large geographical area of Islamic rule, the book will not cover the Mamluks, Ottomans, Safavids or Spain, India, Mali and Indonesia among others, all of which would merit further examination). One major difficulty will remain unsolved, however, that being that medieval history is a completely patriarchal one, and the stories of women and the institutions around them were reported by male historians. Even poetry and stories of female slave singers (*qiyan*) and their musical settings were also reported to us, unfortunately, by men only. So, we are looking through the optics of male chroniclers into women and gender in history to try to examine what those chroniclers wanted us to believe.

Although during this period most women and eunuchs had no proper names, bearing only titles or nicknames, there are records of many women who dominated political life within Shi'i and Sunni Islam. This book will present the historical narratives and cross-examine them with a critical analysis of their role to understand how the sociopolitical process formed and developed around Muslim women's historical subjectivities. The research will be very careful to distinguish between powerful women, such as the wives or sisters of the rulers, concubines/lovers, slaves and *qahramana*s (stewardesses). Furthermore, the book will examine in detail the fully recognised public queens, who held that title in their own right and were de facto rulers on the throne, in Yemen, Syria, Egypt and Iran. Approached from this wider and multidisciplinary perspective, this book intends to provide a comprehensive and systematic historical study of sexual politics, the role of women and eunuchs in the trajectory of history and the running of inner and public policy from the Umayyads and 'Abbasids to the Turkmen – and Ayyubid periods. Hence, it will demonstrate how many areas of the Muslim world looked at women more equally in political leadership than we are accustomed to, both among the elites and the common population. Thus, I hope it will bridge the gap in the field of women and gender studies between the medieval and modern eras, challenging some of the previous conceptions and understanding of how history developed.

A Brief Survey of Previous Studies

There are few books and studies that thoroughly examine the history of women under the various Islamic dynastic powers. In 1946, Nabia Abbott wrote her groundbreaking book, *Two Queens of Baghdad: Mother and Wife of Harun al-Rashid*,[7] in which she analysed the vital roles of the mother and the wife of the legendary 'Abbasid caliph, Harun al-Rashid (786–809). Although neither his mother, Khayzuran, nor his wife, Zubayda, held the official title of 'queen' or have been referred to as such in Muslim chronicles, Abbott wanted to express the de facto power that these two women had. Abbott also wrote *Aishah: The beloved of Muhammad*[8] a detailed religio-political history of one of Muhammad's wives in early Islamic history.

Fuad Caswell's book *The Slave Girls of Baghdad* provides a detailed account about one of the many types of women slaves in the 'Abbasid period,[9] the *qiyan* slave-women singers, as well as poetry under the 'Abbasid dynasty. This volume focuses more on literature than politics, yet it is an illuminating study of the age and its hidden private life. In 2015, Nadia El Cheikh produced the distinguished book *Women, Islam, and Abbasids Identity*. It is a rather short volume, and does not give full attention to the role of women, eunuchs, *qahramana*s, *ghulman* (slave soldiers) and concubines.[10] At the time of writing, a new book has been published: *Concubines and Courtesans: Women and Slavery in Islamic History* (edited by Matthew Gordon and Kathryn Hain).[11] That book is concerned with the development of women and slavery, and concubines and music, and also covers areas such Andalusia, Timurid Iran and Ottoman history; this book and my own study integrate to cover the field. In addition, just as this book is being submitted for editing in 2018, a further volume was published, titled *Celibate and Childless Men in Power: Ruling Eunuchs and Bishops in the Pre-modern World*, by Almut Höfert, Matthew Mesley and Serena Tolino.[12] However, most of its chapters are not related to the book presented here. Certainly, it emphasises the shortage of studies in the field, and the need for further work in order to understand the development of Muslim societies.

There are also the other studies of Nadia El Cheikh, 'The Qahramana in the 'Abbasid Court: Position and Functions', examining the age of the boy caliph al-Muqtadir (d. 932), and 'Servants at the Gate: Eunuchs at the Court of al-Muqtadir'.[13] There is room for further studies on the establishment, evolution and decline of the post of *qahramana*, as well as the evolution of the institution of the eunuch under the 'Abbasids, namely, how they influenced political life in civil and military posts, and the collaboration between them and women, particularly as regards the legendary commander of the 'Abbasid army, Mu'nis al-Khadim (a eunuch, d. 933). Hugh Kennedy's excellent book, *The Court of the Caliphs*,[14] provides insight on the influence of the caliphal entourage, but it covers only the first century of 'Abbasid rule. These are the principal studies dealing with the history and historiography of the period. As the late David Ayalon remarked, 'Islamic history is not written yet.'[15] This is true at least in the area of medieval Islam. It is clear that nothing has been written about and dedicated to the rest of the 'Abbasids from North Africa to Central Asia, and we have to excavate between the lines of dynastic histories to find a few clues about women, eunuchs and power.

Moving to the Fatimids, we are facing the same challenge, with only a few studies having been produced, such as the excellent book by Delia Cortese and Simonetta Calderini, *Women and the Fatimids in the World of Islam*[16] and the article by Farhad Daftary, on Queen Arwa of Yemen.[17] While these are significant studies, much more research is needed into the dynamic issues of gender and sexual politics in Islamic medieval history. In particular, we need to address the question of how women under the 'Abbasid and Fatimid dynasties were able to govern in association with other 'genders' such as eunuchs and *atabeg*s, for instance. The pact between women and eunuchs or *atabeg*s was a major development from Iran to Egypt, later spreading to Yemen under the Ayyubids, and influencing other dynasties, such as the Turkmen.

With regard to the long and complicated Seljuq period in Iran and Central Asia (1038–1194), and their branches in Syria and Asia Minor, we know almost nothing about the role of women in power and politics. That is despite several women having led armies or being directly engaged in political affairs after the death of Sultan Malik Shah in 1092. I have tried to examine the political and social role of the Syrian branch in the twelfth century, and how the *atabeg*s played a fundamental role in association with the Seljuqs,[18] on which I intend to expand here.

On the other Turkmen dynasties, such as the Artuqids, Zengids and the Ayyubid Kurds, who dominated large areas of the Muslim Middle East, we have the works of Carole Hillenbrand.[19] I have tried to explore the relationship between women and power in one Ayyubid case, Dayfa of Aleppo in the thirteenth century,[20] which will be more detailed in this book, and have also looked at the lives of a number of other Ayyubid women. It is hard to imagine that a figure like Shajar al-Durr, who faced the Seventh Crusade in 1249–50, and later declared herself queen of all Muslims on coinage and in mosques, in addition to her challenge to the Ayyubids of Syria, still needs further study.

Regarding the Salghurid Turkmen of Shiraz in Iran (1148–1285), and their relations with the Mongol invaders of the area, we have the unique rise of Queen Abish bint Sʻad in 1265, and her relations with the *atabegs* of Kirman. We have the study in Turkish by Erdoğan Merçil covering the political history of the Salghurid dynasty,[21] and, in addition, the recent distinguished book by Bruno de Nicola, *Women in Mongol Iran: The Khatuns, 1206–1335.*[22]

Also on Turkmen history, but in India, we have the study of Peter Jackson on Queen Radiyya (r. 1236–40).[23] Alyssa Gabbay has also added her examination of the short-lived queen of Delhi,[24] and on the Turkmen Rasulids of Yemen 1229–1454, there is G. Rex Smith's *The Ayyubids and Early Rasulids in the Yemen (567–694/1173–1295)*, which has limited focus on gender and politics.[25]

On the topic of eunuchs and the third gender, there is the study of Shaun Marmon,[26] but it is dedicated to the late Mamluk era only, which is out of our focus in this work. The other major work on this subject is the pioneering book of David Ayalon, *Eunuchs, Caliphs and Sultans*.[27] It is the only long work dedicated to this topic, covering diverse Muslim dynasties. Ayalon guides us to many fields of Islamic history, which he does not cover at all, such as the Fatimid dynasty, or covers only partially, for example, the ʻAbbasids and the Ayyubids; I intend to add to these fields. Actually, while Ayalon's book was still in press, I wrote a study on 'The Influence of Eunuchs in the Ayyubid Kingdom',[28] and presented it to a conference in the same year. Somewhat fortuitously, Ayalon did not cover the whole Ayyubid realm.

Perhaps it can be argued that women enjoyed most academic attention in Islamic history under the Ottoman caliphate, which ended in 1924. Books such as *In the House of Law*, by Judith Tucker,[29] in addition to the work of Amira Sonbol[30] and Fariba Zarinebaf-Shahr have all focused on the diverse roles of Ottoman women and gender politics, but not during the previous period.[31] That is due to the unparalleled achievements of the long-ruling Ottoman empire, which no other dynasty can match, both in legal records and documents.

On the level of encyclopaedic works, there is a very useful book by 'Umar Kahala, *A'lam al-Nisa'*,[32] which lists in alphabetical order hundreds of women in the Muslim world from early Islam to the twentieth century. It counts on the sources with very little analyses. The second is *The Encyclopaedia of Islam*,[33] with thorough studies and entries on very wide topics of Islamic history.

In 2007 Brill also produced *The Encyclopedia of Women and Islamic Cultures*,[34] in five volumes. Volume 2 covers family, law and politics, including medieval Islam, but the major concern of the encyclopedia deals with contemporary topics.

A final word has to be made on the non-historian authors, and their well-appreciated and respected works (but that have misleading titles). There is the book in Arabic, of Najwa Kira, *Al-Jawari wa al-Ghulman fi Misr fi al-'Asrain, Alfatimi wa Alayyubi* (*Al-Jawari and Ghulman in Egypt under the Fatimids and Ayyubids*).[35] Most of the book is dedicated to the military *mamluks/* slaves under the Fatimid and Ayyubid dynasties, considering them as *ghulman* (slave soldiers) in a twist of terminology. She dedicates only ten pages to the *jawari* (female slaves) of the Fatimids and less than three pages to the Ayyubids, without any analyses. Another example is Amal al-Kurdi, with her book *Dor al-Nisa' fi al-Khilafa al-'Abbasiyya* (*The Role of Women under the 'Abbasid Caliphate*).[36] I should mention that Fatema Mernissi's book[37] is a good attempt at exploring the marginalised role of women in Islamic history. However, she covers a very long period of thirteen centuries over a large geographic area extending from Indonesia to Spain. She does not focus on analysing the historiography of the age, or the power relations between different courtesans and institutions as much as she focuses on modern concepts such as democracy in the Islamic city, or the veil, and equality between the two genders. Her book opened the way for some other respected feminists who are neither historians nor using a clear methodology for analysing early and medieval Islamic history to follow her, despite being unaware of the related sources of such ages.

The main task and challenge of this book is to unearth many sources and documents that remain unexamined to date, in order to reveal how a great number of women and their advisors influenced and shaped Islamic history. This will lead to a better understanding of events that took place and will challenge a number of conventional concepts still held by many scholars and feminists today about Islam, its history and its politics. I also aim to illustrate how chroniclers of those respective periods, despite having the chance to criticise women and gender, were in fact much more liberal than many politicians and philosophers during the same periods, and even today.

In this book, the material and data drawn from the extensive selection of medieval primary sources and documents are interpreted through the methods of textual, socio-historical and contextual analyses.

Chapter Outlines

This long introduction covers the aim of this study, the survey of previous works and a selected examination of the status of women and gender in pre-Islamic civilisations, as well as in the Qur'an and Hadith. In addition, it looks at the changes that took place under the four rightly guided caliphs who followed Muhammad.

- Chapter One looks at women and power in political and social life under the Umayyads.
- Chapter Two covers the role of 'Abbasid women in politics and society from 749 to 1055. I investigate how the royal wives and royal concubines came into political life, and the influence they had on the state; how women interacted with other courtesans and male members in the army and administration; and how political marriage was used during the age.
- Chapter Three focuses on the rise of 'Abbasid eunuchs, from their domestic work in the harem and palace to their role in politics and the military during the tenth century, as well as their interaction with the harem, courtiers and elite members of the state.
- Chapter Four considers sexual politics under the Fatimids (909–1171), and examines the first queens in Islamic history, in Egypt and Yemen,

and their interaction with the other genders. I investigate the rise of the first three women to queenship under the Fatimids and their influence on politics, society and religion, and consider whether political marriage affected the politics of the state.

- Chapter Five looks at the development of the realm of eunuchs, following on from the 'Abbasids. I study the rise of the deputy of the Fatimid caliphs in North Africa, a eunuch whose unique biography was well documented. I examine the unusual situation of the Fatimids in that they started their rule in North Africa with a eunuch deputy, and ended in Egypt with another, thus influencing the Ayyubids afterwards. I also explore how eunuchs collaborated with Fatimid women.

- Chapter Six analyses the Seljuq age (1038–1194), in particular the power relations between royal wives, their *atabeg*s and eunuchs. I study the introduction of the Turkic post of *atabeg* under the Seljuqs and its political–military influence on the state in the Middle East. It also covers how *atabeg*s and royal wives governed through political collaboration, and how the post of *atabeg* contributed to the disintegration of the Seljuq state and the rise of other Turkic dynasties with similar Turkic traditions. The decadent relationship between some sultans and their *ghulman* (servant boys), and how it affected the rule and the state, changing the concept of the harem, is also considered. In addition, this chapter covers political marriage and how it was put to use in the state.

- Chapter Seven is concerned with the Ayyubid Kurdish state from 1171 to 1260, with a focus on the first Sunni queens of Islam and their castrated *atabeg*s. Here I examine the rise of the first Sunni queen in Aleppo, and how she ruled in collaboration with military commanders and eunuchs, and the rise of the queen of Muslims in Cairo during a very critical time, both politically and militarily, and its influence on the Middle East. I investigate how the post of *atabeg* developed, establishing a new paradigm under the Ayyubids, borrowed from the Seljuqs, and its profound influence on the state. I also look at political marriage and the granting of legitimacy to male rulers.

Beautified for men is the love of desires; women and male children (Q. 3:14).

Women and Gender in the Qur'an: Different Interpretations of the Sacred Book

Did Islam, as a religion, improve the status of women from the *jahiliyya* (pre-Islamic period) to the age of Islam, and make them equal to men? If so, where, and when? We should first look at the background of the Prophet of Islam and the circumstances in which he received the message of that religion.

Muhammad b. 'Abd Allah b. 'Abd al-Muttalib b. Hashim was born in about 570 in Mecca, Hijaz, on the Western Arabian Peninsula. He was a member of the Hashim clan that, together with the 'Abd Shams clan, formed the tribe of Quraysh.[38] Muhammad's father died before he was born, and his mother Amina died when he was six years old. As an orphan, his clan took good care of him. His grandfather 'Abd al-Muttalib raised him until his death, when Muhammad was eight, and his uncle, Abu Talib (father of 'Ali, the future imam of all the Shi'a), took the responsibility for Muhammad's upbringing.[39] As a member of the Quraysh, Muhammad took part in the Battle of al-Fijar against other Arab tribes to secure the north and western commercial routes of Arabia, which was vital for Meccan trade. He took up a career in commerce, ending up working for a wealthy widow, Khadija. She admired his qualities, and proposed marriage to him. At that time, she was about forty years old, while he was approximately twenty-five.[40] Such a marriage granted Muhammad financial and spiritual support from his wife, especially after he became a prophet. Khadija gave birth to their four daughters, Zaynab, Um Kulthum, Ruqaiyya and Fatima.

The details and chronology are not clear, but almost all the sources agree that in about 610, when Muhammad was forty years old, and had taken to practising solitary meditations in the caves of Mecca's mountains, he started to receive the revelation of the Qur'an through the angel Gabriel. Muhammad was instructed by Gabriel to recite a series of verses of divine commandments.[41] Muhammad returned, terrified, to his wife, and shared with her what had happened to him. She took him to her cousin Waraqa b. Nawfal, a Christian with knowledge of Hebrew writings. According to Muslim sources, he explained to them that Muhammad was a true messenger of God.[42]

From 610 to 622 Muhammad was active in his preaching of the revelations he continued to receive in Mecca. His wife was the first convert to Islam, followed by their daughters and his adopted son, Zayd b. Haritha, and then Muhammad's cousin, 'Ali b. Abi Talib. Muhammad's uncle, Abu Talib, did not convert, but as chief of the clan, he gave Muhammed moral support, unlike his other uncle, Abu Lahab, who was a strong enemy of Muhammad.

Khadija's well-off financial status gave Muhammad the freedom to stand against the enemies of the new religion. In 619 Muhammad lost both his devoted wife and his uncle Abu Talib.[43] As a result, the social and economic pressure on Muhammad in Mecca became unbearable for him and his few followers. He decided to immigrate to Yathrib, some 450 km to the north of Mecca, after its leaders invited him there. In 622 Muhammad made the migration to Yathrib, which was renamed Medina. This year was the start of the Muslim calendar, or Anno Hegira (AH). The new Muslim community in Medina, under the authority of the Prophet, gained some momentum after Muhammad achieved a landmark victory at the Battle of Badr (about 135 km south of Medina) in 624. He attempted to intercept a commercial caravan led by Abu Sufyan, the grand merchant of Mecca, and confiscate it as booty. However, Muhammad failed due to Abu Sufyan's skilful tactics. Abu Sufyan called the Meccan leaders to march in arms to protect their vital trade and confront Muhammad. A battle ensued, resulting in victory for Muhammad's forces.[44] Badr was both a vital moral and military victory over the well-established Qurayshi forces. Most probably, Islam would have not survived if Muhammad had lost this battle.

Between Badr and Muhammad's conquest and forced submission of Mecca in 630, Ibn Hisham lists some fifteen *ghazwa* (invasions) by Muhammad on the neighbouring Arab tribes of Medina and the Hijaz, including several Jewish Arab tribes, such as Banu Qurayza, who suffered great brutality by the Prophet's forces, for different political reasons.[45]

In 632, after Muhammad had declared that the revelation of the Qur'an was complete, and having created a semi-established confederation in most of the Arabian Peninsula, headed by him, he died in Medina.

Having looked at this sketch of Muhammad and his message, we will now discuss the status of women in the Qur'an and Hadith, as regards equality and submission.

1. Muslim Eve

'O peoples, be dutiful to your lord who created you from the same soul (*nafs*)' (Q. 4:1). Here, Allah is stressing the equality of men and women, who were created from the same soul. Ironically, in the same sura (chapter) that is named 'Al-Nisa" ('The Women'), Allah mentions in the scriptures: 'Men are the protectors of women, according to God's preference of some over the others' (Q. 4:34). It continues in another *aya* (verse), 'As to those women on whose part you see ill-conduct, admonish them first, then after refuse to share their beds, then after that, beat them' (Q. 4:34).

Here Allah makes it clear that men have a higher status than women. In addition, men may discipline women by way of beating them. In the same sura, it reads, regarding sexual desires: 'And if you fear that you shall not be able to deal justly with orphan girls, then marry as many women as you please, two, or three, or four. If you fear that you shall not be able to deal justly with them, then keep only one, or have slaves as many as your right hands possess' (Q. 4:3). The Qur'an also states, 'Allah commands you that when it comes to inheritance, a male gets twice as much as what a female gets' (Q. 4:11).

Being feminine in any form in the Qur'an is considered an abuse, even if those mentioned were angels: 'And they make/consider the angels who themselves are slaves of the Most Gracious (Allah) females ... They will be questioned' (Q. 43:19).

It is clear that women in the Qur'an are less equal to men. Apologists (Muslim defenders of these verses) try to defend the verse of beating women, and include in their translation ('beat them lightly if it is useful'). Who decides what is useful and how far to go? Here, too, apologists from early Islam up to modern times have tried to read the verse of multiple wives to the favour of the man, without any restrictions. Although a deeper interpretation of the verse shows that a second wife must be a widow with young orphans, so the man can help economically and socially with the care of this family.[46]

When it comes to marrying more than one wife or having many women slaves for sexual pleasure, they defend taking slaves through *sabaya* (prisoners of war) or through slave purchase. This was especially boosted by Prophet

Muhammad's practices, known as Sunna (tradition), as will be discussed. Moreover, no one is trying to give exegesis to the following verse. Some try to translate it according to their own views; it reads: 'Tell the believing women not to reveal their adornment except to their husbands, or their fathers ... or what their right hands possess (*ma malakat aymanuhunna* – feminine)' (Q. 24:31).

Women, too, were granted the same right of having freedom with what their right hands possessed, if we interpret this verse in the same way as with verse 4:3, above. Apologists could not allow that, and translate it as 'female slaves'.[47] So, 'right hands possess' for men means female slaves, and for women, female slaves as well, which is a patriarchal reading par excellence. In some cases, it might change the sexual orientation of some women.

If we follow the theory of Amina Wadud in her book *Qur'an and Woman*, when she writes: 'From my perspective on the Qur'an, every usage of the masculine plural form is intended to include males and females, equally, unless it includes specific indications for its exclusive application to males',[48] that will complicate the matter even further.

2. Muslim Perception of Paradise

The Qur'an describes and promises the believers in paradise the following: 'Round amongst them go boys of perpetual youth, whom when one sees, he thinks them pearls unstrung' (Q. 76:19). Therefore, these boys signify both genders. Another example can be found in Q. 44:54: 'We shall marry them to *hur* (fair females).' Moreover, 'These will be the nearest to Allah, in paradise, immortal boys will go around them, and *hur* (fair females) like preserved pearls' (Q. 56:17–23).[49] On the same notion, the Qur'an promises to male believers in paradise, *hur* who have not been deflowered (Q. 55:72–4). While very few have given a clear reason as to why Allah promises his believers in paradise the company of beautiful *ghulman* (young boys), we have to say that, from the rise of the 'Abbasids in the eighth century onwards, many Islamic dynasties bought hundreds or thousands of *ghulman* for pleasure, as will be discussed later.

I am sure that there are many traditional interpretations by orthodox jurists, from medieval to modern times, who try to defend the ethical/social right for a man to be more preferable to God than a woman, because men have better minds and richer knowledge. Also, beating her is part of women's submission to her man's will.[50]

On the issue of polygamy, many apologists follow the exegesis of al-Tabari in his *Jamiʿ*, and Ibn Kathir's, *Tafsir*[51] among others, which state that if the man fears that he will not be capable of being just to his many wives, it is better to marry only one. The question here is how a man will keep or have relationships with indefinite numbers of concubines and female slaves and still be able to do justice to his sole wife, socially or biologically. I agree with Asma Barlas in her opinion that 'a patriarchal exegesis of the Qur'an often results from applying the Hadith to interpret it'.[52]

3. Misogyny

'And when the news of (the birth of) a female (child) is brought to any of them, his face becomes dark, and he is filled with inward grief. He hides himself from the people as a result of what he has been informed' (Q. 16:58–9).

Continuing with the misogynic discourse in the Qur'an: 'Is it for you the males, and for Him (Allah) the females?' (Q. 53:21). This kind of hatred towards women expressed in the Qur'an reflects the male Arab mentality. Yet it is not clear – does it include all Arabia, or does it depend on certain tribes at a certain time?

In the same discourse, the Qur'an emphasises that a woman is less equal to a man when it comes to giving legal witness. For example, 'And get two witnesses out of your own men. And if there are not two men (available), then a man and two women, so that if one woman errs, the other can remind her' (Q. 2:282).

This interpretation has been universalised by conservatives.[53]

4. What is a Veil?

The debate is ongoing as regards the Muslim Eve dress, and whether she should be fully or partially covered. In 33:59–60 the Qur'an reads: 'O prophet! Tell thy wives and daughters, and the believing women, that they should draw their *jilbab* (cloak) over their persons when they go out. That is most convenient, that they should be known, so as not to be molested.' This verse, according to Bou Hdeiba among others, is concerning only the Prophet's women. The Qur'an tries to distinguish and protect the free women, and is not concerned with slave women in the early years of Islam. As Muslim societies have developed through the centuries to modernity and modern constitutions, the rule no longer applies. One should add that free women only were using such practices in the surrounding civilisations of the Arabian Peninsula, such as Assyria in Iraq, as will be explained.[54] The other verse about the veil reads:

> Say to the believing men that they should lower their gaze, and guard their private parts. That is purer for them ... Tell the believing women to lower their gaze and protect their private parts, and not to show off their adornment except that which is apparent. They should draw their *khumur* (veils) over their bosoms. (Q. 24:30–1)

Here, men and women were equal in resisting temptation, as both were ordered to lower their gaze to avoid temptation. Thus, each one was capable of recognising the other, and women were not fully covering their faces. 'Believing women' here includes female slaves. The Prophet himself did not follow this order, and was tempted by looking to Zaynab bint Jahsh, wife of his adopted son, Zayd b. Haritha.[55] According to Yedida Stillman, not everyone in early Islamic Arabia could afford separate undergarments. Men and women used to 'drape themselves in a fashion known as the *shamma*, whereby one end of the mantle was pulled up on the shoulder, leaving the other side of the body exposed, apparently in the style of the Greek Chiton'.[56] In addition to the problem of identifying the definition of *zinatahunna* (adornment), is the hair an organic part of the body, or something to add or attached to it? The problem continues with the variety of items that are used by different Arabs in different areas to veil. There is the '*qinaʿ*, which is a rectangular piece of fabric, made to cover the head and fall down over the face. There is also the '*burquʿ*, which is a kind of shroud that hides the entire body, including the feet.[57] Covering the hands is an added problem to consider.

The literal '*hijab*', with the meaning of 'screen' or 'curtain' is mentioned in the Qur'an only to stop visitors to the Prophet's house from intruding into his privacy when he married Zaynab bint Jahsh:

> O you believers, do not enter the Prophet's house unless permission is given to you for a meal. When you have taken your meal, disperse without sitting

> for a talk ... When you ask (his wives) for anything you want, ask them from behind a screen; that is purer for your hearts and for their hearts. It is not right to annoy the messenger of God, and you should never marry his wives after his death. (Q. 33:53)[58]

So the *hijab* here is used to give privacy to certain women (wives of the Prophet) and to avoid any visitor from having any desire for any of them. This is why it says that it is purer for both sides, and it continues in the same *aya*, forbidding anyone to marry the wives of the Prophet after his death.

Traditionalists and conservatives always follow the literalist readings or interpret these verses as a legitimate divine licence to force Muslim Eve to cover her head or head and face. This misused mandate condemns Muslim men, as they could not resist the temptation or desire towards a woman's body, considering it as pudendum, so it is safer to hold her prisoner to her cover and hide her altogether. The topic is far from being a matter of dressing, but it shapes the social environment and interaction of the whole society, leading to different levels of segregation and isolation.

It is ironic that men perform the pilgrimage and *'umra* (shorter pilgrimage) to Mecca, covering themselves mainly from the waist to the knee, while women are fully covered. They ignore the fact that women had to lower their gaze, especially as the only story of seduction in the Qur'an with some picturesque details was from a woman to Joseph (Q. 12:23–31).

Such debate will probably continue for a long time, especially given that conservative scholars in institutions such as al-Azhar in Egypt, or Saudi Arabia or Indonesia are fast to accuse anyone who denies that veiling means covering the head is denying what is clearly known in Islam, thus he or she is an apostate,[59] even though any Muslim is obliged to perform *ijtihad* (critical hermeneutics) as there is no clergy in Islam (theoretically).

5. Veiled and Unveiled Desire; the Marriage of Pleasure

> [Y]ou (the Prophet) said to him (Zayd): 'Keep your wife for yourself.' But you (the Prophet) concealed your desire, although God will reveal it. You feared the people, although you should fear God ... When Zayd had accomplished his desire from her (Zaynab) we gave her to you in marriage, so the believers could follow such an example. (Q. 33:37)

His first wife, Khadija, gave Muhammad a marriage gift in about 595. The gift was a male slave, Zayd. Muhammad freed him, and adopted him as his son. Years later in Medina, Muhammad went to visit his married son. Zaynab, Zayd's wife, opened the door, lightly dressed. She invited the Prophet in, but he refused when he knew that Zayd was not in the house. As he left, he said repeatedly: 'We ask God to divert our hearts.'[60] Clearly, the messenger of God was inflamed by her. When Zayd returned, he was told by Zaynab what had happened. When he went to see his father, Zayd asked the Prophet why he had not remained in the house. Then he asked him: 'If you like Zaynab, I can divorce her, so you can marry her.' The Prophet said: 'Keep your wife for yourself.' Ibn Sa'd wrote that after that, Zayd could not touch Zaynab as a husband would.[61] Then came the revelation of God with the above verse. The Qur'an itself explained the situation of the shy Prophet. He feared losing his moral status as a leader of the community when he admired and married his daughter-in-law. In addition, it was forbidden by the Qur'an in 4:23 for a man to marry his daughter-in-law (the wife of his biological son).[62]

I believe that the Qur'an considers women as chattels more than as humans with sentiments and will, which leads us to the following and final example from the Qur'an about 'the marriage of pleasure', which is confined to a certain period of time, and with known financial benefit in return for the woman.

> So with those of whom you have enjoyed sexual relations, give them their reward as prescribed; but if after a reward is prescribed, you agree mutually (to pay more), there is no sin on you ... Whoever of you has not the means wherewith to marry free, believing women, they may wed believing girls from among those (slaves) whom your right hands possess. (Q. 4:24–5)

Here, we can clearly see how the revelation portrayed the woman as an object that could be used for a short time, as long as it was negotiated between the two parties. Yet it is humiliating for the woman. Most Sunni and Kharijite Muslims no longer follow such practices, although most Shi'i followers do. I believe that the Sunnis have been influenced by the second caliph, 'Umar (d. 644), who forbid such a practice during his rule and punished those who ignored his order,[63] despite it being dictated by God.

On the same discourse, the Qur'an and Hadith do not allow a woman who has been divorced by the same husband three times to remarry him, unless she marries another husband first: 'And if he has divorced her (the third time), then she is not lawful unto him thereafter until she has married another husband' (Q. 2:230). The Prophet explained this in a Hadith, saying to a woman: 'You (the woman) cannot return to the divorced husband, until your new one had tasted your honey, and you have tasted his.'[64] Why did the woman in such cases have to be exchanged like an object? Yet, traditionalists insist that Muslim Eve is honoured under Islamic law, and elevated to a higher status than the one she had in pre-Islamic times.

Until now, in most Muslim countries, the shari'a (Islamic law)[65] has been adopted and incorporated into modern laws, which use the term *nafaqat al-mut'a* – the cost/gift of pleasure paid by the man when he divorces his wife. That is influenced by the interpretation of Qur'an 2:236, which deals with this matter.

Influential Women in the Qur'an

The Qur'an, influenced by the Old Testament, dedicates and names five suras after male prophets, from Abraham to Joseph,[66] in addition to the sixth, which is named Muhammad. Only one woman is mentioned by name in the whole 114 suras of the Qur'an, and she has a sura named after her: Maryam (Mary), mother of Jesus. However, there is an error about the family of Mary in the Qur'an when it reads: 'O Mary, sister of Aaron. Your father was not a sinful man, nor was your mother an unchaste woman' (Q. 19:28). According to the Christian faith, Mary did not have any brothers.[67]

Despite Muslim Eve being considered less equal to a man in the Qur'an, as explained, we see a few verses, also influenced by the Old Testament, about the unnamed Queen of Sheba, who was in contact with King Solomon: 'I found a woman ruling over them: she has been given all things that could be possessed by any ruler on earth. She has a great throne' (Q. 27:23). I think that this is the only signal in the Qur'an about a queenship in pre-Islamic times, given to Muslim believers to learn or take as an example of the Qur'an's purpose, especially as this queen was in Arabia. Unfortunately, not much more is said in the Qur'an about women in the public sphere of influence to teach the believing Muslims about the role of Eve.

All of the above examples are from the one Qur'an, which we have today in several editions and prints, but with the same order and number of chapters. Nevertheless, the history and historiography of the Qur'an, and the decoding of its verses, might lead us to a different understanding and interpretation of its textuality, which scholars of Qur'anic studies have pointed out. Thus, a number of points here are important.

'Qur'an' is not an Arabic word. It is a Syriac one and written as 'Keryana', meaning 'scripture' or 'lessons'.[68] We do not know the precise meaning of *aya* (verse). The same applies to 'sura', a Syriac word, given to the 114 chapters of the book. As Arthur Jeffery writes:

> The great part of the religious vocabulary and most of the cultural vocabulary of the Qur'an is of non-Arabic origin. One of the principal difficulties before us is to ascertain whether an idea or expression was Muhammad's spiritual property or borrowed from elsewhere. How he learnt it, and to what extent it was altered.[69]

That is why, in early Islam, Muslims were beset about how to interpret or understand these foreign words, during and after the death of the Prophet, as well as the collection of the scattered *aya* of the scripture.[70] J. D. Pearson states: 'The history of the text and the recitation of the Kuran after the death of Muhammad is still far from clear.'[71] This why we find al-Sajistani (d. 864) naming his book *Kitab al-Masahif* (the 'Book of Qur'ans' (plural of Qur'an)), and Ibn al-Nadim in the tenth century mentioning more than ten different versions of the Qur'an. One mention was for Ibn Mas'ud who was a companion of the Prophet. He did not include the first chapter, or the last two in his version. The Qur'an of Ibn Mas'ud was used in Baghdad until the eleventh century and was cited during civil unrest between Sunni and Shi'i Muslims. Ubayy b. K'ab was another companion whose copy of the Qur'an had 116 chapters.[72] There is also the Qur'an of 'Ali, one of the first men to convert to Islam, a close cousin of the Prophet, the fourth caliph and grand imam to all Shi'a.[73]

Another problem with reading the Qur'an is that the early Arabic script had only six distinguishable consonants; the remaining twenty-two were very similar and could only be understood from the context. The so-called diacritical dots were only added and widely used centuries later.[74] If we apply them to the Qur'an we have now, nearly every single line will see changes to the style of writing, and if we introduce the grammar introduced centuries later, the verses will change again.

The first caliph, Abu Bakr, refused to collect the Qur'an in one book, because the Prophet did not request such collection. By the time of the third caliph, 'Uthman (d. 644), he worried about the different readings and interpretations of the Qur'an, thus he commissioned its collection in one book, and ordered five copies to be made and ordered all other scattered chapters and fragments to be burned. Not everyone obeyed such orders, and that is why we have different versions[75] by the closest companions to the Prophet, which were dictated by him after the revelation. Also, it is not clear why Abu Bakr and 'Umar had selected one man for the collection, Zayd b. Thabit, who was less knowledgeable than other authorities, such as 'Abd Allah b. Abbas, 'Ali b. Abi Talib or Ibn Mas'ud.

The logic of classification of the suras in the Qur'an is not clear. We have Meccan suras but with some *aya* revealed to the Prophet in Medina, for example, suras 13, 55 and 57. We have many suras about which it is unknown where the revelation was made to the Prophet, Mecca or Medina. This is a very important matter to resolve, as scholars and jurists who write Islamic laws always claim that many *aya* in the Qur'an were given by God for a specific time and reason, then other *aya* abrogate the earliest, for example, the allowing and forbidding of wine-drinking. In addition, there is no solution for the mysterious letters at the beginning of the twenty-ninth sura. And we have no idea who gave names to the 114 sura and why?

Although it is widely believed that Gabriel was the medium between God and Muhammad for the revelation only, we have stories about Gabriel bringing special food for the Prophet (which will be discussed later), or appearing to the Prophet as a human being to fight with him against Banu Qurayza.[76] Of course, this is not the place to study the historiography of the Qur'an in detail, yet it is important to know the nature of the scripture that greatly affects the place and status of women in Muslim society, and to distinguish between the verses that were meant to last and others that were abrogated.

Staying with the nature of the revelation, al-Tabari writes of the famous story of Sura al-Najm: 'Have you then considered Al-Lat and Al-'Uzza (two idols of the pagan Arabs), and Menat, the other third? These are the great *gharaniq* (goddesses), whose their patronage is desired.' It was Satan who made Muhammad praise the three Goddesses of Mecca, glorified by his enemies in Mecca. The non-believers of Mecca were very pleased with Muhammad's shift towards their gods, instead of his Allah, and this was echoed in other areas. Later Gabriel came to Muhammad and blamed him for what he had recited. He told Muhammad that praising the ancient Goddesses of Quraysh in Mecca was a deed of Satan. As a result, the verse was abrogated and changed to: 'Have you then considered Al-Lat and Al-'Uzza, and Menat the other third.? Is it for you the males and for Him the females?'[77]

In other parts of the Qur'an, it mentions that Muhammad could forget some of the verses (Q. 2:106).[78] Christoph Luxenberg mentions how two men were arguing about how to read a certain verse, so they went to Ubayy, one of the companions of the Prophet. He contradicted both of them, and so they all went to the Prophet for a solution. Each man read to the Prophet the same verse in a different way, yet the Prophet said that all three were correct. Ubayy was in great doubt; Muhammad noticed this, and he told Ubayy: 'Pray to God for protection from the accursed Satan.' Ubayy broke into a sweat. It was the habit of the Prophet not to interpret anything from the Qur'an with the exception of a few verses. That is a thorny issue for the apologists.

As a result, we are captives to the traditional exegesis, on which later Qur'anic commentators drew.[79] We are yet to unravel many of meanings and misreadings that rule and dominate a large part of Muslim minds and societies. For example, sura 55:56 reads: 'In them are "damsels" of restricted glance, whom deflowered before them has neither man nor jinn.' If it is understood according to the Syro-Aramaic it reads: 'Therein (are found) drooping fruits (ripe for the picking), which neither man nor genie (an invisible being) before them has ever defiled.'[80] Also, sura 108 states: 'Verily, we have given thee (Muhammad) the Kauthar (river in paradise). So pray to thy Lord and sacrifice. Verily, it is he who hated thee who is the docked one.' The Syro-Aramaic reading reads: 'We have given you the (virtue of) constancy. So pray to your lord and preserve (in prayer). Your adversary (the devil) is then the loser.'[81]

We can say that the Qur'an is a fixed scripture, but our understanding of it is changeable and indefinite according to time, place, language and culture. The topic of gender is at the heart of it.

Muhammad and his Harem in Early Islam

> The Prophet said, 'I was one of the feeblest men when it came to love-making with women. That changed when Allah gave me al-Kafit. The angel Gabriel gave it to me. From then onward, when I needed it, it was made available for me. It is a pan with some kind of meat. Al-Kafit gave me the power to copulate equivalent to forty men at once'.[82]

Ibn Sa'd repeats this story in different forms, mentioning Gabriel as the one who brought down this type of food. What is important here is not the authenticity of the story as much as its influence on the traditionalist scholars and Muslim public mind and culture. Muslims believe in this and other such stories, which form a major part of Muhammad's biography. It is a thorny issue and confusing to have Gabriel, with three missions, delivering the revelation, fighting with Muhammad, as already mentioned, and giving him divine food.

The history and historiography of the Prophet Muhammad is no less problematic than that of the Qur'an. We have no documents or accounts from his time. What we do have, however, is the famous biography of Ibn Hisham (d. 833), written two centuries after the death of Prophet, and widely based on the accounts of Ibn Ishaq. There is also Ibn Sa'd (d. 845), who wrote a voluminous work on the biographies (*tabaqat*) of the Prophet and the hundreds of men and women around him. I should note that the prime source of the first three centuries of Islamic history, al-Tabari (d. 923), was a Persian. There are three centuries separating him from the Prophet, yet no historian can afford to ignore it, and it has not yet been annotated.

Adding to the confusion, we have the six main books of Hadith (sayings and practices of the Prophet), collected by Persian scholars, the earliest of them being al-Bukhari (d. 870), and the last being al-Nasa'i (d. 915).[83] None of the six collectors of Hadith were Arab natives, and we have very little knowledge about their early careers, such as where and how they studied the Arabic language. They collected tens of thousands (in other accounts, hundreds of thousands) of Hadith on every aspect of Muhammad's life, from food habits to prayers, and from jihad to medication and sexual habits. That created a chaotic ocean of facts, fiction, truth and misconceptions. There are Hadith and anti-Hadith in these books, covering all topics. In addition, many Hadith contradict several verses of the Qur'an. We cannot distinguish between Muhammad the person and Muhammad the Prophet, in order to properly understand his gendered practice.

The fundamental question here is: how can a human being who comes two centuries after someone else, let alone a prophet, transmit precisely thousands of oral undocumented traditions, which is then later used as a founding nucleus of a religion?

Al-Bukhari left no original manuscript, and nor did the other five, which adds to the confusion of the historicity of Hadith.

In a recent book by Rashid Ilal (which has been banned in Morocco), the author argues that there are thirteen different versions of al-Bukhari, amounting to approximately 650,000 Hadith.[84]

We have no record of the Prophet ordering the writing and collecting of the Qur'an or Hadith. On the contrary, the Prophet was quoted as saying: 'Anyone who quoted me with anything other than the Qur'an, should obliterate it.'[85]

In this section we will discuss the roles of significant women close to Muhammad in his harem and in society, and how he used political marriage to serve his socio-political career. We will also consider whether or not the status of women was improved by adopting Islam. "Aisha, wife of the Prophet, said: "The Prophet admired three things in this world: perfumes, women and food."'[86]

Muhammad had a large entourage of women: twelve wives, including some who were *sabaya* (prisoners of war); six others from whom he was separated (but it is not clear when or how); nine others, who were either engaged or devoted to him; and, in addition, at least two concubines and several *jawari*.[87]

One might agree partially with Laila Ahmed that 'Muhammad's wives, Khadija and 'Aisha, encapsulate the kinds of changes that would overtake women in Islamic Arabia'.[88] We cannot apply the models witnessed in the Hijaz to the whole of Arabia, from Yemen to the desert of Syria. Even within the Hijaz, there are different social–tribal hierarchies, evolving through time.

Khadija, First and Sole Wife

Khadija, who employed Muhammad in her business in pre-Islamic times, was the one to propose marriage to him. She was about forty years old, while he was twenty-five. Khadija remained with Muhammad until she died in 620. She had male slaves at her home in her service before and during her marriage to Muhammad. When the revelation of the Qur'an to Muhammad started, he was afraid, and it was Khadija who believed his story and pacified him. She also helped Muhammad by taking him to her Christian cousin Waraqa b. Nawfal, who admitted, according to the sources, that this was the divine word of Allah.[89]

We can only imagine how Muhammad would have felt or what he would have done if Khadija had disbelieved him or deserted him at the dawn of Islam. Khadija's business provided Muhammad with solid financial security during his early preaching period in Mecca, when he faced strong opposition from local tribes. Khadija gave birth to Muhammad's four daughters: Zaynab, Ruqaiyya, Um Kulthum and Fatima. All four daughters were to follow their mother in converting to Islam and believing in their father as a prophet of the new religion.[90]

It seems that Khadija was a strong and even dominant person and, as a result, Muhammad did not marry a second wife during her lifetime, nor did he have any concubines or female slaves. During the fierce opposition of Quraysh to Muhammad, she would pray in public at the Ka'ba with her husband and their slave. However, as soon as she died in 620 after twenty-five years of marriage, the situation changed dramatically.

Two Wives at the Same Time: Sawda and 'Aisha

Soon after Khadija's death, a relative of Muhammad's, Khawala, approached him with a recommendation of new brides for him – Sawda and 'Aisha.

Sawda had previously been married to a Muslim convert, al-Sakran, who had subsequently converted to Christianity. According to Islamic law, Sawda could not remain in such a relationship and divorced al-Sakran. A few weeks after her marriage to the Prophet in Mecca, the Prophet asked to marry 'Aisha, the six-year-old daughter of his close friend Abu Bakr. The marriage was consummated in Medina two years later in 1/622. How the

Prophet, at the age of 52, married a girl at the age of nine, has been a topic of great debate. 'Aisha was literally a child, and recalling her marriage, she said:

> My mother came to find me while I was playing with my friends on a swing. She called me and I went to her, not knowing what she wanted of me. She took me by the hand and stopped me on the threshold. I cried out until I was out of breath. She took me into a house in which were some women of Medina, who said, 'Happiness and blessing.' My mother gave me into their keeping and they washed my head and made me beautiful. I was not frightened, except in the morning, when the messenger of God came and they gave me to him.[91]

'Aisha was not mature, biologically or psychologically. Many apologists have tried to defend such a marriage until the present day. For example, during the one-year rule of President Muhammad Morsi (of the Muslim Brotherhood) in 2012/13, the Egyptian Parliament, dominated by his party, attempted to pass a law reducing the age of marriage from eighteen to nine, guided by the Prophet's tradition;[92] the move was supported by many Salafi parties. This practice exists in a number of Muslim societies in Africa and Asia, including Yemen and Afghanistan. The Muslim Brotherhood in Egypt wanted to legalise and broaden it.

The Qur'an, in sura 4:3, allows the believers to marry up to four wives (Muhammad is exempted from this number), on the condition that they treat them all fairly. It seems that with other wives added to Muhammad's harem, he was not able to deal justly with his wives. Some of them asked his daughter Fatima to go and talk to him on that matter, as he was spending more time with 'Aisha.[93] Sawda took the initiative and offered her days to 'Aisha to keep Muhammad happy, fearing he would divorce her.[94]

'Aisha is known for being the most beloved of Muhammad; however, it is notable that there is a Hadith about the only four perfect women in humanity: 'Asia, wife of Pharaoh; Mary, daughter of Imran; Khadija, wife of Muhammad; and Fatima, daughter of Muhammad – 'Aisha is not included.[95] On the other hand, the Prophet believed that there were many perfect men. 'Aisha's religious–political role following the Prophet's death will be discussed later.

Muhammad and the Practice of Political–Tribal Marriage

Muhammad was keen to strengthen relations with his close companions and allies through marriage. After he married 'Aisha, daughter of Abu Bakr, he married Hafsa, a divorced daughter of 'Umar b. al-Khattab, in 625. This step meant that there were four marriages between the Prophet and his close companions, who would all later succeed him as leaders/caliphs of the Muslim community and empire. Previously, in about 621, 'Uthman b. 'Affan, one of the wealthiest merchants from the strong Umayyad tribe, married Ruqaiyya, the Prophet's daughter.

'Ali, cousin of the Prophet, married Fatima bt. Muhammad in 624. When Muhammad's daughter Ruqaiyya died in 624, Muhammad gave 'Uthman his other daughter, Um Kulthum, to marry (in 624/5).[96] So, marriage gave legitimacy to the four rightly guided caliphs, who were either the Prophet's fathers-in-law (Abu Bakr and 'Umar), or his sons-in-law ('Ali and 'Uthman). We cannot ignore his marriage of Ramla bint Abi Sufyan. Her father, Abu Sufyan of the Umayyads, was Muhammad's arch enemy. Ramla joined Muhammad in Medina, when he was fighting her father.[97] It could be that Muhammad entered into this relationship for political purposes.

Invasions of the Prophet and Divine Assistance

There is no mention in the sources of the Prophet's profession following the revelation, and we don't know how he supported himself and maintained a house with several wives, concubines and slaves. The only indication in the sources is that (in accordance with Q. 8:41) he would have been entitled to one-fifth of the booty from the various invasions (*ghazwa*) that he initiated against his enemies. Al-Tabari lists about twenty-five *ghazwa* commanded or dispatched by Muhammad in Medina, including the conquest of Mecca.[98] Therefore, he was able to live on the booty given to him by revelation.

Female Captives ('Those Whom Your Right Hand Possesses') and Forced Marriage

In the year 626 the Prophet invaded the Jewish tribe of Banu Qurayza. According to the account of al-Tabari, the angel Gabriel appeared to the Prophet on horseback, and fought with him alongside other angels against the tribe.⁹⁹ After Muhammad defeated Banu Qurayza, he had trenches dug, and ordered all of the some 900 male captives to be slain and buried in those trenches. The women and children were taken as slaves. Muhammad took one Jewish woman named Rihana as a concubine, after killing all her family.¹⁰⁰ All the other women and children were distributed among the army commanders of the Prophet.

In the year 627 Muhammad invaded Banu al-Mustaliq, to the south of Medina, and took as a female war captive (*sabiyya*) a woman named Juwayriyya. Originally, she was the 'booty' of another man named Thabit, but when the Prophet saw how beautiful she was, he bought her from her new master.

Following the same pattern, in 628 Muhammad invaded a Jewish tribe in Khaybar, north of Medina. After defeating them, he surveyed the women captives. A Jewish woman, named Safiyya, charmed the Prophet with her beauty. He threw his gown at her, as a mark that she had become his captive. Safiyya had witnessed her husband being killed by Muhammad; despite that, the Prophet sent her immediately to be beautified for him, and the marriage was consummated in or near Khaybar a few days later.¹⁰¹ Muhammad was not concerned with Safiyya's feelings or her grief over the deaths of her husband and father. In this instance, the Prophet was acting against the clear commands of the Qur'an, in that when a woman is divorced or becomes a widow, she cannot remarry unless four months and ten days have passed (in order to ensure there is no pregnancy from the previous relationship) (Q. 2:234).

The following year, at the conquest of Mecca, Muhammad did the same thing again, capturing and marrying a woman called Malika al-Laythiyya after killing her father. Muhammad later divorced her; it is not clear from the sources how long they were married.

Such acts by the prophets, blessed and supported by the Qur'an ('what your right hand possesses'), created a tradition and industry of war and expansion by the later Muslim leaders. During the Wars of Apostasy (Ridda Wars) in 632–4, Caliph Abu Bakr approved of such behaviour by his commanders. Political dynasties, from the Umayyads, 'Abbasids and Fatimids to the Ottomans, followed the same pattern and owned tens of thousands of female and male slaves of different categories.

Such a mentality continues to exist in the twenty-first century because of that tradition. For example, Salwa al-Mutairi, who ran for the Kuwaiti Parliament in 2011, called for the introduction of a law to regulate the ownership of Russian *jawari* (female slaves) captured during the Chechen war. She offered US$10,000 for each female captive, arguing that this would protect men in a Muslim society from adultery.[102] In 2014, Suad Salih, a female professor of Islamic studies at al-Azhar University in Egypt, proudly declared on television that Islamic law allows Muslims to invade non-Muslim countries and enjoy the *sabaya*.[103] This idea was echoed in Tunisia by a member of parliament, al-Bahari al-Ghallas, in 2017. He wanted to incorporate such a law into the modern state.[104] This practice was also reflected in the savage and inhumane conduct of the Islamic state of Iraq and Syria (IS) in 2014–17, who would parade their female slaves on camera. The same thing is still committed by the Islamic movement of Boko Haram (lit. Western education is forbidden) in Nigeria and West Africa.

The Prophet was fearful about the fate of his harem (a haven or protected place where certain acts or persons are not allowed. The harem became a reference to the women's sector of the house or palace in medieval times). When he marched out of Medina for invasions he would gather his entire harem and keep them locked at the fort of his close and trusted friend, Hasan b. Thabit, in Medina.[105] The Prophet's custom of keeping his wives together, and under protection while he was away, set the pattern for future dynasties, where the harem would be surrounded by a curtain (*hijab*).

Concubines, Slaves and Eunuchs of the Prophet

Slavery is accepted by the three Abrahamic faiths. Muhammad was probably following his own needs, as well as being influenced by other cultures around him, such as the Persian or the Byzantine. As the Qur'an narrates the stories of several Jewish prophets, Muhammad probably knew about the life of Solomon and the hundreds of wives and concubines that he had had,[106] and he wanted to replicate this model.

In 626 Muhammad took his first concubine, the charming war captive, Rihana. When she refused Muhammad's request to convert to Islam, he kept her as a concubine (a woman used by only him for sexual pleasure, but without any of the rights of a wife).[107] It is not clear when she converted to

Islam, but it was only then that the Prophet married her, elevating her from a concubine to a wife.

In the year 627 the Byzantine ruler of Egypt, Cyrus, sent a gift to the Prophet in Medina, after the latter had invited him to become a Muslim. The gift was two slave females, Mariyya bt. Sham'un and her sister Sirin, in addition to an old eunuch named Mabur.[108] The Prophet accepted the gift. He took Mariya as a concubine, and gave Sirin as a concubine to his close friend Hasan b. Thabit. Both concubines converted to Islam, and Mabur also converted later.

Ibn Sa'd wrote: 'The Prophet copulated with Mariya according to the rule of *milk al-yamin* (those whom your right hand possess), and called her a *sariyya* (one who gives pleasure). Muhammad forced her to wear the *hijab*. Two years later when she gave birth to their son Ibrahim, who died as an infant, the Prophet emancipated her from slavery, but she remained a concubine, not a wife, until the prophet died.'[109]

The Prophet was not equitable in dividing his time and energy among his women. 'Aisha, who was extremely jealous of this concubine, complained that Muhammad was spending nights and days with Mariya. Another wife of the Prophet, Hafsa, was infuriated when she saw the Prophet and Mariyya in her room. Hafsa considered bringing a concubine to her own room and disregarding her privacy as humiliation. Muhammad's reaction was to shun Hafsa for a time.

All wives of the Prophet were elevated to some level of aristocracy in Islam. They were called, in the Qur'an, *ummahat al-mu'minin* (mothers of the believers) (Q. 33:6). All Muslim sources deal with them as a kind of saint; their sayings and deeds are not to be disputed or questioned. That has created a parallel tradition for them, glorified by traditional Muslims who take such narratives as an organic part of Islam.

According to al-Bukhari, the Prophet himself elevated Fatima, but not his other daughters, as 'grand lady of all women in paradise'.[110] All believers, according to Qur'an, are considered equal, and what distinguishes them from one another are their deeds only. So why did the Qur'an and Muhammad create such designations?

Women who Devoted Themselves to the Prophet

The Qur'an states: 'And a believing woman if she gives/devotes (*wahabat*) herself to the Prophet, and the Prophet wishes to marry her – a privilege for you only' (Q. 33:50).

The sources mention several women under the category of *wahabna* giving themselves to the Prophet. Some were accepted by the Prophet for marriage; others were refused. In one case, Khawala bt. Hakim devoted herself to Muhammad, who accepted, but did not marry her. She remained in his house serving him, and subsequently married another man.[111]

Male and Female Slaves

As already mentioned, Muhammad owned a male slave while living with Khadija, called Maysara. He had another called Zayd, who was a gift from Khadija (he was later freed), and a third, Aba Raf'i, who accompanied 'Aisha from Mecca to Medina.[112]

There were at least four female slaves in Muhammad's household: Salma, who was a midwife to several of his wives and daughter, Um 'Ayyash and Maymona bt. Sa'd. In addition, there was Um Ayman, who had taken care of Muhammad as a child and lived a long life.[113] Anwar Hekmat mentions that when the Prophet died, there were fourteen male and female slaves in his possession.[114]

Eunuchs – the Third Gender

The phenomenon of eunuchs (*khisyan*) was known in other civilisations before Islam, as will be detailed later. There is no verse in the Qur'an allowing or forbidding such a practice as castration, but we find the Prophet refusing the request of a man called 'Uthman b. Maz'un to castrate himself in order to avoid temptation. The Prophet said: 'Fasting is the castration of my *umma* (community).' The same answer was given to Muslim troops leaving to invade remote places.[115] Nevertheless, Muhammad had accepted a eunuch from Egypt, as already mentioned.

The sources also mention a man who appeared to serve the house of Mariyya, the concubine of the Prophet. We cannot imagine that such a man would dare to do this without Muhammad's permission. Muhammad's cousin 'Ali was sent to investigate, and he discovered that this man was a eunuch; however, the Prophet continued to employ him to serve Mariyya.[116] It seems likely that this man is the same Mabur from Egypt.

There are two types of eunuch, the first who have only their testicles removed, and the second who have their entire male organ removed.[117] It is important to know that eunuchs of the first type still have strong sexual desires and are capable of copulation. We have no idea which category Mabur belonged to.

The Prophet's ownership of a eunuch in his service held the gate wide open for many Islamic dynasties to use eunuchs to serve the armies of female slaves in the harem. Later, eunuchs were used in other sections of the palace and the state, as will be explained later.

Still on what we might call a 'third gender', we know that the household of the Prophet used or permitted the service of at least one *mukhannath* (transsexual/epicene). When Muhammad was at the house in Ta'if of his wife Um Salama, he heard a *mukhannath* named Hayt speaking in a loud voice, praising the sexual attractions of another transsexual named Ghilan. Muhammad was angered at such talk and banned him from the house.[118] Yet, other dynasties later on adopted the example of the Prophet, and allowed transsexuals in their palaces.

I agree with Anwar Hekmat and Laila Ahmed in their opinions that women in *jahiliyya* (pre-Islamic) Arabia had greater power in marriage or, at least, there was an absence of misogyny. When Muhammad established himself in Medina as Prophet, autonomy and monogamy became absent in his marriage.[119]

On a related topic, we have the important case of Fatima bt. Muhammad. She was married to 'Ali, as previously mentioned. When her husband engaged another woman named Juwayriyya bt. Abi Jahl, she complained to her father. 'Ali had done what the Qur'an allowed a Muslim man to do, and what Muhammad himself had done several times. However, Muhammad went to the mosque of Medina, and gave a very angry speech to the public, denouncing 'Ali's act. Muhammad insisted that if he wanted to marry the second woman, Fatima should be divorced first. He said: 'Fatima is a part of me; whatever angers her, angers me too.'[120] Here we see the father, not the Prophet, acting against the implementation of Islamic law.

Fatima's case well reflects how polygamy, although permitted by the Qur'an, still hurt the dignity, instinct and emotions of a woman. Muslim jurists have always tried to interpret polygamy in the Qur'an as being due to a fatal illness of the first wife or her being barren, or the increased proportion of women to men after wars in certain countries. Fatima was neither ill nor barren, which asserts the inequality of polygamy. The main reason given by Muslim scholars as to why a woman cannot reverse the situation and marry more than one man if she desires is because she cannot accurately identify the biological relationship between the children and their fathers. Of course, that is not an obstacle now, with modern tools such as deoxyribonucleic acid (DNA) testing.

Muhammad's Opinion of Women in Society and the Limited Role They Played

Apart from Muhammad's household, there were some 1,200 women in his community, who had varying levels of contact with him.[121] Muhammad's opinions and practices, which are reflected mainly through his copious Hadith and biography, reflect very limited faith in the equality and capability of the other gender. If we look into and compare the social–political status of pre-Islamic woman in and around Arabia, we will see how Islam either did not add much to the status of women, or gradually caged Muslim Eve in very limited roles in society.[122]

Selected Hadith

Unfortunately, Women are Just Flesh and Bone

1. The Prophet said: 'If a man invited his woman to bed and she refused, the angels would curse her till morning.'[123]
2. 'Aisha said: 'The Prophet used to kiss and *yubashir* (get involved) in sexual acts while fasting. Of all of you, he was the one most likely to control himself.'[124]
3. The Prophet said to Um Hakim, a woman in Medina who would circumcise girls: '*Ashemmi wala tanhaki* (do not cut deeply into the clitoris). That is more preferable to the man.'[125]

The first example reflects the full submission of a Muslim woman to her man, marginalising or totally ignoring her own needs. This is supported by the traditionalist exegesis of the Qur'an, reflecting the following *aya*: 'Your women are a tilth for you, so go to your tilth when and how you wish' (Q. 2:223).[126]

The second example shows how the beloved wife of the Prophet talks proudly about their intimate relationship, reflecting her own understanding of the humble status of Muslim Eve regarding her sexual satisfaction to her man, even during fasting.

The third case, although nothing is mentioned in the Qur'an about male or female circumcision, we see Muslims believing in Muhammad's full right to encourage the mutilation of a vital organ of a woman's body, using the excuse that this is better for her purity according to a man's point of view.[127] This view contradicts the Qur'an, which mentions in many verses how God had created the human being to perfection; yet Muhammad, as a human being, can alter such a creation and dominate a woman's body. The brutal practice of female circumcision took place in East Africa before Islam, yet Muhammad did not prohibit it, and it is still widely practised in many East African countries, as well as in Egypt.[128]

Children of a Lesser Mind

1. The Prophet said: 'I stood at the gate of hell, and I saw that most people there were women.'[129]
2. According to the Qur'an, men have a higher status than women, and two women's testimony is equal to that of one man, as mentioned earlier. The Prophet said: 'Woman's testimony is half of the man, due to her defective mind.'[130]
3. When the Prophet was told about a daughter (Puran) of the Sassanian king in Persia, who became a queen, he said: 'Never will succeed such a nation which makes a woman their ruler.'[131] Al-Bukhari, and other sources, can furnish us with several other examples.

Such Hadith, and there are many others with the same notion, have influenced many Muslim scholars and jurists throughout Islamic history in order to deny *al-imama al-kubra* (supreme political rule for women), simply because the Hadith is the second most important source of shari'a after the Qur'an. For example, Abu Hamid al-Ghazali (d. 1111), considered to be the most influential medieval Muslim scholar, was in favour of women remaining at home, and that they should get permission from their husbands when going out. He was in favour of boys' education, while denying this for girls.[132] His contemporary, the grand vizier of the Seljuqs, Nizam al-Mulk (d. 1092) stated:

> They [women] give orders following what they were told by those who work amongst them; naturally their commands mostly are the opposite of what is right and mischief ensues; the king's dignity suffers and the people are afflicted with trouble; disorder affects the state and the religion.[133]

If we look at contemporary Muslim thinkers, we will see that the founder of the Muslim Brotherhood, Hasan al-Banna (d. 1949), followed the same pattern, believing that God created woman to remain at home to raise children and look after the family. This has had profound effects, as the Muslim Brotherhood organisation has branches in more than eighty countries. The same concept and literal interpretation of the Qur'an regarding gender non-equality and misogyny is still practised to this day in the Wahhabi Kingdom of Saudi Arabia.[134]

Moving to Shi'i Islam, the leader of the Iranian revolution, Ayatollah Khomeni (d. 1989), insisted that a woman's testimony amounted to half of that of a man. Woman, he believed, is a mother above all else. He reinstated the 'marriage of pleasure', one of his many misogynistic beliefs.[135]

This is why we consider the women who became queens or were involved in political–military affairs, among other roles and practices in their societies, pioneers and fighters in such a confining environment. Their societies, or parts of it, were progressive, regardless of the realpolitik behaviour of some of those around them. The scarcity of contemporary material from the early Islamic ages prevents researchers in the field from fully understanding the boundaries of sexual politics in society, and between different areas and different tribes.

Most of the activities of women in Muhammad's time was narrated or transmitted through the Hadith. However, we have several stories about women who emigrated to Medina to follow Muhammad without seeking the permission of their families, or converting to Islam without their husband's permission, which reflects some independence and freedom of movement. For example, there is an account of a woman named Hawwa' bt. Yazid, who declared herself a Muslim in Mecca and joined Muhammad without her husband's permission, and another of Umayya bt. Qays, who joined Muhammad with a group of women who all converted to Islam, and joined some of Muhammad's invasions in order to nurse the wounded.[136]

Muhammad responded to a woman who wanted to join him in his jihad, saying: 'Jihadukunna al-hajj' ('Your jihad is performing the pilgrimage').[137] Muhammad was strict, confining Muslim women to their homes, and any woman had to get the permission of her husband to go out.[138] In saying that, there are examples to the contrary, such as Sajah, who was an Arab tribal military leader in the Jazira at the time of Muhammad's death, or Reqash of the Banu Tayy who was a *kahina* (priestess) who led her tribe in battle in pre-Islamic times.[139]

The Battle of Uhud: A Landmark in Women's Independence

I believe that the most revealing moment as regards the liberty and semi-independence for Muslim and non-Muslim women was the Battle of Uhud in 625. This battle was the second between Muhammad and his enemy, the Quraysh. He won the first battle, which took place the previous year in Badr, when the Quraysh mobilised a very large force to confront him. The men of Quraysh marched north of Medina accompanied by their women, who were there to provide moral support, and to ensure that the men did not desert the battlefield. One woman out for revenge was Hind bt. 'Utba, the wife of Abu Sufyan and mother of Mu'awiya, the future caliph. Hind had lost her father, 'Utba, and her brother, al-Walid, who had both been killed in Badr.[140] She hired a black slave to kill Hamza, Muhammad's uncle (whom she accused of killing her father) during the battle in return for setting him free after the battle. The Qurayshi women were singing during the battle to encourage their men in the fight against the Muslims, saying:

> If you advance we hug you
> Spread soft rugs beneath you
> If you retreat we leave you
> Leave and love you no more.

Muhammad was severely wounded during the battle, and fell to the ground; some of his companions thought he had been killed. While he was on the ground, a Muslim woman named Nusaybah bt. Ka'b came to his defence, fighting with a sword in her hand, and thus saving his life. Another woman, Sulafa, came to Muhammad's rescue, carrying arms. Both women were mentioned later, fighting in other battles during the conquests of Islam.[141]

The behaviour of Nusaybah and Sulafa reflect a pre-Islamic mentality and persona other than the new Islamic one that was yet to develop. We have no idea where they learned their fighting skills.

As for Hind bt. 'Utba, she fulfilled her promise to her black slave, who managed to kill Hamza. She cut open Hamza's body and ate part of his liver on the spot, in revenge for her father. She cried: 'I could not tolerate the loss of my father.' Not only that, but she mutilated his body and many other bodies from the Muslim side, cutting off their ears and noses, and making a necklace out of them.[142] She cried out to the defeated Muslims: 'We have paid you back for Badr.' This oral battle developed with another Hind, Hind bt. 'Uthatha from the Muslim side, who replied: 'O daughter of a despicable man, great only in disbelief. Hamza is my lion, 'Ali [cousin of Muhammad] is my Falcon.'[143]

The dilemma we face here is that we cannot say, based on just a few cases on the model of both Hinds, or the limited numbers of women on both sides, that Arab women at the dawn of Islam enjoyed greater liberty than in later centuries. We have no idea what level of liberty other women had in their societies across Arabia.

However, Laila Ahmed and Nadia El Cheikh both believe that Arab women enjoyed far more liberty during *jahiliyya*, and that Islam put an end to it.[144] Which Islam do we mean – the Qur'an? The Hadith? Or the practices collected by the so-called four rightly guided caliphs of Muhammad? Or the tribal culture, behaviours and mentality that coincided with the Muslim conquests or invasions outside Arabia? That is far from clear.

Yes, several Arab women of Medina in 622 went out in a parade to welcome Muhammad's arrival in their town. Others in Yemen, mainly known as the six harlots of Yemen (*kahena*), sang and danced in jubilation at the death of the Prophet in 632.[145]

Despite the details given about Muhammad's life, we have very little about his first wife, Khadija, and her traditions and teachings, unlike the ample material we have on 'Aisha, although both women lived with him for ten years under Islam. Similarly, there is little information about the daughters of Muhammad, with the exception of Fatima, around whom the Shi'a followers created an aura.

Women: Gender and Politics under the Four Rightly Guided Caliphs, 632–61

> Wives of the Prophet, you are not as other women ... Remain in your houses; and display not your finery, as did the pagans of old. (Q. 33:32–3).

During this short period, four of Muhammad's close companions led the Muslim *umma*. All of them were connected to Muhammad through marriage, as mentioned previously. All of them too were polygamists, following the tradition of the Prophet. In these three decades, the best-known role for women was the narration and teaching of Hadith. The exception was the rare, yet highly influential, interference in political religious affairs, especially by 'Aisha and Ramla, two of the Prophet's wives, and his daughter Fatima. However, this period, as described by Ruth Roded, was 'shrouded in twilight zone between religious–legal precedents and military–political chronicles. Ambivalent messages on women's activities drawn from this period are a case in point.'[146]

Fatima and Royal Legitimacy

The day Muhammad died, Abu Bakr and 'Umar, among other Muslim chiefs, gathered in Medina, and did not attend Muhammad's burial. They were concerned with the political succession of the Prophet. (We have no evidence that any woman attended that gathering.) On the other hand, 'Ali (Muhammad's cousin and son-in-law) was occupied by the burial. When the task was finished, he found that Abu Bakr had been selected as caliph. 'Ali then toured around Medina on a camel seeking political support, having with him his wife and beloved daughter of Muhammad, Fatima. The chiefs of Medina told him he was too late.

Fatima and 'Ali's house became a base for those who did not support Abu Bakr,[147] on account of Fatima's status. For the next six months, until Fatima died, 'Ali refused to support and recognise the new caliph. When Abu Bakr and 'Umar marched to Fatima's house, and called him out to talk, 'Ali refused. 'Umar was so angry, he threatened to burn the house down with all the people inside. Abu Bakr reminded him that Fatima was inside. 'Umar replied: 'Even so, I will.'[148]

Under such pressure, other Muslim chiefs had recognised the new caliph, but 'Ali continued to refuse. Fatima blamed Abu Bakr and his followers for seizing the moment during the burial of her father to take control, saying: 'We were not consulted and it was 'Ali's right to succeed Muhammad.' 'Umar continued with his threats to Fatima and her husband, and many in the public sympathised with her plight. Fatima's protection of her husband, and their claim of political legitimacy against the caliphate, ended the day she died. As 'Ali was now alone, he immediately declared his support for Abu Bakr. Abu Bakr had always said he could not force 'Ali as long as Fatima was with him.[149]

Fatima did not only influence the political affairs of the Muslim *umma*, she had also criticised the first caliph publicly for his denial to give to her her inheritance from the Prophet's share of land at Fadak, a village near Medina.[150] When Abu Bakr said to her that prophets are not to be inherited Fatima reminded him of the Qur'anic verse (27:16) that mentioned how Solomon had inherited David.[151] The Muslim Shi'i followers adopted Fatima's stance and amplified it as political–religious female leadership. Al-Mas'udi wrote that the famous 'Abbasid scholar al-Jahiz (d. 868) wrote a book immortalising the argument between the two figures.[152]

Fatima's political activities were happening during the same time as a non-Muslim queen, Sajah (mentioned earlier), of the Arab tribes of the Jazira, marched out to fight Abu Bakr. She was in command of an army, and led several male tribal chiefs.[153] The status of both women, the Muslim and the non-Muslim, reflects a high level of liberty among the different Arab tribes, both in the north or west of Arabia.

During the two-year caliphate of Abu Bakr (d. 634), he was fully concerned with the Ridda Wars, fought against those Muslims who had deserted Islam after the death of the Prophet. Although Abu Bakr proudly announced that he would continue to apply Muslim laws introduced by Muhammad, he was very weak at implementing such laws against one famous Muslim commander, Khalid b. al-Walid. Khalid was a genius military commander, and the caliph depended heavily on him through military campaigns to save the infant fragile unity of Arabia. During such campaigns, Khalid had killed local Muslim chiefs, and had taken their wives as war captives, forcing them into copulation soon after, without first marrying them.[154] Abu Bakr and 'Umar condemned Khalid for his deeds, but they applied none of the punishments mentioned in the Qur'an against him.

Under 'Umar's caliphate (634–44), the Muslim Arabs started their rapid conquests outside Arabia, in Iraq and Syria at the same time, and then in Iran and Egypt. During these conquests, there were a number of women taking up arms and fighting, such as Asma' bt. Abu Bakr, who fought with her husband in 636 at the Battle of Yarmouk against the Byzantine forces in Jordan, and Um Eban bt. 'Utba, who fought with her husband in Ajnadayn, Syria, in 634.[155] The sources mention several other cases, but this is not the place to expand on this in detail. Although women fighting on the battlefield was against the misogynist persona of the caliph, 'Umar was the one to ban women from performing the hajj (one of the five duties that Muslims have to perform). In addition, he agreed with the opinion of 'Aisha, who deprived women from praying at mosques. That is despite, in the Prophet's time, both genders performing the ablutions together. In addition, there are reports about women becoming imams (Um Waraka, to name but one) and leading the prayers for women, and even for men, according to Laila Ahmed.[156] One of the revealing characteristics of 'Umar's misogynistic persona was demonstrated in 624 when Ruqaiyya, daughter of the Prophet, died. During the burial ceremonies, he flogged the weeping women, until the Prophet asked him to stop.[157] He also stormed the house of Caliph Abu Bakr when he died in 634 to stop the caliph's sister from screaming, and he beat her. 'Aisha was in the house and told him to respect their privacy, but such advice was ignored.[158]

Under the third caliph, 'Uthman (d. 656), gender and politics played a substantial role in early Islamic history. The *fitna* (revolt) during this period, which ended with 'Uthman's murder at the hands of a group of angry Muslims, witnessed a higher level of female interference in politics. Um Habiba, wife of the Prophet and daughter of Abu Sufyan, went to 'Uthman's house during the crisis. She, as a mother of the believers, as described by the Qur'an, asked the angry crowd to withdraw and end the siege. Some of the crowd flogged her mule, and she was almost killed. When the *fitna* escalated, 'Aisha felt she could not stay in Medina, and decided to go on pilgrimage to

Mecca. Some Muslim leaders asked her to remain and interfere in this crisis. She refused and commented: 'Do you want me to suffer what Um Habiba suffered?' and marched out to Mecca. She returned only after the assassination of the caliph.[159]

'Aisha's Political–Military Ambitions

'Aisha's status was prestigious, both politically and religiously. She was the widow of the Prophet and daughter of his most trusted friend and successor, as well as being the mother of a believer. She challenged the fourth rightly guided caliph, 'Ali (the grand imam of the Shi'a). The sources provide detailed accounts from both the Sunni and Shi'i sides on the significant political–religious role she took in leading the community. She said after the murder of 'Uthman in a public speech: 'He was unjustly treated. I will seek revenge.'[160] 'Aisha was not only fighting 'Ali for the sake of the murdered caliph, but also to punish him for not recognising her father as the caliph during the first six months of his caliphate. Many Muslims from different backgrounds are said to have gathered around her seeking advice. She formed a pact with two of the most prestigious Muslim companions, Talha and al-Zubayr, in addition to many leading Umayyads, as 'Uthman was an Umayyad.

When 'Aisha, acting like a true generalissimo, decided to march out from the Hijaz to Basra in Iraq to fight the caliph, at least two of Muhammad's widows, Hafsa and Um Salama, advised her to remain at home, as the Qur'an had ordered the women of the Prophet to do. In addition, 'Abd Allah, son of the second caliph, 'Umar, rejected her. She ignored him and marched for war.[161] 'Aisha led her army, comprising tens of thousands of men, into southern Iraq in 656, and actually went into battle herself, riding her camel. The Arabic chronicles written more than a century and a half later differ about the numbers of casualties, but al-Tabari reports that 10,000 men were killed trying to protect 'Aisha, who was sat astride her camel, hence the battle being named 'the Battle of the Camel'.[162]

The most important question here is: did 'Aisha act according to the newly formed and evolving Islamic tradition, or did she act according to pre-Islamic customs? In *jahiliyya* there are a few examples, such as the Queen of Sheba, who was alleged to have been a great ruler and is referenced in the Qur'an (Q. 27:23) as an example given to Muslims, but with no historical evidence to back it up. Mawiyya bt. 'Afzar was another of the few Arab queens in *jahiliyya* who would lead her tribe and select men for marriage.¹⁶³ If we add Queen Sajah, mentioned above, we can see that 'Aisha's act was influenced by pre-Islamic tradition, but also driven by a strong persona and political ambition. The outcome of the battle was disastrous, resulting in the deaths of thousands of Muslims and the capture of 'Aisha by 'Ali. It should be noted that he treated her with extreme honour and sent her back to Medina.¹⁶⁴ 'Aisha did not only participate directly in warfare, but she also acted as a mediator between her chief allies, Talha and al-Zubayr, who would quarrel about who was to lead the prayers (a symbol of tribal–political leadership); she alternated this duty between them. Such ambition and domination continued up to the Umayyad age, as will be discussed later.

The literature written in the ninth and tenth centuries regarding gender and politics, such as the account of Ibn Hanbal (d. 855), strongly rejected 'Aisha's model, and any participation of women in Islamic government. The example of the Battle of the Camel has been used to warn against all women's involvement in state affairs by traditionalists from medieval through to modern times.¹⁶⁵ It is reported that some of 'Aisha's contemporaries, such as Um Af'a, accused 'Aisha of causing the death of 20,000 men.¹⁶⁶ The same sources that are critical of 'Aisha are not denying or criticising the women who fought in early Arab conquests in Syria and Iraq or with the Prophet himself. It may be assumed that such chronicles were against women in positions of leadership.

In 657, when Mu'awiya challenged the caliphate of 'Ali at the battle of Siffin in Syria, sources mention al-Zarqa' bt. 'Udayy and Bakkara al-Helaliyya as two articulated women who gave rousing speeches in order to encourage the army of the caliph, and they took up arms as well.¹⁶⁷

I strongly believe that 'Aisha's actions with her supporters resulted in an unbridgeable crack between Sunni and Shi'i Muslims of the community from that time onwards. Her daring fight challenged the status and authority of the caliph much further than the *fitna* during 'Uthman's caliphate (which had no clear leader). We see the model of Sajah, as an Arab leader of the community, replicated here by 'Aisha.

Ironically, scholars like al-Bukhari, who reported negatively on the role of 'Aisha in the Battle of the Camel, depending heavily on her narrative of the

Hadith. She is said to have narrated some 1,200 Hadith, of which al-Bukhari selected 228, and Muslim 242.[168] Nearly 1,000 women from the early Islamic period were considered as Hadith transmitters. Their educational testimonies were well taken, although, of course, female testimony is equal to half that of a man!

Therefore, women were not welcomed in the political arena, yet they were partially appreciated for their religious role, probably because of the first-hand information they took from the Prophet. Having said that, we do not know why not one single woman of that age wrote down or dictated her knowledge or thoughts. Indeed, early Arabs continued from pre-Islamic times to depend on their orality, but with the problem of collecting the Qur'an, maybe it would have elevated the status of women in society as prominent interpreters or thinkers who should have contributed to the intellectualism in society, especially after the establishment of Islam. This tradition of the non-written word continued until the production of the first book written by a woman in late Mamluk Damascus, 'Aisha al-Ba'uniyya (d. 1516), who produced a book on the divine love of Muhammad.[169]

It is worth pointing out here that all the four caliphs were polygamists like Muhammad, and 'Ali certainly had more than seven wives and three concubines, on which the sources are reluctant to elaborate.[170]

After surveying woman and gender in the Qur'an, during Muhammad's life and the period of the four rightly guided caliphs, it is important to review briefly the status of women and gender in surrounding civilisations in Arabia before Islam, to ascertain whether the new religion elevated the status of women or not, especially given that Islam went on to conquer most of these ancient civilisations.

Women and Gender in Ancient Egypt

Egypt was the exception to other ancient civilisations in the Near East, in that women enjoyed the same legal status as men, whether unmarried, married, divorced or widowed. A woman could propose marriage to a man, could initiate a divorce and could also include conditions in her marriage contract if she wished. Polygamy was legal, but it was practised mainly by the very wealthy and royals. Most royal courts in ancient Egypt had concubines, not just for sexual pleasure, but as artisans and musicians, too. A woman was equal to a man in the ownership of properties and could also inherit equally.[171] Egyptian women were unveiled regardless of their social class. They moved about freely at social events and could travel independently of men. In addition, they could own their own businesses and conduct business on an equal basis to men, as the records show.[172] Up until the Greek invasion of 332 BCE, women in ancient Egypt enjoyed a better position than many of their contemporaries and those in the modern world. Will Durant states: 'Women's position was more advanced than in most countries today. No people, ancient or modern, has given women so high a legal status as did inhabitants of the Nile Valley.'[173] Through the 3,000 years of Egyptian history, several queens have come to power in their own right and have led the political and military affairs of the kingdom. For example, during the fourth dynasty (2680–2560 BCE), Princess Khint Kaws took the throne and ruled the country. She had a tomb and temple built by her ancestors equal to that of men in religious and political affairs. Arguably the most renowned queen was Hatshepsut (r. *c*.1493–1479 BCE), who dispatched military campaigns into East Africa, and had diplomatic relations with ancient Iraq.[174] One of the most revealing areas of women's liberal identity could be found in the Egyptian arts, for example, paintings and statues of female musicians and dancers dressed in liberal fashion, which challenge any modern style in the West today.[175] Another aspect worth mentioning is women as goddesses and priestesses. Women played a pivotal role in myth and religion, shaping Egyptian doctrine through three millennia, such as the goddess Isis, sister and wife of the god Osiris, and mother to Horus.[176] It could be argued that the status of women in Egypt deteriorated after the Arab Muslim invasion of 640, bringing a mix of Arab nomadic cult and confusing readings of the Qur'an and Hadith.

Women and Gender in Ancient Iraq

Between the Kingdom of Assyria in the north and the Kingdom of Babylonia in the south, the two major kingdoms of ancient Iraq were established in about the nineteenth century BCE, following several centuries of struggle between the inhabitants of earlier city-states, such as the Sumerians and the Akkadians.[177] The Mesopotamian society was generally a patriarchal one, due to increasing military struggles between the different powers in the valley of

Tigris and Euphrates. The diversity of economic life in urban society had increased women's subordination to men, and the seclusion of women.[178] Both the laws and codes of King Hammurabi in the eighteenth century BCE in Babylonia, and the Assyrian laws, permitted a husband to beat his wife, pull out her hair and mutilate her ears. A man could easily divorce his wife, especially if they had no children, but they had to return the dowry and pay divorce money. In very limited conditions only could women ask for divorce.[179]

Having said that, monogamy was the norm in society, except among the royal class, as in ancient Egypt. Adultery by the wife and her partner was punished by death. (Muslim laws regarding beating of the wife and offering a dowry or a price for the woman were influenced by the practices of ancient Iraq, as was the death penalty for adultery, introduced by 'Umar when he became caliph.) The royalty of Iraq maintained a harem with tens of concubines, but this was no match for the Sassanian realm in Iran in the sixth and seventh centuries CE, which had thousands of them.[180] Women could own, purchase and inherit property and could also serve as a witness in court. They were accepted to work in the field alongside men of the family, too.

The law of Isin in eighteenth-century BCE northern Iraq denied the children of a freed slave woman to inherit from their father, unlike his children from his wife. Concubines' children on the other hand could inherit, if the wife was barren.[181] Regarding the veil in ancient Iraq, article 40 of the Assyrian law codes speaks clearly about who should be veiled:

> Married women, widows and Assyrian women must not have their heads uncovered when they go out into the streets. Daughters of status must be veiled, whether by a veil, a robe or a mantle; they must not have their heads uncovered. When they go into the street (alone) they are to be veiled. A concubine on the street with her mistress is to be veiled. A hierodule who has got married must be veiled on the street, but a single hierodule must have her head uncovered; she may not be veiled. A harlot is not to be veiled; her head must be uncovered. Any man who sees a veiled harlot is to apprehend her, produce witness and bring her to the palace entrance. Although her jewellery may not be taken, the one who apprehended her may take her clothing. She will be caned (fifty stripes) and have pitch poured on her

head. If a man sees a veiled harlot and lets her go rather than bringing her to the palace entrance, he will himself be caned (fifty stripes). The one who turns him in may take his clothing. His ears will be pierced, threaded with a cord tied behind him, and he will be sentenced to a full month's hard labour for the king.

Slave girls are not to be veiled either. Any man who sees a veiled slave girl is to apprehend her and bring her to the palace entrance. Her ears will be cut off, and the man who apprehended her may take her clothing. If a man sees a veiled slave girl and lets her go rather than bringing her to the palace entrance, and he has been charged and convicted, he is to be caned (fifty stripes). His ears will be pierced, threaded with a cord tied behind him, and he will be sentenced to a full month's hard labour for the king.[182]

I believe that such a law was aimed at separating society into different social classes at the time, as a mark of prestige and symbol of status. It had to be observed very rigidly. Due to the organic geographical extension of Arabia into southern Iraq, it was not only the Syriac language from which the Arabic language was derived, but we see a strong geo-cultural influence of these traditions on Arabs, Christians and Muslims alike. I would add that facial veiling was not evident in Assyrian art.[183]

Babylonian society did have queens involved in some political affairs of the kingdom, such as Queen Semiramis, wife of Shamshi Adad (824–810 BCE), among others, but they were not governing fully independently in their own right.[184]

The Mediterranean and the Status of Women

These Mesopotamian traditions, mainly the veiling and, to a certain extent, female seclusion according to different social classes, could be found in other ancient Mediterranean societies and religions. There are some veiling references in the Torah from 500 BCE, probably influenced by the Babylonian captivity of the seventh century BCE (Gen. 38:13–19). In Christianity, too, there is evidence of a letter of St Paul regarding the veiling of women.[185] Germaine Tillion states that the tradition of veiling and variable degrees of seclusion was practised in European countries on the Mediterranean shores until the early twentieth century, especially in the countryside.[186] (In my own country, Egypt, Christian women, especially in Upper Egypt, continue to wear various styles of the head veil in everyday life, particularly when they go to church.)

We can see that these two Abrahamic faiths, which are very evident in many chapters in the Qur'an and hundreds of Hadith, influenced the early Arab Muslims through the Jewish and Christian Arabs living among them, and directed the interpretations of the Qur'an in a monogamist way.

Regarding ancient Greece, after Alexander the Great defeated King Darius of Persia in 333 BCE, he seized hundreds of women, slaves and concubines, and assimilated the royal Persian model of harem. Eunuchs were used widely to serve and guard this large harem.[187] More than a century before this war took place, the free women of Athens usually lived in seclusion, and only their close relatives could have access to them. The great Greek philosopher of the age, Aristotle, was proud to state that the purpose of marriage and the function of women was to provide children and successors. He was proud to theorise that 'women were subordinate by social necessity and biologically inferior in both mental and physical capacities'.[188] This is why, when Alexander died in Egypt in 323 BCE and was succeeded by the Ptolemaic Greek dynasty that ruled until 30 BCE, the Greeks were astonished by the equality between the genders in Egypt and started to make changes to their mentality and traditions. That led to the coming of Queen Cleopatra VII (d. 30 BCE) to the throne of Hellenic Egypt.[189]

Under the Eastern Roman Empire and early Byzantine Empire there was a development in women's powers in the first centuries of Christianity. St Helena, mother of the legendary Constantine I (d. 337), was a royal mother and empress, and secured from her son authority to officially grant toleration to Christianity. That had led other women from the ruling class to become acting empresses, such as Eudoxia (r. 395–404), wife of Arcadius, especially after Christianity became the official faith of the empire in 390. Theresa Earenfight argues that women were influenced by the Virgin Mary, considering her as an idol and role model.[190] Female right of inheritance gave women the power to install certain candidates to the throne of Byzantium; for example, when Emperor Leo I died in 474, his widow, Empress Verina, crowned her brother Leo II as emperor, despite the political–military turbulence in the empire.[191] Other empresses who could not directly command the army married military commanders or secured loyalty from such commanders. Maybe one of the outcomes of the newly forming Christian society in Eastern Europe was that it had produced queens soon after the fourth century CE due to the entrenched pre-Christian tribal traditions, while it took the Muslim East some 400 years to produce the first one.

The Status of Women in Syria and Ancient Israel

If we look panoramically, we will see that in Roman Syria, an exceptional woman came to power for five years, the Syrian-Aramaic Zenobia in Palmyra, north east of Damascus. After her husband Odenathus was killed in 268, she assumed power as queen, and ruled over all of Syria and Egypt until 272, a clear revolt against the Roman Empire. Nabia Abbott names her as the most prominent pre-Islamic Arab queen, but Mark Whittow considers her as an authentic Syrian women, and not an Arab, a view that I would support.[192] In a recent study by Yasmine Zahran, the author describes the multi-ethnicity of Zenobia saying: 'Zenobia was a Roman to the Romans, an Arab to the Arabs, a Panhellenist to the Greeks, but in fact she was a Hellenised Arab', although she did not speak Arabic, and worshipped the Syriac Goddess Allat, which also influenced pre-Islamic Arabia.[193] Nabia Abbott tried to dig up examples of pre-Islamic Arab queens in a much-appreciated attempt; however, it did not yield very sound results. For example, she alluded to Zabibi as the first Arab queen in the eighth century BCE. She wrote: 'Though listed as queen of the Arabian land, the locality of her kingdom within Arabia is not specified.' Her short study is more hypothetical with a few elusive incidental examples included in the Assyrian records or the Old Testament, like the Queen of Sheba.[194]

We do not have sufficient materials about ordinary life and gender in pre-Islamic Arabia. However, Laila Ahmed argues that Arab women enjoyed more freedom than during the early Muslim times. For example, women were more able to move around and leave their homes and they were freer to have sexual relations outside the institution of marriage. Islam made the female less human and subordinate to the male as an object, increasing the 'protection' and seclusion around her for the benefit of the ever-growing patriarchal society. Ahmed adds that Muhammad was influenced by traditions in surrounding lands, such as Syria and Iran, which marginalised and secluded the women.¹⁹⁵ In Iran, while Muhammad was Prophet, there was a queen in power named Puran, daughter of Khosrau II; she had her image and name on the coinage in 629–30 and was succeeded by another queen, her sister, Azarmedukht (630–1).¹⁹⁶ In Syria there was the model queen, Queen Zenobia. The problem is that we have very little data or details about other Arab societies around Arabia, with the prime image being mainly from the Hijaz. Within that model, we have different social classes and tribal traditions of which we hardly have enough evidence due to the oral nature of the Arabic language.

Finally, we shall look briefly at the ancient Israeli society, according to the theory of Niels-Erik Andreasen. He argues, from the perspective of the Hebrew Bible, that mothers of Israelite kings were considered queens in ancient Israel. They held their position independently of the king. The queen acted as regent upon the king's death and during his extended absence. She was involved in the political, military and economic affairs of the realm, for example, Bathsheba and King Solomon (1 Kings 2:13). That was a continuation of civilisations prior to the Israeli one, such as the Ugaritic and Hittite.¹⁹⁷ As for the usage of hundreds of concubines, as mentioned earlier, we have no historical details about their social roles.

Notes

1. Al-Tabari, *Ta'rikh al-Umam wa al-Muluk*, Amman, 2000, compiled edition, pp. 509–10; Ibn Taqataqa, *Al-Fakhri fi al-Adab al-Sultaniyya*, Beirut, 1986.
2. Al-Tabari, *Ta'rikh*, p. 510.
3. Anna Comnena, *The Alexiad*, London, 1985.
4. Farhad Daftary, 'Sayyida Hurra: the Ismaili Sulayhid Queen of Yemen', in *Women in the Medieval Islamic World*, ed. Gavin Hambly, London, 1999, pp. 117–30.
5. Taef El-Azhari, 'Dayfa Khatun: Ayyubid Queen of Aleppo 634–640/1236–1242', *Annals of Japan Association for Middle East Studies*, 2000, Vol. 15, pp. 27–56. In medieval Western Europe, queenship was introduced as early as the sixth century, for example, the Frankish queen, Clotilde (d. 545), who was the wife of King Clovis I (d. 511). Also, in medieval Eastern Europe, there was the Byzantine empress, Irene (r. 797–802). See Theresa Earenfight, *Queenship in Medieval Europe*, London, 2013, pp. 56, 87.
6. C. E. Bosworth, *The Islamic Dynasties*, Edinburgh, 1980, p. 179.

7. Nabia Abbott, *Two Queens of Baghdad: Mother and Wife of Harun al-Rashid*, Chicago, 1946.
8. Nabia Abbott, *Aishah: The Beloved of Muhammad*, Chicago, 1942.
9. Fuad Caswell, *The Slave Girls of Baghdad: The Qiyan in the Early Abbasid Era*, London, 2011.
10. Nadia El Cheikh, *Women, Islam, and the Abbasid Identity*, Cambridge, MA, 2015.
11. Oxford, 2017.
12. Based on papers presented at a conference at Zurich university in August 2013.
13. Nadia El Cheikh 'The Qahramana in the 'Abbasid Court: Position and Functions', *Studia Islamica*, No. 97, 2003, pp. 41–55. Also, Nadia El Cheikh, 'Servants at the Gate: Eunuchs at the Court of al-Muqtadir', *Journal of the Economic and Social History of the Orient*, Vol. 48, No. 2, 2005, pp. 234–52.
14. Hugh Kennedy, *The Court of the Caliphs: The Rise and Fall of Islam's Greatest Dynasty*, London, 2004.
15. Said in a conference discussion.
16. Delia Cortese and Simonetta Calderini, *Women and the Fatimids in the World of Islam*, Edinburgh, 2006.
17. Daftary, 'Sayyida Hurra'.
18. Taef el-Azhari, 'The Role of Salguqid Women in Medieval Syria', in *Orientalia Lovaniensia Analecta*, eds U. Vermeulen and J. Van Steenbergen, Leuven, 2005, Vol. IV, pp. 111–26.
19. Carole Hillenbrand, 'The Career of of Najm al-Din Il-Ghazi', *Der Islam*, Vol. 58, No. 2, 1981, pp. 250–92; 'Jihad Propaganda in Syria from the Time of the First Crusade until the Death of Zengi: The Evidence of Monumental Inscriptions', in *The Frankish Wars and Their Influence on Palestine*, eds K. Athamina and R. Heacock, Birzeit, 1994, pp. 60–9; *The Crusades: Islamic Perspectives*, Edinburgh, 1999.
20. El-Azhari, 'Dayfa Khatun', pp. 27–56.
21. Erdoğan Merçil, *Fars atabegleri Salgurlular*, Ankara, 1991.
22. Bruno de Nicola, *Women in Mongol Iran: The Khatuns, 1206–1335*, Edinburgh, 2017.
23. Peter Jackson, 'Sultan Radiyya bint Iltutmish', in *Women in the Medieval Islamic World: Power, Patronage and Piety*, ed. Gavin Hambly, London, 1999, pp. 181–98.

24. Alyssa Gabbay, 'In Reality a Man: Sultan Iltutmish, His Daughter Raziya and Gender Ambiguity in Thirteenth-century Northern India', *Journal of Persianate Studies*, Vol. 4, 2011, pp. 45–63.
25. G. Rex Smith, *The Ayyubids and Early Rasulids in the Yemen (567–694/1173–1295)*, Oxford, 1978.
26. Shaun Marmon, *Eunuchs and Sacred Boundaries in Islamic Society*, Oxford, 1995.
27. David Ayalon, *Eunuchs, Caliphs and Sultans: A Study of Power Relationships*, Jerusalem, 1999.
28. Taef el-Azhari, 'The Influence of Eunuchs in the Ayyubid Kingdom', in *Orientalia Lovaniensia Analecta*, eds U. Vermeulen and J. Van Steenbergen, 2005, Vol. IV, pp. 127–42.
29. Judith Tucker, *In the House of Law: Gender and Islamic Law in Ottoman Syria and Palestine*, Cairo, 1998.
30. Amira Sonbol (ed.), *Beyond the Exotic: Women's Histories in Islamic Societies*, Cairo, 2006.
31. Fariba Zarinebaf-Shahr, 'Women, Patronage and Charity in Ottoman Istanbul', in *Beyond the Exotic: Women's Histories in Islamic Societies*, ed. Amira Sonbol, 2006, pp. 8–101.
32. 'Umar Kahala, *A'lam al-Nisa' fi 'Alami al-Arab wa al-Islam*, 5 vols, Damascus, 1959.
33. *Encyclopaedia of Islam*, 2nd edition, Leiden, 2002.
34. Suad Joseph *et al.* (eds), *The Encyclopedia of Women and Islamic Cultures*, 5 vols, Leiden, 2007.
35. Najwa Kira, *Al-Jawari wa al-Ghulman fi Misr fi al-'Asrain, Alfatimi wa Alayyubi*, Cairo, 2007.
36. Amal al-Kurdi, *Dor al-Nisa' fi al-Khilafa al-'Abbasiyya*, Amman, 2014.
37. Fatema Mernissi, *The Forgotten Queens of Islam*, Minneapolis, 1993.
38. Ibn Hisham, *Al-Sira al-Nabawiyya*, 2 vols, Beirut, 2014, Vol. 1, p. 93.
39. Ibid., p. 100.
40. Hugh Kennedy, *The Prophet and the Age of the Caliphate*, London, 1986, p. 30.
41. Ibid., p. 31.
42. Al-Tabari, *Ta'rikh*, p. 310.
43. Ibid., pp. 314–17.
44. Ibn Hisham, *Al-Sira*, Vol. 1, p. 360.
45. Al-Tabari, *Ta'rikh*, pp. 398–400; Ibn Hisham, *Al-Sira*, Vol. 2, pp. 70–242.

46. Muhammad Shahrur, *Fiqh al-Mar'a*, Beirut 2016, pp. 288–9.
47. Ibid., p. 635.
48. Amina Wadud, *Qur'an and Woman*, Oxford, 1999, p. 4.
49. Christoph Luxenberg, in *The Syro-Aramaic Readings of the Koran: A Contribution to the Decoding of the Language of the Koran*, Berlin, 2007, argues that *hur* has a double meaning; *hur* can also mean 'white grapevines of paradise', see pp. 253–62.
50. Jalal al-Suyuti and Jalal al-Mahalli, *Tafsir al-Jalalayn*, Damascus, 1995, pp. 77–8.
51. Al-Tabari, *Jami' al-Bayan fi Tafsir al-Qur'an*, Beirut, 2002, Vol. 5, p. 122; Ibn Kathir, *Tafsir al-Qur'an*, Beirut, 1984, Vol. 4, p. 88.
52. Asma Barlas, *Believing Women in Islam: Unreading Patriarchal Interpretations of the Qur'an*, Austin, 2002, p. 63.
53. There are ample examples of how the Taliban in Afghanistan has treated women in the twenty-first century. Another example is the parliamentary election in Egypt in 2012, during the rule of the Muslim Brotherhood, when conservative (Salafi) parties used a picture of a rose instead of female candidate photos.
54. A. Bou Hdeiba, *Sex in Islam*, trans. H. Alouri, Beirut, 2001, p. 78; see also Laila Ahmed, *Women and Gender in Islam*, New Haven, 1992, pp. 14, 56.
55. Anwar Hekmat, *Women and the Koran: The Status of Women in Islam*, Amherst, 1997, p. 193.
56. Yedida Stillman, *Arab Dress: A Short History: From the Dawn of Islam to Modern Times*, Leiden, 2003, p. 11.
57. Ibid., p. 20.
58. The same concept can be found in Q. 19:17.
59. Fatwa by Ali Jum'a, former mufti of Egypt and member of the supreme council of Azhar's scholars, 4 May 2015.
60. Ibn Sa'd, *Al-Tabaqat al-Kubra*, Beirut, 2004, Vol. 10, p. 98.
61. Ibid., pp. 98–9.
62. Hekmat, *Women and the Koran*, pp. 56–7.
63. Murtada al-'Askari, *Ma'alim al-Madrasatine*, Beirut, 2010, pp. 348–9.
64. Al-Bukhari, *Sahih al-Bukhari*, Beirut, 2015, p. 977.
65. Literally, 'digging a path for animals to get to a water source'. In Jordan until today, the locals call River Jordan 'shari'a'.
66. Arthur Jeffery, *The Foreign Vocabulary of the Qur'an*, Leiden, 2007, reprint of 1938 first edition in Cairo, pp. 1–2.
67. Hekmat, *Women and the Koran*, p. 11. The word 'Allah' is also of Syriac origin.

68. J. D. Pearson, art: 'Al-Kuran', *EI²*; Jeffery, *The Foreign Vocabulary*, p. 1.
69. Jeffery, *The Foreign Vocabulary*, p. 2.
70. Luxenberg, *The Syro-Aramaic Readings of the Koran*, p. 23; Jeffery, *The Foreign Vocabulary*, p. 3.
71. Pearson, 'Al-Kuran'.
72. Ibn al-Nadim, *Kitab al-Fihrest*, 4 vols, ed. A. al-Sayyed, London, 2014, Vol. 1, pp. 64–8; al-Sajistani, *Kitab al-Masahif*, Beirut, 1988, pp. 20–1.
73. Ibn al-Nadim, *Al-Fihrist*, vol. 1, p. 70; Ibn Sa'd, *Tabaqat*, Vol. 2, p. 338.
74. Luxenberg, *The Syro-Aramaic Readings of the Koran*, p. 31; Pearson, 'Al-Kuran'.
75. Ibn S'ad, *Tabaqat*, Vol. 3, p. 107; Pearson, 'Al-Kuran'.
76. Ibn S'ad, *Tabaqat*, Vol. 10, pp. 182–3; Ibn Hisham, *Al-Sira*, Vol. 2, p. 146.
77. Al-Tabari, *Ta'rikh*, p. 322; Q. 53:20–1. Allat the Goddess has a close similarity in writing and pronunciation of the word Allah, which is also Syriac, and has other forms like اله, الاله, اللاه, الله ; Hekmat, *Women and the Koran*, p. 18.
78. Pearson, 'Al-Kuran'. It is important to mention that although Menat was one of the Quraysh pre-Islamic goddesses, the name is still used today for one of the pilgrimage ceremonies, pronounced Mena.
79. Luxenberg, *The Syro-Aramaic Readings of the Koran*, pp. 36, 64–5.
80. Ibid., p. 272.
81. Ibid., p. 300.
82. Ibn Sa'd, *Tabaqat*, Vol. 10, pp. 182–3.
83. W. Montgomery Watt, *Muhammad at Mecca*, Oxford, 1991, p. 20; T. Ehlert, art. 'Muhammad', *EI²*. Malik b. Anas (d. 795) wrote his own book on Hadith before them, *Al-Muwatta'*. Yet, al-Bukhari is considered by the majority of Muslim scholars as the most knowledgeable one.
84. Rashid Ilal, *Sahih al-Bukhari: Nehayat Austora (Al-Bukhari, the End of a Myth)*, Rabat, 2017, pp. 18–19.
85. Ahmad b. Hanbal, *Al-Musnad*, Cairo, 2002, n. 10,731.
86. Ibn S'ad, *Tabaqat*, Vol. 2, p. 342.
87. Ibid., Vol. 10, pp. 52–170.
88. Ahmed, *Women and Gender*, p. 42.
89. Al-Tabari, *Ta'rikh*, pp. 310–11.
90. Ibid., pp. 311–12.
91. Hekmat, *Women and the Koran*, pp. 43–4.
92. *Al-Masry Al-Youm* (newspaper), 25 September 2012.
93. Kahala, *A'lam al-Nissa'*, Vol. 3, p. 9.
94. Ibid.

95. Ruth Roded, *Women in Islam and the Middle East: A Reader*, London and New York, 1999, p. 62.
96. Kahala, *A'lam al-Nissa'*, Vol. 1, pp. 274, 457; Vol. 4, p. 108. There is very little mention in the sources as regards the marriage of Muhammad's daughter Ruqayya to 'Uthman, despite the volume of detail about the Prophet's life.
97. Kahala, *A'lam al-Nissa'*, Vol. 1, p. 464.
98. Al-Tabari, *Ta'rikh*, p. 397.
99. Ibid.
100. Ibid., p. 400. Al-Tabari mentioned that, on his return to Medina following this marriage, the Prophet missed the dawn prayers on a number of occasions.
101. Ibn Hisham, *Al-Sira*, Vol. 2, pp. 210, 211.
102. *Al-Siyasa al-Kuwaitiya* (newspaper), 4 June 2011.
103. *Al-Shorouk* (newspaper), 21 October 2014.
104. *Al-Sarih* (newspaper), 9 March 2017.
105. 'Kahala, *A'lam al-Nissa'*, Vol. 2, p. 341.
106. 1 Kings 11:3.
107. Al-Tabari, *Ta'rikh*, p. 398.
108. Ibn S'ad, *Tabaqat*, Vol. 10, pp. 201–2.
109. Ibid., pp. 202–3.
110. Al-Bukhari, *Sahih al-Bukhari*, Vol. 10, p. 856.
111. Ibid., pp. 145–53.
112. Kahala, *A'lam al-Nissa'*, Vol. 3, p. 11.
113. Ibid., Vol. 1, p. 18; Vol. 2, p. 254; Vol. 3, p. 380.
114. Hekmat, *Women and the Koran*, p. 150.
115. Abu 'Amr al-Jahiz, *Al-Hayawan*, Beirut, 1990, Vol. 1, pp. 128, 129; Hekmat, *Women and the Koran*, p. 86.
116. Ibn S'ad, *Tabaqat*, Vol. 10, p. 203.
117. Al-Jahiz, *Al-Hayawan*, Vol. 1, pp. 106–19; Maxime Rodinson, *Muhammad*, London, 2002, p. 49.
118. Bou Hdeiba, *Sex in Islam*, p. 78.
119. Hekmat, *Women and the Koran*, p. 41; Ahmed, *Women and Gender*, p. 42.
120. Kahala, *A'lam al-Nissa'*, Vol. 4, p. 108.
121. Roded, *Women in Islam*, p. 33.
122. M. Montgomery Watt, *Muhammad at Medina*, London, 1956, p. 375.
123. Al-Bukhari, *Sahih al-Bukhari*, p. 955.
124. Ibid., p. 330. *Yubashir* is Arabic for to involve directly, but it is not clear exactly to what limits.

125. Abu Dawud, *Sunan*, Beirut, 1998, p. 422.
126. In the translation it mentions wives, although the word *nisa'* applies to all females.
127. Christine Schirrmacher, *Islam and Politics*, Bonn, 2008, p. 98; Bou Hdeiba, *Sex in Islam*, p. 260.
128. Schirrmacher, *Islam and Politics*, p. 98.
129. Al-Bukhari, *Sahih al-Bukhari*, p. 654.
130. Ibid., p. 460.
131. Roded, *Women in Islam*, p. 57.
132. Abu Hamid al-Ghazali, *Ihya''ulum al-Din*, Cairo, 1985, pp. 78–9.
133. Nizam al-Mulk, *Siyasat Nameh*, trans. H. Darke, London, 1978, p. 65.
134. Bernard Lewis, *The Crisis of Islam*, London, 2003, pp. 112–13. Until very recently, women could not drive cars in Saudi Arabia. Every woman must secure the permission of a male, even from her adult son, if she wants to travel abroad.
135. Lamia Shehadeh, *The Idea of Women in Fundamentalist Islam*, Gainsville, 2003, pp. 18, 84–6.
136. Kahala, *A'lam al-Nissa'*, Vol. 1, pp. 91, 304.
137. Al-Bukhari, *Sahih al-Bukhari*, p. 506. A Muslim has to fulfil the pilgrimage once in his/her life if he/she can.
138. Ibid., p. 961.
139. Kahala, *A'lam al-Nissa'*, Vol. 1, p. 452.
140. Al-Tabari, *Ta'rikh*, pp. 371–2.
141. Ibid., pp. 374–8; El Cheikh, *Women, Islam*, pp. 20–1.
142. Al-Tabari, *Ta'rikh*, pp. 378–9.
143. Ibn Hisham, *Sirat*, Vol. 2, pp. 82–3; Roded, *Women in Islam*, p. 35.
144. Ahmed, *Women and Gender*, pp. 42–3; El Cheikh, *Women, Islam*, pp. 26–7.
145. Al-Abshihi, *Al-Mustatraf fi kul fan mustazraf*, Beirut, 2016, Vol. 2, p. 245; El Cheikh, *Women, Islam*, pp. 1–2.
146. Roded, *Women in Islam*, p. 76.
147. Ibn S'ad, *Tabaqat*, Vol. 10, pp. 180–1.
148. Ibid., p. 183.
149. Ibid., p. 185.
150. Hekmat, *Women and the Koran*, p. 65.
151. Al-Mas'udi, *Muruj al-Dhahab*, Beirut, 2005, Vol. 3, p. 198.
152. Ibid.; al-Askari, *Ma'alim*, pp. 96–100.
153. Al-Tabari, *Ta'rikh*, pp. 509–10.

154. Ibid., p. 512.
155. Kahala, *A'lam al-Nissa'*, Vol. 1, pp. 18, 20–1.
156. Bou Hdeiba, *Sex in Islam*, p. 78; Ahmed, *Women and Gender*, p. 61.
157. Kahala, *A'lam al-Nissa'*, Vol. 1, p. 457.
158. Kahala, *A'lam al-Nissa'*, Vol. 3, p. 43.
159. Kahala, *A'lam al-Nissa'*, Vol. 1, p. 465; Vol. 3, p. 30.
160. Al-Tabari, *Ta'rikh*, p. 802.
161. Ibid., pp. 807–8.
162. Al-Mas'udi, *Muruj*, Vol. 2, pp. 284–5.
163. Al-Abshihi, *Al-Mustatraf*, Vol. 1, p. 122.
164. Al-Tabari, *Ta'rikh*, p. 840.
165. Denise Spellberg 'Political Action and Public Example: 'Aisha and the Battle of the Camel', in *Women in Middle Eastern History*, ed. Nikki Keddie, New Haven, 1991, pp. 45–56, 50–1; Nabia Abbott, 'Women and the State on the Eve of Islam', *The American Journal of Semitic Languages and Literatures*, Vol. 58, No. 3, July 1941, pp. 259–84, 268.
166. Kahala, *A'lam al-Nissa'*, Vol. 1, p. 73.
167. Al-Abshihi, *Al-Mustatraf*, Vol. 2, p. 143.
168. Roded, *Women in Islam*, p. 49.
169. Th. Emil Homerin, 'Living Love: The Mystical Writings of 'A'ishah al-Ba'uniyah (d. 922/1516)', *Mamluk Studies Review*, Vol. 7, 2003, pp. 211–34, 211; it was also mentioned by al-Isfahani in *Kitab al-Aghani*, Vol. 18, ed. I Abbas, p. 47, Beirut, 2008, that Dananir, a beloved singer of al-Rashid the 'Abbasid, wrote a book, but it was lost.
170. Al-Mas'udi, *Muruj*, Vol. 3, p. 58; Kahala, *A'lam al-Nissa'*, Vol. 4, p. 17.
171. Janet Johnson, 'The Legal Status of Women in Ancient Egypt', in *Mistress of the House, Mistress of Heaven: Women in Ancient Egypt*, eds Betsy M. Bryan *et al.*, New York, 1997, pp. 175–86, 177.
172. Hekmat, *Women and the Koran*, p. 95.
173. Ibid.
174. Abd al-Aziz Saleh, *Misr wa al-Iraq (Egypt and Mesopotamia in the Ancient Near East)*, Cairo, 1982, pp. 184, 293.
175. Ibid, pp. 388–9.
176. Joyce Tyldesley, *Daughters of Isis: Women of Ancient Egypt*, London, 1995, p. 66.
177. Abd al-Aziz Saleh, *Misr wa al-Iraq*, pp. 650–70.
178. Ahmed, *Women and Gender*, p. 12.

179. Ibid., p. 13.
180. Ibid., p. 14.
181. Abd al-Aziz Saleh, *Misr wa al-Iraq*, p. 683.
182. Ibid., p. 680.
183. Beatrice Brooks, 'Some Observations Concerning Ancient Mesopotamian Women', *The American Journal of Semetic Languages*, Vol. 39, No. 3, 1923, pp. 187–94, 188.
184. Ahmed, *Women and Gender*, p. 15.
185. Germaine Tillion, *The Republic of Cousins*, trans. E. Khatabi, Beirut, 2000, p. 160.
186. Ibid, pp. 192–3.
187. Ahmed, *Women and Gender*, pp. 17–18.
188. Ibid., pp. 28–9.
189. Ibid., pp. 30–3.
190. Earenfight, *Queenship*, pp. 42–5.
191. Ibid., p. 46.
192. Nabia Abbott, 'Pre-Islamic Arab Queens', *The American Journal of Semitic Languages and Literatures*, Vol. 58, No. 1, 1941, pp. 1–22, 21–2; Mark Whittow, 'The Late Roman/Early Byzantine Near East', in *The New Cambridge History of Islam*, ed. Chase Robinson, Cambridge, 2010, Vol. 1, pp. 72–97, 76–7.
193. Yasmine Zahran, *Zenobia: Between Reality and Legend*, London, 2010, pp. 18, 25.
194. Abbott, 'Pre-Islamic Arab Queens', pp. 4, 7, 8, 15.
195. Ahmed, *Women and Gender*, pp. 19, 34, 42.
196. Josef Wiesenhoffer, 'The Late Sasanian Near East', in *The New Cambridge History of Islam*, ed. C. Robinson, Cambridge, 2010, Vol. 1, pp. 98–151, 150.
197. Niels-Erik Andreasen, 'The Role of the Queen Mother in Israelite Society', *The Catholic Biblical Quarterly*, Vol. 45, No. 2, April 1983, pp. 179–94, 180–2.

1

The Umayyad Empire and the Establishment of a Royal Court, 661–750

When the Umayyad caliph al-Walid b. Yazid [al-Walid II] (r. 743–4) came to power, he was in pursuit of drinking, singing and hunting. He brought many singers from Medina to him in Damascus.

One day when he was in a bad state of drunkenness, and had just finished copulating with Nawwar, a concubine of his, the caller of the dawn prayer came to him asking permission to call the prayer. Al-Walid swore that no one would lead the Muslims as an imam except for his concubine, Nawwar. In shock, and after a moment's silence and hesitation, she veiled her face and prayed as an imam for all the men of the palace [the concubine was under the influence of drink, and was *junub* (unwashed) after having copulated, when she performed the prayer].[1]

This anecdote reflects the decadence of the Umayyads. It also reflects a major shift in lifestyle from the age of the rightly guided caliphs and it paved the way for the 'Abbasid realm of pleasure after them.

Despite the extreme modesty of the military, cultural and political tradition associated with the early Arab Muslims, in particular those of Western Arabia, we find extraordinary military successes with the early Arab conquests from Western Iran to Egypt under the rightly guided caliphs. That led to a change in the Arab modesty culture in the Hijaz, where the capital Medina is located. Many elite men, including close companions of the Prophet, such as al-Zubayr b. al-'Awwam (d. 656), the son-in-law of the first caliph, owned 500 concubines as a result of their enslavement through conquest.[2]

When the Umayyads came to power, they eagerly abandoned the Arabian desert, and made Damascus, the heart of Syriac-Byzantine culture, their capital. The Umayyads' swift military expansion was a phenomenal success, mainly on land, but also in the Eastern Mediterranean Sea. By the year 711 they had reached the pinnacle of their military–political expansion, which no other Islamic dynasty could even attempt to follow. In that year the Umayyad armies seized the Iberian territories in Western Europe and, at the same time, seized the Sind Valley in present-day Pakistan. This led to an enormous number of female and male slaves being taken (as the Qur'an states: 'what your right hand possesses'), in accordance with the practice of the Prophet, as set out in the Introduction. The institution of slaves and their various categories opened the way for a luxurious lifestyle in the newly formed Umayyad court, especially after Mu'awiya ruled that inheritance would be passed from father to son.

The Umayyad aristocracy also imitated the pattern of life led by their rulers. That model of political rule continued in practice under almost all Muslim dynasties until the early twentieth century. The huge Umayyad expansion would lead to a vital question: what kind of Islam did we have then? Did we have an Arab tribal tradition galvanised by some Muslim beliefs introduced through the conquests as the new faith? The Umayyads lacked any mechanism to introduce the message of the new faith, especially as regards education. They did not translate the Qur'an into the main written languages of the newly invaded territories, such as Persian, Coptic and Greek. In fact, no Muslim power took on this task, and it was only carried out by the French during the Crusades in the twelfth century. In addition, they did not put any effort into making copies of the Qur'an available in the conquered territories for those who could read Arabic and wanted to know about the new religion. The early Arab Muslims in their humble numbers might have started to Islamicise and Arabise the countries they invaded in a modest tedious pace over centuries, but they were under much superior cultural influence from those countries – Persia, Iraq, Byzantine Syria and Coptic Egypt – that the Arabs had proudly emulated.

The Umayyad expansion resulted in the enslavement of a very large number of men and women who had submitted to the authority of the new Arab rulers, creating an embryo of slave realm (within which there were different categories), which led to further expansion and developments after the eighth century, mainly under the 'Abbasids. It is appropriate here to give a definition of the main categories of slaves of both genders, which are relative to the period of study, and used throughout this book.

1. Categories of female slaves
- *jariya* (lit. runner for service (pl. *jawari*)): the most commonly used term for an enslaved female, brought to Muslim lands through captivity in warfare and from slave markets.[3] The owner, a man or a woman, of this type would use her in domestic labour. A man owner could copulate with her and offer her to other men for sexual pleasure. The *jariya* could be sold or inherited as a chattel, or freed upon her owner's wishes. Other synonyms of *jariya* in the sources are *ama* and *khadima*.
- *um walad* (lit. mother of a son) was a *jariya* who gave birth to a child by her master. With this new status she could not be sold and would remain a slave under her master's authority.[4] Most caliphs' mothers, especially under the 'Abbasids, were from this category – of the thirty-eight 'Abbasid caliphs in Iraq, only al-Saffah and al-Amin were born to free woman (*hurra* (pl. *hara'ir*)), with the remaining thirty-six caliphs having *um walad* mothers.[5]
- *mahziyya* (concubine (pl. *hazaya* or *mahziyyat*)): a female slave owned especially for sexual pleasure and who could not be shared with another man, unlike the *jariya*.[6] The price for a *mahziyya* could reach hundreds of thousands of dirhams. She played a major role as a foe to the wife of the master.
- *qina* (pl. *qiyan*): a female slave who was a musician and a singer, or sometimes a poetess.[7] They could reach very high prices, and could become concubines. They appeared in small numbers with the Umayyad dynasty.
- *qahramana* (stewardess, Persian for 'strong'/'keeper'):[8] this term applied to a female slave who supervised some of the financial affairs within the caliph's palace. Moreover, she was in charge of the domestic section of the caliph's sleeping quarters.[9] Her position in the palace, close to decision-making circles, enabled her to influence political affairs in many cases. The *qahramana* appeared with the Abbasid dynasty. Very few of them were free women.

2. Categories of male slaves
- *khadim* (pl. *khadam*): a male slave used in domestic service. This term had been used since pre-Islamic times and continued to be used throughout different Islamic ages.
- *mawla*: synonym of *khadim*, which some sources use, in addition to *'abd*.
- *ghulam* (pl. *ghulman*): a servant for civil services; the term was used from the tenth century under the 'Abbasids, and also applied to those in the military.
- *ghulam amrad*: a pre-pubescent boy (*amrad* means 'without a beard'). They are mentioned in the Qur'an as servants in paradise, as previously mentioned. It is important to note that the word *ghulumiyya*, derived from *ghulam*, means 'libido' or 'sexual urge' in Arabic.[10]
- *mamluk* (pl. *mamalik*): a person owned by his master. *Mamluks* appeared mainly in the ninth century under the 'Abbasids, and the term was applied mainly to military slaves.
- *khasiyy* (pl. *khisyan*): a eunuch. Eunuchs were introduced into domestic service in small numbers under the Umayyads. Under the 'Abbasids they were used to serve the harem section, but soon were also used in the military. From the tenth century onwards, they were elevated to vice-sultan, commanders of the armies and even de facto rulers of kingdoms. This type of eunuch had their testicles removed (castrated), but were still capable of copulation, and they could own concubines.[11] From the tenth century, medieval sources referred to them by other terms like *khadim*, *shaikh*, *ustadh* and *tawashi* (Turkish for 'servant').[12]
- *majbub*: a eunuch who was not only castrated, but had his entire sexual organ removed. This type of eunuch was mostly used in domestic service in the harem section of the palace.[13]
- *atabeg*: a Turkish word – '*ata*' meaning 'father', and '*beg*' meaning 'military emir' or 'prince'. They were introduced by the Seljuqs into the Islamic administration as tutors and regents for future kings. They developed by establishing their own dynasties, such as Tughtekin in Damascus (r. 1104–28), or Zengi in Mosul and northern Syria (r. 1127–46); Saladin (d. 1193) also claimed this title early in his early career.[14] Some Ayyubid *atabeg*s, among others, were eunuchs, and the post underwent several developments, namely that the *atabeg* was originally appointed from

mamluk military circles, but later some of them were from among the freemen.

All of the above were slaves under Islamic law, which sanctioned slavery. The *jariya* and *khadim*, concubine and *qina*, *ghulam* and *khasiyy* could be bought, hired or sold, or inherited like chattels. Under Islam, children of slave fathers and mothers are slaves as well, while children of a slave mother and a free father is a free person. Having said that, the latter are considered less equal, or inferior, such as the co-founder of the 'Abbasid dynasty, al-Mansur (d. 775). His mother was an *um walad*, so she could not be sold. Thirty-six of the thirty-eight 'Abbasid caliphs in Iraq had *um walad* mothers, and this was replicated in the other dynasties in Islamic history.

The history of the Umayyads was written during the period of their rivals, the 'Abbasids, who had toppled them. From the seventh century to the tenth, religious and legal works established what would be considered orthodox Islam. Unfortunately, not a single woman wrote, dictated or asked for her story to be told, and so we are fully dependent on and held hostage to the male Muslim historians' perspectives of women. The early generation of chroniclers included al-Jahiz (d. 868), who wrote *Al-Taj fi akhlaq al-Muluk* (*The Crown in the Manners of Kings*), Ahmad b. Taifur (d. 893), who wrote *Balaghat al-Nisa'* (*Eloquences of Women*) and the famous Abu al-Faraj al-Isfahani (d. 967), who wrote *Kitab al-Aghani* (*Book of Songs*).[15] These works furnish us with a great wealth of orality and poetry attributed to women in various situations, including erotic/sexual contributions on heterosexuality, and homosexuality, too. The history of al-Tabari contains several stories of the first two books mentioned here.

The second category of books consists of biographies of women, written by twelfth–thirteenth-century chroniclers. For example, Ibn 'Asakir of Damascus (d. 1176) wrote 196 biographies, ranging from Sara, wife of Abraham, to Zumurrud Khatun, the Seljuqid princess of Damascus, with clear evidence of biblical influence. He was proud that he was licensed to teach Hadith (*ijaza*) by tens of women in his time, but he did not give details of them, and how he received these teachings. As the madrasa, introduced in Damascus in 1097 under the Seljuqs, was for male education only, we have to wonder where Ibn 'Asakir met these women. The second example is

Ibn al-Sa'i (d. 1217), who wrote *Nisa' al-Khulafa'* (*Women of the Caliphs*). This Iraqi historian ignored the Umayyad women, seeing no role for them, and started his work with the 'Abbasid royal wives and concubines. There was also the grand Hanbali conservative scholar, Ibn Qayyim al-Jawziyya (d. 1350), who, despite his fame in the field of religious studies, wrote *Akhbar al-Nisa'* (*Stories of Women*). The book contains stories from pre-Islamic to post-Umayyad times, with a focus on poetry and the eroticism of both genders.[16] Both categories of work provide a wealth of information, yet we wonder about their rationality and methodology. Many events mentioned appear to be fiction rather than reality. Who documented these intimate details, and to what extent were they exaggerated?

Royal Women under the Umayyads

The only queen who existed in Islamic history during the Umayyad dynasty was the non-Muslim Dihya (also known as Kahina) of Berber North Africa in the Aures area, as will be covered later. In order to protect their own interests, royal women during the short reign of the Umayyads began gradually to interfere in political affairs.

After the assassination of Caliph 'Ali in 661, his son, al-Hasan, was nominated as the new caliph in Iraq, but his reign only lasted for six months. Mu'awiya in Syria had refused to accept al-Hasan's rule and lured him to relinquish his power in return for a substantial financial reward. Al-Hasan agreed to the deal and signed his abdication in the Kufa mosque; Mu'awiya was declared the new Umayyad caliph.[17] Mu'awiya wanted to ensure that al-Hasan would not go back on his word, especially under pressure from the Shi'a, who remained supportive of their imam. Mu'awiya contacted al-Hasan's wife, Ja'da bt. al-Ash'ath, and offered her 100,000 dirhams and marriage to Yazid b. Mu'awiya if she poisoned al-Hasan. Ja'da, tempted by this offer, agreed and poisoned her husband, who died as a result. Mu'awiya did fulfil his financial promise to her, but he ignored the marriage part. He told her in a letter: 'We would like Yazid to live.'[18] This act by Ja'da had eliminated a major political rival to the Umayyad caliph, and it contributed to the stability of his rule.

Another woman who contributed to the hereditary rule of the Umayyads and gave the dynasty a consolidated legitimacy was 'Aisha, wife of the Prophet and mother of the believers. In the year 675 Muʿawiya decided to make his son Yazid his successor, thereby creating the first political dynasty in Islam. To ensure that Yazid would not be challenged in the way that ʿAli had been, Muʿawiya travelled to the Hijaz to see ʿAisha. He asked her to give the *bayʿa* (oath of allegiance) to Yazid; she did not object to this request.[19] ʿAisha's stance here was essential for political legitimacy, not only to an individual ruler but to a new shift in political Islamic rule. Her seal of approval was essential for the Umayyads, so as not to repeat the scenario of ʿAli.

Political–tribal marriage was common under the Umayyads. One of the most influential wives of Muʿawiya was Maysun bt. Bahdal of the Yamani tribe. When Yazid was declared heir to his father, Maysun's tribe played a key role in support for their candidate, pushed by the royal mother. Not only that, she influenced her husband, the caliph, in the appointment of her brother Hasan as a governor of one of the Muslim provinces, despite his questionable administrative qualities. We see a poet criticise this corrupt caliphal policy, and assert that the power was only granted due to Maysun's political weight.

> If Hasan became a powerful governor
> That is due to Maysun not his father
> It is only because of her son [Yazid]
> That you remained a governor.[20]

The Umayyad dynasty was shaken by the murder of al-Husain b. ʿAli in the mayhem of Karabalaʾ in Iraq in 680, during the first year of Yazid's caliphate. Al-Husain believed that he deserved the caliphate more than Yazid, but the latter's army killed and decapitated him, sending his head to Damascus. Many of his sisters were taken as prisoners to the Umayyad capital.[21] To contain the negative effects and repercussions of this massacre, Um Kulthum, one of Yazid's wives, took responsibility of orchestrating an official mourning ceremony in the Umayyad court to deflect any accusations as to Yazid's role in the catastrophe; other Umayyad royal women joined her in this ceremony.[22]

A thorny topic in medieval Islam relates to the daughters of ʿAli who survived Karbalaʾ being taken as war captives to Caliph Yazid in Damascus. Among them were Zaynab, the eldest of ʿAli's daughters, and her younger sister, Fatima. When they were paraded before the caliph, one of Yazid's companions requested to have Fatima, daughter of al-Husain, as a concubine. Zaynab publicly challenged the caliph, accusing him of taking the granddaughters of the Prophet as *sabaya*, as though they were non-Muslims; not only that, but she claimed that such a deed would make him a non-Muslim, and said to him: 'You are the enemy of Allah.'[23] Yazid responded by insinuating that her father and brother were the apostates. The Shi'i followers have glorified the courageous political stance of Zaynab, exaggerating the fiery confrontation between the war prisoner and the caliph.[24] In addition to her prestigious ancestry, and her political stance against Yazid, Zaynab's mausoleum in Cairo, which became a shrine, witnesses a great annual celebration on her birthday, and is visited by several million people from all over Egypt.[25]

Perhaps one of the rarest cases of the intervention of Umayyad royal wives in political affairs was the case of Fakhita, wife of Yazid. She was ambitious enough to suggest to Yazid to declare their son, Mu'awiya II (d. 684), as *wali al-'ahd* (heir apparent). After Yazid had consulted his uncle Hasan on the matter, he agreed. Al-Baladhuri mentions that Fakhita continued to interfere in politics. She would consult with her son when he ascended the caliphate, and when he wanted to leave his post, she castigated him harshly. Moreover, when Mu'awiya II was adamant that he should be caliph, she strongly suggested to him that his brother Khalid should be the new ruler.[26] When Mu'awiya died mysteriously after only a few weeks in office, we find that the chief of the Marwanid branch of the Umayyads, Marwan b. al-Hakam, marries Fakhita on the condition that he will act as a regent for her son Khalid, and will install him as *wali al-'ahd*.

Marwan did not fulfil his promise and instead installed two of his sons, 'Abd al-Malik, and then 'Abd al-'Aziz, as heirs. We should take into consideration that at this time there was a revolution against the Umayyads in the Hijaz and in other parts of the state, led by 'Abd Allah b. al-Zubayr. Fakhita did not hesitate to kill her husband, the caliph Marwan, when he slept in her section of the palace, by suffocating him with a pillow over his face, aided by some of her trusted *jawari*.[27] Here we see an ambitious royal wife who manoeuvered to install her favoured political candidates in power, and was given legitimacy as a widow of the caliph by her political marriage to Marwan. She did not hesitate to end his life after nearly ten months as caliph.

The Umayyad dynasty did not see another example like Fakhita, but after Marwan, the sources start to refer to a certain wife of the caliph as *um al-Banin* (mother of the sons). What we do understand is that the woman with this particular status became more powerful in the hierarchy of the Umayyad palace, surpassing any other woman and concubine. Such a title became more common than the woman's birth name, and we can see many examples where the chronicles have ignored the original name. For example, there was Um al-Banin, whose name was 'Aatika, wife of the powerful 'Abd al-Malik b. Marwan (d. 705). She was referred to by name in the sources because she was the granddaughter of Mu'awiya I.[28] Another example is Um al-Banin, wife of al-Walid b. 'Abd al-Malik (d. 715); he had married sixty-three wives in his ten years in office.[29] It is believed that this term applied to free Umayyad women from prestigious descent and it was their sons who were groomed for future caliphate. Although they had no political rules, these women enjoyed some liberty in meeting with men of governance, and their harsh opinions and manners were tolerated. Um al-Banin, wife of al-Walid, asked her husband to meet al-Hajjaj, the Umayyad governor of Iraq and Iran, and friend of the caliph. The reason for this request was that one of her *jawari* had reported to her how al-Hajjaj, while meeting the caliph, would say: 'Women are just for pleasure, and not to be trusted with a secret or to be consulted about affairs of the state.' Um al-Banin, dismayed by what she heard, deliberately made al-Hajjaj wait for a long time outside her door to see her. When he was admitted, she told him in a cynical way: 'The caliph will not take your opinion about his women seriously. You are the most trivial person living, and this is why God has chosen you to destroy the Ka'ba [during the revolt of Ibn al-Zubayr], and kill the grandson of caliph Abu Bakr.' Then she ordered one of her *jawari* to dismiss him.[30]

In addition to having the liberty of stating her personal political opinions directly to an Umayyad politician, al-Isfahani accuses her of having a degree of sexual liberty. He mentions that she committed adultery in Mecca with a poet named Waddah, to whom she was attracted. When the caliph found out about this affair, he buried Waddah alive, but he did not punish her.[31]

Umayyad royal women also enjoyed some financial independence, and could own property. 'Atika, wife of Caliph 'Abd al-Malik, was free to declare her will according to her own free wishes. She owned land to the south of

Damascus and had a palace there, where her husband died.[32] Um al-Banin, wife of Caliph al-Walid, owned two houses in Damascus.[33] It seems that some of the houses of these women were used for charitable purposes; for example, Fatima, wife of Caliph 'Umar b. 'Abd al-'Aziz (d. 720) had a house in Damascus dedicated to helping the blind.[34] We cannot say that this was a phenomenon in Umayyad Syria, as there was also female ownership of property and patronage of charitable buildings in Umayyad Spain from 756 to 1031.[35] The real phenomenon was the rise and expansion of little desert palaces for caliphs, dotted mainly around the Syrian desert.

While the Arab–Muslim side did not have or produce a queen or de facto female ruler during the Umayyad reign, there was an enigmatic Christian or Jewish Berber queen of North Africa, Dihya (better known as Kahina, 'the Sorceress'). She led all the Berber tribes of the Aures in several military campaigns in response to Umayyad invasions of her lands, especially from 695 to 700. Her legendary resistance and command of the Berbers meant that the Umayyads could not take control of North Africa until she herself was killed in battle: 'The Kahina, queen of the Berbers defended all of North Africa, and defeated the Arab commander Hasan.'[36] It is important that the perspective of Muslim medieval chronicles of her was positive, and that she was referred to as *al-malika* (queen); they spoke highly of her courage in defending her land and her wisdom in leading a huge number of male troops.[37] There is no mention in the sources as to how or why the Berbers allowed a woman to rule, but at the same time, her success did not persuade Muslims to follow this example (see Figure 1 – the statue of Kahina, which stands in Algeria today, commemorating her legacy).

Royal Concubines and their Influence: Realm of Desire

> Caliphs Mu'awiya, Marwan, 'Abd al-Malik, al-Walid I, Sulayman and Hisham would listen to music separated by a curtain from their *nudama'* (drinking companions). The companions would not be able to see what the caliphs were doing, such as the different movements when they were raptured by singing, shaking and dancing to music, or taking off some of their robes. Only their very intimate *jawari* would be able to see that. The rest of the Umayyad caliphs did not avoid dancing and getting naked in the presence of their companions and singers. Caliph Yazid II and his son

al-Walid II had their own extravagant style; they would shamelessly dance and get naked, paying no attention to their jesting deeds in front of others.³⁸

We might not believe all the details in this anecdote told to al-Jahiz by the grand Persian/Iraqi musician Ishaq al-Mosuli (d. 850), who was a very close companion to four 'Abbasid caliphs, and involved in entertainment circles. Yet, it reflects the inner surroundings of the Umayyad palace. The Umayyad rulers continued to have concubines for pleasure, just as the Prophet and his companions had; the major difference is the large numbers of them, and the exaggerated prices they paid to buy them, sometimes reaching thousands of dinars. That led to the creation of a body or institution for them, especially with the large number of palaces built by different caliphs in Syria, Jordan and Palestine, mainly for pleasure.

The most significant development with the Umayyad concubines was the start of their interference in political–administrative affairs of the state, taking advantage of the caliph's infatuation with some of them. This began with the pioneer of Arabisation and builder of several iconic buildings in the empire, Caliph 'Abd al-Malik b. Marwan. He would have more than one concubine attending his council with his advisors. These concubines acted as domestic aids to the caliph, but were well aware of the state's secrets.³⁹

Under the caliphate of his son, Yazid II, one concubine, Habbaba, took matters further towards clear intervention in politics. She was a slave of non-Arab origin, and was taught to sing and play music in Medina, a renowned centre for the profession. She was brought to Yazid by his wife S'ada, after she realised that her husband was fascinated by this *qina* and concubine. (The caliph had seen her on a previous trip to the Hijaz; 4,000 dinars was her price.)⁴⁰ Habbaba's influence on the caliph was immense, to the extent that he delegated to her some of his powers, including hearing the complaints of members of the public. This role developed and she dismissed the assistant appointed by the caliph to aid her. The caliph was castigated by his brother Musallama, who thought that the concubine had occupied Yazid's seat for too long and that the complaints of the locals were being neglected by the caliph.⁴¹

Habbaba's influence grew, and she was able to install certain men as governors to the Umayyad provinces. For example, she managed to appoint

'Umar al-Fazzari as governor of Iraq. On other occasions, she was in direct contact with the governor of Medina without consulting the caliph. When Yazid found out about that, he did not blame or punish her.[42]

Like his father, Caliph al-Walid owned a large number of concubines, many of whom were *qiyan*. In his almost one year in power, none of them was empowered to influence political affairs. However, as quoted above, one of his favourite concubines, Nawwar, once led the men of the Umayyad palace for the dawn prayer, upon the strict orders of al-Walid. The caliph was drunk, and so Nawwar had to dress as a man and mask her face for this unusual task; although she could not mask her voice, she managed to complete the job, according to al-Isfahani.[43] The world authority on Islamic art, Robert Hillenbrand, has described this caliph's age: 'In response to the increasingly extravagant ambitions of the playboy caliph al-Walid II, greatly enlarged multi-functional palaces were built.'[44] Hillenbrand speaks of several Umayyad palaces that were built in the Syrian desert and around the Jericho valley, starting in the late seventh century, such as Qusayr 'Amra in Jordan, for example, which has wall paintings of (naked) human figures celebrating the pleasures of wine, women, song and dance (see Figures 2 and 3).[45] These little palaces were built away from the locals' eyes, to accommodate the craving behaviour of many caliphs, among other reasons.

It was a humble beginning for the royal concubines under the Umayyads. The main differences between their time and that of the concubines of the Prophet or Caliph 'Ali was their large numbers and association with music and widescale entertainment and flagrant behaviour. Although the exception was their interference in politics, they had no noticeable influence on social life, unlike their counterparts, the Umayyad concubines in Spain, who played a significant role in the patronage of architecture, mainly in the ninth–tenth centuries[46] (a topic that would benefit from further study). Eunuchs and their rise to power influenced power relations. The same was experienced in Muslim Spain, which was contemporary to the 'Abbasids.

The Umayyad Eunuchs and the Establishment of their Institutions

> One day, Caliph Mu'awiya I visited his wife Fakhita in her chamber, with a *khasiyy* (eunuch) in his company. Fakhita had no cover on her head, so when she was surprised by the presence of the eunuch, she hurried to cover

her head. Muʿawiya said: 'He is only a eunuch.' She replied: 'Did God allow him what was forbidden for the others?' Muʿawiya was convinced by her opinion, and from then onwards stopped eunuchs from entering his wives' section, even if they were old and time-worn.[47]

Eunuchs were used in the Umayyad dynasty from the first to the last caliph in different numbers and capacities. We know that the Prophet had owned one eunuch, although we do not know if he was a castrated eunuch or a *majbub* (the difference is significant as the first type is still capable of copulation, as will be analysed later). The chronicles do not mention any use of them under the four caliphs succeeding the Prophet.

With the huge military expansion under the Umayyads, and the formation of a large empire, we find that the number of female slaves and concubines grew quickly, forming the harem in the Umayyad palaces and many other houses of the aristocracy and upper classes. Consequent to that came the need to employ eunuchs, the third gender, permitted to service the areas of the palaces where no foreign males were allowed. Eunuchs were also the keepers of the keys to the harem 'cage'. The phenomenon of eunuchs was known in other civilisations before Islam. The Assyrians, Chinese, Persians, Romans and Byzantines used them, especially in the harem.[48] In these civilisations they were natives, not outsiders.

Under Islam, eunuchs were also employed for several other purposes, especially with the trend of polygamy and the inflated numbers of female slaves for the rulers or the aristocracy. Eunuchs enjoyed full freedom to move around different sections of the palace, unlike the sons of the ruler or the emir, who had different mothers and were prohibited after a certain age to enter the harem; but eunuchs were allowed.[49]

Although castration was forbidden in Islam, as the Prophet rejected the concept of resisting desire, as already mentioned, it was not prohibited to own one or more eunuchs. The act of castration was carried out mainly in early Islamic history in Spain and Byzantium from where white eunuchs were imported, and also in Abyssinia and Takrur, Africa, from where black eunuchs were bought.[50] This savage, inhumane practice was not condemned by Muslim laws at any age or time, which is surprising, given that it was an act of alteration to God's creation; the Qur'an had emphasised that the human being was created to best stature (mould) (Q. 95:4). The Prophet's approval of female genital cutting, as mentioned earlier, may be compared here as approval to mutilate the human body permanently, resulting in dire psycho-physical consequences. In the tenth century we start to see that euphemisms were applied to eunuchs in the chronicles. In Arabic, they were called *khadim* (servant), *mu'allim* (instructor), *shaikh* (teacher/chief) and *tawashi* (servant); in Turkish, *khodja* (teacher), *agha* (master); and in Persian, *khawadja* (teacher/lord), *agha* (master). Muslim Spain used different terminology, such as *fata* (youth) and (*ghulam*).[51] It is sometimes confusing and open to different interpretation when these terms are used interchangeably, according to the context.

We can confidently say from the information about Mu'awiya mentioned above that there was a body of eunuchs used by the caliph to serve in the Umayyad palaces. How large was that body? In what capacity did these eunuchs serve – domestic service, bodyguards or otherwise? These questions remain unanswered.

David Ayalon mentions that Mu'awiya, in the year 656 while he was a governor of Syria, had threatened the Arab tribes of Mudar (on the lower Euphrates) by dispatching an army to fight them, which included 4,000 eunuchs. Ayalon himself states that not only were the numbers exaggerated, but also that it is not known if eunuchs were used in the army at that point in the newly formed Arab state.[52] However, we do understand that Mu'awiya may have employed eunuchs as early as this time, probably influenced by the Syro-Byzantine tradition.

The role of eunuchs progressed significantly; for example, Caliph 'Abd al-Malik used them as *hajib* (chamberlains).[53] That was an important position to be given or entrusted to a eunuch, who had the power to admit or deny access to the caliph for the majority of the members of the administration. At the same time, the Umayyad custom of using eunuchs as a medium between the male and female sections of the palace continued. Sometimes they were the eyes of the caliph as regards a certain concubine, with whom the caliph may be fascinated, or they were employed as messengers between the two sides of the palace.[54] Other Umayyad governors followed the pattern of their caliphs in the use of eunuchs. One example is Ibn Qutn, the governor of Andalusia in 733; he owned some 700 female slaves and a number of eunuchs.⁵⁵ Clearly, the larger the harem became, the more eunuchs were employed for their service and protection.

There is a well-known anecdote that is often repeated in the chronicles, about Caliph Sulayman, who ordered his governor in Medina to 'ahsi' or calculate the number of transsexuals in the city, after he had been informed that the best singers were the transsexuals of Medina. For some reason, in the message to the governor a dot had been added to the letter *ha*, to become *kha*, readable as 'akhsi', meaning 'to castrate'; as a result of this unfortunate error, nine transsexuals were castrated. In another story, it is mentioned that Caliph al-Walid I was annoyed by the poor manners of a certain transsexual in Medina named al-Dallal, who moved freely into women's houses, so he ordered his castration. There is also a case of a full male castration that took place under Caliph Hisham, who was angered by a singing guard in the palace, and so he ordered his castration.⁵⁶ Perhaps the most interesting aspect here is that castration could be carried out in Medina, the second most holy place in the Muslim lands, or in Damascus, within the Muslim lands. Later dynasties, such as the Zengid dynasty, carried out castrations on military commanders as a punishment.

At the very end of Umayyad rule, we see new developments in the use of eunuchs, with a certain eunuch who was in the company of the harem of the last caliph, Marwan II (d. 750). Marwan and his royal women tried to escape to Egypt from the 'Abbasid army; however, the Abbasids managed to kill Marwan. When the 'Abbasid forces stormed the church where the female royals were hiding, a eunuch bodyguard tried to kill the Umayyad royal women. He was stopped by the forces, and asked why. He said: 'Marwan ordered that if he was killed, I should decapitate his daughters and the rest of his women.'⁵⁷ Clearly, Marwan wanted to avoid his daughters being taken captive by his enemies, and entrusted this gruesome task to a eunuch, who should show extreme loyalty to his master. It also seems that the Umayyads quickly imitated the Byzantine pattern of using eunuchs in the military. Muslim chronicles tell us of many Byzantine senior commanders who were used against the Arabs, including Manuel the eunuch who, in 645, led the attack on Alexandria;⁵⁸ the chronicles do not indicate that using a eunuch as a commander was an abnormal practice.

Finally, on trust and employing Umayyad eunuchs in the immediate circles around the caliph, we see that the last Umayyads entrusted a eunuch with keeping the caliphal insignia, as well as the Prophet's mantle and stick passed down to the Umayyads. This insignia was used by the caliph as a sign of royalty and supreme authority.[59] No state document was considered authentic without it. That of course shows how eunuchs were now holding significant administrative and military posts. They were more preferable in service as they had no children, and thus no heirs or political ambitions, as was perceived then. That situation would change gradually and entirely under the 'Abbasid dynasty, as we will see in the following chapter.

Notes

1. Al-Isfahani, *Kitab al-Aghani*, Vol. 7, p. 38; Ibn 'Asakir, *Tarikh Madinat Dimashq: Tarajim al-Nisa'*, ed. S. al-Shihabi, Damascus, 1981, pp. 411–12.
2. Al-Mas'udi, *Muruj*, Vol. 2, p. 284.
3. Ahmad Ateyya, *Al-Qamus al-Islami*, Cairo, 1972, p. 541.
4. Bou Hdeiba, *Sex in Islam*, p. 161.
5. Jalal al-Suyuti, *Ta'rikh al-Khulafa'*, Beirut, 1997.
6. Ibn al-Sa'i, *Nisa' al-Khulafa'*, ed. M. Jawad, Beirut, 2011, p. 64.
7. Caswell, *The Slave Girls*, pp. 1–2.
8. 'Abd al-Na'im Hasanain, *Persian–Arabic Dictionary*, Cairo, 1982, p. 520.
9. 'Abd al'Aziz al-Duri, *Al-'Asr al-'Abbasi al-Awwal*, Beirut 1998, p. 70.
10. Al-Isfahani, *Al-Aghani*, Vol. 4, p. 192; Elias A. Elias, *Arabic–English Dictionary*, Cairo, 1994, p. 483.
11. Al-Jahiz, *Al-Hayawan*, Vol. 1, pp. 115–20.
12. Ch. Pellat, art.: 'Khasi', *EI²*.
13. Ibid.
14. Taef el-Azhari, art. 'Atabeg', *The Crusades: An Encyclopedia*, ed. Alan Murray, Santa Barbara, 2006, Vol. 1, pp. 116–17.
15. Abu 'Amr Al-Jahiz, *Al-Taj fi akhbar al-Muluk*, ed. A. Zaki, Cairo, 1914; Ahmad b. Taifur, *Balaghat al-Nisa'*, Tehran, 1997.
16. Ibn 'Asakir, *Tarajim*; Ibn al-Sa'i, *Nisa' al-Khulafa'*, ed. M. Jawad, Beirut, 2011; Ibn Qayyim al-Jawziyya, *Akhbar al-Nisa'*, Beirut 1998.
17. Al-Tabari, *Ta'rikh*, pp. 900–1.
18. Al-Mas'udi, *Muruj*, Vol. 3, p. 6.
19. Kahala, *A'lam al-Nissa'*, Vol. 3, p. 65. We do not know when 'Aisha died precisely, but estimate that it was in about 678. This lack of accuracy demonstrates

how complicated the history of women was in Muslim chronicles, even a grand woman such as 'Aisha.
20. Al-Baladhuri, *Futuh al-Bildan*, Cairo, 1965, Vol. 5. p. 157.
21. Al-Tabari, *Ta'rikh*, pp. 994–5.
22. Ibn 'Asakir, *Tarajim*, pp. 438–45.
23. Taifur, *Balaghat*, pp. 34–5.
24. Al-'Askari, *Ma'alim*, pp. 454–5.
25. In addition to the Zaynab mausoleum, there have been other Shi'i shrines built for leading females, like the wives and daughters of Shi'i imams such as Nafisa, Ruqayya and Sakina, who all had an immense spiritual influence over ordinary Sunni Muslims in Egypt, especially the Sufis.
26. Al-Baladhuri, *Futuh*, Vol. 5, p. 383.
27. Ibid., Vol. 6, pp. 275–80; al-Tabari, *Ta'rikh*, pp. 1,069–70.
28. Ibn 'Asakir, *Tarajim*, p. 203.
29. Taifur, *Balaghat*, p. 191.
30. Ibid., pp. 172–3.
31. Al-Isfahani, *Kitab al-Aghani*, Vol. 6, p. 312; see also al-Tha'alibi, *Thimar al-Qulub*, Beirut, 1993, p. 96.
32. Ibn 'Asakir, *Tarajim*, p. 203.
33. Yaqut al-Hamawi, *Mu'jam al-Buldan*, Beirut, 1989, Vol. 4, p. 242.
34. Ibn 'Asakir, *Tarajim*, p. 290.
35. Glaire D. Anderson, 'Concubines, Eunuchs and Patronage in Early Islamic Cordoba', in *Reassessing the Role of Women as Makers of Medieval Art and Architecture*, ed. T. Martin, Leiden, 2012, Vol. 2, pp. 633–70, 664.
36. Eduardo Moreno, 'The Iberian Peninsula and North Africa', in *The New Cambridge History of Islam*, ed. C. Robinson, Cambridge, 2010, Vol. 1, pp. 581–622, 590–1. Ibn 'Abd al-Hakam, *Futuh Misr wa al-Maghrib*, Cairo, 1961, Vol. 1, p. 270.
37. Ibn 'Adhara al-Marakishi, *Al-Bayan al-Mughrib*, ed. L. Provencal, Beirut, 2009, Vol. 1, pp. 30–9; Ibn Khaldun, *Al-'Ibar*, Vol. 1, Amman, 2003, p. 1,604.
38. Al-Jahiz, *Al-Taj*, p. 30; al-Isfahani in his *Al-Aghani*, Vol. 7, pp. 5–64, details similar stories about the self-indulgent and fancy lifestyle of al-Walid II.
39. Abu 'Amr al-Jahiz, *Rasa'il*, Cairo, 1996, Vol. 1, p. 160.
40. Al-Isfahani, *Kitab al-Aghani*, Vol. 15, pp. 98–9.
41. Ibid., p. 100.
42. Al-Baladhuri, *Futuh*, Vol. 8, pp. 270–4.

43. Al-Isfahani, *Kitab al-Aghani*, Vol. 7, p. 38. Interestingly, in Berlin in June 2017 a female imam named Siran Atish prayed in the Ibn Rushd-Gut Mosque, leading men and women together in the same line, without any segregation. Women had their hair uncovered. Available at: <http://www.Almasryalyoum.com>, 27 June 2017 (last accessed 16 September 2018). This daring move was negatively received by al-Azhar in Egypt, among other conservative Muslim institutions.
44. Robert Hillenbrand, *Islamic Art and Architecture*, London, 1999, p. 32.
45. Ibid., pp. 30, 32.
46. Anderson, 'Concubines', pp. 665–6.
47. Al-Masudi, *Muruj*, Vol. 3, p. 177.
48. David Ayalon, *Outsiders in the Land of Islam: Mamluks, Mongols and Eunuchs* (Variorum Reprints), London, 1988, p. 68; Pellat, 'Khasi'.
49. Pellat, 'Khasi'.
50. Bernard Lewis, *Race and Slavery in the Middle East: An Historical Enquiry*, Oxford, 2014, p. 14.
51. Pellat, 'Khasi'.
52. Ayalon, *Eunuchs*, p. 66.
53. Kahala, *A'lam al*-Nissa', Vol. 3, pp. 216–17.
54. Al-Isfahani, *Kitab al-Aghani*, Vol. 9, p. 105.
55. Ayalon, *Eunuchs*, p. 68.
56. Al-Isfahani, *Kitab al-Aghani*, Vol. 4, pp. 194–5.
57. Al-Masudi, *Muruj*, Vol. 3, p. 206.
58. Ibn 'Abd al-Hakim, *Futuh*, Vol. 1, p. 237.
59. Al-Masudi, *Muruj*, Vol. 3, p. 206; Ibn al-Athir, *Al-Kamil fi al-Tarikh*, Beirut, 1982, Vol. 5, pp. 430–1.

2

Princesses, Concubines and *Qahramanat* under the 'Abbasids: Gender and Politics, 749–1055

The Umayyad Arab dynasty declined fast despite its brilliant military expansion. Among the reasons for this decline was their racism towards various groups, including non-Arab Muslims (*mawali*) of the conquered countries, religious discord among the Muslims and the lack of efficient administration in running this vast empire and unjust economic policies against the non-Muslim majority, even the newly converted Muslim minority.

The 'Abbasids, who descended from the uncle of the Prophet, al-'Abbas, managed to harness the anger of the *mawali*, especially in Iran, and to revolt against Umayyad rule, bringing it to an end in 749. As Hugh Kennedy states: 'The 'Abbasids were Islam's greatest dynasty,'[1] even though they ruled smaller territories than those of the Umayyads. The 'Abbasids ruled in Iraq from 749 to 1258, and this period is divided into the following eras:

- 749–847: the golden, or Arab, age
- 847–945: the first Turkish age of domination
- 945–1055: the Persian Buwayhid Shi'i age
- 1055–1258: the Seljuq Turks and Mongol invasion

In this chapter, I will examine the first three eras as one unit, although we know that the 'Abbasid caliphate had practically lost all its symbols of powers by about 936; however, I aim to study the start and evolution of gender and politics throughout this period, especially as the Buwayhids did not have a paradigm shift from the previous administrations. The Seljuq period, due to its distinct character, will be discussed separately in Chapter Six.

Most historians refer to the first period as 'the golden age' for several reasons, for example, the huge financial wealth, urbanisation and grand architectural achievements, like Baghdad and Samarra',[2] in addition to the legacy of Harun al-Rashid (d. 809) and his grandiose lifestyle on which the *Arabian Nights* (*Alf Layla wa Layla*) was founded. He was portrayed as protecting the daughter of the king of the Franks who had defected to his court and converted to Islam.[3] Also the foundation of the Dar al-Hikma (House of Wisdom) in 829, which saw the start of the massive movement of translation of science and knowledge from other civilisations into Arabic.[4] Having said that, it was an age of instability, too. Just five years into the start of the dynasty, there was a bloody civil war between the second caliph, al-Mansur, and his uncle, 'Abd Allah b. 'Ali, both declaring themselves the legitimate caliph. The same thing happened later between the two sons of Harun al-Rashid from 810 to 813, which ended with the decapitation of the caliph and the destruction of Baghdad.[5] A few years after the 'Abbasids came to power, large parts of the empire pulled out of their orbit, including Spain and most of North Africa; only Egypt was left under their direct rule for the majority of the 'Abbasid period.

The relocation of the Muslim imperial capital under the 'Abbasids from the Umayyad Mediterranean capital of Damascus to the new metropolis of Baghdad, founded by the 'Abbasids in the heart of Mesopotamia, meant that the 'Abbasids broke with the dominant Western Roman–Byzantine cultural–political influence and established a new dynastic identity aligned to the dominant Iranian heritage in the East. After all, Baghdad was built in 762 near the Sasanian capital Ctesiphon (al-Mada'in). Nearly all other capitals of the 'Abbasid Empire, and the other powers who gained autonomy from them, remained orbiting the geopolitical and cultural influence of the Persian and Turko-Persian identity in the East, such as Samarra', Merv, Isfahan, Nishapur and Tabriz.

The early 'Abbasids, with their humble Arab numbers and modest culture, had emulated and depended on the Iranian culture and heritage from administration to architecture, and from costumes to music and court culture – a tradition that would remain and grow for centuries to come.[6] Among this was the establishment of the harem, emulating pre-Islamic Iranian court culture. Over the years, the harem played a very significant political role under the 'Abbasids.

The harem, derived from *hurum* (sing. *haram*), is a masculine word meaning 'sanctum' or 'forbidden area', like a religious temple. It was applied to the part of the palace or house where family members like queen mothers, wives of the caliph or sultan, his unmarried sisters, daughters, children, aunts and divorced and widowed princesses resided. There was a defined administrative hierarchy, which developed over the years, with female servants for housekeeping duties, female slaves owned by some of the princesses and young boys (*ghulam*). There were also female *qahramanat*, musicians, singers, concubines and, most importantly, eunuchs to guard and serve the harem, and to spy on them and report to the master of the palace. The harem, which started on a smaller scale at the beginning of the 'Abbasids' reign, reached a legendary level of extravagance and lavish spending on concubines and palace-building. For example, al-Mahdi (d. 785) commissioned one palace for his leisure at 'Isa Abad, some hours outside Baghdad, costing 10 million dinars (at that time an average family of four would have been able to live on four dinars per month).[7] His son al-Rashid owned hundreds of concubines, one bought for the price of 100,000 dinars.[8] More astonishing is the case of al-Mutawakkil (d. 861), who built one palace in Samarra' for 1.7 million dinars. He owned 4,000 concubines, and it is said that he had copulated with all of them.[9] Al-Muqtadir (d. 932) had in his palace 11,000 eunuchs, as well as thousands of other *jawari* and concubines, the cost of which depleted the state treasury.[10] These astounding prices are all the more shocking when we consider that an average married man and his wife needed 300 dirhams a year for their living costs at that time.[11]

The 'Abbasid rulers arranged the harem in such a way as to segregate the genders and prevent the women from interfering in any affairs of the state; the only roles expected from them were to provide leisure and entertainment for the men, and to give birth to children.

In this chapter I will investigate how different women, from royals to concubines and *qahramanat*, and also eunuchs, managed to influence and interfere in political affairs of the state. Sometimes they liaised with one another, forming different levels of allegiance to penetrate the harem walls and encroach on the world of men and state affairs in order to protect their own interests, and aspire to a better status.

I will look at four different categories here: royal women – mothers, wives, daughters and sisters; concubines; *qahramanat*; and eunuchs, with their unique world of secret missions, military service, conspiracies and political rule.

Royal Women

> Do not change Baghdad for any other city; I do not think you will follow this advice. Take extreme care of the people of Khurasan, as they are your real supporters who sacrificed their souls and wealth for the state; I do not think you will follow this advice. Never involve your women in your political affairs; I think you will involve them.[12]

That is the advice of Caliph al-Mansur to his son and heir, al-Mahdi, at the end of his caliphate. The co-founder of the 'Abbasid dynasty and builder of Baghdad was against any role for women in public state affairs and public life in general. The 'Abbasid caliphate did not have any queens on the throne, or as heads of state ruling from the caliphate capital. Nabia Abbott metaphorically uses the term 'two queens of Baghdad' to assert the power that two particular royal women enjoyed: Khayzuran (d. 789), concubine of Caliph al-Mahdi and mother of Caliphs al-Hadi and al-Rashid; and Zubayda (d. 831), wife of al-Rashid and mother of al-Amin.[13] Hugh Kennedy applies the term 'queen mother' as a metaphor to Zubayda's status in the 'Abbasid court.[14] He does not mention 'queen wife', and it is understood that the queen mother had a prestigious social status, in that they might contribute to works of piety without having effective political power. I should add that the queen mother had a better chance of intervening in the affairs of her caliph/ruler son, for example, if he was too young, or in the absence of a regent or capable advisor nominated by the passing ruler to his successor. However, this did not happen until the early tenth century.

In reality, the 'Abbasid empire had two local queens (but not from within the 'Abbasid House) who took the title literally, and are described as such in medieval chronicles. The first was Dayfa of Ayyubid Aleppo (d. 1242); after six years in power she delivered the *khutba* (when the official declaration of the ruler would have been made or renewed) to the 'Abbasid caliphate in her realm as a sign of political–religious assertion, and she faced no rejection from the caliphate. The second was Shajar al-Durr (d. 1257), from Ayyubid Egypt, who declared herself as queen of all Muslims (albeit for a period of less than three months), and delivered the *khutba* to the 'Abbasids as a sign of homage. The last 'Abbasid caliph, al-Musta'sim (d. 1258), strongly denied her ascendency to the throne, and she was forced to marry a slave Mamluk military commander who became king. Both will be discussed under the Ayyubids (see Chapter Seven). It should be noted that '*malika*' (queen) is derived from the masculine '*malak*', meaning 'the one who seizes by force, thus dominates and rules'. It is often written as *malik* (king).

The first 'Abbasid century did not witness direct and significant influential interference in state affairs by free women of the 'Abbasids or their princesses. Slave women, on the contrary, were the exception, in particular Khayzuran, who was a concubine from 757 until 775/6, when she became a wife.[15] She will be discussed under the section on concubines in this chapter, in which I will investigate the gradual rise and evolution of her career.

During this period the main role of the 'Abbasid princess revolved around political marriage with various 'Abbasid caliphs, their relatives and close confidants, and among other Sunni and Shi'i political powers under the nominal 'Abbasid authority. The great majority of these marriages were arranged and agreed by men, not by the women themselves. Romance was not an organic part of the process, and politicians used women as a means to cement or boost their political relations. The exception known to us was the case of Princess 'Abbasa, sister of al-Rashid, and her comical marriage to Ja'far of the Barmakids, as we will see later. It is important to review the status of royal women in order to see and understand the differences between them and the concubines and *qahramanat*.

Consider the following sketches: the two brothers al-Saffah and al-Mansur, founders of the 'Abbasid dynasty, married Princess Rayta, daughter of the first, to al-Mahdi, son of the second. That helped the succession of power from al-Mansur to his son,[16] and assisted in the war against al-Mansur's uncle. Rayta played a minor role when her husband, as caliph, arrested a noble Hashemite and his harem. The women were given to Rayta to torture; she accomplished the mission by killing them.[17] Rayta also enjoyed the trust of her father-in-law during his last year in power. He gave her the keys of the treasury and caliph's palace as he headed to Mecca where he died, while Rayta's husband and heir was in Iran, and she handed her husband the keys upon his return with specific instructions from al-Mansur.[18] Rayta was probably the only princess of true Arab blood. Despite that, she was not strong as her mother, Um Salama, or her mother-in-law, Arwa, who forced al-Saffah and al-Mansur to write into their marriage contracts that they would not marry any other woman or have concubines.[19]

The following story concerns the marriage of al-Rashid to his cousin Zubayda, which took place in 776.[20] Zubayda, who was considered a free woman of royal 'Abbasid blood, was the daughter of a slave mother, Salsal, concubine of Ja'far (another son of al-Mansur).[21] Therefore, she was in fact a *hajin* (of mixed parentage). Despite her humble social background on her mother's side, Zubayda enjoyed more prestige and fame in the medieval chronicles than Rayta. Zubayda expressed well her mentality towards gender and politics in 813, when her only son, Caliph al-Amin, was decapitated in Baghdad by an army sent by his half-brother al-Ma'mun. Her remaining courtesans rushed to her. One said: 'What are you waiting for, when the commander of the faithful, al-Amin, has been murdered?' She replied, 'What can I do?' The man replied: 'March out and seek revenge like 'Aisha, who marched out to avenge Caliph 'Uthman's murder.' She said, angrily: 'Women should not get involved in revenge affairs or confronting leaders.' To the contrary, she wrote a few lines of poetry expressing her pain to the new caliph.[22]

J. Renate and Hugh Kennedy both see Zubayda playing only a social role, mainly relating to her philanthropic projects, especially the water supplies of Mecca and the pilgrim road. Zubayda spent lavishly on this act of piety to serve Muslim pilgrims, who commemorated her name around Mecca with 'springs of Zubayda'. Word of her deeds came down to Ibn Jubayr, who saw these springs in 1182 on his way from Mecca to Iraq.[23] On the other hand, Nabia Abbott, who names Zubayda as one of the two queens of Baghdad, sees very little evidence of her as a political partner. Most of her argument focuses on Zubayda's romantic relationship with al-Rashid, and her growing jealousy of his concubines.[24] Abbott argues that there was a *diwan* (special office) for Zubayda, but she presents no evidence, and does not examine the nature of that *diwan*.[25] On the other hand, Zubayda seems to have been a woman of trade, as mentioned in the stories of Ibn Taqataqa about a commercial agent of hers running and looking after her business,[26] but with no direct interference in politics.

Zubayda's limited involvement can be seen in two accounts: (1) her securing succession of the throne for her son; and (2) her role in bringing down the Barmakids. Regarding the first, when al-Rashid appointed al-Ma'mun as a second heir with a large military force in Khurasan and the eastern provinces, Zubayda expressed her resentment. Al-Rashid castigated her strongly, saying: 'How dare you (interfere), this is *ummat* Muhammad (the state of Muhammad, the Prophet). I'm the one accountable before God to govern it accordingly.'[27] Al-Mas'udi has a similar response, quoting al-Rashid denying her interference, saying: 'Who are you to interfere in the affairs of the provinces, and the judgements of men.'[28] It could be said that al-Rashid did not pay attention to Zubayda's discomfort with Yahya of the Barmakids, vizier of the caliph who was entrusted for a long time with the keys of the harem and its supervision. The caliph continued to count on his vizier for that matter,[29] and Zubayda's concern was ignored.

It is believed that al-Rashid did not wish to repeat the experience of his mother, Khayzuran, who brought him to the caliphate and dominated his rule during the first three years of his reign until her death in 789.[30] We find Zubayda gaining some social independence under the short caliphate of her son, and having a palace of her own in Baghdad, but we have no details about its milieu.[31]

The second account relates to the contribution of Zubayda to the downfall of the Barmakids. The Barmakids were Persian officials who joined the 'Abbasids at the beginning of their rule. Three successive generations of Barmakids served the dynasty as high political officials, the most significant and powerful being Yahya, who was the vizier of al-Rashid who delegated all power to him, including the insignia. Yahya empowered two of his sons, Ja'far and Fadl, with the title of the vizier as well and they became the de facto rulers of the entire realm.[32]

Several chroniclers mention the growing anger of al-Rashid towards the Barmakids, for political, religious and financial reasons. Their role also fuelled Zubayda's anger. She was opposed to the Barmakid attempt to relegate her son, al-Amin, from first to second heir. She revealed to her husband the secret love affair between Ja'far and al-Rashid's sister, Princess 'Abbasa, a relationship that produced at least one child, and possibly two.[33]

The crisis of the Barmakids is not our focus here, as we are concerned more with political marriage and power. It was mentioned earlier that the exception to almost all political marriage, dry of romance, was that of Princess 'Abbasa. She was allowed to attend some of the poetry meetings organised and attended by her brother the caliph. She captivated the vizier Ja'far by her charm. Ja'far took the forbidden step of asking al-Rashid if he could marry 'Abbasa.[34] We must remember that this is a Persian man, although a vizier and commander of a private army of tens of thousands of troops and wealth exceeding tens of millions of dinars, yet he is of humble origin compared to the (assumed) royal blood of the 'Abbasid Arab caliph.

Al-Rashid could not refuse the proposal, and finalised the political marriage; a bizarre marriage like no other, as al-Masudi reports it:

> The caliph said to Ja'far in the presence of many courtiers, 'I marry 'Abbasa to you, a marriage to permit you only to sit and look at her in a meeting at which I will be your third partner, not anything else'. Al-Rashid concluded the marriage after partial defiance from Ja'far to these terms. The caliph held his close private assistants as witness to this and took the strongest of oaths from the groom that he would never meet or sit under any ceiling [with 'Abbasa] unless al-Rashid was their third companion. Ja'far swore to honour this contract.[35]

Princess 'Abbasa was enamoured by him, and according to many accounts was the one to take the initiative and break this sacred contract, because of her love for her man. The result was her murder by al-Rashid in Mecca, together with her child/two children in 803, and the massacre of the Barmakids in the same year, ending their monopoly of power.[36]

Under the rule of Caliph al-Ma'mun b. al-Rashid (r. 813–33), two significant cases of political marriage took place, using the woman as a bond to his political targets, and with one of them managing to expand the caliph's authority over his realm. Al-Ma'mun was entrenched in a civil war with his brother and predecessor, al-Amin. During this war, al-Ma'mun's vizier was al-Fadl b. Sahl, and his brother al-Hasan was one of the leading assistants who had managed to bring al-Ma'mun to the caliphate.

In 817 al-Hasan became the vizier of the caliph, who was residing in far eastern Merv in Khurasan, while Baghdad was in turmoil. Al-Ma'mun badly needed the influence of al-Hasan on the Iranian elements, in addition to his strong administrative skills to overcome many domestic political–military challenges. The caliph proposed to marry his eight-year-old daughter Puran (the caliph was thirty-one at the time). The 'Abbasid contemporary chronicler and official, al-Jahshyari (d. 945), provides a rare account of al-Ma'mun's perspective of political marriage. He mentions that Caliph al-Ma'mun put great effort into marrying one of his daughters to his vizier, al-Fadl. The vizier kept apologising for accepting such proposal and said, 'Even if you crucify me, I will not accept.'[37] This shows how the caliph needed to build trusting relationships through political marriage. He failed with al-Fadl, but succeeded with his brother and successor, al-Hasan.

The marriage was consummated eight years later.[38] His father-in-law managed to secure Baghdad and the caliphate for al-Ma'mun against two other 'Abbasid royal contestants for the throne.[39] The political marriage/pact proved successful, not just for the interests and security of the caliph, but for Puran's father, who consolidated his grip over Khurasan, which in turn led to her brother Talha b. Tahir taking power in about 825, laying the foundations for the Tahirid dynasty there. Carrying the name of the caliph's father-in-law, it was one of the first autonomous states in the eastern 'Abbasid provinces.[40]

The marriage itself was lavish and epic-like; we can get a feel for it from the following:

> A marriage that surpassed any others from *jahiliyya* to date, Puran's father had prepared a large number of leather patches kept in little perfumed shells. On these patches were names of towns, provinces and concubines, among other presents. All were scattered on the military commanders and the 'Abbasid royals. Whoever had a patch was given what was written on it. Special runners were made, brocaded with gold. The amount spent on the wedding exceeded fifty million dirhams.[41] Precious pearls were scattered on 'Abbasid princesses. Trays made with golds and precious stones and jewellery were used for carrying drinks for the guests. A candle made from saffron weighing more than fifty pounds was put in the bride and groom's apartment.[42]

Al-Ma'mun used other political marriages to bring stability to his empire. The schism between Sunni and Shi'i Muslims had never been bridged since the early caliphate, which had resulted in many military–political revolts against the state led by different Shi'i leaders. We find al-Ma'mun taking the unprecedented step of naming a Shi'i leader, 'Ali al-Rida, as heir to him in 817.[43] Such a daring reconciliatory step had never taken place in Islam before then, and most probably never will in future. Al-Ma'mun wanted to have greater bonds with the new heir, so the caliph gave his daughter, Um Habiba, to marry al-Rida, and another daughter, Um al-Fadl, to marry Muhammad b. al-Rida.[44]

We cannot judge how successful the marriages were, as 'Ali al-Rida died the following year.[45] Yet al-Ma'mun used gender as a tool to bond relations with his historic political enemies, hoping to create a different generation in the future combining both of the main elements of the Muslim doctrine.

If one of the results of the political marriage of al-Ma'mun to Puran was the establishment of the Tahirid autonomous state, the political marriage of Caliph al-Mu'tadid (r. 892–902) managed to rectify the relationship between the 'Abbasids and the rebellious Egyptians, under the Tulunids, who had declared independence from the caliphate in 868 under Ahmad b. Tulun.[46] Khumarawayh, who succeeded his father Ahmad in Egypt, managed to secure a political–financial accord in 893 with Caliph al-Mu'tadid. He declared the *khutba* again for the 'Abbasids; however, he would continue to have a semi-independent political system for three decades in Egypt.[47] To boost this agreement, al-Mu'tadid married Khumarawayh's daughter Asma', who was given the title '*qatr al-nada*' (dew drop) in 895, after negotiation on the financial arrangements. The caliph provided a dowry of one million dirhams.[48] The bride's father would pay a yearly tribute to the central treasury in Baghdad, the amount being 200,000 dinars.[49] Although Khumarawayh was killed by his eunuchs just a few months after the marriage, Qatr al-Nada lived as a princess for five years in Baghdad; the caliph was very attached to her until she died in 900.[50] As a result, we see the caliph refrain from interfering in the turbulence that followed the death of his father-in-law – that is despite many Tulunid commanders asking him for help. The Egyptian chronicler Ibn Taghri attributes this to Qatr al-Nada's position in the caliph's heart.[51]

The institutionalised political marriage continued up to the tenth century, when the Shi'i Buwayhids dominated the 'Abbasid Sunni caliphate. We know that several marriages took place between different 'Abbasid caliphs and the daughters of several Buwayhid kings. However, we do not see the reverse, that is, where an 'Abbasid princess married a non-Arab lord or king, as they were considered to be of inferior blood. Although the great majority of the caliphs' mothers were slaves from different parts of the world, they were considered to be noble Hashemite Arabs from the paternal side.

Among those marriages was that of Caliph al-Ta'i' (r. 974–91), who married the daughter of Bakhtiar, the Buwayhid king of Iraq in 977.[52] In addition, his successor, al-Qadir, married the daughter of King Baha' al-Dawla the Buwayhid, king of Iran, in 993.[53] These types of marriage were just symbolic, but do not reflect much political interests. The chronicles paid no attention to them, writing barely one or two lines about them. We do not know even the name of the bride, unlike the earlier cases of Puran or Qatr al-Nada.

As we have seen from the examined cases of political marriages, 'Abbasid women in general did not have a direct and influential role in politics and the affairs of the state. However, political marriages, especially in the first century of 'Abbasid rule, contributed to a smoother transition of power. They enabled caliphs like al-Ma'mun to have a stronger grip of power over his realm due to his tactful selections of the other gender. In addition, rebellious Tulunid Egypt was restored to 'Abbasid authority due to the amicable relations and marriage between Caliph al-Mu'tadid and a Tulunid princess, among other factors. Under the Buwayhids, marriages were just prestigious ceremonies between politically crippled caliphs and dominant Buwayhid lords of the realm. This is important to mention and monitor because we will witness a paradigm shift of sexual politics under slave women, mainly concubines and *qahramanat*.

Before moving to that topic, I should mention that the shadow of Queen Sajah of the seventh century reappeared in the tenth century through two women from her Arab tribe, Taghlib. It is mentioned briefly by Ibn al-Athir about the military and political direct intervention in the rule of two Taghlibi Arab women under the Hamdanids in Mosul and the Jazira. The Hamdanids were from the Arab tribe of Taghlib in the Jazira. For most of the tenth century they established their rule semi-independently from the 'Abbasids, first in Mosul and parts of the Jazira from 905. They had a branch in Aleppo from 945, which lasted for six decades.[54]

Their founder in Mosul was Nasir al-Dawla (r. 929–69). Ibn al-Athir provides this anecdote:

> His wife, Fatima al-Kurdiyya (the Kurd) was in control of his affairs. She planned with her son, Abi Taghlib, to arrest the father. They managed to achieve that in 968/9. From his jail, Nasir managed to send a message to his other son, Hamdan, asking for military help. The message was intercepted and Nasir was removed to the mountainous citadel of Kawashi.[55] Nasir remained in prison for a few months and then died. Abi Taghlib managed to defeat his half-brother Hamdan in battle and became the new ruler.[56]

This is a brief and rare exception of gender and politics in the third 'Abbasid period. Ibn al-Athir wrote that Fatima was in control of her husband's affairs. Unfortunately, he did not give details about the type of control, or if it was through the entire reign of her husband. One strongly believes that Fatima took advantage of her ageing husband and interfered, together with her son Abi Taghlib, to remove him from power. She wanted to seize power from Abi Taghlib's half-brother from his father's side.

Another rare exception was in 968 when the Hamdanid prince of a number of areas in the Jazira, Abu al-Barakat b. Nasir al-Dawla, wanted to expand and seize Mayyafariqin. Mayyafariqin was under the authority of Prince Sayf al-Dawla II, the Hamdanid of Aleppo. When Abu al-Barakat appeared with his forces at Mayyafariqin, while its lord was absent from the city, his wife ordered the military commanders to close the gates of the city and resist the siege. This anonymous wife reached an agreement to surrender several villages around Nasibin, and paid a donation of 200,000 dirhams in return for the attackers abandoning their siege.[57]

When she realised that Abu al-Barakat was secretly contacting some commanders in the city with a view to surrendering it, and could not wait for military help from her son, who was fighting a rebellion in Aleppo, she marched out in person, leading a force at night in a surprise attack on her enemy, defeated Abu al-Barakat and looted his camp.[58] We can see here two tribal Arab princesses fighting for their interests, changing the rule in the first case and leading a military force in person in the second.[59]

The grand poet al-Mutanabbi (d. 965) failed to praise these two women as he had done with another Hamdanid princess from their dynasty some years earlier, the mother of the founder of the Aleppo branch. When she died, he wrote:

> If women were like the one we lost
> People will prefer women than men
> Giving the sun a feminine name is not a shame
> Neither giving a masculine one to the crescent will bring glory

These two cases, considered rare during this period, had their parallels later with other ethnicities, such as the Kurds and Turkmen under the 'Abbasids in the fourth period. Although these models or paradigms appear mainly in the dynasties connected to the 'Abbasids, we do not see similar examples from within the core 'Abbasid house in Iraq.

The Realm of Royal Concubines and *Qahramanat*

The 'Abbasid empire witnessed great extravagance and opulence with the increasing numbers of *jawari*. They were brought from slave markets from the four corners of the earth, in addition to the *sabaya* (war captives). The more of them that were brought to Baghdad, the more harm was done to the *hara'ir* (sing. *hurra*) (free women). As already mentioned, slave women were formed from four main categories: *jawari*, *qiyan* (singers), *mahziyyat* (concubines) and *qahramanat* (stewardesses). In some cases, a *jariya* or *qina'* could be elevated to the status of concubine. The latter was used as the personal exclusive pleasure-maker/giver to the 'Abbasid caliph. Concubines became the anti-wife, and experienced a great deal of jealousy from the wife. Also, in some cases, a concubine could be freed and elevated to the status of a wife. Such a practice was emulated by the aristocracy or entourage of the caliph on a smaller scale. The patriarchal society had used the licence given in the Qur'an ('what your right hand possesses') and completely ignored what woman's right hands possess (*ma malakat aymanuhunna*) (Q. 24:31). Therefore, free women were only allowed to own female slaves. Some of them owned *ghulman* and eunuchs, too. Numbers of concubines were on the rise under the 'Abbasids, reaching phenomenal figures due to the sexual obsession of different caliphs, and also associated with economic prosperity. Moreover, they had no legal rights, unlike the wife.

The 'Abbasid age was saturated with literature descriptive of female slaves and their sexual merits. For example, the famous Iraqi scientist al-Jahiz (d. 868) wrote about the world of *al-jawari wa al-ghilman*.[60] The famous Persian physician al-Razi (d. 923) produced a manuscript called *Al-Bah* (copulation).[61] The most famous Arab poet, Abu Nuwas (d. 814), dedicated copious poetry to the sexual attraction of *ghulman*.[62] There was also the significant works of al-Aghani, with a large body of poetry celebrating love and sexuality composed by caliphs, poets, courtesans and singers.

With the growing industry of the slave trade, we find the Iraqi physician Ibn Butlan (d. 1038) producing an auction catalogue for the purchase of female slaves. This was categorised according to their ethnicities, nationalities and characteristics, as follows:

Indians:	Good figure; swarthy complexion; great beauty; clear yellowish skin; sweet breath; delicate, but tendency to age early; faithful and amiable.
From Medina:	Swarthy; well-proportioned; combination of good speech and good figure; charming and flirtatious. They feel no jealousy towards their men. Fit for singing.
From Mecca:	Soft and feminine; soft wrists; white complexion tinged with brown. Their eyes are unattractive.
From al-Ta'if:	Golden swarthiness; braided hair; exceedingly light-hearted, pleasant and fun-loving. Do not make good mothers.
Berbers:	Mostly of black complexion, but some of paler hue; obedient, faithful and energetic. Very caring towards their children. If any of them with a good physique are brought at the age of nine to Medina, trained there for three years, then sent to Mecca for another three, brought to Iraq at age of fifteen for training and education, then she will combine all merits of the women of Medina, Mecca and Iraq in addition to her good Berber physique. Thus, she will deserve a very special place.
Yemenis:	Like the Berbers or Medinese and combining the femininity of the Meccans; generally with pretty faces.

Zanj/sub-Saharan:	Many faults: the blacker the uglier, the sharper the teeth, the less desirable. Dancers by instinct. Very hard labourers.
Abyssinians:	Mostly slender and soft; some close to being consumptive; useless for singing or dancing. Loyal and trustworthy.
Nubians:	Resemblance to the blacks; self-indulgent and delicate.
Turkic:	Combination of beauty with white skin; charming eyes despite their smallness; tendency to sullenness. They are the treasures for child birth.
Byzantines:	Straight blond hair, blue eyes; obedient and amiable.
Armenians:	Would be pleasing were it not for their monstrous legs; enjoy rude health and strength. Chastity is rare among them. Cleanliness is not known to them.[63]

This male discriminating mentality of Ibn Butlan was echoed in later centuries; for example, al-Suyuti (d. 1505) provided a similar description in his book *Al-Idah fi'Ilm al-Nikah* (*The Distinct Book in the Science of Copulation*).[64] Neither of them had a catalogue for male slaves explaining the differences between full men and eunuchs, for example, and the services for which they were needed, demonstrating that society looked at women more as commodities than as humans.

The Rising Power of Concubines

Concubines were part of this slave trade. The first 'Abbasid caliph had a small palace called al-Hashemiyya built in al-Anbar, east of the Euphrates. Al-Anbar became his capital during his short rule.[65] Although we know very little about his court life, there is no evidence that he had any concubines. Perhaps that was due to his strong wife, Um Salama, who proposed marriage to him, and literally provided him with money, as he was poor, to conclude the ceremonies (taking place before the establishment of the 'Abbasid state). She insisted that they write into their marriage contract that al-Saffah would not marry any other woman, a pledge that he honoured.[66]

Arwa, the wife of his successor al-Mansur, insisted on the same condition, but added that there would be no concubines. He tried hard to annul this condition, but failed. When she died, he was free to marry others. Afterwards he owned two concubines, but their names are not mentioned in the chronicles. It is mentioned, however, that he was presented with 100 virgin slaves on the very same day of Arwa's death.[67]

Both caliphs had a small number of boon companions, who would sit separately from the caliph, behind a curtain. Neither of them was interested in music or singing gatherings, and neither of them was a drinker.[68] It was during the rule of the third caliph, al-Mahdi b. al-Mansur, that we see the start of lavish spending on palaces and entertainment. He built the Rassafa Palace in Baghdad and al-Salam Palace in 'Isa Abadh (less than a day trip from Baghdad), which cost him 10 million dinars.[69] Through these palaces, we learn about the first concubine to intervene in politics. Khayzuran ('reed' – her real name is unknown, as is the case with most other concubines of the age), was bought by al-Mansur from the slave market of the Hijaz in about 761. He gave her to his son and heir, al-Mahdi, as a good candidate for childbearing.[70]

Concubines and politics under the 'Abbasids is encapsulated mainly in two individuals: Khayzuran of al-Mahdi, mother of the two caliphs al-Hadi and al-Rashid; and concubine Shaghab of al-Mu'tadid, mother of the boy caliph al-Muqtadir in the tenth century. Immediately after his reign, the 'Abbasid state and administration collapsed due to severe financial difficulties and the domination of the Buwayhids, among other political factors.

Starting with Khayzuran, her career could be divided into three main stages: (1) when she was a concubine for al-Mahdi as heir from 761 to 775; (2) when he became caliph (r. 775–85), freed and then married her;[71] and (3) when she was mother of two caliphs, al-Hadi, who succeeded his father for a year, and then al-Rashid. She was active until she died in 789.

Khayzuran: Concubine of Prince al-Mahdi

Khayzuran joined the court of Prince al-Mahdi, who was deputy to his father in Iran; she was not the only woman in his life as he was newly married to his cousin, Princess Rayta.[72] In 764 she gave birth to their first boy, al-Hadi, and the following year gave birth to another, al-Rashid. Al-Mahdi already had two sons by Rayta, 'Abd Allah (b. 762) and 'Ali, born the following year.[73] It is not clear in the sources when Khayzuran disclosed the secret that she was related to her master, Prince al-Mahdi. However, she must have told him soon after she joined his court. Prince al-Mahdi sent the 'Abbasid deputy of Yemen to bring to him her two sisters, Salsal and Asma', in addition to her brother Ghitrif; all joined her in Iran.[74]

Khayzuran's ambition, aided by good fortune, helped her to weave a power base for herself in the court. Her sister Salsal won the admiration of al-Mahdi's brother. She became his concubine, and soon after gave birth to their daughter Zubayda.[75] Nabia Abbott argues that Khayzuran did not tell her master about the existence of her family in Yemen until her own position was secured through the birth of their two sons.[76] I consider that to be highly unlikely, as Zubayda, daughter of Khayzuran's sister Salsal, was born just a few months after al-Rashid, in about 765, which would give very little time for the family to arrive from Yemen, and for Salsal to get pregnant and have her daughter.

At any rate, Khayzuran made use of this connection, and years later created the holy alliance. Her son al-Rashid married her niece Zubayda. Going back to her early years, she had to survive in polygamous royal surroundings in Prince al-Mahdi's court. In addition to his wife, Rayta, he owned many concubines. One of his favourites was the concubine Bakhtyar, who was captured during the suppression of a revolt in Khurasan in 767.[77] Another favourite concubine of Prince al-Mahdi was Muhayyat, who was competing with Khayzuran for the prince's heart. The prince was fond of Muhayyat, and bought a Persian slave girl, named Shakala, as a present for her. She was groomed and educated to perform music and sing in Muhayyat's quarters of the palace.[78] When al-Mahdi became caliph years later, he expressed his attraction towards Shakala. Muhayyat did not hesitate to present her to the caliph as a concubine. Shakala gave birth to Ibrahim, who was declared caliph briefly in and around Baghdad in 817, challenging al-Ma'mun.[79] We have virtually no information about her. However, it is clear that she played no role in Ibrahim's attempt to seize power. The only influence she had on her son was to train him to become one of the best musicians and singers of the 'Abbasid age. He even challenged and competed with the legendary court musician of the age, Ishaq al-Mosuli.[80]

In the same court milieu, Khayzuran kept her patience with two other competing concubines whom Prince al-Mahdi admired. One was Maknuna, from Medina. She gave birth to their daughter 'Ulayya, who also had a passion for singing and music. Khayzuran expressed extreme jealousy towards her saying: 'No one is more threatening to my position than her.'[81] The other was Basbas, of whom al-Mahdi was so fond that he paid 120,000 dirhams to buy her. He had to conceal the price from his father, who would certainly have accused him of extravagance.[82]

Khayzuran: From Concubine of a Prince to Wife of a Caliph

In 775 al-Mahdi succeeded his father al-Mansur as the new caliph. The transition of power was not smooth as he faced a challenge from an 'Abbasid prince, 'Isa b. Musa. Al-Mahdi forced 'Isa to accept his caliphate in return for installing him as heir.[83] In 776 al-Mahdi decided to secure the caliphate for his son, al-Hadi, son of Khayzuran. He elevated his favourite concubine to the status of wife, after emancipating her. Then he held 'Isa, his heir, as hostage in the palace in Baghdad until he declared his abdication as heir apparent.[84] Al-Mahdi then nominated al-Hadi as heir in 776. Six years later al-Rashid, their other son, was nominated as a second heir.[85]

Both al-Tabari and Ibn al-Athir mentioned another competitor to Khayzuran, whom al-Mahdi had married at about the same time, Um 'Abd Allah, daughter of one of his close officials.[86] It seems that moving to al-Khuld Palace in Baghdad, which was the official palace of the caliph, had increased the appetite of al-Mahdi for more wives; the following year he married another woman named Ruqaiyya while performing the hajj.[87]

The sources fail to provide any more information about these most recent marriages, but they continue to report on Khayzuran, which reflects her strong presence in the corridors of the palace and political circles. The question at this stage is: why did al-Mahdi not nominate his two sons from his cousin and first wife, Princess Rayta, as heirs, or his son from the concubine, Shakal? I believe that this is down to the strong influence of Khayzuran over her husband, who accommodated his wife's ambitions. Mernissi describes the nomination of Khayzuran's sons as heirs as a coup.[88] Caliph al-Mahdi was sometimes weak in the face of the fiery persona of Khayzuran, who, on one occasion, treated him very harshly, as al-Waqidi tells us: 'One day the caliph went to see Khayzuran in the harem. Khayzuran was angry with him, tore his clothes and shouted at him: "O you picker of left-overs; what good have

I ever received at your hands?"' Al-Mahdi told al-Waqidi: 'She was bought from a slave trader. I have made her two sons heirs to my throne. Am I, then, a picker of left-overs?'[89]

Clearly, she had asked for one of her frequent demands and favours, which the caliph had declined. The result was that angry reaction, which the caliph, surprisingly, tolerated, and did not conceal it from al-Waqidi. Unfortunately, we have no information as to when that incident took place.

Khayzuran's influence in public and political life increased gradually from limited incursions during the reign of her husband to more powerful ones during the reigns of her two sons. Under al-Mahdi, she owned a private business, manufacturing cloth and producing embroidery. She had agents who looked after her commercial activities and interests. Sometimes she wrote directly to governors with orders to facilitate the tasks of her agents.[90]

It is likely that Khayzuran had established connections with the successive viziers of al-Mahdi in order to protect her own interests. The poet Bashshar b. Burd (d. 785) accused the vizier Yaʿqub b. Dawud of corruption, and accused the caliph of neglecting his rule in favour of his extravagant life. He wanted al-Hadi to succeed the caliphate, even though he would be under the influence of Khayzuran.[91]

Al-Mahdi died under suspicious circumstances in 785 in Masabadhan, Iran. He was poisoned by one of his favourite concubines, Husna, who poisoned some pears in a tray, aiming to kill another concubine in al-Mahdi's company, of whom she was jealous. By mistake, the caliph ate this poisoned fruit and died.[92]

Khayzuran: The Influence of a Royal Mother

The ʿAbbasid state was in a very delicate situation, both militarily and politically. Al-Mahdi had died suddenly in Iran, while his first heir, al-Hadi, was leading a military campaign in Jurjan, eastern Iran. Al-Rashid was in his father's company. Many commanders had advised al-Rashid to conceal the news of al-Mahdi's death until they had brought him back to Baghdad, as they feared that the troops would riot. Al-Rashid, upon the advice of his mentor and secretary, Yahya the Barmakid, buried al-Mahdi in Iran, and sent the caliphal insignia to al-Hadi with his condolences and congratulations.[93]

When al-Rashid entered Baghdad with the troops, riots broke out in the city, and prisoners were sent free, in addition to some other acts of sabotage. The troops asked for more money. Khayzuran summoned al-Rabi' b. Yunus, *hajib* of al-Mahdi, and Yahya the Barmakid for a consultation as to how to resolve this political crisis, especially as the new caliph was still away from Baghdad.[94] This is the first time that we see an 'Abbasid woman intervening directly in state affairs on that level. It was she who called the state officials for political consultation amid the crisis.[95] Yahya declined the invitation, fearing an angry response from al-Hadi, especially as Yahya was the mentor of al-Rashid. On the other hand, al-Rabi' saved the situation, and with Khayzuran's financial support, managed to give the rioting troops two years' pay, which contributed to the end of the crisis.[96]

Nearly all of the chronicles mention how dominant Khayzuran became during the first four months of the reign of her son al-Hadi. Beginning during the rule of al-Mahdi, she continued to interfere in state affairs. Unfortunately, the sources only provide a small amount of detail about her influence, which had the full approval of her son, the caliph. Khayzuran met at her quarters of the palace with state officials, such as the chief of police,[97] and commanders, among many others, who welcomed her interventions, for a variety of reasons. People were flocking to her with their requests and petitions.[98] In addition, she had her own palace,[99] had a free hand in her trade and business and took a share of state revenues. As a result, she would earn in the region of 260,000 dinars annually.[100]

Regarding the loyalty of al-Hadi to Khayzuran, consider this: 'Caliph al-Hadi was in full submission to his mother, Khayzuran. He responded positively to all the requests and demands coming to her from the locals. They used to come to her door in convoys, due to her influence.'[101] That mood changed when Khayzuran requested that her son, the caliph, should install her brother Ghitrif, who was also the uncle of al-Hadi and his father-in-law, as governor of Yemen. Al-Hadi was reluctant and divorced his wife, 'Ubayda, daughter of Ghitrif.[102] Khayzuran tried to get al-Hadi to go back on his oath of divorce, explaining that her maid who was sent with the request of Ghitrif's appointment did not explain it well, but al-Hadi was adamant.

Matters then took a lethal turn between Khayzuran and her son when she asked him for a favour on behalf of the chief of police, 'Abd Allah b. Malik, who had failed to ask for it himself. We can see the high status of Khayzuran, who intervened to help the chief of police, from this anecdote of the caliph and Khayzuran arguing:

> Khayzuran: You must meet my request.
> Caliph: I will not do it.
> Khayzuran: I already assured the chief of police that it will be done.
> Caliph: He is a son of a harlot. I will not do it for him.
> Khayzuran: Then I will never ask you for any more favours.
> Caliph: I do not care.
>
> Then he said angrily as she was leaving: 'Stay where you are and perceive these words. I swear by Allah if I hear that any one of my commanders, retainers or servants is at your door, I will decapitate him and confiscate his wealth. Let anyone dare to take that chance. What is the meaning of all these daily processions back and forth to your door? Have you no spindle to keep you busy, or a Qur'an to remind you of God? Or a house to shelter you? Beware and again beware. Open not your doors hereafter to either Muslim, or non-Muslim.'
>
> Khayzuran departed in absolute anger, and never had any words with him again, sweet or bitter.[103]

This situation between the royal mother and her son was never resolved and it remained an open wound. Nabia Abbott attempted a psychoanalysis of al-Hadi, stating that he felt bitter as Khayzuran had always favoured his brother al-Rashid. In addition, al-Hadi suffered from a slight defect with his upper lip, which made his mother think that al-Rashid was the right person for the caliphate.[104] Such assumptions have no evidence to support them in the chronicles and, as previously mentioned, al-Hadi was very welcoming of his mother's wishes in the first few months of his caliphate.

> Al-Hadi gatherered his commanders and asked them: 'Who is better, my mother or your mothers?' They replied: 'Yours, commander of the faithful.' Al-Hadi asked: 'Which one of you would like the men to talk about or mention his mother, and keep saying, she did this and that?' They replied: 'None of us would like that.' Al-Hadi said: 'Why do some men visit my mother, then spread the news about their talk with her?' When the

assembled commanders heard this, they completely boycotted his mother afterward. Khayzuran was very depressed because of that.[105]

The remaining few months of the very short reign of al-Hadi were spent in galvanising support from his commanders, in order to replace his brother, al-Rashid, as his heir with al-Hadi's son, Ja'far.

The 'Abbasid state was split into two camps, each fighting for their own candidate. Not surprisingly, Khayzuran and Yahya the Barmakid, mentor and secretary of al-Rashid, took the side of the latter.[106] Al-Tabari wrote: 'Khayzuran sent for Yahya to consult with him. She told him that al-Hadi would not prevail. Khayzuran was in charge of all al-Rashid's affairs and supervising the shifting of the caliphate to al-Rashid.'[107]

It seems that this anecdote came in the final week of al-Hadi's life, when the confrontation between the mother and son turned ugly. There are several stories with slightly different details, but they all portray how al-Hadi and Khayzuran tried to end the life of each other. Al-Hadi started by sending poisonous food as a present to his mother, but the conspiracy was discovered. Khayzuran then seized her opportunity when al-Hadi suddenly fell ill; she commissioned some of her *jawari* to suffocate him, which they successfully did.[108] The sequence of events is not clear. We do not know if these *jawari* were in al-Hadi's palace at 'Isa Abadh near Baghdad as part of his entourage as agents of his mother, or if they were dispatched by her from Baghdad. How could they be trusted in this hostile atmosphere? How were they able to move freely to the caliph's chamber, bypassing all his guards, *jawari* and, most importantly, his *hajib* and *qahramanat*?

At dawn on 17 September 786, Khayzuran dispatched a trusted servant to Yahya the Barmakid, who was imprisoned in al-Hadi's palace. He asked Yahya to go and meet the (Lady) Khayzuran. When he went to see her, she told him that the caliph was dead, and, as she was a woman (with limitations on her movements), he should take the lead for al-Rashid and do what was best for him.[109] The commander of the army, Harthama, was also summoned to her and told about the news. On the same day, diplomas for the new caliph, Khayzuran's other son, were written and made ready to be dispatched to the 'Abbasid provinces.[110]

These measures by Khayzuran had never been witnessed in Islamic history in such magnitude. She had managed to topple a caliph and install another. Al-Tabari mentioned that 'al-Rashid had delegated all powers to his vizier, Yahya. Khayzuran was in charge and supervising all affairs of the state. Yahya would tell her about all matters, and take the final decision upon her approval.'[111] That went on for three years during her son's rule until she died in 789. Khayzuran and Yahya had come together as a team to look after their interests. Together they planned how to avenge the commanders who had supported the removal of al-Rashid as heir for the benefit of al-Hadi's son, Ja'far.[112] Thirsty for more power and her growing business, we see a personal private secretary, named 'Umar b. Mahran, being hired by her.[113] It is not clear if she had her own *diwan* in her palace, or if she looked after her business from her quarters in the caliph's palace. Abbott, who tried to prove the might of Khayzuran, mentions that her annual income reached approximately 160 million dirhams, while she herself stated that it equalled half of the entire 'Abbasid state income in one year.[114] I believe that this reflects the power of a mighty woman, although that figure is probably exaggerated, and it is not found in al-Tabari, Meskawayh or Ibn al-Athir. In addition, the chronicles do not give details of how that amount was translated to properties, estates, jewellery and other items. Fatima Mernissi describes her as a 'presidentess who shared the rule with al-Rashid, who did not feel shame sharing power with a talented woman'.[115] We have seen earlier how al-Rashid did not believe in gender equality and warned his wife Zubayda from interfering in state affairs. Moreover, we cannot consider this example of tolerance between a son and his mother as a general case of appreciation of gender and politics under the 'Abbasids.

The rise of Khayzuran from a slave bought in the market to a favourite concubine to Caliph al-Mahdi, and mother of his two sons, to her modest interference in political matters from behind the curtain during her husband's life, to her achievement in installing her two sons as heirs to the caliphate (and not the sons of the free woman and first wife of the caliph, Rayta), to her excessive interference during the reigns of her two sons, al-Hadi (who was killed by her) and then al-Rashid, reflects an extraordinary case of gender and politics. However, she always required certain male leading figures to collaborate with. She did not frequently come to the front line to face the officials of the state or the public. Rather, she would remain behind the veil, leaving her male agents or representatives to guard and follow her interests.

Khayzuran may have succeeded in her career to rise from slavery to shared power, especially during al-Rashid's reign, but she failed to convince most, if not all, chroniclers that her husband had freed her. All chroniclers refer to her right up to the end of her life as *um walad*, not a free woman. I believe that the shadow of slavery always followed politicians of that origin, and could form an obstacle to their career. For example, al-Mansur, who was older than his brother al-Saffah, was not nominated as first 'Abbasid caliph because his mother was a Berber slave. When he became caliph he was ridiculed by one Shi'i leader, and labelled an enemy of the 'Abbasids because of his slave mother.[116] The same fate followed other caliphs, including al-Ma'mun, who was born to the concubine Marajil (lit. boilers). He was ridiculed by his half-brother and caliph al-Amin in 812 during their civil war about the slave origin of his mother.[117] This is probably why Khayzuran was trying to gain some prestige through her acts of piety. She bought the house of the Prophet in Mecca and transformed it into a mosque, in addition to other charitable projects.[118] One event of that age to note was the naming of an area in Baghdad, al-Khayzuraniyya, which was named after her during the reign of her son al-Rashid.[119] Such an honour was not given to any other 'Abbasid concubines or free women. If we look panoramically, we will see that concubines in ninth-century Andalusia were replicating the same acts and projects,[120] trying to eclipse their past.

The category and calibre of Khayzuran would not occur again until the reign of al-Muqtadir in the tenth century. There were only one or two minor cases of powerful women in between. Before we examine them, it is important to mention that the 'Abbasid caliphs, high officials and aristocracy around them increased tremendously the number of concubines, *jawari* and singers in their palaces, reaching about 2,000 under al-Rashid. Al-Mutawakkil had 4,000.[121] In addition, the prices of some concubines reached an inflated level. For example, the concubine Hilana of al-Rashid was bought for 100,000 dinars;[122] the concubine Dananir reached approximately the same figure. Al-Isfahani is the only one to note that 'she wrote a famous book of songs'.[123] As previously mentioned, we have no books written by women in medieval Islam until the sixteenth century, and yet we are told by a man, not a woman, about this contribution, which sadly has been lost.

Having said that, none of these concubines had any influence on public life and politics, but they did have influence on the hearts of their lords. The realm of the harem became a separate world of pleasure and desire. Consider these anecdotes from al-Rashid and his son al-Muʿtasim, which give a taste of the milieu in which the concubines were living and making.

1. al-Rashid and his *jawari*:
   On very hot days, a silver bowl would be placed in the room and filled with perfumes, saffron and rosewater. Each day seven slave girls were brought in. They undressed and put on specially provided linen tunics which had been dipped in the perfume. Then they would sit on a pierced chair with incense burning under it until the garments were completely dry and the girls fragrant with perfumes. Only then were they ready for their master's pleasure.[124]

2. the famous concubine, singer, musician veteran of four caliphs, from al-Maʾmun (d. 833) to al-Mutawakkil (d. 861) – ʿArib al-Maʾmuniyya (named after Caliph al-Maʾmun) (d. 890).[125] During the caliphate of al-Muʿtasim b. al-Rashid, Ibn ʿAsakir described the following:
   Al-Muʿtasim (d. 842) would visit ʿArib often, but he became occupied with some matters and neglected her. She was involved in a love affair with a young man. She brought him one day, and they sat together drinking and singing. The commander of the faithful, al-Muʿtasim, unexpectedly paid her a visit. She hid her lover in one of the chambers. The caliph inquired about the drinks and music instruments. ʿArib said that she was emulating the sitting of the caliph when they would sit together; she explained how much she was missing him. She brought the caliph his favourite drink, and sang him his favourite tunes and songs. The caliph was happy with the gathering until he became drunk. When he left, she recalled her lover from the place of hiding and continued with their love affair until the morning.[126]

This royal and princely culture was manifested in the wall paintings of the new ʿAbbasid capital, Samarraʾ, built by al-Muʿtasim in 836, especially for his Turkish troops. Some of the paintings show the images of women dancers with wine bottles, symbolising luxury and festivity.[127] His son, al-Mutawakkil, had twenty-two palaces built, one of them at the cost of 1.7 million dinars.[128]

He had an army of concubines and *ghulman*, as mentioned. This was the start of the second 'Abbasid age, or the Turkish age, when the caliphs wanted to remodel their army on the Turkish troops. They bought thousands of Turkish troops and bought thousands of Turkish female slaves for them, as they preferred their own ethnicity, especially during battles.[129] Al-Mutawakkil gave his mother, Shuja', a degree of financial power, to the extent that she had about 500,000 dinars and several pieces of land;[130] however, there is no mention in the sources that she had any political power.

Concubine Qabiha and her Son, Caliph al-Mu'tazz

Qabiha (lit. ugly) was a Rumi/Greek concubine to Caliph al-Mutawakkil. She gave birth to their son, Muhammad, who later became Caliph al-Mu'tazz.[131]

The killing of al-Mutawakkil at the hands of his son and successor, al-Muntasir, opened the gate for strong interference from and domination by leading Turkish commanders in the caliphate until the end of the second 'Abbasid century. Ibn Taqataqa described the character of the age, saying: 'The Turks had seized the realm since the killing of al-Mutawakkil. They dominated the caliphs. A caliph in their hands was like a prisoner. Upon their wishes, they could keep him, dismiss him, or kill him.'[132] It was the start of the age of *iqta'* (feudal system), where leading commanders were allocated large areas of the empire to run for themselves with little control from Baghdad, leading to autonomous provinces in Egypt and parts of Iran.

During this period of instability and quickly changeable pacts among different powers, al-Musta'in, nephew of al-Mu'tasim, became caliph. A group of Turkish commanders brought him to power in 862.[133] By 865 the caliph was facing growing opposition from several Turkish commanders in Iraq, which led to a civil war across Iraq. Some commanders declared the toppling of al-Musta'in and the appointment of al-Mu'tazz.[134] The mother of the deposed caliph, the Saqlabi concubine, Makhariq (lit. awkwardness), offered him one million dinars to defend his caliphate. Having this huge amount of money indicates that she had some level of influence. In February 866 al-Musta'in finally abdicated in favour of al-Mu'tazz.[135]

A group of leading commanders of al-Mutawwakil feared the return to power of the abdicated caliph. They consulted with Qabiha, mother of the new caliph, as regards the protection of her son. After several meetings with them, she ordered her secretary to write to the Turkish commander Ahmad b. Tulun, who was guarding al-Musta'in. In her letter, she wrote: 'When you read this message of mine, kill al-Musta'in and send me his head. Then I will install you as governor of Wasit [in Iraq].'[136] Ibn Tulun replied: 'God will not see me killing a caliph to whom I once gave an oath.' This passive reply persuaded Qabiha to replace Ibn Tulun from guarding the deposed caliph. Soon after, the head of al-Musta'in was sent to Qabiha and her son.[137] Here we have a woman who held meetings with leading generals, coordinating with them and corresponding with others, and who could allocate certain *iqta'*.

Qabiha's role in securing the caliphate for her son did not stop at this stage. She was at war with other concubines who wanted to install their sons as heirs. Al-Mu'tazz had nominated his half-brother al-Mu'ayyad from another concubine named Habashiyya (Abyssinian) as his heir in the same year. Months later he was imprisoned, and found dead in mysterious circumstances in August 866. Then Isma'il, the other son of Qabiha, was nominated as heir to al-Mu'tazz.[138] We cannot rule out the role of Qabiha in these violent changes for her sons' interests. It is worth pointing out that it was one of the women in the harem who reported the conspiracy between some Turkish commanders and the imprisoned al-Mu'ayyad.[139]

Due to the mounting tension between the diverse ethnic Turkish commanders and troops in Iraq from 866 to 868, and to the competition between the Turkish troops and the Maghribi/North African troops, al-Mu'tazz experienced great difficulty in keeping law and order in his realm, especially now that the treasury was almost empty.[140] The result of that was a military revolt against the caliph, with troops demanding an advance in their salaries. The caliph sent to his mother asking her for money to solve the crisis, but she said she had no money to offer.[141] It is likely that the caliph would not ask his mother Qabiha for help in these pressing times unless he knew that she had substantial wealth, which was probably collected due to her influence in her son's realm, with commanders and high officials, in addition to her commercial activities.

In July 869 her son was toppled by his commanders and killed after being severely tortured. Surprisingly, Qabiha escaped with her daughter from the palace through an underground tunnel. Two months later, she surrendered herself, and also surrendered her massive wealth, which she had denied to her son earlier. Among that wealth was 1.8 million dinars and several precious stones. The commander who captured her, humiliated her, saying: 'You had your son killed for the sake of only 50,000 dinars, while you have all this wealth.'[142]

The biography of women by Ibn al-Sa'i (d. 1217) gives us information about different women in medieval Islam. There is a brief mention of Fatima bt. Al-Fath, one of al-Mu'tazz's wives, but with no further details of her life.[143] This demonstrates how difficult it can be to trace and have a fuller picture of the role of women in history.

Between this time and the reign of al-Muqtadir four decades later, which witnessed the pinnacle of gender and power, we could say that the 'Abbasid caliphate witnessed a sharp decline in the number of women in the harem in general. Al-Muhtadi, who ruled for one year (869–70), had exiled all female slaves and banned luxurious lifestyles. Not a single concubine or *qahramana* was mentioned in the records relating to him.[144] The harem institution was restored but in a smaller scale for socio-economic reasons during the reign of two out of three of al-Muhtadi's successors.

Concubine Shaghab and her Boy Caliph, al-Muqtadir, 908–32

Shaghab (lit. disorder) was of Rumi ethnicity, bought by caliph al-Mu'tadid (r. 289–902) for the price of 40,000 dirhams.[145] She was one of three concubines of al-Mu'tadid. The other two were Jijank, mother of Caliph al-Muktafi (r. 902–8), and Fitna, mother of Caliph al-Qahir (r. 932–4).[146]

Shaghab was a phenomenal person, and her period was an exceptional one, encapsulating the relationship between power and gender under the 'Abbasids. She brought her son to power at the age of thirteen, and dominated his entire long caliphate. She died from being tortured a year after the death of her son, accused by al-Qahir of gross financial corruption. Shaghab had a sister named Khatif and a brother named Gharib, who had a son, Harun. She created a team or network, including them, to run the caliphate with other leading figures like the viziers, the eunuch commander of the army, *qahramanat* and *hajib*.

I believe that she eclipses the power of Khayzuran due to her long career, and her usage of *qahramanat* to dominate the rule. There was, however, one thing that she did not manage or attempt to do: lead a military force in person like the Seljuqid princess in the last 'Abbasid period in Iraq, as will be discussed later. Before I examine the age of al-Muqtadir and his harem, and the eunuch commander of the entire 'Abbasid army, I should note that many regional and political changes took place at this time, which affected and challenged al-Muqtadir, his harem and his courtesans.

Three political powers emerged in the Middle East, which posed a threat and challenge to the 'Abbasids. First, the radical Shi'i Qaramita, who established themselves in eastern and central Arabia from 894 and lasted for a century;[147] they often attacked southern and central Iraq during the time of al-Muqtadir. The second was the rise of the Shi'i Isma'ili Fatimids in North Africa in 909, who launched annual attacks on 'Abbasid Egypt during the caliphate of al-Muqtadir, aiming to seize it. The third was the declining 'Abbasid grip of power over Iran, with the rise of the Daylami ethnicity in Iran, and then the rise of Shi'i Buwayhid Twelvers, who were leading an ambitious military rise during al-Muqtadir's reign until they declared their dynasty during his final year in power, taking the Sunni 'Abbasid government under their control.[148]

> You should know as a reader, that the state of al-Muqtadir was a weak one, due to his young age, and his mother, Shaghab's, domination of state affairs with other women and courtesans. He was only occupied with his pleasures. As a result, the rule was bankrupt, the treasury became empty. He was toppled, then reinstated and finally killed.[149]

That is the opinion of Ibn Taqataqa in *Al-Fakhri fi al-Adab*, who summarises the reign of al-Muqtadir and how his mother brought the state down. Such opinion was shared by almost all other chroniclers of the age. After the death of her master, Caliph al-Mu'tadid, in 902, Shaghab was sent with her sister, brother and many other *jawari* of her husband to live in a house called Ibn Tahir in western Baghdad. That was upon the order of the new caliph al-Muktafi, half-brother of her son. Al-Muktafi refrained from having *jawari*, concubines and *qahramanat*.[150] The house of Ibn Tahir was considered a place of punishment, unlike most of the palaces built in the eastern part of the city.

Al-Muktafi had been suffering from a long serious illness during his final year in 908, which affected his grip on power. His vizier, al-'Abbas b. al-Hasan consulted with four leading figures in the administration (chiefs of *diwans*) to select a successor. This was despite the will of al-Muktafi to install his brother al-Muqtadir after him.[151]

With the presence of eight sons of al-Muktafi, and another half-brother, named al-Qahir, and in addition to the strong concerns of some of the leading men in the administration of the dying caliph, we cannot rule out the role of Shaghab in securing the caliphate for her son through much persuasion with the vizier and his advisors.

When al-Muktafi died in September 908, al-Muqtadir was declared as the new caliph on the same day. Meskawayh, among others, wrote that the sultan (here meaning the supreme authority) had delegated the financial affairs to the vizier to secure and complete the *bay'a* (oath) for him.[152] The question here is: al-Muqtadir was a thirteen-year-old boy, so who really did have the power to delegate such authority to the vizier? In my opinion, it was Shaghab. It should be noted that the treasury at that time had 15 million dinars.[153]

Only five months later, in January 909, the vizier of the boy caliph, al-'Abbas, in collaboration with the *qadi* of Baghdad and some other commanders, decided to topple al-Muqtadir and install Prince 'Abd Allah, son of the former caliph al-Mu'tazz. A large public council was held that was attended by most of the men in the administration, civil and military, in addition to nobles and elite figures. The prince was declared as Caliph al-Murtadi b. Allah. The new caliph selected a new vizier after the head of the plot was murdered mysteriously. A new chief of the *diwan* was also nominated.[154] I should point out that the civil administration represented in the several *diwans* were run by a small number of influential families, like Ibn al-Furat, al-Jarrah and Ibn 'Isa, who rotated around the posts frequently, bringing instability and corruption to the 'Abbasid state.

The new caliph wrote to al-Muqtadir, ordering him to evacuate the caliphal palace and retreat to Ibn Tahir's house in the west of Baghdad. The boy caliph agreed to this order. It seems that the different military groups around the new caliph (al-Murtadi) were disunited and had no clear plan. Al-Muqtadir was left with his mother, maternal aunt, uncle, eunuch commander of the army (Mu'nis al-Khadim), Mu'nis al-Khazin, and a large number of *jawari*, *ghulman* and courtiers.[155] A certain commander, al-Husayn b. Hamdan, launched a lone attack on al-Muqtadir in his palace, without coordinating with other powers. He surprisingly failed, and withdrew. That lifted the morals of Shaghab and her camp. The following day, all the courtiers, led by Mu'nis al-Khadim, sailed along the Tigris River and made a surprise attack on al-Murtadi. Surprisingly, he was terrified by their approach, and fled to the desert; his chief, al-Husayn b. Hamdan, had already deserted him, fleeing to Mosul in northern Iraq. The commander of police also changed sides and declared his support for al-Muqtadir. Ibn al-Athir, among others, expresses his astonishment at the luck of al-Muqtadir, who had few supporters and yet was reinstated in the caliphate less than two days after the coup.[156]

Shaghab and the eunuch Mu'nis al-Khadim took their revenge out on al-Murtadi and his men. She appointed Mu'nis al-Khazin as commander of police. He arrested and killed al-Murtadi on the spot, as well as his vizier and most of the men who had supported his plot with the help of *hajib* Sawsan. Only the *qadi* and chief of the *diwan* were spared. A special force was dispatched to Mosul to arrest al-Husayn b. Hamdan, who had helped al-Murtadi. That reflects strong political–military will to extend her power over Iraq, and not just Baghdad. She contacted, in her son's name, al-Hasan b. al-Furat and appointed him as a vizier to her son. He was one of the few men who did not take part in the plot against her son.[157]

Meskawayh comments on the outcome of this failed coup: 'Al-Muqtadir's rule became unshakable, and those who were conspiring against him (due to his young age) ended their treasons.'[158] From this moment onward, the 'Abbasid state was run by Shaghab, in close coordination with the eunuch Mu'nis al-Khadim, and other close courtiers, like a kind of small political council. She was acting as a regent for al-Muqtadir at the age of thirteen, but even when he became mature enough, she continued her domination until the end of his caliphate (at the age of thirty-seven). The question here is: how did Shaghab manage to control or dominate the rule of her son?

Shaghab was contented to depend on the eunuch chief of the 'Abbasid army, Mu'nis al-Khadim, as long as he looked after the best interests of her son and showed absolute loyalty. However, she supervised the budget of the army and delegated to him general policy matters, leaving it to him to decide on details and tactics.

The sources repeatedly mention the following phrases: 'Mu'nis was ordered' to march to invade the Byzantine front, such as in 909, or: 'It was bestowed upon him.'[159] Who had the power to instruct the commander in chief of the entire 'Abbasid caliphate? Also, who had the power and legitimacy of the caliph to grant or bestow honours? That was certain to be Shaghab.

Again, in 910, the 'Abbasid ruler of Fars, Qinbaj al-Khadim, died. Fars was given to the new ruler, 'Abd Allah b. Ibrahim, to govern in addition to Kirman.[160] Who decided to appoint an 'Abbasid deputy to run one or more provinces? Also, in 913, for example, the four-year-old Prince 'Ali b. al-Muqtadir (Shaghab's grandson) was installed as governor of Egypt and North Africa, but Mu'nis al-Khadim was representing him there as a deputy. 'Ali was also installed in Qazwin and Rayy in Iran in the same year.[161] Again, the fingerprints of Shaghab were all over the political–military and financial affairs of the empire. It seems that she was keen to have a clear declared successor for her son. Al-Muqtadir was thirteen when he had his son 'Ali. Shaghab had depended on her political arms inside the palace to monitor every movement; I mean, of course, her *qahramanat*.

During the twenty-four years of al-Muqtadir's caliphate, Shaghab played a vital role in appointing and dismissing his viziers. The post witnessed great instability, and the viziers became more like secretaries to her. Twelve different changes were made during that caliphate. Ibn al-Furat served five years, interrupted over three different cycles; Ibn 'Isa served six years over two periods; others served for only a few weeks. Nevertheless, all of them recognised Shaghab's power.[162] For example, in 916 the indispensable judge and historian al-Tannukhi wrote that Ibn al-Furat sought the support of Shaghab's secretary, Ibn 'Abd al-Hamid. Ibn al-Furat asked him to mediate with the royal mother for his return to the post.[163] Ibn 'Abd al-Hamid was offered the vizierate by Shaghab in 919, but he refused, preferring to be close to his mistress; this shows how Shaghab enjoyed full power in her son's realm.[164]

Also, in 925, when the vizier al-Khasibi was newly appointed, he would continually correspond with her, expressing his loyalty and wishing for her blessing.[165] The post of vizier, among other posts, was associated with financial corruption. For example, in 928 Ibn Muqla had offered 500,000 to the royal mother and the caliph to be given such a post.[166]

Such domination had made the chief of the army, the eunuch Mu'nis, a traditional ally of Shaghab, express his dissatisfaction about her to the caliph in 929:

> Mu'nis wrote to al-Muqtadir, expressing the dissatisfaction of the army about Shaghab, the harem and her courtiers, for their gross financial mismanagement and their continuous interference in the decision-making of the state. Mu'nis demanded an end to this, and the removal of Shaghab's nephew, Harun, from the palace.[167]

Shaghab had used her financial power to boost her position. After her son became caliph, she started to acquire many fiefs and agricultural lands with high revenues. She was keen to buy land to expand her wealth right up until her son's murder. The annual revenues from these lands exceeded 700,000 dinars.[168] In addition to properties, Shaghab had other commercial activities, such as shops and storehouses. She would receive a very large amount of money from the state treasury, given to her by the vizier. For example, in 918 Ibn al-Furat delivered to the *sayyida* (mistress) (as she is often referred to in the sources), the sum of 2.5 million dinars for expenditure for her and the harem.[169]

Shaghab owned her own palace, and had her own independent *diwan* and private secretary.[170] It was a kind of parallel administration. Vizier Ibn al-Furat, for example, was always paying visits to the harem, to get Shaghab's instructions. He was replaced in 924 by al-Khaqani, who was brought to the office upon the strong recommendation of her nephew, Harun. That is despite the discomfort of al-Muqtadir towards the vizier.[171]

With the wealth and domination by the royal mother, we also see clear signs of absolute wealth in those people around her. Her *qahramana*, Um Musa, had acquired a fortune of one million dinars.[172] She is but one of the many figures in the court. Shaghab herself had a massive wealth, and was a big spender, along with her son. When the Qaramita invaded southern Iraq, the caliph asked his mother for money to pay the army. She gave him 3,000,000 dinars.[173] In another attack by the Qaramita on Iraq in 927, al-Muqtadir again sought help from his mother. She paid him from her private purse the amount of 500,000 dinars.[174] The lines between the public and private purse were not always clear, otherwise how would the royal mother have collected all this wealth.

Another important example here is what took place in 919. Baghdad and other parts of Iraq had witnessed food shortages and soaring prices. The result was serious civil and military riots, even by some military battalions of the caliphal palace, demanding a salary increase. In his attempt to contain the situation, al-Muqtadir ordered that the shops and stores that were owned by the royal mothers and his relatives should be opened and the merchandise distributed and given to the locals at much reduced prices.[175] The royal mother was profiting tremendously from her position, which helped her to buy and pay for her harem and entourage who aided her in her semi-revealed co-rule.

She was obsessed with gathering money to the extent that she would hide or save hundreds of thousands of dinars in one place, such as in her tomb, which she had prepared for herself.[176] That explains how she could supply her son instantly during times of need, such as those outlined above, with huge sums of money. This massive wealth was not only used to service political–military operations; it was also used to fund her extravagant lifestyle, reflecting the splendours of the court. For example, al-Muqtadir owned in his palace 11,000 eunuchs, in addition to thousands of *ghulman, jawari* and 700 *hajib*.[177] Kennedy compares the royal palace during the time of al-Muqtadir and his father to the Forbidden City of Beijing.[178]

No wonder that the palace of the caliph was of exorbitant style, competing with some of the stories in *The Arabian Nights*. Al-Suyuti reports that in 917, when the Byzantine envoy of the emperor was received in Baghdad by the caliph, the court of the caliph had 38,000 curtains hanging on the walls, made from *dibaj* (silk) brocades, and 22,000 carpets.[179]

Among other splendours reflecting the exorbitant spending of al-Muqtadir, was the silver tree in his palace made from 500,000 dinars, implanted in a round pool, with gold branches and different birds made from gold and silver as well[180] (one dirham makes approximately 4.2 grams of silver, so 500,000 dirhams would make about two million grams or two tons of silver). There was also the silver village commissioned by Shaghab, which was a miniature of a village made from silver and other precious stones, and that was one of the wonders of the palace.[181] Such a prodigal lifestyle would have dire consequences with the downfall of the caliph and his royal mother. Shaghab had founded in 918 a hospital named after her in Baghdad, as an act of piety, and probably in order to make herself more popular. The annual expenses of the hospital amounted to only 7,000 dinars[182] – no match for her other lavish private spending.

The caliph's mother remained the supreme authority for the elite officials of the court in times of need and consultation. For example, in 923 when al-Muqtadir was almost thirty years old, the vizier, Ibn al-Furat, and chief of the army, Mu'nis al-Khadim, were on bad terms with each other. Each was trying to get the caliph to side with him. Finally, Mu'nis was ordered by the caliph to leave Baghdad on a military campaign to different provinces to collect unpaid taxes, after he had just returned from another expedition to the Byzantine borders. Mu'nis believed that this decision was made on the opinion of Ibn al-Furat, delivered to the caliph.[183] After Mu'nis left for his mission, the vizier started to suspend various high-ranking officials, like secretaries in the *diwan*, in addition to Nasr, the chief *hajib* of the caliph. The vizier convinced the caliph that the *hajib* was receiving too much income from his private properties. Nasr went to Shaghab pleading for help. She contacted her son, and said to him:

> Ibn al-Furat sent Mu'nis away from you, because he is your sword, and he is extremely loyal to you. Now he turns on your *hajib* to harm him, so he can pay you back and seek revenge on you; that is because Ibn al-Furat was dismissed from office twice before [in 911 and 918] and was imprisoned, humiliated, and his harem disgraced. Who will then stand to assist you against him, if he has conspired against you and planned to topple you from the caliphate, especially as he has carried out evil acts before, and his son, al-Muhsin, does not hesitate to commit evil acts.[184]

Here we see how the royal mother continues to advise her son the caliph, and to analyse the political situation around him. As a result of that intervention, the caliph waited a few months until Mu'nis had returned to Baghdad; he then ordered the removal of the vizier from office and his arrest, along with his son. Both father and son had their money and wealth confiscated, and were brutally slain in 924.[185]

Continuing with our quest to reveal how Shaghab dominated the 'Abbasid state of her son, we should look at her family and relatives who were empowered by her to guard her interests. Shaghab had a sister called Khatif, who does not appear much in the sources, but we know that she did meet with some officials and received petitions from locals in the palace of Rassafa in Baghdad.[186] On one occasion, in 925, she and her sister, the royal mother, recommended the appointment of vizier al-Khasibi to al-Muqtadir.[187] On the other hand, Gharib, her brother, and his son, Harun, were key players in al-Muqtadir's administration. However, all of them would be addressed like Shaghab by official letters on different occasions, and with a prestigious prelude ranked higher than the 'Abbasid governors of the provinces.[188]

At the beginning of al-Muqtadir's career in 909, we find Gharib interfering and fighting in opposition to the coup against his nephew.[189] During 918/19, Baghdad witnessed several serious riots by the locals as a result of food shortages and soaring prices. Al-Muqtadir appointed his uncle Gharib as a commander of an army to deal with this crisis. Gharib managed to end the riots, in a brutal manner.[190]

In 924, when the vizier Ibn al-Furat was dismissed from office and arrested, Harun, the nephew of Shaghab, together with Mu'nis, the chief of the army, strongly recommended the new vizier al-Khaqani, and Harun guaranteed financial promises made by al-Khaqani.[191] How could Harun guarantee the financial promises in millions made by the new vizier, unless he made use of his relationship with the caliph and his mother?

In the same year, Gharib, together with Mu'nis, decided to brutally kill the deposed vizier, Ibn al-Furat, and his son. They first slew Ibn al-Furat's son, bringing his head to the father to look at before slaying him, too. Harun then went to tell the good news to the new vizier, who fainted from hearing of the brutal killing. Harun did not leave until he received 2,000 dinars for delivering this news.[192] If Gharib was in a position to decide with the chief of the army that a certain political opponent should be killed and how that execution should be carried out, was that power not gained though the relationship or connection with Shaghab?

Harun served not only in political and mediation administration, he also participated, in 928, in the fight against the Qaramita under the command of Nasr, the *hajib*. When the latter died during the campaign, Harun took the lead and managed to push the invaders back to the desert, and returned victorious to Baghdad.[193] That boosted his confidence and ambitions, to the extent that he went into a confrontation with the chief of police in Baghdad, Nazuk, in the same year. A fight broke out between the horse groomers of Harun and Nazuk over an attractive boy whom they both craved. Some of Harun's men were arrested, so he sent his men to storm the police headquarters; they attacked the deputy commander, and released the men. Nazuk complained to the caliph, but al-Muqtadir refrained from interfering between the two.

Who, other than someone well connected to the royal mother, would dare to attack the headquarters of the police in the capital? When Nazuk dispatched some of his men to Harun's house, they were killed. The locals of Baghdad feared this unrest. Some started to refer to Harun as *amir al-umara'* (chief of commanders).[194] Mu'nis al-Khadim was alarmed by the growing influence of the cousin of the caliph. He was at Raqqa on the Euphrates at this time, but returned immediately to Baghdad. The caliph kept Harun close to him to protect him from any future confrontation with Mu'nis.

The rising power of Harun, and the financial mismanagement of Shaghab and her courtiers, made Mu'nis direct a stern warning to the caliph in February 929. Mu'nis requested an end to Shaghab's influence with her harem and relatives in state affairs. He demanded that Harun should no longer be attached to the caliphal palace.[195] When the caliph did not fully respond to the requests of his chief commander of the army, the latter staged a coup d'état against the caliph, on 1 March 929.

I will detail and analyse further these events within the section on eunuchs. However, I am concerned here with the influence of Shaghab and her relatives. Mu'nis arrested the caliph, his mother, aunt, children and all their courtiers, and imprisoned them at his house. He installed al-Muqtadir's half-brother, al-Qahir, as the new caliph.[196] Harun was not arrested, and he disappeared. He then led an anti-coup movement, and less than two days later, the deposed caliph al-Muqtadir was brought back to his throne upon the demand of the majority of the troops.[197]

Here we have a caliph, his mother and their relatives being arrested by the chief commander of the 'Abbasid empire. Yet they managed to reverse the situation after only two days in captivity. One of the reasons was the cry of the soldiers: 'Muqtadir ya mansur' ('Muqtadir, you are the victorious').[198]

We can see the long-established influence of Shaghab on the courtiers. Her lavish spending on them and her reputation among the different troops probably had a bearing on the coup that lasted only two days, which resulted in the reinstatement of her son.

The failed coup had totally broken the trust between the caliph and his family on one side, and Mu'nis on the other. Due to Mu'nis's power, he could not be removed from office. However, we see that the caliph depended more on his cousin Harun during major military challenges. In 931 al-Muqtadir sent Harun to Iran, commanding a large army to fight Merdawij, who had rebelled against Baghdad.[199] During this strange political situation, we see another concubine appearing on the political stage: Dimna, concubine of the caliph and mother of his son, Prince Ishaq. She was entrusted by her master to deliver messages between him and his new vizier, al-Husayn, in 931.[200]

It is worth pointing out that the chronicles furnish us with details about different concubines in addition to the royal mother, but fail to give us any details about other females of the harem, such as the caliph's sisters. We know of at least one princess, the sister of al-Muqtadir named Maymuna (d. 921).[201]

During the final year of al-Muqtadir's caliphate, Harun became an even more important political figure in the state. He established with the vizier a pact to curb the influence of Mu'nis.[202] After failing to face the financial crisis in the administration, the caliph took the advice of Harun and appointed a new vizier.[203]

In 932 when Mu'nis, as the commander of the army, decided to remove al-Muqtadir from office, the caliph called on his cousin Harun to help him against the attack. Harun tried, but it was a lost battle, and the caliph was slain.[204] Hugh Kennedy's description of the turbulent situation in the caliph's palace neatly sums it up: 'No one's political position was secured in the snake-pit of al-Muqtadir's court.'[205] We could add that this applied to the caliph himself. Here we see how the nephew of Shaghab drew his power from his blood relationship with her. She, too, was satisfied with his loyalty and his collaboration with her.

The power of Shaghab and her relatives and entourage was well expressed by Mu'nis and some leading officials after the murder of al-Muqtadir. Mu'nis suggested installing Prince Ahmad, son of al-Muqtadir, 'to gain the forgiveness of Shaghab'. Some other high officials commented: 'After all this suffering and agony, we finally got rid of a caliph who had a dominant mother, aunt, and assistant who dominated him, and we do the same again? No, we need a mature capable person who governs for himself.'²⁰⁶

It seems that al-Muqtadir's father, Caliph al-Mu'tadid had anticipated years earlier that his son's life would be dominated by the women around him, due to his weak persona. It was during a visit to Shaghab in the harem by her father, when al-Muqtadir was only a boy of five years old, that Caliph al-Mu'tadid was shocked to see his little son surrounded by ten little *jawari* of the same age. In his hand, he held a bunch of grapes, and it was not the season of this fruit. He would eat one berry and feed the rest to his companions in turn. Every time his turn came, he would eat one berry and give the rest to his *jawari* until the bunch was finished. The father said to his *hajib*, Safi:

> If it was not for the shame and punishment of God, I would have killed this boy and saved the Muslim state from his recklessness. I'm getting old and I rebuilt the state after great suffering. People will bring to the throne my son, al-Muktafi, who will not rule for long due to his illness. Therefore, al-Muqtadir will come to power, and with such an attitude and behaviour towards the other gender, women will dominate him, as they are the closest to him in his young age. He will spend the wealth and money as he spent the grapes.²⁰⁷

We could say that al-Mu'tadid was also anticipating the ambitious and dominant persona of his concubine, Shaghab.

The *Qahramanat* of Shaghab and al-Muqtadir: Gendered Politics

Before discussing the *qahramanat* and their highly distinguished and unique role during the reign of al-Muqtadir and his mother, we should see how the role developed in Islamic history and the courts before the time of al-Muqtadir. Ibn al-Nadim mentions that the pre-Islamic Persian courts would have the office of *qahraman*, which was a job given to a male or female in charge of the ruler's household or his/her private quarters of the palace.²⁰⁸ Michael Cook argues that the Prophet did not have this court culture.²⁰⁹ There are no signs of any *qahraman*, male or female, appearing in the sources under the early caliphate, too.

The earliest appearance of a male and two female *qahramanat* was during the reign of Caliph al-Mansur. He had one male called Sab' al-Durar, but nothing is mentioned about his role or influence, or his dates of service.[210] There were two other female *qahramanat*, Helana (d. 762), who was a concubine before becoming a *qahramana*, and then Risana (d. 767); however, nothing is known about the nature of their tasks and duties.[211]

Meskawayh mentions briefly that Caliph al-Mahdi had a male Persian *qahraman* named Wadih, who was in his company in his final days.[212] Again, nothing is known about the nature of his work or its duration. The male or female *qahramana* comes from slave origins, like *jawari*, concubines and singers. Despite the large number of slaves under the 'Abbasids, especially from the age of al-Rashid onwards, we do not see much mention about their positions in the growing 'Abbasid court, until the golden age in the tenth century under al-Muqtadir. In the age of al-Muqtadir and his mother Shaghab, the 'Abbasid court and political life witnessed five female *qahramanat*: Fatima, Um Musa, Thumal, Zaydan and Nazm. Some high officials also emulated their rulers and had *qahramanat*.

Qahramana Fatima

The first *qahramana* to Shaghab, she moved with her to the caliphal palace at the start of al-Muqtadir's reign. She aided her mistress in taking care of the financial affairs of the court. She died in 911 in a boating accident on the River Tigris in a storm.[213] Due to her close connection with Shaghab and the caliph, her funeral was attended by chief commanders and judges and the elites of the state,[214] a sign of distinguished respect of her and her mistress, Shaghab.

Qahramana Um Musa

She was a free Hashemite woman (against the norm),[215] and in 922 replaced the previous *qahramana* attached to Shaghab. However, she was not the only *qahramana* in the palace at that time, as the terrifying *qahramana*, Zaydan, was also present. The official jailer and torturer of high-ranked officials, she was attached directly to al-Muqtadir.[216] Um Musa's principal duty was to carry or deliver messages from Shaghab and the caliph to the vizier of the state.[217] In addition, she was in charge of the harem's purse, and was responsible for paying the servants in the 'Abbasid palace.[218] Meskawayh mentions that the allowance to the harem had exceeded half a million dinars per year in her time.[219]

We can assert that Um Musa exceeded her role. She would ride in her own parade around Baghdad and its markets, with knights and soldiers in her company.[220] In some cases she was empowered and commissioned by her mistress as her representative in the public sphere, which included delivering presents from Shaghab on behalf of her nieces, the daughters of Gharib, to their new husbands for their marriages. In that parade, Um Musa had twelve horses decorated with gold and silver saddles and bridles, in addition to guards and servants carrying forty containers of highly luxurious brocaded clothes and 100,000 dinars.[221] Such a display of power around Baghdad by the *qahramana* as an envoy of the royal mother was extraordinary at that time. Um Musa had immense power in the state. Consider this:

> In the year 917 she went to talk with the vizier Ibn 'Isa about certain financial demands regarding the harem and the approaching feast of sacrifices. The *hajib* of the vizier very deeply and politely apologised that he could not wake up his master. She left at once very angry, and when the vizier knew of what had taken place, he sent an apology and invited her back, but she adamantly refused. She went and complained to the caliph and Shaghab, and invented some fictitious stories condemning the vizier. As a result, seven days later, on the eve of the feast, the vizier was dismissed upon the order of the caliph and jailed at *qahramana* Zaydan's quarters.[222]

Here we have a *qahramana* representing the royal mother, and who could dismiss the vizier or prime minister of the entire 'Abbasid state and be the cause of his imprisonment. The caliph entrusted another woman, the *qahramana* Zaydan, to jail the former vizier.

As a messenger of the royal mother and the administration and high officials, the following anecdote is told by al-Tannukhi:

> Abu al-Hasan 'Ali b. al-Qadi (judge) Abu Talib told me that the mistress (Shaghab) asked my grandfather for a *waqf* (endowment) deed for a village she had bought. The deed was in the *diwan* of justice and she wanted to retrieve it in order to tear it up and cancel the *waqf*. My grandfather, not knowing her intent, brought it to the palace and told the *qahramana* Um Musa: 'I have brought the deed as she has ordered. What does she want?'

They answered: 'We want to keep the deed.' He realised what they were up to and told Um Musa: 'Please tell the *sayyida* (mistress) that this, by God, is totally out of the question.' The *qahramana* conveyed the letter to Shaghab, who complained to al-Muqtadir.[223]

This *qahramana* was the prime mediator between the royal mother, her son, and large numbers of courtiers, high officials and bureaucrats.

There is another example, in 912, when a high official, Muhammad b. Khaqan, wanted to replace the acting vizier, Ibn al-Furat. Ibn Khaqan contacted Um Musa, and told her about the vizier's hidden sympathy with the Shi'i followers who were conspiring against the caliph. He asked her to tell this news to the caliph and his mother. As soon as Um Musa passed this story to her mistress and the caliph, the vizier was dismissed, arrested and his family severely humiliated.[224] That encouraged another high official, Ibn Baghl, to contact Um Musa from his prison, seeking her help to recommend him as a vizier to her mistress and the caliph. He promised her a large sum of money if she succeeded. Um Musa managed to convince Shaghab and the caliph of her candidate, but vizier al-Khaqani knew about her plot. He managed to soften the caliph's heart and keep his office. As for Um Musa, she failed to appoint Ibn Baghl, but succeeded in releasing him from prison, thereafter he safely returned to Isfahan. Not only that, but the vizier who challenged her plan 'feared her revenge in future and sought her pardon by appointing two of her relatives as financial officers over some districts in Iran'.[225] From what is mentioned, we can observe how influential and pragmatic this *qahramana* was. The following anecdote will reassert such a view.

When the vizier al-Khaqani (served 924–5) faced great financial difficulties in his administration, especially as regards the army's salaries, one ambitious high official in the *diwan*, Ibn Ruh, wrote a letter to the caliph recommending himself as a vizier, and gave this letter to *qahramana* Um Musa to deliver. Indeed, she did deliver it, but according to her own interests: she gave it to the vizier instead. Al-Khaqani dismissed Ibn Ruh from office and arrested him.[226]

Um Musa had great freedom of movement within the forbidden areas of the palace. We understand that she might have collaborated with or at least had an exchange of information with the other *qahramana*, Zaydan. That is because we find her visiting the imprisoned vizier, Ibn al-Furat, who was in Zaydan's custody.²²⁷

In another revealing situation about her unrestricted movement, we see Um Musa storm into a council of war, shouting and demanding her budget to be increased. That meeting was attended by top officials of the 'Abbasid state, like the commander of the army, Mu'nis al-Khadim, and the vizier 'Ali b. 'Isa, among others. They gathered to discuss the crisis of the Fatimid invasion of Egypt.²²⁸ How did Um Musa manage to get into that meeting despite the presence of the caliph's *hajib*? It seems that this was the norm because she was representing the royal mother, so no restrictions were applicable to her, even to an official council of political–military importance. In the public sphere outside the court, we see her often visit the local markets in Baghdad, sometimes disguised as a normal *jariya*, and sometimes as a *qahramana* with prestigious attire, accompanied by some of her servants.²²⁹

The influence of Um Musa was extended to her relatives. In her final year in office, she succeeded in getting her brother Ahmad appointed as commander to the official pilgrimage campaign. In addition to that, Ahmad would sit at a certain place in the palace to meet the public and collect their petitions.²³⁰ Um Musa's sister, Um Muhammad, worked as her assistant, primarily looking after her private financial affairs.²³¹ Normally such a prestigious task was bestowed by the caliph upon a senior 'Abbasid prince from the Ashraf or the nobles, and not a sister of a *qahramana*. Yet her closeness to the royal mother had contributed to this position. As a result, Um Musa accumulated a wealth in excess of 100,000 dinars during her office. Such socio-political and economic power led Um Musa to a new level of ambition. In 922 she married her niece to the 'Abbasid prince, Ahmad b. Muhammad b. Ishaq b. al-Mutawakkil, the former caliph. He was a popular figure and had previously been nominated for the throne or caliphate. Um Musa spent lavishly on the wedding ceremonies, which led to other courtiers and elites of society spreading gossip about her political ambitions. Stories were transmitted to al-Muqtadir (and certainly to Shaghab) that Um Musa took the oath from the military commanders to Prince Ahmad, and that she was seeking his appointment as the new caliph.²³²

Shaghab and her son ordered the arrest of Um Musa, and the confiscation of all her properties and wealth. The royal mother summoned her, and said to her: 'You tried to conspire against my son by this marriage.'[233] The royal mother then ordered Um Musa, her brother and sister to be sent to Thumal to be jailed at her quarters.[234] As soon as that happened, the officials who had been appointed in the administration of Iran at Um Musa's behest were dismissed. *Qahramana* Thumal, well-known for extreme brutality, managed to interrogate and torture her and extort a huge amount of money and property from her.[235]

We can see here that it was neither the wedding itself nor the status of the groom that resulted in such a reaction by the caliph and the royal mother. Certainly, Um Musa had asked for their blessing for such an ambitious step. It was a change of mind driven by fear and warning from surrounding courtesans that led to her arrest and downfall.

It is worth mentioning that after five years in prison, during which the brother and sister of Um Musa died, she was released from jail, and some of her lands and farms restored to her, but certainly not her post.[236]
This realm of harem, and the network of several *qahramanat*, was a landmark of the age of al-Muqtadir and his mother.

Qahramana Zaydan

Zaydan was a Rumi slave, bought for 10,000 dinars from the slave market in Samarra' before joining the court of al-Muqtadir.[237] It seems that Zaydan was directly attached to the caliph as Um Musa was attached to Shaghab, but we have no clear date as to the start of her office. She had two important tasks, as jailer and torturer of high state officials handed over to her by the caliph, and as keeper of the precious jewellery of the 'Abbasid court.

If we look into her first role, that of jailer and torturer, we see that she executed her job very successfully and benefited greatly from it. When the caliph dismissed his vizier, Ibn al-Furat, in 911, he gave him to Zaydan to imprison inside the palace at her quarters. When he was reinstalled for a second time as vizier in 916, he realised her power within the court and he rewarded her by allocating to her various lands around Wasit and Basra.[238] He would count on her influence to defend his own interests, even when she jailed him until his death.

Consider this revealing anecdote:

There was a debate or confrontation around 918 between Hamid b. al-'Abbas, 'Ali b. 'Isa and the deposed vizier, Ibn al-Furat,²³⁹ about Ibn al-Furat's unsatisfactory administrative–financial conduct. The debate took place in the caliph's palace. Nasr, the *hajib* of the caliph, the elite commanders and chief judges attended. Ibn al-Furat greeted the attendees in a very confident manner and with little respect, although he was the accused person. The vizier Ibn al-'Abbas said to him privately: 'You disdained the crowd, and depended fully on *Qahramana* Zaydan to be your advocate and defend your situation at the caliph's court.'²⁴⁰

Here we see how this *qahramana* had the ears of the caliph and the royal mother, and could have equal, or even greater, influence than the vizier and military commanders, and even the personal *hajib* of the caliph.

Several viziers were jailed at Zaydan's quarters after their dismissal. In 923 Ibn al-Furat was jailed at her quarters, and then was released and installed as a vizier in place of 'Ali b. 'Isa, who was jailed at her place instead.²⁴¹ Zaydan and the royal mother tried hard to protect 'Isa from interrogation, which Ibn al-Furat sought to conduct at her jail. Both women warned the caliph that Ibn al-Furat wanted to transfer 'Isa from Zaydan's authority to the son of Ibn al-Furat in order to extract more financial secrets and information from him.²⁴² That move by Zaydan was partly to retain her power, and also to be rewarded in the future by 'Isa if he was to be released, as was the way at that time.

In 926 Vizier al-Khasibi was jailed at her quarters. When he was interrogated upon the orders of the caliph, he confessed about the tens of thousands of dinars he had given as presents to Zaydan.²⁴³ It should be pointed out that not every political opponent was given to Zaydan to jail, only the top officials. She was entrusted to jail the rebellious leader of Azerbaijan, Yusuf b. Abi al-Saj, and the rebellious leader of Mosul, al-Husayn b. Hamdan, who died in her jail.²⁴⁴ Here we have a woman entrusted with the top political opponents to the state, which added to the iron and gendered circle of the *qahramanat* under al-Muqtadir and his mother.

Zaydan's high status enabled her to have her own private physician, 'Isa, a prestige normally enjoyed by royals and viziers only. That physician was sometimes the messenger who carried messages between her and several viziers in the administration.²⁴⁵ I support the opinion of Nadia El Cheikh when she says that Zaydan greatly benefited from her diverse relations with different high officials of the state.²⁴⁶

Zaydan's other duty was to keep the precious priceless jewellery that al-Muqtadir had inherited from previous Umayyad and 'Abbasid caliphs. She was given a unique rosary worth more than 300,000 dinars by the caliph, which became known as the 'rosary of Zaydan'.²⁴⁷ Among other known items was a topaz stone worth 300,000 dinars, and the *durra al-Yatima*, a precious and unique pearl worth 120,000 dinars. Most of these jewels were given as gifts by al-Muqtadir to his concubines and his mother until there were none left.²⁴⁸ His vizier al-'Abbas, during the first year of al-Muqtadir's caliphate, advised the caliph: 'These are the grace and elegance of Islam. It is harmful to give them away.'²⁴⁹

We do not know how the career of this *qahramana* came to an end, but it is likely that she was killed or imprisoned with her master, the caliph, at the end of his caliphate in 932.

Qahramana Thumal

Thumal, in Arabic, means 'poison', or 'the one who takes the challenge to the end'. It is worth mentioning that this term was also used for women and eunuchs during that age.

Before she joined the service of Shaghab, Thumal was working for a commander named Abu Dulaf in the service of Caliph al-Mu'tadid as a discipliner of his slave girls.²⁵⁰ She appears in the sources in 918. It has been previously mentioned that when the royal mother ordered the imprisonment and punishment of *Qahramana* Um Musa and her family in 922, she selected the quarters of her *qahramana* Thumal as the jail.

It seems that Thumal joined the service of Shaghab before 918 and gained her trust and admiration, which she retained until her death in 929. Because of that, Shaghab appointed Thumal to a unique post that had never been occupied by a woman before or after her. That post was head of the *mazalim* court in Rassafa, Baghdad. *Mazalim* is a state judicial institution by means of which the state takes direct responsibility for enforcing justice and considering complaints lodged against administrative and judicial misuse.²⁵¹

At the quarters of Rassafa in eastern Baghdad, Thumal would sit for *mazalim* court each Friday. The locals disagreed that a woman should take such a position, and their opposition was so strong to the extent that the first day was a failure. The royal mother did not reverse her decision, however, and sent Thumal the following Friday in the company of the judge Aba al-Hasan. Although we have no details of what Aba al-Hasan's role was during the session, his moral support of the other gender proved important.

Thumal took full charge of the court and signed the decrees and documents on her own. The locals started to accept this and were satisfied by her performance.[252] This is the only *qahramana* to work outside the palace in the public sphere. The tenth-century chronicler al-Mas'udi, and Ibn Aybak, were critical of Thumal's role and considered her work to be a mark of the deterioration of the 'Abbasid state in general, and the rule of al-Muqtadir in particular.[253]

Among the duties of the *mazalim* court, listed by al-Mawardi (d. 1058), over which *Qahramana* Thumal was ruling were: acts of injustice committed against people by officials and governors, oppression in tax collection, claims by regular troops in respect of a reduction in or a withholding of their pay and restoring properties seized by force.[254]

Since the second guided caliph 'Umar created the post of *qadi* (judge), it has always been occupied by males. The court of the *mazalim* is an administrative court with significant responsibility and requirements, devised from the main court system. The *nazir* (judge) should have full knowledge of Qur'an, Hadith and shari'a, which are the primary tools for him/her. Where did Thumal study these fields, when the madrasa was introduced only in the twelfth century? And even after that, women were denied education in such an institution. I cannot offer an answer to this question.

Al-Mas'udi's anti-women in politics was really a common view, if not a doctrine of the age, in the Muslim East or West. The first condition given by the eleventh-century al-Mawardi necessary for a person to become a judge was that it could not be a woman, but only a mature man.[255] That condition is based on the four Sunni schools of law that deny such posts for women, in addition to the various Hadith discussed in the Introduction. Even the Shi'i Zaydi school of law supports this opinion, while the majority of the Twelvers go the same way. Other male theorists of politics, like Ibn Abi Rabi' of Iraq

(d. 842), who wrote the *Siyasat al-Malik* for al-Muʿtasim, was anti-women. The same applies to the grand Seljuqid vizier, Nizam al-Mulk (d. 1092), and his book *Siyasat Nameh*, and the Moroccan/Andalusian Ibn Ridwan al-Milqi (d. 1380), with his *Siyasat al-Nafiʿa*. All were strongly against any interference in the public sphere and political life by females, because they were simply not qualified.[256] Even poets of the age shared the same opinion, with sarcastic lines. Ibn Bassam, contemporary to al-Muqtadir, wrote:

> What do women have to do with duties like writings, deputies, or secretariats
> Such jobs are for us, men
> They, women, should only expect that at night, they go to sleep with a janaba.[257]

This contemporary look at the other gender, among other opinions mentioned, explains why Shaghab never tried to seize power herself, and preferred to remain behind a curtain using her political agents. I should add that such hostile opinion towards the other gender still finds its echoes in several Muslim societies, while, on the other hand, the Muslim women in Pakistan and Bangladesh in particular have produced more than one female political leader of the state.

The judicial power given or entrusted to Thumal was a landmark in Muslim history, despite the opposition by the locals then, or some chroniclers who criticised the move afterward, based on their understanding and interpretation of the Qurʾan and Hadith that women are less equal to men. A similar case to that of Thumal took place in tenth-century ʿAbbasid Egypt but with a eunuch, Kafur, who did the same thing. Also, in twelfth-century Ayyubid Egypt, the eunuch Qaraqush, deputy of Saladin, sat for *mazalim* for al-ʿAziz b. Saladin.[258] No locals or chroniclers commented on the illegality of a eunuch or 'incomplete male' holding the office, as will be discussed later.

Going back to the ʿAbbasid age, we do not see the chroniclers or the locals putting in writing strong religious or legal criticisms against the male judges who supported a thirteen-year-old boy like al-Muqtadir assuming the caliphate, or the chief judge Ibn Aktham of the ʿAbbasid state during al-Maʾmun's caliphate being a declared homosexual.[259] Their superior gender played a role in social favouritism towards their cases.

The influence of Thumal extended to the political affairs of the state like the *qahramanat* Um Musa and Zaydan. She played a major role in recommending and appointing viziers in al-Muqtadir's administration in collaboration with other elite courtiers. In 924, during the third and last vizierate of Ibn al-Furat, we see al-Khaqani, a top official in the administration, contacting Thumal and Nasr (the *hajib* of the caliph) in order that they recommend his appointment rather than Ibn al-Furat. Such a recommendation was boosted by the commander of the army, Mu'nis, and Harun, cousin of the caliph. Al-Khaqani was indeed installed as a new vizier and Ibn al-Furat and his son were arrested and killed in prison, as previously mentioned.[260] It is believed that Thumal was handsomely rewarded for her mediation. The following year, Thumal, in collaboration with Shaghab, recommended her own former private secretary, al-Khasibi, who had now become a secretary to the royal mother, to be appointed as a vizier, and succeeded in this quest.[261]

These four *qahramanat*, with Mu'nis, the chief of the army, Nasr, chief *hajib* of the caliph and the relatives of the royal mother, formed an iron network of interests and meddling in political affairs dominating the caliph, viziers and the administration to a great extent. Caliph al-Muqtadir on the other side, even when he grew up, prioritised his leisure time with his concubines more than state affairs and political matters.

Among the thousands of concubines of that age in the palace, we see a very brief appearance of two of al-Muqtadir's concubines: one at the very end of his career in 931, when the rift between him and commander in chief of the army became unbridgeable – Concubine Dimna, mother of one of his sons, who was used on several occasions to carry his secret messages to some of his courtesans and viziers;[262] and Dastanwayh, who was mentioned among those who recommended the appointment of al-Khaqani to the vizierate. He promised her a reward of 100,000 dinars if he got the post.[263]

Ibn al-Jawzi mentions very briefly a midwife named Nazm, who was made a *qahramana* to the royal mother, but neither him nor any other sources mention any details about the nature of her role.[264] It is worth pointing out that we know nothing about the other important women who have been mentioned briefly, for example, Princess Maymuna, sister of al-Muqtadir (d. 921).[265]

Maaike Van Berkel asks the question: did Shaghab and her harem contribute to the disintegration of the 'Abbasid caliphate? Julia Bray suggests that many chroniclers of the age blamed Shaghab and her protégées for the disaster of al-Muqtadir's reign.[266] I believe that it is not the gender, as much as the policy and practice, which brought the state down – the corrupt administration of the royal mother, her son who turned his back to the rule and dedicated his time to his leisure pursuits, thus allowing his immediate surrounding entourage, including the commander of the army, police, *hajibs*, viziers, *qahramanat* and his relatives to run the show.

The previous 'Abbasid male caliphs, as discussed, such as al-Rashid, al-Amin, al-Mu'tasim and al-Mutawakkil, among others, were male and had largely contributed to the depletion and sapping of the state. They made a modest political contribution, but with their extravagant and legendary lifestyles, paid more attention to their singers and concubines, surpassing, on occasion, the narrative and imagination of the *Arabian Nights* stories. As a result, al-Muqtadir's caliphate became the breaking point of a decadent unaccountable style of rule, which had started in the early 'Abbasid period and maybe even before them.

Al-Jahiz, the analytical 'Abbasid writer, noticed the gradual interference of the other gender in the rule. He blamed it on the weakness of different caliphs' personalities and minds to resist the charm and ambition of the women around them.[267] Yet he was not anti-women like the chroniclers mentioned earlier, and never suggested or questioned the possibility of a female in power. Those chroniclers were not alone in their negative feelings or perceptions. Sometimes these anti-women sentiments surfaced, such as in 1013 when Caliph al-Qadir b. Allah totally forbade the other gender from going out in the streets of Baghdad.[268] He thought the other gender always brought affliction, and that it was better for them to remain 'caged' at home.

The age of al-Muqtadir had witnessed the pinnacle of gender and politics, represented and concentrated in the five *qahramanat* of Shaghab and her feeble son, the caliph.

The use and hiring of female and male *qahramanat* continued in the following decades, but on a smaller scale, as we can see in the sources.

We have discussed the influence of Shaghab and her different companions. It seems suitable here to discuss how her career and life ended, before we continue with the evolution of the 'Abbasid *qahramana*.

In 932 al-Muqtadir was slain in a coup by his eunuch commander in chief, Mu'nis al-Khadim, as previously mentioned. The army commanders brought to power the half-brother of the killed caliph, giving him the title of '*al-Qahir*'. He arrested the royal mother and her harem, and interrogated her about her money and jewellery.[269] By then she already was suffering from severe illness and depression over how her son's life had ended.

Shaghab told al-Qahir about her luxurious embroideries and richly manufactured clothes, but not the money. Al-Qahir, of course, was not convinced by the outcome of her revelations, so he had her hanged upside down and ordered a brutal beating to make her confess. In addition to that, he held a public council and brought the judges of Baghdad to force her to give up or cancel the *waqfs* (endowments) she had devoted to numerous charities in Iraq and the Hijaz.[270] According to Islamic law, these endowments were considered sacred and could not be abrogated. Thus, al-Qahir surprisingly declared that all her *waqfs* would be for sale, and were distributed among his men and entourage.[271]

Shaghab died the following year after suffering very poor health and was buried in the tomb she had prepared for herself. Of her relatives and others who had supported her, we know that her nephew, Harun, disappeared for a while, and then paid al-Qahir 300,000 dinars for his safety; he was pardoned and installed as a deputy in Kufa in 933. Her grandson, 'Abd al-Wahid, escaped, as did many other commanders from Baghdad. Later in 933 his safety was assured by his uncle, the caliph. He returned to Baghdad and was given some of the confiscated properties of his grandmother, Shaghab.[272]

The indispensable chronicler Meskawayh blamed al-Muqtadir, his royal mother and her harem for the economic crisis that contributed to the collapse of their rule. He wrote in detail that 70,000,000 dinars were wasted during his caliphate, while another contemporary, al-Suli, puts it at 80,000,000. He compares him to al-Rashid, who saved 48,000,000 dinars and who had also ruled for a quarter of a century. Meskawayh notes that al-Muqtadir could have saved at least one million dinars every year after all financial demands of the state were covered, as had other 'Abbasid caliphs before him.[273]

'Abbasid *Qahramanat* after the Age of al-Muqtadir

The office of *qahramana* continued to play a key role in 'Abbasid politics up to the Buwayhid era, but the number of *qahramanat* decreased after the age of al-Muqtadir and his royal mother, which was the golden age for that post. In addition, there was only one *qahramana* at one time, and not a team of them like in Shaghab's era.

In 933 during his first year in the caliphate, Caliph al-Qahir was in conflict with the army chief Mu'nis, vizier Ibn Muqla and Ibn Yalbaq, the *hajib*,[274] about how to run the realm. Mistrust and fear between the two sides increased quickly. As Mu'nis's pact was well connected to other allies due to his long commandership of the army, we see that the new caliph stood helpless against them. However, he used the services of his *qahramana*, Ikhtyar (lit. choice). This *qahramana* advised the caliph to contact her old adherent, Muhammad b. al-Qasim, to aid him against Mu'nis, in return for appointing him later as a vizier.[275]

Qahramana Ikhtyar became the secret envoy between the caliph and his new allies in his battle. Sometimes Ikhtyar would pretend that she was going out to purchase items for the caliph's harem, but, in reality, she was working undercover against Mu'nis, arranging and negotiating different pacts.

Caliph al-Qahir managed to trick all his enemies into attending his palace, whereby he had them all arrested; he decapitated Mu'nis and Yalbaq, but the vizier managed to escape from captivity. His collaborator, recommended by *Qahramana* Ikhtyar, was appointed as the new vizier.[276] Here we see how this *qahramana* managed to arrange with others the end of this military commander to pave the way for her lord, Caliph al-Qahir, to win the political battle against his enemies. Ikhtyar was arrested with the caliph when he was toppled in 934 by his troops.[277]

If we take a wider view, we will see that the institution of the caliphate was suffering a paralysing financial crisis, which affected the entire 'Abbasid administration. This led to the rise of the Shi'i Buwayhid forces and their seizure of Shiraz in 934.[278] This victory was the start of a chain crisis leading to the arrival of the Buwayhids in Baghdad in 944, and the de facto end of the 'Abbasid caliphate. During this period, we see the disappearance of the harem institution as we know it, and along with it the singers, concubines, *jawari* and eunuchs.

During this unstable transitional period, Caliph al-Muttaqi b. al-Muqtadir (r. 940–4) was toppled from power by Commander Tuzun, in collaboration with a certain woman known as Husn, the widow of the secretary of Tuzun.[279] This woman was present when Tuzun arrested and gouged out the eyes of al-Muttaqi. Commander Tuzun needed to closely monitor and control the new caliph, al-Mustakfi, so he used Husn, who had the title, "*alam*' (flag), as a *qahramana* to the newly appointed caliph. Ibn al-Athir describes her influence: "Alam became the *qahramana* of Caliph al-Mustakfi, and she dominated all his affairs.'[280] It is likely that the alliance between the post-holder of the *qahramana* and commander of the army continued to serve their mutual interests, such as in the time of al-Muqtadir. 'Alam seemed to dominate the affairs of the state during that year.

Consider this anecdote by Meskawayh:

> The court of al-Mustakfi suffered the most humiliating times among the eras of caliphs, because it became under the domination and influence of a Persian woman named Husn. Several corrupt and evil people gathered around her, forming her entourage. She would inspect the *hajib*s and *ghulman* of the caliph in a council called the Hudan, where only the vizier had access. As a result of that, the prestige and dignity of the caliphate was torn apart. The court ceremonies were lost, and the palace of the caliph became approachable by many (allowed by her). She wanted to reward Tuzun, so she made the caliph treat him with ceremonies unheard before this time. Tuzun would eat with the caliph at the same table, and used the caliph's parasol.[281]

Meskawayhh lamented the collapse of the caliphate and blamed it on the interference of a certain woman in political affairs, but he was more accommodating to the wild behaviour of the many 'Abbasid caliphs who were the principal contributors to the collapse.

'Alam (Husn) tried to establish good relations with the various Daylami Iranian commanders who worked under the Buwayhids. She held several banquets in their honour, in the hope they would support the caliph against any opposition.[282]

As a result of her influence, the Buwayhid leader, Mu'izz al-Dawla

Ahmad, when he entered Baghdad in 945, accused her of working and collaborating against him, so he cut her tongue out and seized her money (her ally Commander Tuzun had died a few months earlier). She was arrested with her caliph, who was then replaced by another, ironically titled '*al-Muti°* (the obedient).[283] At the same time in Ikhshidid 'Abbasid Egypt, there were some minor cases of *qahramana* intrusion in state affairs, such as Sumaya, who had instructed the chief judge, Ibn Shu'ayb, in the late 930s.[284]

The 'Abbasid realm under the Buwayhids witnessed tremendous change to the *qahramana* office and the institution of the harem in general. Due to the financial crisis, to which Caliph al-Muqtadir had contributed greatly, from 945 to the end of the Buwayhid rule at the hands of the Seljuq Sunni Turks who entered Baghdad in 1055, there was no administrative–political roles given to *qahramanat* or other women. Hugh Kennedy states: 'The Buwayhids' seizure of power caused the 'Abbasid court to be much reduced in numbers and wealth, and effectively restricted it to a domestic role.'[285]

Caliph al-Muti' (d. 974) had no court or courtiers and would take only 100 dinars a day as his stipend from his real master, the Buwayhid king.[286] His successor, al-Ta'i' (d. 991), followed the same model, but he had a few *jawari* (without political influence) for pleasure. Matters became bizarre when Caliph al-Qadir (r. 991–1031) exiled all singers, *jawari* and *ghulman* from Baghdad. His misogynous acts went even further, namely that in 1013 he inhibited females from going out into the streets of Baghdad.[287] Interestingly enough, this mental virus (as one might define it) also infected the Shi'i Fatimid caliph in Cairo, al-Hakim (r. 996–1021), who implemented the same idea in the same year. Women were completely forbidden from stepping out of their habitats, by day or night. Shoemakers were even ordered not to manufacture any shoes for them.[288]

I would have to agree with Hugh Kennedy's statement about the end of 'Abbasid harem: 'The fall of the mistress (Shaghab) in 932 meant the end of the 'Abbasid harem as it had developed since the informal days of Mansur, nearly two centuries before.'[289]

A number of points here are noteworthy:

1. Aspects of the harem, mainly their eunuch keepers, continued to operate in a different capacity. They progressed from humble domestic service to

become elite commanders of the state, and in Ikhshidid 'Abbasid Egypt and Syria in 966, one became the official declared lord; this will be examined later.
2. The harem and its influence resurfaced again under the later 'Abbasids with the Seljuqid rule from 1055 and the associated Turkmen dynasties; this will be discussed in Chapter Four.
3. Concubines continued to play key political roles under several Muslim and non-Muslim dynasties, such as the Ottoman harem, mainly in the sixteenth century, but also in some parts of South East Asia up to the nineteenth century, and in the Chinese court from 1644 to 1911.[290]
4. The segregation of the sexes under the 'Abbasids, and the marginalisation of women failed. On the contrary, it created a distinguished society with its own powerful hierarchy and power, which interfered and sometimes dominated the whole state with key offices in and outside the harem, as mentioned.
5. The 'Abbasid harem and its tens of thousands of subjects throughout certain periods had its legacy and reflections in literary works, like the tenth-century *Kitab al-Aghani* (*Book of Songs*). It was also reflected in *Alf Layla wa Layla* (*Thousand and One Nights/Arabian Nights*), which, interestingly, started to be written at about the ninth century in Baghdad, or translated from the Persian *Hazar Afsan* at about the same time, as al-Mas'udi points out.[291] After all, King Shahrayar travelled the 1,001 nights between his desires and eroticism, and his threats to his concubine Shahrazad, who had three children by him.[292]
6. For reasons set out below, I do not agree with the feminist opinion of Fatima Mernissi, who describes this age of the 'Abbasid harem with her question: '*Jawari* or the revolution of the harem?' Mernissi believes that the *jawari* under the 'Abbasids revolted against their masters and avenged their enslavers who had humiliated them. She even compares the harem revolution with the Zanj revolution under the 'Abbasids.[293]

- Eliyahu Ashtor, who studied the revolutions under the 'Abbasids, including the black slaves (Zanj) from 870 to 883, did not, along with other scholars, refer to what Mernissi called '*jawari*' revolt.[294]

- The anatomy of the revolution in Mernissi's definition does not exist. There is no period, or a body, mass or leadership to such a revolution. In addition, there are no certain claims, demands or targets by the alleged *jawari* or revolutionaries. Mernissi makes distinct historical errors within the same framework, including describing the Buwayhid rulers as Shi'i-Ibadi.[295] We know that Shi'i doctrine is totally separate and independent from the (Khariji) Ibadi creed.
- Mernissi does not differentiate between domestic *jawari*, such as keepers, cooks, cleaners, servants, maids and messengers, and *qahramanat*, concubines and *qiyan*. She counts them all as one, which is not the case at all.
- Mernissi, an anthropologist and not a historian, but as a spokesperson for Arab women, provides no clear line between what is Arab and what is Islamic. She inveighs against the sombre conditions of women in present-day (Arab) societies, and places the blame for it at the door of the *qiyan* and *jawari*, or their historical phenomenon of their introduction into diverse Muslim dynasties from the Umayyads onwards.[296] A recent study by the feminist historian Wafa' al-Deresi points out that *jawari* in medieval Islamic history used as their main weapon seduction and the pretence of being upset against their masters in order to receive unlimited amounts of money and jewellery; for example, Khayzuran among others.[297] There is no mention of a unity and revolution by the other gender.

Mernissi certainly has a case about the marginalisation of the other gender in different Muslim societies from West Africa to Indonesia in modern times, but her readings of medieval Islamic history do not support her argument convincingly.

Notes

1. Kennedy, *The Court of the Caliphs*.
2. Hillenbrand, *Islamic Art*, pp. 39–42.
3. *Alf Layla wa Layla* [*The Arabian Nights*], Cairo, 2006, Vol. 4, Story 894, p. 691.
4. Dominique Sourdel, art. 'Dar al-Hikma', *EI²*.
5. Al-Tabari, *Ta'rikh*, p. 1,494, 1,723–56.

6. Bernard Lewis, art. "Abbasids', *EI²*; Adam Metz, *The Renaissance of Islam*, trans. M. Abu Rida, Cairo, 2008, Vol. 1, pp. 2–12.
7. Al-Hamawi, *Muʿjam*, Vol. 4, p. 172; Eliyahu Ashtor, *A Social and Economic History of the Near East in the Middle Ages*, trans. A. Abla, Damascus, 1985, p. 223.
8. Ibn al-Athir, *Al-Kamil*, Vol. 6, p. 91.
9. Al-Suyuti, *Taʾrikh*, p. 411.
10. Ibid., p. 454.
11. Metz, *Renaissance*, Vol. 2, p. 172.
12. Ibn al-Athir, *Al-Kamil*, Vol. 6, pp. 18–19.
13. Abbott, *Two Queens*.
14. Kennedy, *The Court of the Caliphs*, p. 189.
15. Al-Masʿudi, *Muruj*, Vol. 3, p. 369.
16. Ibn Aybak, *Kanz al-Durar*, Cairo, 1965, Vol. 5, p. 56; Kahala, *Aʿlam al-Nissaʾ*, Vol. 1, p. 479.
17. Abbott, *Two Queens*, p. 40.
18. Ibid., p. 41.
19. Kahala, *Aʿlam al-Nissaʾ*, Vol. 2, p. 235; Kennedy, *The Court of the Caliphs*, p. 166.
20. Other dates are mentioned, including 781 and 782.
21. Abbott, *Two Queens*, p. 30.
22. Al-Masudi, *Muruj*, Vol. 3, p. 341.
23. J. Renate, art.: 'Zubayda bt. Djaʿfar' *EI²*; Kennedy, *The Court of the Caliphs*, p. 167; Ibn Jubayr, *Rihla*, Beirut, 1986, p. 165.
24. Abbott, *Two Queens*, pp. 138, 142.
25. Ibid., p. 164.
26. Ibn Taqataqa, *Al-Fakhri fi al-Adab*, p. 187.
27. Kahala, *Aʿlam al-Nissaʾ*, Vol. 2, p. 18.
28. Al-Masudi, *Muruj*, Vol. 3, p. 292.
29. Ibid., p. 311.
30. Al-Tabari, *Taʾrikh*, p. 1,656; Ibn Aybak, *Kanz al-Durar*, Vol. 5, p. 154.
31. Kennedy, *The Court of the Caliphs*, p. 164.
32. W. Barthold and Dominique Sourdel, art. 'Al-Baramika', *EI²*.
33. Abbott, *Two Queens*, p. 195.
34. Al-Tabari, *Taʾrikh*, pp. 1,684–6; al-Masudi, *Muruj*, Vol. 3, p. 310; Abu ʿAli Meskawayh al-Razi, *Tarajib al-Umam*, ed. Abu Al-Qasim Imami, Tehran, 2001, Vol. 3, pp. 531–2.

35. Al-Masudi, *Muruj*, Vol. 3, p. 310.
36. Meskawayh, *Tarajib*, Vol. 3, pp. 532–3; al-Masudi, *Muruj*, Vol. 3, pp. 310–11.
37. Abu Abdulla Ibn Abdus al-Jahshyari, *Kitab al-Wuzara' wa al-Kuttab*, Cairo, 1980, p. 307.
38. Ibn al-Sa'i, *Nisa' al-Khulafa'*, p. 85; Al-Tabari, *Ta'rikh*, p. 1,789; Meskawayh, *Tarajib*, Vol. 4, p. 141.
39. Ibn al-Athir, *Al-Kamil*, Vol. 6, pp. 341–50.
40. Bosworth, *Islamic Dynasties*, p. 99.
41. Ibn al-Taqataqa, *Al-Fakhri fi al-Adab*, p. 222.
42. Tha'alibi, *Thimar*, pp. 140–1; Suyuti, *Ta'rikh*, p. 364; al-Masudi, *Muruj*, Vol. 4, p. 26.
43. Al-Tabari, *Ta'rikh*, p. 1,784; Ibn Aybak, *Kanz al-Durar*, Vol. 5, p. 189.
44. Ibn Aybak, *Kanz al-Durar*, Vol. 5, p. 178; Meskawayh, *Tarajib*, Vol. 4, p. 141.
45. Meskawayh, *Tarajib*, Vol. 4, pp. 141–2.
46. T. Bianquis, 'Autonomous Egypt from Ibn Tulun to Kafur, 868–969', in *The Cambridge History of Egypt*, ed. C. Petry, Cambridge, 2006, pp. 86–119, pp. 86–8.
47. Ibid., pp. 105–6.
48. T. Bianquis mentions the dowry being one million dinars; however, Ibn Taghri, among others, puts it at one million dirhams, see Ibn Taghri Bardi, *Al-Nujum al-Zahira fi Muluk Misr wa al-Qahira*, Cairo, 1963, Vol. 3, p. 53.
49. Ibn Sa'i, *Nisa' al-Khulafa'*, pp. 128–9; Al-Tabari, *Ta'rikh*, p. 2,116; Meskawayh, *Tarajib*, Vol. 4, p. 494.
50. Al-Tabari, *Ta'rikh*, p. 2,116.
51. Ibn Taghri Bardi, *Al-Nujum*, Vol. 3, pp. 90–1.
52. Ibn al-Athir, *Al-Kamil*, Vol. 8, p. 688.
53. Ibn al-Athir, *Al-Kamil*, Vol. 9, p. 101.
54. M. Canard, art. 'Hamdanids', *EI²*.
55. Kawashi is an inaccessible mountain citadel in the Kurdish area, East of Mosul. Al-Hamawi, *Mu'jam*, Vol. 4, p. 486.
56. Ibn al-Athir, *Al-Kamil*, Vol. 8, pp. 593–6.
57. Ibid., p. 599.
58. Ibid., p. 600.
59. Al-Tabari, in *Ta'rikh*, mentions in one line two 'Abbasid princesses, Um 'Isa and Lubaba, sisters of Salih b. 'Ali, who were commissioned by al-Mansur in 756 to lead the summer invasion of Byzantine Eastern Anatolia. They took part

in this campaign, but we believe that their roles and contributions were very limited, as there is no more information on this, p. 1,505.
60. Al-Jahiz, *Rasa'il*, p. 51.
61. Abu Bakr Muhammad al-Razi, 'Al-Bah', in *Nisa'*, ed. H. Abd al-Aziz, Cairo, 1999, pp. 149–75.
62. Ibn al-Nadim, *al-Fihrest*, Vol. 1, p. 504.
63. Metz, *Renaissance*, Vol. 1, pp. 271–2; Caswell, *The Slave Girls*, pp. 15–16.
64. Bou Hdeiba, *Sex in Islam*, p. 87.
65. Al-Suyuti, *Ta'rikh*, p. 306.
66. Kahala, *A'lam al-Nissa'*, Vol. 2, p. 235.
67. Kennedy, *The Court of the Caliphs*, p. 166.
68. Abu 'Amr al-Jahiz, *Tahdhib al-Akhlaq*, Cairo, 1989, pp. 31–2.
69. Al-Hamawi, *Mu'jam*, Vol. 4, pp. 172–3; Kennedy, *The Court of the Caliphs*, p. 145.
70. Abbott, *Two Queens*, pp. 23–5.
71. Ibid., p. 38.
72. Al-Ya'qubi, *Ta'rikh al-Ya'qubi*, Baghdad, 1989, Vol. 2, p. 439; Al-Tabari, *Ta'rikh*, p. 1,512.
73. Al-Suyuti, *Ta'rikh*, pp. 331, 336. Dates vary among different sources.
74. Ibn al-Athir, *Al-Kamil*, Vol. 8, pp. 82–3.
75. Abu 'Amr al-Jahiz, *Al-Mahasin wa al-Addad*, Cairo, 1906, pp. 233–4.
76. Abbott, *Two Queens*, p. 29.
77. Al-Tabari, *Ta'rikh*, p. 1,574.
78. Al-Isfahani, *Kitab al-Aghani*, Vol. 10, p. 58; 'Ali Kharbotly, *Al-Mahdi al-Abbasi*, Cairo, 1966, pp. 59–60.
79. Abbott, *Two Queens*, p. 34; Al-Tabari, *Ta'rikh*, p. 1,786.
80. Al-Isfahani, *Kitab al-Aghani*, Vol. 10, pp. 79–119.
81. Al-Isfahani, *Kitab al-Aghani*, Vol. 6, p. 74; Abbott, *Two Queens*, p. 36; Kahala, *A'lam al-Nissa'*, Vol. 5, p. 72.
82. Abbott, *Two Queens*, p. 36.
83. Ibn al-Athir, *Al-Kamil*, Vol. 6, pp. 34, 44.
84. 'Ibn Taqataqa, *Al-Fakhri fi al-Adab*, p. 179. Isa was the cousin of al-Mansur and also his heir, until he was deposed in 764 in favour of al-Mahdi.
85. Ibn al-Athir, *Al-Kamil*, Vol. 6, pp. 43–4, 69; Al-Tabari, *Ta'rikh*, p. 1,610; al-Suyuti, *Ta'rikh*, p. 323; Abbott, *Two Queens*, p. 38.
86. Al-Tabari, *Ta'rikh*, p. 1,610.
87. Ibid., p. 1,615.

88. Mernissi, *The Forgotten Queens*, p. 84.
89. Abbott, *Two Queens*, p. 45.
90. Ibid., p. 58.
91. Ibn al-Athir, *Al-Kamil*, Vol. 6, pp. 86–7.
92. Sibt Ibn al-Jawzi, *Mir'at al-Zaman*, Damascus, 2013, Vol. 12, p. 404. Ibn al-Athir, *Al-Kamil*, Vol. 6, p. 82; Meskawayh, *Tarajib*, Vol. 3, p. 480; Al-Tabari, *Ta'rikh*, p. 1,632. The same sources mention also that the caliph was killed during a hunting trip, but I support the story of the poisoned fruit.
93. Al-Tabari, *Ta'rikh*, p. 1,635.
94. Meskawayh, *Tarajib*, Vol. 3, p. 486.
95. Ibn Taqataqa mentions that some concubines had minor roles, with the permission or order of the caliph. He wrote that al-Mahdi had commissioned one of his concubines to spy on his vizier, Ya'qub b. Dawud, as the caliph suspected him of favouring the Shi'i doctrine. See Ibn Taqataqa, *Al-Fakhri fi al-Adab*, p. 167.
96. Meskawayh, *Tarajib*, Vol. 3, p. 486.
97. Al-Mas'udi, *Muruj*, Vol. 3, p. 272.
98. Meskawayh, *Tarajib*, Vol. 3, p. 488.
99. Kennedy, *The Court of the Caliphs*, p. 164.
100. Al-Khatib al-Baghdadi, *Ta'rikh Baghdad*, Beirut, 1993, Vol. 3, p. 45.
101. Al-Mas'udi, *Muruj*, Vol. 3, p. 272.
102. Abbott, *Two Queens*, p. 89.
103. Al-Tabari, *Ta'rikh*, p. 1,646; al-Mas'udi, *Muruj*, Vol. 3, p. 272; Meskawayh, *Tarajib*, Vol. 3, pp. 488–9.
104. Abbott, *Two Queens*, pp. 60–3.
105. Meskawayh, *Tarajib*, Vol. 3, p. 490.
106. Ibid., pp. 492–3; Al-Tabari, *Ta'rikh*, pp. 1,646–7.
107. Al-Tabari, *Ta'rikh*, p. 1,648; Anon., *Al-'Uyun wa al-Hada'iq fi Akhbar al-Haqa'iq*, Leiden, 1869, Vol. 3, pp. 283–6.
108. Ibn al-Athir, *Al-Kamil*, Vol. 6, p. 100; *Al-'Uyun*, Vol. 3, p. 287; Editor, art.: 'Al-Khayzuran', *EI²*.
109. Abu 'Ali al-Tannukhi, *Al-Faraj B'ad al-Shidda*, Beirut, 1987, p. 285; *Al-'Uyun*, Vol. 3, p. 288.
110. *Al-'Uyun*, Vol. 3, p. 289; Ibn al-Athir, *Al-Kamil*, Vol. 6, p. 106.
111. Al-Tabari, *Ta'rikh*, p. 1,656; al-Jashyari, *Kitab al-Wuzara'*, p. 177.
112. Sibt Ibn al-Jawzi, *Mir'at*, Vol. 12, p. 412; Abbott, *Two Queens*, p. 115.
113. Abbott, *Two Queens*, p. 121.

114. Ibid., p. 124.
115. Mernissi, *The Forgotten Queens*, pp. 77–8.
116. Caswell, *The Slave Girls*, p. 19.
117. Al-Suyuti, *Ta'rikh*, p. 359. Al-Amin wrote the following verse:

> If men are getting proud of their origins
> You should withdraw, as you have no chance
> God has granted you what you wished
> But against your wish you have Marajil (his mother)

118. Editor, 'Al-Khayzuran'.
119. Ibn al-Jawzi, *Al-Muntazam fi Ta'rikh al-Muluk wa al-Umam*, ed. M. Ata, Beirut, 2007, Vol. 9, p. 197; see also al-Tabari, *Ta'rikh*, p. 1,746, a poem written during al-Amin's reign glorifying that area of Baghdad.
120. Anderson 'Concubines', pp. 633–70, 644, 664–5.
121. Kennedy, *The Court of the Caliphs*, p. 165; al-Suyuti, *Ta'rikh*, p. 411.
122. Ibn al-Sa'i, *Nisa' al-Khulafa'*, p. 71; al-Baghdadi, *Ta'rikh Baghdad*, Vol. 3, p. 120.
123. Al-Isfahani, *Kitab al-Aghani*, Vol. 18, p. 47.
124. Kennedy, *The Court of the Caliphs*, p. 145.
125. Ibn al-Sa'i, *Nisa' al-Khulafa'*, p. 80.
126. Ibn Asakir, *Tarajim*, p. 231. Some of the royal 'Abbasid princess were no stranger to at least expressing their drinking habits, or their frank sexual desires, such as 'Ulayya, sister of al-Rashid, and Khadija, daughter of al-Ma'mun. See Caswell, *The Slave Girls*, pp. 197–8, 206.
127. Hillenbrand, *Islamic Art*, pp. 46–7; Eva Hoffman, 'Between East and West: the Wall Paintings of Samarra and the Construction of Abbasid Princely Culture', *Muqarnas*, Vol. 25, 2008, pp. 107–32, 109–13.
128. Kennedy, *The Court of the Caliphs*, pp. 147–8.
129. Meskawayh, *Tarajib*, Vol. 4, pp. 297–8; al-Ballawi, *Sirat Ahmad b. Tulun*, Cairo, 1999, p. 32.
130. Ibn Aybak, *Kanz al-Durar*, Vol. 5, p. 230.
131. Al-Ballawi, *Sirat*, p. 40.
132. Ibn Taqataqa, *Al-Fakhri fi al-Adab*, p. 243.
133. Al-Suyuti, *Ta'rikh*, p. 423; Ibn al-Athir, *Al-Kamil*, Vol. 7, p. 117.
134. Ibn al-Athir, *Al-Kamil*, Vol. 7, pp. 137–43.
135. Ibid., p. 167; al-Mas'udi, *Muruj*, Vol. 4, p. 117. For further details, refer to al-Tabari's *Ta'rikh* and Ibn al-Athir's *Al-Kamil* on this long civil war.

136. Al-Ballawi, *Sirat*, p. 40. Wasit is a province in southern Iraq, al-Hamawi, *Mu'jam*, Vol. 5, p. 347.
137. Al-Ballawi, *Sirat*, pp. 40–1; Ibn al-Athir, *Al-Kamil*, Vol. 7, pp. 172–3.
138. Al-Mas'udi, *Muruj*, Vol. 4, p. 142; Ibn al-Athir, *Al-Kamil*, Vol. 7, p. 172.
139. Meskawayh, *Tarajib*, Vol. 4, pp. 370–1.
140. Ibn al-Athir, *Al-Kamil*, Vol. 7, pp. 173–86.
141. Meskawayh, *Tarajib*, Vol. 4, p. 386.
142. Ibn al-Athir, *Al-Kamil*, Vol. 7, pp. 199–200.
143. Ibn al-Sa'i, *Nisa' al-Khulafa'*, p. 121.
144. Al-Mas'udi, *Muruj*, Vol. 4, pp. 151–2; al-Suyuti, *Ta'rikh*, p. 428.
145. Al-Suyuti, *Ta'rikh*, p. 447.
146. Ibid., pp. 444, 456.
147. Bosworth, *Islamic Dynasties*, p. 69.
148. Ibid., p. 94.
149. Ibn Taqataqa, *Al-Fakhri fi al-Adab*, p. 261.
150. Kahala, *A'lam al-Nissa'*, Vol. 5, p. 67.
151. Ibn al-Athir, *Al-Kamil*, Vol. 8, pp. 8–9.
152. Meskawayh, *Tarajib*, Vol. 5, p. 54.
153. Ibn al-Jawzi, *Al-Muntazam*, Vol. 13, pp. 60, 62; Ibn al-Athir, *Al-Kamil*, Vol. 8, p. 8.
154. Ibn Taqataqa, *Al-Fakhri fi al-Adab*, p. 163; Meskawayh, *Tarajib*, Vol. 5, pp. 55–6; K. V. Zettersteen and C. E. Bosworth, art.: 'Al-Muktadir', *EI*².
155. 'Arib al-Qurtubi, *Silat Ta'rikh al-Tabari*, Cairo, 1999, p. 24; Ibn al-Athir, *Al-Kamil*, Vol. 8, p. 15.
156. Ibn al-Athir, *Al-Kamil*, Vol. 8, pp. 17–18.
157. Meskawayh, *Tarajib*, Vol. 5, pp. 56–7.
158. Ibid., p. 59.
159. Ibn al-Athir, *Al-Kamil*, Vol. 8, p. 54.
160. Ibid., p. 61.
161. Ibid., p. 76.
162. Dominique Sourdel, *Le Vizirat 'Abbasid*, Damascus, 1960, Vol. 2.
163. al-Tannukhi, *Al-Faraj*, p. 129.
164. Ibn al-Jawzi, *Al-Muntazam*, Vol. 13, p. 192.
165. Ibn al-Athir, *Al-Kamil*, Vol. 8, p. 158.
166. Ibn Taqataqa, *Al-Fakhri fi al-Adab*, Vol. 8, p. 272.
167. Ibn Taqataqa, *Al-Fakhri fi al-Adab*, Vol. 8, p. 200.
168. Kennedy, *The Court of the Caliphs*, p. 194.

169. Meskawayh, *Tarajib*, Vol. 5, p. 111.
170. Kennedy, *The Court of the Caliphs*, p. 192.
171. Ibn al-Athir, *Al-Kamil*, Vol. 8, pp. 150, 151.
172. Meskawayh, *Tarajib*, Vol. 5, p. 325.
173. Kahala, *A 'lam al-Nissa'*, Vol. 5, p. 67.
174. Ibid., p. 255.
175. Meskawayh, *Tarajib*, Vol. 5, pp. 129–30.
176. Kennedy, *The Court of the Caliphs*, p. 195.
177. Al-Suyuti, *Ta'rikh*, p. 454.
178. Kennedy, *The Court of the Caliphs*, p. 152.
179. Al-Suyuti, *Ta'rikh*, p. 450.
180. Ibn al-Jawzi, *Al-Muntazam*, Vol. 13, p. 68; Metz, *Renaissance*, Vol. 2, p. 182.
181. Ibn al-Jawzi, *Al-Muntazam*, Vol. 13, p. 157.
182. Al-Suyuti, *Ta'rikh*, p. 450.
183. Meskawayh, *Tarajib*, Vol. 5, pp. 177–8.
184. Ibid., p. 179.
185. Ibn al-Athir, *Al-Kamil*, Vol. 8, pp. 151–3.
186. Al-Tannukhi, *Al-Faraj*, p. 366.
187. Ibn al-Jawzi, *Al-Muntazam*, Vol. 13, p. 112; Meskawayh, *Tarajib*, Vol. 5, p. 210.
188. Al-Hilal al-Sabi', *Tuhfat al-Umara' fi Ta'rikh al-Wuzara'*, Beirut, 2012, pp. 172–3.
189. Ibn al-Athir, *Al-Kamil*, Vol. 8, p. 14.
190. Ibid., pp. 116–17.
191. Ibid., pp. 150–1.
192. Ibn al-Jawzi, *Al-Muntazam*, Vol. 13, p. 150; Ibn al-Athir, *Al-Kamil*, Vol. 8, pp. 153–4.
193. Ibn al-Athir, *Al-Kamil*, Vol. 8, p. 182.
194. Meskawayh, *Tarajib*, Vol. 5, pp. 262–3.
195. Ibid., pp. 264–5.
196. Ibn al-Athir, *Al-Kamil*, Vol. 8, pp. 200, 201.
197. Ibid., pp. 203–4.
198. Meskawayh, *Tarajib*, Vol. 5, p. 272.
199. Ibn al-Jawzi, *Al-Muntazam*, Vol. 13, pp. 187–8; Ibn al-Athir, *Al-Kamil*, Vol. 8, pp. 227–8.
200. Meskawayh, *Tarajib*, Vol. 5, p. 300.
201. Ibid., p. 142.

202. Ibn al-Athir, *Al-Kamil*, Vol. 8, pp. 231–2.
203. Ibid., p. 238.
204. Ibn al-Jawzi, *Al-Muntazam*, Vol. 13, p. 220; Ibn al-Athir, *Al-Kamil*, Vol. 8, p. 241.
205. Hugh Kennedy, 'Mu'nis al-Muzaffar: An Exceptional Eunuch', in *Celibate and Childless Men in Power: Ruling Eunuchs and Bishops in the Pre-modern World*, eds A. Höfert, M. Mesley and S. Tolino, London, 2018, pp. 79–91, 85.
206. Ibn al-Athir, *Al-Kamil*, Vol. 8, p. 244.
207. Ibn al-Jawzi, *Al-Muntazam*, Vol. 13, p. 240.
208. Ibn al-Nadim, *Al-Fihrest*, Vol. 1, p. 423; Maaike van Berkel, 'The Young Caliph and His Wicked Advisors: Women and Power Politics under Caliph al-Muqtadir (r. 295–320/908–932)', *Al-Masaq, Journal of the Medieval Mediterranean*, Vol. 19, No. 1, March 2007, pp. 3–15, 8.
209. Michael Cook, 'Did the Prophet Muhammad Keep Court?', in *Courts Cultures in the Muslim World: Seventh to Nineteenth Centuries*, eds A. Fuess and J.-P. Hartung, New York, 2011, pp. 23–9, 23.
210. Sulaf Hasan, *Dawr al-Jawari wa al-Qahramanat fi dar al-Khilafa al-'Abbasiyya*, Damascus 2013, p. 61.
211. Ibid., pp. 62–3.
212. Al-Qurtubi, *Silat*, p. 136; Meskawayh, *Tarajib*, Vol. 3, p. 485.
213. Ibn al-Jawzi, *Al-Muntazam*, Vol. 6, p. 255.
214. Ibid., p. 256.
215. From a minor branch or clan of the Hashemites.
216. El Cheikh, 'The Qahramana', pp. 43–4.
217. Kahala, *A'lam al-Nissa'*, Vol. 5, p. 123; Kennedy, *The Court of the Caliphs*, p. 192.
218. El Cheikh, 'The Qahramana', p. 46.
219. Meskawayh, *Tarajib*, Vol. 5, p. 199.
220. Ibn al-Athir, *Al-Kamil* Vol. 8, p. 240.
221. Kahala, *A'lam al-Nissa'*, Vol. 5, p. 124.
222. Al-Qurtubi, *Silat*, p. 168; Meskawayh, *Tarajib*, Vol. 5, p. 95.
223. El Cheikh, 'The Qahramana', p. 47.
224. Hilal al-Sabi', *Ta'rikh*, p. 272.
225. Meskawayh, *Tarajib*, Vol. 5, p. 74; al-Sabi', *Ta'rikh*, p. 273.
226. Sibt Ibn al-Jawzi, *Mir'at*, Vol. 16, p. 406; Meskawayh, *Tarajib*, p. 48.
227. Meskawayh, *Tarajib*, Vol. 5, p. 76.
228. Al-Sabi', *Ta'rikh*, p. 354; van Berkel, 'The Young Caliph', p. 9.

229. Al-Tannukhi, *Al-Faraj*, pp. 406–7.
230. Ibid., p. 271.
231. Hasan, *Dawr al-Jawari*, p. 126.
232. Ibn al-Athir, *Al-Kamil*, Vol. 8, p. 137; Kennedy, *The Court of the Caliphs*, p. 193.
233. Kahala, *A'lam al-Nissa'*, Vol. 5, p. 124.
234. Meskawayh, *Tarajib*, Vol. 5, pp. 141–2.
235. Ibid., p. 142; Ibn al-Athir, *Al-Kamil*, Vol. 8, p. 140
236. Kahala, *A'lam al-*Nissa', Vol. 5, p. 123.
237. Hasan, *Dawr al-Jawari*, p. 128.
238. Ibid., p. 129.
239. A confrontation (*munazara*) between two dismissed officials took place among high officials where they revealed the financial corruption of each other. That style of interrogation took place all through al-Muqtadir's rule.
240. Al-Sabi', *Ta'rikh*, p. 132.
241. Al-Qurtubi, *Silat*, p. 187; Ibn al-Athir, *Al-Kamil*, Vol. 8, p. 140.
242. El Cheikh, 'The Qahramana', p. 45.
243. Meskawayh, *Tarajib*, Vol. 5, pp. 217, 226.
244. Van Berkel, 'The Young Caliph', p. 9.
245. Al-Sabi', *Ta'rikh*, p. 240.
246. El Cheikh, 'The Qahramana', p. 45.
247. S. al-Munajjid, *Bayna al-Khulafa' wa al-Khula'a' fi al-'Asr al-'Abbasi*, Damascus, n.d., p. 15.
248. Al-Suyuti, *Ta'rikh*, p. 453.
249. Al-Munajjid, *Bayna al-Khulafa'*, p. 61.
250. Kennedy, *The Court of the Caliphs*, p. 193.
251. Van Berkel, 'The Young Caliph', p. 10; El Cheikh, 'The Qahramana', p. 52.
252. Kahala, *A'lam al-Nissa'*, Vol. 1, p. 185; Ibn Arnus, *Ta'rikh al-Qada'*, Cairo, 1972, p. 75.
253. Al-Mas'udi, *Al-Tanbih wa Ishraf*, Beirut, 2003, p. 320; Ibn Aybak, *Kanz al-Durar*, Vol. 5, p. 330.
254. El Cheikh, 'The Qahramana', p. 52.
255. Ibid., p. 53.
256. Ibn Abi al-Rabi', *Siyasat al-Malik fi Tadbir al-Mamalik*, Cairo, 1930, p. 88; Ibn Ridwan al-Milqi, *Siyasat al-Nafi'a*, Beirut, 1976, p. 123; Nizam al-Mulk, *Siyasat Nameh*.

257. Metz, *Renaissance*, Vol. 2, p. 145. *Janaba* means 'unwashed after copulation' according to the shari'a.
258. Ibn Taghri Bardi, *Al-Nujum*, Vol. 3, p. 326; Al-Maqrizi, *Al-Suluk le M'arifat Duwal al-Muluk*, Beirut, 1997, Vol. 1, p. 248.
259. Al-Isfahani, *Kitab al-Aghani*, Vol. 20, pp. 158–9.
260. Meskawayh, *Tarajib*, Vol. 5, pp. 190–1.
261. El Cheikh, 'The Qahramana', p. 52.
262. Meskawayh, *Tarajib*, Vol. 5, p. 300.
263. Hasan, *Dawr al-Jawari*, p. 130.
264. Ibn al-Jawzi, *Al-Muntazam*, Vol. 13, p. 70.
265. Meskawayh, *Tarajib*, Vol. 5, p. 142.
266. Van Berkel, 'The Young Caliph', p. 4; Julia Bray 'Men, Women and Slaves in Abbasid Society', in *Gender in the Early Medieval World, East and West, 300–900*, ed. L. Brubaker, Cambridge, 2004, pp. 121–46, 145.
267. Al-Munajjid, *Bayna al-Khulafa'*, p. 6.
268. Ibn al-Jawzi, *Al-Muntazam*, Vol. 14, p. 115.
269. Ibn Taqataqa, *Al-Fakhri fi al-Adab*, p. 276; Suyuti, *Ta'rikh*, p. 456.
270. Ibn Taqataqa, *Al-Fakhri fi al-Adab*, p. 277; Ibn al-Athir, *Al-Kamil*, Vol. 8, p. 245; Kennedy, *The Court of the Caliphs*, pp. 196–7.
271. Ibn al-Athir, *Al-Kamil*, Vol. 8, p. 246.
272. Ibid., p. 250.
273. Meskawayh, *Tarajib*, Vol. 5, p. 322; Ibn Taghri Bardi, *Al-Nujum*, Vol. 3, p. 234.
274. Meskawayh, *Tarajib*, Vol. 5, p. 348.
275. Ibid., p. 350.
276. Ibid., pp. 353–4.
277. Ibn al-Jawzi, *Al-Muntazam*, Vol. 14, p. 142.
278. Ibn al-Athir, *Al-Kamil*, Vol. 8, p. 275.
279. Ibid., p. 420; Meskawayh, *Tarajib*, Vol. 6, p. 100.
280. Ibn al-Athir, *Al-Kamil*, Vol. 8, p. 421.
281. Meskawaih, 'Kitab al-'Uyun', in A. Metz, *The Renaissance*, Vol. 1, pp. 239–40.
282. Al-Qurtubi, *Silat*, p. 148.
283. Ibid., p. 150; Meskawayh, *Tarajib*, Vol. 6, pp. 119–20.
284. Al-Kindi, *Al-Wulat wa al-Quda*, Beirut, 1908, p. 568.
285. Kennedy, 'Mu'nis', p. 79.
286. Al-Suyuti, *Ta'rikh*, p. 464.
287. Ibid., p. 487.

288. Al-Maqrizi, *Itti'az al-Hunafa' bi Akhbar al-A'imma al-Fatimiyyin al-Khulafa'*, ed. M. Hilmi, Cairo, 1971, Vol. 2, pp. 102–3.
289. Kennedy, *The Court of the Caliphs*, pp. 198–9.
290. Leslie Pierce, 'Beyond Harem Walls: Ottoman Royal Women and the Exercise of Power', in *Servants of the Dynasty: Palace Women in World History*, ed. A. Wathhall, Oakland, 2008. pp. 81–95, 88; Shuo Wang, 'Qing Imperial Women: Empresses, Concubines and Aisin Gioro Daughters', in *Servants of the Dynasties,* , ed. A. Wathhall, Oakland, 2008, pp. 137–58, 138; William Smith, 'Eunuchs and Concubines in the History of Islamic South East Asia', *Journal of Humanities*, Vol. 14, 2007, pp. 8–19, 9–10.
291. Richard Van Leeuwen, *The Thousand and One Nights: Space, Travel and Transformation*, London, 2007, pp. 2–3.
292. *Alf Layla wa Layla* [*The Arabian Nights*], Vol. 4, pp. 942–3, Story 1,001.
293. Mernissi, *The Forgotten Queens*, pp. 55–60.
294. Ashtor, *Social and Economic History*, pp. 152–8.
295. Mernissi, *The Forgotten Queens*, p. 60.
296. Caswell, *The Slave Girls*, pp. 46–8.
297. Wafa' al-Deresi, *Al-Jawari wa al-Ghulman fi al-Thaqafa al-Islamiyya*, Rabat, 2016, pp. 363–5.

3

The Kingdom of Eunuchs under the 'Abbasids

> The full moon describes the beauty of your face (Kawthar)
> I become confused: am I looking at the moon or at you?
> If the soft narcissus flower breathes
> I imagine it as the scent of your mouth
> Kawthar is my religion and my world
> My illness and cure
> The most failing people are
> Those who blame a lover for his beloved.[1]

This rare romantic poetry by the 'Abbasid caliph al-Amin (d. 813) was written to his lover, Kawthar. Kawthar was not a woman, but a eunuch. The evolution of the phenomenon of the eunuch under the 'Abbasids influenced almost all other dynasties that followed, from the medieval Fatimids, Turkmen and Ayyubids to the modern Ottomans and Qajars. David Ayalon states in his pioneering book, *Eunuchs, Caliphs and Sultans*, that further studies are needed in this field; he mentions that he did not cover the entire 'Abbasid and Ayyubid periods, and that he intentionally did not cover the Fatimid dynasty as 'it was saturated with eunuchs, and deserves a separate study'.[2] I intend to take up his invitation to uncover the influence of eunuchs in the political affairs of these periods. Shaun Marmon's study on eunuchs in Islamic history, *Eunuchs and Sacred Boundaries*, covers the Mamluk dynasty onwards.[3]

The phenomenon of eunuchs started mainly in the harem, and in very small numbers at the time of the early 'Abbasid caliphs, but it accelerated rapidly to the point that eunuchs controlled various positions, both civil and military, in the state. It peaked with the appointment of a eunuch as official ruler of 'Abbasid Egypt under the Ikhshidids in the third 'Abbasid era. That eunuch ruler was Kafur (r. 966–8). He had been de facto ruler of Egypt and parts of Syria during the previous two decades.[4]

We have seen earlier how the Prophet owned a eunuch named Mabur, given to him as a gift by the Byzantine ruler of Egypt. The Prophet used him as a servant for his Egyptian concubine, Mariya, in her house, which the Prophet would visit. Under the Umayyads, eunuchs were used as servants in the harem, until Caliph 'Abd al-Malik employed them as *hajibs* at his palace doors; with such an important office, this was the beginning of their introduction to the world of politics and power. As we seen, the last Umayyad ruler, Marwan II, entrusted a eunuch to carry the insignia of the caliph, and act as a bodyguard to his harem during his escape from 'Abbasid forces.[5]

Eunuchs in Islam and Other Civilisations

Eunuchs (*khisyan*) had existed in other civilisations before Islam. There is sufficient evidence to prove that the Chinese, Byzantines and Persians, among others, used eunuchs in their palaces for the rulers and aristocracy. They were used mainly in the harem section of the court.[6]

Al-Jahiz pays great attention to the phenomenon in his great work, *Al-Hayawan* (*The Animal*). He mentions that the castration carried out by the Byzantines was done in order to donate their sons to the church, hoping they would become priests in the future. The families of the little boys carried out the castration (removing the testicles without cutting the male organ) to limit the male temptation from impregnating the nuns. Having said that, the Council of Nicaea held in 325 CE had already prohibited eunuchs from entering the priesthood, but the door was open to them in the Eastern oriental churches.[7] There were two eunuchs who became Patriarch of Constantinople in the tenth century.[8]

From the period of the Umayyads onwards, surrounding empires, including those of the Sasanids and Byzantines, were assimilated into Islamic civilisation. The service of eunuchs was required for several purposes, such as serving, guarding and protecting the harem, especially with the rapid increase of polygamy, and the flood of *jawari*, concubines and *qiyan* accompanying the early Arab/Muslim conquests across three continents. Three main characteristics made a eunuch preferable to a 'normal' male for certain administrative, political and military offices:

1. He had no family, no children and no biological future, so, therefore, no personal ambitions. As a result, it was assumed that his loyalty to his master or mistress was absolute, and unquestionable.
2. A eunuch enjoyed freedom of movement inside and around the palace or residence. They were the medium or go-between who could enter any gendered space prohibited to others, whereas the sons of the ruler or the emir, who had different mothers, were prohibited after the age of puberty to enter specific places.[9]
3. Due to their early castration, eunuchs developed differently physically, and were more tolerant of difficult tasks, such as those in the military. For that last reason, they were sold at prices three or four times higher than normal males of the same age and race.[10]

One major difference that distinguished eunuchdom in Islam from other civilisations is that, under Islam, eunuchs belonged to the *mamluk* slave institution, while in other civilisations they were free persons, natives, and they did not need to change their religion.[11]

Castration was prohibited in Islam in order to resist lust, influenced by the Prophet's Hadith: 'fasting is the castration of my *umma*. It is better for the body.' He said that when a man named 'Uthman b. Maz'un asked the Prophet to castrate himself as he could not control or resist sexual desire.[12] Although Metz points out that the Qur'an prohibited human and animal castration, he does not cite a specific verse.[13] Yet, we understand that God did forbid the changing or alteration of his creation. Since the Prophet owned and used a eunuch in the service of one of his houses, we see Muslim dynasties and rulers trying to be deceitful around the clear Hadith and the spirit of the Qur'an. They were keen to buy and import ready-castrated slaves from other places and markets, as long as they were not involved directly or physically in such a crime. In other words, Muslim rulers and dynasties needed the products (castrated men), so they allowed the continuation of this barbaric savage process in other territories, and then reaped the benefits. We have no evidence in any source of a Muslim ruler or jurist who clearly condemned the ownership of eunuchs and refrained from purchasing them. The 'Abbasid caliph al-Mansur refused the service of one particular eunuch, not out of sympathy or mercy, but because that eunuch was an Arab, and the caliph could not tolerate humiliating him in this way.[14]

Classification of Eunuchs and their Markets

The tenth-century al-Mas'udi classified eunuchs into four types: Sudanese/African blacks, Saqaliba/Eastern European–Slavic, Rum/Byzantine, and Chinese. The blacks were castrated in Abyssinia in East Africa, and Takrur in West Africa.[15] As for the white eunuchs, in particular the Saqaliba, they were brought mainly to Spain, to the town of Pechina in Almeria, and in some other towns in France, where certain Jewish physicians specialised in the operation.[16] There were other centres for castration in the vast Byzantine Empire, with its sophisticated medical practices.[17]

Individual non-regular castration sometimes took place in Muslim areas or under Muslim rules, such as under the Umayyads, when the transsexuals in Medina were castrated, as mentioned in Chapter One, or when the Umayyad caliph Hisham b. 'Abd al-Malik punished a slave who sung in his palace by castrating him.[18] In addition, the 'Abbasid caliph al-Rashid used this practice on one occasion. When he discovered that his *jariya*, Kharshi, married her sister to a man without his permission, he was angered as he considered them to be his property or capital, so he castrated the new husband of Kharshi's sister.[19] Some political enemies were castrated inside the 'Abbasid palace itself as a punishment; the Turkish lord Zengi (d. 1146) used castration as a punishment against one of his deputies, as well as some of his prisoners of war, as will be discussed in detail later.

Due to the huge numbers of eunuchs owned by different Muslim rulers from the ninth century onwards, it is likely that castration did take place in various territories under the rule of Islam, but Muslim chroniclers avoid mentioning this practice.

It is important to note that there were two categories of eunuchs: first, *khasiyy* (pl. *khisyan*), who had his testicles (*khisya*) removed; and, second, *majbub*, who had his entire sexual organ removed or mutilated. Unfortunately, the sources do not distinguish between the two and refer to both as *khasiyy*.[20]

In trying to understand the nature and behaviour of the eunuchs, without straying too much into the medical aspects, we will see that castration resulted in the following, according to Jahiz, who wrote about them in terms of a third gender:

> Larger bones and larger feet. Strong sexual desire. Great appetite. Eunuchs will grow no beard if the operation was performed before adolescence. They will not go bald.
>
> Eunuchs suffer quick changes of mood due to hormone imbalance. They can endure longer riding distances than the ordinary person, and can run longer distances than an ordinary person. If the eunuch has had his organ removed, he has a change of voice, and will sound like a child. Eunuchs will have a distinctly different walk from a normal person, due to the damage of castration to some of the body's nerves and cords in the lower body. A *majbub* will suffer later in life from significant flatulence of their stomach and deformation of their eyes.
>
> Both categories share a bad odour, and later in life they suffer from bending limbs.[21]

It is important to point out that the *khasiyy* of the first category owned concubines and had a strong desire for women, as they were capable of copulation.[22]

These descriptions by al-Jahiz are supported by the descriptions in the Byzantine chronicles.[23] Al-Jahiz's story is supported by Ibn al-Athir's stories that some eunuchs of that type (*khasiyy*) were married, such as Shukr of the Buwayhid ruler 'Adud al-Dawla. Others had affairs with the *jawari* of the rulers, like the eunuchs of the Tulunid ruler of Egypt, Khumarawayh.[24] That is why we see several cases in Islamic history of rulers and clergy owning eunuchs to a certain age and then either dismissing them or prohibiting them from entering the harem. Al-Shafi'i (d. 820), founder of the school of law bearing his name, was one of these cases.[25] Also, the Ayyubid sultan al-'Adi I (d. 1218) never allowed a eunuch in his palaces after they reached puberty, out of jealousy and fearing their behaviour.[26]

It seems strange and illogical to buy and have a eunuch within a Muslim administration to use in the services and jobs that could be trusted or permitted to a normal male to conduct, especially in the harem; then, that eunuch might endanger the harem, sexually. But al-Jahiz explains that the medical operation was not always successful and was carried out in a variety of ways. As a result, a eunuch might escape his fate with an undescended testicle; for example, he mentions a eunuch called al-Tayyan who had a son.[27]

On the psychological side, which al-Jahiz does not ignore, we find that 'full' men or 'stallions' scorned the eunuchs and looked down on them as being inferior, while the eunuchs themselves could discriminate against, or be racist towards, one another, depending on their ethnicity or appearance, which could cause the eunuchs to become depressed.[28]

These rare descriptions and analyses are important, so we understand the general mentality of eunuchs and the environment in which they lived and interacted. It is worth mentioning here that the last eunuchs in Saudi Arabia serving at the Mosque of the Prophet at Medina up to 1982 confirmed, when interviewed in 2014,[29] some of what was said by al-Jahiz. The eunuchs in Medina even had a street named after them, where they lived.

Following on from what has been discussed above, it is believed that most *khisyan* eunuchs were used in the military, police, *barid* (messenger/intelligence service), as well as other public offices, as they made good warriors and guards, while the *majbub* were used mainly inside the palace and around the harem due to the medical and physical conditions they developed, in addition to their feminine voices.

It is unfortunate that Michel Foucault, in *The History of Sexuality*, does not give any answer or analyses as to why the phenomenon of eunuchs started and developed, at least in Western culture. He focused this work on Victorian society and seventeenth-century Western Europe.[30] The same could be said about the *Encyclopedia of Women and Islamic Cultures* (eds. Suad Joseph et al.), Volume 1 of which is concerned with 'Methodologies, paradigms and sources for the study of women and Islamic cultures'. Frederic Lagrange's work on 'Sexuality and Queer Studies' concentrates on homosexuality and lesbianism, but ignores the study of the third gender and the phenomenon of eunuchs in Islamic history and societies across the ages, and how it influenced the history of women.[31]

On the other hand, we see echoes in some societies under Muslim rule in medieval Islam that did develop some rules and regulations devised from *fiqh* (understanding of religious texts). There were several fatwa regulating copulation with eunuchs, and how to purify oneself after sex.[32] Thus, such fatwa looks to eunuchs as a third gender. The fifteenth-century Egyptian historian and religious scholar al-Suyuti dedicates a chapter on copulation with the eunuch (*nikah al-khasiyy*).[33] Having said that, we know that jurists in medieval Islam focused more on the stance and position of hermaphrodites vis-á-vis shari'a, and paid little attention to examining the situation and position of eunuchs under the same shari'a.[34]

I should add that there is a connection between eunuch-hood and homosexuality in some eras of Muslim history. That may be linked to a love of *ghulman* (young beardless boys) (which are mentioned several times in the Qur'an, as discussed in the Introduction), and eunuchs who are also beardless, or raised as *ghulman*, like the 'Abbasid caliph al-Amin and Kawthar. Consider this about the Turkmen lord Zengi (d. 1146): 'When Zengi desired and adored a *ghulam* in his service, he emasculated him by keeping him beardless (to enjoy him).'[35]

This research is concerned mainly with the political influence of eunuchs in Islamic history, and it might be the interest of other researchers to study the social attire of the period and its literature.

Titles and Names of Eunuchs

The medieval chronicles refer to the eunuch by the word *khasiyy*. From the late ninth century CE and early tenth onwards, we see the chroniclers use titles like *khadim* (servant), *shaikh* (teacher), *ustadh* (teacher), *atabeg* (regent) and *tawashi*, from the Turkish *tabushi*, which means servant.[36] We find some sources naming some of them as *ghulam* (lit. young boy), but that term is used for an adult slave eunuch and a full man too. I should add that, from the sources, it is difficult to distinguish between a eunuch and a non-eunuch under the titles of *ustadh* or *shaikh*, and *ghulam*. It is from the context and name of the person that we understand if the source means a eunuch or not, whereas the usage of *tawashi* makes matters easier as it is only applicable to eunuchs.

As for the names given to eunuchs, the great majority had strange names, or names that enjoyed less respect and that were not given to full men – for example, Masrur (happy), Kafur (camphor), Nawfal (beautiful), Thumal (drunk), Najih (successful), Mu'nis (good companion), Shukr (thanks), Jawhar (essence) and Rihan (basil), among many others. Feminine names like Raja' (hope), Sawsan (name of a flower) and Kawthar were also given to eunuchs. In addition, they shared names applicable to men and women, asserting their third-gender classification, or at least reflecting gender irregularity – for example, Badr (full moon), Bishara (good omen) and Wafa' (faithful). In some eras, their names were associated with al-Din (religion), like Baha' al-Din, or Shihab al-Din, but it is extremely rare to find a eunuch in medieval Islam named Muhammad or 'Umar, as such names carry more respect than a eunuch is considered to deserve.

Eunuchs in the 'Abbasid State up to the Caliphate of al-Amin (749–809)

The dawn of the 'Abbasid state witnessed limited employment or use of eunuchs in offices outside of the harem. Very few were used during these six decades with five different caliphs. Ibn al-Athir mentions that the first 'Abbasid caliph, al-Saffah (d. 754), had a eunuch named Sabiq al-Khuwarizmi. He was in the service of al-Saffah's elder brother, Ibrahim, before being passed to him. It seems that this eunuch was fully trusted to the extent that he knew where the 'Abbasid imam (leader) was hiding from his Umayyad enemies, who were vigorously hunting for him. When the chief 'Abbasid *da'i* (political/religious propagandist) took al-Saffah and ten other 'Abbasid princes into hiding, one commander asked Sabiq about the hiding place of al-Saffah, as he wanted to consult with him. The eunuch refused to tell without first asking his master's permission.[37] Clearly, any treason from that eunuch could endanger the whole 'Abbasid *da'wa* (movement). The nature of Sabiq's job is not mentioned in the source.

Due to the short reign of al-Saffah and his shift of the kingdom's capital from the grand city of Damascus to the new and humble Anbar, we do not see any more evidence of eunuchs in his court. His successor and co-founder of the state and of Baghdad, the legendary al-Mansur (d. 775), also had limited employment of eunuchs in his new court. Like the Umayyads, we do not find him having eunuchs as *hajib*s, or holders of the insignia. However, he entrusted a eunuch named Salma, in collaboration with another servant (not a eunuch), to keep the key to one of the caliph's most important locked chests. In this chest, al-Mansur kept his political guidelines that he wrote himself for his son and successor, al-Mahdi.[38]

When al-Mansur died during the pilgrimage season in Mecca, only his vizier, al-Rabi', and a few eunuchs were present. It was one of these eunuchs, a black man named Abu al-'Anbar, who delivered the news of the caliph's death to his public. However, it was al-Rabi' who was the one in charge of all the processions.[39] Another eunuch, Manara, was dispatched to Baghdad upon the orders of Musa b. al-Mahdi and the vizier to inform al-Mansur's son and successor, al-Mahdi. Manara was entrusted with the caliphal insignia and carrying the *bay'a* (diploma) of the caliphate.[40]

Caliph al-Mahdi, as understood from medieval chroniclers, followed the pattern of his father, with one significant difference. He used several eunuchs as his *hajibs*, their chief being al-Abrash, and he had another as his *qahramana*, named Wadih, who was with him on his final day.[41] We can see that from the time of al-Mahdi onwards, nearly all 'Abbasid caliphs who had courts used eunuchs in the position of *hajib* and chief *hajib*. We don't know why al-Mansur in particular did not follow this Umayyad tradition, especially as he was the founder of Baghdad and had been influenced by Iranian court heritage. It should be noted that the *hajib* in Muslim administration was one of the closest posts to the ruler. He regulated, supervised and permitted and denied access to the caliph or sultan. His job was to coordinate with the vizier, commander of the army and chief of police. As a result, his position was always of high political influence.

Al-Hadi, who succeeded his father in 785, learned of his father's death in faraway Maha Abadh through a eunuch sent by his brother, al-Rashid. The political situation in Baghdad was fragile, as the capital had been left without a ruler. Al-Rashid was in the company of his father, while al-Hadi was involved in a campaign in Jurjan.[42] Therefore, the mission entrusted to the eunuch to deliver such news promptly was crucial for the 'Abbasids. Al-Hadi, who ruled for only a year, did not have the time to develop the institution of the eunuchs any further. Nevertheless, under the long reign of his brother al-Rashid, there was a significant increase in the number of eunuchs, as well as the numbers of *jawari*, concubines and *qiyan*.

The most significant development to this institution was the elevation of one eunuch as a commander in the 'Abbasid army, at a crucial time. It was the first time that a eunuch would appear in public, away from the palace, leading large numbers of troops, and he had to earn their respect. That took place during a difficult period, when the 'Abbasid governor of Khurasan, 'Ali b. 'Isa, revolted against his caliph. Al-Rashid could not afford for the 'Abbasids to lose the strategically important Khurasan. He dispatched two commanders to arrest 'Ali in 806.[43] One was the grand commander Harthama b. A'yan, and the other was the eunuch commander Raja'. Both went to Merv, to meet 'Ali, pretending that they were sent to support his rule. They had letters sent from al-Rashid to 'Ali. After meeting with him, they arrested him and his deputies, after Raja' had given him the caliphal letter.[44] It could be perceived that sending a eunuch commander in the company of a grand commander like Harthama was a test by the caliph of the troops' reaction to his soldiers about how they would react and interact with a eunuch.

Another major development in al-Rashid's administration was the appointment of several eunuchs as chief of the *barid*. The eunuch Masrur was in charge of the *barid* in Baghdad, and his deputy was another eunuch named Thabit.[45] More significant was the appointment of a eunuch named Hammawayh as chief of the *barid* in Khurasan in 806.[46]

The caliphal post was considered by Caliph al-Mansur as the most important job in the state. He once said:

> 'The kingdom needs four pillars; if one is missing it collapses. One is a courageous judge who fears no one but God. The second is a police chief who attains the rights of the vulnerable from the aggressor. The third is a chief of finance who is just with the locals.' After some hesitation and regret, he said: 'The fourth is a chief of *barid* who will report justly and in detail of those previous three to me.'[47]

It was the first time in Islamic history that we see a eunuch appointed as a commander of intelligence in a vast significant area like Khurasan, during the same year that al-Rashid saw a challenge to his authority there.

Since the hiring and employment of eunuchs was associated with secretive positions or concealed affairs, like *hajib*, bodyguards or the *barid*, al-Rashid resorted to one of his chief eunuchs, Masrur, to help him get rid of the significant political and malign influence of the Iranian Barmakids, of which al-Rashid was the maker in the first place.[48]

The Barmakids joined the service of the 'Abbasids from the time of al-Mansur. Yahya al-Barmaki, as already mentioned, was the secretary of al-Rashid when he was a crown prince, and orchestrated his coming to power. As soon as al-Rashid became caliph, he appointed him as a vizier to the entire 'Abbasid realm. He delegated all powers to Yahya, and gave him his insignia too, in addition to keeping the keys to the caliph's harem. Even when Zubayda, wife of the caliph, expressed discomfort at that, al-Rashid continued to use him, rather than a eunuch, as guardian to the harem. Yahya and his two sons, especially Ja'far, became de facto rulers of the state.[49]

When Caliph al-Rashid decided to end the Barmakid state within a state, as described in the chronicles, and to end Ja'far's life too, he trusted no one but a small network of his eunuchs to protect himself and win the realm back. In 802 the caliph entrusted his chief eunuch, Masrur, to bring him the head of Ja'far. Masrur was confused about such an order from the caliph, due to Ja'far's status, but he went ahead and executed the man in his palace, and brought his head to the caliph.[50]

After this successful start to the caliph's 'plot' against his old friend, he sent Masrur, accompanied by other commanders, including some trusted eunuchs, to arrest the remainder of the Barmakids and their affiliates. The caliph dispatched the eunuch Raja' to the summer 'Abbasid capital of Raqqa to seize all the treasures kept there by the Barmakids.[51]

Also at this time, another eunuch was sent by the caliph to summon the Baghdad police chief, al-Sindi; at this critical moment the caliph trusted no one else with this task. Also, a distinguished trusted eunuch was entrusted with jailing Yahya al-Barmaki.[52] David Ayalon states that the caliph had much more confidence in eunuchs than in non-eunuchs. The function of eunuchs under al-Rashid became very discernible as arresters and torturers.[53]

However, eunuchs could not yet be given the commandership of an army or the police. Why was this? It could be that this was due to the social surroundings, with people being unready to accept them in these elite public offices. Consider this anecdote:

> In 806 al-Rashid appointed Harthama b. A'yan as commander of the summer campaign against the Byzantines. He gave him 30,000 Khurasani soldiers under his command. Eunuch Masrur was in the company of Harthama, and he was in charge of the expenses, and all affairs (*jami' al-umur*), but not the presidency/leadership.[54]

We see here that Masrur was de facto in command of almost all affairs, but denied military command. That would, however, dramatically change in later 'Abbasid periods.

Also under al-Rashid, there was some minor participation of eunuchs in the raids against the Byzantines in the Thughur (the Syrian-Anatolian frontiers between the 'Abbasids and Byzantium). David Ayalon believes that it was al-Rashid who used eunuchs as commanders in such seasonal warfare for the first time.[55] He provides no evidence for such a claim, but as we see that eunuchs were indeed part of the inner circle of the caliph, it would be natural for them to be in his company at these moments, such as in 805 at Heraklion. They could participate as soldiers/commanders under full men, but not as absolute commanders themselves.[56]

When al-Rashid died in Tus in 809, he had three of his eunuchs around him: Masrur, Husain and Rashid (it is strange to have a eunuch sharing the same name as his caliph), in addition to two commanders, al-Fadl (his vizier) and Isma'il. It was eunuch Hammawayh, chief of *barid* in Khurasan, who dispatched the news to al-Rashid's son and successor, al-Amin, in Baghdad, with the written *bay'a*. The new caliph first knew about the death of his father and his succession from the *barid* agent. However, Salih b. al-Rashid who was in Tus too, sent Raja' separately with the news, just to guarantee that al-Amin knew of the situation. Raja' arrived a few days after the *barid*,[57] but he was carrying more than just news. He also carried the insignia of the caliph, and the stick and cloak of the Prophet.[58] It was only then that al-Amin took his decision to move to the caliphal official palace.[59] Here we see how the eunuchs under al-Rashid occupied with efficiency some important posts of the state.

Caliph al-Amin and his Exotic Eunuchs

All you Muslims should praise Allah
Always say, repeat and do not get tired
Oh Almighty, please keep our al-Amin
He elevated the eunuchs to the highest places
Until impotence became a religion in the state
So all the public followed that model
Of the commander of the faithful.[60]

This poetry was by the famous homoerotic poet, Abu Nuwas (d. 814), who was a friend of al-Amin. He was a very libidinous homosexual, just like the caliph criticised by him here. The Abu Nuwas lines mentioned by al-Tabari, among other similar lines by others, express how the 'Abbasid state expanded through the employment of eunuchs during this period. The five years of al-Amin's reign was consumed politically by the civil war with his brother, al-Ma'mun. On the administrative and social front, it was certainly consumed by his infatuation with his eunuch Kawthar, who became like a declared spouse for him.[61]

The political arrangement made by al-Rashid during his life was to have al-Amin as first successor with the rule of Iraq and western provinces, and al-Ma'mun as a second successor with the rule of provinces east of Iraq. Third would come their brother, al-Mu'tamin, who would rule the Jazira. As soon as al-Amin became caliph, he worked towards deposing al-Mu'tamin, and appointing his own young son, Musa. When that took place in 810, al-Ma'mun condemned the caliph's decision, and then declared himself as caliph in his eastern territories.[62] Al-Amin expressed clearly to his mother that only men were capable of governing when she tried to advise him during this crisis. He said: 'The crowns and governance are not kept by the worries of women. The politics of the caliphate are bigger than what women can accommodate or understand – no breast feeders can get into this.'[63] Interestingly enough, the caliph was not interested in running his own realm, and left most of the political affairs to his vizier and advisor, al-Rashid, and al-Fadl b. al-Rabi'.[64]

As for the caliph himself, he had other desires to pursue. He made his eunuch Kawthar the bearer of the insignia, and the Prophet's stick and cloak, in addition to the sword.[65] The insignia, which was one of the most important symbols of authority in the realm, was probably kept by Masrur under al-Rashid's rule, and then delivered to al-Amin by Raja', and held by Kawthar. Al-Amin became so enamoured by Kawthar, to the extent that he wrote love poetry to him, such as the lines quoted at the start of this section. The caliph described his eunuch lover as his religion and world, his illness and cure.[66]

This signalled a shift for 'Abbasid administration and politics, where the bearer of the sword as a chief bodyguard, and bearer of the insignia, was the beloved of the caliph – that is, mixing business with pleasure. The following extract concerns Caliph al-Amin, as quoted by several chroniclers:

> When he became caliph, and secured the *bayʿa* of al-Maʾmun for himself, he sought out eunuchs and purchased them for the highest of prices. He took them as his boon companions for night and day, and in his seclusion too, during his dining and drinking. He gave them power, as they represented him.
>
> He created two eunuch regiments: one called the Jaradiyya (locusts), made up of white Saqlabi eunuchs, and the other composed of blacks, called the Ghurabiyya (crows). He despised all women, free or slave, to the extent that he was accused of homosexuality.'[67]

The nature of these two regiments is not clear. Were they military regiments or honorary ones for the court and pleasure, or both? This unprecedented public behaviour by a Muslim caliph spawned several bitter and sarcastic poems about al-Amin. Consider the following few lines, in which some of his locals reflect their anger in a kind of social media of the medieval age. The poet directs his lines at al-Amin:

> You kept the hungry eunuchs
> It only brought the evil omen
> You prefer the company of eunuchs Nawfal or Badr
> Half of your life is dedicated to them
> The other half is dedicated to drinking
> Even harlots have no luck with you
> If only al-Rashid could hear about this misery.[68]

We can see here how the caliph became infatuated with his eunuchs and neglected all state affairs. As this study is concerned with gender and politics, not the history of sexuality, we will not go into further detail here about al-Amin's activities with his eunuchs.

The caliph ignored completely the civil war that had started in 810 with his brother al-Maʾmun and that raged in the ʿAbbasid empire for four years. He counted on his vizier, al-Fadl, and his military commander, ʿAli b. ʿIsa, to conduct this war. As for his lustful affairs, Ibn al-Athir reports how the caliph sent to all corners of the empire seeking entertainers to have around him. He bestowed upon them regular stipends. He alienated himself from his family and brothers. He had no respect for his commanders and took their concerns lightly. He spent all the money and state treasures, and bestowed the jewellery he owned to his eunuchs, boon companions and partners of his private councils. The caliph ordered the construction of several amusement and leisure areas in his various palaces for his private distasteful affairs with his eunuchs, in addition to five ships to sail in the Tigris, on the building of which he spent lavishly.[69]

In addition to the social media of that age (that is, poetry), which criticised the caliph's behaviour, we see al-Ma'mun, brother of al-Amin and self-declared caliph in the eastern provinces of the empire, use the caliph's carnal behaviour to condemn and discredit him and his administration by way of counter-propaganda.[70]

Fearing the careless and failing political conduct of the caliph, and the alarming military superiority of his enemy al-Ma'mun, the royal mother, Zubayda, tried to interfere to help the image of her useless son. She established, for the first time in the Muslim court life, a regiment carefully selected by her of 100 very charming maidens, and dressed them up as boys with short haircuts, like *ghilman*. She made their posteriors stand out so they would look like eunuchs. They were called the Shakiriyya[71] or Ghulamiyyat (fem. pl. of *ghulam*). This influenced later 'Abbasids to follow the same model, namely Caliph al-Qahir in 933.[72]

To the disappointment of his mother, al-Amin did not give up his unnatural love for eunuchs. When he was told about the defeat of his army and the murder of his chief commander in 811, he was fishing in a pool in the palace with Kawthar. Instead of being shocked by the news carried to him by a special agent of the *barid*, the caliph replied: 'Get away from me, Kawthar just caught two fish and I have none.'[73]

The Shakiriyya regiment continued to serve in the palace with other eunuchs in different services in the harem under the authority of Zubayda.[74] The name remained until the rule of Caliph al-Musta'in in 863, but it was now a male military unit.[75] As for al-Amin, he surrendered to the forces sent by his brother, which had besieged Baghdad for fifteen months, and then he was decapitated.[76]

With the end of al-Amin's dramatic reign, some points should be mentioned:

1. The sources that furnish us with much of the poetry on the unusual behaviour of al-Amin with his preferred and dominant eunuchs, fail to mention any eunuchs in key positions, apart from Kawthar. We have no mention of eunuchs appointed as deputies in other states, commanders in the army, police or the *barid*.
2. Ayalon writes: 'The accession of al-Amin to the throne reveals, quite by accident, the existence of a very impressive body of eunuchs in the eastern part of the realm, a clear inheritance from his father's reign.'[77] However, we do not see much political influence of eunuchs inherited by al-Ma'mun, who was ruling these eastern provinces. Al-Ma'mun had a very modest number of eunuchs in his service. One was Masrur, the long-serving eunuch of his father. He was in charge of other eunuchs serving in the harem.[78] Another, called Nawfal, was used occasionally for delivering al-Ma'mun's messages to his commanders.[79] There was also a eunuch called Rushd, who undertook (undocumented) domestic service for al-Ma'mun.[80] It seems that al-Ma'mun was opposed to the service of eunuchs, apart from the few inadvertently mentioned in the sources; for example, he requested his aunt, Princess 'Aliyya bt. al-Mahdi, to dismiss her eunuch, Tall.[81]
3. Al-Ma'mun, who condemned the homosexuality of his enemy and brother al-Amin, had installed a chief judge to the 'Abbasid empire, Yahya b. Aktham. He was known by the chroniclers as a famous man who loved only young beardless *ghulman*. He was described as being gayer than a sodomist, and was once warned off by the caliph when he caught him gazing in admiration at his nephew, al-Wathiq, the future caliph. The caliph told him: 'Oh judge, gaze around us, not at us.'[82] In addition to that, al-Ma'mun himself and his brother and successor al-Mu'tasim were clearly accused of bisexuality and their love of *ghilman* by al-Tha'alibi. He said that the latter caliph owned 8,000 of them, and some jurists allowed such a practice with their own interpretation of shari'a.[83] After all, the *ghilman* were seen as a prize in paradise for Muslim believers.
4. The chronicles, which are saturated with stories about the regiments of al-Amin's eunuchs and their large numbers, unfortunately do not supply us with any information about the fate of these eunuchs following the

decapitation of their lord. Only Ibn al-Jawzi mentions in one line that all eunuchs were dispersed in the streets of Baghdad.[84] The keeper of the insignia and bearer of the sword, the famous Kawthar, followed al-Amin until he surrendered to the commander of the 'Abbasid forces, Tahir b. al-Husayn. He took it from Kawthar and dispatched it to al-Ma'mun along with the head of al-Amin.[85]

5. All eunuchs under Umayyad or 'Abbasid rulers until the beginning of ninth century had absolute and undisputed loyalty to their masters, like a shadow following a person, which was exactly what was expected of them. They were not yet tempted to follow their own political ambitions, avenge their bitter conditions or inflict on their surroundings the anger they felt as a result of their castration.

For reasons that are unclear, the tradition of employing eunuchs in key areas and positions in the 'Abbasid state under al-Mansur, al-Rashid and al-Amin was interrupted for some 160 years. Eight 'Abbasid caliphs came to power during that period, which witnessed a huge expansion in the hiring and buying of various Turkish ethnic soldiers into the army.

This process started under al-Mu'tasim b. al-Rashid (d. 842) and his son al-Mutawakkil (d. 861). It was the latter who established what is known as the 'Turkish era' within the 'Abbasid state, when Turkish commanders started to hold provinces and large *iqta'*.[86] There is very little mention in the sources about the function of eunuchs at that time. For example, we know that al-Mu'tasim continued to use the veteran eunuch, Masrur, as a chief to a prison built inside a royal palace called Bustan Musa in Baghdad, where his political enemies were held;[87] however, there is very limited information on this.

As regards his son, al-Mutawakkil, he owned 4,000 concubines, in addition to other *jawari*. Was it the case that eunuchs were used only at the harem, and banned from politics? The sources tell us of only one eunuch, who was in charge of carrying messages for this caliph to his advisors.[88] Another anecdote reveals that Caliph al-Musta'in (d. 866) had used a eunuch named Shahak for his harem and private treasures and affairs.[89] This leads us to believe that eunuchs were excluded from political circles during this century and a half.

The Realm and Evolution of Eunuchs in the 'Abbasid State, 870–968

With the coming of Caliph al-Mu'tamid (d. 892), we do not only see a comeback by eunuchs in politics, but also their occupation of positions of greater responsibility, with eunuchs finding themselves being quickly elevated to elite offices. This practice influenced the 'Abbasid caliphs who followed, as well as other dynasties in the Muslim world, like the Sunni Seljuqs and Ayyubids, as well as enemies of the 'Abbasids, such as the Fatimids; this use for eunuchs became the norm in medieval history.

It has been mentioned that during the rule of al-Rashid (r. 786–809), all of North Africa to the west of Egypt pulled out of the 'Abbasid orbit, being ruled by diverse Shi'i, Khariji and Sunni powers. In 868 a Turkish slave commander, Ahmad b. Tulun, was appointed as an 'Abbasid governor over Egypt. Within three years he declared a rebellion against Baghdad, and Egypt became independent.[90]

Ibn Tulun's short-lived dynasty in Egypt and Syria (it came to an end in 905) witnessed developments in the use of eunuchs, which opened the gate for their successors, the Ikhshidids in Egypt and the 'Abbasids in Iraq, to follow them.

Ibn Tulun had used eunuchs in his northern Syrian territories, around the Taurus Mountains, as commanders in his army and deputies to his authority. In 882 one of them called Yazman became ruler of the town of Tarsus in Anatolia, and withdrew his loyalty to Ibn Tulun.[91] This was a very critical time for the new rebellious ruler of Egypt, because he could not afford to see parts of Thoghur or the Syrian marshes, close to Byzantium and the 'Abbasid controlled territories in the Jazira, being removed from his control, especially as the de facto ruler of the 'Abbasid state, al-Muwaffaq (brother of the caliph), was an arch-enemy of Ibn Tulun.[92]

The sources mention that Ibn Tulun besieged Yazman in Tartus, but failed to seize Tarsus or end the rebellion. One of the reasons for this was the popularity of that eunuch commander among the military. Another reason was the great military skills of Yazman, who diverted part of the Baradan River, flooding the Tulunid camp.[93]

Yazman remained in power until he died in 891. Ibn Tulun had died in 884. His son and successor, Khumarawayh, recognised Yazman's authority over Tartus following difficult negotiations in 890 to secure Khumarawayh's nominal (ceremonial) authority of Tulunid Egypt.[94]

For six long years, neither the 'Abbasids in Iraq nor the Tulunids in Egypt and Syria managed to end Yazman's power. He continued the tradition of *fida'* (annual exchange of prisoners of war) with Byzantium. This tradition was started by al-Rashid,[95] following three successful *sa'ifa* (summer raids) on Byzantine forces. He also managed to defend a strong Byzantine attack on his limited territories in 883.[96]

The case of Yazman shows us the following: Ibn Tulun and Khumarawayh, in their efforts to keep their infant independence from the 'Abbasids, installed eunuchs as elite military commanders, especially in the frontier areas. At these frontiers, they would stay for longer periods, especially over the winter, as they had no families to return to.

The eunuch-hood of Yazman did not stop him from rebelling against his master. Although he was bought for a higher price to assure loyalty, Yazman was probably the earliest eunuch on record to rebel against his authority.

In the same year that Yazman died, another 'Abbasid eunuch commander called Raghib appeared in Tarsus. He was a very close servant of al-Muwaffaq, the caliph's brother and de facto ruler of the state. He was dispatched to Tarsus to perform jihad against Byzantium in this frontier area.[97] (The 'Abbasid caliphate had already reconciled with Khumarawayh. As already mentioned, the latter's daughter was married to the 'Abbasid caliph.)

The influence of eunuchs reached its peak in Tulunud Egypt, which officially recognised the 'Abbasid caliphate under Khumarawayh. In 896 eunuchs did not revolt against their lord, like in the case of Yazman, but instead killed him. A group of more than twenty eunuchs, who were in the service of Khumarawayh in Damascus, decapitated him. The reason, as mentioned by Ibn al-Athir, was that

> Khumarawayh was told that his *jawari* in his palace in Egypt would have eunuchs as lovers, and enjoyed affairs with them like a husband would. He ordered his deputy to investigate the matter with the *jawari*. The eunuchs close to him in Damascus feared his reaction if the truth of their situation was revealed and so decided collectively to kill him.[98]

From this anecdote, three remarks are to be made:

1. For the first time within the 'Abbasid realm, with its semi-autonomous states, we see eunuchs influence the political rule by eliminating the ruler himself. This act influenced other Muslim dynasties, for example, the Aghlabids in neighbouring Tunisia, to do the same: in 901 several eunuchs were commissioned by Prince Ziyadat Allah III to kill his father, 'Abdallah II.[99]
2. Eunuchs were no longer as loyal as they had been during the first decades of the 'Abbasids, or previously under the Umayyads, and could now follow their own interests. In this case, the only capable Tulunid lord was removed, and his successor was too young to govern, which contributed to the swift decline of the Tulunids.
3. Some eunuchs were capable of copulation with women (as mentioned before), and their service in the ruler's palace was not always loyal, in both metaphorical and physical terms.

During the last two years of the rule of Caliph al-Mu'tamid, we see the frequent appearance of Wasif al-Khadim in Iraqi affairs, as a commander of Ibn Abi al-Saj, 'Abbasid deputy of Mosul and parts of Azerbayjan, who rebelled against Baghdad.[100] David Ayalon considers Wasif to be a eunuch because he is described in the sources as a *khadim*.

Wasif contacted the new caliph, al-Mu'tadid (r. 892–902) to appoint him as his deputy at the Syrian frontiers. The caliph refused and marched to arrest Wasif in 900 in northern Syria, which he managed to do after he dispatched a separate force ahead of him, led by Rashiq al-Hurami, his close and trusted eunuch.[101] Unfortunately, Wasif could not be counted as a eunuch as he had 'sent his children and the children of his fellows to safety in Mar'ash before the caliph went to confront and arrest him'.[102] We have to note the term *khadim* with extreme caution here, as it is used differently according to context in the ninth and tenth centuries – in this particular case, it would not be possible to be a eunuch if he had children.

Ironically, the same source describes other commanders of the caliph as *khadim* during the same campaign, including Mu'nis, the legendary commander of the future caliph al-Muqtadir, who was known to be a real eunuch, and Mu'nis al-Khazin.[103] It is unique during this era to find a eunuch, Mu'nis al-Khadim, appointed as chief of police of the 'Abbasid army (a term rarely used before, or after), especially as the caliph was marching in person to maintain unity in his territories in the Syrian marshes, very close to Byzantium; this would add to the prestige and trust given to such eunuchs. The caliph trusted Mu'nis al-Khadim with the imprisonment of Wasif.[104]

The Legendary Mu'nis al-Khadim and his Realpolitik Relationship with the Royal Mother, Shagab, her qahramanat and Caliph al-Muqtadir[105]

The twenty-four year reign of the boy caliph al-Muqtadir b. al-Mu'tadid, which began in 908, witnessed the collapse of the Aghlabids in North Africa and the rise of the powerful Fatimid Shi'i state that dominated the whole of North Africa.[106] Their continuous obsessive invasions of 'Abbasid Egypt took place during al-Muqtadir's reign. That reign also saw the early rise of the Shi'i Buwayhids in Iran, who intimidated the 'Abbasids, leading to the fall of al-Muqtadir. Domestically, there was the first serious collaboration between eunuchs and the harem, represented by the royal mother, Shaghab, and her *qahramanat*. We could call it the 'trio of powers' among elite eunuchs, the caliph and the mistress Shaghab with her harem. That trio dominated the 'Abbasid Empire, in all domestic and foreign affairs.

I have highlighted the name of Mu'nis al-Khadim, the eunuch commander of the whole 'Abbasid army, due to his paramount power, role and extraordinary achievements during that era. However, there were other key eunuchs, such as Sawsan, the chief *hajib* of the caliph, and Muflih, the black *khasis* (close confidant) of al-Muqtadir, who was a private companion of the caliph but had no specific office mentioned; we could say he was a trusted advisor. In addition, eunuchs were employed as police, military commanders and governors of provinces around the empire.

During the reign of al-Muqtadir (which merits its own study), who was the youngest caliph to come to power, at the age of thirteen, his court held the largest number of eunuchs in Islamic history. The 'Abbasid court contained about 11,000 eunuchs: approximately 7,000 black eunuchs and approximately 4,000 white Saqaliba (Slavs), in addition to more than 4,000 *jawari*.[107] A large number of these eunuchs were used in the harem for the domestic services of the mistress and her *jawari*, as well as the *jawari* and concubines of the caliph.

The chief eunuch, Safi al-Hurami (lit. the one belonging to the harem), headed that section, and had held the same post during al-Muqtadir's father's reign. The non-harem or non-domestic eunuchs were used in key offices, like the army, police, finance, guards and ceremonies, in particularly the office of the *hajib*. The number in this last office soared to 700, and was headed by chief *hajib*, Sawsan, among others.[108]

Due to the authority of Mu'nis al-Khadim in almost all affairs of the state, and also his long career, we will look at his influence in two parts: his activities and contribution to domestic affairs within Iraq, and his military–political contribution outside Iraq. I will cover each one independently, as they are different in nature, although sometimes they influenced each other.

Mu'nis and his Role in Iraq's Inner Politics

Mu'nis (lit. good companion) al-Khadim is referred to in the sources with the title '*al-muzaffar*' (lit. the ever-victorious), although he only earned that title from the caliph in 918.[109] As mentioned previously, he was the chief of military police to al-Mu'tadid in 900. When the boy al-Muqtadir was installed as caliph by the vizier of the 'Abbasids, al-'Abbas b. al-Hasan in 908, under the close direction of Shaghab, Mu'nis was already commander of the 'Abbasid army, and his approval was needed and secured.

Four months later in 909, the vizier, Abu al-'Abbas b. al-Hasan, along with other elite personnel, including the chief of police in Baghdad, launched a coup and brought in a new caliph. He was the son of the former caliph, al-Mu'tazz, and was given the title of '*al-murtada*'.[110] Only Mu'nis al-Khadim, Mu'nis al-Khazin (who was chief of police), Shaghab, her brother Gharib and his son Harun, together with their entourage, remained loyal to al-Muqtadir. Mu'nis al-Khadim managed to defend the caliph's palace against the attack by the commander al-Husayn b. Hamdan and his followers.[111]

Al-Murtada had no organised forces around him, and many of his supporters were scattered around Baghdad and its suburbs. Commander Mu'nis seized this opportunity and marched with his limited number of supporters, attacking al-Murtada and arresting all of his collaborators, who were then surrendered to Mu'nis al-Khazin to be punished. It seems that a number of eunuch commanders were among those arrested, such as Yumn (a name often given to the third gender).[112] Due to the courage and experience of Mu'nis and the strong support of the locals of Baghdad, the coup was reversed and al-Muqtadir reinstated to his thrown. Hugh Kennedy sees Mu'nis's act as a loyalty to his masters,[113] but we could assume that Mu'nis was fighting for his own career too.

One of the courtesans of al-Muqtadir knew where al-Murtada was hiding, so Safi al-Hurami was dispatched with a force to arrest him. Al-Murtada, once in Safi's custody, was killed by a rare and telling method: his testicles were squeezed until he died.[114] Was that the revenge of some eunuchs for their castration years ago? Was that deed carried out by direct order from Mu'nis? What is important here is that the eunuch commander of the army, Mu'nis, saved the caliphate for his candidate in collaboration with other leading eunuchs, as well as the royal mother. Mu'nis and Shaghab enjoyed taking revenge on the plotters of the previous coup.

Mu'nis's influence and opinion as to how the caliphal administration should run cannot be ignored. At times it was he who decided whom should serve as a vizier, especially after Safi al-Hurami died in 910 and additional powers were handed to Mu'nis. For example, in 910 the caliph wanted to dismiss the inefficient vizier al-Khaqani, and reappoint Ibn al-Furat. Mu'nis refused, as the latter had ignored Mu'nis's opinion in military affairs in Iran. Mu'nis suggested the name of 'Ali b. 'Isa as a vizier; al-Muqtadir accepted this recommendation.[115] Again, in 924 during the third vizierate of Ibn al-Furat, Mu'nis tried to dismiss him and recommend al-Khaqani. Ibn al-Furat was arrested and handed over to Mu'nis. The latter surrendered him to the eunuch Nazuk, chief of police, who brutally killed him and his son, as mentioned earlier.[116] Not only that, but Mu'nis interfered in the affairs of the office of al-Khaqani, and strongly suggested to him that the former vizier, 'Ali b. 'Isa, should supervise the governorate of Egypt and Syria. His suggestion was accepted without question.[117]

We can see that Mu'nis tried to create and maintain a chain of supporters in key offices and places to consolidate his own power. This practice continued to the end of the caliph's rule.

After the failed coup orchestrated by Mu'nis against the caliph in 929, mistrust between the two parties became apparent. In 931 the caliph wanted to dismiss the vizier Sulayman, upon the recommendation of the new chief of police, Muhammad b. Yaqut. Mu'nis objected to this idea. The caliph, in return for keeping Mu'nis as an ally, gave the chief of police more power as a *muhtasib* (a person who monitors the markets). According to Meskawayh:

> Mu'nis assembled his supporters. As a result, Yaqut and his son assembled their supporters at the caliphal palace. Mu'nis was told that Yaqut's party would attack his house at night. Mu'nis demanded the dismissal of the police chief and his father, and their exile from central Iraq. Al-Muqtadir yielded to the pressure, and installed Yaqut as deputy of Fars and Kirman, and his son as deputy of Isfahan.[118]

When the caliph was finally able to dismiss Sulayman, he was compelled to replace him by Mu'nis's choice, al-Kuludhani. The caliph sent his personal eunuch, Muflih, with the diploma to the new vizier who was at Mu'nis's house.[119]

A few months later, the caliph decided to stand up to his real enemy, Mu'nis, by dismissing al-Kuludhani and appointing Ibn Qasim. Tensions between the two parties escalated quickly; as a result of pressure from Mu'nis, the caliph was forced to dismiss his new vizier, but he refused to confiscate his money.[120]

All these sketches prove how Mu'nis, although a military commander, was heavily involved in the administration, which continued to be in financial difficulty. That was a major concern to Mu'nis, as it affected his military budget. He maintained his close relationship with the highly influential royal mother, as mentioned before, which gave him an additional layer of protection.

On the domestic front, social stability had become an issue, with the caliph having to contend with riots, as well as trying to protect Iraqi lands from outside threats. It was the task of the chief of police to keep law and order in the capital, and for the governors to do the same in other major cities. Yet during the reign of al-Muqtadir, which witnessed continuous financial difficulties, we see him, his mother and his administration resort to Mu'nis to save the rule on several occasions, or restore law and orders after rebellions or revolts. Mu'nis was always the saviour of the caliphate.

In 915 al-Husayn b. Hamdan rebelled in Mosul and northern Iraq against ʿAbbasid authority, while Muʾnis was fighting the Fatimids in Egypt. The vizier, ʿAli b. ʿIsa, dispatched a eunuch commander, Raʾiq al-Kabir, to fight Ibn Hamdan. The rebellion was not put down until Muʾnis returned to the Jazira and arrested Ibn Hamdan. He brought him to Baghdad, where he was imprisoned at the quarters of the *qahramana* Zaydan.[121] Here we see a pact between a eunuch commander and the harem, represented in the person of this *qahramana*, to guard the political enemy of the caliphate.

Muʾnis dealt with several instances of unrest around Iraq through his military skills, but also through his network of trusted eunuchs. In 918 the leading knights in the army rioted as their salaries had not been paid in time. Muʾnis, as their commander, calmed them down and duly dismissed and arrested the vizier, Ibn al-Furat, for his inefficiency.[122] On another occasion, when the Qaramita invaded Kufa in southern Iraq in 924, Muʾnis marched out to confront them and quickly defeated them. Before returning to his base in Baghdad, he installed another eunuch, commander Yaqut, as a deputy there.[123] Muʾnis had collaborations with other leading eunuchs in key positions. For example, he coordinated affairs with Muflih, the closest eunuch of the caliph. The police commander was the eunuch Nujh al-Tuluni (d. 923). It was Nujh who ended the religious–Sufi dispute involving the Sufi leader al-Hallaj in Baghdad; he brutally killed him in 922.[124] Nujh was succeeded by another eunuch, Nazuk (d. 928), also a key figure. Another important eunuch was Shafiʿ al-Luʾluʾi, who was in charge of the *barid*. It was he who was given Ibn al-Furat by Muʾnis to imprison after his final dismissal in 924.[125] It is interesting that the name Luʾluʾ (pearl) is given to this eunuch. It is associated with the beardless *ghulman* in paradise as mentioned in the Qurʾan, and eunuchs were beardless too. When Shafiʿ died in 924 he was replaced by another eunuch, Shafiʿ al-Muqtadiri.[126]

In foreign affairs, too, eunuchs were in key positions. When the king of the Saqaliba in the Volga Basin, Almashi b. Yaltiwar, wrote to al-Muqtadir requesting political help, the ʿAbbasid embassy comprised four people headed by the eunuch Sawsan al-Rassi, and included the geographer Ibn Batlan. Sawsan was also instructed to visit the king of the Bulgars.[127] We can see here how a eunuch was appointed as representative of the caliph himself.

In addition to this network, it is important to bear in mind the close collaboration between the royal mother and Mu'nis. She described Mu'nis in 923 as the 'sword of the caliph', and contributed millions of dinars to support Mu'nis and the army against the threat of the Qaramita.[128]

Mu'nis as Champion of the Empire and Governor of Several Provinces

During his long military career, we can count twelve major military campaigns around the 'Abbasid empire in which Mu'nis bravely fought to defend the caliphate against the Fatimids, Qaramita, separatists in Iran and the traditional enemy, Byzantium. In all these campaigns, Mu'nis never lost a single confrontation, always emerging victorious. That is why he was given the title of '*al-muzaffar*' (always victorious) in 918.

In all these campaigns, Mu'nis coordinated with the royal mother and the caliph, especially while the caliph was still young. The following list highlights his exceptional military ability and successes:

1. Year 909   Invasion of Byzantium, sacking of Malatya
2. Year 910   Campaign in Iran to put down a rebellion by al-Layth b. 'Ali and the recapture of Shiraz
3. Year 913   Campaign against the Fatimid invasion of Egypt
4. Year 914   Campaign against the Fatimids who occupied Alexandria, expelling them
5. Year 915   Campaign against the Fatimids in Egypt, expelling them
6. Year 916   Invasion of Byzantium frontiers
7. Year 916   Crushing a rebellion in Qazwin and Zanjan in Iran, led by Ibn Abi al-Saj
8. Year 918   Campaign against the Fatimids in Egypt, defeating al-Qa'im, son of the Fatimid caliph who was in command; resulted in Mu'nis restoring most of Upper Egypt and Alexandria
9. Year 923   Invasion of Byzantium frontiers
10. Year 924 Defence of southern Iraq from the invasion of the Qaramita
11. Year 927 Invasion of Byzantium frontiers, attacking the Qaramita
12. Year 928 Attack on the Qaramita on the Euphrates around Raqqa[129]

A few remarks should be made here: the frequent Qaramita raids on the 'Abbasids in Iraq and Syria represented a real military threat until 903.[130]

Mu'nis managed to confront them, whereas other commanders before him in such campaigns had failed.

The frequent 'Abbasid invasions of Byzantium was not aimed at occupying large lands of the enemy, or at eliminating them. It was part of the seasonal frontiers campaigns, which started under the Umayyads and continued under the 'Abbasids. They were aimed at emphasising their authority over the frontiers area. A significant number of eunuch commanders, who were resident in the area as governors or deputies of the 'Abbasid administration, aided Mu'nis.

Such as with the internal affairs of Iraq, where we see Mu'nis surrounded by various eunuchs in elite positions, the same situation was reflected in warfare. He was instructing significant numbers of eunuch commanders across the empire. For example, in the campaign of 916 in Iran, the eunuch Nihrir was fighting there before Mu'nis arrived. Nihrir had previously served in Mosul in 913, together with the eunuch Yumn.[131] In addition, Mu'nis used the eunuch Wasif in Egypt against the Fatimid invasions, and he appointed Thumal the eunuch to lead the naval warfare from Tarsus.[132] Also, in 916 he appointed several eunuch commanders in the Jazira.

In the decisive Fatimid campaign in Egypt in 918, Mu'nis saved Egypt from a prominent Fatimid attack led by the heir apparent. When Mu'nis remained in Egypt, he asked for military aid from Iraq, which arrived, led by the eunuch commander Jenni.[133] The eunuch commander Sulayman led the Fatimid fleet of that campaign. He was captured and displayed around Fustat in disgrace.[134]

So, eunuchs were used on both sides of the Muslim caliphate: the 'Abbasids and the rising Fatimids. That paved the way for wider powers being granted to the third gender in the decades to follow.

Mu'nis's twelfth campaign was his last outside of Iraq, when he staged a coup against his master, the caliph; their relationship became very strained after that.

In the early years of al-Muqtadir's caliphate, when he was an immature youth, it is likely that it was the royal mother, Shaghab, who instructed Mu'nis on foreign campaigns. We have already discussed the term 'sultan', meaning 'supreme authority' in the context of instructing and empowering Mu'nis to march to fight Byzantium, for example. In addition, Shaghab trusted Mu'nis to conduct such warfare for the benefit of her son's best interests.

Another important department of the 'Abbasid administration witnessed a significant increase in the numbers of eunuchs in use. That was the *wali*, or provincial governors of the 'Abbasid state. The following list shows how these third-gender governors were entrusted with highly important provinces at a time when many enemies were attacking the empire from different directions. That office was closely linked to the military commandership, as the *wali* acted as the local military commander too.

1. Takin al-Khadim — Egypt (910)
2. Qinbaj al-Khadim — Persia (910)
3. Demyana — Tarsus (912)
4. Bishr — Tarsus (912)
5. Mu'nis al-Khadim — Mecca and Medina (912)
6. Mu'nis al-Khadim — Byzantine frontiers (912)
7. Mu'nis al-Khadim* — Egypt (913)
8. Mu'nis al-Khadim* — the Maghrib (913)
9. Bishr al-Khadim — Tarsus (914)
10. Thumal — Byzantine frontiers (917–31)
11. Subuk — Basra (923)
12. Yaqut — Kufa (923)
13. Nujh — Isfahan (924)
14. Yaqut — Persia (927)
15. Mu'nis al-Mu'nisi — Mosul (928)
16. Mu'nis al-Khadim* — Egypt, Syria and the Maghrib (930)

* as deputy of Abu al-'Abbas b. al-Muqtadir[135]

Owing to the scarcity of information about eunuchs, and the unknown date of dismissal of most governors, a given *wali* (governor) is listed as being in service. Mu'nis al-Khadim and Thumal are known to have served long terms, while the others served for about one year. They could be reinstalled again in the same location at a later date.

It is interesting that in some of these campaigns led by Mu'nis, he had the power to install new governors according to his evaluation of the military–political situation, for example, in 916 in Iran, when he installed new governors in Rayy, Qazwin, Zanjan, Isfahan, Qum and Kashan.[136] The Iranian provinces at the time were experiencing the start of the erosion of 'Abbasid authority in the face of several rising nationalist movements, such as the Buwayhids.

The appointment of Mu'nis as *wali* in Egypt during the Fatimid military threats was nothing out of the ordinary as he was the chief of the army during times of significant threats, such as the one the Fatimids represented. Nevertheless, it was extraordinary and unprecedented to mention him in the *khutba* after the caliph in the mosques of Egypt.[137] It was also unusual for a eunuch to be appointed as a governor in the prestigious holy places of Mecca and Medina. This practice later encouraged the Seljuq/Zengid dynasty to use eunuchs in these places in the twelfth century.

From among the eunuch military *wali* emerged a unique person. He was Thumal, who served for fourteen years at the Byzantine frontiers, as shown above. Al-Jahiz had pointed out in the ninth century that the Muslim powers would deliberately appoint eunuch commanders in Tarsus and Adana against Byzantium, in order for these eunuchs to take revenge for their castration, as castration had originated in Byzantium. Tarsus therefore became a well-established military base under the 'Abbasids, with powerful commanders.[138] Despite al-Jahiz's belief, castration did not actually originate in Byzantium; it was known to have taken place in ancient China, India and Persia too, but he was right in saying that the Muslim frontiers with Byzantium had a large number of eunuch commanders with authority, especially Tarsus. Thumal was a very clear example of that. Tarsus was disputed during early Islamic conquests with Byzantium up until the age of al-Rashid, who was the first to fortify it under the 'Abbasids.[139] Thumal, who carried the same name as one of the caliph's *qahramanat*, was a master of the north-eastern Mediterranean under the 'Abbasids. While Thumal fought at sea, another eunuch commander, Bishr, was leading a land campaign in 918.[140]

He fought under the banner of Mu'nis in the same year and the following one, in the Mediterranean against the Fatimid fleets. He managed to capture the two fleet commanders of the Fatimids, who were also both eunuchs.[141] He earned the honour of having his name minted on the 'Abbasid bronze coins of Tarsus and the frontiers. On the obverse we have 'the Emir Thumal', and on the reverse we have 'Muhammad is the apostle of God'. Silver and gold coins were reserved to carry the caliph's name,[142] but it was an exceptional privilege to have the name and title of a eunuch put on an 'Abbasid coin. Even Mu'nis did not enjoy that prestige. This was a new positive development in accepting eunuchs in the public sphere.

When Thumal retired at the end of al-Muqtadir's rule, he was replaced by the eunuch commander Bishr, who served until 938. Thumal's distinguished career led to a number of eunuch commanders carrying his name; they were referred to as al-Thumali – for example, Nasr al-Thumali, who fought against Byzantium in 947. He rebelled against the authority of another eunuch commander, Kafur the Ikhshidid in Cairo, which will be discussed later.[143]

From what has been examined of the domestic and foreign affairs of Mu'nis and the different offices occupied by eunuchs in the al-Muqtadir administration, we can say that he had a circle of power in the state, composed of eunuch military commanders, eunuchs in the police, eunuchs in the *barid*, eunuchs as governors and eunuchs in the caliphal palace, especially Muflih.[144] These officers collaborated and coordinated closely and frequently with the royal mother, Shaghab.

Mu'nis: The Killing of one 'Abbasid Caliph and Appointment of Another

The last three years of al-Muqtadir's rule witnessed dramatic events in the state, especially between him, his royal mother and Mu'nis. In February 929 Mu'nis wrote a very grave letter to the caliph, as he could no longer tolerate the power of Shaghab and her courtiers. He wrote to his caliph: 'The army is alarmed by the extravagant spending of the royal mother, the harem and associated courtesans, and their distribution of wealth and lands among themselves.' Mu'nis then denied the harem interference in political affairs of the state and decision-making in the caliphate.

Mu'nis demanded the expulsion of those mentioned from the palace, and the confiscation of most of what they owned.[145] He sent this letter after he gathered the army and was joined by the chief of police and many other supporters in a show of strength. He was most concerned with the growing influence of Harun, the nephew of Shaghab, as previously examined.

The caliph replied with a very long letter, after he had also amassed his supporters in his palace. He wrote to Mu'nis:

Oh Mu'nis, may God always allow me to enjoy your company, and always keep you close to me. The harem are my supporters and their behaviours are in my best interests. As for you, al-Muzaffar Aba al-Hasan (father of Hasan, an honorary name given to a childless eunuch), you are my mentor, my respected elder, without whom I would never dream of ignoring or conducting the affairs of the state. I looked into the matter of the harem and their associates personally, and I do not see wrongdoing. As for you and your company, you will see that I bestow most of your prosperities. I have never treated you unjustly. I did not stop Nazuk from attacking my cousin, Harun.

You should rethink and reconsider what you have done and disperse your crowds. If you refuse, I will not initiate any hostility towards you, but I will ask God to help me and I will remain in my house, just as Caliph 'Uthman remained and was besieged in his.[146]

It is not only rare, but unprecedented, that a caliph should declare to his eunuch commander that he considers him as a mentor and tutor.

Mu'nis's reply was not in words; rather, he marched with his forces and sacked the caliphal palace. Most of al-Muqtadir's courtesans escaped, like the *hajibs*, servants and the vizier.

At night Mu'nis arrested the caliph, his mother, his aunt and his private *jawari* and took them to his house. Harun, the cousin of the caliph, went into hiding. Nazuk took the insignia of Mu'nis and went to summon Muhammad, the brother of the caliph, to install him as the new caliph. Kafur, the chief of Muhammad's house, surrendered him to Nazuk after he saw the insignia. Kafur was also a eunuch.[147]

Before the dawn broke, Muhammad was installed by Mu'nis as the new caliph, and given the title of '*al-qahir*' (vanquisher). Mu'nis released the former vizier 'Ali b. 'Isa from prison, and appointed him as the new vizier to the puppet caliph. To guarantee full control over al-Qahir, Mu'nis appointed the eunuch Nazuk, chief of police, as *hajib* to the new caliph.[148]

Why did Mu'nis, who at this time was about seventy years of age,[149] with no offspring, turn so viciously against his master? It was probably a matter of survival, to protect himself from the power of the harem and the weakness of al-Muqtadir vis-á-vis the powerful cousin, Harun. Ibn Aybak wrote: 'All affairs were dominated by Shaghab. She alone was in control of all finances. She stopped and interrupted the pay and stipends.'[150] In addition, there was an assassination attempt against Muʾnis, planned in the palace in 928, from which Muʾnis escaped due to him being warned by a eunuch from inside the palace.[151] So the mistrust was mounting between the two sides.

Three days after the coup, some of the troops who defected from al-Muqtadir to Muʾnis demanded their pay and reward. Before negotiations on the matter took place, they broke into violence, encouraging others to join them, and shouted: 'Ya Muqtadir ya mansur' ('Oh Muqtadir, you are the victorious').

Sources supply us with unconvincing stories about the drunk chief of police who avoided them, and the enigmatic absence of Muʾnis from the army. The result of that was the return of al-Muqtadir to power and the jailing of his brother al-Qahir at the harem, all under the supervision of Shaghab.[152]

While al-Muqtadir replaced the vizier, reinstating Ibn Muqla, he could not replace the commander of the army. On the contrary, he raised the stipends of all commanders and soldiers to appease them. In 930 al-Muqtadir tried to mend his broken trust in Muʾnis by appointing Aba al-ʿAbbas b. al-Muqtadir as deputy in Egypt, Syria and the Maghrib. He installed Muʾnis as deputy to Aba al-ʿAbbas there.[153]

Why did the caliph retain the commander who had conspired against him and toppled him from office? If he was so strong, why did some rebellious troops manage to force Muʾnis to release al-Muqtadir, who was jailed at Muʾnis's house? During these events, we see that Muʾnis had a battalion in the army bearing his name. They were called the Muʾnisiyya; it was a novel concept to name a battalion after a eunuch.[154] Despite that, he failed to enforce his will on al-Muqtadir.

The mistrust between the two men remained until 932. Muʾnis tried to appear as a champion of jihad. He had commissioned Thumal to invade Byzantium in a massive campaign the previous year. He reached as far west as Ankara, but the Byzantines forced him back to Sumaysat.[155] In January 932 Muʾnis left for Mosul, declaring his dissatisfaction with the caliph's policy and his courtiers, especially the royal mother having firm control of the state finances, and soldiers having had their pay deferred. Al-Dhahabi mentions that 'the treasures were spoiled'.[156] Mu'nis sent his trusted eunuch commander Bushra with a personal message to the caliph, in an attempt to rebuild trust. He asked about the growing influence of Harun, cousin of the caliph. Bushra was badly humiliated, and the caliph refused to receive him. The vizier, Ibn Qasim, insulted, beat and jailed him. Then he sacked Bushra's house in Baghdad. The vizier, in collaboration with al-Muqtadir, went on to sack and loot many of Mu'nis's lands and farms, and also the farms of his supporters.[157]

That was the final straw, resulting in the end of the caliph's rule and his life. In November 932 Mu'nis took over Mosul, gathered his forces, assembled many Arab tribes in his pact and marched to seize Baghdad, with the full intention of arresting the caliph. The popularity of Mu'nis surpassed that of the caliph. When al-Muqtadir asked his cousin for military support, Harun said: 'I cannot. I fear that my troops will desert me for Mu'nis's side.'[158] That is how great and powerful Mu'nis was, despite his old age.

Al-Muqtadir, who had coordinated with his mother and advisors, decided to march out to fight Mu'nis. In Baghdad, the caliph marched wearing the Prophet's gown, and was surrounded by raised copies of the Qur'an in a parade. That spiritual show did not stop the army of Mu'nis fighting and slaying the caliph. Mu'nis, who remained close to Baghdad, received the head of his caliph, claiming that he did not order his killing. The caliph's corpse was left naked on the ground for some time. Ibn al-Athir splendidly analyses this step of Mu'nis:

> Mu'nis's actions were the cause and origin of many provincial governors rebelling against the caliphs in future times, and of being too ambitious. They could never have imagined what Mu'nis did to the caliph. After that, the caliphal prestige and dignity were torn apart.[159]

Mu'nis, who had protected al-Muqtadir at the beginning of his rule and fought against those who toppled him in 909, was the same one who toppled him in 929, and then dared to fight and kill him. I believe that the real challenge for Mu'nis was his rebellion and march to fight his master. Since he was the commander of the army, it was his responsibility to see his strict orders being observed, not to claim that he did not order the killing of the caliph.

Mu'nis suggested installing Aba al-'Abbas b. al-Muqtadir as the new caliph, in order to pacify the lamenting royal mother and her courtiers. Only then, would she release her hidden money for her candidate. Mu'nis's supporters were against that and said:

> After so much suffering from a caliph who had a dominant mother, aunt and influential courtiers who dominated him, we finally had an end to this; do you want us to return and have a repeat of the same situation? No. We need a mature man who can take control of himself and the rule.[160]

Eunuch Fa'iq al-Hurami, chief of the harem, came to Mu'nis and told him that he had convinced the royal mother not to escape after the killing of al-Muqtadir. He mentioned that both 'Abbasid princes, Muhammad b. al-Mu'tadid and Muhammad b. al-Muktafi, had been imprisoned by him. Mu'nis ordered Fa'iq to bring both of them to him. In addition, he ordered that his arrested commander, Bushra, should be immediately released.

After Mu'nis had negotiated the position of the caliph with both princes, he selected Muhammad b. al-Mu'tadid, who had been previously installed during the failed coup. He was given the same , 'al-qahir', in December 932, and was declared the new caliph.[161]

If we draw a comparison between Tulunid Egypt and Syria in 896, when some twenty eunuchs killed their ruler Khumarawayh, and the situation with Mu'nis, we can see distinct differences. The first was a criminal act without any plan or political ambition, and the Tulunid eunuchs were not involved in any affairs of the state after that date. On the other hand, we see Mu'nis, other eunuchs and normal men topple the caliph and arrange the political transition and future of the state by selecting a new caliph. That is a significant development in the eunuch institution and in medieval Islamic history.

Mu'nis asked (practically imposed) al-Qahir to recognise him as chief of the army, and his friend, Baliq and his son 'Ali b. Baliq as *hajib*s, and Ibn Muqla as vizier.[162] All his political team were naturally accepted by the new caliph. Mu'nis closely monitored the caliph. I should add that the powerful eunuch of al-Muqtadir, Muflih, had disappeared.

For nearly ten months al-Qahir was mercilessly torturing Shaghab to force her to confess to the whereabouts of her money and jewellery. She adamantly refused. Hugh Kennedy describes al-Qahir as 'a psychopath, whose cruelty went way beyond the harsh norms'.[163] Al-Qahir ordered her to relinquish her endowments. She adamantly refused. He held a public council, summoning the chief judges; he declared that she had agreed to sell all her endowments to him, which the judges approved, despite its contradiction of the shari'a. As previously mentioned, Shaghab died following her torture, and in depression for the way that her son was killed in June 933.[164]

What happened to the huge harem and the thousands of eunuchs and *jawari* in the caliphal palace? Where did they go? It is not clear. Interestingly enough, one of the leading eunuchs of the royal mother, Sapur, was set free (which was a mistake), while several of al-Muqtadir's sons were arrested.[165] Although Mu'nis showed deserved loyalty to his new caliph by marching out in force to fight Prince 'Abd al-Wahid b. al-Muqtadir, who rebelled in southern Iraq in 933,[166] tension and mistrust between Mu'nis and al-Qahir quickly grew. Al-Qahir, who wanted to create his own trusted circle around him, elevated the commander Muhammad b. Yaqut and enabled him to assemble a large force. Mu'nis and the *hajib* of the caliph arrested the physician of the caliph, 'Isa, who was collaborating with the caliph to recruit new elements to the caliph's side. Not only that, but Mu'nis attacked Muhammad b. Yaqut, while his friend Ibn Baliq, the *hajib*, encircled the caliph's palace. Everyone was thoroughly searched; even women who covered their faces were ordered to remove their veils. Al-Qahir was described as 'a bird in a cage'.[167]

In about June 933 al-Qahir appointed his *qahramana* in the harem, Ikhtyar, to be his secret messenger. She had more freedom of movement around Baghdad than others and she would meet his supporters at al-Qahir's former residence. She recommended her old adherent, Muhammad b. al-Qasim, to al-Qahir as an ally who would help him against Mu'nis. In return he would be rewarded with the vizierate.[168] Ikhtyar also was the messenger of the caliph to the wife of Sandal, one of the leading commanders of the army, trying to recruit him and his followers to al-Qahir's side.[169] Al-Qahir succeeded in bribing the trusted eunuch of Mu'nis, Bushra, to his side, together with the commander, al-Subkuri.

Mu'nis again took the daring step of attempting to change the rule and the caliph. He contacted Prince Ahmad b. al-Muktafi to install him as the new caliph. Al-Qahir dismissed Mu'nis as chief of the army, and appointed his unsatisfied general, al-Subkuri, as the new chief. In September 933 Mu'nis was arrested in his house by the new chief, and led to the caliph.[170] Later that month, al-Qahir ordered and attended the slaying of Mu'nis, and his ally Ibn Baliq; their heads were displayed in public.[171] The caliph rewarded Bushra with the rule of Damascus and Aleppo.[172]

Why was Mu'nis captured so easily, and why did he not fight to defend himself? I believe it was for the following reasons:

1. Al-Qahir managed to penetrate the military circles around Mu'nis, and managed to get leading commanders, such as Sandal, on his side.
2. Al-Qahir also recruited the loyal eunuch of Mu'nis, Bushra, who helped in the efforts against his commander.
3. The Sajiyya brigade in the army, dissatisfied with their poor pay compared to that of the pay of the Hujariyya brigade, had been promised better financial rewards. Their leader, Sima, was recruited through Sandal. In addition, they were badly treated by Mu'nis's ally, Ibn Baliq.[173]
4. The efforts of the *qahramana* Ikhtyar and her associate Ibn al-Qasim, who was installed as a vizier, helped in galvanising support around al-Qahir. She also carried out successful undercover liaisons.
5. The swift act of the experienced new chief of the army against Mu'nis.
6. Finally, Mu'nis was now old, and his attempt to pull political strings failed.

With the disappearance of this unique eunuch commander of the army, a few remarks are due here: Islamic medieval history and the 'Abbasid period in particular had not previously witnessed a long-serving eunuch in an office such as chief of the army. This eunuch dominated and even replaced caliphs. He saved vital provinces from falling to the enemy, especially Egypt. Through his network of eunuchs and coordination with the harem,[174] he managed to resolve the problem of the seclusion of the caliph, who rarely appeared in public, or received his administrators. Mu'nis and other eunuchs became the medium in the state for making decisions and transmitting caliphal messages around the empire.

Almost the same year in which he left the political stage in the Muslim East (934), another very dominant eunuch rose to the rank of 'deputy caliph' in the Islamic West under the Fatimids in North Africa. That was Jawdhar, deputy to three Fatimid caliphs. The 'Abbasid influence was not just on the Fatimids, but also on their autonomous provinces. In 946 the eunuch Kafur became de facto ruler of Ikhshidid Egypt and Syria, regent to two rulers, and then became the sole master of Egypt in 966. That was, I believe, down to the influence of the development of the 'Abbasid institution, especially under al-Muqtadir.

H. Bowen states that Mu'nis did not have the intelligence needed to save the caliphate from deterioration.[175] On his defensive military campaigns against Byzantium and the Fatimids, in addition to the Qaramita, he did his best. On domestic political affairs, it was not his job alone to accomplish that. He did give some stern warnings against the harem. However, he was ambitious and keen to have power within his grasp, as we discussed in his relations with the several viziers of the caliphate.

It seems that the 'Abbasids were not just influenced by the Greek–Byzantine heritage they started to translate from the mid-ninth century. They also were influenced by the way that the Byzantine state was administered, and they tried to assimilate it. While Mu'nis was chief of military police of the 'Abbasid army, the Byzantines had a eunuch admiral named Eustace, who was a very successful and powerful commander under Emperor Leo VI. There was also another eunuch named Samona who, in 906, was made a godfather to Emperor Leo VI's son and heir, Constantine.[176]

On the confrontation between the 'Abbasids and Byzantium, Mu'nis was absent from the military–political scene, which resulted in the domination of Byzantium at the frontier area with the 'Abbasid Empire and the capture of the 'Abbasid naval base at Tartus.[177]

As mentioned in the previous chapter, the institution of the caliphate collapsed on the eve of the coming of the Buwayhids to Baghdad in 945. The harem institution and the lavish lifestyle of *jawari*, singers and eunuchs almost disappeared, due to severe financial difficulties, among other factors. There is mention in the sources of cases of eunuchs serving at the frontier of Tartus in 941 under Thumal, and in 965 under the command of Rashiq. In addition, Aleppo was briefly governed by the eunuch Yannas al-Mu'nisi in 944.[178] These cases had no direct tangible influence on the political affairs of Baghdad or the centre of power.

The Buwayhids dominated the 'Abbasid caliphate until the coming of the Turkmen Seljuqs in 1055. There is no detailed account in the sources of their court during this period, although we know that the rulers were Iranian. They did not, however, use the vast and sophisticated court cultures of the Iranians; perhaps that was due to their nomadic nature, coming from the Qazwin area.

The endless strife between the three branches of the Buwayhids, in addition to their warfare with the separatist Hamdanids in the Jazira and northern Syria, left them little chance to settle down and produce a sophisticated court. Also, the rise of the autonomous Ikhshidids in Egypt and Syria in 935, and the coming of the Fatimids to Egypt and Syria in 969, added to the destabilisation of the Buwayhid rule.

While the political–military influence of eunuchs declined under the Buwayhids in Iraq and Iran, we see it appear strongly in Egypt and Syria at the same time, manifested in the unique rule of Kafur the Ikhshidid.

Eunuch Kafur: The First Recognised Sole Ruler of a Muslim Country, 946–68

Kafur was a Nubian eunuch who rose to power during the short-lived Ikhshidid dynasty of Egypt and southern Syria. The Ikhshidids ruled Egypt and southern Syria from 935 to 969.[179] Their founder, Muhammad b. Tughj al-Ikhshid, was a Turkish commander in the 'Abbasid army. In 935 he was appointed as an 'Abbasid governor to Egypt. With the rapid decline of the 'Abbasid caliphate, in 944 Caliph al-Muttaqi granted al-Ikhshid (an Iranian local title for 'prince of the rulers of Farghana') the right to rule Egypt with his descendants for a period of thirty years.[180]

Therefore, al-Ikhshid, who was a Tulunid commander, did not repeat the Tulunid experience of rebelling against the 'Abbasids and declaring full independence, but rather he enjoyed autonomous rule with full 'Abbasid approval. The Ikhshidid mint bore the names of the 'Abbasid caliphs, and the *khutba* was declared in their names, followed by the name of the Ikhshidids.[181] We have further evidence of the Ikhshidid vassalage relationship with the 'Abbasids, with the second ruler, Unujur (d. 961) asking, in 949, the permission of the Buwayhid king, the de facto ruler of Baghdad, to make Unujur's brother his heir, which was granted.[182]

Al-Ikhshid emulated the 'Abbasid court and military tradition of his masters in acquiring eunuchs at different levels of the state. Ibn Sa'id mentions that he employed a large number of eunuch military commanders, including Badr al-Kabir, Shadin al-Saqlabi, Munjih al-Saqlabi, Bushra, Fatik al-Rumi and Kafur al-Aswad.[183] It was this last eunuch, Kafur al-Aswad (lit. camphor the black), who had landmark achievements in Ikhshidid/'Abbasid Egypt and Syria.

Coming from Nubia and sold in the slave markets of Egypt like many other eunuchs, he was bought by al-Ikhshid, and soon came to his attention due to his loyalty and intelligence. Kafur was trusted by his master to command several military campaigns in Syria, such as in 938 against Ibn Ra'iq in Aleppo, and in 944 against the Hamdanids, also in Aleppo.[184] These campaigns, among others, managed to consolidate Ikhshid authority over southern Syria in particular.

Due to the resourcefulness of Kafur, al-Ikhshid, in the final year of his rule, installed him as regent for his two young sons.[185] That was a serious political move by al-Ikhshid, who did not trust his brother Abu al-Hasan to act as regent; he preferred Kafur. I believe that Kafur was the first eunuch in Islamic history to be installed as a regent to two princes and heir to the rule of an 'Abbasid province, with full 'Abbasid approval. That is a step further to the one taken by the mother of al-Muqtadir when Mu'nis al-Khadim was appointed in Egypt in 913 to rule in the name of the four-year-old son of al-Muqtadir. Nevertheless, he was not called a regent.

The Regency of Kafur

Kafur acted as regent for Unujur b. al-Ikhshid from 946 to 961, and then for 'Ali b. al-Ikhshid from 961 to 966. He had to get the blessing of the 'Abbasids for each new ruler in Egypt.[186] We can divide the achievements and challenges of Kafur during this period into 'domestic' and 'foreign'.

On the domestic front, Kafur was in Damascus in the company of his master, al-Ikhshid, when the latter died in August 946. Kafur managed to arrange the administration of Damascus and its defences before returning to Egypt to assume the regency of the fourteen-year-old Unujur.[187] Kafur, who was about forty years old, managed to secure the recognition of the 'Abbasid caliph al-Muti' of his regency, according to the will of the late al-Ikhshid. Not only that, but he committed himself to the annual financial tribute al-Ikhshid had paid to the central treasury in Baghdad.[188]

The first challenge within Egypt was the revolt of Ibn Ghalbun in Upper Egypt against the boy prince Unujur. In 946 Ibn Ghalbun advanced on Fustat (the functioning capital of Egypt at that time) and defeated Unujur while Kafur was fighting the Hamdanids in Syria. After Kafur returned to Egypt in the same year, he managed to fight and kill Ibn Ghalbun and secure Egypt for his boy ruler.[189] Ibn Taghri Bardi mentions that Kafur then became the de facto ruler of Egypt, dominating all affairs of the country, while Unujur was just a facade. Kafur was the one to decide the annual stipend paid to Unujur, which was 400,000 dinars. The spending of the remainder of the annual income of Egypt, more than 2.1 million dinars, was in Kafur's gift.[190]

Five years into his regency, in 951, Kafur managed to include his name in the official *khutba*, which was given first to the 'Abbasid caliph, then Unujur, then himself.[191] This prestigious political move reveals how dominant and respected Kafur was in Egypt by the army and elites, including the uncle of Unujur. How did Kafur manage to consolidate this position? It could be that it was a combination of successful financial administration and military power. As regards the former, Kafur succeeded in increasing the annual income of Egypt from an average two million dinars under al-Ikhshid, to three million dinars.[192] That is a 50 per cent increase in Egypt's revenues, which would be used for securing political–military power. Using this revenue Kafur established an army brigade called the Kafuriyya, carrying his name and comprising black Sudanese slaves of his own ethnicity.[193] Such a move was designed to consolidate his power against the Ikhshidiyya troops of his previous master, especially as Fatimid Isma'ili propaganda had infiltrated some of their ranks and some of their commanders became supporters of the Fatimids, and thus could not be trusted.[194]

In addition to that, Kafur owned 4,000 black and white slaves.[195] It is not clear from the sources how many of the Kafuriyya or his slaves were eunuchs, but it is likely that a substantial proportion of them were.

Kafur's achievements as regards security and finance enabled him to stand against the legitimate political challenge of Unujur in 954. In that year, Unujur was twenty-two years old, and had tried to assume power himself through force. Some of his followers told him: 'Kafur has dominated all financial affairs of the state. He became the sole commander of the army. He took over the wealth and properties of your father and you have been subdued.'[196] There was a street fight in Fustat between the supporters of the two sides, but the Kafuriyya ended the challenge to their side quickly. Unujur left the capital to a place in the country called al-Mahalla (the exact location is not clear). His mother pleaded to Kafur to forgive him, and the latter responded positively.[197] After this failed attempt, no one had any doubts about who the real master of Egypt was. The 'Abbasid caliphate, occupied with the Buwayhids, Hamdanids and other lords, had no power to rectify and interfere in Egyptian politics.

In 961 Unujur died, and Kafur installed in his place 'Ali b. Muhammad al-Ikhshid, in accordance with the will. It was Kafur who held a council attended by military commanders and secured the oath of allegiance to the new twenty-three-year-old puppet lord of Egypt. Caliph al-Muti' recognised him as lord of Egypt, Syria and the Hijaz.[198] The question here is: why did Kafur continue to be a regent for a mature ruler? The ambitious and powerful Kafur forced his political will in the absence of any real challenge. He continued to pay 400,000 dinars annually to 'Ali, as he had done with his late brother. However, Kafur became more dominant of the new ruler. He banned him from appearing in public, and banned him from contacting or meeting any state officials, especially after an attempt to seize power himself and get rid of Kafur. He was permitted only to meet with his boon companions for leisure.

As the domestic and foreign affairs reflect each other, we see Kafur managing to keep his grip on power despite a severe economic crisis, which coincided with Fatimid military pressure and the Nubian Christian invasion of southern Egypt. Consider this anecdote:

> Egypt experienced high prices and food shortages. The administration across Egypt suffered, particularly in Alexandria because of Fatimid Maghribi supporters coming from the west. Prices continued to soar, and wheat became scarce. Qaramita forces attacked the Ikhshidid territories in Syria in 963. The Ikhshidids could not confront them due to the economic crisis and were occupied with resisting the Fatimids. During these years, the Nile water decreased, resulting in severe price inflation. The countryside and

villages of Egypt were severely affected due to the situation with the Nile. The king of Nubia saw an opportunity and invaded Aswan in Upper Egypt and progressed to Akhmim (600 km south of Cairo) and sacked and looted the land.[199]

Kafur managed to survive these multiple crises and pushed back the Nubians and Fatimids.

In addition to commanding the army, and being in charge of the politics of Egypt, Kafur sat for the *mazalim*. He was the first eunuch to do so in Islamic history. As we have seen in the previous chapter, one of Shaghab's *qahramanat* did the same in Baghdad, and Kafur was probably encouraged by this. According to al-Kindi: 'Kafur would sit every Saturday for the *mazalim*. The vizier, all jurists, witnesses and elites of society would attend his court. The chief judge looked like a marginalised persona due to the regularity of Kafur practising these judicial affairs.'[200] Kafur never encountered opposition to this post like the initial opposition the *qahramana* faced in Baghdad as a woman.

In 966 'Ali died and Kafur refused to install Ahmad b. 'Ali. Instead, he took the daring step and declared himself the ruler of Egypt.[201]

Moving to the foreign policy of Kafur, he faced three main challenges: the Hamdanid Arabs who dominated the 'Abbasids in northern Iraq, and ruled Mosul, Aleppo and the Jazira; the Fatimids who constantly attacked western Egypt from the west with their active agents inside Egypt; and the Nubians, who invaded Upper Egypt. In 946 al-Ikhshid died in Damascus. In his company was his military commander, Kafur. After the latter returned to Egypt to assume the regency of Unujur, Sayf al-Dawla, the Hamdanid who had come to power in Aleppo the previous year, invaded Damascus.[202]

In Egypt, Kafur received a message from the locals of Damascus asking him for help against the Hamdanids. For more than a year Kafur had been commanding the army in Syria, and in his company was the boy prince Unujur. Kafur managed to save Damascus for the Ikhshidids, and then followed Sayf al-Dawla to Hims, where he defeated his forces. Kafur then followed Sayf al-Dawla to Aleppo (he had fled there following the defeat at Hims). Kafur's military skills forced Sayf al-Dawla to surrender Aleppo and escape to the Jazira.[203] Kafur and his prince returned to Egypt after he forced Sayf al-Dawla into a truce, which secured the Ikhshidid's territories in Damascus and southern Syria, while handing over Aleppo to the Hamdanids.²⁰⁴ This demonstrates the brilliance of Kafur, who had just assumed the regency in a newly established political autonomous system; he managed to retain power in Egypt and easily defend Syria.

The second foreign danger to Kafur and his administration was the powerful Fatimids to the west of Egypt. He managed to halt their advances, which had, at times, penetrated the Nile Delta.²⁰⁵ In addition to that, Kafur was pursuing the agents of the Fatimids inside Egypt who were preaching the Isma'ili doctrine, and managed to get some support from the Ikhshidiyya troops in the army. The Fatimid agents wrote to the Fatimid caliph, al-Mu'izz: 'If the black stone (meaning Kafur) is removed, our caliph al-Mu'izz will seize all the lands. Only the black stone separates us from you.'²⁰⁶

Ibn Taghri Bardi mentions that Kafur adopted realpolitik in his policy with the Fatimids:

> Kafur was a real expert of politics. He was brilliant, with good judgement, and behaved with great astuteness. He sometimes would reach a truce with al-Mu'izz of the Fatimids, and show some sympathy to his rule. At other times he showed full submission to the 'Abbasids. He maintained this cunning policy until he dominated Egypt.²⁰⁷

Delia Cortese and Simonetta Calderini observe that Kafur's master, al-Ikhshid, tried to use political marriage with the Fatimids to secure his new seat, while maintaining his relations with the 'Abbasids.²⁰⁸

It could be considered that in times of economic crisis with no hope of any military help from the devastated 'Abbasid caliphate, Kafur forged a pragmatic way of saving himself and his rule. When he was a regent for twenty years, or sole ruler for two years, the Fatimids never managed to seize Egypt, despite their enormous manpower and finance. When Kafur died in 968 the Fatimids seized the opportunity and captured Egypt the following year.²⁰⁹

In addition to keeping the eastern and western borders of Egypt well guarded, as well as maintaining his rule of southern Syria, Kafur managed to defend southern Egypt from the numerous invasions of the Nubian Kingdom. The Nubians invaded Upper Egypt in 950, and Upper Egypt and the Western Oasis of Egypt in 955. Kafur managed to confront them, and push them back across the borders to Ibrim.[210]

Kafur was a very pragmatic person, even in dealings with his masters. In 958 the Buwayhid king of Iraq, Muʿizz al-Dawla, dispatched an envoy to Kafur ordering him to pay a certain ransom to him. Kafur deliberately kept the envoy under house arrest, but treated him kindly. Meanwhile, Kafur dispatched his spies to ascertain the political situation in Iraq. He was trying to get an idea of the real power of Muʿizz al-Dawla. When Kafur received the news that Muʿizz al-Dawla was preoccupied with domestic strife in the Buwayhid house, he released the envoy back to Iraq without any money.[211]

Kafur: Sole Ruler of Egypt, 966–8

In 966 Kafur refused the succession of Ahmad b. ʿAli, who was nine years old,[212] and declared himself the master of Egypt with the title '*ustadh*' (ruler). Al-Ikhshid's brothers, Ubaid Allah (who had been ruling Ramla in Palestine) and al-Hasan b. Tughj, died in 944 and 953, respectively.[213]

Kafur, who rose to prominence under al-Ikhshid, and dominated the rule as a regent for his two sons for two decades, had now successfully taken control of Egypt, southern Syria and the Hijaz, despite the socio-economic, military and political challenges outlined above.

As a result, there was no real challenge to the eunuch who assumed power, representing himself in the Ikhshidid territories. Caliph al-Mutiʿ recognised the rule of Kafur in Egypt, and sent an envoy to him with the robe of honour and presents. He was given the title of '*abu al-misk*'.[214] As a result, Kafur's name was declared in the official *khutba* over the mosques of Egypt, after that of the caliph. Here we see the Islamic shariʿa being ignored and the permitting of a eunuch, who was not a full capable man, to rule Muslim territories and represent the caliphate. However, the shariʿa was also ignored when a child such as al-Muqtadir was allowed to rule as a caliph, or Unujur in Egypt, among many other examples. The ʿAbbasids saw in Kafur the only hope for keeping Egypt out of Fatimid control.

Kafur was the first eunuch to be a regent for a ruler's sons and to direct the rule; he also was the first eunuch to be declared as sole ruler of a Muslim state in early and medieval Islam. His example influenced and encouraged the Fatimids, Seljuqs and Ayyubids to install eunuchs as regents, but never as a sole ruler. In addition to declaring the *khutba* in his name as a sign of supremacy, he also had coins minted in his name in Mecca in 968. On the reverse of a one dinar coin it reads 'Li Allah. Muhammad rasul Allah. Al-Muti' li Allah. Kaf-for Kafur'.[215]

His name did not appear on coins minted in Egypt, however, but his keenness to have his name on Meccan coins gave him more prestige and religious legitimacy, as it was the most holy place for Muslims.

There is little evidence in early and medieval Islamic history, up to the period of the Ayyubids, of eunuchs being eulogised by poets. Kafur was the exception. His memory was kept in the public mind, thanks to the grand Iraqi Arab poet, al-Mutanabbi (d. 965). Al-Mutanabbi is arguably the most famous and influential Arab poet of the medieval period. He came to Egypt to visit Kafur in 957, escaping from his rivals, the Hamdanids. He remained in Egypt until 961,[216] during which time he praised Kafur, saying:

> The king master prospered in rule
> He dominated the affairs from Egypt to Eden to Iraq, and Nubia[217]
> I am today one of his *ghulman* bonded by a clan
> He is like a father to us.[218]

Al-Mutanabbi was determined to be rewarded by Kafur, hoping that he would be appointed to his administration. When he lost hope of this happening, he turned against him, with strong racist satire verses ridiculing him as a eunuch:

> The eunuch became the imam (chief) of slaves in Egypt
> Free men are enslaved while the slave (Kafur) is worshipped
> Do not buy a slave unless you buy a stick with him (for beating)
> Slaves are nasty and miserable
> Who taught the black eunuch good behaviour?
> His white people or his prestigious ancestors?
> The white stallions are unable to do good
> So how will the black eunuchs do it?[219]

Apart from these racist and anti-eunuch lines, the contemporary or post-contemporary sources who had the chance to criticise Kafur without fear attempted to do so. Indeed, the thirteenth-century scholar Ibn Khallikan, who specialised in writing biographies of the elite, described the physical ugliness of Kafur: 'Kafur was a black eunuch, with an ugly appearance. He had a big belly, and a massive body which moved slowly. Kafur had disgusting feet, and his lower lip was pierced.'[220] On the other hand, the contemporary judge al-Kindi (d. 966), or chroniclers such as Ibn al-Athir (d. 1233) and al-Dhahabi (d. 1348), among others, never criticised Kafur for his appearance. On the contrary, they praised his wisdom, and admired his power. Ibn al-Athir had no disrespect for the third gender in Muslim territories, or elsewhere. He mentioned in 979, for example, the eunuch minister of Emperor Romanos I Lekapenos of Byzantium with clear neutrality during the power struggle there.[221]

With the end of Kafur's rule, the 'Abbasid eunuchdome had completed its circle, from humble beginnings as a bearer of the insignia to the caliph or serving and protecting the royal harem, to being employed as caliphal bodyguards and *hajib*s and governors, to becoming commanders in the army, and then commander of the army, ending with regent to the ruler's children and becoming officially recognised by the caliphate as sole ruler of Egypt, with the blessing of their powerful associates, the Buwayhids. The Buwayhids continued to use the services of eunuchs in their administration, but on a much smaller scale.

It is unlikely that the example of Kafur was replicated again in medieval Islamic history; however, other dynasties, such as the Fatimids who took over Egypt after his death, employed the third gender on a wider scale, as will be discussed in Chapter Four.

Notes

1. Al-Suyuti *Ta'rikh*, p. 359, as reported by al-Suli.
2. Ayalon, *Eunuchs*, p. 139.
3. Marmon, *Eunuchs and Sacred Boundaries*.
4. A. S. Ehrenkreutz, art.: 'Kafur', *EI*².
5. Ayalon, *Eunuchs*, p. 68.
6. Ayalon, *Outsiders in the Land of Islam*, p. 68.
7. Al-Jahiz, *Al-Hayawan*, Vol. 1, p. 124; Ch. Pellat, art. 'Khasi', *EI*².
8. Metz, *Renaissance*, Vol. 2, p. 129.
9. Ayalon, *Outsiders in the Land of Islam*, pp. 68–9.

10. Metz, *Renaissance*, Vol. 2, pp. 129–31.
11. Lewis, *Race and Slavery*, p. 14; Pellat, 'Khasi'.
12. Al-Jahiz, *Al-Hayawan*, Vol. 1, p. 128.
13. Metz, *Renaissance*, Vol. 2, p. 127.
14. Ayalon, *Eunuchs*, p. 75.
15. Al-Mas'udi, *Muruj*, Vol. 4, p. 243; Ibn Hawqal, *Surat al-Ard*, Leiden, 1890, Vol. 1, p. 110; al-Qalqashandi, *Subh al-'Asha*, Beirut, 1987, Vol. 5, p. 295.
16. Metz, *Renaissance*, Vol. 2, p. 129; Pellat, 'Khasi'; Lewis, *Race and Slavery*, p. 51.
17. Al-Jahiz, *Al-Hayawan*, Vol. 1, p. 83.
18. Al-Tabari, *Ta'rikh*, p. 1,320.
19. Muwaffaq al-Din Ibn Abi Usabi'a, *Tabaqat al-Atibba'*, Beirut, 1987, Vol. 2, p. 140.
20. Pellat, 'Khasi'.
21. Al-Jahiz, *Al-Hayawan*, Vol. 1, pp. 78, 106–16, 119, 135–6.
22. Ibn Aybak al-Safadi, *Tuhfat Dhawi al-Albab*, ed. I. Khulusi, Damascus, 1992, Vol. 2, p. 105; al-Jahiz, *Al-Hayawan*, Vol. 1, pp. 166–7.
23. Kathryn Ringrose, *The Perfect Servant: Eunuchs and the Social Construction of Gender in Byzantium*, Chicago, 2003, pp. 20, 33.
24. Metz, *Renaissance*, Vol. 2, p. 129.
25. Ayalon, *Eunuchs*, p. 62.
26. Ibn Aybak, *Tuhfat*, Vol. 2, p. 105.
27. Al-Jahiz, *Al-Hayawan*, Vol. 1, pp. 81–2. I did consult two professors of medicine, one in the field of eternal medicine, and one in the field of psychiatry, and they supported most of what al-Jahiz had observed.
28. Ibid., pp. 85–6.
29. 'Al-Aghawat fi al-Madina (The Eunuchs in Medina)', in *Meka* (newspaper), 6 February 2014.
30. Michel Foucault, *The History of Sexuality*, trans. R. Hurley, New York, 1978, Vol. 1.
31. Frederic Lagrange, art.: 'Sexuality and Queer Studies', *Encyclopedia of Women and Islamic Cultures*, ed. S. Joseph, Leiden, 2003, Vol. 1.
32. Bou Hdeiba, *Sex in Islam*, p. 88.
33. Al-Suyuti, Jalal, *Nawadir al-Iyk fi Ma'rifat al-Naik*, ed. T. Hasan, Damascus, 2004, p. 50.
34. Paula Sanders, 'Gendering the Ungendered Body: Hermaphrodites in Medieval Islamic Law', in *Women in Middle Eastern History: Shifting Boundaries in Sex and Gender*, ed. N. Keddie, New Haven, 1991, pp. 74–95, 77.

35. 'Imad al-Din al-Isfahani, *Ta'rikh Dawlat al-Saljuq*, Beirut, 1980, p. 190.
36. Pellat, 'Khasi'; Ayalon, *Outsiders*, p. 74; Metz, *Renaissance*, Vol. 2, p. 130.
37. Ibn al-Athir, *Al-Kamil*, Vol. 5, p. 410.
38. Ayalon, *Eunuchs*, p. 73.
39. Al-Tabari, *Ta'rikh*, p. 1,595; Ibn al-Athir, *Al-Kamil*, Vol. 6, p. 33.
40. Ibn al-Athir, *Al-Kamil*, Vol. 6, p. 34; Ayalon, *Eunuchs*, p. 96.
41. Al-Qurtubi, *Silat*, p. 136; Meskawayh, *Tarajib*, Vol. 3, p. 385.
42. Ayalon, *Eunuchs*, p. 97.
43. Al-Tabari, *Ta'rikh*, p. 1,698.
44. Ibid., p. 1,699.
45. Ayalon, *Eunuchs*, p. 98.
46. Ibn al-Athir, *Al-Kamil*, Vol. 6, p. 26; al-Tabari, *Ta'rikh*, p. 1,699. Khurasan is now eastern Iran, Turkmenistan and most of Afghanistan. It was the centre of 'Abbasid power, and controlled access to the Turkmen area of natural horse warriors, who crossed the River Oxus in massive numbers.
47. Ibn al-Athir, *Al-Kamil*, Vol. 6, p. 26; al-Tabari, *Ta'rikh*, p. 1,562.
48. W. Barthold and D. Sourdel, art.: 'Al-Baramika', *EI²*..
49. Ibid.; al-Masudi, *Muruj*, Vol. 3, p. 311.
50. Al-Tabari, *Ta'rikh*, p. 1,686; Ibn Taqataqa, *Al-Fakhri fi al-Adab*, pp. 208–9; Ibn al-Jawzi, *Al-Muntazam*, Vol. 9, p. 133.
51. Al-Masudi, *Muruj*, Vol. 3, p. 312; al-Tabari, *Ta'rikh*, p. 1,686. Al-Tabari, among others, gave different accounts and details about 'the night of the long knives' against the Barmakids.
52. Ibn al-Athir, *Al-Kamil*, Vol. 6, p. 179.
53. Ayalon, *Eunuchs*, pp. 90–1.
54. Ibn al-Jawzi, *Al-Muntazam*, Vol. 9, p. 194.
55. Ayalon, *Eunuchs*, pp. 108–10.
56. Ibid., pp. 109–12. Ayalon mentions that in 787 Abu Sulayman al-Khadim was a eunuch who commanded a raid on Tartus, but it is not clear if Abu Sulayman (father of Sulayman) here is a eunuch, and also the word *khadim* was synonymous to eunuch from the tenth century onwards, as Ayalon himself states. Before that, we cannot assert such an opinion.
57. Al-Tabari, *Ta'rikh*, pp. 1,705, 1,712.
58. Ibid., p. 1,714.
59. Ibn al-Athir, *Al-Kamil*, Vol. 6, p. 221.
60. Al-Tabari, *Ta'rikh*, p. 1,769. This free translation of mine is concerned only with the meaning, not the articulation and rhyme.

61. Al-Masudi, *Muruj*, Vol. 3, p. 340.
62. Ibn al-Athir, *Al-Kamil*, Vol. 6, pp. 227–30.
63. Al-Masudi, *Muruj*, Vol. 3, p. 326.
64. Al-Tabari, *Ta'rikh*, pp. 1,717–20.
65. Al-Masudi, *Muruj*, Vol. 3, p. 341.
66. Al-Suyuti, *Ta'rikh*, p. 359.
67. Al-Tabari, *Ta'rikh*, p. 1,771; Ibn al-Athir, *Al-Kamil*, Vol. 6, p. 293; al-Masudi, *Muruj*, Vol. 3, p. 342.
68. Ibn al-Athir, *Al-Kamil*, Vol. 6, pp. 293–4. This free translation of mine is concerned only with the meaning, not the articulation.
69. Ibid., p. 294.
70. Al-Tabari, *Ta'rikh*, p. 1,775.
71. Abbott, *Two Queens*, p. 212; Editor, art.: 'Liwat', *EI²*.
72. Abbott, *Two Queens*, p. 254.
73. Ibn Taqataqa, *Al-Fakhri fi al-Adab*, p. 213; al-Suyuti, *Ta'rikh*, p. 352.
74. Ayalon, *Eunuchs*, p. 129.
75. Ibn al-Jawzi, *Al-Muntazam*, Vol. 12, p. 20.
76. Al-Tabari, *Ta'rikh*, p. 1,756.
77. Ayalon, *Eunuchs*, p. 132.
78. Ibn al-Jawzi, *Al-Muntazam*, Vol. 10, p. 267.
79. Ayalon believes that Nawfal was in Baghdad during the civil war, looking after two sons of al-Ma'mun, *Eunuchs*, p. 133.
80. Ibn al-Jawzi, *Al-Muntazam*, Vol. 9, p. 223, Vol. 10, p. 65.
81. Al-Isfahani, *Kitab Al-Aghani*, Vol. 10, p. 200.
82. Al-Isfahani, *Kitab Al-Aghani*, Vol. 20, pp. 158–9; al-Tha'alibi, *Thimar*, p. 132; al-Masudi, *Muruj*, Vol. 4, p. 19.
83. al-Tha'alibi, *Thimar*, p. 123; Metz, *Renaissance*, Vol. 2, p. 133.
84. Ibn al-Jawzi, *Al-Muntazam*, Vol. 10, p. 45.
85. Al-Tabari, *Ta'rikh*, p. 1,760.
86. Kennedy, *The Court of the Caliphs*, pp. 218–28.
87. Al-Tannukhi, *Al-Faraj*, p. 138.
88. Ibn al-Jawzi, *Al-Muntazam*, Vol. 11, p. 192.
89. Ibn al-Jawzi, *Al-Muntazam*, Vol. 12, pp. 20–1.
90. Bianquis, *Autonomous Egypt*, pp. 90–2.
91. Ibid., pp. 100–1; Ibn al-Athir, *Al-Kamil*, Vol. 6, pp. 396–7.
92. Bianquis, 'Autonomous Egypt', p. 101.
93. Al-Tabari, *Ta'rikh*, p. 2,080.

94. Ibn al-Athir, *Al-Kamil*, Vol. 7, pp. 439, 449; Ibn Taghri Bardi, *Al-Nujum*, Vol. 3, p. 76.
95. Ayalon, *Eunuchs*, p. 115; S. M. Stern, 'The Coins of Thamal and of Other Governors of Tarsus', *Journal of the American Oriental Society*, Vol. 80, No. 3, 1960, pp. 217–25, 220.
96. Ibn al-Athir, *Al-Kamil*, Vol. 7, pp. 406, 411, 420, 427, 449.
97. Ibid., p. 450.
98. Ibid., pp. 474–5. Ibn Taghri Bardi mentioned different reasons related to another sexual behaviour, *Al-Nujum*, Vol. 3, pp. 63–4.
99. Ibn al-Athir, *Al-Kamil*, Vol. 7, pp. 520–1.
100. Ibid., pp. 439, 441.
101. Al-Tabari, *Ta'rikh*, p. 2,132; Ayalon, *Eunuchs*, p. 124.
102. Al-Tabari, *Ta'rikh*, p. 2,132.
103. Ibid.
104. Ibid.
105. Less than two decades before the reign of al-Muqtadir, the sources mention several commanders who may have been eunuchs due to their names, or the course of events: for example, Yunis al-Khadim, commander of al-Mu'tadid, who was entrusted by that caliph to secure the succession to his son, al-Muktafi, in 902, Ibn al-Athir, *Al-Kamil*, Vol. 7, p. 515; Tughj, the 'Abbasid deputy of Damascus in 903, who dispatched a commander called Bishr to fight the Qaramita, Ibn al-Athir, *Al-Kamil*, Vol. 7, p. 523; and Commander Zarafa (giraffe), who was stationed in Tarsus in 904, Ibn al-Athir, *Al-Kamil*, Vol. 7, p. 533. However, we will not consider them as eunuchs and their cases will not be studied, as more evidence is needed.
106. Ibn Adhara al-Marakishi, *Al-Bayan*, Vol. 1, p. 149. He mentioned that the last Aghlabid ruler, Ziyada, owned hundreds of eunuchs in his court.
107. Al-Suyuti, *Ta'rikh*, p. 454.
108. Meskawayh, *Tarajib*, Vol. 5, p. 58.
109. Ibn al-Athir, *Al-Kamil*, Vol. 8, p. 113.
110. Meskawayh, *Tarajib*, Vol. 5, pp. 56–7; Ibn Aybak, *Kanz al-Durar*, Vol. 5, p. 324.
111. Al-Dhahabi, *Ta'rikh al-Islam*, ed. A. Tadmuri, Beirut, 1991, Vol. 22, p. 25; Meskawayh, *Tarajib*, Vol. 5, pp. 56–7.
112. Al-Qurtubi, *Silat*, p. 156; Meskawayh, *Tarajib*, Vol. 5, p. 57.
113. Kennedy, 'Mu'nis', p. 82.
114. Ibn al-Athir, *Al-Kamil*, Vol. 8, p. 18.

115. Ibid., p. 68; Sibt Ibn al-Jawzi, *Mir'at*, Vol. 16, p. 392.
116. Ibn al-Athir, *Al-Kamil*, Vol. 8, pp. 150–1.
117. Ibid., p. 151.
118. Meskawayh, *Tarajib*, Vol. 5, pp. 288–9.
119. Ibid., pp. 290–1.
120. Ibn al-Athir, *Al-Kamil*, Vol. 8, p. 232.
121. Ibid., pp. 92–3.
122. Meskawayh, *Tarajib*, Vol. 5, pp. 110–11.
123. Ibid., p. 213.
124. Ibn al-Athir, *Al-Kamil*, Vol. 8, pp. 126–9.
125. Ibn al-Athir, *Al-Kamil*, Vol. 5, p. 190.
126. Ibn al-Athir, *Al-Kamil*, Vol. 8, p. 157.
127. Ignati Krachkovski, *Istoria Arabskoi Geograficheskoi Literatury*, trans. S. Hashem, Cairo, 1963, Vol. 1, pp. 186–7.
128. Meskawayh, *Tarajib*, Vol. 5, p. 179; Kahala, *A'lam al Nissa'*, Vol. 5, pp. 67, 255.
129. Ibn al-Athir, *Al-Kamil*, Vol. 8, pp. 54, 56, 85, 89, 92, 101, 106, 113, 140, 156, 169, 181.
130. T. Bianquis, 'Autonomous Egypt', p. 107.
131. Ibn al-Athir, *Al-Kamil*, Vol. 8, p. 76.
132. Ibid., pp. 107–8.
133. Ibn Taghri Bardi, *Al-Nujum*, Vol. 3, p. 196.
134. Ibn al-Athir, *Al-Kamil*, Vol. 8, p. 113–14; al-Maqrizi, *Itti'az*, Vol. 1, p. 104.
135. Ibn al-Athir, *Al-Kamil*, Vol. 8, pp. 59, 61, 65, 74, 76, 77, 86, 106, 107, 121, 143, 144, 156, 179.
136. Ibid., pp. 99–100.
137. Al-Kindi, *Al-Wulat*, p. 194.
138. Al-Jahiz, *Al-Hayawan*, Vol. 1, p. 83.
139. Stern, 'Coins of Thamal', p, 218; Aly Mohamed Fahmy, *Muslim Sea-power in the Eastern Mediterranean from the Seventh to the Tenth Century* AD, Cairo, 1966, pp. 126–7.
140. Ibn al-Athir, *Al-Kamil*, Vol. 8, p. 121.
141. Ibid., pp. 113, 121.
142. Stern, 'Coins of Thamal', p. 223.
143. Ibn al-Athir, *Al-Kamil*, Vol. 8, p. 468
144. El Cheikh, 'Servants at the Gate', p. 244. In this study El Cheikh studies the role of two eunuchs, Safi al-Hurami and Muflih. She mentions (based on

al-Qurtubi's *Silat*, p. 244), that in 923 Muflih was all powerful. As we have seen, Mu'nis was very dominant and was called 'the sword of the caliph' by the royal mother. Although Muflih was the special eunuch of the caliph (*khasis*) we have no clear information on the nature of his post. He managed to defend himself against the racist comments of the vizier Hamid in 923, but that cannot be generalised to all positions at all times. As for Safi, he died as early as 910, Al-Dhahabi, *Ta'rikh*, Vol. 22, p. 33.

145. Meskawayh, *Tarajib*, Vol. 5, p. 264; Ibn Aybak, *Kanz al-Durar*, Vol. 5, p. 361.
146. Meskawayh, *Tarajib*, Vol. 5, pp. 266–8. The third caliph, 'Uthman, was besieged and killed in his house by rebels who thought his conduct was unfair.
147. Ibid., p. 269.
148. Al-Qurtubi, *Silat*, p. 140; Ibn al-Athir, *Al-Kamil*, Vol. 8, pp. 201, 202.
149. Al-Sabi', *Ta'rikh*. He puts the age of Mu'nis at ninety years with sixty years of service in the military, p. 94.
150. Ibn Aybak, *Kanz al-Durar*, Vol. 5., p. 361.
151. Ibn al-Athir, *Al-Kamil*, Vol. 8, p. 169.
152. Ibid., pp. 203–7.
153. Ibid., p. 223.
154. Meskawayh, *Tarajib*, Vol. 5, p. 289.
155. Ibn al-Athir, *Al-Kamil*, Vol. 8, p. 232.
156. Al-Dhahabi, *Ta'rikh*, Vol. 22, p. 27; Ibn Aybak, *Kanz al-Durar*, Vol. 5, p. 361.
157. Ibn al-Athir, *Al-Kamil*, Vol. 8, pp. 237–40.
158. Ibid., p. 241.
159. Ibid., pp. 242–3.
160. Ibn al-Jawzi, *Al-Muntazam*, Vol. 13, pp. 306–7; Meskawayh, *Tarajib*, Vol. 5, p. 327.
161. Meskawayh, *Tarajib*, Vol. 5, p. 328.
162. Ibn al-Athir, *Al-Kamil*, Vol. 8, p. 245.
163. Kennedy, 'Mu'nis', p. 89.
164. Ibn Aybak, *Kanz al-Durar*, Vol. 5, p. 364; Ibn al-Athir, *Al-Kamil*, Vol. 8, pp. 245–50.
165. Ibn al-Athir, *Al-Kamil*, Vol. 8, pp. 246, 279.
166. Ibid., p. 248.
167. Al-Dhahabi, *Ta'rikh*, Vol. 24, p. 5; Ibn al-Athir, *Al-Kamil*, Vol. 8, p. 253.
168. Meskawayh, *Tarajib*, Vol. 5, pp. 348–50; Ibn al-Athir, *Al-Kamil*, Vol. 8, p. 250.
169. Ibn al-Athir, *Al-Kamil*, Vol. 8, p. 258.

170. Ibid., *Al-Kamil*, Vol. 5, pp. 355–7.
171. Ibid., p. 357.
172. Ibn al-'Adim, *Zubdat al-Halab fi Ta'rikh Halab*, ed. S. al-Dahhan, Damascus, 1959, Vol. 1, p. 138.
173. Ibid., *Zubdat al-Halab fi Ta'rikh Halab*, Vol. 5, p. 350; Ibn al-Athir, *Al-Kamil*, Vol. 8, p. 259.
174. Murtaza al-Naqib, 'The Political and Military Career of Mu'nis al-Muzaffar at the 'Abbasid Court', unpublished master's dissertation, McGill University, Montreal, 1969. This is a good study on the detailed military and political career of Mu'nis and the 'Abbasids during that period. However, it does not focus on the complicated relations of the gendered politics of Shaghab, her *qahramanat* and Mu'nis, which are intertwined. We cannot fully understand Mu'nis's career without such coverage.
175. H. Bowen, art.: 'Mu'nis al-Muzaffar', *EI²*.
176. Ringrose, *The Perfect Servant*, p. 101; Shaun Tougher, *The Eunuch in Byzantine History and Society*, London, 2008, p. 66.
177. Ibn Taghri Bardi, *Al-Nujum*, Vol. 3, pp. 288–348.
178. Ibn al-Athir, *Al-Kamil*, Vol. 8, pp. 392, 445, 562.
179. Sayyeda al-Kashif, *Misr fi Ahd al-Ikhshidiyyun*, Cairo, 1950, p. 55; C. E. Bosworth, art.: 'Ikhshid', *EI²*.
180. Al-Kashif, *Misr*, pp. 81–2, 86; Bosworth, *Islamic Dynasties*, p. 45.
181. Al-Kashif, *Misr*, p. 90; Bianquis, 'Autonomous Egypt', pp. 112–13.
182. Ibn Taghri Bardi, *Al-Nujum*, Vol. 3, p. 298.
183. Ibn Sa'id, *Al-Maghribi fi Huliyy al-Maghrib*, ed. S. Daif, Cairo, 1955, Vol. 1, p. 190.
184. Ehrenkreutz, 'Kafur'; Ibn al-Adim, *Zubdat al-Halab fi Ta'rikh Halab*, Vol. 1, pp. 154, 156.
185. Ibn al-Athir, *Al-Kamil*, Vol. 8, p. 457. Ibn al-Athir, among others, used the eleventh-century Seljuq Turkish term '*atabeg*' for the position of regent in tenth-century Egypt, which is not exact.
186. Ehrenkreutz, 'Kafur'.
187. Al-Kindi, *Al-Wulat*, p. 294.
188. Ibn Taghri Bardi, *Al-Nujum*, Vol. 4, pp. 1–2, 10.
189. Ibid., p. 2.
190. Ibid.; al-Maqrizi, *Al-Mawa'iz wa al-I'tibar bi Dhikr al-Khitat al-Athar*, Cairo, n.d., Vol. 1, p. 321.
191. Al-Maqrizi, *Al-Khitat*, Vol. 1, p. 321; Vol. 2, pp. 26, 27.

192. Al-Kashif, *Misr*, p. 343.
193. Al-Maqrizi, *Al-Khitat*, Vol. 1, p. 94.
194. Al-Kindi, *Wulat*, pp. 287–8.
195. Al-Kashif, *Misr*, p. 137.
196. Ibn Taghri Bardi, *Al-Nujum*, Vol. 3, p. 292.
197. Bianquis, 'Autonomous Egypt', p. 116; al-Maqrizi, *Al-Khitat*, Vol. 2, p. 28.
198. Ibn Taghri Bardi, *Al-Nujum*, Vol. 3, pp. 325–7; al-Kindi, *Al-Wulat*, p. 296.
199. Ibn Taghri Bardi, *Al-Nujum*, Vol. 3, p. 326.
200. Al-Kindi, *Al-Wulat*, pp. 583–4.
201. Al-Kindi, *Al-Wulat*, Vol. 4, pp. 1–2; al-Kashif, *Misr*, p. 127.
202. Ibn al-Athir, *Al-Kamil*, Vol. 8, p. 457.
203. Ibn al-'Adim, *Zubdat*, Vol. 1, p. 370.
204. Ibid., p. 372.
205. Al-Maqrizi, *Al-Khitat*, Vol. 2, p. 28.
206. Ibn Taghri Bardi, *Al-Nujum*, Vol. 4, p. 22.
207. Ibid., p. 6.
208. Cortese and Calderini, *Women*, p. 63.
209. Ibn al-Athir, *Al-Kamil*, Vol. 8, p. 590.
210. Ibn Taghri Bardi, *Al-Nujum*, Vol. 3, pp. 326–7. Ibrim is in the far south of Egypt, and has been largely flooded by Lake Nasser.
211. Meskawayh, *Tarajib*, Vol. 6, p. 211.
212. Ibid., *Tarajib*, Vol. 4, p. 9.
213. Al-Kindi, *Al-Wulat*, p. 292; Ibn Taghri Bardi, *Al-Nujum*, Vol. 3, p. 298.
214. Al-Maqrizi, *Al-Khitat*, Vol. 1, p. 330; al-Kindi, *Al-Wulat*, p. 297.
215. Jere Bacharach, *Islamic History through Coins*, Cairo, 2006, p. 85.
216. Al-Mutannabi, *Diwan*, Cairo, 2005, pp. 18–19.
217. Kafur did not rule any areas of Yemen, but the poet exaggerates his influence. He also did not hold the title of 'king'.
218. Al-Mutannabi, *Diwan*, p. 95.
219. Ibid., pp. 101–2. The poet here tries to compensate the childless eunuch with assumed children.
220. Ibn Khallikan, *Wafayat al-A'yan*, Beirut, 1985, Vol. 1, p. 547.
221. Ibn Taghri Bardi, *Al-Nujum*, Vol. 4, pp. 1, 6; Ibn al-Athir, *Al-Kamil*, Vol. 8, p. 703.

4

Fatimid Royal Women and Royal Concubines in Politics: The Rise of the First Queens of Islam

In the name of God, the merciful, the compassionate. From the lady, the queen, the eminent, the kind, the mother of Imam/Caliph al-Musta'li b. Allah, commander of the faithful, son of Imam al-Mustansir b. Allah, to al-Hurra, the queen, the lady, the righteous, the faithful, the powerful, the preserver of religion, the chief of the believers, the cave of the followers, the supporter of the commander of the faithful; and the protector of his blessed followers. The Almighty may keep her rule, grace, and assist her. I would like to convey to you, how our Imam al-Musta'li became victorious over the people of evil, like his delusional brother, Nizar. As al-Hurra occupies the highest of places and ranks of loyalty, we wanted to keep her informed of the affairs of the state, so she will continue her pride in the state. We are always keen to hear her news and achievements, as the Almighty distinguished her above the rest of the people of her time.[1]

This is part of a long epistle from the Fatimid chancery sent by the queen mother of the Fatimid caliph al-Musta'li (d. 1101) to Queen Arwa the Sulayhid of Yemen in 1095. It is one of three Fatimid epistles/documents, and probably the only case of queenship in medieval Islam where we have two queens corresponding independently with each other.

The Fatimid Shi'i dynasty takes its name from Fatima, daughter of the Prophet, and wife of his cousin, 'Ali. It is the only Muslim political dynasty to carry the name of a woman. The Fatimids, who ruled for six decades from 909 to 969 in North Africa, in Egypt from 969, and expanding into Syria, the Hijaz and Yemen later, claimed their direct descent from Fatima and 'Ali.[2]

The Fatimids were the enemy of the Sunni 'Abbasids and represented only the Isma'ili Shi'i faith, who believe in the seventh Shi'i imam, Isma'il b. Ja'far al-Sadiq (d. 755). That is why they are called the Isma'iliyya. Other Shi'i factions, such as the Zaydis and Twelvers do not follow the Isma'ili doctrine. The main doctrinal difference between the Fatimids and the 'Abbasids was that the Isma'ili caliph came to power through the *nass* (declared religious–political will) of the previous caliph. In most cases the post of caliph transmitted from father to the eldest son, who inherited religious knowledge, just as the Prophet had passed his knowledge to the first imam, 'Ali.[3]

The main aim of the Fatimids was to uproot their Sunni 'Abbasid enemies and replace them as the sole religious–political authority. For that reason, they had a sophisticated large underground *da'wa* (movement) active in several places across Muslim territories, in order to spread their teachings. Fatimid history is divided into two periods. The first period spanned 909 to 1063; that period witnessed the military and political expansion of the Fatimid state during the rule of eight caliphs. They took Sicily, Egypt, most of Syria, the Hijaz and Yemen from the 'Abbasids, and the *khutba* was given to al-Mustansir (d. 1094) in some areas of Iraq, including Baghdad itself, the heartland of the 'Abbasids, in about 1055.[4]

The second period, until their downfall at the hands of the Zengids, witnessed a severe famine and civil wars from 1063 that lasted for nearly seven years, referred to as the Mustansiriyya Crisis. That had dire consequences for their rule; thereafter the caliphs were dominated by their viziers and military commanders. There were also two significant regional political and military developments during that period that negatively affected the Fatimids. The first was the coming of the powerful Sunni Seljuq Turkmen to the Middle East, who stripped the Fatimids of cities including Aleppo, Jerusalem and Damascus during and immediately after the famine;[5] the second was the coming of the Crusaders to the Levant in 1097, and within a decade they had seized most of the Fatimid coastal cities, with the exception of Tyre and Ascalon, which were captured several decades later. Losing such key coastal centres was a severe blow to the Fatimids as regards commerce and revenues in the Eastern Mediterranean.[6]

It was in the second Fatimid period that we see the title 'queen' being applied to royal mothers and sisters of some caliphs. We also see the influence of some royal aunts in political and religious affairs. It was the age that witnessed the rise of the first undisputed queen in medieval Islam, Arwa the Sulayhid of Yemen (1099–1138), as a political ruler and supreme religious authority (*hujja*: undisputed proof), coming second only to the religious authority of the caliph.

This chapter will address the following questions: how did the royal sisters and mothers interfere in the political affairs of the Fatimid state, and in the Fatimid doctrine? What challenges did they meet? Why did the Fatimids not have a fully publicly declared queen in their centre in Egypt, yet have the first declared queen in Yemen? Why was this model not repeated by the Fatimids? What are the reasons for the Fatimids being more tolerant than the ʿAbbasids in elevating women to a high religious status? What role in state affairs did concubines play under the Fatimids?

The First Fatimid Age, 909–1063

The harem in the Fatimid courts in North Africa and Egypt differed significantly from the harem of their counterparts, the ʿAbbasids. While the ʿAbbasids had an entourage of concubines and *jawari* for pleasures and entertainment, the Fatimids possessed smaller numbers. This was likely due to the Fatimid state being smaller than that of the ʿAbbasids. Does the absence of a voluminous book such as *Kitab al-Aghani*, among others from the Fatimid age, contribute to our limited knowledge of the details of the age? Or has the destruction of the Fatimid libraries, during the Mustansiriyya Crisis, and then the deliberate and systematic dispersal of the libraries by Saladin (d. 1193), deprived us of tens of thousands of valuable documents and chronicles?[7] In addition, the personal conservative behaviours of caliphs such as al-Muʿizz and the unusual al-Hakim contributed to minimising the harem and its associated activities. While there were large numbers of female poets in the ʿAbbasid court, and in Andalusia, the limited nature of the Fatimids, in comparison to other dynasties, is reflected in the observation of Cortese and Calderini: 'As far as the Fatimid courts are concerned, the names of their poetesses have remained unknown, except for one woman.'[8]

Ibn Khaldun (d. 1406), the great North African historian, mentioned that the native Berbers of North Africa did not create large sophisticated urban centres for themselves,[9] so maybe the Fatimids were influenced by the rigid nature of the majority of their subjects. In addition, the small numbers of Arab Fatimids who claimed descent from Fatima had no precedent with court culture, and very little is known about their nature and customs.

However, the Fatimids followed the 'Abbasid pattern or practice of choosing future rulers from among children born of concubines, rather than wives and free women. The great majority of Fatimid caliphs were born to concubines who had no political roles or a *jariya* who became *um walad* after giving birth, including the founding imam, al-Mahdi.[10] We have difficulty in identifying the mother of the first Fatimid caliph, as the beginnings of the dynasty are shrouded in legend. Regarding the numbers of concubines, al-Mahdi had about six, and his son and successor, al-Qa'im, had seven.[11]

The first Fatimid caliph in Egypt, al-Mu'izz, had only one wife, Taghrid. He would advise his commanders and the chiefs of his Berber tribe, Kutama, to follow his example. On the other hand, his son and successor, al-'Aziz, owned several thousand *jawari*, mainly as domestic servants. Some of them were concubines, including the mother of his successor, al-Hakim.[12] The elite officials of the state followed the example of their caliphs. Al-'Aziz's vizier, Ibn Killis, owned some 800 concubines, in addition to a large number of *jawari*.[13] Not surprisingly, the chief eunuch of al-'Aziz, Barjawan, also owned several *jawari*, who would provide musical entertainment for him.[14]

There are few details regarding the *qahramana*'s office. It is mentioned that Prince al-Qa'im b. al-Mahdi was raised for some time by a *qahramana* named Um 'Ali,[15] but this was a domestic palace task, and had no political significance.

It is important to have these sketches in order to envisage the size and nature of the harem during the first Fatimid period. None of the women mentioned had any role in political affairs, with the exception of the slave mother of Prince al-Mansur b. al-Qa'im, as mentioned by Heinz Halm. Her name was Karima, and she, together with his wet nurse, Salaf, aided her son in his power struggle against al-Mansur's half-brothers to succeed their father to the caliphate.[16] That took place in collaboration with the trusted eunuch Jawdhar; together, with al-Mansur, they concealed the news of al-Qa'im's death in 946 until they could secure the throne for al-Mansur.[17] (Chapter Five focuses on Fatimid eunuchs.)

Sitt al-Mulk, Sister of al-Hakim and Regent of his Son, al-Zahir

During the reign of the first two caliphs in Egypt, al-Muʿizz and his son al-ʿAziz, it appears that there was no influence in politics by women. Nevertheless, when the latter died suddenly in Belbais to the east of the Nile Delta in 996, we see the first daring attempt by a Fatimid princess. She was Sitt al-Mulk, the eldest daughter of al-ʿAziz, born in 970 in al-Mansuriyya in North Africa to a Christian slave woman.[18] Her original name was Sultana (feminine form of sultan), and her title 'Sitt al-Mulk' (lit. lady of the rule). She was half-sister of al-Hakim b. al-ʿAziz, and had two sisters, Rashida and ʿAbda.[19]

Sitt al-Mulk was the beloved daughter of her father. He built for her a separate palace in Cairo, known as the Western Palace; he did not do this for her sisters. She had about 4,000 slave girls in her service, in addition to several eunuchs, including ʿUtuf, who had a battalion in the palace named after him.[20] Sitt al-Mulk attempted twice to interfere in the political affairs of the state. The first was when the eleven-year-old al-Hakim was succeeding their father in 996, and the second was some twenty-five years later when she is thought to have collaborated in the killing of her brother, the caliph, in 1021.

As regards the first attempt, in 996 Sitt al-Mulk was in the company of her father in the Delta, where he died. Also present was the chief *qadi*, al-Nuʿman, and the bearer of the parasol, Raydan. Ibn al-Qalanisi (d. 1160) wrote that Sitt al-Mulk had become ambitious to seize the rule for her cousin and husband-to-be, ʿAbd Allah.[21] That was, of course, against the basic Ismaʿili teaching of passing the caliphate from father to the eldest son, and it is not clear why Sitt al-Mulk preferred her cousin over her brother. The eunuch Barjawan, faithful servant of al-ʿAziz, who was appointed by him in 993 as regent and guardian for al-Hakim, was also in the camp. When Barjawan found out about her conspiracy and her attempt to march to the royal palace, he dispatched a battalion of 1,000 knights to arrest and detain her in her palace in Cairo, to where she had returned.[22] Barjawan swiftly returned to Cairo, carrying the coffin of the dead caliph, and in his company was the caliph-in-waiting. He entered Cairo in a parade, revealing al-Hakim as the new caliph, and secured the oath of allegiance from the elite chiefs and commanders of the state.[23]

Throughout the twenty-one years of al-Hakim's caliphate, Sitt al-Mulk had no power over her young brother, due to the domination of Barjawan, until al-Hakim took over the leadership himself in the year 1000. Cortese and Calderini write: 'As long as Barjawan was in power, Sitt al-Mulk either kept a low profile or was sidelined.'[24] Al-Hakim had a history of discriminating against the Christian population of Egypt, who represented the majority at that time, and against Sunni Muslims and Jews, too. He also displayed misogynous behaviour against women; in 1013 he forbade them from going outside their houses into the streets (see Chapter Two – coincidentally, the 'Abbasid caliph, al-Qadir, had taken similar action in that same year). He also persecuted female members of the Fatimid family, which made Sitt al-Mulk take his own son, the future caliph al-Zahir, into her custody, along with his mother.[25]

Al-Hakim attempted to burn Fustat, the centre of the Sunni population, when they expressed their rejection to his policies. Upon the rejection of such measures by some women in Fustat (but not in the royal city of Cairo), al-Hakim ordered the street merchants to sell their merchandise to women at their homes by way of a long spoon-stick, in order to stop them from seeing one another.[26]

In the same year, 1013, al-Hakim took the controversial decision of installing his cousin, 'Abd al-Rahim Ilyas as *'wali 'ahd al-Muslimin'*, and his successor. He ordered that a diploma should be read in the mosques of Egypt. The caliph shocked his followers when he minted Ilyas's name on the currency as well.[27] Now al-Hakim had gone against the Isma'ili doctrine by not naming his own son, al-Zahir, but appointing his cousin. The royal family, including Sitt al-Mulk, could not have been happy with such a step.

Al-Maqrizi wrote: 'Killing became the norm to him, against all kinds of peoples: vizier, judge or secretary; Jew or Christian. He ordered the amputation of the hands of some of his *jawari* in his palace.'[28]

This disastrous policy forced Sitt al-Mulk to interfere, advising her stubborn brother by saying: 'Oh my brother, be warned. The collapse of our ruling house might be caused by your deeds.'[29] Al-Hakim was angry by her intervention, and he persecuted anyone associated with her. In 1014 he killed the long-serving chief judge al-Fariqi, accusing him of collaborating with her. He was not the only official to be punished. He enjoyed cutting, in an act of insanity, the body of his police chief, Ghayn.[30] In addition to that, al-Hakim was declared as God by more than one *da'i*, for example, in 1017 by al-Durzi, which added to the strife in society.[31]

The result of such caliphal policies was that the political and military elites and commanders of the state resorted to Sitt al-Mulk for help or a way out, in order to prevent the Fatimid administration collapsing. Ibn al-Qalanisi reports:

> They complained to Sitt al-Mulk about the gross misconduct of al-Hakim's policies. She accepted what they said to her, and rejected the dangerous policies of her brother. She promised and assured them that she would seek a way to stop his conduct and protect them. Sitt al-Mulk found no other way but to get rid of him by assassination. That was her only way to stop his harm. She kept that idea to herself until she had the opportunity to hire the one who later killed him.[32]

It seems that Sitt al-Mulk tried to repeat her advice to al-Hakim to stop his bizarre policies for the sake of the state and the people. However, matters became ugly when he accused her of having sexual affairs with several men who were admitted to her palace. He accused her of losing her virginity, having received reports of all her affairs, and threatened to kill her.[33] The question here is: why did the political elites of the state resort to Sitt al-Mulk, and not to other members of the ruling family, such as her sisters, Princess Rashida and Princess 'Abda, who both lived until 1050 and enjoyed great financial wealth?[34] Why did the envoy not seek help from the Fatimid princes? Clearly they considered Sitt al-Mulk as a leading political figure who had the power and tools to implement her will. This situation is reminiscent of that of the North African queen, Kahina (see Chapter One).

A large number of medieval chronicles, including those of al-Musabbihi (d. 1029), Hilal al-Sabi' and Quda'i (d. 1062), on which the fifteenth-century al-Maqrizi and Ibn Taghri Bardi heavily depended, accused Sitt al-Mulk of orchestrating the disappearance and killing of al-Hakim. She had corresponded secretly with Ibn Dawwas, the chief of the largest Berber tribe in the Fatimid state, Kutama. Ibn Dawwas had also been threatened by al-Hakim.[35] Sitt al-Mulk went to meet him, and said to him, after demanding the strongest of oath from him:

I have come to you regarding an important matter which will save both of us. You know what al-Hakim thinks of you, and when he has his chance he will not keep you alive, and the same goes for me.

Al-Hakim has called for his divinity, tearing up all rules of the shari'a, and all established commands of his predecessors. The Muslims have become intolerant of his madness and deeds, and I fear their revolt, which will be the end of him and us as well. As a result, our dynasty will be uprooted.

Ibn Dawwas replied: 'What is your opinion our *mawlatuna* (highness)?' She said:

> We kill him to stop his evils, and install his son, and distribute a large amount of money among the men and commanders for their loyalty. You will be his regent, and commander of the army. I'm only a woman who stays behind the curtain and seeks nothing but safe conduct.[36]

Despite the power of Sitt al-Mulk, she is reported by male historians as being of 'weak gender', with limited access to public political life.

The details of the killing of al-Hakim are contradictory, and are not our concern here. It is thought that on 13 February 1021 al-Hakim disappeared during one of his frequent visits outside Cairo to Muqattam Hill to enjoy the astronomy. He only had one or two servants in his company. What was found was his gown, holed and blood-stained. Al-Maqrizi, in one of his stories, reported that the servants brought the corpse of al-Hakim to Sitt al-Mulk, who quickly buried him.[37] It is believed that Sitt al-Mulk was one of the prime beneficiaries of his demise, together with Ibn Dawwas.

How did Sitt al-Mulk manage to run the affairs of the state afterwards? What achievements and changes did she make? For forty days until 25 March 1021, Sitt al-Mulk was the de facto ruler of Egypt, in collaboration with other commanders. She managed to distribute one million dinars among her supporters and commanders to secure their loyalty. When people expressed their worries about the absence of their caliph, she would assure them that he had told her that he would be absent for a week. Afterwards she designated certain men to pretend that they were her messengers to him in his place, and that they would come back to her with his orders.[38]

She summoned Ibn 'Ammar, al-Hakim's vizier, and revealed the situation to him, and took his oath of allegiance to her. She also summoned Ibn Dawwas and ordered him to march out in a splendid royal parade after forty days, in the company of sixteen-year-old al-Zahir b. al-Hakim. She made al-Zahir wear the crown of her father. Ibn 'Ammar shouted: 'Oh slaves and followers of the state; her highness tells you, this is your new caliph, commander of the faithful. Come and greet him.'[39] Ibn Dawwas was the first to recognise the new boy caliph, and everyone followed him in his deed, while drums and trumpets were playing. For hours the palace was opened to receive the Berber inhabitants of the royal city, Cairo, who came to see and greet the new ruler. Only one soldier of al-Hakim's entourage said: 'I will not give my oath until I know what happened to my lord.' He was quietly taken out, and later was found dead at the Nile. Afterwards, the might was restored to the caliphate.[40]

That was the first success of Sitt al-Mulk: killing a caliph, selecting another and managing to secure recognition and the oath for him. Al-Maqrizi reports:

> Al-Sayyida (Sitt al-Mulk) had killed a group of men who knew her secrets and that she killed al-Hakim. Afterwards, her might increased among those who were near or far. She started with Ibn Dawwas. She visited him in his palace and promised him to keep him as a regent, and said: 'You know the trust between us. I'm a woman, and I need to keep the rule for that youth (al-Zahir). You are the leader of the state, and you will be appointed as head of all sections of the state.'[41]

Why did Sitt al-Mulk always consider her gender to be unqualified to rule directly? Indeed Fatima, daughter of the Prophet, did not seek the caliphate; however, as discussed, she publicly toured around Medina and other places with her husband, 'Ali, for support for his rule.

Sitt al-Mulk was counting on other people to maintain her rule and gather information, like Mi'dad, the closest and trusted eunuch commander, and also the eunuch Nassim, holder of the sword and leader of a powerful elite military battalion. In other words, the coordination and pact between the harem represented by Sitt al-Mulk and the eunuchs was very strong. While Sitt al-Mulk admitted to Ibn Dawwas that because of her gender she was not destined to lead the Fatimid state, she secretly ordered Nassim to invite him to the palace. Then, when the crowd was gathered to hear the investiture of Ibn Dawwas, Nassim shouted: 'Oh slaves and followers of our lord. Ibn Dawwas is the one who killed al-Hakim.' On the spot, Nassim and his troops killed Ibn Dawwas. His head was brought to Sitt al-Mulk. She ordered the killing of his secretary and the confiscation of all his wealth. No one showed any objection.[42]

Al-Zahir, who had lived with his aunt Sitt al-Mulk and his mother since he was nine years old in 1014, continued to live with her as caliph until she died in February 1023. During that period, there was no doubt that she was the leader of the Fatimid state. After she had Ibn Dawwas killed, she relied on the vizier Ibn 'Ammar for about seven months and then she ordered his killing, and appointed Ibn al-Hasan.[43]

In addition to such strong measures, she made sure that her cousin, Ilyas, who had been appointed as successor to al-Hakim in 1013, and had his name on the mint, was also eliminated. She contacted men around Ilyas, who was ruler of Damascus, and managed to get him arrested and sent back to Egypt. He was killed in the town of Tinnis in the Eastern Delta on his way to Cairo, upon her orders.[44] It is far from clear why Sitt al-Mulk was so eager to secure the rule for her cousin when her father died, and then adopted a different political stance.

Sitt al-Mulk managed to restore order to major cities in Syria, especially Aleppo, where the Fatimid deputy there, Fatik, had rebelled against al-Hakim. She managed to gain the trust of Fatik using astute measures, until replacing him with one of his commanders, Badr, for two years, before appointing the eunuch commander Mawsuf as Fatimid deputy of the city.[45]

Sitt al-Mulk also restored freedom of movement to women who had been held hostage in their houses, as well as restoring respect to the *dhimmi*s of Egypt by way of returning confiscated land to them.[46] She was keen to improve the damage to international relations caused by her brother when he ordered the destruction of the Church of the Holy Sepulchre in Jerusalem. She sent an envoy to the Byzantine emperor, Basil II (d. 1025), to inform him of her policy towards the Christians of Egypt, and that she would restore the Holy Sepulchre and all damaged monasteries. She also sent an envoy with some precious gifts to the emperor, including some valuable items that had belonged to her maternal uncle, Arsenio, the Patriarch of Jerusalem.[47] It is believed that Sitt al-Mulk achieved all of that by spending lavishly on her trusted followers, having a large organised network of loyal men inside Egypt and Syria, and by depending on key eunuch commanders, like 'Utuf, Mi'dad and Nassim, in addition to elite battalions that would execute any orders from her against her various enemies. All of that was achieved contrary to the prime Isma'ili doctrine of not involving women in public affairs.

Despite the considerable details given in the sources about Sitt al-Mulk, there is nothing mentioned about al-Hakim's wife or his sisters, which show how the chronicles were concerned with gender and politics more than reporting the stories of Fatimid royals in general.

A Concubine, a Royal Mother and a Fatimid Queen: Rasad, Mother of Caliph al-Mustansir

Unlike the concubinage of the 'Abbasid ages, concubines under the Fatimid age had a very limited political role, or at least that is what the chronicles tell us. I agree with Delia Cortese and Simonetta Calderini, who write:

> While there is almost no information on the identities of most of the Fatimid court concubines, on the lifestyle they enjoyed, even the language they spoke, there is a relative abundance of references to the few who became famous. These references in most cases are presented in anecdotal form, even though the historical value of these anecdotes is limited.[48]

There are differing interpretations as to the numbers of concubines in the Fatimid court. For example, the eleventh-century Shi'i traveller Nasir Khisraw reported that the court of al-Mustansir had a massive number of *jawari*, too many to count. The total number of inhabitants in al-Hakim's palace was said to be 10,000.[49] We have no idea how many of these were concubines.

In the first Fatimid age, the governor of Damascus, Sa'd al-Dawla (d. 991), owned in the region of 400 concubines; other state dignitaries had concubines, too. In the second Fatimid age, when viziers became the de facto rulers of the state, the powerful and extremely wealthy commander of the armies, the vizier al-Afdal (d. 1121), owned only fifty concubines.[50] In all these cases, concubines were associated with music, entertainment and poetry, in addition to sexual pleasure, but they had no involvement in politics.

The exception to this was the extraordinary concubine, Rasad, mother of the seven-year-old caliph al-Mustansir. Rasad (lit. observed) resembled the 'Abbasid concubine and royal mother, Shaghab. She was the second women to heavily influence politics in Fatimid Egypt.

Rasad was a regent for her seven-year-old boy caliph, and co-ruler with her son for more than forty years. She created an army comprising troops of her own ethnicity in order to accomplish her policies and defend her interests. She was declared in one state document as a queen. She also exceeded the accomplishments of Sitt al-Mulk, in the title, her period of rule, and also in that she had her own insignia: 'Thanks to Almighty. He is the lord of every grace.'[51]

Rasad had a very humble background, as a black Sudanese slave. She was sold by the merchant Abu Sa'd al-Tustari to Caliph al-Zahir, and became his concubine. She gave birth to their son, al-Mustansir, in 1029, and at the age of only eight months al-Mustansir was declared *wali al-'ahd*.[52] Rasad was not mentioned in the sources during the life of her master al-Zahir, who also had other concubines. When he died in 1036 her son was installed as a boy caliph under the supervision of the strong vizier al-Jarjara'i, who remained in office until he died in 1044.

Ibn Khallikan wrote that 'Ali al-Jarjara'i, who had previously had his hands cut off by al-Hakim,

> summoned the elite, and commanders of the state, while the child caliph al-Mustansir was sitting behind a curtain in the palace. When the elite eunuch commanders were ordered by the vizier to raise their swords, the vizier took the *bay'a* for the new caliph.[53]

It is thought that Rasad was present during these ceremonies. However, we do not see any attempt by Rasad to intervene in state affairs using her son's young age, until the death of al-Jarjara'i.[54]

When al-Mustansir was fifteen years old, Rasad started to intervene in state affairs in her son's name, and remained influential until the famine and civil war that started in 1063, and even after that until 1087. According to al-Maqrizi: 'When al-Jarjara'i died, the mother of al-Mustansir became very influential, and dominated the state.'[55] We can divide the career of Rasad into two parts: internal policy and external policy.

Rasad and Her Role in the Domestic Political–Military Affairs of the Fatimid State

In 1044 Rasad, who has been described by H. A. R. Gibb as 'evil genius mother',[56] established her own *diwan*, and appointed her old master who sold her, Abu Saʿd al-Tustari, as its head, and also as her financial and commercial agent. He enjoyed unlimited trust by the royal mother for three years, and when he died, she replaced him for a short time by his brother, Abu Nasr.[57] The post of the vizier was second only to the chief of Rasad's *diwan*, but she had the final say. Ibn Muyassar wrote: 'Vizier al-Falahi, who succeeded al-Jarjuraʾi for two years, had no power in the state. He enjoyed the title only, but the real executive was al-Tustari.' When al-Falahi orchestrated the assassination of al-Tustari, out of jealousy, in collaboration with Turkish elements in the army, Rasad ordered his dismissal and had him arrested, jailed and then killed.[58] As the caliph could not identify the assassin of al-Tustari, and sought to avoid punishing a large number of Turkish soldiers, Rasad opted to boost her ethnicity in the army through an increase in Sudanese soldiers. That led to future strife and civil war between the two sides.[59] Rasad ordered all viziers of the state to buy more Sudanese slave soldiers to curb the Turkish influence in the army. When the vizier al-Husayn al-Jarjaraʾi, who succeeded al-Falahi, objected to their numbers in 1050, she dismissed him and appointed al-Yazuri, head of her *diwan*, as a new vizier. He remained in office for eight years and was keen to implement her policy and vision.[60] If the sources are to be believed, the number of black soldiers exceeded 50,000.[61]

Al-Yazuri was ordered by the royal mother not to stand to greet anyone in the state, irrespective of his rank, as he was representing her. When he attended the caliphal councils, while sitting behind a curtain following the discussion, she would send out a eunuch who would always support the opinion of al-Yazuri.[62] She appointed him as chief judge in addition to his office as vizier, which was rare in Islamic administration. As a result, he sent his two sons to work as their father's deputies at Rasad's *diwan*, in order to keep his special place close to her. He would kiss the ground before her as a sign of full submission and gratitude for her grace.[63]

When her trusted vizier was killed in 1058, the Fatimid state witnessed a rapid deterioration in the economy and administration. The office of the vizier experienced a long unstable period, where some of the viziers kept their post for only a few months, some even for one day only. Rasad was in charge of appointing and dismissing them; according to the sources, more than fifty people held that post from 1059 to 1072.[64] That would make her responsible for the political instability as well. Why did al-Mustansir, who was mature enough by now, not take command of the situation? It could be that he had a feeble character, and avoided confronting his dominant ambitious royal mother, especially as she had a well-established network of advisors and commanders, and tens of thousands of Sudanese slaves.

Sunni and Shi'i theorists share the same misogynist suspicious opinions of women's involvement in political affairs. I have previously made reference to al-Mawardi, the 'Abbasid theorist who was contemporary to Rasad. We see here the Shi'i equivalent, al-Mufid of the early eleventh century, who objected to any involvement of women in politics, suggesting that they should be confined to their houses. He ignored Fatima's role after the death of the Prophet in seeking the caliphate for her husband.[65] Here, Rasad followed the pattern of several 'Abbasid women, in addition to Sitt al-Mulk, in forcing her agenda and interests on the rule in a realpolitik fashion.

If we look panoramically for brief comparisons with Rasad's case, we will see that royal mothers in Muslim Spain had an influence on politics, in addition to the empresses of Byzantium during the same period. In Umayyad Spain in 976, a nine-year-old, Hisham II b. al-Mustansir (d. 1013), was installed as caliph. His mother, Subh, a favourite concubine of his father, pressured the father to declare her infant son as a *wali al-'ahd*. Subh formed an alliance with Ibn Abi 'Amir, her powerful secretary and agent, and al-Mushafi the vizier, to administer the caliphate of the boy caliph.[66] Concubine Subh, now a royal mother, lavishly distributed a large amount of monies among her supporters to guard her interests against the opposition of the chief judge, Muhammad b. al-Salim and the Saqaliba eunuch commanders who wanted to dominate the state themselves. She was the source of legitimacy over whom officials around her quarrelled in order to win her trust.[67]

Rasad must have been encouraged by the Spanish case two decades before her, as well as the 'Abbasid cases before her time. In contemporary Byzantium also, there were women in power, with Empress Zoe and

Empress Theodora, as free women, ruling exceptionally together briefly in 1042. Empress Theodora then ruled as sovereign until 1056. Also contemporary to Rasad was Eudoxia Makrembolitissa (d. 1078) who was appointed by her late husband Constantine X as regent for their son in 1067.[68] The difference here is, in Muslim cases, no man had believed the other gender, whether royal or slave, to be capable of becoming a regent, let alone a ruler, like in Byzantium.

The second stage in the domestic policy of Rasad coincided with the ravishing civil war, associated with severe famine, from 1063 to 1071. Al-Maqrizi, one of several chroniclers who wrote about it, referred to it as 'al-shidda al-Mustansiriyya' (Mustansiriyya Crisis); it reached its peak with acts of cannibalism among the locals, in addition to the looting of the Fatimid caliphal palaces.[69]

Al-Maqrizi accused Rasad of having favoured the Sudanese slaves since she came into politics in 1044, and of trying to marginalise the Turkish elements of the army. That had led to strife between the three army elements: the Turks, the Berbers and the Sudanese. It is not my concern to examine the civil war here, but it could be said that Rasad was wholeheartedly supporting the Sudanese, despite complaints to the caliph about their misconduct. She supplied them with arms and money until Egypt collapsed financially and politically in 1068. The Turkish elements in the army held Cairo and its surrounding areas, while the Sudanese held Upper Egypt and the Berbers took the land west of the Delta.[70]

There is little mention of Rasad after that in the chronicles. Ibn Khallikan and Ibn Taghri Bardi both commented that 'the mother of al-Mustansir and his daughters took refuge in Baghdad in 1067'.[71] Although the 'Abbasids were the enemies of the Fatimids, when it came to the caliphal harem and their honour, they set aside their differences and acted with humanity.

The Fatimids had started to reorganise themselves and restore their state to order when al-Mustansir appointed the capable commander Badr al-Jamali in 1074 as a vizier of Egypt.[72] The coming of Badr al-Jamali to the office of vizier marked a new age of Fatimid administration, where the vizier *tafwid* (delegated) was the de facto ruler of the realm and commander of the armies to the end of the Fatimid era. Despite that, we see the exceptional appearance of Rasad in 1078, which will lead us to the second aspect of her career.

Rasad and External Relations

In 1054 the Fatimids of Egypt had asked Empress Theodora for urgent food supplies due to the severe famine in the country at that time, and she had offered to form a military pact between the two states,[73] especially as the Merdasids of northern Syria were a threat to both realms. The vizier who was in charge of the Egyptian administration at that time was al-Yazuri, Rasad's darling, who was also chief of her *diwan*. We cannot rule out that he consulted with her regarding seeking help from the empress of Byzantium, especially as Theodora had exchanged presents before with Rasad.[74] In addition to that, we must not forget that while the sources mention the name of al-Mustansir and his conduct, it was Rasad who dominated his administration, as previously discussed. In addition, she was following the pattern set by Sitt al-Mulk as regards her communication with Basil II.

The following year an Egyptian envoy arrived in Constantinople led by al-Quda'i, the judge of Egypt, to attend to some common matters between the two realms. At the same time, the envoy of the Seljuq sultan Tughril Beg (d. 1063) arrived, seeking the approval of Theodora to declare the *khutba* in the mosque of Constantinople for the 'Abbasid caliph. She agreed to this request.[75]

It is worth mentioning that Muslim chroniclers, including al-Maqrizi, narrated Theodora's story in the same manner paid to other male rulers, while Ibn al-Athir mentioned that her husband was elevated to power due to his marriage to her.[76]

Rasad as Queen of Diplomacy

Rasad's other foreign relationship was the most exceptional and influential to Fatimid royal women who followed her. This took the form of her only official correspondence sent to another queen: Arwa the Sulayhid of Yemen.

The Sulayhids were a Yemeni Isma'ili dynasty that ruled large parts of Yemen as vassals to the Fatimid caliphate from about 1060 until their collapse in 1138.[77] (They will be discussed in detail under Queen Arwa later in this chapter.) Here, I will focus on the political role of Rasad, and its significance. After the famine and civil war during the reign of al-Mustansir, the remains of any caliphal power ended, and thereafter started the second Fatimid age, which was the beginning of the militarisation of the office of the viziers. Having said that, we see in 1078, despite the power of the mighty vizier Badr al-Jamali, Rasad forces herself into diplomacy, on behalf of herself and her caliph son, who was almost fifty years old at that time.

Rasad was responding to a letter by the then queen consort, Arwa the Sulayhid, who was ruling on behalf of her paralysed husband, Ahmad; she had been queen consort since approximately 1074 (the date is disputed).[78]

Queen Arwa, in an epistle directed to the Fatimids (although it is not clear to whom it was addressed – the caliph or Rasad), probably at the end of 1077, updated the Fatimids on her new situation in Yemen, and how she was in control as a loyal vassal to the Fatimids, both on political and religious affairs.[79] Rasad responded by this letter:

> In the name of God, the merciful, the compassionate. Thanks to Almighty, lord of every grace. (That was the official insignia of Rasad.)
>
> From the lady, the queen, mother of Imam al-Mustansir, commander of the faithful. What you have sent has been submitted to us, you al-Hurra (lit. the independent; it is the Sulayhid term for queen), the righteous, the powerful, the preserver of religion, the chief of believers, the cave of the followers, the supporter of the commander of the faithful. May God aid and grant you success, and protect you.
>
> We saw your letter, which was sent from Yemen, including all successful conducts of you and your followers, God protect them all.
>
> We witnessed how loyal you are to our Imam al-Mustansir, God bless him and his righteous fathers and his honoured sons. Your deeds are exactly what the Qur'an had ordered us to do 'and hold fast all of you, to the rope of Allah and not be divided' (Q. 3:103) Your endless valuable loyal service to us, night and day, revealed and concealed, made your followers submit to your will, and your affairs became straight and reliable. Almighty had rewarded you with the prayers of the imam, which will open the gates of happiness and eminence to your rule.
>
> We attended to the holy caliphate, God always illuminates its proof to the believers, and multiply its might and rule; to enquire from our son about your status. The imam was fully convinced and satisfied with your loyal service and is full of hope about your future service too, to him. In this

glorious letter sent to you by us, you will find all the support and confidence in your rule, which you hoped for. You should realise and recognise, God protect and aid you, what confidence we put in yourself, and continue to send to us your news and reports about your affairs and needs, which delight us, God willing.[80]

Here we have a document in which Rasad named herself as a queen for the first time, near the end of her career. Why medieval chronicles did not use or apply this term to her is unclear. Cortese and Calderini believe that using such a term was more of an honorary title as a member of the royal family.[81] I do not support this view, and ask: why did Sitt al-Mulk, among other free royal princesses, not use such a term, or be described by it in the sources? It is clear that Rasad, the dominant concubine, had elevated herself to the status of queen mother, and associated herself with her son's name for more legitimacy, when she wrote 'mother of al-Mustansir', following the title 'queen'. In addition to that, she allowed herself the right to discuss and evaluate the Isma'ili *da'wa* in addition to political affairs, but with the ceremonial reference to the name of her son and his 'holy caliphate'.

Although the influence of women had significantly decreased in the second Fatimid age, we still see such a letter, which encouraged three other Fatimid women to follow the model of Rasad, and issue their own letters naming themselves as queens too. The Mustansiri *sijillat* are sixty-six letters found in India at one of the Isma'ili archives, mainly sent from al-Mustansir, and a few by his son al-Musta'li, to their Sulayhid vassals in Yemen from 1053 to 1096, as stated by Majid.[82]

We have to ask: why did Rasad write this letter to the queen consort of Yemen at that time? The political–military situation in the region was going against the Fatimids. The Sunni Seljuqs had seized the main inland cities from the Fatimids, including Aleppo and Jerusalem in 1070, and Damascus in 1075. Not only that, but in 1077 the Seljuqs invaded Egypt; however, Badr al-Jamali forced them out.[83]

Rasad tried using diplomacy to secure Yemen for Egypt as a crucial Fatimid province, dominating a vital commercial route to the Indian Ocean; this was critical for the Egyptian economy, which was suffering from Seljuq domination of the Syrian cities. In addition, securing Yemen meant securing nearby Mecca in the Hijaz, the holiest Muslim town; this was essential for the religious leadership of the Fatimids, and for Rasad's son, especially after the famine and civil war, which had dire consequences on the economy and the rule in general.

Finally, despite the tens of letters sent by al-Mustansir himself to the Sulayhids, we see Rasad trying to retain her status as a key figure in Fatimid politics. Rasad's letter had encouraged three other Fatimid princesses to correspond with Queen Arwa.

The first letter was sent in 1085 from an unnamed sister of al-Mustansir to the Sulayhids. She did not use the title 'queen', but used '*al-sayyida*' (the lady), sister of the imam'.[84] The letter praised her brother the caliph, and the great policy of his sword (the vizier Badr, commander of the armies). In addition, the princess conveyed to the Sulayhids how the Fatimids were overcoming their enemies, and how pleased the imam was with the loyalty and the conduct of Arwa.[85]

Why did this anonymous sister of al-Mustansir write such a letter? Clearly, she was powerful enough to use the Fatimid chancery. The Fatimids in Egypt were at that time in a much better economic and military position; this letter was concerned with the domestic political situation in Yemen, as, in 1084, Arwa's husband died, to be followed by a political–tribal debate about his succession, as will be examined later in this chapter. This letter could be seen as a message of solidarity between the women, with some significant political weight.

The second letter was sent in 1087 from the queen, daughter of the previous caliph, al-Zahir, to Queen Arwa. Was she the same sister of al-Mustansir who had sent the previous letter? It is a unique situation in Muslim history to have correspondence between two queens, one ceremonial and one with sovereignty. The daughter of al-Zahir was clearly supporting the political status of Queen Arwa in Yemen, which could be used by the latter domestically. In addition, it showed how the daughter of one caliph believed in the political capability of another woman to rule, although not in Egypt.

The third letter was sent in 1096 by the queen, mother of the new caliph al-Musta'li, and former concubine. This is the letter cited at the start of this chapter. In this letter to the queen of Yemen, the queen in Egypt was trying to defend the interests of her son, the new caliph, after his elder brother,

Nizar, had been removed by the vizier, al-Afdal, from the caliphate. That of course led to a schism in the Isma'ili faith.[86]

These four letters, from two royal mothers of two caliphs, who named themselves as queens, in addition to one or two sisters of al-Mustansir, are a unique phenomenon in Fatimid–Islamic history, where women would use the official state chancery to express their political–doctrinal opinions and wishes. In addition, they were directed to another queen, in a show of support and encouragement. The term 'queen' did not appear again afterwards until the end of the rule of the Fatimids.

The Second Fatimid Age, 1074–1171: Princess versus Viziers

Although the second Fatimid age is associated with the decline of caliphal powers in favour of their viziers, we have already seen how Fatimid royal women participated in the diplomacy of the state, by way of the four letters discussed above.

When Caliph al-Mustansir died in 1094, the Fatimid state experienced a bloody and endless debate about the legitimacy of his successor, his youngest son al-Musta'li. This debate led to a schism in the Isma'ili doctrine, inside Egypt and around the Fatimid Empire.[87]

Ibn Muyassar and al-Maqrizi mentioned that al-Mustansir, in his final days, was not on good terms with some of the mothers of his sons. Every mother tried to pressure al-Mustansir to nominate her son as his successor. As a result, he only trusted his sister (whose name is unknown) with his nomination, one day before he died.[88]

Immediately after the death of al-Mustansir, the powerful vizier al-Afdal (d. 1121), who had inherited the post from his father, Badr, installed al-Musta'li b. al-Mustansir as the new caliph. Al-Musta'li was the son-in-law of the vizier, having married his daughter, Sitt al-Mulk. That was a clear coup d'état, as the Isma'ili doctrine stated that only the eldest son should succeed the father–imam, or by *nass*, as M. Canard believes.[89] Nevertheless, the political marriage between the vizier and the caliph played into the hands of al-Musta'li. As a result, Nizar, the eldest son of al-Mustansir, refused to recognise his brother as caliph, and declared that he was in possession of a document from his father that stated that Nizar was the rightful *wali al-'ahd*. Nizar escaped to Alexandria with his brother 'Abd Allah. There, Nizar was declared caliph, and named al-Mustafa, with the help of the governor there.⁹⁰

The information in the sources are blurred about the end of Nizar's life, but when he disappeared the following year the founder of the Assassin sect in Iran, al-Hasan al-Sabbah, declared that he was informed by al-Mustansir himself about the nomination of Nizar as a successor. ⁹¹

The debate continued until the caliphate of al-Amir b. al-Musta'li, when the Fatimid state suffered strong attacks from the Nizariyya. In 1122 a royal council was held in the caliphal palace, arranged by the new vizier, al-Ma'mun. He invited one Fatimid princess, the daughter of al-Mustansir and aunt of al-Amir, along with many of her female cousins and relatives, in a rare gathering for royal testimony. The vizier also invited the male elite of the royal family, elite officials of the state and chief eunuch commanders to the palace. After the vizier had introduced the sister of Nizar, who was standing behind a curtain, she declared:

> Oh people who are attending. Be my witness, and tell the Muslims on my behalf, that my full brother, Nizar, never was nominated for the imamate. I fully refute his claims, and condemn everyone who believes his claims. That is because I knew the truth from my father and heard it from my mother. Al-Mustansir told my mother and the mother of my brother, 'Abd Allah, that none of their sons will be a successor. I witnessed my father in his final illness, when he summoned al-Musta'li.
>
> He took him in his bed, and conveyed to him several matters, and they both wept. The following day, which was the final one of my father, he summoned my aunt, daughter of al-Zahir, and conveyed only to her who will be his successor. When he died, the following morning came vizier al-Afdal, together with the commanders, soldiers and chief *da'i* to the palace. He asked my aunt: 'Oh Your Highness, whom was nominated by al-Mustansir for the caliphate?' She replied: 'It is a trust, for which I gave him the oath. His commandment to me was that his son Ahmad (al-Musta'li) will succeed him.' When al-Afdal called for al-Musta'li, my aunt was the first to give him the oath as caliph, then my brother 'Abd Allah. Nizar rebelled, not because he was seeking the caliphate, but because of an old hostility with the vizier, and he wanted to end the influence of al-Afdal.⁹²

Here we have a Fatimid princess influencing religious–political discourse, and was believed as single witness, despite a sole female witness being invalid according to shari'a. As a result, the vizier ordered his secretary to write what the princess had testified, and that it be declared in the mosques of Egypt. The document was called 'The Amiri guidance in refuting the Nizari claims'.[93] Such royal testimony by the sister of Nizar consolidated the disputed legitimacy of the caliphate of al-Amir b. al-Musta'li, and also consolidated the position of the caliph in arresting and prosecuting the Nizariyya followers. We should remember that this royal intervention came after what had taken place in 1095 when the mother of al-Musta'li wrote to the queen of Yemen, defending the legitimacy of her son's caliphate, as already mentioned.

The last four decades of the Fatimid caliphate saw a further decline in the caliph's power and erosion to their prestige. In 1130 Caliph al-Amir was assassinated, and another Fatimid Isma'ili crisis of succession ensued. The Fatimid state was divided between the claimed infant son of the murdered caliph, al-Tayyib (whose very existence is disputed), and the coming to power of al-Hafiz, the eldest cousin of the murdered caliph, which went against all basic teaching of the Isma'ili and Shi'i faith.[94] Al-Hafiz (lit. the guardian) ruled first as a caretaker, and then as caliph until 1149, among strong schisms, especially from Yemen, concerning his legitimacy.[95] The last three caliphs, al-Zafir, al-Fa'iz and al-'Adid, were from the al-Hafiz line of descent, and were all young when they came to the throne, which contributed to the weakness of the rule. In addition to the domination of the viziers since Badr al-Jamali, several military commanders and provincial governors now quarrelled with one another for the post of vizier, and became even more dominant in state affairs. They found effective resistance from the royal harem, represented in the royal aunts of the caliphs. The aunts here, we could say, had recalled in some way the spirit of Sitt al-Mulk and al-Zahir's case. The oppressive conduct of the viziers made the Fatimid aunts of the caliphs resort to other powerful provincial commanders for help, in return for elevating them to the post of vizier to look after their nephews. That was the political game practised by the harem, and they mastered it on occasion.

Caliph al-Zafir b. al-Hafiz, who came to power at the age of seventeen in 1149, was dominated by the Berber vizier Ibn Massal. The governor of Alexandria and Western Delta, the Sunni Kurd Ibn al-Salar, and his Berber son-in-law, 'Abbas al-Sinhaji, governor of Gharbiyya in the Delta, collaborated to oust the vizier and have Ibn al-Salar seize the post for himself.[96] In December 1149 Ibn al-Salar appeared before the royal palace in Cairo with his forces, while Ibn Massal escaped to Upper Egypt.

> Ibn al-Salar sent to the caliph, and to the royal princess who conducted his affairs, declaring his presence. After long negotiations between him and the harem, the palace gate was opened and the robes of the vizierate were bestowed upon him, and he was given the title 'the grand master, commander of the armies, honour of Islam'.[97]

Here, we see that Ibn al-Salar knew about the impotent status of the caliph and negotiated directly with the Fatimid princess in the harem, who finally agreed to install him as the new vizier. Ibn al-Salar rewarded 'Abbas al-Sinhaji with a leading position in the army, especially after he managed to kill Ibn Massal some months later.[98]

In March 1153 'Abbas and his son Nasr, according to the contemporary chronicler and eye witness, Ibn Munqidh, collaborated to kill Ibn al-Salar; 'Abbas replaced him as a vizier. The following year, the father and his son conspired and killed the caliph himself. 'Abbas installed the four/five-year-old al-Fa'iz b. al-Zafir as the new caliph.[99] That bloody move was followed by a further bloodbath, with several of al-Fa'iz's brothers being murdered by 'Abbas, who falsely accused them of killing the caliph. The aunts of the new boy caliph, al-Fa'iz, could not trust this homicidal vizier, and they wanted revenge. Led by the elder princess, they contacted al-Salih b. Ruzayq, the Armenian governor of Ashmunin in Upper Egypt. The Fatimid princesses cut their hair and dispatched it, with a letter, to Ibn Ruzayq as a call for help. They promised him the vizierate if he got rid of 'Abbas and his son.[100]

A few weeks later, in June 1154, al-Salih b. Ruzayq entered Cairo with a large force in a parade, raising his flags with the hair of the Fatimid princesses atop them, as a sign of legitimacy. 'Abbas and his son escaped to Syria with a large amount of money.[101] The Fatimid princesses declared al-Salih the new vizier. Al-Maqrizi and other chroniclers mentioned that al-Fa'iz had bestowed upon al-Salih and his two sons several ropes of honour, and issued a long diploma with his appointment as vizier with the new title *'malik'* (king), used for the first time.[102] Naturally, that was the work of the harem, only ceremonially presented by the boy caliph.

The eldest aunt of the caliph, who was conducting the resistance against 'Abbas, had no limit to her revenge. She contacted the Crusaders in Ascalon, a town that they had captured from the Fatimids the previous year. She sent to them several messages through the caliphal post, and requested them to capture 'Abbas and his son and surrender them to her. In return for fulfilling this task, she promised the Crusaders a large amount of money. She also permitted them to take what ever 'Abbas and his son had in their possession. They had taken with them 400 camels carrying what 'Abbas had looted and owned.[103]

The Crusaders acted positively and swiftly, especially as Nur al-Din had seized Damascus in April 1154, posing a tremendous challenge to Jerusalem. The Crusaders killed the fugitive vizier 'Abbas (or Habeis to William of Tyre) during a confrontation and captured his son, Nasr al-Din (Nosceredinus). The Knights Templar put him in an iron cage and sent him to Cairo, as requested by the harem, who had offered a reward of 60,000 dinars, even though Nasr had 'learned the Roman letters and professed an ardent desire to be reborn in Christ'. Nasr al-Din, who declared his dismay to the old princess, was brutally killed upon the order of the aunts, by their *jawari*. He was first beaten by clogs, and then they cut flesh from his body, grilled it and fed it back to him until he died. That was not the end of the drama; he was then brought to the Zawila Gate of Cairo, where he was crucified and then burned.[104]

The pragmatism of the Fatimid princesses led by the eldest aunt, and her contacts through which she was able to ask for help from the Crusaders (who just seized Ascalon from the Fatimids), shows how determined they were to avenge their brother, al-Zafir, and to interfere in the political affairs of the state.

One question is due here: why did none of these princesses come forward and declare herself as sovereign queen or ruler of Egypt, especially since Fatimid Yemen had already proved a worthy case by Queen Arwa (d. 1138). Why, instead of counting on viziers and granting them the title of king, did they not rule the country directly? No princess came forward even as a ceremonial queen, using the same vizier as commander of the armies. If the rule of the other gender is against the shari'a, why was it recognised in Yemen by the very same Fatimids?

Farhad Daftary, the Isma'ili scholar, admires the progressive and even equal education of the Isma'ili tradition of teachings – *majalis al-hikma* (sessions of wisdom) – from the early Fatimid periods, and provides proof of the influence of those teachings by way of the roles played by Sitt al-Mulk and Rasad, who dominated the state.[105]

Accordingly, why did no woman, princess or royal concubine, dare to rule publicly and directly, as a result of such education? Why did no Fatimid princess in Egypt, who received the religious teaching, occupy any post in the Isma'ili *da'wa*, like Arwa of Yemen?

If we widen the scope for comparison, we will see that from 1131 to 1153, Queen Melisende of Crusader Jerusalem was ruling independently, then as a regent for her son, Baldwin III (d. 1161).[106] Such a nearby case must have influenced and encouraged the Fatimid princesses to follow this example, but perhaps they did not have enough faith in their gender to rule independently.

It was also against the same shari'a to bring young boys to the caliphate, such as al-Hakim, al-Mustansir or al-Fa'iz – the latter was epileptic, so was he unfit to rule? If these princesses were observing the Isma'ili teachings, it is clear that these rules were broken and ignored for long periods and on several occasions, as already explained.

In 1160 the eleven-year-old Caliph al-Fa'iz died. He was replaced upon the choice of the vizier al-Salih, in co-ordination with the harem, by another eleven-year-old, al-'Adid, grandson of al-Hafiz. The following year, the powerful and ambitious al-Salih forced the boy caliph to marry his daughter: 'Al-Salih intended, from this marriage between his daughter and the vizier, to have a boy, so Banu Ruzayq would enjoy both the caliphate and kingship.' The eldest aunt of the caliph did not like the behaviour of the vizier and planned to assassinate him. She distributed 50,000 dinars among her loyal commanders to kill the vizier, but al-Salih discovered the plot and arrested and killed her. I believe that one of the main reasons for the princess's objection was that al-Salih was not an Isma'ili, but a Shi'i Twelvers fanatic. Therefore, she was guarding the doctrine of the state, in addition to the political prestige.[107] Cortese and Calderini mention that the vizier al-Afdal intended to have a political marriage between his daughter and Caliph al-Amir, but the marriage was never consummated.[108]

The younger aunt of the caliph, Sitt al-Qusur (the lady of the palaces), managed to orchestrate a better plot to murder the vizier, in collaboration with some of the guards of the palace. Al-Salih was wounded, and died later in 1160. Sitt al-Qusur sent a message to his son, Ruzayq, informing him that those who killed his father were the agents of his adversary Shawar, the governor of Qus in Upper Egypt.[109] Ibn al-Athir wrote that the terrified caliph surrendered Sitt al-Qusur to al-Salih before he died from his lethal wounds, to deflect any suspicion away from him; while al-Maqrizi mentioned that Ruzayq, the son of al-Salih, was the one who ordered the arrest of the aunt from the harem, and suffocated her with his own hands.[110]

The final decade of Fatimid rule witnessed a rapid decline due to the weakness of the caliph and the fight between his two viziers, Shawar and Dirgham, both of whom invited the Crusaders and Nur al-Din b. Zengi of Damascus to intervene in Egyptian affairs. For the first time since the Crusaders had arrived in the Levant, we hear, in 1168, of King Amuri in Cairo, who was called upon earlier by the vizier Shawar.[111] The Fatimid caliph, who had lost all hope, and witnessed the Crusaders in the heart of his capital, sent a message of distress to Nur al-Din: 'If you do not intervene immediately, Egypt will be lost'; he dispatched with the message the hair of his women as a sign of complete submission and fragility.[112] The hair of the harem, as the highest sign of honour, was sent before to al-Salih b. Ruzayq, as previously mentioned. On this second occasion, the commanders, sent by the Sunni Nur al-Din, seized Egypt in 1169, bringing to an end the Fatimid state.

The First Queen and Female Religious Leader in Islamic History: Arwa the Sulayhid of Fatimid Yemen

> The goddess of the noble palace has departed
> No one can hope for victory anymore
> The evil times had uprooted her garden
> Punishing humankind; oh goddess of the age
> They all became blind (after you), like those living in Egypt.[113]

These lines lament the first queen in Islamic history, Arwa the Sulayhid of Isma'ili Yemen (d. 1138), after more than half a century of ruling as queen. Qadi al-Yami had the spirit and courage to praise his queen, while his contemporary, the grand poet of Iran, Omar Khayyam (d. 1130), only mentioned the other gender in his famous philosophical *Ruba'iyyat* as a source of pleasure. When he praised Iranian rulers, they were all kings, with no mention of queens.[114]

The Isma'ili Sulayhids, who ruled Yemen from 1047 to 1138, introduced the first sovereign undisputed queen in Islamic history. As geography is the main maker of history in the first place, we see the remoteness of Yemen in the far corner of the southern Arabian Peninsula, with its steep challenging mountains, away from the 'Abbasid powerbase of Iraq. Thus, it forms an inviting place for several Shi'i movements, led by the Zaydis. Yemen held a mosaic of Muslim religious doctrines in addition to the Zaydis, including Isma'ilis, Kharijis and, of course, a large Sunni following. In addition to this, there was a substantial Jewish population, which rose significantly after the second caliph, 'Umar, expelled them to Yemen from most of Arabia.[115] It could also be said that the land of Yemen, from Hadhramaut to Tihama on the Red Sea, was a tribal society par excellence, which hardly engendered civil peace.

The Fatimids, who established themselves in Egypt in the tenth century, started to widen their *da'wa* in Yemen to their doctrine. The Sulayhid tribe was part of the Hashid tribe in Haraz, south-west of Sana'a. They all were part of the larger tribe of Hamadan, which dominated several areas of Yemen.[116] Sulayhid political–religious history is difficult to examine due to the rarity and secrecy of Isma'ili sources.

The founder of the dynasty, 'Ali al-Sulayhi (d. 1067), was a Shafi'i Sunni follower like his father, who was a local judge. Due to the active propaganda of his friend, the Isma'ili *da'i* Sulayman al-Zawahi, 'Ali adopted the Isma'ili doctrine early in his life. In 1047 he declared his vassalage to the Fatimid caliph in Cairo, and launched a remarkable offensive against most areas of Yemen, but details about this are rare. By 1063 he had managed to subdue the Sunni Najahid Abyssinian slave dynasty in Tihama, and the Shi'i Zaydis in Sa'da and Sana'a. He captured Aden from the Banu Ma'n, in addition to Hadhramaut, and then marched to invade the Hijaz. To maintain these vast mountainous and tribal areas, he installed his deputies in key cities, citadels and provinces.[117]

Before moving to the history of Queen Arwa, within the Isma'ili context, I will briefly say a word about the sources covering her, which will illuminate her surroundings and situation, as well as the limited resources available to historians and researchers. According to A. Sayyed:

> Until quite recently the legacy of the Fatimid Ismailis was considered an unknown aspect of the Islamic past. The reason is that this was a secret legacy to which no one had access except those approved by the agents (*da'is*) of the Ismaili mission (*da'wa*) for their loyal adherence. A greater portion of this legacy has remained inaccessible and therefore unknown in modern Islamic studies.[118]

Still until today, Isma'ili libraries in Yemen, western India, Iran and Central Asian countries contain a large number of manuscripts belonging to Fatimid Isma'ili history, but unfortunately made available only to followers of the *da'wa*,[119] or through them, such as the Institute of Ismaili Studies in London. From Arwa's time, during which the *da'wa* was separated from politics, many sources found their way to Gujarat in India – for example, the *Sijillat al-Mustansiriyya*, which comprises sixty-six epistles from the Fatimid chancery to the Sulayhids.[120] As a result of that, future revelation of new manuscripts might invite new researchers to re-examine parts of the history of Arwa.

The sources of Queen Arwa's era are really confined to the following: the Yemeni Sunni historian 'Umara al-Yamani (d. 1174), who wrote *Ta'rikh al-Yaman* (*History of Yemen*). He was a Fatimid sympathiser, despite being a Sunni follower, and settled in Egypt in 1164, becoming close to many high officials in Cairo. His book covers the Sulayhids and their contemporary Yemeni dynasties. It influenced other later Yemeni chroniclers to use copious materials from him, such as Taj al-Din al-Yamani (d. 1342), 'Ali al-Khazraji (d. 1409) and Yahya b. al-Husayn (d. 1687).[121]

The second source is *'Uyun al-Akhbar wa Funun al-Athar*, by 'Imad al-Din Idris, the nineteenth Isma'ili Tayyibi *da'i mutlaq* (absolute missionary) (d. 1468/9). The importance of this book is that Volume 7 was dedicated to the religious doctrinal history of Arwa and the Sulayhids. He was a passionate Isma'ili, who used different information, sources and documents that only a *da'i* would have access to; his chronicles are indispensable, despite his clear favouritism to the doctrine, as al-Hamdani observed.[122]

Finally, we have the Fatimid–Sulayhid Sijillat, which are crucially important as contemporary documents, exchanged between the Fatimid caliph al-Mustansir, and the Sulayhids and Arwa. They focus on the political affairs between the Fatimid caliphate and the rulers of Sulayhid Yemen, the issue of their succession to power and their religious hierarchy in the religious *da'wa*. There are sixty-six epistles. We have no idea why they were not edited in chronological order. However, they are as follows:

- al-Mustansir to the founder 'Ali al-Sulayhi, nos 1–13.
- al-Mustansir to Lady Asma', wife of 'Ali, nos 55, 65.
- al-Mustansir to Ahmad b. 'Ali, nos 29–34, 39–42, 54 and 56–62.
- al-Mustansir to 'Abd al-Mustansir 'Ali b. Ahmad and Arwa, nos 14–19, 23–7 and 37.
- al-Mustansir to 'Abd al-Mustansir, his mother, Arwa, and all Sulayhi sultans, nos 22, 38.
- al-Mustansir to Arwa as the Noble Lady, without the title of queen, nos 20, 21, 44, 46, 48, 66.
- al-Mustansir to Queen Arwa, nos 36, 45, 47, 49, 50, 53.
- queen mother of al-Mustansir to the Noble Lady Arwa, without the title queen, no. 51.
- queen, daughter of al-Zahir to Queen Arwa, no. 52.
- queen mother of al-Musta'li to Queen Arwa, no. 35.
- al-Musta'li to Queen Arwa, no. 43.

Egyptian historians, such as Ibn Muyassar, al-Maqrizi and Ibn Taghri Bardi, paid very limited attention to Fatimid Yemen during that period. The same could be said about Iraqi chroniclers, including Ibn al-Athir. That in itself shows how male chroniclers dealt negatively with the first queenship in medieval Islam.

The political–religious career of Arwa could be divided into four periods:

1. from her marriage to *wali al-'ahd*, Ahmad b. 'Ali al-Sulayhi, in 1065 and his ascendancy to the throne in 1067 until the death of her mother-in-law, Asma', in 1074.

2. from 1074, when her husband, King Ahmad, delegated all powers and affairs of the state to Arwa until his death in 1084.
3. when she became queen–regent to her young boy king, 'Abd al-Mustansir. When he died, she was forced by the caliph to marry Prince Saba' al-Sulayhi, a cousin of her husband who became a king (at least ceremonially). Saba' became regent for her son, and then remained her deputy of the realm until his death in 1097/98. Caliph al-Mustansir ordered Arwa to marry Saba', a marriage that was not consummated. Arwa was queen consort, and was referred to by the caliph in Egypt as *malika* (queen).
4. from 1097/8 until her death in 1138, when Arwa became sole sovereign in her own right, without any regency or ceremonial marriage.

The First Period: Arwa's Early Days until 467/1074

Arwa (lit. female ibex) was born to Ahmad b. al-Qasim al-Sulayhi and his wife al-Raddah the Sulayhid in 1047/48. The early death of Arwa's father and the second marriage of her mother made 'Ali al-Sulayhi and his wife Asma' take Arwa (a relation of 'Ali al-Sulayhi) to their palace and bring her up.[123]

Sources provide only brief sketches about her early years in the palace; however, these are based on her later status, thus praising her personality and wide knowledge, but without providing further detail. In 1065, when Arwa was eighteen years old, she was married to *wali al-'ahd* Ahmad b. 'Ali al-Sulayhi. Her dowry was the revenues of Aden, which equalled 100,000 dinars per year.[124]

In 1066 her father-in-law was killed by his Sunni rivals, the Najahids of Tihama, while heading to Mecca for pilgrimage. (There is some disagreement about the date in the sources; it is sometimes cited as 1080.) Her mother-in-law was taken captive during the battle and held for a year, until her son Ahmad, now the new Sulayhi king, freed her.[125]

In 1068 the caliph in Cairo sent to Asma' two epistles (the only two sent to her), congratulating her on her safe return from captivity. It was very rare for a caliph to address a letter directly to the other gender. It would have been considered a great honour to receive a letter directly from the caliph; these particular letters were ceremonial ones. Both started with the following:

> From Imam al-Mustansir, commander of the faithful, to al-Hurra (lit. the free – it was used by most Yemeni tribes for their elite women), the noble, the pure, the pious, the honoured, guardian of the faithful, mother of the loyal princes, God protect her.[126]

Asma', who had her husband's head hanging outside her window during her captivity, was praised for her endurance, and her son, the new King al-Mukarram Ahmad was praised for his loyalty and courage.[127] Until the death of Asma' in 1074, there is no evidence of any political or religious role for her or Arwa, who was now wife of the Sulayhid king. Only in 1074 did the chronicles mention that, due to the paralysis of King Ahmad from illness and previous war injuries, he delegated all powers to his wife, Arwa.[128]

Before moving to the second period of Arwa's career, I will try to answer the following question: was Asma' politically influential during her husband's, and then her son's rule? Did that, in turn, influence Arwa?

Fatema Mernissi refers to Asma' as a queen, who was side by side with her husband in dealing with all state affairs. Her husband gave her the royal gift of gender equality. She adds that Asma' had created a new tradition by bringing up her son, Ahmad, with the idea that a wife has power that should not be confined to the harem.[129] Husain al-Hamdani also refers to Asma' with the title 'queen', based on her title '*al-hurra*' (the noble), as mentioned in different chronicles, following the tradition of Yemeni tribes at that age.

Regarding the title, we see that *al-hurra* was a title used differently to that of queen. The caliph al-Mustansir, in his epistles to Arwa from 1078 until 1087, never called her al-Malika, and just used *al-hurra*.[130] I should point out that neither 'Umara al-Yamani nor *da'i* Idris called Asma' 'queen'.

In addition to that, both of the above scholars mentioned that Asma' was involved in ruling the state with her husband, without giving any evidence, details or reason to support their arguments. Asma' was praised in a few lines as a noble generous lady, trusted by her husband, and enjoying his respect, according to the mentality of the chroniclers who would praise a person after they had died.[131]

The only case concerning the involvement of Asma' in any political affairs was in 1063, when she advised her husband to appoint her brother As'ad as deputy over Tihama. He took her advice.[132]

In addition to that, epistle no. 20, which was sent by al-Mustansir and his vizier to Arwa – queen consort – later in April 1080, mentioned how the caliph 'had selected Asma' due to her loyalty, to play a role in political affairs'.[133] The problem is that this epistle gives no details or reasons for this caliphal selection, and in what capacity: political or religious concerning the da'wa? Was it during her husband's rule or her son's rule? Chroniclers were also silent about that.

Clearly, she was a distinguished person, especially as she did not always hide her face when she appeared before other males in the palace, which was against the norm. In addition, the court poet of her husband compared her to the ancient Queen of Sheba (known mythically as Bilquis).[134] That might have cemented her name in the Yemeni public mind. We do not encounter any activity by Asma' after she was freed by her son, until she died. Thus, her influence on Arwa as a political model should not be given much credit.

The Second Period, 1074–1084: Empowerment During her Husband's Life

Arwa had four children by her husband, King Ahmad: Fatima (d. 1140), who was married to 'Ali b. Saba', the future deputy and ceremonial second husband to her mother, after Ahmad's death; and Um Hamdan (d. 1122), who was married to her cousin, Ahmad al-Zawahi. She also had two sons, Muhammad and 'Ali, who both died in early childhood in about 1087.[135]

When King Ahmad's mother died in 1074, he empowered Arwa with all state affairs, due to his paralysis. She dominated the state,[136] and took two major political–religious decisions.

The first was her order to move the Sulayhid capital from Sana'a south to Dhu Jibla. She said to her husband: 'Moving to Dhu Jibla is more stabilising and secure for the realm, and better for governing and controlling it. Dhu Jibla is in the middle between Upper and Lower Yemen, and better for administering the resources of the realm.' The new capital had been founded a few years earlier during the rule of her father-in-law. She enlarged the city, and supervised in person the foundation of her royal palace Dar al-'Izz. Taj al-Din and 'Umara al-Yamani reported that she marched in person, leading a large army, to her new capital.[137] Why did Arwa take such a strategic decision at that time? It is possible that there was some opposition to the

Sulyahids in Sana'a, mainly from the large Zaydi Shi'i, in addition to other separatist movements in other parts of Yemen, such as the Najahids who retook Tihama, and the Zuray'ids in Aden, who reduced their annual tribute. This move took place at the beginning of Arwa's co-rule in a relatively newly united tribal Yemen.[138] As a result of these developments, Arwa's realpolitik move was a saviour to her new, but challenged, administration.

It seems that she was prepared for such delegation from her husband. She decided to stay in Dhu Jibla most of the year, while her husband would stay in the fortified al-Ta'kar citadel, close to her capital.[139] She proudly said to King Ahmad: 'A woman desired for bed is unfit for ruling, so leave me to my mission.'[140] Maybe his health was too poor for a healthy marriage to continue – she was about twenty-six years old at this time.

The second major religious–political step by Arwa was shrewdly ambitious. She declared her name in the *khutba*, after those of the caliph and her husband.[141] That was a historical paradigmatic shift in Islamic society, Sunni and Shi'i alike, whether located in Damascus, Baghdad, Cairo or European Cordoba. Why had tribal or urban Islamic society not produced a queen or a queen consort like Arwa, who dared for the first time to declare her name in the *khutba*? Even within the Isma'ili house Sitt al-Mulk and Rasad had not dared to take such a move. Was it the patriarchal interpretation of the Qur'an and the limitations imposed by the shari'a in the ninth century, as discussed in the introduction? Or was it more to do with political necessity and the particular nature of some tribal societies that were more liberal than others?

A brief comparison with other societies with a strong tribal background might be due here. The first queen consort in medieval Islam appeared under the Arab–Berber tribal Isma'ili rule, after four and a half centuries from the beginning of Islam. We see in Europe from 700 to 1100 several societies with varying levels of tribal background, and a different pace of conversion to Christianity, legitimising the king's wife and accepting the other gender as queen consort or queen regent. That took place in societies that valued warrior kingship and preferred adult males as rulers.

The seventh century witnessed Christian missionaries entering Anglo-Saxon England. In addition, Charlemagne of Carolingian France (d. 814) led several campaigns against German and Saxon tribes to spread Christianity, while the Viking north and Kievan Rus' in Eastern Europe remained pagan until the tenth century.[142] However, we see, for example, by the eleventh century, queen consort Emma (d. 1052), wife of the Anglo-Saxon King Aethelred (d. 1016), and then wife of his killer, the Danish king Cnut.

Another case contemporary to Arwa was that of Queen Sancha of Leon (d. 1067) in northern Spain, wife of King Fernando I of Castile (d. 1065). She played a major role in the preparation for the Reconquista movements against the Muslims.[143] There are plenty of other cases in Scotland, England and among other European realms. It seems that European feudal societies with tribal backgrounds, especially in Western Europe, were quicker than the medieval Middle Eastern societies to recognise women as queens. This is probably due to their interaction with the Roman and Byzantine Empires, with their long history of women in power, and despite their patriarchal readings of Christianity, which also originated in the East, with passive results as regards gendered politics.

Returning to Arwa, in about 1075 Arwa orchestrated a major plot to kill the leader of the Najahids, Sa'id al-Ahwal. She contacted her commanders in Sana'a and deputies in other key castles, and designated the number of troops who would march for battle. The outcome was 'the mother of all battles', as described by 'Umara al-Yamani. The Najahids were devastated. Arwa ordered the head of Sa'id to be displayed directly under her room window in her palace in Dhu Jibla.[144]

This political–military success, initiated by Arwa, was not only to avenge 'Ali al-Sulayhi, but would also show her strength and determination domestically, in addition to eliminating the Najahids in her western territories.

Naturally, Arwa would depend on other key figures when ruling during this era. The chronicles are silent on detail during the decade before her husband died, which affects our evaluation of her methods. However, we do know that she relied on the *qadi* 'Umran al-Yami and Abu al-Futuh b. As'ad in ruling Sana'a, and 'the mother of all battles'.[145] There is no indication that she made significant changes to the men who had served her husband. She also counted on the *da'i* Lamak (d. 1098) for the *da'wa* affairs.[146]

Why did she not use in her administration Prince Saba' al-Sulayhi, a close cousin of her husband, who surfaced after 1084 with prominent political tribal weight? The same could be said about the husband of her mother and future assistant, 'Amir al-Zawahi, and also his son, and her half-brother,

Sulayman al-Zawahi. We can only deduce that the chronicles might have neglected them as they did most of the information of this decade.

Moving now to queen consort Arwa and her relations with the Fatimids in Cairo. How did they perceive her in this new situation? The Fatimid caliphate, emerging from the long Mustansiri calamity, had witnessed dramatic administrative changes on all fronts. Vizier Badr al-Jamali, who came to power in 1073, became commander of the armies and de facto ruler of Egypt. He also occupied the highest religious post in the *da'wa* as 'guide to the *da'is* of the believers', and became chief judge, second only to the caliph.[147]

The Fatimid chancery, in the name of the caliph, and practically the deed of Badr, had sent during this long period three epistles directly to Arwa, one in August 1078, the second in April 1080 and the third without a date, but we believe it was also in 1080.

In all of the letters, Arwa was referred to as 'the noble, the faithful, the wise, the capable, the treasure of religion, chief of believers, and cave of the followers, deputy of commander of the faithful',[148] but without the title 'queen'. In the first and third there was no mention of her husband, Ahmad, who was still the Sulayhi king, which reflects her powerful status. The second epistle mentioned Arwa, and then briefly her mother-in-law Asma', 'mother of the King Ahmad', as the epistle described her. It is likely that the mention of Asma' here, four years after her death, was out of courtesy, rather than for any other reason; otherwise, why would the chief *da'i* and chroniclers such as Idris never elaborate on the reole of Asma?

In the first epistle, the caliph and his vizier both show their great trust in the religious knowledge of Arwa and her loyalty to the Fatimids. The caliph reported to Arwa what the vizier told him about her, saying:

> Aba al-Najm al-Mustansiri, God bless him, keeps reporting to our eminence how you (Arwa) are the guardian of the believers, male and female, in Yemen; how you are keen to keep the orderliness of religion, until the banners of truth shine. As a result, the followers are organised in their obedience to the Alawite (Fatimid) state. And as a result, the commander of the faithful has issued this letter to you, to honour you and distinguish you among your peoples. Do exaggerate in enforcing your justice in Yemen, so your news can spread around to the furthest of corners.[149]

These details show clearly that the administration in Cairo recognised Arwa as the powerful leader in Yemen and depended on her completely to keep and protect the Isma'ili *da'wa*, and rule Yemen as a vassal to the Fatimids. The question is: why did they accept a queen consort at that time? With the loss of Syria to the Seljuqs in the 1070s, and their failed invasion of Egypt itself in 1078, and the fragile domestic political–economic situation after the calamity, the acceptance of a female co-ruler in Yemen was vital not only for religious reasons, but because Yemen and the Red Sea were the main gates to the trade routes to the Indian Ocean.[150] Thus, the Fatimids could not afford to lose these geo-commercial interests.

The Third Period, 1084–98: Arwa as Queen Regent, and Then as Wife of King Saba'

King Ahmad died in the citadel of al-Ta'kar in October 1084. He left a will stating that his cousin, Prince Saba' al-Sulayhi, should succeed him.[151] Arwa shrewdly concealed the news of her husband's death, and wrote to the caliph in Cairo, requesting the appointment of her ten-year-old son, 'Abd al-Mustansir 'Ali, as the new king in Yemen. When the caliphal letter came with approval of the caliph and his vizier, she declared her son as the new king.[152] The long epistle, dated July 1085, clearly mentioned the noble lady (Arwa), mother of the new king, as the one on whom the caliph would depend to guard the *da'wa*, and to loyally serve Fatimid affairs.[153]

The question here is: why did the caliph and his vizier prefer to recognise a boy as king, rather than recognising the legitimate Prince Saba'? It could be that the power and influence that Arwa had shown since her empowerment had convinced the Fatimids in Cairo that challenging her ambition would lead to instability in the Sulayhid realm.

However, if Arwa's husband did not see her, as a female, as a good candidate for his succession and overcome the fatherly instinct to name his boy to succeed him, it could be the case that the caliph held the same opinion. Soon after that, the realm faced turbulent challenges. Aden and a number of other areas separated completely from the Sulayhids, posing economic–commercial difficulties.

Prince Saba' and 'Amir al-Zawahi competed with each other for leadership, which affected the unity of what remained under Arwa. Thus, the caliph sent a rare epistle in 1087, directed to 'all sultans of the Sulayhids, Zawahids, Hijazid chiefs, and other leading believers', ordering them to unite under the banner of the boy king 'Abd al-Mustansir, and his queen mother al-Malika.[154] A caliphal order for all tribal kings to obey the queen was not the only positive development for Arwa. The caliph elevated her to the rank or status of *hujja* (absolute proof). She became second in the Isma'ili religious hierarchy to the caliph himself, which was unprecedented in Islamic history.[155]

Arwa appointed Saba' as deputy to her son for a short while. He was a failed commander, and had lost almost all military confrontations against Arwa's enemies. Yet he remained as a commander of her army until he died in 1097.[156]

In about 1090 the younger son of Arwa, Muhammad, became king, when 'Abd al-Mustansir died suddenly. It was at this point that Saba' started to demand his right to be king. Some chronicles mention, in an exaggerated way, that Arwa and Saba' entered into a military confrontation for several days, as she had refused his proposal for marriage.[157] This is highly improbable, but it reflects the power of this queen. The caliph in Cairo then ordered Arwa to marry Saba'. As the survival and stability of the Sulayhid realm became vital to Cairo, the caliph sent a high-ranked envoy, a eunuch named Yamin al-Dawla, to meet Arwa in person. Yamin al-Dawla went to Dhu Jibla with an entourage. When he arrived, Arwa received him with all her advisors and secretaries. He conveyed to her: 'The commander of the faithful greets the lady of the kings of Yemen.' He then recited the following from the Qur'an:

> It is not for a believer, man or woman, when Allah and his messenger have decreed a matter that they should have any option in their decision. And whoever disobeys Allah and his messenger, he has indeed deviated from the true path – Islam. (Q. 33:36)

He went on to say: 'the caliph has wedded you to the commander of the princes, Saba' al-Sulayhi, and the caliph has sent 100,000 dinars as a dowry, in addition to the value of 50,000 dinars in presents, gowns and other items'.[158]

Queen Arwa, if she refused the caliphal order, would be classified as a deviator from the true path, which would threaten her legitimacy and rule. She therefore had to agree in the presence of this council, and the marriage contract was concluded, but there is doubt over the consummation of the marriage.[159]

Why did Arwa have to be associated with a male to remain in power – be it her ill husband, boy son or ceremonial new husband who had been forced on her? It was, of course, out of political necessity, more than a profound belief in gender equality, which had made the Fatimids in Cairo accept Arwa previously, especially as she was dependent on a male of some kind or capacity. When the moment of truth came after the death of her two sons, the traditional patriarchal mentality was recalled to dominate the scene. (The same scenario took place when the Sunni Ayyubid queen Shajar al-Durr (d. 1257) came to power in Egypt, as will be discussed later.)

The *da'i* Idris described Arwa, saying: 'She was a savant in the sciences of the Qur'an, and its interpretation, in addition to her wide knowledge of the Hadith. The Isma'ili *da'is* would learn from her.' Farhad Daftary asserts the same view about the distinction of the female education under the Isma'ilis, and the vast knowledge of Arwa,[160] but neither could comment about the caliphal decree of literary forcing her to marry. She was simply denied the opportunity to be a sovereign queen, and in order to keep her status as queen consort she had to marry, or she would be designated a non-believer, despite having been classified as a *hujja* by the same caliph.

In 1094 Caliph al-Mustansir and his vizier Badr died, leading to a deep Isma'ili schism, as mentioned earlier. Queen consort Arwa was contacted by the queen mother of Caliph al-Musta'li in 1096, in a rare epistle between two queens.[161] As mentioned before, the mother of al-Musta'li realised the geopolitical weight of Yemen, and tried to keep Arwa as a loyal vassal. The mother of al-Musta'li tried to defend her son's case against his brother Nizar, and his supporters' claims for the caliphate.

King Saba', who was commander of the Sulayhid army, and now officially a king, never received any letters from the Fatimid chancery, which reflects Arwa's political prominence. The question here is: why did Arwa support al-Musta'li against his elder brother Nizar as caliph? It is believed that she was pragmatic in such a move, realising the strength of the vizier of Egypt, al-Afdal b. Badr, who had installed the new caliph. Therefore, it was wiser for her not to call for confrontation with Cairo so long as she kept her power.

We should take into consideration that the great Seljuq sultan Malik Shah had dispatched the Turkmen commander Tarshak with a Turkmen army to invade the Hijaz and Yemen in 1092, just months before Malik Shah died. Chroniclers, including Ibn al-Athir and Yahya b. 'Ali, mention the partial success of this Turkmen invasion. They both refer to the seizure of the Hijaz and Aden by the Turkmen.[162] I believe that Arwa had kept her territories safe from this Turkmen incursion, which faded away with the death of Tarshak, and the Seljuq sultan. The annual tribute from Aden to Arwa had not been affected. After that, the Seljuqs were mired in civil wars in Iran and Iraq, and did not repeat the attempt on Yemen.

The Final Period, 1097/8–1138: Queen Arwa as Sovereign and Sole Ruler

While the Musta'li–Nizari schism was raging in 1097, King Saba', the ceremonial husband of Arwa, died.[163] Arwa became sole queen of Sulayhid Yemen. It was the first time in Islamic history to date that a woman was publicly named *al-malika*, to rule directly without any association with marriage or regency. In addition, she was a religious leader, as a *hujja*, until she died four decades later in 1138.

Why, despite earlier caliphal attempts to cosmetically keep Arwa's queenship associated with a male (of any age and capacity), was her absolute sovereignty now approved? There are two reasons behind that. First, the schism within the Isma'ili doctrine altered the priority of the Fatimid administration. Second, there was the new intense geopolitical regional changes brought to the Middle East by the arrival of the First Crusade in northern Syria in September 1097. The Crusaders besieged Seljuq Antioch for nine months, and were contacted by the Fatimids in Cairo to form an alliance against the Sunni Seljuqs. By June 1098 the Crusaders had established the principality of Edessa, and then Antioch,[164] and the Fatimid vizier was fully occupied with military campaigns in Syria for years to come.[165] Therefore, the Fatimids had their priorities in the Levant and not in Yemen, and the coming of a woman to the throne was secondary to that. This is probably why the chroniclers did not pay attention to the coming of Queen Arwa to power.

The death of King Saba' had negative effects on the rule of Arwa. Sana'a pulled away completely from Sulayhid control, and Arwa had to accept the new de facto situation due to her limited resources.[166]

After depending on Saba' as her deputy and commander of the army for many years, Queen Arwa appointed al-Mufaddal b. Abi al-Barakat in his place. He was very loyal to her; he and his father before him had been in the service of the Sulayhids. He tried to fight the Najahids without much success, but at the same time he managed to deter them from leaving Tihama for Dhu Jibla.[167]

Queen Arwa's trust in al-Mufaddal was unconditional. She submitted to his advice while she was in al-Ta'kar, the place where most of the Sulayhid treasures were kept. He said to her: 'Your Majesty, you can take all the treasures from this citadel to Dhu Jibla, and leave al-Ta'kar to me to govern as your deputy.' She replied: 'The citadel is yours. You are the man of the Sulayhid house, and there are no restrictions between you and me, due to your eminence.'[168]

Al-Mufaddal had led numerous campaigns around Yemen to retain what was left of Sulayhid influence, but his most significant achievement was his restoration of Sulayhi authority over Aden. The Zuray'id lords there agreed to pay 50,000 dinars as an annual tribute, half of what they had paid before. According to 'Umara al-Yamani, Arwa trusted the loyalty of al-Mufaddal, to the extent that she gave him the revenues of Aden to use according to his administrative needs. She would reward him by sending him presents of *jawari*, *qiyan* and eunuchs for his court.[169] That was an unusual thing for a queen to do for her commander.

Arwa's rule with the military commandership of al-Mufaddal was effective. For example, in 1109 the Tihama chief, Fatik, died, leaving an infant successor, al-Mansur. The result was a struggle and division within Tihama. Some of the Tihama commanders went to al-Mufaddal seeking military help, in return for paying a quarter of Tihama's annual revenues to Queen Arwa.[170] Although the Najahid behaviour shown here was conducted by political necessity towards their traditional enemy (Arwa), it reflects her reputation and strong rule as well.

The following year, following months of campaigning in Tihama, a number of Sunni jurists, supported by the Khawlan tribe in the vicinity of al-Ta'kar, launched a coup against al-Mufaddal's deputy and took control of the strategic citadel. On his way back to his citadel to confront the rebels, al-Mufaddal died.[171] As soon as Queen Arwa heard of the death of her chief commander, and that al-Ta'kar was out of control, she marched in person from Dhu Jibla leading a large army, and camped in the foothills of the citadel. Queen Arwa negotiated in person with the chief jurists and exchanged letters with them, some in her own handwriting.

After agreeing to some of their demands, mainly financial ones, she appointed a new deputy there, Fath b. Muftah.[172] Due to the fragile political–military situation following the death of al-Mufaddal, Queen Arwa made this rare military appearance as a generalissimo leading an army, and was successful in restoring that key citadel.

The death of al-Mufaddal marked the beginning of the end for Queen Arwa. Although she replaced him with his cousin, Prince As'ad Abu al-Futuh (who was killed in 1120), the Sulayhid grip of power over Yemen became much weaker, and she lost several key citadels that were vital for communications and military support. Other territories, such as Aden, reduced their levy to her, and then stopped paying completely. She even lost al-Ta'kar again for a time, and the Sunni opposition there led a seasonal challenge to the queen.[173]

Again, we see silence by the chroniclers as to details and information during the office of Prince As'ad, which lasted a whole decade.

In 1119, at the age of sixty-five, Queen Arwa asked the Fatimids in Egypt to send an advisor to assist her in running the affairs of her declining realm. She did that despite the presence of Prince As'ad as her deputy,[174] which reflects his inefficiency. The vizier al-Afdal (not al-Ma'mun, as named by Ibn Muyassar and al-Maqrizi), dispatched Ibn al-Muwaffaq b. Najib al-Dawla with twenty knights to Arwa in Yemen in an attempt to control Arwa, according to Farhad Daftary. When he arrived to meet Queen Arwa, she installed him as chief of the army.[175]

Why did al-Afdal respond swiftly to Arwa's request, but did not dispatch an army with al-Muwaffaq? By 1119 the Crusaders had dominated all the coastal areas of the Levant, stripping the Fatimids of all their valuable commercial centres, with the exception of Tyre and Ascalon. Thus, Fatimid commercial activity to Yemen, and then to the Indian Ocean became a substitute for their Mediterranean trade routes. If Arwa supplied al-Muwaffaq with troops, he would need to enforce her authority; that means that she had the military resources, but had no trust in her Yemeni chiefs, including her deputy.

Al-Muwaffaq served Queen Arwa until 1125. During this time he restored some authority to the queen over several key castles, but failed to subdue any major significant city, for example, Aden, Sana'a or Zabid. In 1123 the new vizier, al-Ma'mun, dispatched to him some 400 Armenian archers and 700 knights. Yet he failed to improve the military situation, and the tribal kings loyal to Arwa expressed some discomfort as to his presence.[176]

By 1125 al-Muwaffaq's relationship with the queen had become strained; he accused her of being old and weak, and planned to arrest her. She contacted her allies who came in their thousands to fight him. Al-Muwaffaq was arrested and jailed in Dhu Jibla, although we don't know for how long. He was badly treated and humiliated, especially after the news came that Caliph al-Amir had dispatched an elite commander with a battalion of a hundred knights to take al-Muwaffaq back to Cairo.

Queen Arwa sent a personal messenger to the caliph with several precious gifts, apologising for arresting al-Muwaffaq.[177] The messenger travelled with al-Muwaffaq back to Egypt on the same ship, after Arwa decided to send him back to Egypt in a wooden cage. Al-Muwaffaq never made it to Egypt as the ship sank. Arwa was accused of paying the commander of the ship to scupper it,[178] but that is unlikely, as her envoy, who was also her trusted secretary, al-Azdi, was on the same ship with the precious gifts for the caliph.

Caliph al-Amir did not respond to Arwa's arrest of his commander who was sent to Yemen to assist her, as he was preoccupied with dealing with his rebellious vizier, among other domestic challenges.

The fourth and final deputy to Queen Arwa, after al-Muwaffaq, was 'Ali b. 'Abd Allah al-Sulayhi, nephew of the founder of the realm.[179] There is no mention in the chronicles about any of his achievements or administrative affairs until Arwa's death.

Queen Arwa and her Influence on the Da'wa and Religious Affairs

Under Arwa's queenship, it is impossible to separate the religious from the secular and political. They are bonded together and influence each other, especially as her name was declared in the *khutba* in the Friday prayer, and then she was nominated as early as 1087 as a *hujja* by the caliph. In addition to that, Arwa allied or supported one caliph against the other after al-Mustansir died, with all the religious–political consequences mentioned before.

On 20 March 1130, a few months before he was killed, Caliph al-Amir had a son called al-Tayyib. According to al-Maqrizi, Cairo was decorated for the newly born son who was declared *wali al-'ahd*. The royal celebrations went on for two weeks.[180] Queen Arwa was honoured when al-Amir sent to her a special envoy telling her the good news of al-Tayyib. The envoy had an epistle sent to the queen, which was read among the locals of the realm.[181]

Eight months later, in November 1130, al-Amir was killed, and his infant son mysteriously disappeared. Prince 'Abd al-Majid, the cousin of al-Amir, who was in jail, was released from prison with the help of some commanders of the state; he was declared '*al-hafiz*' (keeper or regent) of the caliphate until the reappearance of al-Tayyib.[182] It is not our concern to get into the long debate about the existence of al-Tayyib, or if he was murdered by al-Hafiz. However, in 1131 al-Hafiz no longer was an interregnum-regent ruler, and declared himself as a caliph. That move created yet another schism within the Fatimid state and its Isma'ili *da'wa*, which was now divided into Hafiziyya and Tayyibiyya.[183]

Queen Arwa, in Yemen, categorically refused to recognise the caliphate of al-Hafiz, and continued to declare the *da'wa* in what remained under her authority in Yemen to Imam al-Tayyib in his hiding place as the awaited caliph. She summoned her chief *da'i* in Yemen, al-Dhu'ayb b. Musa, to be on his guard about any counter-*da'wa* coming from Egypt, especially as the vizier of al-Hafiz, 'Ali Kutayfat b. al-Afdal was, ironically, not an Isma'ili follower but a Twelver Shi'i.[184]

Caliph al-Hafiz was keen to secure Arwa's loyalty to his new rule. He sent to her special envoys with several letters, but she replied: 'He occupied a place which is not his, and claimed a matter that is remote from his position.' She announced to her followers that he had violated his promises, and lost his reason. Al-Hafiz was too weak to send an army to fight Arwa, or coordinate through his allies in Yemen an attack against her. It is worth mentioning here that despite Arwa's strong opposition to al-Hafiz, he did not abrogate her status as a *hujja*, which had been given to her by a previous caliph, and that could only be taken away by another.

The enemies of Queen Arwa, the Zuray'ids in Aden and Hadhramaut, and the Hamdanids in Sana'a, supported al-Hafiz after the latter sent several *da'i*s to their cities promoting his opinion.[185] The result of Arwa's stance in this religious schism was her religious independence from Egypt, added to her sovereignty as a queen. From 1131 until she died in 1138 she did not need the recognition of the caliphate in Cairo, and she bravely depended on her power to maintain her authority as queen and *hujja* in the absence of her infant caliph, who might have been killed or was in a state of concealment (*satr*), to appear later.

At about that time, Arwa decided to make the Tayyibi *daʿwa* independent in its affairs from the political affairs of her Sulayhid realm, according to al-Hamdani, but there is no evidence of that, and the *daʿi* Idris did not mention that.[186] In fact, Arwa as a queen and a *hujja* continued to appoint the *daʿi*s. She empowered the *daʿi* al-Dhuʾayb as absolute *daʿi* (*mutlaq*), who with this high rank could be deputy to the imam himself.[187] It was unprecedented for a woman to install a *daʿi mutlaq*, and this never occurred again under the Ismaʿili *daʿwa*.

Here, I will examine the religious status of Arwa as a *hujja*, and her religious education based on Fatimid *daʿwa*. Heinz Halm and Farhad Daftary both mention how the Fatimid *daʿwa* from its early days in North Africa had paid attention to the education of women in *majalis al-hikma* (sessions of wisdom on Ismaʿili doctrine). The lessons took place mainly in Fatimid royal palaces where the genders were segregated, but some sessions took place in al-Azhar mosque.[188]

We should consider a number of points here. To whom was this education aimed? Was it aimed only at royalty and their close elites, or at the locals as well? How long did it continue, given the political instability? How was it influential, if the madrasa was not introduced under the Fatimids? Why did these sessions not produce a female teacher if they continued over a long period, since Fatimid education was distinguished? We should bear in mind that the ʿAbbasid education system was male dominated as well. The Dar al-Hikma (House of Wisdom), commissioned by al-Maʾmun (d. 833) in Baghdad, was a meeting place and research arena for males only. The same could be said about the Seljuq institution of the madrasa, introduced in the eleventh century by Nizam al-Mulk (d. 1092), which continued as a male institution under subsequent dynasties. If the Fatimid education system was highly distinguished, as Daftary argues, using the cases of Sitt al-Mulk and Rasad as proof, why did they not see themselves as eligible to rule directly, and why did they not produce any kind of writings of their own, or an earlier *hujja* than Queen Arwa, or indeed a later one, as well as lesser ranks in the hierarchy?

Arwa grew up in the palace of 'Ali al-Sulayhi and his wife Asma', according to the *da'i* Idris, who looked to Arwa as a devoted Isma'ili. He described how Queen Arwa became the religious authority, to whom all male *da'i*s would refer when in need for any religious interpretation or problem. He added that she became a savant in the Qur'an and Hadith, but he does not say anything about how that was achieved, or about the 'sessions of wisdom'.[189] At the same time, Idris and other chroniclers did not mention anything about Arwa's education. More importantly, why did Arwa not produce any religious writings during those years, or dictate to others to write her thoughts; as an educated *hujja*, who was trying to state and spread her thoughts and philosophy about the *da'wa* (especially after 1131), like any other chief male *da'i*, why was she not quoted in any chronicles on science and knowledge?

The prominent Isma'ili *da'i*, Sultan al-Khattab b. al-Hasan (d. 1138), a deputy to al-Dhu'ayb and one of the entourage of Arwa, tried to defend the caliph's appointment of Arwa as a *hujja*. That was because there was some resentment in Yemeni society; he tried to come up with a suitable solution, writing:

> The human bodily *qumus* (shirts, sing. *qamis*) are not vitally important, and are not the real indication of a person's gender, but their deeds which generated from their souls. We can see some who appear in female shirts, and occupy the most honourable ranks, like Fatima bt. Muhammad, Khadija, wife of the Prophet, and Maryam (Mary). We also see other cases of some appearing in female shirts, who are despicable. The male and female, who appear in the bodily shirts do not reflect their true substance. It is only their deeds which guide us to determine their gender. Therefore, if a woman appears in a female shirt, yet she achieved all good and praised deeds, she is actually a male, enveloped in a female body. On the other hand, if a male appears in a male shirt, and shows no merits and excellence, in this case he is definitely a female. Men and women are not what appears in the bodies or shirts, but classified only according to their benefits and good deeds.[190]

This exotic and pragmatic new theory was a way out by al-Khattab to Arwa, who became a male according to his opinion. That was not only degrading to his queen, but to the wife and daughter of the Prophet. In addition, it contradicts the direct meaning of the Qur'an about the creation of two different genders. It is clear how the patriarchal interpretation, Sunni or Shi'i was politicised. Otherwise, why did other women, according to the same theory, appear within the *da'wa* hierarchy? Samer Traboulsi argues that the philosophy of al-Khattab did exist in other pre-Fatimid theology, especially the Brethren of Purity and their philosophy of the hidden soul and the revealed body.[191]

With the appointment of Arwa as a *hujja*, the caliph instructed her to be in charge of the *da'wa* in Gujarat in western India, which was established a few decades earlier. All Fatimid epistles to Arwa, with the different levels of her queenship, stressed her vital religious–political role as an active person for the *da'wa*.[192]

During her long reign, she depended on several *da'is*. She appointed Qadi Lamak as chief *da'i* until he died in 1116, and then she replaced him with his son Yahya (d. 1126). Under both *da'is*, Gujarat witnessed a significant spread of the Musta'lian Isma'ili *da'wa*.[193]

With the crisis following the murder of al-Amir in 1130, Queen Arwa appointed al-Dhu'ayb as absolute *da'i* to look into the affairs of the *da'wa* with new challenges, like spreading the new Tayyibi *da'wa* in India, and facing the counter Hafizi *da'wa* within Yemen.

In 1138, at the age of ninety-two years, Queen Arwa died and was buried in her mosque in Dhu Jibla (see Figure 4). She left a will stating that she devoted all her wealth to the hidden imam, al-Tayyib.[194]

With the death of Queen Arwa, the Sulayhid rule in Yemen also ended. The Zuray'ids in Aden expanded north and seized Ta'iz and Dhu Jibla itself,[195] which was a victory of the Hafizi Isma'ilis over her Tayyibi creed. Other parts of Yemen, such as Sana'a and Zabid, remained under their lords until the coming of the Ayyubids to Yemen in 1174.[196]

A few remarks here, on Queen Arwa's career: Arwa's biggest achievement was that she became the first queen in Islamic history, with her name declared in the *khutba*. She managed to remain in power for six decades, as queen consort, and then as queen. In addition to that, she is the only female in Islamic history who has occupied a religious post and who could practice religious interpretation like male jurists and scholars and interpret and teach men on the Qur'an and in other religious fields. That post was the *hujja*, which comes second in religious authority in the Fatimid realm, thus she was in charge of appointing *qadi*s and *da'i*s, and was literally in charge of making religious policy.

The other major achievement was that she was the one who separated her rule politically and religiously from Egypt, and planted the seeds of the Tayyibi creed in western India, and her influence continued after her departure. Until the present day we have a community of a few million Tayyibi followers in India, Pakistan and Yemen.[197] (Living in Cairo, I have witnessed since the early 1980s several thousand Tayyibi followers, living in medieval Cairo. They are known as 'Buhara' and have the mosque of al-Hakim as their centre despite him being the imam of the Druz.)

Queen Arwa had inspired another Yemeni female (this time a Sunni), to declare herself as a queen. Details on this are scarce, but Yahya mentioned in his chronicles that the Najahids had witnessed a power vacuum in 1125, after their ruler Mansur was killed. His concubine, 'Alam, declared herself as queen consort to protect her infant son, Fatik, and the throne from the killers of her master. Despite being a slave originally, we find her also assuming the traditional Yemeni title of '*al-hurra*'.[198] She appointed viziers and created a ruling council of men to speak in her name and that of her son, and to represent them.[199] Unfortunately, chroniclers did not pay attention to 'Alam after that, and we do not know how long she lived. In addition, what was the opinion of the Sunni 'Abbasid caliph then, on a queen declaring the *khutba* to him?

Queen Arwa's legacy influenced other women to interfere in Yemen's political affairs, like in Ayyubid Yemen, when their rule witnessed a power vacuum in 1215. The queen mother, Um al-Nasir, kept the rule under her authority, and wrote to Cairo for assistance. When the new king, al-Mas'ud, entered Zabid, she surrendered the rule to him.[200] Later, under the Turkmen Rasulids, we see al-Dar al-Shamsi (d. 1295), who defended Zabid after the death of her father. Her brother, al-Muzaffar (d. 1294), made her queen of Zabid.[201] Also contemporary to her was the Seljuq queen mother Zumurrud Khatun of Damascus (d. 1161), who will be discussed in Chapter Six.

Arwa's influence on her daughters was remarkable, and it is telling about how she perceived women. In 1101, her daughter Fatima sent to her asking for help, as Fatima's husband, 'Ali, had married a second wife. Queen Arwa objected categorically to her son-in-law's actions (just as the Prophet had done when he refused 'Ali's wish to take a second wife after Fatima, his daughter). Arwa dispatched a force led by her deputy, al-Mufaddal, to punish her son-in-law. When her forces arrived at the citadel of Qaydan, where her daughter lived, Fatima was already dressed in male clothing waiting for the force. She joined al-Mufaddal, and they besieged her husband until he surrendered. Later in the same year, al-Mufaddal poisoned 'Ali;[202] we one cannot rule out Arwa's role in that murder. This anecdote shows her immense respect for the dignity of women, in addition to her mercilessness.

Why Arwa declared her name on the *khutba*, but refrained from minting the coinage in her name, is unknown. She continued to use the coinage of her deceased first husband. R. Darley-Doran mentions that she minted a half dinar in 1135 in her name. However, what was actually written on that picture of the coin used in that study was, on the obverse, 'al-Malik al-Sayyid al-Mukarram 'Azim al-'Arab Sultan Amir al-Mu'minin',[203] and not her own name.

Why did Queen Arwa not appoint women to any post or capacity during her long rule, despite her dual secular–religious authority? Why were all her assistants and deputies male, and why did she not bring up any female, even her own daughters, through the claimed Isma'ili teachings to learn and participate in affairs of the realm? Unlike the queen mother Shaghab, who used more than one woman around her as she believed in their capabilities, I believe that Arwa herself did not believe in gender equality. I believe that she herself was inhibited by Yemini tradition against the female gender, despite her own exceptional achievements. It is worth pointing out here that, unlike the 'Abbasid courts and state in Baghdad and the Fatimid courts and state in Cairo, which used eunuchs in political–military affairs as the medium between queen mothers and other royal females and the outside world, that did not take place during Queen Arwa's long rule. That changed, however, when the Ayyubid Kurds came to Yemen in 1174, bringing with them the culture of eunuchs in the administration, a model adopted from their masters, the Turkmen Seljuqs.

This inhibition of women extended to the chroniclers and epistles reporting her rule. None of them ever used her given name, Arwa; instead they used titles such as 'the lady' and 'the queen', among others – as though it was shameful to call her by her own name.

Notes

1. 'Abd al-Mun'im Majid, *Al-Sijillat al-Mustansiriyya*, Cairo, 1954, no. 53, pp. 109–18. '*Al-hurra*' is a title used by Yemeni female royals, meaning 'the free and independent'. 'Imam' is a title given to the religious chief. Interesting enough, it originates from the word Um (mother). Al-Fairuz Abadi, *Al-Qamus al-Muhit*, Cairo, 2003, Vol. 1, p. 167.
2. M. Canard, art.: 'Fatimids', *EI²*.
3. 'Abd al-Mun'im Majid, *Al-Hakim bi Amr Allah*, Cairo, 1982, p. 12; M. Canard, 'Fatimids'.
4. Ibn Muyassar, *Al-Muntaqa min Akhbar Misr*, ed. A. al-Sayyed, Cairo, 1981, p. 19; Canard, 'Fatimids'.
5. Taef el-Azhari, *The Saljuqs of Syria during the Crusades, 463–549 AH, 1070–1154 AD*, Berlin, 1997, pp. 30–7.
6. Hillenbrand, *The Crusades*, pp. 76–80.
7. Abu Shama, *Al-Rawdatayn fi Akhbar al-Dawlatayn*, Cairo, n/d, Vol. 1, p. 507.
8. Cortese and Calderini, *Women*, p. 87
9. Ibn Khaldun, *Muqaddimah*, Beirut, 2008, p. 231.
10. Ibid., pp. 46–8.
11. Ibid., pp. 49–50.
12. Al-Maqrizi, *Itti'az*, Vol. 1, p. 96; Ibn al-Qalanisi, *Dhayl Ta'rikh Dimashq*, ed. S. Zakkar, Damascus, 1983, p. 44.
13. Ibn Aybak, *Kanz al-Durar*, Vol. 6; Ibn Aybak, *Al-Durra al-Mudi'a fi Akhbar al-Dawla al-Fatimiyya*, ed. S. al-Munajjid, Cairo, 1961, p. 266.
14. Al-Maqrizi, *Al-Khitat*, Vol. 2, p. 4.
15. Cortese and Calderini, *Women*, p. 49.
16. Heinz Halm, *The Empire of the Mahdi: The Rise of the Fatimids*, trans. M. Bonner, Leiden, 1996, p. 311.
17. M. 'Abd al-Hadi Sha'ira, *Sirat al-Ustadh Jawdhar*, Cairo, 1954, pp. 39, 44.
18. Yahya Ibn Sa'id al-Antaki, *Ta'rikh*, ed. U. Tadmuri, Tripoli, 1990, p. 131; Heinz Halm, art.: 'Sitt al-Mulk', *EI²*. Mernissi, incorrectly, wrote that she was born in Cairo, *The Forgotten Queens*, p. 245.
19. Ibn Taghri Bardi, *Al-Nujum*, Vol. 4, pp. 177–8.
20. Al-Maqrizi, *Al-Khitat*, Vol. 1, pp. 291, 457; Ibn Muyassar, *Misr*, p. 50. 'Utuf is an area in medieval Cairo, close to al-Azhar Mosque, which still bears the same name.
21. Ibn al-Qalanisi, *Ta'rikh*, p. 74.

22. Ibid., p. 74.
23. Ibn al-Athir, *Al-Kamil*, Vol. 9, p. 118; Halm, 'Sitt al-Mulk'; Bernard Lewis, art.: Bardjawan, *EI²*.
24. Cortese and Calderini, *Women*, p. 121.
25. Yaacov Lev, 'The Fatimid Princess Sitt al-Mulk', *Journal of Semitic Studies*, 1987, Vol. 32, pp. 319–28, 325.
26. Ibn al-Athir, *Al-Kamil*, Vol. 9, p. 540.
27. Al-Maqrizi, *Itti'az*, Vol. 2, pp. 100–1.
28. Ibid., pp. 120–1.
29. Ibn Taghri Bardi, *Nujum*, Vol. 4, p. 188.
30. Al-Maqrizi, *Itti'az*, Vol. 2, pp. 106–7.
31. Majid, *Al-Hakim*, pp. 108–9.
32. Ibn al-Qalanisi, *Ta'rikh*, p. 127; Mernissi documents the worries of Cairo with fourteenth-century details of Mamluk Cairo, recorded by Ibn Battuta's journey as a grand urban place, although during al-Hakim's time it was a confined royal city, p. 257.
33. Ibn Zafir al-Azdi, *Akhbar al-Duwal al-Munqati'a*, ed. F. Andrea, Cairo, 1972, p. 57; Ibn Aybak, *Kanz al-Durar*, Vol. 6, p. 301; Lev, 'Sitt al-Mulk', p. 324.
34. Kahala, *A'lam al-Nissa'*, Vol. 1, p. 447; Vol. 3, p. 239.
35. Ibn Taghri Bardi, *Nujum*, Vol. 4, pp. 185–9; A. al-Sayyed, *Al-Dawla al-Fatimiyya fi Misr*, Cairo, 2000, p. 180.
36. Ibn al-Athir, *Al-Kamil*, Vol. 9, pp. 315–16; Ibn Taghri Bardi, *Nujum*, Vol. 4, p. 188; al-Maqrizi, *Itti'az*, Vol. 2, p. 115; Ibn al-Jawzi, *Al-Muntazam*, Vol. 7, p. 298.
37. Al-Maqrizi, *Itti'az*, Vol. 2, p. 116; Ibn Taghri Bardi, *Nujum*, Vol. 4, pp. 185–9.
38. Ibn Taghri Bardi, *Nujum*, Vol. 4, p. 189; al-Maqrizi, *Itti'az*, Vol. 2, p. 128.
39. Al-Maqrizi, *Itti'az*, Vol. 2, p. 125; Lev, 'Sitt al-Mulk', p. 325.
40. Ibn al-Jawzi, *Al-Muntazam*, Vol. 7, p. 310.
41. Al-Maqrizi, *Itti'az*, Vol. 2, p. 126.
42. Ibn al-Jawzi, *Al-Muntazam*, Vol. 7, p. 312.
43. Halm 'Sitt al-Mulk'.
44. Ibn Sa'id al-Antaki, *Ta'rikh*, p. 305; Ibn Aybak, *Kanz al-Durar*, Vol. 6, p. 312; al-Maqrizi, *Itti'az*, Vol. 2, pp. 131–2.
45. Al-Maqrizi, *Itti'az*, Vol. 2, pp. 129–30.
46. Ibid., p. 130.
47. Ibn Sa'id al-Antaki, *Ta'rikh*, pp. 237–8; Cortese and Calderini, *Women*, p. 125.

48. Cortese and Calderini, *Women*, pp. 75–6.
49. Ibid., p. 79; al-Maqrizi, *Itti'az*, Vol. 1, p. 295.
50. Cortese and Calderini, *Women*, p. 77.
51. Majid, *Al-Sijillat*, no. 51.
52. H. A. R. Gibb, art.: 'Al-Mustansir', *EI²*; Ibn Muyassar, *Misr*, p. 3; al-Maqrizi, *Itti'az*, Vol. 2, p. 179.
53. Ibn Khallikan, *Wafayat*, Vol. 5, pp. 229–30.
54. Al-Maqrizi, *Itti'az*, Vol. 2, p. 183.
55. Ibid., p. 266.
56. Gibb, 'Al-Mustansir'.
57. Ibn Muyassar, *Misr*, p. 4.
58. Ibid., pp. 4–5.
59. Ibn al-Athir, *Al-Kamil*, Vol. 9, p. 580; al-Maqrizi, *Al-Khitat*, Vol. 1, p. 335; 'Abd al-Mun'im Majid, *Al-Imam al-Mustansir*, Cairo, 1982, p. 77.
60. Ibn al-Sairafi, *Al-Isharah ila man nal al-Wizara*, ed. A. Mukhlis, Cairo, 1924, p. 39; Al-Sayyed, *Al-Dawla*, p. 199.
61. Ibn al-Sairafi, *Al-Isharah*, p. 50; Al-Maqrizi, *Itti'az*, Vol. 2, p. 267.
62. Al-Maqrizi, *Itti'az*, Vol. 2, p. 203.
63. Majid, *Al-Mustansir*, pp. 205–6.
64. Ibn Muyassar, *Misr*, p. 58; Muhammad al-Manawi, *Al-Wizara wa al-Wuzara' fi al-'Asr al-Fatimi*, Cairo, 1970, pp. 307–11.
65. Cortese and Calderini, *Women*, p. 105.
66. Ibn 'Azara al-Marakishi, *al-Mughrib*, Vol, 2, pp. 230–48.
67. Ibid., pp. 255–8; Ahmad al-Maqarri, *Nafh al-Tib min Ghusn al-Andalus al-Ratib*, ed. I. 'Abbas, Beirut, 2008, Vol. 3, pp. 353–5; Al-Derisi, *Al-Jawari*, p. 373.
68. Earenfight, *Queenship*, p. 90.
69. Gibb, 'Al-Mustansir'.
70. Ibn Muyassar, *Misr*, p. 38.
71. Ibn Taghri Bardi, *Nujum*, Vol. 5, p. 2; Ibn al-Athir, *Al-Kamil*, Vol. 10, p. 86 mentioned that Rasad was arrested in Egypt. However, detail on this is unclear; Paul Walker, *Exploring an Islamic Empire: Fatimid History and Its Sources*, London, 2002, p. 66.
72. Ibn al-Athir, *Al-Kamil*, Vol. 10, p. 87.
73. Ibn Muyassar, *Misr*, p. 13; H. A. R. Gibb, 'Al-Mustansir'; Cortese and Calderini, *Women*, p. 102.
74. Ibn al-Zubayr. *Al-Dhakha'ir wa al-Tuhaf*, ed. M. Hamid, Kuwait, 1984, p. 81.

75. Ibn Muyassar, *Misr*, p. 14; al-Maqrizi, *Itti'az*, Vol. 2, pp. 230–1.
76. Ibn al-Athir, *Al-Kamil*, Vol. 9, pp. 603–4.
77. Ibn Khallikan, *Wafayat*, Vol. 3, pp. 360–1; W. Madelung, art.: 'Isma'iliyya', *EI*².
78. 'Umara al-Yamani, *Ta'rikh al-Yaman*, Kay edition, Cairo, 1957, p. 62.
79. Majid, *Al-Sijillat*, no. 51.
80. Ibid.
81. Cortese and Calderini, *Women*, p. 109.
82. Majid, *Al-Sijillat*, pp. 17–18.
83. El-Azhari, *The Saljuqs*, pp. 36–43.
84. Majid, *Al-Sijillat*, no. 28.
85. Ibid., no. 28.
86. Ibid., no. 35; Canard, 'Fatimids'.
87. Farhad Daftary, *The Isma'ilis: Their History and Doctrines*, Cambridge, 1990, p. 44.
88. Al-Maqrizi, *Itti'az*, Vol. 3, p. 86.
89. Canard, 'Fatimids'.
90. Ibn Muyassar, *Misr*, pp. 59–60, 70; Irene Bierman, *Writing Signs: The Fatimid Public Text*, Oakland, 1998, p. 133.
91. Ibn Muyassar, *Misr*, p. 47.
92. Ibid., pp. 100–1; al-Maqrizi, *Itti'az*, Vol. 3, pp. 86–7.
93. S. M. Stern, 'The Epistle of the Fatimid Caliph al-Amir (al-Hidaya al-Amiriyya): Its Date and Purpose', *Journal of the Royal Asiatic Society*, No. 1/2, 1950, pp. 20–31, 23; Jamal al-Din al-Shayyal, *Majmuat al-Watha'iq al-Fatimiyya*, Cairo, 2001, pp. 211–15.
94. Walker, *Exploring an Islamic Empire*, p. 73.
95. Ibid.
96. Al-Maqrizi, *Itti'az*, Vol. 3, pp. 193, 196.
97. Ibid., p. 197; Ibn Aybak, *Kanz al-Durar*, Vol. 6, p. 553.
98. Ibn al-Athir, *Al-Kamil*, Vol. 11, p. 142; al-Maqrizi, *Itti'az*, Vol. 3, pp. 197–8.
99. Usama Ibn Munqidh, *Al-I'tibar*, Beirut, 2003, p. 73; Ibn Aybak, *Kanz al-Durar*, Vol. 6, pp. 564–6; al-Maqrizi, *Itti'az*, Vol. 3, pp. 205–6, 209, 213–15.
100. Usama Ibn Munqidh, *Al-I'tibar*, p. 74; Ibn al-Athir, *Al-Kamil*, Vol. 11, p. 193.
101. Usama Ibn Munqidh, *Al-I'tibar*, pp. 80–1.
102. Al-Maqrizi, *Itti'az*, Vol. 3, pp. 217–19; Ibn al-Athir, *Al-Kamil*, Vol. 11, p. 193; Ibn al-Qalanisi, *Ta'rikh*, p. 507. Al-Maqrizi mentioned the term '*kafala*'

(guardianship); the boy al-Fa'iz's grandmother was his guardian, but she had no political role, unlike his aunts.

103. Ibn Taghri Bardi, *Nujum*, Vol. 5, pp. 310–11; al-Maqrizi, *Itti'az*, Vol. 3, p. 220; Usama Ibn Munqidh, *Al-I'tibar*, p. 86.
104. William of Tyre, *A History of Deeds Done Beyond The Sea*, Vol. 2, trans. E. A. Babcock, New York, 1976, pp. 251–3; Ibn Taghri Bardi, *Nujum*, Vol. 5, p. 311; al-Maqrizi, *Itti'az*, Vol. 3, p. 220, 221; Ibn Aybak went further in his story to write that the queen of the Crusaders selected Nasr for herself as she liked him, but later upon the advice of her commanders surrendered him for 25,000 dinars, *Kanz al-Durar*, Vol. 6, p. 567.
105. Daftary, 'Sayyida Hurra', p. 118.
106. William of Tyre, *A History of Deeds*, Vol. 2, pp. 205–10.
107. Ibn Khallikan, *Wafayat*, Vol. 1, p. 270; al-Maqrizi, *Itti'az*, Vol. 3, pp. 246, 249.
108. Cortese and Calderini, *Women*, p. 56.
109. 'Umara al-Yamani, *Al-Nukat al-'Asriyya fi Akhbar al-Wazara al-Misriyya*, Cairo, 1991, pp 34–7; Ibn al-Athir, *Al-Kamil*, Vol. 11, p. 275.
110. Ibn al-Athir, *Al-Kamil*, Vol. 11, p. 274; al-Maqrizi, *Itti'az*, Vol. 3, p. 253.
111. Ibn al-Athir, *Al-Ta'rikh al-Bahir fi'l-Dawla al-Atabekiyya*, ed. A. A. Tulaymat, Cairo, 1963, p. 137.
112. Ibn al-Athir, *Al-Kamil*, Vol. 11, p. 337.
113. Qadi Muhammad al-Yami (d. 1145). Husain b. Fayid Allah al-Hamadani, *Al-Sulayhiyyun wa al-Haraka al-Fatimiyya fi al-Yaman*, Cairo, 1955, p. 209. Sad about the death of his queen Arwa in 1138, he calls the Egyptians blind, due to the religious schism between Egypt and Arwa after 1130.
114. Jalal Zankabadi, *Diwan Omar al-Khayyam*, Baghdad, 2010.
115. G. Rex Smith, art.: 'Sulayhids', *EI*; C. E. Bosworth, *Islamic Dynasties*, p. 74; Werner Daum, 'From Aden to India and Cairo: Jewish World Trade in the 11th and 12th Centuries', in *Yemen: 3000 Years of Art and Civilization in Arabia Felix*, ed. W. Daum, Frankfurt, 1987, pp. 167–73, 168.
116. Husain b. Fayid al-Hamdani, 'The Life and Times of Queen Saiyidah Arwa the Sulaihid of the Yemen', *Journal of the Royal Central Asian Society*, Vol. 18, No. 4, 1931, pp. 505–17, 506; Smith, 'Sulayhids'.
117. G. Rex Smith, 'The Political History of the Islamic Yemen down to the First Turkish Invasion (1–945/622–1538)', in *Yemen: 3000 Years of Art and Civilization in Arabia Felix*, ed. W. Daum, Frankfurt, 1987, pp. 129–40, pp. 132–3; al-Hamdani, *Sulayhiyyun*, pp. 86–8; Daftary, 'Sayyida Hurra', p. 120.

118. Idris Imad al-Din. *'Uyun al-Akhbar*, Vol. 7, ed. A. Sayyed, London, 2002, p. 1; Smith, 'Sulayhids'.
119. Al-Din, *'Uyun al-Akhbar*, Vol. 7, p. 1.
120. Majid, *Al-Sijillat*, pp. 11–13.
121. Al-Yamani, *Ta'rikh al-Yaman*.
122. Al-Hamdani, *Al-Sulayhiyyun*, pp. 4–5.
123. Al-Yamani, *Ta'rikh al-Yaman*, p. 61.
124. Ibid.
125. Smith, 'Sulayhids'; al-Hamdani, *Al-Sulayhiyyun*, pp. 129–30.
126. Majid, *Al-Sijillat*, nos 55, 65.
127. Taj al-Din al-Yamani, *Bahjat al-Zaman fi Ta'rikh al-Yaman*, ed. A. Habashi. Sana'a, 1988, p. 77.
128. Al-Din, *'Uyun al-Akhbar*, Vol. 7, p. 122.
129. Mernissi, *The Forgotten Queens*, pp. 211–13.
130. Majid, *Al-Sijillat*, nos 20–1, 46, 49–50; al-Hamdani, *Al-Sulayhiyyun*, pp. 66–7.
131. Ibn Zafir al-Azdi, 'Akhbar', p. 67.
132. Yahya b. Ali, *Ghayat al-Amani fi Akhbar al-Qutr al-Yamani*, ed. S. Ashur, Cairo, 1968, p. 255.
133. Majid, *Al-Sijillat*, no. 20.
134. Al-Hamdani, 'Arwa the Sulaihid', pp. 506–7; al-Hamdani, *Al-Sulayhiyyun*, p. 67.
135. Al-Yamani, *Ta'rikh al-Yaman*, p. 61.
136. Ibid., p. 62.
137. Al-Din, *'Uyun al-Akhbar*, Vol. 7, pp. 149–50; al-Yamani, *Bahjat*, p. 79; Al-Yamani, *Ta'rikh al-Yaman*, p. 62.
138. Al-Yamani, *Bahjat*, p. 79; Smith, 'The Political History', p. 133; Cortese and Calderini, *Women*, pp. 130–1.
139. Al-Din, *'Uyun al-Akhbar*, Vol. 7, p. 151; al-Hamawi, *Mu'jam*, Vol. 2, p. 34.
140. Al-Yamani, *Bahjat*, pp. 79–80.
141. Daftari, 'Sayyida Hurra', p. 122.
142. Earenfight, *Queenship*, pp. 79, 100, 117–19.
143. Ibid., pp. 104, 107, 115–16.
144. Abd al-Rahman al-Zabidi, *Qurrat al-'Uyun bi Akhbar al-Yaman al-Maymun*, ed. M. al-Akwa, Sana'a, 1988, p. 188; al-Yamani, *Ta'rikh al-Yaman*, p. 64.
145. Al-Yamani, *Ta'rikh al-Yaman*, p. 64.
146. Daftary, 'Sayyida Hurra', p. 124.

147. Al-Manawi, *Al-Wizara*, pp. 67–8; S. Dadayan, art.: 'Badr al-Jamali', *EI³* online, 2010.
148. Majid, *Al-Sijillat*, nos 44, 20–1.
149. Ibid., no. 44.
150. Shelomo Goitein, 'New Lights on the Beginning of the Karim Merchants', *Journal of the Economic and Social History of the Orient*, Vol. 1, No. 2, 1958, pp. 175–84, 175.
151. Al-Yamani, *Ta'rikh al-Yaman*, p. 66.
152. Al-Din, *'Uyun al-Akhbar*, Vol. 7, pp. 156–61.
153. Ibid., p. 160; Majid, *Al-Sijillat*, nos 14, 26.
154. Majid, *Al-Sijillat*, no. 38; al-Din, *'Uyun al-Akhbar*, Vol. 7, p. 168; Samer Traboulsi, 'The Queen was Actually a man: Arwa Bint Ahmad and the Politics of Religion', in *Arabica*, T. 50, Fasc. 1, 2003, pp. 96–108, 100.
155. Al-Din, *'Uyun al-Akhbar*, Vol. 7, pp. 161–2.
156. Al-Hamdani, *Al-Sulayhiyyun*, pp. 151–4.
157. Al-Zabidi, *Qurrat*, p. 191.
158. Al-Yamani, *Ta'rikh al-Yaman*, pp. 67–8.
159. Ali, *Ghayat*, p. 276; Al-Din, *'Uyun al-Akhbar*, Vol. 7, p. 176.
160. Al-Din, *'Uyun al-Akhbar*, Vol. 7, p. 161; Daftary, 'Sayyida Hurra', pp. 118, 122.
161. Majid, *Al-Sijillat*, no. 35.
162. Ibn al-Athir, *Al-Kamil*, Vol. 10, p. 204; Ali, *Ghayat*, p. 277.
163. Al-Din, *'Uyun al-Akhbar*, Vol. 7, pp. 214–15.
164. Hillenbrand, *The Crusades*, p. 56.
165. El-Azhari, *The Saljuqs*, p. 92.
166. Al-Zabidi, *Qurrat*, p. 192; Ali, *Ghayat*, pp. 277, 280; al-Hamdani, *Al-Sulayhiyyun*, pp. 161–2.
167. Al-Zabidi, *Qurrat*, pp. 280–1.
168. Al-Yamani, *Ta'rikh al-Yaman*, pp. 70–1.
169. Ibid., pp. 71–3; Al-Din, *'Uyun al-Akhbar*, Vol. 7, p. 215; al-Zabidi, *Qurrat*, pp. 194–5.
170. Ali, *Ghayat*, pp. 282–3.
171. Al-Yamani, *Ta'rikh al-Yaman*, pp. 72–3.
172. Ibid., p. 73.
173. Ali, *Ghayat*, p. 284; al-Yamani, *Ta'rikh al-Yaman*, p. 74; al-Hamdani, *Al-Sulayhiyyun*, pp. 165–6.
174. al-Hamdani, *Al-Sulayhiyyun*, p. 168.

175. Al-Yamani, *Ta'rikh al-Yaman*, p. 76; Ibn Muyassar, *Misr*, p. 106; al-Maqrizi, *Itti'az*, Vol. 3, p. 119; Daftary, 'Sayyida Hurra', p. 124.
176. Al-Din, *'Uyun al-Akhbar*, Vol. 7, pp. 238–9; Al-Yamani, *Ta'rikh al-Yaman*, p. 76; al-Maqrizi, *Itti'az*, Vol. 3, p. 103.
177. Al-Yamani, *Ta'rikh al-Yaman*, pp. 79–80.
178. Al-Din, *'Uyun al-Akhbar*, Vol. 7, p. 242; Al-Yamani, *Ta'rikh al-Yaman*, p. 80; al-Maqrizi, in *Itti'az*, Vol. 3, p. 119, mentions that al-Muwaffaq arrived in Cairo in 1127 and was paraded around the city in a very humiliating manner.
179. Al-Din, *'Uyun al-Akhbar*, Vol. 7, p. 243.
180. Al-Maqrizi, *Itti'az*, Vol. 3, p. 128; Ibn Muyassar, *Misr*, p. 109.
181. Al-Din, *'Uyun al-Akhbar*, Vol. 7, pp. 247, 254–5; al-Shayyal, *Majmuat*, pp. 92–3.
182. Al-Shayyal, *Majmuat*, pp. 94–100.
183. Ibid., p. 101.
184. Al-Din, *'Uyun al-Akhbar*, Vol. 7, pp. 264–5; Daftary, 'Sayyida Hurra', p. 125.
185. Al-Din, *'Uyun al-Akhbar*, pp. 271–4; Daftary, 'Sayyida Hurra', p. 126; Smith, 'The Political History', p. 133.
186. Al-Hamdani, *Al-Sulayhiyyun*, p. 180.
187. Al-Din, *'Uyun al-Akhbar*, Vol. 7, p. 301; al-Hamdani, *Al-Sulayhiyyun*, pp. 192–3.
188. Heinz Halm, *The Fatimids and Their Traditions of Learning*, London, 1997, trans. S. Qusair, Damascus, 1999, pp. 48–9; Daftary, 'Sayyida Hurra', p. 118.
189. Al-Din, *'Uyun al-Akhbar*, Vol. 7, p. 161.
190. Sultan al-Khattab, 'Ghayat al-Mawalid', quoted in al-Hamdani, *Al-Sulayhiyyun*, pp. 144–5; Daftary, 'Sayyida Hurra', p. 122; Traboulsi, 'The Queen', p. 105.
191. Traboulsi, 'The Queen', p. 106.
192. Majid, *Al-Sijillat*, nos 41, 50; Daftary, 'Sayyida Hurra', p. 123.
193. Al-Hamdani, *Al-Sulayhiyyun*, p. 180.
194. Al-Din, *'Uyun al-Akhbar*, Vol. 7, p. 307.
195. Ibid.
196. Ibid., pp. 308–9; Smith, 'The Political History', p. 133.
197. Farhad Daftary, art.: 'Al-Tayyibiyya', *EI²*.
198. Ali, *Ghayat*, pp. 289–90.
199. Al-Yamani, *Ta'rikh al-Yaman*, p. 107.

200. 'Ali b. Hasan al-Khazraji, *Al-'Uqud al-Lu'lu'iyya*, Vol. 1. Cairo, 1983, p. 39.
201. Ibid., pp. 245–6.
202. Ibid., pp. 69–70.
203. R. E. Darley-Doran, 'Examples of Islamic Coinage from Yemen', in *Yemen: 3000 Years of Art and Civilization in Arabia Felix*, ed. W. Daum, Frankfurt, 1987, pp. 182–203, 201.

5

The Fatimid Eunuchs and their Sphere[1]

Peace be upon you, Jawdhar. You know your eminent place in our hearts. You enjoyed the graciousness of all of the guided imams. How great is my affliction. I count only on you after God in what I'm facing.

Jawdhar, be on your guard and practise restraint to the best of your ability to prevent those apes from getting to us, or even stepping out of their houses. Conceal all secrets completely, particularly from relatives, assistants and the public. If they discover any matter, deny it and frighten them as much as you can.[2]

These lines were written in 953 by al-Muʿizz (d. 975), the *wali al-ʿahd* and custodian of the imamate, when his father caliph al-Mansur died. Al-Muʿizz entrusted his confidant servant Jawdhar with the task of controlling the Fatimid relatives of the caliph. They represented a political threat to the caliphate of al-Muʿizz, as any of them could rebel or declare a coup against his succession. Thus, al-Muʿizz referred to them as 'apes'.

It was not the first time that Jawdhar had enjoyed such prestigious trust during a critical transitional political period within the Fatimid caliphate. When al-Mahdi died in 934 Jawdhar was entrusted at his graveside during the funeral by his successor al-Qaʾim with highly secret information concerning the appointment of the *wali al-ʿahd* to lead the Ismaʿili creed. Jawdhar kept the secret for seven years.[3]

Jawdhar, the person with this privileged status, was a eunuch. David Ayalon writes that the Fatimid dynasty was saturated with eunuchs and they deserve a separate study, as they effectively administered the realm for long periods. Ayalon has written but a few pages,[4] leaving this mission to other researchers, which is what this book is seeking to accomplish. Indeed, Serena

Tolino has recently written a chapter on 'Eunuchs in the Fatimid Empire: Ambiguities, Gender and Sacredness',[5] although she focuses on eunuchs in the North African stage of Fatimid history, omitting the long Egyptian period.

The Fatimids, unlike the 'Abbasids, used eunuchs on a wide scale and employed them in very influential offices from the beginning of their dynasty. The 'Abbasids, as previously discussed, took longer to promote them to such offices, for example, the cases of Mu'nis al-Muzaffar and Kafur of Egypt. The Fatimids surpassed the 'Abbasids by having a eunuch as a deputy to the caliph. In addition, the Fatimids employed eunuchs as chief treasurer of the empire, chief of the army, police, provincial governors and viziers.

Like the previous Muslim dynasties, mainly the 'Abbasids and the Umayyads in Spain, the demand for eunuchs under the Fatimids was met from two main sources. White eunuchs, predominantly Saqaliba, were imported overland via France and Spain, where they were castrated or captured by Muslims in Spain. There were also Venetian slave merchants who controlled part of this lucrative trade. In addition, large numbers of Saqaliba came from the Byzantine Empire.[6] Black eunuchs were imported from West Africa across the Sahara to Morocco, from East Africa down the Nile to Egypt, and from sub-Saharan Africa across the desert to Tunisia and Libya.[7]

The Fatimids applied titles used before them to eunuchs, like *khadim*, *ghulam* and *ustadh*. This last title was the most widely used, associated with *muhannak* (a term used to describe a man who wears a turban, part of which covers his jaw). Like the 'Abbasid eunuchs, they had recognisable names, such as, Mi'dad, Sandal, Wafa', Raydan and Barjawan. Such names were associated with their third gender and would have been insulting to call a normal male by a eunuch's name. Tolino does not view Fatimid eunuchs as being of the third gender, as they were used in different posts including the military;[8] however, she does not provide an alternative term for them.

Eunuch Influence on the Isma'ili Faith and Politics

The Fatimid dynasty depended on eunuchs in political life from Jawdhar, under the first Fatimid caliph al-Mahdi, to Jawhar, under the last Fatimid caliph al-'Adid. Jawdhar, who was a Saqlabi eunuch, was brought from Spain and entered the service of al-Mahdi in his early years. He enjoyed the highest of influence among the eunuchs of the Fatimids. Under the second caliph, al-Qa'im, Jawdhar became a deputy to his caliph master. Jawdhar's influence rose significantly when al-Qa'im was occupied with the strong revolt of Ibn Kindad, the Khariji, in Tuzar in the far west of the Maghreb. This revolt spread to most of the Atlas Mountains and lasted for almost the entire reign of al-Qa'im.[9] At this point, the revolt threatened the Fatimid capital of al-Mahdiyya itself, which was besieged in 944.

Moreover, Jawdhar was installed in charge of the whole Fatimid realm as a keeper of all treasuries and *diwan*s by al-Qa'im's successor.[10] Al-Qa'im died in 946, but his death was concealed by his son, al-Mansur, with the help of the loyal Jawdhar. Ibn Kindad's revolt increased the pressure on the Fatimids during that year and, as a result, al-Mansur appointed Jawdhar as his deputy: 'Al-Mansur left Jawdhar in control of the realm and gave him keys to all the treasuries. The correspondence between them was made in the name of deceased al-Qa'im.'[11]

No eunuch ever had such responsibility as that given to Jawdhar. He was not only in charge of administering the affairs of the realm, he also managed to conceal the death of Caliph al-Qa'im upon the orders of his new master. That prevented a rupture in the unity of the Fatimid house, and maintained support to the Fatimid rule among most of the Maghrebi tribes. Caliph al-Mu'izz, who succeeded al-Mansur, instilled the same trust as his fathers in Jawdhar. In 969 he departed from Tunisia to fight the Khariji Zanata chief, Abu Khazar in the west, and appointed Jawdhar as his deputy in al-Mahdiyya.[12]

After the Fatimids moved to Egypt and founded Cairo as their new capital, the influence of the eunuch institution on politics and creed continued up to the Mustansiriyya Crisis. During the first year of the rule of the eleven-year-old boy al-Hakim (we have already discussed how he managed to confront and stop Sitt al-Mulk from installing her cousin as a caliph, and put her under house arrest, a pivotal move that influenced religious–political affairs), we see Barjawan (d. 1000) in charge of the state. Barjawan started as a tutor for al-Hakim in the royal palace, appointed by Caliph al-'Aziz. Before he died, al-'Aziz installed Barjawan as a regent for al-Hakim. That move created a power struggle in the caliphate of his successor.[13] Barjawan tried to subject the rule of Egypt to his authority. He was a white eunuch, probably of Turkish origin, who refused to submit to the leader of the grand tribe of the Kutama Berbers in Egypt, Ibn 'Ammar, who was the *wasita* (lit. medium; prime minister) of al-Hakim.

Ibn 'Ammar's economic and political policies discriminated against non-Berber elements, so Barjawan created a Turkish pact to confront the Berbers. He conspired with the eunuch Shukr, a distinguished Turkmen commander who had escaped Buwayhid Iraq and entered the service of al-Hakim's father. Barjawan also allied with Menjutakin, the Turkish deputy of Damascus, against Ibn 'Ammar in 996.[14]

After bitter military confrontations in Syria, Libya and Egypt, Ibn 'Ammar was ousted from office by Barjawan, who prevailed as the dominant commander of the Fatimid state. Ibn al-Athir wrote: 'When Barjawan prevailed, he declared al-Hakim as caliph, sat him on the throne, and renewed the oath of sovereignty to him.'[15] Barjawan gave orders to his Turkish allies in Damascus to attack all Berber Kutama elements there. To achieve civil peace in Egypt, Barjawan returned the confiscated land of Ibn 'Ammar and guaranteed his personal safety in return for not interfering in political affairs again. Barjawan achieved this victory, not only by creating a Turkish military pact, but by penetrating the Kutami pact and planting spies inside the palace of his foe, Ibn 'Ammar. As a result, Barjawan seized the office of the *wasita* for the boy caliph, and became de facto ruler of the Fatimid dynasty until he died in 1000.[16]

For four years Barjawan dominated state affairs. He planted a spy named 'Aqiq, a eunuch, inside the caliph's palace to report to him personally on news of the commanders of the Fatimid army,[17] who might influence the boy caliph. One of the elite commanders feared by Barjawan was Raydan, bearer of the parasol for al-'Aziz and al-Hakim. He was ranked fourth in the military hierarchy of the army,[18] and his closeness to al-Hakim disturbed Barjawan. Al-Maqrizi, the indispensable source on Fatimid history, wrote that Raydan feared the domination of Barjawan, and wanted to remove him from his position. Raydan urged al-Hakim to assassinate Barjawan, saying to the caliph: 'Barjawan wanted to dominate you like Kafur did his Ikhshidid lords.' Al-Hakim replied: 'If that is your opinion, Raydan, and you believe in its validity, I will seek your help to prevent that from happening.' Al-Hakim then ordered Raydan to assassinate Barjawan swiftly. Raydan carried out his master's order and decapitated Barjawan in the presence of the caliph.[19] As a result, the caliph restored his authority from the eunuch prime minister and held absolute power in his realm, and Raydan inspired his master to place more confidence in him.

The paramount importance of Barjawan among the ruling circles in Egypt was reflected in al-Hakim's fear of a potential revolt in his state, especially from the Turkish elements. As a result, al-Hakim took the exceptional step of issuing a declaration that was read throughout Cairo, Fustat, Giza and all the Fatimid provinces, justifying his murder to Barjawan: 'O, peoples, Barjawan was a slave of mine, who once served the caliph sincerely. When he abused his services, the commander of the faithful did as he wished with him and covered him in wrath.'[20]

Clearly, such a step by the caliph reflected how powerful that eunuch had been in his administration. I should mention that Barjawan's name lived on through the centuries due to his legacy. From medieval times until today, close to the Northern Gate of Cairo, a street bears his name.

Because politics and religious affairs of the Fatimids were closely connected and influenced each other, we can see how eunuchs protected the continuation of the religious tradition, thus ensuring the continuation of the dynasty. In 934, while Caliph al-Mahdi was being buried by his son and *wali al-'ahd*, al-Qa'im, who was also heir to the throne, whispered to Jawdhar:

> 'You know, Jawdhar, that it is forbidden for the new *hujja* after the deceased imam to bury him, and not to choose a new *hujja* for himself (*wali al-'ahd*). I will not be considered a legitimate new imam until I do so. Out of all the people, I selected you for revealing this trusted matter. Come closer, and give me your hand.'

Jawdhar gave him his hand. Al-Qa'im said: 'I take the oath of Almighty that you will keep the secret I will tell you. My son Isma'il (the future al-Mansur) is my *hujja*.' Jawdhar reported in his biography that he honoured his promise and kept the secret for seven years.[21]

The same situation reoccurred when al-Mansur died in 953. Al-Mu'izz revealed to Jawdhar, alone, his selection of his son 'Abd Allah as successor. Again, Jawdhar honoured him and kept the secret for seven months.[22] This reflects the immense trust that Jawdhar enjoyed by several imams or caliphs.

If he had revealed to other members of the royal family the secret he was entrusted to keep, a political challenge to power might have erupted in the state. Indeed, Jawdhar was entrusted due to his devotion, and because, being a eunuch, he did not pose a personal threat to the rule. Having said that, many other eunuchs were not selected to keep the secret, and were politically ambitious despite having no families, like Kafur in Egypt (prior to the Fatimids), or Barjawan, for example. The behaviour of Jawdhar in both cases enhanced the rule of the caliphs.

Under al-Mansur, and during the early reign of al-Mu'izz, there were serious domestic disputes; Jawdhar's ability to keep secrets gave stability to the caliphate in these transitional periods. Furthermore, according to Shi'i creed, al-Mu'izz should have selected his eldest son Tamim as his successor; therefore, Jawdhar, concealing the knowledge of the different choice by al-Mu'izz, contributed to the religious–political stability and avoided a coup d'état by members of the family who would have been in support of the neglected Tamim.

Caliph al-Mansur entrusted Jawdhar with all the precious manuscripts of his rule as well those of the previous Shi'i imams.[23] This put Jawdhar in the position of the guardian of the fundamental Isma'ili sources, elevated above any other Fatimid prince or commander; he was therefore able to alter those sources if he wished to do so or use them to his advantage with other ambitious Fatimid royals. He never did. His loyalty was well valued, and when the Fatimids founded their capital, Cairo, they named a street and an alley after him, which still exist today.[24]

In the mysterious and vague period before al-Mahdi became the first Fatimid caliph, he was seized by the 'Abbasid authorities with his eunuch, Ja'far, in Sijilmasa (in modern-day Morocco). The eunuch did not say a word about his master's secrets. When the Fatimid dynasty was declared, Ja'far became the *hajib* of the caliph.[25] However, we should deal with the pre-foundation of the state and its data with caution.

From Tunisia to Egypt, the influence of eunuchs continued. During the reign of Caliph al-'Aziz, Barjawan was appointed as regent of his young son and successor al-Hakim, as mentioned. When al-'Aziz died suddenly in 996 in Belbais in the Nile Delta, Barjawan had in his company the caliph's powerful daughter Sitt al-Mulk, the *qadi* and the eunuch Raydan, bearer of the parasol. According to Ibn al-Qalanisi, Sitt al-Mulk tried to hijack the caliphate for her cousin 'Abd Allah, who was her husband-to-be. Barjawan knew of the conspiracy and ordered 1,000 knights to detain her in her palace in Cairo. Barjawan swiftly installed al-Hakim, revealed him to the leaders of the realm and secured their oath of obedience to him.[26]

The following day Barjawan escorted the young caliph in a procession with armed guards across Cairo in the presence of another prominent commander, the eunuch Raydan, who continued to serve al-Hakim as bearer of the parasol.[27] The public parade across the capital was essential to reveal the new caliph, thus protecting the creed from the ambitious Sitt al-Mulk and her cousin; in addition, Barjawan fulfilled the will of the deceased imam.

Before resuming analysis of the influence of eunuchs on politics, I will briefly abandon chronological order to follow the influence of eunuchs on the Fatimid religious doctrine.

As pointed out in the previous chapter, when the queen consort Arwa of Yemen lost her two male children, the Fatimid caliph and his vizier were keen to secure the Isma'ili creed in Yemen, which was inseparable from the Sulayhi state. They therefore dispatched a high-level envoy representing them, to convince and force Arwa to marry Prince Saba' in order to preserve the *da'wa* and the state. That envoy was the eunuch *ustadh* Yamin al-Dawla, who read the caliphs threatening letter to her and witnessed the conclusion of the marriage contract.[28]

Also, in 1122 during the caliphate of al-Amir, a dispute arose again about the authenticity of the succession of Nizar, son of Caliph al-Mustansir, instead of his younger brother al-Musta'li. As discussed in the previous chapter, the vizier al-Ma'mun, the de facto ruler of Egypt, held a royal council and summoned the eldest sister of Nizar to give her testimony. This testimony, crucial for renewing the legitimacy of the rule of al-Amir, was given in the presence of some of the elite eunuch commanders known as *ustadhin* (plural of *ustadh*).[29] Such witnesses were not only prestigious but also vital in terms of persuading the ruling circles of the Fatimids to continue supporting al-Amir.

Three years later, the vizier al-Ma'mun was in full control of the state together with his brother al-Mu'taman, governor of Alexandria. Al-Ma'mun tried to shift his religious alliance to the Nizari creed, as reported in some sources.[30] In that case, the vizier was supporting the enemies and religious–political opposition of the caliph himself. Al-Amir was alarmed by this move from al-Ma'mun and started to question his loyalty. Al-Amir summoned a eunuch *ustadh* and instructed him to infiltrate the service of the vizier and his brother and secretly persuade the commanders to support the caliph and weaken al-Ma'mun's position.

As a result, the vizier and his brother were both arrested,[31] and the caliph remained without a vizier for the remainder of his rule. After al-Amir was killed in 1130, followed by a long dispute about the existence of his infant son, al-Tayyib, we see a report that Yanas, chief commander of the army, who was a eunuch, had killed al-Tayyib in collaboration with al-Hafiz. In return, al-Hafiz, who became caliph, rewarded Yanas by appointing him as a vizier.[32]

In 1160 when Caliph al-Fa'iz died, his grand vizier al-Salih headed desperately to the Fatimid royal palace in search of a quick replacement for him. A powerful eunuch inside the palace assisted him in the selection of young al-'Adid, who was a relative but not a son of the deceased caliph. From all the reports and anecdotes mentioned above, we can see how eunuchs were influential in the affairs of the Isma'ili doctrine.

Returning to the political influence of eunuchs, we note the first appearance of al-Zahir, the sixteen-year-old son of the murdered al-Hakim. In 1021 he was escorted to Cairo by the vizier, and the eunuch Nassim, holder of the caliphal sword, and one of the leading military commanders in the state; that took place upon the orders of Sitt al-Mulk, as mentioned.[33]

That same eunuch commander, Nassim, was the one who had collaborated fully with Sitt al-Mulk to arrest her cousin, Ilyas, who had previously been declared as *wali al-'ahd* by al-Hakim. This represented a threat to al-Zahir's rule. In addition, when Sitt al-Mulk wanted to end the life of Ibn Dawwas, her powerful partner in the killing of al-Hakim, she found no one better than the Saqlabi eunuch, Nassim. It was a complicated operation, as Ibn Dawwas was not only the regent of the caliph, but the chief of the powerful Kutama Berber tribe. As a result, Nassim collaborated with another eunuch, Mi'dad, a teacher of al-Zahir and a close confidant of Sitt al-Mulk. Together they ambushed Ibn Dawwas with a battalion of Saqlabi eunuchs to avoid arousing suspicion; they murdered Ibn Dawwas, fearing a violent response from his tribe.

Mi'dad appointed another person to replace Ibn Dawwas as keeper of the treasury. That person was the eunuch Rifq.[34] The collaboration between the harem institution represented by Sitt al-Mulk and the eunuch institution, which became her arms or tools to control the realm, was the main feature of that time. Mi'dad continued to gain more power in the Fatimid state, particularly from 1024, when Sitt al-Mulk died. Among the several signs indicating the rise of Mi'dad's influence, as detailed by al-Maqrizi, is his title 'most glorious commander'. To administer the realm, Mi'dad formed and led a supreme council of four persons, including the vizier, to run the state. He even prohibited the rest of the commanders, including the eunuch who carried the parasol from the meeting with Caliph al-Zahir, who had led a dissolute life. That of course shows that not all eunuchs were united or had the same agenda.

Mi'dad successfully dispatched an army to put down a revolt in Palestine by the Arab al-Jarrah. On the domestic front, he coordinated his efforts with the eunuch Nassim to punish the slaves who looted Cairo and Fustat during a particularly difficult economic year.[35] Such influence by eunuchs, it could be said, was a continuation of Jawdhar and Barjawan's influence, despite the different political circumstances, namely, the power of the caliphs.

The Fatimids used eunuch commanders as personal envoys and representatives of the caliph in transitional times that affected the stability of the state. In 1085 Caliph al-Mustansir and his vizier had commissioned the eunuch commander Jawhar to travel to Yemen to give the caliphal condolences to Queen Arwa after her husband died, to look into the new political situation of Yemen, and report it back to Cairo.[36]

When al-Afdal, the grand Fatimid vizier, was killed in 1121, there was a revolt by the Armenian community in Cairo. Caliph al-Amir entrusted a eunuch *ustadh* to put down that revolt because al-Afda's sons coveted their father's post. More importantly, al-Amir trusted Rihan (lit. basil plant), the chief eunuch and keeper of all treasures, to count the huge financial resources left by al-Afdal, some of which had not been put on record by the previous vizier. Rihan found approximately twelve million dinars – an unbelievable amount, more than double the annual production of Egypt.[37] This particular task of counting the wealth left by the murdered vizier, which was left to the chief eunuch, was maybe part of his job, but it also reflects how powerful and trustworthy eunuchs became.

In 1134 Caliph al-Hafiz became fearful of his violent son Hasan, who had acted as vizier since 1131. Al-Hafiz wanted to kill his influential son, so he ordered Wafyy Ishaq, one of the chief *muhannak* eunuchs, to confront Hasan. Wafyy went to Upper Egypt and contacted the Rihaniyya eunuch battalion for help.[38] Here, we see the unprecedented level of trust in the eunuch institution to fight the caliph's own son and heir.

The conspiracy against Saladin that was led in 1170 by the last eunuch commander, Jawhar, illustrates further the immense influence of eunuch commanders in the Fatimid state. This conspiracy will be examined under the military system described below. Yaacov Lev states that eunuchs did not form a majority in the state and did not control or dominate the ruling circles.[39] I can agree with the first part, but given the evidence examined here, they consistently dominated the ruling circles, whether in North Africa or in Egypt. More evidence on that will be presented later.

Eunuchs and the Military System

Commanders

If the use of eunuchs under Muslim rule began with assignment of miscellaneous duties inside the palace, it was not long before they were used in other posts and sections of society, including the army. There were several reasons for such a development. First, eunuchs wanted to elevate themselves from domestic posts in the palace as they became rivals to the outer bureaucracy. Second, caliphs assumed that they could rely on the loyalty of eunuchs, believing that without families or a biological future, eunuchs would be less ambitious. In addition, eunuchs enjoyed greater physical strength than ordinary soldiers, giving them an advantage in terms of rising through the ranks.

According to David Ayalon, a large number of eunuch commanders were present in North Africa from the beginning of the Fatimid era.[40] As soon as Caliph al-Qa'im came to power, he was faced with a dangerous revolt led by the Khariji leader Ibn Kindad in the Maghreb area around Fas and all the way down to what is Senegal today. Al-Qa'im sent a huge army to restore order to that region, led by his trusted commander, Maysur. Maysur was a eunuch who managed to restore order to the area.[41] He enjoyed the full trust of his master and remained in his service as the chief commander until his death in 944. During his last year Maysur had to confront an approximately 100,000-strong Berber army that captured al-Qayrawan and threatened the very existence of the Fatimids. He was provided with a large army by the caliph to defend the state, and managed to delay the Berber advance.[42]

When Maysur died, he was succeeded by another eunuch commander, Bushra, who had fought Ibn Kindad in an earlier confrontation. It is worth comparing here the 'Abbasid case of Mu'nis, who was the first eunuch chief commander of the army after about 160 years from the beginning of the dynasty. The Fatimids were much quicker to use eunuchs in high offices, probably learning from the 'Abbasid evolution. Bushra was able to defeat the Khariji revolt and protect the Fatimid capital of al-Mahdiyya.[43] In Jawdhar's biography, we find stories or anecdotes of other eunuch commanders, such as Shafi' in Tunisia under al-Qa'im,[44] who were in the service of the caliphs, but this research cannot cover all such stories; they deserve a separate study.

While fighting in the Maghreb, al-Qa'im continued the Fatimid attack on Egypt and sent in another massive army, according to Ibn al-Athir. The caliph spent lavishly on that army in order to seize Egypt. Raydan, the faithful eunuch commander, was the leader of this military project, which managed to seize Alexandria; however, he was defeated by the Ikhshidid army in 934.[45] Clearly, the Fatimids depended on eunuch commanders in important crises, missions and projects.

Al-Mu'izz moved all of his family and treasures to Egypt in 974; he faced a threatening invasion of the Nile Delta region by the Qaramita, who dominated most of its eastern and central areas. The caliph dispatched his eunuch commander Raydan, a Saqlabi, to confront them and save the newly established Fatimid realm in Egypt.[46] The chronicles emphasise al-Mu'izz's great trust in Raydan's ability and loyalty. We can only imagine what the situation would have been had the Qaramita managed to bribe him to join their side.

The caliph had dispatched Raydan earlier in that year to Tripoli, where he defeated a Byzantine army dispatched by Emperor John I Tzimiskes (d. 976). Raydan was then ordered to march to Damascus to restore the authority of the Fatimids there by defeating Abu Mahmud, a rebellious commander. Raydan was successful in all of these missions.[47]

In early 975 major parts of southern Syria and Lebanon, including Beirut, Sidon, Acre and Damascus, were not under the full authority of the Fatimids. The Fatimids were confronting diverse Turkish elements venturing out of their 'Abbasid–Buwayhid sphere of influence, and there was also a revolt of several Arab chiefs and the presence of Byzantine forces in these areas. Al-Mu'izz had no choice but to order the eunuch commander Nusay' to march to Beirut and restore it to Fatimid rule.[48]

This unstable political–military situation continued until the end of the tenth century in Syria. Under the administration of Barjawan, who became *wasita* (prime minister) to al-Hakim, an army was sent to fight and defeat the Byzantines and restore order to Damascus. According to Ibn Sa'id al-Antaki, Barjawan was engaged in a series of negotiations with the Byzantines in 999 and received their ambassador in person to conclude a truce between the two sides.

In North Africa, Barjawan failed to save Barqa and Tripoli from rebellious tribal separatists during his administration,[49] yet we can see here a total domination by Barjawan of military and political affairs. We should take into consideration the multi-fronts and challenges he was facing, in addition to Sitt al-Mulk, who was constrained by him for a while.

Under al-Hakim's caliphate in 1020, the caliph wanted to punish the people of Fustat for being loyal Sunnis. He sent Sudanese battalions to burn and loot their properties. The result was disastrous, as the rage and rebellion in Fustat threatened to spread to Cairo. The caliph selected Ghadi, a Saqlabi eunuch commander, to confront this crisis and resolve the critical situation. Ghadi successfully put down the rebellion.[50] Considering the large population of Fustat, with its traditional anti-Shi'i sentiments, in addition to its urban extension to the southern walls of Fatimid Cairo, we can see the great importance of the task that Ghadi was commissioned with.

Under the caliphate of al-Zahir, the black eunuch commander Mi'dad monopolised political affairs. In 1024 he enjoyed the highest of titles: "*izz al-dawla wa mustafaha*' (glory of the state and its most distinguished one).[51] In addition to that, he was chief of the prestigious Kutama *diwan*, the most influential Berber tribe, thus controlling the main Berber elements. Despite the famine of 1024/5 and the revolt of some battalions of the army in protest about not receiving their pay, they were motivated by some military commanders; Mi'dad succeeded in keeping the capital and Fustat from any harm that might have been caused by those rebellious military elements.[52]

Mi'dad was determined to assert his authority over other elements of the army, including the Turks. He marched in a triumphal parade across Cairo, heading for Giza, west of the Nile. At the same time, he dispatched several forces across Egypt and to Palestine to enforce his authority.[53] That reflects his confidence and ability in running the affairs of the state. While Mi'dad was in command of the army, he used Rifq, the black eunuch, as commander of the Nile Delta. It seems that Mi'dad wanted to increase the number of eunuch commanders in the state; in one year he installed three eunuch *muhannak ustadh* in the service of the caliph. In 1049, in an illuminating anecdote on the status of eunuchs in the army, al-Mustansir marched out in a farewell ceremony given in honour of his commander Rifq, 'the victorious, glory of the rule, pillar of the state'.

Under his command a massive 30,000 soldiers were dispatched to Aleppo. The commanders in Syria received orders to strictly submit to his commands and to dismount from their horses when they saw him.[54] The caliphal trust in Rifq, and his dispatch to Syria with a huge force, reflected the distinguished status of eunuchs in the Fatimid military.

Fighting the Crusaders was another demonstration of Fatimid confidence in eunuchs, as well as using them as chief commanders in critical and challenging times. Immediately after the First Crusade, when Jerusalem was captured from the Fatimids in 1099, the vizier al-Afdal launched major campaigns against the Crusaders. In 1100 he led the war himself, and in 1102 he dispatched Sa'd al-Dawla, the trusted *tawashi* of his father, to fight King Baldwin I (d. 1118) near Jaffa. The army led by Sa'd comprised approximately 5,000 knights.[55] When that eunuch commander was defeated, al-Afdal dispatched his own son, Husayn, to fight the Crusaders the following year.[56] With the new geopolitical situation in Syria, created by the arrival of the Crusaders and their rapid expansion, we do not see any discrimination against eunuch commanders in these critical times; they were relied upon in the same way as other commanders.

Actual evidence of some sources and anecdotes in others imply that political–military power was in decline after the first century of Fatimid rule in Egypt. It can be argued that the viziers who became de facto rulers of the

Fatimid state after 1074 had a role in excluding a large number of eunuch commanders from powerful positions in order to eliminate any chance of confrontation with them. Eunuchs were used, but in smaller numbers and scale; cases like Jawdhar, Barjawan and Mi'dad did not occur again. Maybe the economic decline of the state and the high prices of eunuchs had contributed to the decrease in their numbers. The last strong eunuch commander appeared at the end of the dynasty. This was the famous Mu'taman al-Khilafa ('the one entrusted by the caliphate') – Jawhar. He was in charge of the royal palace, and rejected the vizierate of the Sunni Kurdish commander Saladin, who posed a real threat to his office and to the entire state. In 1169 Jawhar orchestrated a plot to contact the Crusaders to march into Egypt to fight Saladin. While Saladin was distracted by confronting the Crusaders, Jawhar and his supporters would attack the followers of Saladin in Egypt, and then would follow him and attack him from the rear while he was confronting the Crusaders. However, the plot was discovered, and Saladin ordered the decapitation of Jawhar. In order to control the Fatimid caliph in his palace, Saladin replaced Jawhar with his own trusted eunuch, Qaraqush, a white eunuch who was in the service of Saladin's deceased uncle, Shirkuh.[57]

Qaraqush was empowered by Saladin to run the affairs of the caliphal palace and, of course, became his eyes and ears there. The Sudanese battalions of the Fatimid army revolted in anger to the killing of Jawhar. In the region of 50,000 of them revolted, which Saladin and Qaraqush could not handle. Saladin gave an order to set fire to their area, al-Mansuriyya, where they lived with their families. Only then, when the revolt was under control, did Saladin annihilate most of the rebels.[58] Such massive defiance as a result of Jawhar's killing can be understood as an action to avenge a popular and prominent commander.

Eunuch Battalions

Despite the high price of slave eunuchs, which was about four times higher than the price of a normal slave, the Ikhshidids and then the Fatimids had eunuch battalions on the battlefield by virtue of their physical abilities. Such battalions were named after eunuch commanders. During the Fatimid invasion of Egypt, the Kafuriyya battalion (named after Kafur the Ikhshidid) of about 5,000 soldiers was apparently under two eunuch commanders who resisted the Fatimids. In fact, there was more than one eunuch battalion, as we see the Kafuriyya in Damascus revolting in 974 against the new Fatimid rule.[59] Under al-Hakim, there was the Yanisiyya battalion named after the eunuch Yanis, chief of the royal palace and later governor of Barqa, until he died in 1004. There was also the Muzaffariyya, named after the eunuch commander al-Muzaffar, bearer of the parasol.[60]

In 1021, when Mi'dad wanted to assassinate the powerful Ibn Dawwas, he commissioned the eunuch Nasim to execute the task. Nasim headed a battalion called the Sa'diyya, the personal guards of the caliph, the majority, if not all, of whom were eunuchs.[61] According to al-Sayyed, there was an influential army division in the early years of al-Mustansir's rule, named the Rihaniyya. It was founded by the eunuch 'Aziz al-Dawla Rihan, a commander in the royal court. The Rihaniyya had their own dwelling in Cairo. This unit, then the Jeushiyya of Badr al-Jamali, were the most important divisions in the army in the second half of the eleventh century. Their influence continued to the end of al-Hafiz's rule.[62]

There was another Rihaniyya battalion under Caliph al-Hafiz in 1134, commanded by Rihan al-Khadim, who led this battalion to Upper Egypt against Prince Hasan, son of the caliph, during the famous strife between the father and son.[63] From the sketches discussed here, we can see the trust that was put into slave eunuchs during critical situations. While there was one eunuch battalion under the 'Abbasids (during the reign of al-Muqtadir) – the Mu'nisiyya, the Fatimids expanded their number of eunuch battalions, and this tradition was passed to the Ayyubids. In Saladin's army in 1181, 7,000 out of 11,000 soldiers were *tawashi* or eunuchs, as noted by the Latin chronicler, William of Tyre, as will be examined.[64]

Eunuchs in Maritime Activities

The Fatimids were influenced by the Aghlabids (800–909) who ruled Tunisia before them, and had a formidable navy consisting of hundreds of ships. The Aghlabids had managed to capture Sicily during their expansion in the Mediterranean. The constant Fatimid skirmishes with the Byzantine fleets made them more eager to increase their naval power. By the early tenth century, the Fatimid navy had inherited the bases of the Aghlabids in Tunisia, Susa and Palermo.[65]

The Fatimid caliphs of North Africa pursued an expansionist policy towards the east, and were active in the Mediterranean with a fleet of about 600 ships. The Fatimid caliph personally supervised the navy and appointed one of his leading commanders to be in charge of it.[66]

In 918 Caliph al-Mahdi dispatched his son, Abu al-Qasim, with a huge force to attack Egypt. Abu al-Qasim was accompanied by a large fleet of eighty ships commanded by the eunuch Sulayman, who managed to seize Alexandria. Later in the year, the 'Abbasid caliph sent a fleet from Syria to confront Sulayman. Bishr, the commander of the 'Abbasid navy and also a eunuch, managed to defeat Sulayman.[67] The following year, the Fatimids repeated their attempt, with another eunuch commander of their fleet. The Fatimid commander was defeated and taken captive by the famous 'Abbasid eunuch commander Thumal.[68] We should remember here that Egypt was governed then by another eunuch, Mu'nis al-Khadim (see Chapter Three).

Under Caliph al-Qa'im the Fatimids continued using eunuchs as commanders in their navy. In 934 Raydan was in command of a campaign targeting Egypt; he managed to seize Alexandria for a short period.[69] From information provided in the sources, we can say that Fatimid eunuchs led major maritime activities to capture coastal strongholds in Egypt; they were partly successful. Interestingly, their 'Abbasid counterparts were also eunuchs. That shows how eunuchs had been elevated to prominent positions on both the Sunni and Shi'i sides at the same time.

As the eunuch Jawdhar was deputy to several Fatimid caliphs in North Africa, he was put in charge of the navy as well. When the Byzantine fleet attacked Fatimid Sicily in 948, for example, the governor there asked the caliph for help. Caliph al-Mansur commissioned Jawdhar to prepare all supplies needed for the fleet.[70] Again, in 951, the Fatimid governor of Sicily asked for help against Byzantine raids. Jawdhar supervised the dispatch of the Fatimid fleet headed by the eunuch commander Farah.[71]

In selected cases, we see eunuchs in charge of naval resistance against the Byzantines, which reflects their military ability, in addition to their ruler's confidence in them. At the end of the tenth century, in 998, the Fatimids under Barjawan, faced a rebellion in Tyre, Lebanon. In that year, al-'Allaqa, the unknown leader of the rebellion, defeated the Fatimid garrisons and asked the Byzantine emperor, Basil II, for help. Tyre received military aid from Byzantium. When the situation was about to spread to other Fatimid cities on the coast, a Fatimid fleet under the command of a Saqlabi eunuch, Fa'iq, managed to enter Tyre and defeat al-'Allaqa, restoring the city to Fatimid authority.[72]

Despite the numerous maritime activities against the Fatimids in the first half of the twelfth century, there is no clear evidence of eunuch commanders being involved in such operations as seen before. The only evidence is that when the last remaining Fatimid port in the Levantine coast, Ascalon, was under siege by the Crusaders in 1153, the eunuch Maknun, lord and *qadi* of the city, exhumed the buried head of al-Husayn – grandson of the Prophet Muhammad and the second Shi'i imam – and sent it to Cairo, where it is still buried.[73] It was not a military task, but considered a highly sacred mission by Muslims, especially by Shi'i followers.

Eunuchs in the Police and *Hisba*

According to the book of *Khitat* (streets) of al-Maqrizi, the Fatimid capital developed into a larger metropolis decades after the foundation of Cairo. It was divided into four sections: Fustat, Cairo, Rawda Island in the Nile and Giza. The most important was Fustat,[74] probably because of its large urban area and condensed population. There were two *shurta* (police) authorities: one for the north covering Cairo, and one for the south covering the other three sections. The sources make little mention of the commander of the police serving under the Fatimids, but it is nonetheless appropriate to use such sources.

Under Caliph al-'Aziz, we see that Yannas, a Saqlabi eunuch, was commander of the *shurta* in Fustat in 990.[75] In 1011 Caliph al-Hakim appointed Ghayn (a very strange name, even by eunuch standards – it is the nineteenth letter in the Arabic language, ع), as commander of both the northern and southern districts of *shurta*. He added to him the post of *hisba* (the person who inspected the quality and prices in the markets, and observed the implementation of Islamic laws in public).

The caliph granted him full liberty in terms of jurisdiction, although one of Ghayn's hands had been amputated upon al-Hakim's orders the previous year. Aside from that, he was a eunuch, and therefore occupying a job that observed the implementation of shari'a was highly questionable. In 1012 al-Hakim appointed al-Hasan al-Wazzan, an assistant to Ghayn, to the post of *wasita*. Although al-Hakim was famous for his unpredictable acts, promoting one of his eunuch's assistants to the post of prime minister was utterly strange; yet it reflects how he trusted Ghayn.

In 1013 Ghayn was dismissed from the *shurta* and replaced by a Saqlabi eunuch commander, Muzaffar. He had been the bearer of the parasol for the caliph.[76] Ghayn was promoted to 'qa'id al-quwwad' (commander of all commanders). At the same time, however, his other hand was cut off together with his tongue, at the order of al-Hakim. Ghayn remained chief commander, and received splendid gifts from the disturbed caliph, marching in great ceremony to receive them at the royal palace.[77] It is difficult to understand such behaviour on the part of the caliph, that is keeping a disabled eunuch in this powerful post, unless that particular eunuch displayed exceptional ability, or the caliph was mercurial.

In 1024, during the administration of Mi'dad, we find the black eunuch Nafidh in charge of both offices of the *shurta*. When he was dismissed, the eunuch Baqi replaced him.[78] We should take into account that during this time another eunuch, Rifq, was in command of the Nile Delta region. I would have to agree with Yaacov Lev that the *shurta* and *hisba*, the most powerful posts of the Fatimid capital, were frequently given to eunuchs who were in charge of daily life, fighting crimes and observing the markets and commercial activities. In addition, they were responsible for the strategic wheat trade and supply of it to the bakeries around the vast capital.[79]

Eunuchs as Provincial Governors

Under Fatimid rule eunuchs were trusted and relied upon to govern provinces and large cities with strategic importance to the state. About nineteen eunuch *wali*s held the post in different provinces either in North Africa or Syria. Some of them held the post for more than one term (see Table 5.1). Most of these eunuchs were military commanders before their appointment, and they continued in military service afterward.

In North Africa, the most well-known *wali* was Jawdhar, who governed Ifriqiya (western Libya, Tunisia and eastern Algeria) on behalf of the Fatimid caliphs while they were preoccupied by fighting the numerous rebellious Berber tribes in the Maghreb. In 969 al-Mu'izz appointed Jawdhar as *wali* of al-Mahdiyya, the capital of Ifriqiya. Meanwhile, al-Muʿizz had left to fight the chief of the large Berber tribe of Zanata.[80] There are several aspects of the long period that Jawdhar served as *wali* under three caliphs (al-Qaʾim, al-Mansur and al-Muʿizz) that deserve separate study. Jawdhar was limitless in his power as a *wali*, from political to financial and military. Due only to his extreme loyalty to his masters, North Africa remained under one banner; he could have separated from the Fatimids as he had all the tools, but he did not have the ambition. Al-Qayrawan, the second most important city after the Fatimid capital, had had two eunuch governors. One was in office before 962 when Nasim, who was dismissed in that year, was replaced by the eunuch Sabir,[81] whose duration of office is not clear in the chronicles.

After the Fatimids moved to Egypt we find only a few lines referring to the *wali* of Libya and none referring to the rest of the Maghreb. In 998 Barjawan feared the political influence of another eunuch commander, Yanis, in Egypt. As a result, he appointed him as *wali* to Barqa, more than 1,000 km west of Alexandria. After the murder of Barjawan, al-Hakim extended Yanis's authority to include Tripoli further west, in view of the unrest of the Berber tribes there.[82] In 1004 the *wali* of Barqa was Sandal, a eunuch commander who appeared suddenly in the chronicles fighting the Khariji chief, Abu Rikwa.[83] The principal task of the *wali* was to bring the city or province under Fatimid control, especially during periods of strife and instability.

Looking to the east, as the Fatimids always aspired, we see that they apparently appointed no eunuchs as governors of the Hijaz as the ʿAbbasids had done with Muʾnis. Most, if not all, of their eunuch governors were in Syria and Palestine, where confrontations between the Byzantines and the ʿAbbasids were frequent and unavoidable. From the time of their capture of Damascus under al-Muʿizz to Caliph al-Mustansir, the Fatimids allocated the governance of their largest city in Syria, Damascus, to successive commands of eunuchs. In 974, three years after the Fatimids seized the city, there was a bloody confrontation between the Berber tribes on the Fatimid side and the local powers, bringing continuous civil unrest. Al-Muʿizz was alarmed and ordered his governor of Tripoli (Lebanon), the eunuch Raydan, to lead his forces to Damascus and dismiss the Fatimid ruler there. Raydan was instructed to assess the situation and send his evaluation of the locals' needs and demands directly to the caliph.[84]

Due to the efficiency of Raydan's administration, he remained in office for a year, governing both Damascus and Tripoli despite strong anti-Shi'i sentiment, especially in Damascus. In 988 Caliph al-'Aziz installed his eunuch commander Munir, a Saqlabi eunuch of his vizier Ibn Killis, as ruler of Damascus. Munir was dispatched in a massive army to calm the locals after the violent rule of the Turkish governor, Bekjur. Another eunuch commander, Bishara, marched under his authority. For two years Munir remained in office and extended his authority to other Fatimid governors in Syria upon direct orders of the caliph. This made him a supreme *wali*,[85] mostly of southern and central Syria. Barjawan, the de facto ruler of Egypt, who saw constant Byzantine incursions in Fatimid Syria, decided to dismiss Abu Tamim, the ruler of Damascus, and restore the eunuch Bishara al-Ikhshidi as a governor there.[86] Needless to say Bishara enjoyed the trust and confidence of the caliph and Barjawan, evidenced not only by his reinstatement but also by the task to which he was appointed – to protect Damascus from Byzantine raids.

In 1049 Caliph al-Mustansir installed the *amir al-umara'* (commander of commanders/chief commander), the eunuch Rifq, as governor of Damascus. After one month in office with absolute power, he was ordered to march north to govern Aleppo and punish the rebellious Arab Mirdasids. Rifq became supreme *wali* over all Fatimid *wali*s in Syria.[87] The Fatimid policy of militarising the administration continued until the end of their rule and the coming of the Seljuqs in 1055 to Baghdad, and remained for all the dynasties that came after them down to the Ottomans. Prior to Rifq's appointment in 1023, when Mi'dad was the supreme commander of Egypt, he appointed the eunuch Mawsuf as governor of Aleppo and its citadel. He managed to secure the second largest city in Syria after the unrest, which followed the disappearance of al-Hakim.[88] The control of the citadel by a eunuch reflected great trust and ability in his rule. The citadel was the strongest military position in any medieval city, especially a large one. Any city could not be considered seized by a counter-force without submitting the citadel. The ruler of a large city like Aleppo, in command of its citadel, could declare his independence from the authority in Cairo with much confidence; that reflects the trust that these eunuchs enjoyed by the Fatimids. Appointing eunuchs to govern the citadels in Syria became a tradition, and influenced the Seljuqs, Zengids and Ayyubids to follow that model.

In Fatimid Syria, Beirut and Tripoli were among the medium-sized cities with commercial significance allocated to eunuch governors. In 975 al-Muʿizz appointed Nusayr as *wali* of Beirut and gave him a massive force to protect the city from the rebellious Turkish commander Aftakin. Nusayr failed to govern the city for more than a few months.[89] Again we see in the sources that Saʿd al-Tawashi, the commander of the 1102 campaign against the Crusaders, had previously been *wali* of Beirut, but for how long it is not clear.[90] Raydan al-Khadim, who was governor of Tripoli prior to the year 974, was installed by al-Muʿizz as governor of Damascus as well to restore law and order in this strategic metropolis. Al-Muʿizz then placed Damascus under Raydan's authority.[91]

The chronicles mention that in the time of Caliph al-ʿAziz a number of eunuchs were governing small towns in Syria and Palestine. In 981 Bishara was *wali* of Tabaria and may have been *wali* of Hims a few years earlier; Raqyy was *wali* of Acre, Qaysariyya and Jaffa. In 993 Aphamia was under Wafaʾ, and Shayzar was under Sawsan (see Figure 5, which shows what is assumed to be a eunuch during the Fatimid era drinking wine – the beardless face with long hair around the ears, and feminine features, would suggest this is a eunuch).[92]

The number of eunuchs appointed as *wali*s was evidently not the only factor that determined their influence within the Fatimid rule; as argued by Yaacov Lev earlier, their influence and power were also derived from the offices that they occupied. With regard to numbers, there were about 10,000 eunuchs and concubines under al-ʿAziz. Al-Qalqashandi noted that the *muhannak ustadh* (the elite eunuchs in the Fatimid palace at the time), numbered more than a thousand.[93] So we may assume that eunuchs of lesser ranks numbered several thousands. Furthermore, if the caliphs and viziers were convinced that the use of eunuchs in civil and military posts would enhance their rule, they would not hesitate to purchase large numbers of them, notwithstanding their high prices, as long as they were good military elements. This lavish spending by the Fatimids is demonstrated well in the case of al-Afdal, the grand vizier; the chronicles describe the huge number of eunuchs during his time.

Interestingly, Ibn Taghri Bardi refers to the time of al-Hakim when he murdered Husayn b. Jawhar al-Siqilli: 'We mention Husayn here so Jawhar would not be counted as *khasi* like the others, but *fahl* (stallion), unlike

Table 5.1 Eunuchs holding the office of wali *under the Fatimids*

Wali/Governor	Province	Year of Rule
Bishara	Hims	975[b]
Bishara	Tabaria	981[a]
Bishara	Damascus	998[b]
Jawdhar	North Africa	969[b]
Mawsuf	Aleppo	1023[c]
Maysur	Tripoli – east	998[c]
Muflih	Damascus	1003[c]
Munir	Damascus	988–90[c]
Nasim	Qayrawan	926[b]
Nusayr	Beirut	975[c]
Raqi	Acre	981[a]
Raqi	Jaffa	981[a]
Raqi	Qaysariyya	981[a]
Raydan	Tripoli – east	974[b]
Raydan	Damascus	974–5[c]
Rifq	Damascus	1048[c]
Sa'd al-Dawla	Beirut	1102[b]
Sabir	Qayrawan	926[a]
Sandal	Barqa	1004[b]
Sawsan	Shayzar	993[b]
Wafa'	Aphamia	993[b]
Yanis	Barqa	996–8[c]
Yanis	Tripoli – west	1000[a]
Yumn	Ascalon	998[c]
Yumn	Ghazza	998[c]

Note: Owing to the scarcity of information about eunuchs, and the unknown date of appointment or dismissal of each governor, a given *wali* (governor) is listed as being in service as follows:

[a] held office after that year
[b] held office before that year
[c] known to have held office during that year

khadim (eunuch) Qaraqush, *ustadh* Kafur al-Ikhshidi, *khadim* Raydan, and others.' The same historian on other occasions repeats the distinguishing term '*ghayr khasi*' (not castrated), because of the huge numbers of eunuchs who were employed by the Fatimids.[94]

If we look panoramically, we will see that these large numbers of eunuchs in the Fatimid state, in addition to their rule of Sicily after the Aghlabids in Tunisia, had some kind of influence over the Norman court in Sicily in the twelfth century, and the significant use of Muslim eunuchs there. Ibn Jubayr, who visited the island in 1182, mentioned that King William II (d. 1189) had used a large number of *majbub* eunuchs (the type with their entire sexual organ removed) in his court, most of them Muslims.[95] Certainly, Sicily was part of the Roman–Byzantine heritage long before the short period of Muslim rule, but eunuchs under Byzantium were free citizens. So why did we see a majority of Muslim slave eunuchs in Norman Sicily, unless it was the Fatimid influence?

Titles of Eunuchs and their Ranks

Here I will try to survey the titles reflecting the status of each post holder as well as the positions held by powerful eunuchs in the state. Caliph al-Mansur wrote to his faithful eunuch Jawdhar in 946, when al-Mansur freed him: 'Do not precede your name with any other names except your lord Tamim (the future al-Mu'izz).' Also, al-Mansur bestowed upon Jawdhar the great honour of wearing the same gowns as the caliph, with an embroidered name, as only caliphs would have done.[96] That was an exceptional honour. If other eunuchs, such as Barjawan or Mi'dad, had a similar custom, it was because they seized it due to the weakness of the caliphate.

Throughout the first century of Fatimid rule (969–1073), titles such as '*al-quwwad*' (commander of all commanders) were given, for example, to Ghayn, in 1011, and Sana', who was called 'glory and majesty of the state'. 'Father of knights' was granted to the commander 'Izz al-Dawla. Granting a eunuch a title like 'father of knights' denoted more than just lingual prestige to a patrimonial authority, to compensate for his physical deficiency. Rifq enjoyed the titles 'chief commander, the victor, glory of the rule, pillar of the state'.[97] Such titles were applied to other elite eunuchs, and the titles were always associated with the state or the caliphate, like the last eunuch. His title was '*mu'taman al-khilafa*' (he who is trusted by the caliphate). The Fatimid titles surpassed the 'Abbasid ones granted to eunuchs, as well as those of other Muslim dynasties in medieval Islam.

The care and attention paid to some eunuchs was remarkable; for example, when Caliph al-Qa'im was on his deathbed in 946, the only advice he gave to his successor concerned Jawdhar. Al-Qa'im ordered al-Mansur to keep his eunuch in his high position. Al-Mansur replied: 'My lord, we count

Jawdhar only as one of us.' Al-Qa'im said: 'Indeed he is.' This exceptional prestigious treatment of Jawdhar continued under al-Mu'izz, who wrote to him: 'O, Jawdhar, we never differentiate between you and ourselves.'[98]

Some eunuch commanders won the honour of being visited by caliphs when they were ill. For example, al-Mu'izz visited Jawdhar more than once; Caliph al-Amir visited his veteran eunuch, Lami'; al-Hakim marched to visit Ghayn in his house in 1011. In addition to his unusual gesture, al-Hakim installed Ghayn as chief of police and *hisba*, as well as supervisor of finance and the treasury.[99]

Although the division of duties and responsibilities among the *hisba* officer, the judge and chief of police under the Fatimids is somewhat blurred, we can see the high status reached by some eunuchs; however, judicial authorities were denied to most of them, unlike Kafur in Egypt before them, or Qaraqush in Ayyubid Egypt after them. One of these exceptions was Barjawan who would sit for the *mazalim*, an office that required judicial knowledge[100] and commanded respect from the public. Some eunuchs had so much power and responsibility concentrated in their hands that they had to appoint deputies or viziers. Jawdhar had a deputy in al-Mahdiyya named Nusayr, who was also a eunuch. In 996 Barjawan appointed a secretary with the title of vizier, who continued in his position after the murder of Barjawan. In 1011 a servant in the service of Ghayn, named al-Wazzan, was appointed as *wasita* to the caliph.[101] That simply means that the eunuch became much more prominent than the *wasita*.

The political powers of some eunuchs were extended to commercial activities and private business. Some eunuchs enjoyed full freedom of trade to the degree that they owned their own commercial fleet; Jawdhar, for example, enjoyed the full blessing of al-Mu'izz. On a smaller scale, we find the Gadibu, and Lami', who accumulated considerable wealth from their lucrative trade on the Red Sea at the beginning of the twelfth century.[102]

In addition to the political–military involvement of Fatimid eunuchs, there are two lists: one mentioned by al-Qalqashandi, which shows their prominent positions in the administration; and the second, noted by al-Maqrizi, reflects the eminent position of eunuchs and their influence inside the caliphal palace. It ranks the most powerful leaders in the state after the caliph.

According to al-Qalqashandi, the *ustadhun* (chief eunuchs) occupied the highest status under the Fatimids. The most honourable among them was the *muhannak*. He received the second highest salary after the vizier. Al-Qalqashandi did not attach a certain date or period to his list:[103]

- Sahib al-Majlis – master of the audience, and councils
- Sahib al-Risala – master of correspondence; in charge of passing the caliphal correspondence to the vizier
- Sahib Bayt al-Mal – director of the treasury
- Sahib al-Zimam – major-domo; chief attendant of the palace
- Sahib al-Daftar – keeper of the registry; head of the *diwan*

All of the above were eunuchs with the rank of *muhannak ustadh*. Al-Maqrizi lists the following in his annals of 974 in order of importance, within and outside the palace:[104]

1. The caliph
2. Sahib al-Amwal – chief of finance
3. Sahib al-Shurta – chief of police
4. Sahib al-Mazalla – bearer of the parasol
5. Al-Tabib – Physician
6. Sahib Bayt al-Mal – Director of the treasury
7. Muhtasib – Observer of the markets and behavior of the locals

From the two lists, it is clear that every *mahannak ustadh* inside the palace was deeply involved in state affairs outside the palace, such as correspondence and treasury. Other offices, such as the *shurta* and *hisba*, were occupied by numerous eunuchs. It is worth pointing out that the ceremony of promoting a eunuch to *muhannak* was a prestigious one, and attended by the caliph himself.[105]

From al-Maqrizi's list, we see that the bearer of the parasol was the fourth most important post in the Fatimid state. This post was not a civil one, and it continued as part of the administration to the end of the dynasty. During al-Hakim's era, despite his asceticism, he kept someone in this post throughout most of his rule. The holder of the post was usually a eunuch – as with Shafi',

Raydan and Muzaffar – and they also played a role in the military.[106] That was normal for the parasol bearer, who was also bearer of the sword and acted as a bodyguard to the caliph, hence the holder of this office being one of the very few individuals to be constantly at the caliph's side.

From miscellaneous lines in the sources on the status and tasks of eunuchs, we know that the eunuch Jawdhar was entrusted with the standardisation of the weight of Fatimid coins. This had significant implications for the economic policy of the state. In addition, Jawdhar was also in charge of the royal prison where the Fatimid royals were imprisoned. Barjawan and Mi'dad had the same duty.[107] Such caliphal designation of these eunuchs indicated the caliph's complete confidence that they would control his rivals. Any act of treason from any of them could result in a change of the head of the realm.

In 1004, when al-Hakim had a new son (the future al-Zahir), the eunuch commander Shukr was in charge of the celebratory ceremonies, caring for the child while the caliph received the leaders of the state. Sources show that Caliph al-Amir would refrain from meeting anyone except his eunuch commanders, who guarded the tunnels from his palace inside the capital to the Nile outside the walls.[108]

Owing to their eminence in society, most of the eunuch commanders in the army had streets and avenues named after them (for example, *haret* (avenue) al-Rihaniyya, Yanisiyya and Jawdhariyya). Also mentioned is alley of Barjawan, which still exists today. These sections of Cairo were quite renowned, and the vizier Badr al-Jamali had a house in one of them. Saladin's deputy in Egypt, the eunuch Qaraqush (d. 1198), lived in al-Rihaniyya.[109] One of the gates of the royal palace was named after a eunuch of al-'Aziz. This gate was reserved only for the entrance of the viziers of the state.[110]

From evidence implicit in the sources, we can conclude that the eunuchs discussed here were viewed not with contempt but with esteem during most of the Fatimid period. Even chroniclers who came after the Fatimids and had the chance to criticise their nature and question why they were used in such eminent offices, treated the situation as normal. Nonetheless, poetry written at the beginning and the end of the Fatimid rule contains some defamatory lines relating to Fatimid eunuchs and their domination of the state. Some poets with their natural rebellious minds viewed eunuchs as a third gender and children of a lesser God. Ibn Bishr, a Damascene poet writing in 996 at the end of al-'Aziz's rule, wrote:

> Grant and hinder, and fear no one
> The lord of the palace (the caliph) is not in there
> He is not aware of their deeds and intentions
> Even if he was enlightened, he would still be ignorant.[111]

The poet here is criticising the vizier and the dominant entourage of the caliph, including Barjawan, as the major-domo of the palace.

Other defamatory lines were written at the decline of the Fatimid rule and on the rise of Saladin. Such lines should be viewed with caution as they reflect anti-Shi'i sentiment. They are cited here to present a fuller picture of the period, especially as lines directly concerning eunuchs are very rare. Al-Isfahani, secretary to Saladin, gave the following description of the confrontation between his lord and Mu'taman al-Khilafa Jawhar, the last Fatimid eunuch commander:[112]

> O, Yusuf – Saladin – of Egypt whom we all aspire to emulate
> You overcome the Sudanese by putting swords into them
> Mu'taman of the nation betrayed until death ended his evils
> He treated you with treason, thus his head now hangs from a spear

The poet compares Yusuf of Egypt with the Yusuf (Joseph) of the Bible and Qur'an, who also overcame various difficulties. The poet pours scorn on Mu'taman and the Sudanese troops who revolted with him in defence of the Fatimid rule. In an expression of contempt and disrespect towards eunuchs, Abu Shama mentions the lines of another poet, written at the time of the collapse of the Fatimids:[113]

> The reign, which belonged to the Fatimids
> Became shining with the Ayyubid kings
> The east envied the west for them, and Cairo prided itself over Baghdad
> Honour and integrity are achieved only by determination and the clash of swords
> Not like Pharaoh and Potiphar, and those in Egypt like stallion and eunuch.

Here, the poet equates the Fatimid rulers with the pharaohs as rulers of Egypt, demeaning the eunuchs in the Fatimid state, accusing them of weakness. Ironically, the Ayyubids started using eunuchs in the political–military system from the beginning of their rule. Saladin replaced Fatimid Jawhar with Ayyubud Qaraqush; the tradition continued until 1250 when the eunuch Muhsen imprisoned King Louis IX in Egypt during the Seventh Crusade.[114] Naturally here, the loyal court poet would not criticise the new eunuchs of his master.

Interestingly, when the 'Abbasid caliph al-Mustadi' was informed of the good news of the Fatimid downfall by Nur al-Din, the Zengid sultan of Syria and lord of Saladin, the caliph sent robes of honour to Nur al-Din, and Saladin in Egypt, in celebration of the downfall of the Fatimid dynasty. The caliph's envoy was Sandal, the chief eunuch of the caliphal palace in Baghdad.[115]

At the end of this chapter, we can assert the view that eunuchs were not individual third-gender slaves bought to serve individually at various levels within the Fatimid administration. Instead, they were an institution that grew in number and influence, particularly from Caliph al-Qa'im's rule up to al-Mustansir's era. Was this because of the Shi'i philosophy of *tuqya* (to conceal your true belief), so individuals such as eunuchs were believed by them to be more suitable for the system? They started to fade rapidly from the political–military life in the sources after the vizier al-Jamali's 'dynasty' took over the army and administration. However, they continued to undertake certain domestic tasks in the palace.

Many offices held by eunuchs had dual functions; the holder of the parasol was also holder of the sword and a bodyguard to the caliph. Deputies, such as Jawdhar and Barjawan, had religious–political and military functions.

As with the 'Abbasids, despite the respect shown to most eunuchs on the surface, they were never granted usual names like Muhammad, 'Ali or Ibrahim. Thus, it could be assumed that they were always distinguished as a third gender, which affected their basic humanistic equality. Such inequality, biological or social, was reflected in their personal ambitions and behaviour towards their masters in most cases. Various Muslim rulers used eunuchs because they assumed that they would get their absolute loyalty; however, eunuchs proved otherwise by developing their own ambitions in many situations as Islamic history developed.

I should add that no Shi'i jurist or scholar representing the Fatimid era, or a Sunni one representing the 'Abbasid period, criticised the use of the huge number of eunuchs in the state for civil or military services. Such state practice of charging high prices for eunuchs had encouraged the market to continue the vicious cycle of providing castrated slaves as long as there was a demand for it. This went against the shari'a, on the basis that it altered the creation of God. Eunuchs continued to greatly influence political life after the Fatimids, especially under the Ayyubids.

Notes

1. This study was first presented at the 19th Colloquium on the History of Egypt and Syria in the Fatimid, Ayyubid and Mamluk Eras, Gent, May 2010, organised by U. Vermeulen.
2. Abi 'Ali al-Jawdhari, *Sirat al-Ustadh Jawdhar*, ed. M. Husain, Cairo, 1954, p. 74.
3. Ibid., p. 39; M. Canard, art.: 'Djawdhar', *EI²*.
4. Ayalon, *Eunuchs*, p. 139.
5. Serena Tolino, 'Eunuchs in the Fatimid Empire: Ambiguities, Gender and Sacredness', in A. Hofert et al. (eds), *Celibate and Childless Men in Power: Ruling Eunuchs and Bishops in the Pre-modern World*, London, 2017, pp. 246–67.
6. Ibn Hawkal, *Surat*, Vol. 1, p. 110; F. Dachroui, art.: 'Al-Sakaliba', *EI²*; Lewis, *Race and Slavery*, p. 40; 'Abd Al-Mun'im Majid, *Nuzum al-Fatimiyyin wa Rusumihim fi Misr*, Cairo, 1985, Vol. 1, p. 28.
7. Pellat, 'Khasi'.
8. Serena Tolino, 'Eunuchs in the Fatimid Empire', p. 250.
9. Al-Jawdhari, *Sirat*, pp. 35–40.
10. Ibid., pp. 40–4; Canard, 'Djawdhar'.
11. Al-Jawdhari, *Sirat*, p. 44; Ibn 'Adhara al-Marakishi, *al-Mughrib*, Vol. 1, pp. 216–17.
12. Ibn al-Athir, *Al-Kamil*, Vol. 8, p. 215; al-Jawdhari, *Sirat*, p. 109; Ibn 'Adhara al-Marakishi, *al-Mughrib*, Vol. 1, p. 222.
13. Ibn al-Qalanisi, *Ta'rikh*, p. 74; Ibn al-Athir, *al-Kamil*, Vol. 9, p. 118.
14. Al-Maqrizi, *Itti'az*, Vol. 2, pp. 25, 26.
15. Ibn al-Athir, *Al-Kamil*, Vol. 9, 122.
16. Ibn Sa'id al-Antaki, *Ta'rikh*, p. 240; al-Maqrizi, *Itti'az*, Vol. 2, p. 28.
17. Al-Maqrizi, *Al-Khitat*, Vol. 1, p. 467.
18. Al-Qalqashandi, *Subh*, Vol. 3, p. 483.

19. Al-Maqrizi, *Itti'az*, Vol. 2, p. 26.
20. Ibid., p. 27.
21. Al-Jawdhari, *Sirat*, pp. 39–40.
22. Ibid., pp. 74, 139.
23. Ibid., p. 53.
24. Al-Qalqashandi, *Subh*, Vol. 3, p. 357; al-Maqrizi, *Al-Khitat*, Vol. 3, p. 7.
25. Tolino, 'Eunuchs', p. 255.
26. Ibn al-Qalanisi, *Ta'rikh*, pp. 74–5; Ibn al-Athir, *Al-Kamil*, Vol. 9, p. 118.
27. Al-Maqrizi, *Itti'az*, Vol. 1, p. 291.
28. Al-Yamani, *Ta'rikh*, pp. 67–8.
29. Ibn Muyassar, *Misr*, p. 100.
30. Al-Maqrizi, *Itti'az*, Vol. 3, p. 113.
31. Ibid.
32. Ibn Taghri Bardi, *Nujum*, Vol. 5, p. 240.
33. Ibn Taghri Bardi, *Nujum*, Vol. 4, p. 188.
34. Ibn Sa'id al-Antaki, *Ta'rikh*, p. 373; al-Maqrizi, *Itti'az*, Vol. 3, pp. 127–8, 156–7.
35. Al-Maqrizi, *Itti'az*, Vol. 2, pp. 148, 152, 169.
36. Majid, *Al-Sijillat*, no. 14; al-Hamdani, *Al-Sulayhiyyun*, p. 149.
37. Al-Maqrizi, *Itti'az*, Vol. 3, pp. 62–70.
38. Ibn al-Athir, *Al-Kamil*, Vol. 11, pp. 22–3.
39. Yaacov Lev, *State and Society in Fatimid Egypt*, Leiden, 1991, p. 75.
40. Ayalon, *Eunuchs*, p. 142.
41. Ibn Khaldun, *Al-'Ibar*, Beirut, 1990, Vol. 4, p. 40.
42. Ibid., pp. 47–8.
43. Ibn al-Athir, *Al-Kamil*, Vol. 8, pp. 422–5.
44. Al-Jawdhari, *Sirat*, p. 96.
45. Ibn al-Athir, *Al-Kamil*, Vol. 8, pp. 284–5.
46. Al-Maqrizi, *Itti'az*, Vol. 1, p. 202.
47. Ibn al-Qalanisi, *Ta'rikh*, pp. 19–20.
48. Al-Maqrizi, *Itti'az*, Vol. 1, p. 28.
49. Ibn Sa'id al-Antaki, *Ta'rikh*, p. 248; M. Canard, art.: 'Al-Hakim', *EI²*.
50. Ibn Sa'id al-Antaki, *Ta'rikh*, p. 347.
51. Al-Maqrizi, *Itti'az*, Vol. 2, p. 146.
52. Lev, *State and Society*, p. 74.
53. Al-Maqrizi, *Itti'az*, Vol. 2, pp. 140–57.
54. Ibid., p. 163.

55. Ibn al-Athir, *Al-Kamil*, Vol. 10, p. 364.
56. Al-Maqrizi, *Itti'az*, Vol. 3, p. 36.
57. Ibn al-Athir, *Al-Kamil*, Vol. 11, pp. 345–6.
58. Abu Shama, *Al-Rawdatayn*, Vol. 1, p. 178.
59. Ibn Sa'id al-Antaki, *Ta'rikh*, p. 132; Ibn Taghri Bardi, *Nujum*, Vol. 4, p. 362.
60. Al-Qalqashandi, *Subh*, Vol. 3, p. 363; al-Maqrizi, *Itti'az*, Vol. 2, p. 82.
61. Ibn Taghri Bardi, *Nujum*, Vol. 4, p. 192.
62. Al-Sayyed, *Al-Dawla*, pp. 725–6.
63. Al-Maqrizi, *Itti'az*, Vol. 3, p. 150.
64. Al-Maqrizi, *Al-Suluk*, Vol. 1, p. 187.
65. Aziz Ahmad, *A History of Islamic Sicily*, trans. A. Taibi, Tripoli, 1979, pp. 20–6, 32–3.
66. Al-Sayyed, *Al-Dawla*, p. 728, according to the tenth-century historian Ibn al-Tuwayr.
67. Ibn al-Athir, *Al-Kamil*, Vol. 8, pp. 113–14.
68. Ibid., p. 121.
69. Ibid., p. 284.
70. Al-Jawdhari, *Sirat*, pp. 103–5, 115, 135.
71. Ibn al-Athir, *Al-Kamil*, Vol. 8, p. 494.
72. Ibn Sa'id al-Antaki, *Ta'rikh*, p. 241; Ibn al-Qalanisi, *Ta'rikh*, p. 83; al-Maqrizi, *Itti'az*, Vol. 2, p. 18.
73. Al-Maqrizi, *Itti'az*, Vol. 2, p. 207.
74. Al-Maqrizi, *Al-Khitat*, Vol. 2, p. 45.
75. Al-Maqrizi, *Itti'az*, Vol. 1, p. 267.
76. Al-Maqrizi, *Itti'az*, Vol. 2, pp. 91, 94, 100.
77. Ibn Sa'id al-Antaki, *Ta'rikh*, pp. 309–10.
78. Muhammad b. 'Ubayd Allah al-Musabbihi, *Akhbar Misr*, ed. A. al-Sayyed, Cairo, 2001, Vol. 40, p. 47.
79. Lev, *State and Society*, p. 77.
80. Al-Jawdhari, *Sirat*, p. 109.
81. Ibn al-Athir, *Al-Kamil*, Vol. 9, p. 140.
82. Ibid., p. 154; al-Maqrizi, *Itti'az*, Vol. 2, pp. 17, 34, 37.
83. Ibn Sa'id al-Antaki, *Ta'rikh*, p. 260.
84. Ibn al-Qalanisi, *Ta'rikh*, pp. 19–20; Ibn al-Athir, *Al-Kamil*, Vol. 8, p. 643.
85. Ibn al-Qalanisi, *Ta'rikh*, pp. 52–3; Ibn Taghri Bardi, *Nujum*, Vol. 4, p. 153.
86. Ibn al-Qalanisi, *Ta'rikh*, p. 87; according to the same chronicler, the eunuch Muflih was installed as a *wali* for one year in 1003, p. 101.

87. Ibid., p. 139; Al-Maqrizi, *Itti'az*, Vol. 2, p. 202.
88. Ibn al-'Adim, *Zubdat*, Vol. 1, pp. 227–8.
89. Al-Maqrizi, *Itti'az*, Vol. 1, pp. 218–22.
90. Ibn al-Athir, *Al-Kamil*, Vol. 10, p. 364.
91. Ibid., p. 370.
92. Ibn al-Qalanisi, *Ta'rikh*, pp. 377–87; Ibn Sa'id al-Antaki, *Ta'rikh*, pp. 225–6.
93. Al-Qalqashandi, *Subh*, Vol. 3, p. 481; Lev, *State and Society*, p. 87.
94. Ibn Taghri Bardi, *Nujum*, Vol. 4, pp. 34, 73.
95. Ibn Jubayr, *Rihla*, pp. 266–7.
96. Al-Jawdhari, *Sirat*, p. 52.
97. Al-Maqrizi, *Itti'az*, Vol. 2, pp. 101–2, 140, 146, 202.
98. Al-Jawdhari, *Sirat*, p. 43, 44, 97.
99. Ibn Sa'id al-Antaki, Ta'rikh, p. 309; al-Maqrizi, *Itti'az*, Vol. 2, p. 91, Vol. 3, p. 125; al-Jawdhari, *Sirat*, p. 136.
100. Al-Maqrizi, *Itti'az*, Vol. 2, p. 14.
101. Ibn al-Athir, *Al-Kamil*, Vol. 9, p. 122; al-Jawdhari, *Sirat*, p. 98; al-Maqrizi, *Itti'az*, Vol. 2, p. 94.
102. Al-Jawdhari, *Sirat*, p. 136; al-Maqrizi, *Itti'az*, Vol. 3, p. 125.
103. Al-Qalqashandi, *Subh*, Vol. 3, pp. 481–5, 525.
104. Al-Maqrizi, *Itti'az*, Vol. 1, p. 216.
105. Al-Maqrizi, *Itti'az*, Vol. 2, p. 163; al-Qalqashandi, *Subh*, Vol. 3, pp. 481–5.
106. Al-Musabbihi, *Akhbar Misr*, p. 131; al-Maqrizi, *Itti'az*, Vol. 2, pp. 33, 39, 48.
107. Al-Jawdhari, *Sirat* pp. 91, 141; al-Maqrizi, *Itti'az*, Vol. 2, pp. 127–8.
108. Al-Maqrizi, *Itti'az*, Vol. 2, p. 58, Vol. 3, p. 81.
109. Al-Qalqashandi, *Subh*, Vol. 3, pp. 356–63; Ibn Taghri Bardi, *Nujum*, Vol. 4, pp. 48–51; al-Maqrizi, *Al-Khitat*, Vol. 3, p. 20.
110. Al-Maqrizi, *Al-Khitat*, Vol. 2, p. 45.
111. Ibn al-Athir, *Al-Kamil*, Vol. 9, p. 117.
112. Cited in Abu Shama, *Al-Rawdatayn*, Vol. 1, p. 178.
113. Ibid., p. 200.
114. Al-Maqrizi, *Al-Suluk*, Vol. 1, pp. 455–6.
115. Ibn al-Athir, *Al-Kamil*, Vol. 11, p. 371.

6

The Seljuqs from Syria to Iran: The Age of *Khatuns* and *Atabegs*

> They, women, give orders following what they have been told by those who work amongst them, such as courtesans; naturally, their opinions and commands are the opposite of what is wise and right. As a result, mischief ensues, the dignity of the king suffers and people are afflicted with crisis; disorder affects the state as well as the religion, due to their opinions.[1]

This cynical anti-women view was expressed by the chief architect of the Seljuqid administration, Nizam al-Mulk (d. 1092), in his book *Siyasat Nameh* (*Rules for Kings*). He was a Persian grand vizier for his lords, the Turkmen Seljuqs. The Muslim Middle East from Transoxiana to Anatolia and the Levant underwent a huge transformation in the middle of the eleventh century with the arrival of the Seljuqs.

The Seljuqs were from the Qiniq clan, one of twenty-two clans forming the Oghuz tribe of Turkmen in Mongolia and western China.[2] They were named after their chief, Prince Seljuq. Their history while they were in Mongolia is shrouded in mystery; as they were part of larger and other groups of Turkmen tribes they were mentioned mainly in the Chinese archive, in addition to the eighth-century Orkhon inscriptions of Mongolia.[3]

The Seljuqs, who were Shamanists until the late tenth century and early eleventh, moved westwards to the Steppes of Russia around the Aral Sea, and Transoxania. It was at about this time that they were converted to Sunni Islam. As C. Cahen states: 'It is still to be ascertained what form of Islam had been taught to them and how much of it they did in fact absorb at first.'[4] They, like many Barbarian people before them in the old world, offered their service as auxiliary troops to warring powers in the area, mainly the Ghaznavids and the Qarakhanids in Transoxania and Khurasan. They were very well-trained horsemen (and women) due to their nomadic lifestyle.

In 1038 their chief, Tughril Beg, defeated the Ghaznavids in the decisive Battle of Dandaqan, and claimed himself as sultan.[5] In 1055 he made his triumphant entry to Baghdad, ending the Shi'i Buwayhid domination, and officially establishing the fourth and final 'Abbasid period in Iraq. The Seljuqs, who ruled until 1194, had their power base in Iraq and Iran, with two main branches in Syria and Anatolia.[6] The decisive victory of the Seljuqs over the Byzantine emperor in Manzikert in 1071 had literally created a tsunami of Turkmen emigration from Central Asia to Iran, Iraq, Syria and, especially, to Anatolia. That had contributed to a change in and redistribution of demography and ethnicities such as Kurds, Arabs, Syriacs and Armenians, among others. In addition, it led to a millennium of Turkification of these areas, especially in the military and feudal systems. Many other Turkmen dynasties were born from within their rule, following their traditions, for example, the Burids in Syria, and the Zengids in Iraq and Syria, in addition to the Ahmadilis, Eldiguzids and Salghurids in Iran.[7] The Ayyubids were also Turkicised, and Ottomans were Oghuz, too.

While the Seljuq nomads depended on sophisticated Persian bureaucracy, as the Arabs did before them, the Seljuq political–military administration was characterised by their introduction to the *atabeg* post, which, contrary to the original aims of this post, contributed to the disintegration of their empire. That was associated with the rise of several ambitious mothers or *khatun* (the Turkic–Sogdian word for queen or lady),[8] especially after the death of Malik Shah in 1092.

In this chapter, I will try to examine the women and power twofold: (1) women and their interference in order to seize or secure the rule for themselves or their allies; and (2) the introduction of the *atabeg* office and its association with political marriage, and how it influenced Muslim history for centuries.

Women and their Interference in Order to Seize or Secure the Rule

Khatuns in Iran

'God Ulgen created the world with the help of Goddess Aq-Ana (white mother) (from the Er-Sogotoh Turkic legend)'.[9]

As mentioned by Carole Hillenbrand, the death of the Seljuqid sultan Malik Shah in 1092 was the start of an *annus horribilis*, with a long civil war breaking out in the Muslim Middle East that resulted in many years of instability.[10]

Malik Shah had four sons: Mahmud, Berkyaruk, Muhammad and Sanjar. When Malik Shah died, his wife Turkan Khatun (Turkan is Turkish for queen),[11] was by his side in Baghdad. She concealed the news of his death to prevent her rivals from jumping on the throne. She contacted the commanders of the army and secured their loyalty and oath for her son, in return for lavishly rewarding them.[12]

Turkan was a Turkmen Qarakhanid princess, sister to the lord of Bukhara and Samarqand. During the reign of Malik Shah, she had her own *diwan*, administered by Taj al-Mulk al-Shirazi. That was a sign of power and great distinction compared to the other wives of Malik Shah, such as Zubayda Khatun, mother of Berkyaruk and paternal cousin of Malik Shah. Some chroniclers accused her of hiring assassins to kill Nizam al-Mulk weeks before her husband's death, due to his advice to the sultan to nominate his eldest son, Berkyaruq, as successor, while she wanted to nominate her son. Turkan was eager to nominate one of her sons as successor; she did manage to secure agreement on this from her husband Malik Shah, but both of them died before her wish could be enacted.[13]

Turkan wanted to secure the transition of power to her very young son, Mahmud, who was only four years old.[14] She dispatched a large army to Isfahan, the political seat of government, and managed with the help of Emir Karbugha to seize the citadel and install her own deputy. In addition, she managed to arrest and imprison the half-brother of her son, Berkyaruk, who had threatened her agenda.

Turkan's close involvement with the military was preceded by another Turkmen *khatun*: Ilturinjan (d. 1060), wife of Sultan Tughril, in 1058.

During the havoc that accompanied the Seljuq entry to Iraq, and their confrontations with al-Basasiri, the Fatimid ally, Tughril, was besieged in Hamadan. His wife marched in person with the army, carrying several treasures to him.[15] Nothing else is mentioned about this event, but it reflects the relative independence of Turkmen women in crucial times.

The question here is: how was it that a woman could march with the army and instruct several commanders to follow her orders? The answer is in this anecdote by Abu al-Fida': 'They brought out the treasures, mountains of weapons and arms, and distributed them among her supporters upon the orders of Khatun.'[16] In addition, she had loyal advisors and assistants; she depended on the military chief of the army, Unar, while delegating the administration to the chief of her *diwan*, Taj al-Mulk al-Shirazi, who was installed as a vizier.

Turkan contacted Caliph al-Muqtadi (d. 1094), requesting that he recognise her boy as the new sultan, and declare the *khutba* in his name. It seems that Turkan wanted to become a queen–regent as well; however, but the caliph refused, only agreeing in principle to the *khutba*, but under the guardianship of Unar as commander of the army, and al-Shirazi as vizier, but not her.

Turkan's luck does not end there; she was the mother-in-law of the caliph, as al-Muqtadi had married her daughter, and they had a son named Ja'far who was at that time in Turkan's court.[17] When the caliph was hesitant or reluctant to accept her conditions, she waved the card of Ja'far, suggesting installing him as a new caliph in Isfahan. This daring strategy, only thought of once before by Ibn Tulun in Egypt in the ninth century, made al-Muqtadi dispatch the grand scholar al-Ghazali (d. 1111) in person to meet Turkan. Al-Ghazali met her, and convinced her to send back Ja'far to his father, in return for the Friday sermon being declared in the name of Mahmud in Baghdad and the Hijaz.[18] During these events, some loyal troops of the assassinated vizier Nizam al-Mulk found out about the imprisonment of Berkyaruk. They stormed his prison and freed him. The *khutba* was then declared in Isfahan in his name.

For two years Turkan was involved in the political–military affairs of the state, complicated by bitter civil war. She managed to challenge the male-dominated institutions, with the help of some male advisors. We often see the phrase 'Khatun dispatched the armies to fight'. Having said that, she, like Arwa, her contemporary in Yemen, never used or depended on other women as regards her politics.

When her army was defeated at Barujard in Iran in 1093, Turkan contacted Isma'il b. Yaquti b. Chaghri Beg, maternal uncle of Berkyaruk and ruler of Azerbaijan. She proposed to marry him, and supplied him with money and troops to protect her interests. Not only that, but 'she declared his name in the *khutba* and minted it on the dinar after her son in Isfahan'.[19] For a woman to initiate marriage, or decide to whom the *khutba* should be declared, and to mint the dinar according to the ruler of her selection, was a challenging step at that time. The marriage did not take place, as Isma'il was defeated by his nephew Berkyaruk.

The commander of Turkan's army and chief assistant, Unar, did not welcome the presence of Isma'il. As a result, Isma'il deserted Turkan's camp, and took refuge at the camp of his sister, Zubayda Khatun, mother of his nephew and enemy, Berkyaruk. Zubayda forgave her brother.[20] However, it seems that Isma'il did not appreciate the pardon of his sister, and conspired with some commanders to seize power. He was killed in September 1093 with the knowledge of Zubayda, who turned a blind eye to the matter in the interests of her son.[21]

Turkan Khatun did not lose hope and contacted Tutush, king of Syria and a brother of Malik Shah, in order to form pact with him. Not only that, but at about the same time, in July 1094, she dispatched Unar to fight another Seljuqid royal, Turan Shah, in order to seize most of western Iran from him.[22] Unar failed in his mission, and three months later Turkan Khatun died from illness in Isfahan. She instructed Unar to maintain the shrinking realm of her son. The following month, in November 1094, Mahmud died of smallpox. The political ambition of Turkan as a queen mother had come to a sudden end. Despite the numerous challenges she faced, she did manage to keep the strategic Isfahan for herself and her son. In addition, she was capable of gathering 10,000 knights to be at her service.[23]

C. E. Bosworth states: 'The vizier – Nizam al-Mulk – doubtless had Turkan in mind when, in the *Siyasat Nama*, he denounced the malevolent influence of women at court.' In addition to that, al-Isfahani asked why

Turkan, and not Zubayda (although both of them were princesses), took the lead when her husband died. He reflected some negative remarks on gender and politics, but not as strong as al-Yazdi, who repeated the tradition of the Prophet in describing her interference in politics: 'Turkan is a woman; so naturally of a lesser mind and religion. To obey or follow women is a regret.'[24]

Clearly, several contemporary and medieval chroniclers were anti-women, which made Turkan, who was a contemporary of Arwa in Sulayhid Yemen, or the queen mother of Fatimid al-Musta'li, more liberal, but as mentioned before, it was out of political pragmatism and need more than believing in women in power.

Moving to Zubayda Khatun, mother of Berkyaruk, in addition to agreeing to murder her brother for the benefit of her son, she interfered in 1095 in her son's sultanate by dismissing the vizier Mu'ayyad al-Mulk, and installing Fakhr al-Mulk, who had contacted her about the post and offered a large amount of money to her.[25] There is no sign of her having a *diwan* of her own, nor is there detailed information of a *wakil* (agent) for her, but she did not have long to influence her son as she was mysteriously killed four years later, while Berkyaruk was away fighting in a civil war.[26]

Apart from the two *khatun*s mentioned above featuring in the sources, other women and their influence in Iranian affairs are really no more than fragmented anecdotes, with no fuller picture to provide a better understanding. Nearly all cases are concerned with women as royal envoys, or trying to get to power with local lords in fluid political situations.

For example, in 1064 after the death of Tughril Beg, we see Alp Arslan and his brother, Qawurt, quarrel over Iran. Alp Arslan entrusted his beloved sister, Jawhar Khatun, to be his envoy to Qawurt, and she managed to ease the pressure between the two warlords.[27] In 1114 Sultan Sanjar (d. 1157), lord of eastern Iran, attacked Arslan Shah (d. 1117), Ghaznavid lord of Ghazna. When Sanjar achieved victory, Arslan sent his uncle's wife, Jawhar Khatun, a Seljuqid princess and sister of Sanjar, seeking a pardon. Jawhar Khatun, who was offended by the manner of Arslan Shah and his courtesans towards her, did a deal with her brother. She informed him about the inner situation of the realm. The result was that Sanjar deposed Arslan and appointed Arslan's brother, Bahram, in his place.[28]

Again, in 1119, when Sanjar had heavily defeated his young nephew Mahmud II after a long confrontation in Iran, we see the latter's mother interfering. She wrote to Sanjar asking for a pardon for her son: 'You have seized all lands in addition to Ghazna and its dominions, Transoxiana, and other territories with endless count. You organised and installed their rulers and deputies according to your wishes. Make young Mahmud, your nephew, like one of them.'[29] Sanjar, who of course used realpolitik like any other Turkmen lord, accepted her wish, although family ties to the Seljuqs were not prioritised.

From these two anecdotes, we can say that these two *khatun*s were accidentally involved in politics with no personal ambition. Other incidental lines about women in the chronicles reflect male historian marginalisation of the other gender. Having said that, there was a new shift in the gender of the harem under the rule of some Seljuqid sultans, from women to *ghilman*. This term, as mentioned in the Introduction, is touched on in the Qur'an, meaning 'young beardless beautiful boys to serve the faithful in paradise'. Another very common meaning of the term from the early 'Abbasid period to the Seljuqs, was 'young military *mamluks*'. In some cases, they were private servants in the palaces.

The twelfth-century pro-Seljuqid chronicler al-Isfahani accused some of their sultans of homosexuality, and of empowering some of their young *mamluks* or *ghilman*, creating a unique semi-parallel harem for them. Consider these two anecdotes:

> Sultan Mahmud II owned young *mamluks*, beautiful as the moons. They were guarded by eunuchs, who were watching over them, in addition to other watchers from within themselves. Each one of them had his share of wealth and company around the palace. The sultans created unlimited licentious methods to enjoy these *ghilman*. That was the ninth reason for the decline of the realm.[30]

It was the norm in the sources that when someone was compared to the moon, it indicated beauty and desire. In this case, Mahmud II, the Suljuqid sultan, due to his sexual behaviour, had created a parallel institution, but with an unknown level of influence, as the following anecdote clearly shows.

Zahir al-Din, chamberlain of Sultan Sanjar I, said:

> Sultan Sanjar would follow a habit. He would buy a *ghulam*, which he would select. He would love him passionately, and their relationship would become well known. He would offer him his wealth and his soul, and spend night and day with him. He would empower his rule and sultanate to him. After he took his course with that *ghulam*, he would desert him, and then find his rest in killing him. One of these famous mamluks was Sunqur (note that *ghulam* here is used interchangeably with *mamluk*), who was bought with 1,200 dinars. Sanjar ordered me – the chamberlain:
>
> 'Here is my private *mamluk* Sunqur. Delight of my eye, fruit of my heart, aroma of my soul, and the result of my aim. Here are my treasures and wealth at his will. The taxes of Ghazna and Khwarazm just arrived; give them to Sunqur. Other revenues from far and near realms will be displayed to him.
>
> O, Zahir al-Din, do not refer to me or ask my permission in any matter related to him, just do it. I order you to erect a pavilion for him like mine. Bring him racing horses like mine. Buy him 1,000 *mamluk*s to march in his company when he does, and serve him at night. I delegate you to take any *iqta'* from any holder and allocate it to Sunqur. Or take any town and give it to him too. Bring another treasure like mine; fill it with money, different kinds of jewellery, just for him. Establish a *diwan* for him, with the service of best *katib*s (secretaries) and agents. In two weeks' time, Sunqur should own 10,000 knights.'
>
> I asked the sultan for a three-month period to implement these orders. He refused. He gave me only six weeks, during which time I spent 700,000 dinars, in addition to endless wealth from the sultan's treasure and numerous *iqta'*. After a month, the sultan arrived and saw the new troops of Sunqur in lines, in addition to the horses around the pavilion; he was delighted and embraced me. After two years of domination of most of his commanders and emirs, Sanjar became weary of Sunqur and ordered his assassination in favour of another *ghulam*.[31]

These events took place in about 1123. The difference between these *ghilman* bought for certain sexual pleasure and empowered by the sultan, and the concubines, also bought at the slave market, is that the latter might use her male child by the caliph to gain power, while a *ghulam* had a shorter, but condensed, political life. If we are to believe al-Isfahani, a force of 10,000 knights bought for Sunqur was equal to any large army of most states and provinces of the age, let alone the lavish spending, which might even have surpassed the 'Abbasid model.

This parallel harem for the *ghilman* and *mamluk*s was similar to the eunuchs around the 'Abbasid caliph al-Amin, as already discussed. The *ghilman* and sexuality in some periods of Seljuqid history might be one of the reasons for the marginalisation of women and their interference in politics. That will be discussed later in this chapter.

Khatuns and Other Women in Syria and Iraq

Syria was invaded by the Seljuqs in 1070, who seized Aleppo and Jerusalem from the Fatimids. Five years later Damascus and inland Syria followed the same fate, while the coast remained under the Fatimids until the Crusaders arrived. Syria was ruled by the brother of Malik Shah, King Tutush I (d. 1095). The death of Malik Shah certainly had its impact on Syria as well.

In 1093 King Tutush marched from Syria to Iran seeking his fortune as a sultan as well as a king. He managed to seize the city of Mosul in Iraq from the Arab 'Uqaylids, vassals to the Seljuqs. Within this delicate fluid situation, Tutush appointed his aunt, Safiyya the 'Uqaylid, and her son 'Ali as his deputies.[32] It was very significant to have a woman as a deputy ruler in a major Iraqi city, safeguarding his lines of communication, while he advanced eastwards to protect and keep the link with his dominions in the west. Safiyya was a capable woman who managed to keep Mosul under Tutsh's authority for more than eighteen months. That enabled him to control Diyar Bakr and Azerbaijan while he devoted his efforts to fight his nephew, Berkyaruk.[33] Certainly, Safiyya had achieved that through her powerful status among her Arab tribe, but with the presence of a male figure at her side – her son (unlike Queen Sajah, who appeared in the neighbouring Arab area in Iraq centuries earlier).

In Syria another civil war erupted between two sons of Tutush: Ridwan in Aleppo, and Duqaq in Damascus after Tutush was killed in Iran. Khatun Safwat al-Mulk (d. 1119), wife of Tutush until 1093, married his commander Tughtekin (d. 1128), and became involved in politics. Tughtekin was appointed as an *atabeg* (this will be discussed shortly) for her young son, Duqaq. Just as Khayzuran had behaved before with her son, al-Hadi, under the early 'Abbasids, according to Ibn 'Asakir, in 1104 Khatun Safwat al-Mulk decided to murder her son. Not only that, but she supervised the process in order to secure the realm for her husband Tughtekin and herself. Safwat had ordered a concubine in her court to feed Duqaq poisoned grapes until he perished, while the *khatun* was watching from a distance.[34]

It could be believed that Khatun Safwat al-Mulk, in coordination with her husband, feared Duqaq becoming more independent in his rule, and would no longer need his *atabeg* and influential mother. For three months she had her infant grandson, King Tutush II, king of Damascus and southern Syria, under the guardianship of her husband. Tughtekin removed her grandson from the throne, for unknown reasons, and brought in the half-brother of her murdered son, Artash, who was also a young boy.[35] Due to the strong resistance of Khatun Safwat al-Mulk to that threat to the new boy king, Artash took the advice of his own mother and escaped his realm after only a month on the throne, seeking help from the Crusaders in Jerusalem. Thereupon, Khatun Safwat al-Mulk re-installed her grandson to power.[36]

Here we see a mother who conspired and killed her monarch son, replacing him according to her own wishes, for the political benefit of herself and her husband. When her husband tried to act independently, he was resisted and was forced by her to reinstate her candidate to the throne. The *khatun* continued to influence her husband's career significantly, as will be discussed shortly.

Moving to another case of *khatuns* in Syria and their power relations, during the final year of the Seljuqid realm of Aleppo, a turbulent situation, both militarily and politically, emerged. After the sudden assassination in May 1117 of the powerful regent Lu'Lu', the seventeen-year-old Seljuqid king Sultan Shah was incapable of controlling the chaotic situation in his realm, and this was accompanied by riots and looting by the locals of Aleppo for two days. In addition to that, the Turkmen lord al-Bursuqi of Mosul was hovering to capture the ailing Aleppo,[37] the key to northern Syria and large parts of the Jazira.

In the midst of this turbulence, we find Princess Amina Khatun, daughter of King Ridwan b. Tutush, keeping the citadel of Aleppo under her direct control. The citadel, formidable as it always had been, was the political–military nerve of the city and the realm. Amina contacted the former *isfahsalar* (chief of the army), Yaruqtash, in Damascus, inviting him to come to Aleppo. She installed him as a regent for her incapable brother and monarch, Sultan Shah. As a result, stability was restored in this highly important commercial centre.[38] Just after one month in office, Yaruqtash conspired to seize power for himself. His plot was discovered by the agents of Amina Khatun, who ordered his arrest and exile from Aleppo, in order to minimise any coup from collaborating troops loyal to him. Amina, with her sister, Farkhinds Khatun, installed one of their father's commanders as keeper of the citadel. In addition, they installed another regent for their futile brother–king.[39]

It was a unique case in Seljuqid northern Syria of a *khatun* acting as commander of the formidable citadel of Aleppo. She interfered in the political arena, dictating its course and achieving her aims. The question here is: why did Amina Khatun, after realising the political futility of her brother in the midst of this turbulent situation, not come forward as ruler of Aleppo? We have to take into consideration that she had the tools of controlling the army and diplomacy to contact elite individuals outside her realm, as she did with Damascus. All that took place while the Crusaders of Antioch were sharing the countryside with Aleppo, and were less than a day's march from her dominions.

The last *khatun* in this category is no less significant than the two before her. Zumurrud Khatun bt. Chawli, half-sister of Duqaq through his mother Safwat al-Mulk. Zumurrud was the wife of Buri b. Tughtekin and mother of his sons Isma'il and Mahmud, kings of Damascus.[40]

In 1132 Isma'il b. Buri became king of Damascus, leading a daring and successful war against the Crusaders of Jerusalem, in addition to his fight against the formidable Seljuqid vassal, Zengi, lord of Aleppo and Mosul, who had been attacking Damascus and its dominions for the previous six years.[41] In that year Isma'il conducted a very violent strategy against his and his father's commanders in the realm. He confiscated their wealth, and he killed one of his own brothers for no apparent reason. Strangely enough, King Isma'il had contacted Zengi, inviting him to come and take over Damascus; he threatened Zengi that if he did not come and take his life's ambition (Damascus), Isma'il would surrender it to the nearby Crusaders.

The commanders of the army were alarmed by this move, and naturally feared the rule of Zengi and the threat to their careers. The commanders went and complained to his mother, Zumurrud Khatun, who then ordered the killing of her son.[42] This argument from Ibn al-Qalanisi and Ibn 'Asakir, among other chroniclers, is not convincing as it stands, since Isma'il was victorious against Zengi's deputies. Such a sudden shift in policy could come only from an insane person.

Since our concern here is not the political affairs of Isma'il as much as the role of women in politics, we see a different story by Ibn al-'Adim stating lucidly that Zumurrud Khatun was having an affair with Isma'il's *hajib*, Fayruz. Her son knew of the affair and wanted to take revenge on Fayruz and the commanders under his authority.[43] Therefore, Zumurrud wanted to save her own life, fearing the punishment of her son; in addition, she wanted to secure the realm of Damascus under her control.

The fact that the commanders of the army contacted her for help (as was the case with the commanders who contacted Sitt al-Mulk under the Fatimids) reflects her eminent status and shows that women were not fully isolated from male circles. Zumurrud commissioned her own *mamluk*s (troops) to assassinate her son in the citadel of Damascus on 14 February 1135. Not only that, but she was present while her son was being killed, screaming for mercy and pardon in Turkish: '*Zanhar, zanhar* (peace, peace).' The sources observe: 'She ordered her *mamluk*s to kill him, feeling no mercy for him; then she ordered his corpse to be thrown into a clear spot of the palace to be seen by his *mamluk*s and supporters. As a result, blessings were called upon her.'[44]

The sheer fact that Zumurrud Khatun did not trust her son's *mamluk*s and let her own carry out the murder reflects her capability to manoeuvre within military circles at a critical moment. In addition, her son's spies did not manage to uncover her plot. Afterwards, Zumurrud installed her other son, Mahmud, lord of Tadmur, as king in Damascus, and she sat with him side by side while the commanders of the army, the soldiers, and nobles and elites of the realm were forced to swear their oath of loyalty to both of them. That was a paradigm shift in gender and politics. It was unprecedented in Seljuqid Damascus for a princess to end the career and life of a king, install another and compel the commanders, politicians and religious figures, such as jurists and scholars, to recognise her as a queen–regent:

Mahmud was announced as king in the presence of his mother, the *khatun*. Emirs, soldiers and nobles were forced to recognise him and give the oath of allegiance to both of them, that they would sincerely serve both, and support their supporters and fight their enemies.[45]

Zumurrud Khatun achieved in Damascus what Turkan Khatun had failed to achieve in Iraq some four decades earlier, with no objection from the caliphate. For more than three years Zumurrud dominated the rule of her son Mahmud in Damascus and southern Syria, until May 1138. She invited her former lover, Fayruz, back to Damascus and installed him as regent for Mahmud, and then appointed him as deputy of the city of Hims in 1136.[46] When the queen consort decided to invite him back to Damascus as commander of the army, the serving commander Baswaj and a number of other emirs contacted her, requesting that Fayruz should be kept out of Damascus.[47] That confirms the view that she, and not young Mahmum, was the de facto ruler of the realm.

Due to the successful strong Seljuqid military resistance to the attacks and campaigns of Zengi in Hims and Damascus, Zengi decided to propose marriage to Zumurrud in 1138, as this was the only way in his mind to achieve his political aims. She completely retired from politics and went to live with her new husband in Aleppo; however, when her son was murdered the following year, she asked Zengi to avenge his killing and invade Damascus.[48]

We cannot escape the comparison of Zumurrud with her contemporary in faraway Yemen, Queen Arwa, and with her immediate neighbours in the Crusader Kingdom of Jerusalem, with its European heritage of women participating in power, like Queen Melisende. William of Tyre mentioned that in 1127 King Baldwin II of Jerusalem (d. 1131) had the approval of his commanders to change the law in his kingdom. He made it legal for royal women to inherit the throne through cognate succession. Baldwin had no male children.[49]

Two years later, in 1129, Princess Melisende married Fulk, count of Anjou, and they ruled the kingdom together; thus, Melisende granted him legitimacy to the throne. She ruled the kingdom with him as a real partner, running all affairs, even against his will. For example, she was the one to stop him from interfering in Antioch's domestic affairs in 1136. As a result, she enabled her sister, Princess Alix, to return to the principality of Antioch from exile and assume control of the rule despite the opposition of the barons there.[50] That took place at the same time as queen consort Zumurrud Khatun was the co-ruler of Damascus. Were the Seljuqs influenced by their European Crusader neighbours? Or was it simply a basic political survival instinct flavoured with political ambition for Zumurrud Khatun? We should bear in mind that communication between the two realms was uninterrupted, and no details escaped either of the two co-queens. Perhaps a comparative study of women and power between the Christian and Muslim sides is required to provide a better understanding and to answer these questions.

Women between Political Marriage and the Foundation of the *Atabeg* Institution

Political marriage had always been used as a tool to establish and improve political relations between two competing powers in Islamic medieval times. Between the narrow aims of the individuals and the wider need of the ruling dynasty, there were varying degrees of success and failure. The common feature is that women always traded for the benefit of the men: father, brother or son. As discussed earlier, the Prophet had used it with several allies, and the first four caliphs were attached to him by such marriages.

Under the 'Abbasids, some marriages like the one between the caliph and the daughter of the Tulunid ruler of Egypt, Khumarawayh, had led to the return of Egypt to the 'Abbasid political orbit. Under the Fatimids, the vizier al-Afdal, who gave his daughter Sitt al-Mulk to a younger son of the caliph al-Mustansir, made him use the relationship, and in 1094 he appointed his son-in-law as a new caliph, creating a schism in the Fatimid state.

Under the Seljuqs and their dependants, the situation was different, as they used it to create a new distinguished socio-political institution – *atabeg* – in which women played a key role.

We will look first into the traditional political marriages and their impact before we examine the *atabeg* system. Between the Seljuqs and the 'Abbasids, political marriage continued to be used in numerous cases; Seljuqid women were successful in this endeavour, whereas 'their 'Abbasid counterparts were all but written out of the narrative'.[51] I might add that, while all the marriages since the foundation of the 'Abbasids were confined to 'bride-taking' or where the 'Abbasid male was the one who would marry the foreign bride, the Seljuqs bravely changed this paradigm in Islamic history. In 1063, at the age of seventy, the grand Seljuqid sultan Tughril Beg dared to ask the 'Abbasid caliph al-Qa'im for his daughter's hand in marriage.[52] (The sultan was a free man, and not of slave origin, like the vizier of al-Rashid who wanted to marry al-Rashid's sister, as previously mentioned.) This was considered a calamity to the 'Abbasids, because any 'Abbasid princess was considered a noble aristocratic Hashemite Arab, a descendant of the Prophet, whereas the Seljuqs, or any others, were considered simply as barbaric or inferior (even though only two 'Abbasid caliphs in the entire dynasty were born to free mothers). However, only the male lineage mattered here.

After a long wait and negotiations with the insistent sultan, who would not be angered by the weaker 'Abbasids, the 'Abbasids devised a spoof 'incomplete' marriage (in other words, a sham marriage). They told the sultan: 'The aim of this marriage is to gain the honour (for the sultan), not to be with her alone. If seeing her is necessary, the sultan should do that at the caliph's palace.' The sultan agreed, and saw her once, while she was covering her face; she did not stand to greet him, and he kissed the ground before her.[53] The sultan died shortly afterwards, while the bride died in 1102 in Baghdad.[54]

Why did such a strong sultan like the Seljuqid Tughril Beg accept such humiliation, if indeed he himself considered it as such? What would he gain from this brief, 'visually blurred' encounter, with the bride covering her face? On the other hand, how would the 'Abbasid caliph benefit? The answer is that he would gain social legitimacy.[55] The sultan would claim that the Seljuqs, who were newly converted to Islam, coming from Mongolia, were now bonded to the noble house of the Prophet. That would elevate his dynasty above any others.

According to A. K. S. Lambton, the wife of Tughril Beg, Altunjan Khatun, was the one to propose the marriage of Arslan Khatun, the niece of her childless husband, to the 'Abbasid caliph al-Qa'im at an earlier stage. Tughril's wife aimed to consolidate relations between the two sides.[56] The marriage was consummated upon the advice of a Seljuqid princess on that occasion, not a prince.

As mentioned above, political marriage had certain chances of success. On his departure from the same trip to Baghdad, where the sultan only looked at his 'Abbasid bride, he took with him his niece, Arslan Khatun. She had complained to the sultan about her husband's ill manner, and that the marriage was over.[57] Seljuqid history witnessed several marriages with the 'Abbasids, mainly with the bride from the Seljuqid side. However, they did not result in any political changes on the ground. We should take into consideration that any children, mainly males, from these marriages were considered unworthy for political succession from the side of the Seljuqs. For example, why was Prince Ja'far, son of Caliph al-Muqtadi, and also son to the daughter of Turkan Khatun, never considered an equal candidate in the power vacuum after 1092? He was looked at as merely a caliphal candidate, only a successor to his weak father, as thought by Turkan, as mentioned before. Other cases are not even mentioned by name in the chronicles.

The other model of marriage was between Caliph al-Muqtadi and one of Malik Shah's daughters. Although the caliph offered a certain dowry, he was reminded by the mother of the bride that other rulers were offering much more, and unless the caliph was willing to raise the sum, the bride would not be given to him.[58] This case simply shows how some women were perceived in their society as an item for auction, and no more. It also shows that the honour that would be achieved by marrying the caliph was not always a priority.

Away from political marriage and the power of women, the limited size of the caliphal court during that age has been mentioned. Details about concubines and *qahramanat* are rare. Yet, when al-Muqtadi died, his *qahramana*, Shams al-Nahar, was the one to conceal the death and summon the vizier and leading men to ask them to renew the oath to his son and heir, Abu al-'Abbas. When they did, she revealed the death of her master to them.[59] The level of power she had is not known.

The final model of political marriage was that of Turkan Khatun during the civil war. She proposed to marry Isma'il b. Yaquti, but he took refuge at his sister's camp. However, Turkan never lost hope for power. She proposed to marry King Tutush of Syria, brother of Malik Shah, after he proved himself in Syria and Iraq as a capable commander. Turkan suggested in her letter to him that they would rule the sultanate together.[60] This shows how ambitious this princess was, and that she was really keen to be a queen, or queen–regent. Tutush agreed to the match. It was alluring to marry the widow of the sultan, and to have a large army at his side with significant financial support.

The marriage never took place, however, as Turkan died. Tutush, who was ready to use political marriage in Iran, was the one who used it first in Syria. In 1093, while fighting the lords of Aleppo and Edessa who had made a pact with his enemy, Berkyaruk, Tutush was desperate for military support. He therefore sought the support of Yaghi Siyan in the strategic city of Seljuqid Antioch. Tutush made his twelve-year-old son Ridwan marry the daughter of Yaghi Siyan while the military campaign was underway, in order to unite Syria in his quest for the sultanate.[61]

Political Marriage and the Creation of the Atabegate and its Impact on Muslim Medieval History

'*Atabeg*' or '*atabek*' was the title of an office-holder who acted as a guardian–regent to a Seljuqid prince, grooming and preparing him for future kingship. The word is derived from the Turkish word *ata* (father) and *beg*/*bek* (prince).[62] R. Guseynov mentions that the Ghuzz nomads would use the term *ata* for the tutor to their young princes while they were still in Mongolia. The post started as a civil one, for example, with Ata Yultakin and Ata Belkhan in the eighth century.[63]

The Seljuqs, who were Ghuzz themselves, kept this tribal tradition and brought it with them to the Middle East as part of their administration, which at the time was modelled on the Iranian one. It is thought that this contributed to retaining their Turkmen heritage and character.

From the second Seljuqid sultan, Alp Arslan, onwards, we see the use of the *atabeg* for tutelage, as an essential part of their rule. Chroniclers do not always detail dates, but we know that Alp Arslan had an *atabeg* named Qutb al-Din Kalisargh before his accession to the throne in 1063. He continued to play a military–political role with Alp Arslan after becoming sultan; for example, he participated with him in a war in 1064 against Qutulmish, a Seljuqid prince who contested the sultanate.[64]

C. Cahen, among others, believes that the revival of the post in the Seljuqid administration was achieved in 1072 when Sultan Malik Shah gave the Persian vizier Nizam al-Mulk the honorary title and made him his *atabeg*.

There is no evidence that Malik Shah was tutored by his honorary *atabeg*. Nizam al-Mulk was the rare exception as a Persian to hold the title or office of *atabeg*, a title that was usually only given to the Turkmen.[65]

In the early history of the Seljuqs under Malik Shah, we see two categories of *atabeg*s developing. The first was a social one, such as the case of the appointment of al-Qummi for his son, Berkyaruk. The *atabeg* here was just educating the young prince. The second category was a political–military one, where the *atabeg* assisted the young Seljuqid prince in governing his allocated province.[66]

Seljuqid Syria, as a branch and not the heart of the empire, witnessed the first complete atabegate system and state earlier than Iran. That contributed to other models to follow, leading to the establishment of an institution existing for centuries onward with several modifications.

The Relationship between Women and Atabegs: *The Case of Syria*

Malik Tutush was appointed as ruler of Syria in 1078 at the age of sixteen by his brother, Sultan Malik Shah.[67] It is not known if he had an *atabeg* acting for him before or after he came to Syria. He did not appoint any *atabeg* for any of his five sons until the death of Malik Shah.

It was only after the death of Malik Shah, when King Tutush became deeply involved in the civil war in order to seize the sultanate, that the post of *atabeg* was introduced. Tutush, before marching to Iran in 1093, entered into a cleverly designed network of marriages to secure the rule in Syria for his young and infant boys. Coming back from the war front was not a certainty, so in 1093 Tutush deliberately divorced his wife Safwat al-Mulk Khatun, mother of his son Duqaq, and made her marry his Turkmen elite commander Tughtekin (d. 1128). Tutush allocated him the strategic *iqta'* of Mayyafariqin, and appointed him as an *atabeg* for Duqaq, who was about ten years old, to bring him up with Duqaq's mother according to the Turkmen Ghuzz tradition. The following year King Tutush repeated the same procedure again, and installed Aytakin as *atabeg* to raise his son Ridwan together with another divorcee. Tutush allocated Aytakin the *iqta'* of Hims.[68]

This unique type of political marriage would tie Tutush's relations with his elite commanders. It was considered an honour to marry the divorcee of the king and to raise his son, thus it guaranteed their loyalty. In addition, the marriage was the only way to get the *atabeg* freely into the harem section, which allowed him to have close contact with the young boy in order to exert maximum influence on the candidate child. In other words, the *atabeg* would use the mother as an instrument of rule. We could say that the very nature of the *atabeg* office was highly dependable on the woman. C. Cahen observes that 'the *atabeg* might marry his pupil's mother when she became a widow'.[69]

It is clear from several contemporary chronicles that, in these two particular cases, both *atabeg*s were married off to King Tutush's ex-wives by Tutush himself as a type of honour. It seems that this tradition was brought by the Seljuqs from Mongolia, and they continued with it after converting to Islam. Cahen also believed that whenever there were several sons, there were also several *atabeg*s.[70] This judgement does not agree with the information available, however. For example, Tutush had five sons – Ridwan, Duqaq, Artash, Bahram and Abu Talib – but he only selected two of his sons whom he believed suitable for succession (according to age, among other reasons), and designated an *atabeg* for each one. So, the rule that was introduced here and was carried on later in Syria and Iran, was that there would be one *atabeg* for one son only, the *atabeg* existence being attached to one woman.[71]

Regarding the selection of the *atabeg* who would have the responsibility of passing on the Turkmen traditions, especially the military, language and Ghuzz traditions, he had to be a Turkmen.[72] In addition, he also had to hold a very distinguished position in the army. We see that Tughtekin was one of the close commanders of Sultan Alp Arslan during his campaign to Syria in 1070. Under King Tutush, he served as his deputy in Damascus and *isfahsalar* (commander of the army) before becoming an *atabeg*. Ibn al-Qalanisi sees these qualifications as the reason why King Tutush promoted Tughtekin to this office.[73] They certainly reflect the calibre required for such a post. The *atabeg* was also expected to perform military duty with the king or sultan. For example, both Tughtekin and Aytakin were present at the final confrontation in Iran, where their king was killed, and they were taken captive in 1095.[74]

How long could an *atabeg* remain in this post? Whether he could establish a new family with the mother of his stepson is far from clear. During their two years in office, neither Aytakin nor Tughtekin had much influence due to the presence of King Tutush. That situation changed after Tutush's murder. Aytakin was released from captivity before Tughtekin, and he returned to Aleppo to reunite with the now fourteen-year-old King Ridwan. Soon afterwards, Aytakin ordered the killing of Tutush's vizier in Aleppo, al-Khuwarizmi, in order to eliminate any political challenge to the *atabeg* authority in politics or compete with him over the affairs of the boy king.[75] As King Tutush had not designated a clear successor for the whole of Syria, we see the *atabeg*s using their influence to achieve their own interests through the young kings in their guardianship. Aytakin, who secured the loyalty of the army for Ridwan, advised him to invade Damascus where the latter's brother, King Duqaq, now ruled. In Damascus, Tughtekin had now returned to his boy king, Duqaq. The first thing he did was to kill the commander of the city, Sawtakin, who had secured Damascus during his absence with his master in Iran.[76] This step, following Aytakin's actions, was to eliminate any challenger to his atabegate.

Seljuqid Syria was now divided through the political ambitions of the two *atabeg*s in Aleppo and Damascus, who were using their young kings to achieve their personal gains, instead of meeting to discuss or seek a single successor to their father. They could not refer to a clear Seljuqid sultan in Iran (even if they put the interests of the realm before theirs), due to the chaos of the civil war there.

A war started between the two young kings, led by their *atabeg*s. Ridwan failed to invade Damascus twice in 1096, while Duqaq and Tughtekin tried to subdue Aleppo the following year, but failed.[77] Due to the failure of Aytakin to take Damascus, he escaped with his wife, mother of King Ridwan, to his *iqta'* in Hims, relinquishing the office of the *atabeg*. He continued to rule there as an independent lord until Ridwan hired assassins to kill him in 1103.[78] During this time Aytakin managed to hold on to his designated title, *atabeg*, as he was married to the mother of Ridwan, even though he had no child to raise. Here we see that the woman was the source of legitimacy to the ruler, despite rebelling against his king.

In Damascus the development of the atabegate and the influence of women took a different course. Tughtekin, in the presence of his wife Safwat al-Mulk Khatun, mother of Duqaq, became the de facto ruler of the kingdom of Damascus and southern Syria. He managed to aid his young king against his brother in Aleppo, and defended the interests of Damascus against the arrival of the First Crusade to the Levant and their expansion in southern Syria against Seljuqid dominions, such as Haifa, in 1100–1;[79] he also assisted other Muslim powers against the Crusaders' expansion in the area. He was protecting the geo-commercial and political interests of Damascus.

The *atabeg* Tughtekin and *khatun* Safwat were ambitious to retain their power, but were faced with the dilemma of King Duqaq growing up and assuming the rule. They therefore collaborated to murder him in 1104. The *atabeg* had a free hand in switching the kings of Damascus, and by 1105, with the sudden and mysterious death of infant, King Tutush II b. Duqaq, grandson of the *khatun*, we find the Seljuqid kingdom of Damascus being left without a member of the Seljuqid royal family to sit on the throne. Duqaq's brothers were out of Damascus, and could not interfere for different reasons. Duqaq had no offspring to replace him.[80]

Tughtekin's political office was fully dependent on the physical presence of a royal prince for whom he would act as regent, in the presence of the child's mother. However, in this case, there was no such child. Nevertheless, Tughtekin continued to rule Damascus and southern Syria using the legitimacy of his wife, the former wife of King Tutush and mother of the deceased King Duqaq. She fully supported him in the midst of this vacuum in Syria and in the absence of the new Seljuqid sultan, Muhammad b. Malik Shah, who had assumed the throne that year, but was occupied with domestic problems in Iran and Iraq.[81]

Tughtekin remained in post until 1115, despite not having a diploma recognising his status from the sultan in Iran. He claimed his legitimacy from his wife instead. Ibn al-Qalanisi described Safwat Khatun's support to him, saying:

> Safwat was powerful, with the ability to conduct the affairs of the realm, helping Tughtekin when her son Duqaq died. She supported him until the kingdom became stable and the political affairs were facilitated by Tughtekin, due to her opinion, profound respect and policy.[82]

Tughtekin proved to be a very capable lord in the face of two main challenges. The first was the expansionist Crusaders of Jerusalem. He was engaged with them in a long bloody confrontation over the domination of the Hauran Valley between Damascus and Jerusalem from 1105 to 1108. They attacked his dominions in inland Syria after they captured Tripoli in 1109 and Sidon the following year, putting his dominions under threat.[83] Tughtekin had to collaborate with the Shi'i Fatimids in order to save their main sea port of Tyre, which was under constant attack from the Crusaders. Tughtekin took over the city to protect and defend it with full coordination with Cairo; it was the major outlet for his trade.[84] In 1113 he achieved a landmark victory with his friend and ally, the Seljuqid lord of Mosul, Mawdud, over King Baldwin of Jerusalem, at the Battle of al-Sinnabra.[85] However, Tughtekin refrained from using this surprising victory against the Crusaders, halting his other activities against them.

The second challenge was Tughtekin use of politics of war against the sultanate armies, which were sent to challenge his rule in 1114 and 1115. He proved to be a master of realpolitik; he allied himself with the lord of Antioch and king of Jerusalem against Sultan's Muhammad's colossal army.[86] Tughtekin's policy of survival saved his unrecognised rule from the sultan, even if he had to rebel and fight his forces.

Tughtekin used the politics of jihad against the Crusaders by recapturing a minor town in central Syria later in 1115, appearing as a warrior of Islam.[87] The Seljuqid sultan, who was more concerned with the internal challenges in Iran, ceased dispatching any more troops into the Levant. As a result, he had to come to terms with reality. He issued a *taqlid* (diploma) in 1116 realising the limited role of Iran's geopolitics. He invested in Tughtekin the rule of the territories under his authority in Syria. With this diploma, the sultan empowered Tughtekin with the political and financial governance of his Syrian dominions, with a free hand in spending its revenues according to his discretion.

The long sultanate diploma, of about 1,100 words, bestowed the title of 'emir', which he'd never had before. He was given also the title 'most noble *isfahsalar*' (grand commander of the army). In return, he was ordered to declare his loyalty to Sunnism, and to declare the *khutba* and mint the coins in the name of the 'Abbasid caliph and Seljuqid sultan. He also had to be just to his subjects, and defend his lands against the enemies of God. Most significant was his keeping the title of *atabeg*, despite having no child under his regency. In addition, Tughtekin was granted the right of passing the rule to his own children.[88] Thus, his atabegate was transformed from a temporary office, where the person performing it could be dismissed, to an institutionalised hereditary political dynasty. I believe that the presence of Safwat Khatun at Tughtekin's side at that moment played a role in the wider authority that her husband had secured.

The question here is: how did Tughtekin survive politically from 1105 until 1116, when the diploma was granted. He depended on his de facto power and pragmatism, collaborating with the Crusaders and Fatimids (who were considered prime enemies of the state). In addition, Tughtekin depended on the legitimacy of his wife, the *khatun* (who died in 1119). This development symbolised the start of the deterioration and disintegration of the Seljuqs. This first Turkmen atabegate was the gateway to many others within the Seljuq Empire, including the Ahmadilis, the Zengids and the Eldigizids.

Tughtekin continued in his atabegate with no direct threat to his realm from any power. During this time he was grooming his mature son, Buri, as his successor or *wali al-'ahd*. He appointed him as his deputy, and dispatched him in various challenging campaigns to gain experience. When Tughtekin died in 1128, Buri became the first successor in this atabegate. His power and legitimacy were not only taken from implementing the sultanate diploma; Buri also took his legitimacy through his political marriage to Zumurrud Khatun, daughter of Safwat Khatun (the sister of King Duqaq on his mother's side).[89] What Tughtekin had aspired to before this marriage proved fruitful. It gave his line of successors legitimacy and eminence as descendants of royal blood instead of just ambitious military commanders.

The institution of the *atabeg* in Damascus experienced important changes to its original purpose up until the downfall of the atabegate in 1154, when the Zengid atabegate replaced it. The *atabeg* became more of an honorary title, associated with the leadership of the army. He, the *atabeg*, did not always practise educational or tutorial tasks, as much as being an advisor. He was not always married to a woman. In fact, women sometimes were the one to appoint the *atabeg*. For example, Zumurrud Khatun, after killing her son King Isma'il in 1135, appointed her lover Fayruz as *atabeg* for her son Mahmud, who became the new king. Fayruz also held the office of *isfahsalar* at the same time.[90] There followed two other *atabeg*s for King Mahmud, who also held the office of *isfahsalar* at the same time: Gumushtegin in 1136, and

Bazwaj two months after him, who served for two years. That was upon the order of Zumurrud Khatun.[91]

What is important here is that we see an *atabeg* administering the state affairs of the descendants of another *atabeg*: the grandsons of Tughtekin. That continued with the marriage of Unur to the mother of Mahmud in 1139. Unur had become the last *atabeg* for Mahmud in 1138. After the latter's assassination, Unur installed Mahmud's half-brother Muhammad in 1139 and married his mother, to provide greater legitimacy.[92] This development was significant. The *atabeg* was also the *isfahsalar*, and was the one who would appoint the king and act as his guardian. The legitimacy, which was carried to Unur by his marriage to Muhammad's mother, elevated his status among the commanders and nobles of Damascus, thus enabling him to defend the realm against the dangerous siege of the *atabeg* Zengi in 1140. It also gave Unur more power. When Muhammad died in 1140, Unur was in a position to replace him with his young son, Abaq b. Muhammad (d. 1154) and Unur imposed his atabegate on him until Unur himself died in 1149.[93]

Unur managed to save Damascus from serious attacks from the Zengids through several methods: he allied with the Crusaders of Jerusalem to force Zengi to lift his long siege of Damascus in 1140;[94] and in 1147 he married his daughter, 'Ismat al-Din, to Zengi's son and successor, Nur al-Din.[95] As a result of this marriage, Damascus was never attacked again in Unur's lifetime, although several years afterwards it was seized by the Zengid atabegate, as will be discussed.

Until their downfall in 1118, the Seljuqs of Aleppo underwent a number of changes to the atabegate. King Ridwan (d. 1113) remained without an *atabeg* after his *atabeg*, Aytakin, escaped in 1103. Ridwan did not install an *atabeg* for any of his five sons.[96] Following his death, we see the commander Lu'Lu' al-Baba installing the sixteen-year-old Alp Arslan b. Ridwan as king and Lu'Lu' becoming his *atabeg*. Lu'Lu' controlled the affairs of Aleppo to the extent that he assassinated his mentally troubled king after just a few months and installed his brother, Sultan Shah, as the new king.[97]

Lu'Lu', who was a eunuch, certainly brought a new dimension to this office: not only that there was no woman to marry, such as the mother of the boy king, but there was no man either – only a third gender. It is worth pointing out that of the eunuchs who were beardless, a number of them were given the name Lu'Lu', which is associated in the Qur'an with *ghilman* in paradise, and the sexual desire of young boys (as set out in the Introduction).

Lu'Lu' collaborated with the Crusaders of Antioch against the sultanate army that was dispatched for jihad in 1115.[98] The reason for this was to protect himself and his office, as he was not formally appointed by any Seljuqid ruler. When Lu'Lu' tried to kill his second king, Sultan Shah, in an internal power struggle, he himself was killed, and a power vacuum and instability followed in Aleppo.[99]

Amina Khatun, daughter of Ridwan and sister of Sultan Shah, appointed the *atabeg* Yaruqtash, who was also commander of the army. She dismissed and arrested him a month later when he tried to seize power for himself, as already mentioned. Yaruqtash was succeeded by the *atabeg* Ibn al-Malhi, who was also appointed by Princess Amina.[100] The rule of the Seljuqs collapsed the following year when the Artuqid Turkmen took over the realm.

I have a few concluding remarks here before moving to the other atabegates:

1. The Muslim administration witnessed the concept of the educator of the caliph's children, like many dynasties in world history. Mention has been made of the Iranian Yahya the Barmakid, who was appointed by 'Abbasid caliph al-Mahdi for his son, al-Rashid, in the eighth century. In addition, the Fatimid caliph al-'Aziz appointed the slave eunuch Barjawan as the educator for his son, al-Hakim, in the tenth century. These appointments were different from that of the *atabeg*, in that they were individuals from different ethnic and cultural backgrounds, they were practising civil duties and the presence of a woman was not essential to discharging their duties. On the other hand, the *atabeg* had to be a Turkmen, and an elite military commander, in order to pass on the Turkic–Mongolian culture, which the Seljuqs wanted to preserve for future generations. The *atabeg*, in order to have maximum influence on his pupil, was married to the child's mother, which was never the case under the 'Abbasids or the Fatimids.
2. The atabegate, which was institutionalised and developed into a hereditary dynastic rule initially in Syria, was widespread around the Seljuq Empire

in large numbers and different forms. It actually contributed to the slow eradication of their founders, the Seljuqs, instead of consolidating their power. The children of the *atabegs* needed *atabegs* for themselves.

3. In Syria, unlike Iran, it was the *atabeg*, not the vizier, who held the second most important political role in the state. Even that changed in Iran after 1118.[101]

4. The Seljuqs never appointed *atabegs* for the education of their daughters or *khatuns*. Of course, preparing them for a political career was unthinkable. They were like all other dynasties before them, who viewed women as a lost investment. The Seljuqs reintroduced the madrasa in about 1065, taking it from Iran to the Sunni Muslim world; they allowed *khatuns* to commission some of them, but never allowed women to study in them. Zumurrud Khatun built a madrasa bearing her name in Damascus in 1131,[102] but we still do not know where women did study (if they did) up to the Mamluk period.

We can safely say that the status of Turkmen women depicted in the national epic of the Turks, *Dede Korkut*, did not materialise to near reality on the ground. All the stories in the book about the Turkish heroines had limited coverage, such as in the cases of *khatuns* like Turkan in Iran, or Zumurrud in Syria. The same could be said about the epic of the *Arabian Nights*, between the reality of position and women and what they aspired to have. The exceptional story is that of the slave girl Tawaddud, who was owned by the son of a rich merchant, who decided to sell her to Caliph Harun al-Rashid. For twenty-seven nights, Tawaddud challenged the caliph, and all the scholars and scientists summoned by the caliph, to speak with her about all fields of knowledge, from medicine, and astronomy to jurisprudence, poetry and history.[103] That was of course narrated by the influential Persian, Shahrazad, who achieved in myth what she could not achieve in reality in the mixed Turko-Persian and Arab worlds. Geoffrey Lewis states that Ghuzz women had great freedom of movement and enjoyed financial independence.[104] That was probably before they entered the Muslim world; now they would be framed according to the patriarchal interpretation of Sunni Islam, namely al-Mawardi, Nizam al-Mulk and al-Ghazali, as already mentioned.

The *Atabegs* of Iran and Iraq

The contemporary chronicler of the late Seljuqs in western Iran, Sadr al-Din al-Husayni (d. 1225), marvellously evaluated the state of the Seljuqs after the death of Sultan Sanjar in 1157. He wrote:

> The Seljuq rule in Khurasan came to an end with the death of Sultan Sanjar. It continued in Iraq, as a facade without any substance. That is because the *atabeg*s were dominating the sultans up to the death of Sultan Tughril III in 1194.[105]

Al-Husayni continues with the identity of the dynasties formed from within their body as '*mamluk*s of the Seljuqs'. He lists the atabegate of the Zengids in Iraq and Syria, Ahmadilis in Maragha, Tughtekin of Syria and Eldiguzids in Iraq and Azerbaijan. He wonders how a slave *mamluk* like Eldiguz (d. 1175) became a grand *atabeg* and married the widow of Sultan Tughril b. Muhammad Tapar, and how his line of descendants replaced the Seljuqs.[106]

The history of the Seljuqs in Iran and Iraq produced several atabegates, starting from 1122. I will discuss three of them in chronological order according to their start dates, and consider the diversity and evolution of the post. I will also look at other *atabeg*s who were heavily associated with politics, but had formed no dynasties, to see the difference and impact they made. In addition, I will reflect on how the *atabeg* and princess had to collaborate for political survival, employing political marriage as a tool.

While the original *atabeg* function was to educate and pass on Turkmen culture to the young prince, the *atabeg* in Iran, like Syria, also had to administer the province or *iqta'* in the name of the young prince in order to secure the revenues and maintain the military and its loyalty. They also declared the *khutba*, as a sign of loyalty to the sultan and the caliph to ensure Seljuqid support for Sunni Islam. The other task for the *atabeg* was to monitor the young prince and forbid him from rebelling against the central authority that the sultan represented, for example, like Sultan Berkyaruk, who appointed *atabeg*s for his two other brothers, Muhammad and Sanjar, to guard, but also to dominate, their activities to the benefit of the sultan.[107]

If the death of Sultan Malik Shah in 1092 started a large-scale civil war in the Seljuq Empire, the death of his son, Muhammad Tapar, in 1118 was the start of the decline in western Iran, the Caucasus and Iraq. That created a political–military vacuum, which was filled by the rise of the atabegate, and the attempt of the 'Abbasid caliphate to regain power once again at the expense of the Seljuqs. Their partial success was limited to Iraq.[108]

Like al-Husayni, these atabegates considered Seljuqs their *mamluk*s. Others named them with the new dynastic name of their founding *atabeg*, for ease of reference. I agree with Carole Hillenbrand, who describes them as 'Seljuq successor-states',[109] especially as all of them were Turkmen or Turkicised.

The Ahmadili Atabegate in Azerbaijan

The Ahmadili atabegate (1122–1220) was the second atabegate dynasty to be formed within the Seljuq Empire, in Maragha and the castle of Ru'in Diz in Azerbaijan after the Tughtekinid in Syria. They took their name from Prince Ahmadil (d. 1116), who was a Kurdish lord of Maragha; he participated in the jihad against the Crusaders in 1111 as one of several leading emirs. At the walls of Crusader Tal Bashir in the Jazira, Joscelin, prince of the city, bribed Ahmadil. Ahmadil deserted the Seljuqid campaign; the sultan's son, Mas'ud, was with them.[110]

When Ahmadil was assassinated in 1116, his slave commander, Aq Sunqur, who appears in the chronicles with various names, succeeded him in 1122 as lord and *atabeg* of Maragha in Azerbaijan, and carried the name of his former lord. Maragha had previously been given to the *atabeg* Aq Sunqur al-Bursuqi, who was regent for King Tughril II b. Muhammad. Aq Sunqur al-Ahmadili was appointed by Sultan Mahmud II there, and gave him, as an *atabeg*, his young son, King Da'ud, to raise.[111] Unlike the atabegate of Seljuqid Damascus, Aq Sunqur did not marry the mother of Da'ud, or any other Seljuqid *khatun*. Aq Sunqur's main challenges were to defend his small atabegate against the rise of the Georgians in the Caucasus, and to survive the civil war that followed Sultan Mahmud II's death in 1131. Mahmud II had four sons as kings: Malik Shah III, Da'ud, Arslan II and Muhammad II. They were engaged in a civil war in Iran and Iraq among themselves and against the four surviving sons of Muhammad I Tapar – Mas'ud, Sulayman, Seljuq Shah and Tughril II – who were their uncles.[112]

In 1131, taking the opportunity of Sultan Mahmud II's death, the *atabeg*

Aq Sunqur collaborated with the vizier of the deceased sultan, al-Dargazini, in order to install Da'ud as sultan for the whole of Azerbaijan.¹¹³ The situation in western Iran and Iraq was extremely fluid, and territories and the loyalty of troops for the various kings changed very rapidly; the information covering these warring lords in the sources is sporadic.

Regarding the case of this particular *atabeg*, in 1131–2 there was a war among the three Seljuqid kings and their *atabeg*s looking for military supremacy and symbolic official recognition from the caliph, al-Mustarshid. King Da'ud had his *atabeg*, Aq Sunqur; King Mas'ud allied with Zengi I of Mosul (d. 1146), who was *atabeg* for Alp Arslan b. Mahmud II; and King Seljuq Shah had his *atabeg*, Qaraja al-Saqi of Khuzistan.¹¹⁴ We could say that this was the year of the three *atabeg*s fighting for their own ambitions through their kings (or agents).

Aq Sunqur made a pact with King Mas'ud after realising the strength of his power. As a result, King Tughril II marched to Maragha and seized it from Aq Sunqur. Sultan Tughril appointed Qara Sunqur as the new *atabeg* in Azerbaijan; in addition, he appointed a new *atabeg*, Mankopars, for his son, Alp Arslan III, in Fars. Soon afterwards, King Mas'ud recaptured Azerbaijan from Qara Sunqur, and reinstated Aq Sunqur as *atabeg* there.¹¹⁵

Aq Sunqur was killed by assassins hired by Sultan Tughril II. He was succeeded by his son, who appears in the chronicles with different names, including Aq Sunqur II, Arslan Aba and Nusrat al-Din.¹¹⁶

Aq Sunqur II (d. 1175) ruled for four decades as an *atabeg*, becoming an *atabeg* for Muhammad II b. Mahmud II. The main development in the post of *atabeg* here is that Aq Sunqur II inherited the rule in a remote city of Maragha without a clear *taqlid* (diploma) from the sultan, unlike in the case of Syria in 1115. That was a clear sign of the ailing Seljuqs, and how the *atabeg*s in the Caucasus had moved out of their control: not because the *atabeg*s were strong, but because the Seljuq kings and sultans had no supreme leadership to refer to.

The long career of Aq Sunqur II is not well detailed in the chronicles. However, he was ambitious enough to rule in the name of the king under his guardianship; Da'ud b. Mahmud II. In 1135–6 he marched to Baghdad with Da'ud to support the new caliph, al-Rashid, against the Seljuqid sultan, Mas'ud. In order to achieve this task, Aq Sunqur II coordinated his military efforts with the *atabeg* of Mosul, Zengi, who also was hoping to use the new hostility with Mas'ud in order to declare the *khutba* in the name of Alp Arslan b. Mahmud II in Zengi's custody.[117]

King Da'ud was killed by the Assassins in 1138.[118] The geographical position of Maragha's atabegate compelled the Seljuq Empire, with its numerous warring sultans, to forget about the Ahmadilis. Aq Sunqur II tried to form a pact with the newly established atabegate of Eldiguzids in 1145 in Azerbaijan and Transcaucasia.[119] Aq Sunqur II, who had no king to guard in his custody, united with the *atabeg* Eldiguz (d. 1175) after Sultan Mas'ud died in 1152.

Both *atabeg*s tried to interfere in what remained of the Seljuqis state by trying to install Sulayman, who had been jailed by his brother Mas'ud, as the new sultan in Hamadan. They succeeded in their aim until Sulayman, who was a weak and mysterious ruler, was captured by the *atabeg* of Mosul, Qut al-Din Mawdud b. Zengi, in 1156.[120]

The information about this atabegate shows some collaboration between Aq Sunqur II and Eldiguz in about 1162–3 as regards their fight against the expanding Georgians in order to protect their dominions. Al-Husayni mentioned that during that year, Aq Sunqur joined a pact including Shah Arman of Akhlat and Eldiguz, and they defeated King Giorgi of Georgia.[121]

In 1167 Aq Sunqur II became a guardian to Da'ud II, son of Muhammad II b. Mahmud. He asked the 'Abbasid caliph to recognise him as a sultan, in order to rule in his name, promising that he would never march to Iraq again. He managed temporarily to extend his rule to Tabriz. The feeble caliph, who had received a large sum of money in return, briefly recognised Da'ud II as sultan. Eldiguz's reaction to this was hostile. He dispatched an army led by his son, Pahlawan, to fight Aq Sunqur II. Pahlawan managed to defeat him and besiege Maragha, but they reached a truce and he withdrew back to his father.[122]

Here we see how important it was for an *atabeg* to secure the *khutba*, even for symbolic reasons, as well as having a Seljuq king under his regency in order to claim legitimacy; despite being powerful militarily, he needed the recognition of his neighbours. When Aq Sunqur II died in 1175, his atabegate survived until about 1209 when the Eldiguzid atabegate invaded and captured the Ahmadili capital, Maragha. During this period, the hostility and rivalry between the Ahmadilis and Eldiguzids continued. The *atabeg* 'Ala' al-Din Korp Arslan, grandson of Aq Sunqur II, had used his daughter, Sulafa Khatun, in a political marriage with the last Eldiguzid lord, the *atabeg* Ozbeg.[123] The reason for this marriage was to improve the relationship between the two dynasties, and to unite against the continued raids by Queen Tamar of Georgia (d. 1213), who constantly posed a threat to both atabegate dominions, especially after 1194.[124]

When the Mongols invaded the Caucasus in 1220 and besieged Maragha in April 1221, Sulafa Khatun was the mistress of the city, ruling it from the fortified citadel of Ru'in Diz, half a day's march to the north. Ibn al-Athir, who reported this story, was ashamed of the leadership of a Muslim woman, and repeated the saying of the Prophet: 'No people will succeed if they have a woman as their ruler.'[125] He is reported as saying that when Queen Puran ascended the throne of Iran in 628 (see the Introduction). Ibn al-Athir's hegemony extended to other Georgian female rulers, as will be discussed shortly, under the Eldiguzids.

Sulafa Khatun succeeded in defending and keeping the citadel, and only surrendered it to Jalal al-Din Khuwarazm Shah when he arrived after the Mongols. Apparently, she had divorced her Eldiguzid husband Ozbeg earlier, and she married Khuwarazm Shah.[126] The Ahmadili atabegate ended; Sulafa Khatun, who had conceived a son from the *atabeg* Korp Arslan, but who died in about 1208, passed her symbolic legitimacy to her new husband.

A few remarks about the Ahmadilis are due here:

1. Their atabegate depended on the raising of a boy king without marrying any Seljuqid *khatun*.
2. The Ahmadilis did not have a sultanate diploma stating the passing of power to their line of descents.
3. The core problem of the Seljuqid atabegate was that it was not restricted to a certain period, after which time the *atabeg* should have handed power to his young king. That left the door open for some *atabeg*s to remain holding their young kings for fifteen or twenty years. The relationship became more of a hostage to a master than a king to his regent.
4. The *atabeg* could install and give legitimacy to a new sultan, as in the case of Sulayman.

Finally, we should not rule out the influence of the great Georgian queen, Tamar (r. 1184–1213)[127] on her Ahmadili neighbour, Sulafa Khatun. The latter must have been encouraged by following her example of challenging the patriarchal society, and to rule independently and successfully in the citadel of Ru'in Diz. Queen Tamar, on the other hand, used some Turkmen titles and offices in her kingdom. She had an '*atabeg*' in her administration. His name was Loanne, brother of (the *isfahsalar*) Zakharia.[128]

The Zengid Atabegate in Iraq and Syria

The Zengid atabegate (1127–1234) was the third dynastic atabegate created by the Seljuqs, and was contemporary to the previous two. In 1127 the Seljuq sultan Mahmud II wanted to reward his loyal Turkmen commander Imad al-Din Zengi for his military efforts. The sultan issued a *manshur* (decree) installing Zengi as lord of Mosul, and gave him his young son, King Alp Arslan, to raise. Zengi did not raise Alp Arslan with his mother, but with the widow of Prince Kindaghdi, whom the sultan had forced to marry Zengi two years earlier.[129] Kindaghdi was a leading commander in the sultan's army, and his widow inherited a very large fortune from her husband.[130]

Sultan Mahmud II created a bond with Zengi through this political marriage and by appointing him as an *atabeg*. The atabegate of Zengi did not consist of hereditary rights for his children, nor did it share the same characteristics of the Ahmadilis, as regards when the *atabeg* should return the authority or hand power to his king. However, the Zengid atabegate was famous in medieval Islamic history due to its achievements against the Crusaders, and as the atabegate from which Saladin came. In addition, Ibn al-Athir, their loyal contemporary and native of Mosul, wrote the first book about the atabegate. He entitled it *Al-Ta'rikh al-Bahir fi al-Dawla al-Atabekiyya* (*The Magnificent in the History of the Atabegate State* (of Zengi)). He was the first person to use this term, and made a brilliant link between Zengi's entrance into Syrian politics in 1128 and continuing the achievements of the *atabeg* Tughtekin of Damascus, who died the same year.[131] Zengi also brought Aleppo and parts of the Jazira under his control in that year.

The age of King Alp Arslan under Zengi's custody is not clear, but normally the age would be about ten years old, in order for the *atabeg* to wield influence over their charge. In addition to the prestige that Zengi had gained from his post, he became more involved in Seljuqid politics in the name of his king, and had the *khutba* declared in his name after the caliph and sultan in Zengid dominions. In 1131 Sultan Mahmud II, father of Alp Arslan, died. Zengi tried to secure the sultanate for his candidate from the 'Abbasid caliph al-Mustarshid in Iraq and western Iran, but failed due to the competition with several Seljuqid kings.[132]

Despite the hostilities with the Seljuqid kings and the new sultan, Mas'ud (d. 1152), uncle of Alp Arslan, they could not take the boy king from Zengi, or nullify his atabegate. Thus, the legitimacy of Zengi's atabegate continued. Zengi never lost hope, and in 1135 he briefly secured the *khutba* of the 'Abbasid caliph al-Mustarshid in Syria and Iraq; that is when the caliph needed Zengi's army to fight Sultan Mas'ud.

Again, in the same year and in 1136, Zengi briefly secured the *khutba* for his king, Alp Arslan; that happened while the *atabeg* al-Baqsh was trying to declare the *khutba* for his candidate, King Seljuq Shah, in Iraq. Zengi bribed al-Baqsh to desert his king. That raised the political status of Zengi and his king in Iraq, as he had managed to eliminate the power of another *atabeg*.[133]

In 1145, after eighteen years in Zengi's court, King Alp Arslan, now in his late twenties, tried to assume full power from Zengi, as was logical. Encouraged by some Zengid commanders, he tried to seize Mosul while Zengi was occupied with campaigning in the Jazira. This would have been the natural political course of events: the *atabeg* should hand over power to his grown-up king. Ironically, Alp Arslan was jailed in the Mosul citadel by Zengi's loyal deputy, and Alp Arslan's collaborators were killed upon Zengi's orders.[134] At that time there was no Seljuqid sultan or king in Iran who could provide help for the imprisoned king, not only because of Zengi's military might, but also because of his legendary victory some months earlier in December 1144 over the Crusaders in Edessa. That victory secured his status as a hero of Islam.

Zengi was unexpectedly murdered by his servant in 1146; afterwards the Seljuqid sultanate, represented by Sultan Mas'ud b. Muhammad Tapar, did not interfere or even express objection to his atabegate turning into hereditary model. The original decree of Mahmud II did not empower Zengi with the right of passing power to his successors, unlike Tughtekin in Damascus. However, in reality, two of Zengi's sons succeeded him and continued to declare the ceremonial *khutba* to the caliph and sultan. Ghazi I b. Zengi became lord of Mosul and parts of the Jazira, while Nur al-Din I became lord of Aleppo, central Syria and parts of the Jazira.[135] It is worth pointing out that Zengi did not appoint *atabeg*s for any of his four sons, and did not designate a successor.

During the short reign of Ghazi I in Mosul, King Alp Arslan used the unsettled situation there to try to win support from several commanders to take the throne. However, Ghazi I was powerful enough to end this attempt, and kept Alp Arslan as a kind of hostage, ruling in his name.[136]

The divided Zengid atabegate did not experience serious hostilities between the two Zengid princes who did not assume the title *atabeg*. However, in almost all chronicles, the two Zengid branches were referred to as the atabegate house or dynasty. In 1149 in Iraq, Mawdud succeeded his brother Ghazi in Mosul, and offically assumed the title of *atabeg*, and minted it on the Zengid dirham (see Figure 6). When Sultan Mas'ud died in 1152, his brother Sulayman secured the *khutba* from the caliph in Iraq as sultan. That angered his nephew, Muhammad II b. Mahmud, who sought the support of Mawdud in 1156.[137] Mawdud was attracted by the promises made by Muhammad II. He attacked Sultan Sulayman and defeated him. Not only that, but he took him captive, imprisoning him in the Mosul citadel.[138] Mawdud did not just rebel and capture the official sultan, who still had the *khutba* declared for him in Baghdad, but he also rebelled against the authority of the 'Abbasid caliph who granted Sulayman's legitimacy. This act shows how powerful the atabegate became vis-á-vis the sultanate and caliphate.

Sultan Sulayman was jailed by Mawdud until 1159, which was a long time by any standard, and reflected the decay of the Seljuq realm.[139] In that year, after the sudden death of Mawdud's ally, Muhammad II, and through negotiations, Mawdud released Sulayman. Mawdud would go on to become the *atabeg* for Sultan Sulayman and the de facto ruler of his realm. Mawdud appointed the chief of the army of the sultan and the vizier. Sulayman, and a number of lords in Azerbaijan and western Iran, had accepted these terms.[140] Mawdud did not have time to enjoy the fruits of this political agreement, however, as Sulayman was arrested the following year in Iran, and was killed in 1161.[141]

In 1170 Mawdud died. He had designated his elder son, Zengi II, as successor; however, Dayfa Khatun, mother of the younger son, Ghazi II, wanted to install her son as lord of Mosul. She collaborated with Mawdud's deputy, 'Abd al-Masih, in order to achieve her aim. Dayfa Khatun's wish prevailed, and Mawdud's will was ignored for the benefit of her son.[142] Dayfa Khatun was not an ordinary wife of Zengi, but was the daughter of the mighty Artuqid Turkmen lord of Mardin, Husam al-Din Timurtash (d. 1152).[143] Even when Nur al-Din, uncle of Ghazi II, took over Mosul in 1171, he did not remove him from power. Nur al-Din gave his daughter to Ghazi II to marry.[144]

After Nur al-Din's takeover of Mosul, the two atabegates of Iraq and Syria became entangled and influenced each other. As mentioned before, Nur al-Din, married 'Ismat al-Din, daughter of Unur, the last *atabeg* of the house of Tughtekin.[145] In 1154 he took over Damascus, following Unur's death. Nur al-Din, the son of an *atabeg* himself, ended the first dynastic atabegate, and used his political marriage to boost his new rule there.

The opposition to Nur al-Din's expansion in Iraq came from another atabegate: the Eldiguzids of Azerbaijan. While Nur al-Din was advancing on Mosul, the deputy 'Abd al-Masih dispatched Prince Mas'ud b. Mawdud to the *atabeg* Eldiguz asking for help against Nur al-Din.[146] Eldiguz welcomed this invitation; he dispatched an envoy to Nur al-Din, warning him against interfering in Mosul's affairs. Nur al-Din replied angrily to the envoy, saying:

> Tell Eldiguz this is a family affair. Eldiguz ruled half the Muslim lands, but neglected the frontiers until the Georgians (Gorj) took them over. I, Nur al-Din, on the other hand, have been been left alone to confront the bravest of peoples: the Franks.[147]

The tension between the two atabegates did not materialise into a confrontation. However, it reflects how the atabegates became a separate entity from the Seljuqs, with their own political ambitions.

The sudden illness and death of Nur al-Din in May 1174 was a blow to the relative stability of the Zengid atabegate, after having ruled Syria, Iraq, the Jazira and the Hijaz, and having seized Egypt from the Fatimids in 1169. In his final days, Nur al-Din had to designate his chief commander in his atabegate, Shams al-Din Ibn al-Daya, as *atabeg* for his eleven-year-old only son, al-Salih Isma'il (d. 1181).[148] The problem was that Ibn al-Daya was in Aleppo suffering from gout, while the young King Isma'il was in Damascus, where his father died. As a result, another ambitious commander, Ibn al-Muqaddam in Damascus, declared himself as an *atabeg* for the boy king, and declared the *khutba* in his name.[149] Ibn al-Muqaddam was encouraged by the physical presence of the king alongside him, thus he could claim legitimacy in his name among the army commanders.

A third contender to the atabegate came from Nurid Egypt, a young ambitious Kurdish Nurid commander who had rebelled for five years against his sultan Nur al-Din, yet he continued to declare the *khutba* in Nur al-Din's name, and that of his son, in Egypt. Saladin declared himself as *atabeg* for King Isma'il to gain more legitimacy to his rising rule. Saladin declared the atabegate of Ibn al-Muqaddam illegal or unfit after he, in Damascus, reached a truce with the Crusaders of Jerusalem under King Baldwin IV (d. 1185); Saladin considered this act as a treason to Muslim solidarity.[150]

Saladin did not find his own amicable letter to King Baldwin immoral, while he accused the *atabeg* of Damascus of amicable relations with the Crusaders. Saladin wrote to King Baldwin: 'I wish to confirm to King Baldwin that we (Saladin) will continue the sincere amicable relations we had with his deceased father. You, King Baldwin, should rely on me as a son relies on his father.'[151] The diplomacy of Saladin with the Crusaders in Jerusalem was to avoid any confrontation with them, in order to focus on his expansion in Syria under the banner of his atabegate.

As soon as Ibn al-Muqaddam knew of Saladin's march out of Egypt, he sent for the official *atabeg* in Aleppo, Ibn al-Daya, asking him to send an envoy to take king Isma'il to another location. The commanders in Damascus knew that they could not match Saladin's power, and feared that if he had Isma'il in his custody, he would have more legitimacy.[152] Isma'il travelled with his mother, 'Ismat al-Din Khatun, to Aleppo in the company of the commander Gumushtegin. In August 1174 Isma'il entered Aleppo, but he did not go into the custody of Ibn al-Daya. Gumushtegin launched a coup, arrested the official *atabeg* and declared himself the new *atabeg*.[153] Here, we see that the atabegate of Isma'il was changed three times within a few months. The most important matter in claiming the atabegate is the physical presence of the *atabeg* with their charge.

There are two new developments here: (1) we witness the first non-Turkmen *atabeg*, in the Kurdish commander Saladin, whose father was a *mamluk* to Zengi and Nur al-Din; and (2) an *atabeg* like Ibn al-Muqaddam might leave the post voluntarily or under pressure. As a result, the sources stopped referring to him with that title. It is worth pointing out that the Zengid *atabeg* of Mosul, Ghazi II, cousin of Isma'il, did not interfere in this struggle of the *atabeg*s. Saladin did not give up his ambitions. He seized Damascus in 1174 and declared the *khutba* in the city in the name of Isma'il as his *atabeg*. In addition, he wrote to Gumushtegin in Aleppo threatening him if he did not release Ibn al-Daya.[154] The struggle between the two *atabeg*s reached a new level of realpolitik when Saladin besieged Aleppo in January 1175. Gumushtegin responded by contacting the leader of the Assassins in Syria to kill Saladin. In addition, he wrote to Prince Raymond III of Crusader Tripoli (d. 1187), whom he had released earlier from Aleppo after more than a decade in captivity. Gumushtegin urged him to attack the newly seized dominions of Saladin in central Syria, to ease the siege on his atabegate.[155]

Ghazi II arrived with a large army in Syria to fight Saladin upon the plea for help from Gumushtegin.[156] The fact that Ghazi, the Zengid lord, agreed to form a pact with Gumushtegin, who had hijacked the atabegate, was in itself a recognition of Gumushtegin's office. Saladin defeated the Aleppo–Mosul pact and besieged Aleppo again in April 1175.[157]

By 1177 Isma'il had grown up and wanted to put an end to his *atabeg*'s monopoly of power. He murdered him, and remained ruling Aleppo without another *atabeg* until his sudden death in 1181.[158] Isma'il's cousin, the *atabeg* Mas'ud of Sinjar, took over Aleppo soon after. Saladin marched and besieged the heart of the Zengid atabegate, Mosul, in 1182 in an ambitious move. His aim was to stop the Zengids of Mosul from influencing and interfering in Aleppo's affairs. He succeeded in his aim, and the following year he seized Aleppo, ending the Zengid atabegate in Syria.[159] As a result of such overwhelming success and expansion of Saladin, we see the Zengid *atabeg*, Mas'ud, writing to the Eldiguzid *atabeg*, Pahlawan of Azerbaijan, in 1183–4, urging him for help against Saladin.[160]

It is not the aim here to examine the career of Saladin, but the office of *atabeg* that he claimed for Zengid Isma'il, and how it developed. Saladin tried to win over the 'Abbasid caliph. He wrote to him, accusing the Zengids of declaring the *khutba* for Tughril III, and at the same time contacting the Crusaders to attack his dominions in Syria. He assured the caliph that his aim was not to end the Zengids, but to defend Islam.[161]

Mas'ud did not receive help from the Eldiguzids, and when Saladin approached Mosul, he used the diplomacy of women. He sent an envoy led by his mother, the daughter of Nur al-Din, his deceased sultan and several other women who represented the elite of Mosul. Mas'ud's aim was to make Saladin accept a truce, especially if it was requested from the harem. Saladin received them, but did not respond positively.[162] The following year Saladin submitted Mosul and Mas'ud to his authority, ending the *khutba* to the Seljuqid sultan, and declaring it to Saladin. Saladin managed to seize large territories in the Jazira as well.[163]

Here, we see the Zengid atabegate, created originally by the Seljuqs, became part of the newly founded Ayyubid Turkicised state, borne out of the Zengid dynasty. After Saladin's death in 1193 and the civil war that followed, the atabegate of Mosul tried to restore some independence.[164] However, the Zengid dynasty was declining under the ailing Ayyubid dynasty after 1218, two decades after the Seljuq dynasty had ended in Iraq and Iran.

The result was the rise of a new atabegate in Mosul, founded by Lu'Lu' b. 'Abdallah who was an *atabeg* for the last Zengid prince in Mosul, al-Qahir; he was ten years old. Lu'Lu' founded the Lu'Lu'id atabegate in 1234, which ruled in Mosul and minted the coins in their names until the Mongol invasion of Mosul in 1262.[165]

The Eldiguzid Atabegate in Azerbaijan

The last atabegate to be discussed here was founded by Sultan Mas'ud in Azerbaijan in about 1136, and continued until 1225 when it was ended by the Khwarazmian invasion. The paradigm of this atabegate is unique, like the one in Syria with its political exploitation of the female roles and the political influence of women. By the time the Eldiguzids were founded, there were about twelve *atabeg*s serving at different levels. However, none of them produced a hereditary dynasty, only military chiefs and military governors of provinces and cities. I should point out as well that the different Seljuqid sultans did not learn from the episode of the previous three atabegates discussed above, which all proved to be anti-state, and worked against the basic political interests of the sultanate.

Shams al-Din Eldiguz was a *mamluk*, first of Sultan Mahmud II, and then of Sultan Mas'ud, who appointed him as *atabeg* in Arran, Azerbaijan.[166] Sultan Mas'ud made him marry the widow of his brother Tughril II (d. 1134), Mu'mina Khatun. Eldiguz was given the boy king Arslan III b. Tughril II to raise.[167] Despite our limited knowledge of the early career of Eldiguz, that marriage reflects a great honour to the man, who certainly proved loyal and useful for Mas'ud.

Eldiguz was preceded in Azerbaijan by the powerful *atabeg* Qara Sunqur, who was appointed by Sultan Tughril II. Qara Sunqur had King Seljuq Shah b. Muhammad Tapar under his tutelage. Eldiguz governed Arran, but was overshadowed by Qara Sunqur, who was in command of most of Azerbaijan until his death in Ardabil in 1140.[168] The mountainous nature of Azerbaijan and Transcaucasia, in addition to the endless quarrelling among the three surviving kings, sons of Sultan Muhammad Tapar and their sons and nephews, meant that the chroniclers reported information about this region and period in a sporadic way. Azerbaijan is a vast area that contains major cities such as Arran, Tabriz, Hamadan, Zanjan, Maragha and Jibal. There is often confusion in the sources as regards what is a province and what is a city within a province.

After the death of Sultan Mas'ud in 1152, Eldiguz started to appear in the chronicles as the master of Azerbaijan, with the exception of Maragha. He had formed a pact with his neighbouring Ahmadili atabegate in 1153, represented by Aq Sunqur II, to support the sultanate of Sulayman against his nephew Muhammad II. The pact lasted for some years. When Eldiguz failed in his attempt, he struck the coins in the name of Sultan Sanjar b. Muhammad Tapar in Khurasan.[169]

The rivalry between the Eldiguzids and Ahmadilis atabegates never stopped. In about 1159 the *atabeg* Aq Sunqur II al-Ahmadil was given the infant king Muhammad b. Mas'ud to raise. As a result, he refused the authority of the Eldiguzids in Azerbaijan, and was supported by the 'Abbasid vizier Ibn Hubayra in Baghdad.[170]

Our concern here is the influence of women, and not the detailed political–military history of the Eldiguzids. The new paradigm introduced by

Eldiguz was that he had two sons from his wife, Mu'mina Khatun, mother of King Arslan in his ward (it is not clear when the children were born, but it could be assumed that it was after Mas'ud's death). The elder son was Pahlawan Muhammad, and the younger was Qizil Arslan.[171] Eldiguz was the first *atabeg* to have children from the *khatun* whom he had married, in order to guard the interests of her son. Now he had children by her, we see him establish himself as the hereditary line. In 1161, after the murder of Sultan Sulayman, in which Eldiguz collaborated, he declared himself as '*atabeg* '*azim*' (great *atabeg*), and minted coins in his name.[172] This title was never used by any other *atabeg*s in Syria, Iraq or Iran. Some Seljuqid commanders even declared his stepson, Arslan, as sultan.[173]

Eldiguz marginalised the Seljuqid king Arslan under his tutelage to the benefit of his own two sons. Before his death in 1175, he installed his elder son, Pahlawan, as ruler of Rayy, and Qizil Arslan in north-western Azerbaijan (it is not clear where he was based) and appointed him as *isfahsalar*, too.[174] As previously mentioned, Eldiguz had expansionist and independent ambitions. Al-Isfahani, who was an eyewitness to these events, mentioned that Eldiguz had in his ward two Seljuqid kings: Arslan and Malik Shah III b. Mahmud II. The vizier of the caliph advised him to retreat to Hamadan with only one king.[175] When Dayfa Khatun, mother of Ghazi II of Mosul, contacted him in 1170 to stop Nur al-Din from invading Mosul, he wrote to Nur al-Din, threatening him if he attacked the atabegate of Mosul. In reality, he did not have the military might to support his threat, but through this show of bravado, he widened his influence.

In 1175, Pahlawan Muhammad succeeded his father in the same territories. He declared himself on the dinar as 'the just king, *atabeg* Muhammad ibn *atabeg* Eldiguz'.[176] While his father had named himself the 'great *atabeg*' (in the Seljuqid realm), Pahlawan was the first *atabeg* to declare himself as a king, unlike in the atabegate of Tughtekin, Ahmadil or Zengi. His legitimacy came from his mother, the *khatun*, as much as it came from his father. I should say that the decaying Seljuqid sultanate did not issue any decree for the right of inheritance to the Eldiguzids as they did with Tughtekin in Damascus (that was at the same time, under the Zengid atabegate, as Saladin had installed himself as *atabeg* for Nur al-Din's son in Syria).

According to al-Isfahani, at the beginning of Pahlawan's atabegate his half-brother and king-in-waiting, Arslan III, tried to seize power himself (a legitimate royal coup), although we do not know how he got support. However, Arslan failed in his attempt, and was jailed by Pahlawan, who declared Arslan's young son, Tughril III, as sultan and ruled in his name. Tughril III (d. 1194) was the last of the Seljuqid dynasty in Iraq and Iran.[177] As for Arslan, Pahlawan held him in captivity until both died in 1186.[178]

Pahlawan kept his brother Qizil Arslan as his deputy in Tabriz. The historical significance of the atabegate of Pahlawan is in the following:

1. He managed to continue after his father and declared himself *atabeg* and king; he jailed one sultan, his half-brother, and appointed his own son to rule in his name.
2. He established a special battalion called Pahlawaniyya to protect the atabegate after his death.
3. To consolidate his power in the Caucasus, he resorted to political marriage with Shah Arman in south-western Azerbaijan. He married his daughter so he would inherit his principality. In addition, he had another political marriage with the *khatun* daughter of Inanj, lord of Hamadan.[179]
4. He threatened Saladin while the latter was besieging the Zengid atabegate of Mosul in 1182.[180] That reflects his status in dominating Azerbaijan and its surrounding areas.
5. He managed to dominate the political affairs of the rising atabegate of Salghurid Zengi (r. 1161–78 in Shiraz).[181]

In 1186, Qizil Arslan succeeded his brother Pahlawan in the atabegate. The widow of the latter, Inanj Khatun (as referred to by the chroniclers), interfered to defend the political interests of her two sons, Mahmud Qutlugh and Amir Amiran, against the two sons Abu Bakr and Uzbek from another concubine of Pahlawan, Qutayba. The result was that Qizil Arslan married Inanj Khatun in pure Turkmen fashion, just like inheriting a property. In addition, he declared himself '*al-malik al-mu'azzam*' (the grandest king) and installed himself as *atabeg* for the young Sanjar II b. Sulayman, after Sultan Tughril III tried to 'rebel', encouraged by some ambitious commanders.[182] It is strange that after assuming the title of king, the Eldiguzids were still keen on retaining the title *atabeg*, although originally the same person could not hold both titles, especially as the status of king was higher than any other office.

Qizil Arslan, who was childless, made his eldest nephew Abu Bakr his deputy. Inanj Khatun did not like that her two sons were ignored, and were under the custody of Qizil Arslan.[183] She secretly sent a message from Rayy to the two trusted commanders of her deceased husband Pahlawan in Hamadan, writing:

> How do you accept that a son of a slave concubine came to be in command and to a higher degree than my two sons? I own the money, wealth, treasures and plenty of dinars to maintain all of you for several years ahead. I want you to ride immediately from Hamadan and bring my two sons to me. I will financially support all who will join you in your march, until all the troops of your former lord *atabeg* Pahlawan join your movement.[184]

I do wonder if Inanj Khatun had read parts of the *Shahnameh* of the great Iranian poet Ferdowsi (d. 1010), or if she recalled the spirit of his heroine, Homay. He praised Queen Homay in his epic: 'She succeeded her husband, Behman. She set the crown upon her head, admitted all the army to her court, and opened the portal of her treasures, and gave dinars.'[185] Inanj Khatun tried to follow the same path two centuries later, also in Iran.

The two commanders, Ay Abah and Rus, received her message. Within three days, they were in Hamadan at the service of the *khatun* with her son; a large number of troops from the Pahlawaniyya battalion also joined them. Qizil Arslan had to swiftly put down this rebellion started by the *khatun*. He marched to her in Rayy and besieged her in the citadel, where she was leading the revolt (this occurred in about 1186, although the dates are disputed). Her two chief emirs escaped, and after a few days she surrendered the citadel to her loathed husband.[186] Al-Husayni reports that, despite her surrender to her *atabeg* husband, she encouraged her two sons to join the Seljuqid sultan Tughril III, who had also been marginalised by Qizil Arslan. In 1187, Qizil Arslan, he who referred to himself as the grandest king, had to counter the *khatun*'s measures by contacting the 'Abbasid caliph, al-Nasir (d. 1225), for support; he called himself a *mamluk* of the caliph to gain more legitimacy before his commanders, as well as military support against Tughril and the *khatun*'s sons.[187]

The confrontation between Qizil Arslan and Tughril lasted until 1190, during which time Saladin tried to mediate between the two sides. We could assert the view that Inanj Khatun was supporting Tughril financially in order to elevate the status of her sons during this long period, as she had promised before. Her sons were in the company of Tughril all this time. In 1190 Qizil Arslan captured Tughril and the hopes of Inanj Khatun did not materialise; the following year, however, she had the chance to order some of her *mamluk*s to kill Qizil Arslan in their palace in Hamadan.[188]

Clearly, we can see that the situation of Inanj Khatun depended on her wealth and close commanders around her, like Khayzuran, Shaghab and Sitt al-Mulk. However, she was not of the calibre of Queen Arwa or Turkan Khatun in commanding the forces herself, and appearing courageous in the public sphere.

Inanj Khatun seized her opportunity in the disorder that followed the murder of Qizil Arslan. She wrote to Tughril, who had been set free by the commanders in Hamadan, and proposed to marry him, as he would become the sultan; in addition, she revealed to him that she was in possession of significant wealth, left to her by her first husband, Pahlawan.[189]

Inanj Khatun was hoping that her two sons would occupy leading positions in Tughril's sultanate, and that he was in need of her financial support as much as that of her followers. The marriage was concluded in Hamadan in the same year (1190), but soon after she was mysteriously found dead in her palace.[190] Her two sons appeared in Tabriz, where they were joined by a large force of their father's supporters. In 1191 Qutlugh, son of Pahlawan, became ruler of Tabriz; he killed the last Seljuqid sultan, Tughril III, in 1194.[191] His foe and half-brother, Abu Bakr, ruled large parts of Azerbaijan until 1210.[192] However, his reign was characterised by strife and decay. The Eldiguzids could not resist the constant expansionist invasions into their territories by Queen Tamar of Christian Georgia (r. 1184–1213), who exploited their strife and decline.[193]

In addition to the domestic motives of Queen Tamar to expand in the Caucasus, Prince Amir Amiran b. Atabeg Pahlawan sought military help from her against his half-brother Abu Bakr, in return for becoming a vassal to her afterwards. She welcomed this opportunity and supplied him with an army that marched to Kanja, where he defeated Abu Bakr; he escaped to Tabriz, and soon after Amir Amiran died.[194] The army of Queen Tamar continued to raid the Eldiguzids almost on a yearly basis. Abu Bakr married a Georgian princess in 1203 and submitted parts of his territories to Queen Tamar; he practically became a vassal to her.[195]

As a result of the Eldigizud–Georgian relationship under the powerful Queen Tamar, she took the unusual step by minting a dirham in just the Arabic language, and not Georgian (see Figure 7). It reads on the obverse: 'Malikat al-malikat. Jalal al-dunya wa al-din. Tamara bint Giorgi. Zahir al-Masih' ('Queen of queens. Glory of the secular world and religion. Tamara daughter of Giorgi. Champion of the Messiah'). The coin is dated 1200 CE.

Why was a Giorgian coin, aimed at circulation in the Christian Georgian Kingdom, struck with Arabic letters? It could be that with the expansion of Queen Tamar in Muslim Azerbaijan, she knew that this coin would also be circulated in Muslim territories through trade. She prided herself as the queen of some Muslims, whose caliph's official language was Arabic. Although there were no queens on the Muslim side to be 'queen of queens', perhaps she was referring to those who had come before her as well as her contemporary Seljuqid *khatuns*.

As no coins had ever been minted in the Muslim world bearing the name of a woman, we will shortly discuss how Tamara's dirham, with Arabic writing, had an influence on future Turkmen and Ayyubids.

The Eldiguzid atabegate again witnessed the use of political marriage, this time under their last *atabeg*, Ozbeg b. Pahlawan, who married the daughter of the Ahmadili *atabeg* Korp Arslan after 1210. By 1225 the atabegate had come to an end, with the invasion of the Khwarazmians in Azerbaijan.

Having studied these four Seljuq Turkmen atabegates, I would say that the office of the *atabeg* started as a tutelage post for an individual young prince or son of the sultan and king, but never for the daughter or princess. The use of the king's wife as a political tool to cement the new marriage after she was deliberately divorced to marry a leading Turkmen commander reflects how the office depended on women from its inception. It is telling that the wishes of the woman or princess being forced to marry someone else was not taken into consideration.

The *atabeg* office, which was meant to protect the interests of the young king-to-be, and guarantee the socio-political Turkmen rule, in fact had the opposite effect, mainly because there was no supervision of the *atabeg*, and no clear time limit as to when he should hand power to the king in his guardianship. As a result, we saw kings stay in the wards of their *atabeg*s for very long periods. In addition, the post become hereditary through the line of the *atabeg* and his children, thereby marginalising the original candidate or, in some cases, resulting in their murder. With the various civil wars erupting after Malik Shah's death in 1092, and mushrooming after 1118 when Muhammad Tapar died, with no end, we see the atabegate being recognised as a dynasty within the Seljuqid dynasty. Some, like the Ahmadilis, Zengids and Eldiguzids, survived after their masters, the Seljuqs, and declared themselves as kings.

The following list of *atabeg*s and their wards is constructed mainly from the sporadic information supplied by al-Isfahani, Ibn al-Athir and Nishapuri; we can see that a number of *atabeg*s, some very prominent, did not pass their post on to others or were replaced, or were even killed without a challenge:

Atabeg	*Ward*
Kalisargh	Sultan Alp Arslan (before and after the sultanate).
Nizam al-Mulk	Sultan Malik Shah.
al-Qummi and Gumushtegin	Sultan Berkyaruq (before 1092).
Qimaj	Sultan Sanjar, 1097 for one year.
Qutlugh	Sultan Muhammad I, 1099 (killed by Muhammad in 1102).
Iyaz	Malik Shah b. Berkyaruq, 1105 (killed by Sultan Muhammad I, after Iyaz declared his king as sultan).
Ay Abah or Juyush beg	Mas'ud b. Muhammad (holder of Azerbaijan as an *iqta'*; Mas'ud's mother had a different husband).
Shir Kir	Tughril b. Muhammad I, 1110.
Kindaghdi	Tughril b. Muhammad 1119 (replaced Shir Kir).
Ghurghuli	Mahmud II, 1119.
Juyush Beg	Mas'ud, 1119 (he wanted to install his king as sultan against Mahmud II and his *atabeg*, Ghurghuli).
Juyush Beg	Fought Kindaghdi, 1120 (upon the orders of Mahmud II).
Al-Bursuqi	Son of Mahmud II, 1124–6 (holder of *iqta'*, Mosul).
Qaraja al-Saqi	Seljuq Shah b. Muhammad I, 1131. He fought Zengi and Aq Sunqur. This was the year of the three atabegs fighting for their lords.
Qara Sunqur	Tughril b. Muhammad, after Kindaghdi. He seized Fars from 1135 to 1138, and surrendered half of it to Seljuq Shah. In 1140 Qara Sunqur died after giving his infant son to his commanders to raise.
Al-Baqsh	Seljuq Shah, 1136. He allied with Zengi.

(The dates given here are those mentioned in the sources as regards the existence of the *atabeg*s in office. Start and end dates are often not mentioned in the sources.)

This list shows how *atabeg*s became mostly warlords for the young kings in their custody, but also that they had their own ambitions. Most of them did not manage or have the chance to transform his post into a hereditary one, as was the case with the others discussed. However, the *iqta'* allocated to them was an integral element of their post in order to carry on with their responsibilities, while the woman or mother of the king was never given an *iqta'*, as A. K. S. Lambton observes.[196]

The atabegate as a system continued in several areas in Iran under the Turkmen powers until the Mongol invasion in the mid-thirteenth century. The atabegate of the Salghurids (1148–1282) in Shiraz produced one of medieval Islam's queen consorts under the Mongols, Abish bt. Sa'd (r. 1262–82).[197] In about 1262–3, Abish Khatun, at the age of five, was engaged to the seven-year-old Mongol Ilkhanid prince Mengo Temur, son of Hulegu Khan (d. 1265). Upon Hulegu's order, Abish was declared queen consort, and *atabeg*. She had two significant coins reflecting her political status: a six-pointed star dirham with her name and title on the reverse, '*abateg* Abish', and a dinar, which had on the reverse, '*Khan badh shah/abaqa khan*' (brother of Mengo and successor of Hulegu), and on the obverse: '*La ilaha illa Allah. Abish Bint Sa'd*' (see Figure 8).[198]

Regarding the *atabeg* office, this is a landmark situation, where we have a woman, in fact, a young girl, installed as an *atabeg*. She was the last Salghurid ruler; the *atabeg* post here became synonymous with a leader without any practical duties or anyone in her ward. Having a woman's name minted on the dinar and dirham for an Islamic dynasty with non-Muslim Mongol protection was an exceptional case. Leila Fathi argues that the status of women in pre-Islamic Iran gained much more prestige and respect than after the coming of Islam. Women goddesses, such as Nanaya and Nike, were minted on Parthian coins. In Sassanid Iran, on the eve of Islam, the queens Mouza, Puran and Shapurdakht proudly had their figures on the mint.[199] Clearly, the Mongol Ilkhanid element was behind such changes – again, with the influential two Christian wives of Hulegu. Bruno De Nicola's book, *Women in Mongol Iran*, is a much awaited and valued study, which gives greater focus to this topic.[200] If we look at the same age, in another area, we see that Seljuqid sultan of Anatolia, Kay-Khusraw II (r. 1237–46), who married a Georgian princess, had both his and her figures for a limited time on the currency. Clearly, that was down to Christian Georgian influence. Due to pressure from his domestic advisors, he later substituted her image with that of their son, and his with a lion (see Figure 9).[201]

I believe this was the general milieu of the age, even between the most celebrated and genius, for example, the three Iranian friends in the service of the Seljuqid sultanate: Nizam al-Mulk, Abu Hamid al-Ghazali and Omar Khayyam. Nizam al-Mulk was the Seljuqid vizier who believed that asking the opinion of women on political matters would bring calamity to the state, as already mentioned from his *Siyasat Nameh*. The other two were philosophers and advisors to Malik Shah. Al-Ghazali, influenced by Aristotle, wrote in his book, *Nasihat al-Muluk* (*Advice to Kings*) that women were a major obstacle to proper leadership).[202] Omar Khayyam, the grand poet and close advisor to Sultan Malik Shah, with his Iranian Nishapuri heritage, often praised Iranian kings, such as the seventh-century Parviz or the mythological Kay-Kabad,[203] but he neglected to mention any female Iranian ruling figures, and spoke of women only when talking about pleasure. I should add that Ibn Rushd (or Averroes) of Muslim Spain (d. 1198) took the position of women no further. He did write about the idea of equality between the two genders in power, but it had to be taken with caution within the guidelines of Islamic law.[204] This reflects the dogmatic thinking of apologists in the twenty-first century in most, if not all, Muslim-populated countries.

The Turkmen *atabeg* institution continued and underwent significant changes under the Ayyubids, who were Turkicised, as will be discussed in the next chapter.

Eunuchs and their Influence under the Seljuqs

The Seljuq rule was distinct regarding the nature of their court culture, inherited from their predecessors. The mobility of their nomadic court, or *dargah*, which travelled with the sultan or king wherever he went, made it difficult for the Seljuqs to acquire a large court, and for the chroniclers to observe and be able to tell us more about them. This is what Charles Melville refers to as 'the nomadism of the Seljuq court'.[205] Indeed, the Umayyads and early 'Abbasids were nomads too, and witnessed tremendous military expansion just as the Seljuqs achieved in a relatively short time, but they had a metropolis, like Damascus or Baghdad. Nevertheless, the Seljuqs, with their constant divisions and civil wars among their lords following the death of Tughril Beg in 1063, created local capitals, like Isfahan, Merv, Nishapur, Tabriz, Rayy, Iznik, Aleppo, Damascus and Baghdad. Thus, a smaller-scale multi-court system developed.

The Seljuqs continued to use eunuchs in their state, and its branches from their early days at various military–political levels, as they found that their predecessors, the Buwayhids, or their contemporaries, the Fatimids and what remained of the 'Abbasids, were using them. Having said that, three features do distinguish their age from those before them: (1) the Seljuqs practised castration for sexual and political motives within their dominions – in other words, they did not just depend on importing them from the slave markets from outside the Muslim territories; (2) we see the rise of eunuch–*atabeg*, which influenced other Turkmen and Turkicised dynasties, like the Zengids and the Ayyubids; and (3) the continuation of eunuchs involved in the military, with an emphasis on giving them the office of keeper of citadels in major cities.

Regarding the first feature, the chronicles described how Sultan Tughril was in love with one of his *hajib*s, Khumartakin (d. 1062). He castrated him, and couldn't tolerate being separated from him. Even when the sultan went to see his wives in the harem, Khumartakin was always in his company.[206] Khumartakin, who was killed in his mid-twenties, had the unusual title, '*al-tughrilbi*', simply named after Tughril. This would have been an honour and reflects the close sexual relationship between the two. Ibn al-Athir described the milieu as one that led to total decay, while Sibt Ibn al-Jawzi wrote about how the sultan 'would have the pleasurable company of Khumartakin, alone'.[207]

The eunuch al-Tughrilbi/Khumartakin was not the chief *hajib*, but he was a military commander used by his master in different campaigns around Iraq. He was keeper of the *tughra* (insignia), and was also known as al-Tughra'i. The dual function of this eunuch, as lover and commander, is best described by Abu Bakr al-Bayhaqi (d. 1066):

> They (eunuchs) like women for a placid dweller
> Moreover, act as men if a long campaign calls them.[208]

When Tughril lost his passion for his eunuch in 1962, he simply ordered his murder. Khumartakin was replaced by another commander, Sawtakin; he was also a eunuch.[209] That reminds us of the sexual behaviour of the 'Abbasid caliph al-Amin and his eunuch, Kawthar, and also the behavioural pattern of the Seljuqid sultan Sanjar, with his *ghilman*, although we are not sure if they were eunuchs; however, they all enjoyed powerful political influence in the state.

The second case of castration associated with Tughril was that of his Persian vizier, al-Kunduri (d. 1064). It is reported that al-Kunduri was commissioned by Tughril to be his messenger in completing a marriage to an unnamed bride. Surprisingly, al-Kunduri married this woman instead of his master, so Tughril punished him by castrating him; even more surprisingly, he kept him in his office.[210] Another story in the chronicles is that it was reported to the sultan that al-Kunduri married the woman, so out of fear of what could be awaiting him from Tughril, al-Kunduri castrated himself.[211] It is not convincing that a Seljuqid vizier would be kept in office after betraying the trust of his sultan, and the reason for his castration will probably remain a mystery. However, it is the Seljuqid pattern of castrating normal men for punishment or pleasure within the Muslim territories that is rare. It recalls what was mentioned about castration under the Umayyads in Damascus, and in Medina itself (see Chapter One).

I should point out here that the chief judge of Baghdad under Tughril, al-Mawardi (d. 1058), wrote: 'Castrated men should not be prevented from occupying any office in politics or jurisprudence. Their mutilated sexual organs have no relationship with the capacity of the brain.'[212] That was interpretation of the shari'a, although al-Jahiz, two centuries before him, had noted that their mental capacity was affected by such castration. In addition, out of political necessity, the 'Abbasids preceded the Seljuqs in using eunuchs in leading official positions, even as ruler of Egypt, like Kafur in the tenth century, as previously mentioned.

Al-Kunduri, who tried to execute the will of his sultan by installing his young nephew, Sulayman, as successor, made him a prime enemy of Sulayman's elder and powerful brother, Alp Arslan. In 1063–4 al-Kunduri was severely marginalised by Alp Arslan and his powerful vizier, Nizam al-Mulk. Nizam al-Mulk tried to get rid of his competitor by advising Alp Arslan to assassinate al-Kunduri, which he did in 1064.[213]

This pattern of castration or creating eunuchs in Muslim territories was very clear under the Seljuqid commander Zengi I, who practised it on a wider scale. His contemporary chronicler al-Isfahani wrote this anecdote:

> When Zengi sleeps, a few of his servants sleep around his bed. They attend to his care while awake or asleep. They protect and defend him like lions in battle and almost visit him in his dreams. They are fresh and extremely beautiful *ghilman/mamluk*s, like a morning at sunrise. He loves them as they love him and, despite their loyalty to him, he is sometimes harsh with them. They are the children of the stallions from Turkish, Armenian and Byzantine lords.
>
> It was Zengi's habit if he wanted to punish a leading commander, to dismiss or kill him, while keeping his young son under his authority, and castrate him. If he liked the look of a certain *ghulam*, he castrated him in order to prevent him growing a beard and looking masculine.[214]

It is important to note that the word *ghulumiyya* (lust) is derived from the word *ghulam*. Clearly this sexual taste and behaviour was somewhat known among the Turkmen, from Tughril to Zengi I and Sanjar, as detailed above. In addition to this anecdote, we have the pro-Zengi chronicler, Ibn al-Athir, proudly writing about the firmness and jealousy of Zengi to protect the women of his troops while they were away with him on campaigns.

Zengi castrated Thiqat al-Din, the keeper of the citadel of Jazirat Ibn 'Umar near Mosul. This commander was very close to Zengi, but he would have affairs with the harem of the soldiers, while they are away. Zengi ordered his castration as a punishment for his evil deeds.[215] So, using castration for sexual pleasure or political punishment was known under the Seljuqs, and if three lords practised it, that meant that others would adopt the same practice, but this did not receive attention by chroniclers who reported these anecdotes.

The second feature of Seljuqid eunuchs is that some of them became *atabeg*s, which opened the door for many others to follow under other dynasties. In Aleppo, after the death of the Seljuqid king Ridwan in 1113, the eunuch commander Lu'Lu' became *atabeg* for his sixteen-year-old son, Alp Arslan. He was the de facto ruler of northern Syria, and the following year killed the king and replaced him with his younger brother, Sultan Shah.[216] The eunuch–*atabeg* Lu'Lu' remained in office, leading from his headquarters in the citadel of Aleppo, until he was killed in 1117. In order to retain his office, he led very pragmatic and peaceful relations with the enemies of the

Seljuqs, such as the Shi'i Isma'ilis, and kept his peace with the Crusaders of Antioch and Edessa, who shared his countryside of Aleppo.[217]

Lu'Lu' was replaced by another eunuch *atabeg* for King Sultan Shah. He was Yaruqtash, who was a military commander and became chief of the army during his very short (one month) period of office.[218] In Damascus there was the eunuch commander Sawtakin, who was the deputy of Tutush I in 1095, and was de facto ruler of Damascus after the murder of Tutush in Iran. Sawtakin invited Duqaq to rule Damascus, but soon after the *atabeg* Tughtekin arrived and eliminated all other commanders from the scene so that he alone could dominate the young king.[219]

This move encouraged others to repeat the experience, although the atabegate as an office started with a marriage between a commander and the mother of the boy king. In 1136 the eunuch Amin al-Dawla Gumushtegin, who was commander of the army, became *atabeg* for King Mahmud b. Buri for a period of just two months.[220] That had influenced the Zengids to appoint eunuch *atabeg*s in their administration. In Zengid Mosul the eunuch *atabeg* 'Abd al-Masih, who had been keeper of the Mosul citadel in 1167 under *atabeg* Mawdud, intervened to change the will of his master following Mawdud's death in 1170. Mawdud wanted his son Zengi II to succeed, but 'Abd al-Masih installed Ghazi II.[221] 'Abd al-Masih remained in office as de facto ruler of Mosul until he was deposed by Nur al-Din b. Zengi in 1171. Nur al-Din replaced a eunuch with another eunuch commander, Gumushtegin, as keeper of Mosul citadel.[222] The citadel was the most protected and strategic place in most Muslim cities. It contained the palace of the ruler and his harem, and treasures, and was the last place to fall due to its heavy fortification.

Gumushtegin remained loyal to his powerful master, Nur al-Din. When the latter died in 1174 and competition erupted between three commanders for the atabegate of his son, Isma'il (as previously mentioned), Gumushtegin returned to Aleppo and orchestrated a coup with the vital assistance of the keeper of the Aleppo citadel, the eunuch Shadhbekht.[223] He arrested the legitimate commander whom Nur al-Din had installed after him as *atabeg*, and Gumushtegin became the ruler of Aleppo and *atabeg* for Isma'il. He held this position until his death in 1177, having managed to resist powerful attacks launched by Saladin against the city.[224]

It is believed that most of the Seljuqid and Zengid eunuchs came from a military background and this continued to be the case until the thirteenth century under the Ayyubids. Most of them were chiefs of armies or keepers of strategic citadels. That was the case of our last model, the eunuch commander Mujahid al-Din Qaymaz. In 1180, during the final illness of the *atabeg* Ghazi II, the elite commander Qaymaz convinced him not to appoint as a successor his very young son, Sanjar, and to appoint Ghazi's brother, Mas'ud, in order to resist the ambitious commander Saladin. Qaymaz became 'the true conductor of the realm and the deputy to the *atabeg*. His opinion is the only reference in the state.' That was in addition to being keeper of the citadel of Mosul.[225]

Qaymaz continued to serve Mas'ud, even when Mosul came under the nominal authority of Saladin in 1183. In 1193, before Mas'ud died, he installed Qaymaz as *atabeg* for his son, Arslan Shah I (d. 1211). Qaymaz remained as keeper of the citadel and defender of the interests of Mosul against the Ayyubid successors of Saladin until he died in 1198.[226] We can see how, for nearly two decades, Qaymaz controlled the Mosul citadel and supervised the political succession of two lords of the principality.

Other duties for eunuchs under the Seljuqs were a continuation of the same practices of previous administrations and dynasties. They continued to use eunuchs in key areas, as they had no biological future, and relied on them, believing in their ultimate trust. They held positions such as police chiefs of cities, keepers of prisons and messengers in times of war.

As most Seljuqid sultans resided in Iran, and spent little time in Iraq, they would appoint a *shihna* (prefect of police) to watch over the 'Abbasid caliph, especially if they had political ambitions, like al-Mustarshid (d. 1135). They also represented the sultan in Iraq and ensured the security of Baghdad during the arduous civil wars. One leading eunuch to hold that post was Sa'd al-Dawla Kohra'in (d. 1100). He served for a very long period under Alp Arslan, and then Malik Shah, who dispatched him to get the caliphate diploma of his sultanate from the caliph, with robes of honour.[227] So, dispatching a eunuch to the caliph, representing the sultan on such a very prestigious occasion, tells us that he was not just an ordinary messenger. Again, in 1094, when Caliph al-Muqtadi died, Berkyaruq dispatched his vizier, Kohra'in, and another commander to the new caliph to grant him the sultanate recognition, and receive, at the same time, caliphal recognition.[228]

A eunuch commander, along with two other high officials, witnessed the exchange of the *bay'a* between the new caliph and sultan.

Kohra'in, who later served Sultan Muhammad against his brother, Berkyaruq, enjoyed exceptional influence in Baghdad, and in the middle of the havoc created by the civil war; he had the power of negotiating directly with the sultan's enemies: 'Kohra'in practised and enjoyed such an influence never before given to a eunuch. He was obeyed by the elite and leading commanders, who would serve him.'[229]

Under Sultan Mahmud II, the eunuch Bihruz, *shihna* of Baghdad, succeeded Zengi in that office in 1127. He was influential in his post, especially as Mahmud II was not on good terms with Caliph al-Mustarshid.[230] He was replaced again by Zengi in 1131, after Mahmud II died. Bihruz, who held some *iqta'*, became immensely rich due to his post and lack of supervision over his practices, which al-Isfahani diagnosed as corruption, and categorised it as the second reason for the decay of the state.[231]

The last four decades of the Seljuqs experienced a tremendous power vacuum, and rapid changes of sultan. However, eunuch commanders were part of this element, filling this vacuum and making use of this havoc to their advantage. The following anecdote illustrates the power of eunuch commanders. Sultan Sulayman was jailed upon orders of his brother, Sultan Mas'ud, in Qazwin. After the latter's death in 1152, the eunuch commander, Muwaffaq, released him. As a result, Sulayman declared his sultanate in Hamadan.[232] Sulayman, who established himself in southern Azerbaijan, depended heavily on his eunuch commander, Kardabadhu, largely due to Sulayman's serious alcoholism. One day in 1160, in the company of Kardabadhu and several clowns and entertainers, Sultan Sulayman thought of creating more laughter by revealing the mutilated organs of Kardbadhu. The reaction was lethal. The eunuch killed his sultan and all those who had laughed with him.[233] Kardabadhu contacted the *atabeg* Eldiguz to declare Arslan Shah (who was under Eldiguz's guardianship) as sultan, replacing Sulayman.[234]

There were several cases where eunuchs served as sultanate messengers and representatives of the sultan during political crises; this had been the convention of 'Abbasid and Fatimid caliphs. For instance, in 1058 Tughril I dispatched the eunuch commander Forak to negotiate with al-Basasiri's ally, Quraysh, in Iraq. In 1192 Sultan Tughril III sent the eunuch commander

Faraj to negotiate with Inanj Khatun of the Eldiguzids in relation to their political marriage.[235]

Regarding the status of eunuchs under the 'Abbasid caliphate, as mentioned previously, the 'Abbasids ceased to exist as an effective political power from the mid-tenth century. The 'Abbasid caliphate under the Seljuqs was a grand religious symbol, confined to parts of Iraq. It was very rare for a caliph to dare to assemble an army to challenge the warring Seljuqid sultans. One such case was that of al-Mustarshid (r. 1118–35). However, he paid a heavy price for his actions, as Sultan Mas'ud hired a massive number of twenty-four assassins (normally they moved in groups of no more than four) to kill him, once he had been captured.[236] This was a clear message from the Seljuqs to future caliphs to keep within the limits of their palaces.

Having said that, 'Abbasid caliphs did use eunuchs as their personal representatives in certain situations. For instance, al-Qa'im dispatched two eunuchs to attend the funeral of his wife, Arslan Khatun, in Isfahan in 1064.[237] Al-Mustarshid used several eunuch commanders in a battle against Zengi in 1125. When one of those eunuchs, 'Afif, was defeated and captured, he was released personally by Zengi due to an old friendship between them.[238] This shows that eunuchs could be treated with respect and also had a social status among men.

The following year two eunuch commanders, Nazar and Iqbal, led a caliphal army against Zengi.[239] However, the caliphal army itself had no long-term influence due to the ever-changing pacts with or against him by several Seljuqid sultans. 'Abbasid caliphs would dispatch their elite eunuchs in other missions. In 1145, al-Muqtafi dispatched the eunuch Qaymaz as the leader of the pilgrimage envoy to Mecca. In 1183, while Saladin was besieging Zengid Mosul, Caliph al-Nasir sent his eunuch Bishir as a diplomat to mediate between Saladin and Mas'ud.[240]

Practicality, political necessity or desire accounts for the Seljuqs' continued use of eunuchs. The judge and theorist al-Mawardi saw in them a normal human being. However, there was no book dedicated to the status of eunuchs up to the Mamluk period in Egypt. The chronicler al-Suyuti (d. 1505) was the first to dedicate a short volume to eunuchs: *Akam al-'Iqyan fi Ahkam al-Khisyan* (*The Hills of Gold in the Rules of Eunuchs*).[241] It set out all the opinions in the shari'a regarding the marriage and divorce of eunuchs. Yet it failed to criminalise the act of castration, or promote further restrictions by Muslim dynasties or administrations, which encouraged castration through buying the product: the eunuchs.

Notes

1. Nizam al-Mulk, *Siyasat Nameh*, p. 68.
2. Mahmud Kashghari, *Diwan Lughat al-Turk*, ed. Kilisli Rifat Bey, Istanbul, 1918, Vol. 1, p. 56; C. E. Bosworth, art.: 'Saldjukids', *EI²*.
3. C. Cahen, art.: 'Ghuzz', *EI²*.
4. Ibid.
5. C. E. Bosworth, 'Saldjukids'.
6. C. E. Bosworth, *The New Islamic Dynasties*, Edinburgh, 2004, pp. 185–8, 213–14.
7. Ibid., pp. 185–209.
8. Richard N. Frye, 'Women in Pre-Islamic Central Asia: The Khatun of Bukhara', in *Women in the Medieval Islamic World: Power, Patronage and Piety*, ed. G. Hambly, London, 1999, pp. 55–68, 64.
9. N. Dalkesen, 'Gender Roles and Women's Status in Central Asia and Anatolia between the Thirteenth and Sixteenth Centuries', unpublished PhD thesis, Istanbul, 2007, pp. 50–1.
10. Carole Hillenbrand, '1092: A Murderous Year', in *Proceedings of the 14th Congress of the Union Européene des Arabisants et Islamists*, Budapest, 1995, pp. 281–96.
11. W. Barthold, *Turkestan down to the Mongol Invasion*, trans. H. A. R. Gibb, London, 1958, p. 269.
12. Ibn al-Athir, *Al-Kamil*, Vol. 10, p. 214.
13. Muhammad Ibn al-Nizam al-Yazdi, *Al-'Irada fi al-Hekaya al-Seljuqiyya*, trans. A. Hasanain, Baghdad, 1979, p. 65; C. E. Bosworth, 'The Political and Dynastic History of the Iranian World (AD 1000–1217)', in *The Cambridge History of Iran*, ed. J. Boyle, Cambridge, 1968, Vol. 5, pp. 1–202, 77.
14. Imad al-Din al-Isfahani, *Tarikh Dawlat al-Saljuq*, Beirut, 1980, p. 81; Ibn al-Athir, *Al-Kamil*, Vol. 10, p. 211.
15. Sibt Ibn al-Jawzi, *Mirat*, Vol. 19, p. 72.
16. Abu al-Fida', *Al-Mukhtasar*, Beirut, 1979, Vol. 2, p. 203; A. K. S. Lambton, 'The Internal Structure of the Seljuqid Empire', in *The Cambridge History of Iran*, ed. J. Boyle, Cambridge, Vol. 5, 1968, pp. 203–81, 255.
17. Al-Yazdi, *Al-'Irada*, p. 73; Ibn al-Athir, *Al-Kamil*, Vol. 10, p. 214.

18. Ibn al-Athir, *Al-Kamil*, Vol. 10, pp. 214–15.
19. Ibid., p. 224.
20. Al-Yazdi, *Al-'Irada*, pp. 74–5.
21. C. E. Bosworth (ed.), *The History of the Seljuq Turks, from the Jami' al-Tawarikh: An Ilkhanid Adaptation of the Saljuq-nama of Zahir al-Din Nishapuri*, trans. K. Luther, London, 2001, pp. 66–7; Ibn al-Athir, *Al-Kamil*, Vol. 10, p. 224.
22. Al-Yazdi, *Al-'Irada*, p. 75; Ibn al-Athir, *Al-Kamil*, Vol. 10, p. 239.
23. Ibn al-Jawzi, *Al-Muntazam*, Vol. 9, p. 85; Ibn al-Athir, *Al-Kamil*, Vol. 10, pp. 234, 240.
24. C. E. Bosworth, 'Political and Dynastic History', p. 78; al-Isfahani, *Ta'rikh*, p. 81; al-Yazdi, *Al-'Irada*, p. 75.
25. Al-Isfahani, *Ta'rikh*, p. 84; Ibn al-Athir, *Al-Kamil*, Vol. 10, p. 252.
26. Ibn al-Athir, *Al-Kamil*, Vol. 10, p. 88.
27. Sibt Ibn al-Jawzi, *Mirat*, Vol. 19, p. 169.
28. Ibn al-Athir, *Al-Kamil*, Vol. 10, pp. 504–6; C. E. Bosworth, *The Later Ghaznavids: Splendour and Decay, the Dynasty in Afghanistan and Northern India, 1040–1186*, New York, 1977, pp. 90–1.
29. Ibn al-Athir, *Al-Kamil*, Vol. 10, p. 553.
30. Al-Isfahani, *Ta'rikh*, pp. 117–18.
31. Ibid., pp. 249–50.
32. Ibn al-Athir, *Al-Kamil*, Vol. 10, p. 220–1.
33. El-Azhari, *The Saljuqs*, p. 77.
34. Ibn 'Asakir, *Wulat Dimashq*, ed. S. al-Munajjid, Damascus, 1985, p. 20.
35. Ibn al-Qalanisi, *Ta'rikh*, p. 234.
36. Ibn 'Asakir, *Wulat*, p. 20; Ibn al-Qalanisi, *Ta'rikh*, pp. 234–5.
37. Ibn al-'Adim, *Zubdat*, Vol. 2, p. 516.
38. Ibid., p. 542.
39. Ibn al-Athir, *Al-Kamil*, Vol. 10, p. 531; Ibn al-'Adim, *Zubdat*, Vol. 2, p. 543.
40. Ibn 'Asakir, *Tarajim*, p. 112.
41. In 1132 Isma'il attacked Banyas in the Golan Heights, capturing it from the Crusaders; he also captured Hamah from the deputies of Zengi in Central Syria. In addition, he looted the countryside of Acre, forcing a truce by King Fulk of Jerusalem.
42. Ibn 'Asakir, *Wulat*, p. 22; Ibn al-Qalanisi, *Ta'rikh*, p. 389; Ibn al-'Adim, *Zubdat*, Vol. 2, p. 256. Ibn al-Qalanisi was mistaken in reporting that Safwat al-Mulk was the mother of Isma'il.
43. Ibn al-'Adim, *Zubdat*, Vol. 2, p. 256.

44. Ibn al-Qalanisi, *Ta'rikh*, p. 389; Ibn al-'Adim, *Zubdat*, Vol. 2, p. 256; Ibn 'Asakir, in *Wulat*, p. 10, has conflicting reports in his other book on *Tarajim* regarding this story.
45. Ibn al-Qalanisi, *Ta'rikh*, p. 390; el-Azhari, *The Saljuqs*, p. 242.
46. Ibn 'Asakir, *Wulat*, p. 22.
47. Ibn al-Athir, *Al-Kamil*, Vol. 11, pp. 68–9.
48. Sadr al-Din al-Husayni, *Zubdat al-Tawarikh, Akhbar al-Umara' wa al-Muluk al-Saljuqiyya*, ed. M. Nur al-Din, Beirut, 1985, p. 155.
49. William of Tyre, *A History of Deeds*, Vol. 1, p. 264; Hans Eberhard Mayer, *The Crusades*, Oxford, 1978, p. 85.
50. Jonathan Phillips, *Holy Warriors: A Modern History of the Crusades*, New York, 2009, pp. 69–70; Thomas Asbridge, *The Crusades: The Authoritative History of the War for the Holy Land*, London, 2010, p. 173.
51. Eric Hanne, 'Women, Power, and the Eleventh and Twelfth-Century 'Abbasid Court', *Hawwa*, 2005, Vol. 3, pp. 80–110, 80.
52. Ibn al-Athir, *Al-Kamil*, Vol. 10, p. 25.
53. Ibid.; Lambton, 'Internal Structure', p. 212.
54. Ibn al-Athir, *Al-Kamil*, Vol. 10, p. 366.
55. George Makdisi, 'The Marriage of Tughril Beg', *International Journal of Middle East Studies*, Vol. 1, No. 3, 1970, pp. 259–75, 269.
56. Lambton, 'Internal Structure', p. 212.
57. Ibn al-Athir, *Al-Kamil*, Vol. 10, p. 26.
58. Hanne, 'Women, Power', p. 96.
59. Ibn al-Athir, *Al-Bahir*, p. 13.
60. Abu al-Fida', *Al-Mukhtasar*, Vol. 2, p. 204; el-Azhari, *The Saljuqs*, p. 75.
61. Abu al-Fida', *Al-Mukhtasar*, Vol. 2, p. 204.
62. Kashghari, *Diwan*, Vol. 1, pp. 50, 81.
63. R. Guseynov, 'Institut Atabekov (The Institution of Atabeks)', *Palestinskii Sbornik*, Vol. 15, No. 78, 1966, pp. 181–96, 181–2.
64. Al-Husayni, *Zubdat al-Tawarikh*, pp. 74, 80.
65. C. Cahen, art.: 'Atabek', *EI*²; A. K. S. Lambton, 'Contributions to the Study of the Seljuq Institutions', PhD thesis, University of London, 1939, p. 185; R. Guseynov, 'Institut Atabekov', p. 183.
66. Lambton, 'Contributions', pp. 191–2.
67. El-Azhari, *The Saljuqs*, p. 47.
68. Ibn al-Azraq al-Fariqi, *Ta'rikh al-Fariqi*, ed. B. Awwad, Cairo, 1959, p. 132; Ibn al-Qalanisi, *Ta'rikh*, p. 215; Ibn al-Athir, *Al-Kamil*, Vol. 10, p. 248.

69. Cahen, 'Atabek'.
70. Ibid.
71. El-Azhari, *The Saljuqs*, p. 284.
72. R. Guseynov, 'Institut Atabekov', p. 186.
73. Ibn al-Qalanisi, *Ta'rikh*, p. 214; Ibn al-'Adim, *Bughyat al-Talab fi Ta'rikh Halab*, ed. A. Sevim, Ankara, 1976, p. 27.
74. El-Azhari, *The Saljuqs*, p. 285.
75. Ibn al-'Adim, *Zubdat*, Vol. 2, p. 491; Ibn al-Athir, *Al-Kamil*, Vol. 10, p. 246; R. W. Crawford, 'Ridwan the Maligned', in *World of Islam: Studies in Honour of Philip Hitti*, eds J. Kritzeck and R. B. Winder, London, 1959, pp. 135–44, 138.
76. Ibn 'Asakir, *Tahdhib Ta'rikh Dimash al-Kabir*, ed. A. Badran, Beirut, 1979, Vol. 4, p. 134.
77. Ibn al-Athir, *Al-Kamil*, Vol. 10, p. 269; Ibn al-'Adim, *Zubdat*, Vol. 2, p. 490.
78. Ibn al-'Adim, *Zubdat*, Vol. 2, p. 491.
79. Ibn al-Qalanisi, *Ta'rikh*, p. 225.
80. El-Azhari, *The Saljuqs*, p. 182.
81. C. E. Bosworth, 'Political and Dynastic History', p. 114.
82. Ibn al-Qalanisi, *Ta'rikh*, p. 321.
83. Joshua Prawer, *The Latin Kingdom of Jerusalem: European Colonialism in the Middle Ages*, London 1972, pp. 60, 78.
84. Al-Maqrizi, *Itti'az*, Vol, 3, pp. 46–51.
85. Mayer, *Crusades*, p. 76; A. Murray, art.: 'Al-Sinnabra Battle', *The Crusades: An Encyclopedia*, ed. A. Murray, Santa Barbara, 2006, Vol. 4.
86. Asbridge, *Crusades*, pp. 157–8.
87. Ibn al-Qalanisi, *Ta'rikh*, p. 306.
88. Ibid., pp. 308–13.
89. Ibn 'Asakir, *Tarajim*, p. 112.
90. Ibn al-Athir, *Al-Kamil*, Vol. 11, p. 39.
91. Ibn al-Qalanisi, *Ta'rikh*, pp. 398–400.
92. Abu al-Fida', *Al-Mukhtasar*, Vol. 3, p. 14; Ibn al-Athir, *Al-Kamil*, Vol. 11, p. 68.
93. Sibt Ibn al-Jawzi, *Mir'at*, Vol. 8, Section B, p. 197; Abu Shama, *Al-Rawdatayn*, Vol. 1, p. 64.
94. Ibn al-'Adim, *Zubdat*, Vol. 2, pp. 233–4.
95. Ibn al-Qalanisi, *Ta'rikh*, p. 450.

96. Anne-Marie Eddé, 'Ridwan, Prince d'Alep de 1095 à 1113', *Revue des Études Islamiques*, 1986, Vol. 54, pp. 101–25.
97. Ibn al-'Adim, *Zubdat*, Vol. 2, pp. 536–7.
98. Munqidh, *Al-I'tibar*, p. 81.
99. Ibn al-Athir, *Al-Kamil*, Vol. 10, p. 408.
100. Ibn al-'Adim, *Zubdat*, Vol. 2, pp. 543–5; Ibn al-Athir, *Al-Kamil*, Vol. 10, p. 531.
101. Lambton, 'Contributions', p. 54.
102. 'Izz al-Din Ibn Shaddad, *Al-A'laq al-Khatira fi Dhikr Umara' al-Sham wa al-Jazira*, ed. S. al-Dahhan, Damascus, 1956, Vol. 2, pp. 218–19.
103. *Alf Layla wa Layla*, Cairo, 2001, Vol. 2, pp. 922–60, Stories 438–66.
104. Geoffrey Lewis, 'Heroines and Others in the Heroic Age of the Turks', in *Women in the Medieval Islamic World*, ed. G. Hambly, London, 1999, pp. 147–60, 147, 149.
105. Al-Husayni, *Zubdat al-Tawarikh*, p. 316.
106. Ibid., pp. 319–20.
107. Lambton, 'Internal Structure', pp. 239–40.
108. Bosworth, 'Political and Dynastic History', p. 167; Lambton, 'Internal Structure', p. 240; David Morgan, *Medieval Persia*, London, 1988, pp. 41–2.
109. Carole Hillenbrand, 'Aspects of the Court of the Great Seljuqs', in *The Seljuqs: Politics, Society and Culture*, eds C. Lange and S. Mecit, Edinburgh, 2011, pp. 22–38, 24.
110. Al-Dhahabi, *Al-'Ibar fi Khabar Man Ghabar*, Kuwait, 1961, Vol. 4, p. 9; Sibt Ibn al-Jawzi, *Mir'at*, Vol. 8, p. 36; V. Minorsky, art.: 'Ahmadilis', *EI²*.
111. Al-Isfahani, *Ta'rikh*, pp. 148, 149; Bosworth, 'Political and Dynastic History', p. 170.
112. Minorsky, 'Ahmadilis'; Bosworth, 'Saldjukids'.
113. Ibn al-Athir, *Al-Kamil*, Vol. 10, pp. 669–70.
114. Ibid., pp. 674–6.
115. Al-Isfahani, *Ta'rikh*, pp. 150–3; al-Husayni, *Zubdat al-Tawarikh*, pp. 212–13; Minorsky, 'Ahmadilis'.
116. Bosworth, 'Political and Dynastic History', p. 177; K. A. Luther, art.: 'Atabakan-e Maraga', *Encyclopaedia Iranica*, Vol. 2, London, 2011, pp. 898–900.
117. Ibn Wasil, *Mufarrij al-Kurub fi Ta'rikh bani Ayyub*, ed. J. al-Shayyal, Cairo, 1953, Vol. 1, pp. 62–3; Ibn al-Athir, *Al-Kamil*, Vol. 11, p. 23.
118. Al-Husayni, *Zubdat al-Tawarikh*, p. 219.
119. Bosworth, *New Islamic Dynasties*, p. 199.

120. Al-Isfahani, *Ta'rikh*, p. 209; Ibn al-Athir, *Al-Kamil*, Vol. 11, pp. 205–6.
121. Al-Husayni, *Zubdat al-Tawarikh*, pp. 272–3; Minorsky, 'Ahmadilis'; Luther, 'Atabakan-e Maraga'.
122. Ibn al-Athir, *Al-Kamil*, Vol. 11, p. 332; Bosworth, 'Political and Dynastic History', pp. 169–70.
123. Bosworth, *New Islamic Dynasties*, p. 198; Minorsky, 'Ahmadilis'.
124. Al-Husayni, *Zubdat al-Tawarikh*, p. 304; Ibn al-Athir, *Al-Kamil*, Vol. 12, pp. 204, 240.
125. Ibn al-Athir, *Al-Kamil*, Vol. 12, p. 377.
126. Luther, 'Atabakan-e Maraga'.
127. William E. D. Allen, *A History of the Georgian People from the Beginning down to the Russian Conquest in the Nineteenth Century*, New York, 1971, p. 82.
128. Bosworth, 'Political and Dynastic History', p. 179.
129. Ibn al-Athir, *Al-Bahir*, p. 32; Ibn Wasil, *Mufarrij*, Vol. 1, p. 33.
130. El-Azhari, *Zengi and the Muslim Response to the Crusades*, London, 2016, p. 15.
131. Ibn al-Athir, *Al-Bahir*, p. 38.
132. Ibid., p. 71.
133. Ibn Wasil, *Mufarrij*, Vol. 1, p. 64; Ibn al-Athir, *Al-Bahir*, p. 52.
134. Ibn al-Athir, *Al-Bahir*, pp. 70–2.
135. Al-Isfahani, *Ta'rikh*, p. 65.
136. Ibn al-Athir, *Al-Bahir*, pp. 84–5.
137. Ibn al-Jawzi, *Al-Muntazam*, Vol. 10, pp. 164–5.
138. Al-Isfahani, *Ta'rikh*, p. 222; Ibn al-Athir, *Al-Kamil*, Vol. 11, p. 207.
139. Ibn al-Athir, *Al-Kamil*, Vol. 11, p. 250.
140. al-Husayni, *Zubdat al-Tawarikh*, p. 256; Ibn al-Jawzi, *Al-Muntazam*, Vol. 10, p. 192.
141. Al-Isfahani, *Ta'rikh*, p. 271.
142. Ibn al-Athir, *Al-Bahir*, p. 146; Ibn al-'Adim, *Zubdat*, Vol. 2, p. 331.
143. Ibn Wasil, *Mufarrij*, Vol. 1, pp. 89–90.
144. Abu Shama, *Al-Rawdatayn*, Vol. 1, p. 187.
145. Ibn al-Qalanisi, *Ta'rikh*, p. 450.
146. Ibn al-Athir, *Al-Bahir*, p. 153.
147. Abu Shama, *Al-Rawdatayn*, Vol. 1, p. 188.
148. Ibn al-Athir, *Al-Kamil*, Vol. 11, p. 405.
149. Ibn Wasil, *Mufarrij*, Vol. 2, p. 9.
150. Ibn al-Athir, *Al-Kamil*, Vol. 11, p. 408.
151. Al-Qalqashandi, *Subh*, Vol. 7, pp. 115–16.

152. Abu Shama, *Al-Rawdatayn*, Vol. 1, p. 408.
153. Ibn al-'Adim, *Zubdat*, Vol. 3, pp. 14–18.
154. Ibid., pp. 20–1.
155. Ibn Wasil, *Mufarrij*, Vol. 2, p. 24; Malcolm C. Lyons and D. E. P. Jackson, *Saladin: The Politics of the Holy War*, Cambridge, 1988, p. 88.
156. Ibn Wasil, *Mufarrij*, Vol. 2, p. 33.
157. Ibn al-Athir, *Al-Kamil*, Vol. 11, p. 421.
158. Ibid., pp. 445, 472–3.
159. Ibid., pp. 484–96.
160. Ibid., p. 504.
161. Ibn al-Athir, *Al-Kamil*, Vol. 2, p. 166.
162. Ibn al-Athir, *Al-Kamil*, Vol. 11, p. 512.
163. Ibid., p. 517.
164. Ibn al-Athir, *Al-Bahir*, p. 186.
165. Ibn Wasil, *Mufarrij*, Vol. 3, p. 206; Ibn al-Fuwati, *Al-Hawadith al-Jami'a*, Baghdad, 1931, pp. 45–52; Claude Cahen, art.: 'Lu'Lu'' (Badr al-Din), *EI²*.
166. Ibn al-Athir, *Al-Kamil*, Vol. 11, p. 388.
167. Bosworth, *History of the Seljuq Turks*, p. 110; Al-Isfahani, *Ta'rikh*, p. 152.
168. Al-Isfahani, *Ta'rikh*, pp. 140, 153.
169. Ibid., pp. 214–17; Bosworth, *History of the Seljuq Turks*, pp. 128–30; C. E. Bosworth, art.: 'Eldiguzids', *EI²*.
170. Ibn al-Athir, *Al-Kamil*, Vol. 11, p. 251; Bosworth, 'Political and Dynastic History', p. 171.
171. Bosworth, 'Eldiguzids'.
172. Isfahani, *Ta'rikh*, pp. 271–2; al-Husayni, *Zubdat al-Tawarikh*, p. 258; Bosworth, 'Eldiguzids'; Bosworth, 'Political and Dynastic History', p. 176.
173. Al-Isfahani, *Ta'rikh*, pp. 267–74.
174. Bosworth, *History of the Seljuq Turks*, pp. 142–4.
175. Al-Isfahani, *Ta'rikh*, pp. 233, 260.
176. Al-Husayni, *Zubdat al-Tawarikh*, pp. 284–5; D. K. Kouymjian, 'A Numismatic History of Southeastern Caucasia and Adharbaygan', PhD thesis, Columbia University, New York, 1969, pp. 322–3.
177. Al-Isfahani, *Ta'rikh*, pp. 275–6.
178. Bosworth, *History of the Seljuq Turks*, p. 149; Luther, 'Atabakan-e Maraga'.
179. Al-Husayni, *Zubdat al-Tawarikh*, p. 258; Bosworth, 'Political and Dynastic History', p. 179.
180. Ibn al-Athir, *Al-Kamil*, Vol. 11, p. 487.

181. Al-Husayni, *Zubdat al-Tawarikh*, p. 285; Merçil, *Fars Atabegleri*, pp. 44–5.
182. Al-Husayni, *Zubdat al-Tawarikh*, pp. 288–9.
183. Muhammad b. 'Ali al-Rawandi, *Rahat al-Sudur wa Ayat al-Surur*, trans. A. Hasanain, Cairo, 1960, p. 474.
184. Ibid., p. 475; al-Husayni, *Zubdat al-Tawarikh*, pp. 291–2.
185. Ferdowsi, *Shahnameh*, trans. al-Fath al-Bindari, ed. A. Azzam, Cairo, 1993, p. 376; Mohammad Behnamfar, 'Feminist Criticism of the Story of Homay Cherhzad's Kingdom in Shahnameh', *Theory and Practice in Language Studies*, Vol. 2, No. 9, 2012, pp. 1,980–6, pp. 183–4.
186. Al-Rawandi, *Rahat*, p. 477.
187. Al-Husayni, *Zubdat al-Tawarikh*, pp. 294–5.
188. Al-Rawandi, *Rahat*, p. 501; Bosworth, 'Political and Dynastic History', p. 180.
189. Al-Rawandi, *Rahat*, pp. 503–6; al-Husayni, *Zubdat al-Tawarikh*, pp. 301–2.
190. Al-Husayni, *Zubdat al-Tawarikh*, p. 302.
191. Al-Yazdi, *Al-'Irada*, pp. 167–8.
192. Ibid., pp. 302–3.
193. Mohammad Aziz Nejad and Ali Reza Karimi, 'Eldiguzid–Georgian Relations during the Rule of Attabak Abubakr Eldegizi', *Journal of the History of Foreign Relations*, Vol. 16, No. 63, 2015, pp. 70–95, 80–1; Bosworth, 'Eldiguzids'.
194. Al-Husayni, *Zubdat al-Tawarikh*, pp. 307–8.
195. Ibn al-Athir, *Al-Kamil*, Vol. 12, p. 184; Bosworth, 'Eldiguzids'.
196. Lambton, 'Internal Structure', pp. 224–35.
197. Merçil, *Fars Atabegleri*, pp. 105–11.
198. Ibid., pp. 111–12; Leila Fathi, 'The Study of Statue of Women on Iranian Coins', *Journal of History and Art Research*, Vol. 5, No. 4, 2016, pp. 278–95, 291–2.
199. Fathi, 'Study of Statue', pp. 285–9.
200. De Nicola, *Women in Mongol Iran*, pp. 90–129.
201. Ibid., p. 290.
202. Abu Hamid al-Ghazali, *Al-Tibr al-Masbuk fi Nasihat al-Muluk*, Cairo, 2008, p. 76.
203. Zankabadi, *Diwan*, quatrain 33, p,110.
204. Muhammad al-Jabiri, *Ibn Rushd Sirah wa Fikr*, Beirut, 1998, p. 159.
205. Charles Melville, 'History: From the Saljuqs to the Aq Qoyunlu', *Journal of Iranian Studies*, Vol. 31, Nos 3–4, 1998, pp. 473–82, 474; Morgan, *Medieval Persia*, p. 36.

206. Ibn al-Athir, *Al-Kamil*, Vol. 10, p. 22; Sibt Ibn al-Jawzi, *Mir'at*, Vol. 19, pp. 122–3.
207. Ibn al-Athir, *Al-Kamil*, Vol. 10, p. 22; Sibt Ibn al-Jawzi, *Mir'at*, Vol. 19, pp. 95, 123.
208. Sibt Ibn al-Jawzi, *Mir'at*, Vol. 19, p. 83.
209. Sibt Ibn al-Jawzi, *Mir'at*, Vol. 10, p. 22; Ayalon, *Eunuchs*, p. 153.
210. Sibt Ibn al-Jawzi, *Mir'at*, Vol. 19, p. 150.
211. Ibid.; Ayalon, *Eunuchs*, p. 159.
212. Al-Mawardi, in the manuscript of al-Suyuti, *Akam al-'Iqyan fi Ahkam al-Khisyan*, Cairo, Dar al-Kutub, ms. no. 4991/82, n.d.
213. Sibt Ibn al-Jawzi, *Mir'at*, Vol. 19, pp. 179–83.
214. Al-Isfahani, *Ta'rikh*, p. 190.
215. Ibn al-Athir, *Al-Bahir*, p. 84.
216. Ibn al-'Adim, *Zubdat*, Vol. 2, pp. 531, 536; Ibn 'Asakir, *Tahdhib*, Vol. 3, p. 98.
217. El-Azhari, *The Saljuqs*, pp. 141–2, 150–1.
218. Claude Cahen, *La Chronique Abregree d'al-'Azimi*, Paris, 1938, p. 364.
219. Ibn 'Asakir, *Tahdhib*, Vol. 3, p. 368.
220. Ibn al-Qalanisi, *Ta'rikh*, p. 401.
221. Ibn al-Athir, *Al-Bahir*, pp. 136, 146.
222. Ibid., pp. 153–4.
223. Ibn al-'Adim, *Zubdat*, Vol. 3, pp. 14–18; 'Izz al-Din Ibn Shaddad, *Al-Nawadir al-Sultaniyya*, ed. M. Subhi, Cairo, n.d., p. 81.
224. Ibn Wasil, *Mufarrij*, Vol. 2, p. 8.
225. Ibn al-Athir, *Al-Bahir*, pp. 180–1.
226. Ibid., pp. 189, 193.
227. Ibn al-Athir, *Al-Kamil*, Vol. 10, pp. 295–6.
228. Ibn al-Athir, *Al-Bahir*, pp. 13–14.
229. Ibn al-Athir, *Al-Kamil*, Vol. 10, p. 296.
230. Ibid., pp. 647, 654.
231. Al-Isfahani, *Ta'rikh*, p. 115.
232. Al-Husayni, *Zubdat al-Tawarikh*, p. 254.
233. Ibid., pp. 258–9.
234. Ibid., p. 260.
235. Ibid., p. 302.
236. Ibn al-Athir, *Al-Kamil*, Vol. 11, pp. 27–8.
237. Sibt Ibn al-Jawzi, *Mir'at*, Vol. 19, p. 176.

238. Ibn al-Athir, *Al-Kamil*, Vol. 10, p. 636.
239. Ibid., p. 678.
240. Ibn al-Athir, *Al-Kamil*, Vol. 11, pp. 106, 486.
241. Al-Suyuti, *Akam al-'Iqyan*, ms. no. 4991/82.

7

The Ayyubids: Their Two Queens and their Powerful Castrated *Atabegs*

> I travelled to Cairo from Aleppo as an ambassador to the king of Egypt, to request his permission to allow his aunts to travel to see their sister, al-Malika Dayfa, in Aleppo. King al-Salih Ayyub received me and passed this message to Dayfa: 'You kiss the ground before the queen, and tell her that al-Salih is her *mamluk*, and her status is like that of my late father, King al-Kamil. I offer myself fully to her service, and will follow her orders in any matter.'[1]

These words were written in 1240 by the Aleppan historian, Ibn al-'Adim (d. 1261), who was not only a contemporary of the first publicly acknowledged Sunni queen consort in medieval Islam, Dayfa, daughter of al-'Adil I the Ayyubid, but he was also her trusted advisor, diplomat and negotiator. This was in addition to his original job as chief judge of her realm. The anecdote above is not just telling us about a queen ruling in Aleppo; it also described how the king of a powerful country, such as Egypt, was representing himself as her slave (*mamluk*).

The Ayyubids, who ruled Egypt from 1171 to 1250 and to 1260 in Syria, were ethnic Kurds with a heavy Turkmen influence inherited from their Zengid lords. As regards the military, they could be described as Turkicised Kurds, and in relation to culture, they could be considered to be Persianised. The founders, Najm al-Din Ayyub and his brother Shirkuh, descended from the Ruwadiyya clan, part of the Hadhbaniyya tribe from the suburbs of the Georgian capital Tiblisi in the north-west Caucasus.[2] Ayyub joined the service of Zengi I in Iraq as a *mamluk*, and became very loyal to him and his son, Nur al-Din.

Salah al-Din Ibn Ayyub (Saladin), the legendary hero (1171–93), was a leading figure in the history of this dynasty and in medieval Islamic history due to his overwhelming victory over the Crusaders at Hittin in 1187. However, Saladin was a realpolitik operator who rebelled against his sultan Nur al-Din, who had dispatched him to Egypt with a number of significant emirs. Eager to establish a Kurdish state for himself, Saladin expanded into Yemen in 1174. When his sultan died in that year, Saladin waged a ruthless war to uproot the Zengid dynasty and replace it with the Ayyubids, which he managed to do from 1183 to 1186, dominating Syria, the Jazira and Mosul.[3]

After Saladin's death, the Ayyubids were embroiled in intense civil wars among his several sons, until 1199 when his capable brother, al-'Adil, reunited the Ayyubids and removed all of Saladin's sons from power. However, one son was spared – al-Zahir, in Aleppo – only because he was married to al-'Adil's daughter, Ghaziya Khatun.[4] When al-'Adil died in 1218, the Ayyubids experienced political fragmentation with several independent realms established in Syria, the Jazira, Yemen and Iraq under the nominal authority of the sultan of Egypt, al-Kamil b. al-'Adil, until his death in 1238. Afterwards, open civil wars among the various sons and nephews erupted and continued until the end of the Ayyubid era, with different Ayyubids collaborating with the Crusaders and other powers against their own house.[5] The Ayyubid Kurds, with their limited numbers of warriors, depended heavily on the Turkmen *mamluks*. Their rise within the Zengid dynasty led to them replicating and introducing into their dominions almost all of their administrative practices, the *iqta'* system and the commissioning of religious schools.

The political influence of Ayyubid women is demonstrated in the appearance of two queens in public life during the last two decades of Ayyubid rule. Prior to that, however, Ayyubid women appeared in the socio-political arena in a different guise. This took the form of a very rare Muslim dirham in 1193, when Saladin died. The Turkmen Artuqid lord of Mardin, Husam al-Din Yuluq Arslan (r. 1184–1201), was a vassal of Saladin. When the latter died, he minted this dirham, which showed four mourning women lamenting his death (see Figure 10). On the obverse we see four full-length figures in different postures – one is seated, draped in a long robe and with a covered head, which is turned to the front with a look of dejection. She is surrounded by three standing women, screaming out as they mourn. On the reverse is the name of Caliph al-Nasir, and on the margin is the name of the Artuqid lord, Husam al-Din Yuluq, and the date.

W. F. Marsden and W. G. Spengler describe this dirham bearing female figures as enigmatic of all coins minted in the entire Turkmen figural series,[6] while Robert Hillenbrand states:

> In no area of the visual arts is the flux of cultures represented in the Jazira and the neighbouring areas in the twelfth–thirteenth centuries more apparent than in coinage. Here a decisive break was made with the long-established Muslim tradition that coins should bear inscriptions only and not images.[7]

Wheras we saw on the Zengid dirham, regarding the *atabeg* (see Chapter Six), the face of a man, here we have not one woman, but four, minted on a coin that would be circulated in society and transferred by merchants to other areas. Therefore, there was no problem in presenting women in this way.

It is believed that Byzantine coins bearing human images might have influenced the Artuqids, but there has been no repeat of female figures featuring on Muslim coins.

Queen Dayfa of Aleppo, 1236–42

Dayfa was born in 1185 to al-'Adil, brother of Saladin, while he was governor of Aleppo.[9] Her name means 'guest' in the feminine form. As was typical of the chronicles, and sometimes of the strict harem, nothing is known about her early years. However, it is known that she was one of four daughters of al-'Adil, and that her eldest sister, Ghaziya Khatun, was married in 1186 to her cousin al-Zahir (d. 1216), son of Saladin, lord of Aleppo. She died without giving birth to any male children. After Ghaziya Khatun's death al-Zahir wanted to keep his throne safe from his powerful and pragmatic uncle, so in the same year (1212), he asked his uncle, Sultan al-'Adil, if he could marry his other daughter, Dayfa Khatun.[10] Political marriage was a useful tool for al-'Adil; he also married her other sister off to a Seljuqid prince in Anatolia.[11]

Dayfa was sent in a royal caravan with hundreds of servants to Aleppo that same year; al-Zahir had decorated the city for her entry, and lavished numerous items of jewellery and other gifts upon her.[12]

Dayfa Khatun before Coming to Power

In 1213 Dayfa Khatun gave birth to her only son, Prince al-'Aziz. Nearly three years later her husband, King al-Zahir, died.[13] During her years with al-Zahir, Dayfa did not have the opportunity to interfere in politics in any way, as understood from her two contemporary and indispensable historians, Ibn al-'Adim and Ibn Wasil. It is believed that her powerful husband, who ruled Aleppo for thirty years, did not allow any female interference in public affairs.

During al-Zahir's final illness in October 1216, we see Dayfa appearing for the first time on the political stage. Al-Zahir had already appointed their three-year-old son, al-'Aziz, as his successor in Aleppo, and had appointed the commander Tughril as his *atabeg*.[14] On Sunday 5 October 1216 Dayfa and Tughril, in collaboration, decided to forbid anyone from visiting or seeing the dying king; they were the only two who could have access to his chamber and attend to him. Two days later, when al-Zahir died, Dayfa and Tughril concealed the news from the rest of Aleppo, including the high officials and even the commanders inside Aleppo citadel, where the royal palace was located. This situation continued until the Wednesday.[15]

The question here is: why were such firm and restrictive measures taken by Dayfa Khatun? It is believed that there were two reasons: first, that Dayfa feared any political–military challenge to the power of her infant son from al-Zahir's eldest son, al-Salih, who was twelve years old. He was a son of a concubine of al-Zahir, and he had been declared by his father as second in line to the throne after his half-brother al-'Aziz.[16] Thus, Dayfa wanted to avoid any influence from al-Salih, who was in the citadel as well, to reverse the will of the king who was at the point of death. (I should mention here that Dayfa was interfering in political affairs just as Amina Khatun had done in 1117 in the same city and same citadel; see Chapter Six.)

Dayfa wanted to eliminate any possibility of ambitious commanders in the citadel declaring al-Salih as the new king, on hearing the news of al-Zahir's death. Dayfa managed, through these measures and aided by Tughril, to provide a smooth transition of power to her son, and to keep him there. Since her father was the supreme Ayyubid sultan, there would be no objection to his grandson governing under the regency of his *atabeg*, as Ibn al-Athir described it.[17]

The second reason was to prevent any escalation of the unrest in Aleppo by worried locals, which had started during the last week of al-Zahir's illness. Aleppo was a huge commercial centre, and the market had started to show signs of commercial and financial instability influenced by the political situation. During the last four days of al-Zahir's illness Aleppo's market experienced paralysis and commercial activities came to a complete halt.[18]

After the succession was secured, Dayfa retreated from political affairs and remained inside the royal palace in the citadel with no political ambitions, despite the very young age of her son. It is considered that her full trust in the capability and loyalty of the *atabeg* Tughril, who served until 1231,[19] encouraged her to act in that way. Occasionally, she is reported to have marched in a parade for rare social events. For instance, in 1232 she marched out of Aleppo in the company of the vizier and elite personnel (*a'yan*) to Tal al-Sultan to the south of Aleppo to greet her niece and daughter-in-law, Fatima Khatun.[20] Apart from such events, the chronicles decline to provide any information about Dayfa until the death of King al-'Aziz in December 1236.[21]

Dayfa Khatun in Power as Queen–regent

One month before his death, while suffering from severe pneumonia, al-'Aziz declared that he wanted to install his seven-year-old son, al-Nasir II (by a Turkish concubine), as his successor.[22] This step by al-'Aziz meant that he was reversing the will of al-Zahir, who had decided that al-'Aziz's successor should be his half-brother, al-Salih, and not his son. Al-'Aziz sent Ibn al-'Adim as an ambassador to Prince al-Salih, now lord of 'Ain Tab (west of Aleppo), about two weeks before he died, asking him to swear allegiance to him and his son al-Nasir II as future *malik* (king) of Aleppo.[23] It is believed that Ibn al-'Adim failed in this mission.

While Ibn al-'Adim was still in 'Ain Tab, al-'Aziz died. Dayfa swiftly enforced her son's will and installed her grandson, al-Nasir II Salah al-Din (d. 1260), as the new king. This move was carried out with the support of four leading figures in the realm: the two leading commanders of the deceased al-'Aziz – Emir Shams al-Din Lu'Lu' and Emir 'Umar Ibn Mujalli – and the vizier al-Qifti and influential adviser Iqbal al-Khatuni.[24] (Iqbal held the title '*khatuni*' after Dayfa Khatun, as he was a eunuch; he took great pride in being named after a woman.)

These four leading figures formed a governing council headed by Dayfa Khatun herself. They acted as chancellors and would debate the affairs of Aleppo; then, when they reached an opinion on any matter, they sent Iqbal al-Khatuni, as a eunuch, to Dayfa in the harem to ascertain her opinion and seek her permission to carry out the agreed actions. As Ibn Wasil described it: 'She had the final say on all state affairs, and she put her *'alama* (insignia) on all documents and correspondence.'[25]

As events show, she was not a 'rubber stamp' or ceremonial ruler, but she retained these men as advisors and deputies since they had more experience and freedom of movement. However, she was the mistress, and on numerous occasions she did not refer to them at all. 'She behaved like sultans do.'[26]

This was only the second time in Islamic history, up until that time, where a woman had become a public queen consort, with Queen Arwa of Yemen being the first, as previously mentioned. In fact, medieval Islamic history experienced the rare phenomenon of two queens coming to power in the same year and the same month. While Dayfa became a queen–regent in Aleppo, Queen Radiyya bt. Iltutmish assumed power in Delhi, northern India (r. 1236–40). She was part of the Mu'izzi Turkish slave dynasty that succeeded the Ghaznavids in the early thirteenth century.[27] She forced her way to power, filling the vacuum created by the murder of her brother. The most important matter here is that her father did not nominate her for succession due to her gender, and she faced strong opposition from military commanders and religious scholars.[28] Queen Radiyya imitated Queen Tamar of Georgia by minting coins in her name; for example, on the silver tanka of Delhi. On the obverse we find: '*Al-Sultan al-A'zam shams al-Dunya wa al-Din/al-Sultan al-Mu'azzam Radiyyat al-Dunya wa al-Din*' (Grand sultan (masculine form)/Sun of the world and religion/The glorified sultan Radiyya – of the secular world and religion); and on the reverse we find the title of the 'Abbasid caliph al-Mustansir.[29] However, that was the rare minted tanka; the most common one bore the name of her father (on the obverse: '*Al-Sultan al-A'Azam Shams al-Dunya wa a-Din Il-Tutmish*', and on the reverse, the title of the 'Abbasid caliph al-Mustansir; see Figure 11).

Peter Jackson states: 'She was deposed when she demonstrated signs of independence.'[30] However, the position of the 'Abbasid caliph as regards

Radiyya's queenship is unclear and having his name on her coin was ceremonial, in order to gain legitimacy and support domestically in Delhi.

Returning to Dayfa, why did she not interfere in the rule of Aleppo when her son was only three years old, but did so in the case of her grandson, twenty years later? It is believed that Dayfa had trusted and tested the loyalty of the *atabeg* Tughril, the leading commander of her deceased husband. Since Dayfa was a relatively inexperienced woman in political and state affairs in 1216, at the age of thirty-two, and had no interest or ambition in politics, she relied on the capability of Tughril, as long as he ruled according to the best interests of her son.[31]

Now, in 1236, the political situation had changed. Dayfa, at the age of fifty-two, was much more experienced, having lived in Aleppo's citadel for two decades, and with the deaths of the loyal Tughril and her father the sultan, she had to defend the interests of her grandson against her powerful brother, al-Kamil, whom she saw as a threat.

Dayfa's Titles and Declaration of the Khutba

Queen–regent Dayfa held several titles. In addition to the traditional title, *khatun*, given to most Turkmen and Kurdish princesses from birth, after coming to power she was described by her contemporaries as '*al-malika*' (queen).[32] She was also described by Ibn Wasil as '*al-sahiba*' (lit. possessor of),[33] which asserts the other titles. In foreign correspondence, the Ayyubid lord of Hama, and al-Salih Ayyub, sultan of Egypt, referred to her as '*al-satr al-'ali*',[34] which is Arabic for eminence or highness. These titles clearly reflect the political status of Dayfa in Aleppo.

Queen–regent Dayfa did not put her name on the mint as Radiyya had done in India, and there is no concrete evidence that she included her name in the *khutba*. She only used the name of her grandson in these two matters. However, Queen Dayfa was the one to decide to whom the *khutba* should be given in her realm as a symbolic act of homage. She gave permission to declare the *khutba* to her brother, al-Kamil, in Egypt, along with the 'Abbasid caliph, of course. However, in May 1237 she cancelled the *khutba* for her brother due to a political crisis, as will be discussed. She turned down the request of al-Kamil's son and successor in Egypt, al-'Adil II, and she did not put his name on the dinar.[35] Instead, in 1238, after consulting her political council, she agreed to the request of her powerful ally, the Seljuqid sultan of Rum, Kay-Khusraw II (d. 1246), to declare the *khutba* in his name and to put his name on the dinar along with that of al-Nasir II. The Seljuqs of Rum were always a traditional foe of the Ayyubids of Egypt. On that occasion, a Seljuqid ambassador arrived in Aleppo and ascended the pulpit of the main mosque of Aleppo before the locals in the company of her advisor, Iqbal al-Khatuni. He showered the Aleppans with the new dinars carrying his sultan's name.[36] While Dayfa was on the throne, the *khutba* did not change. It was only after she died that we see al-Nasir II declaring the *khutba* for al-Salih Ayyub of Egypt.[37]

We could assert the opinion that by refusing the *khutba* to an Ayyubid sultan, and declaring it to the Seljuqid one, she shifted the alliance of Aleppo. Giving the *khutba* to the first was merely a ceremonial step, but with the Seljuqs Aleppo had entered into what Cahen describes as 'vassalage relations'.[38] In such a relationship, each side would aid the other militarily.

Queen Dayfa and her Confrontation with her Brother, al-Kamil of Egypt

After Dayfa had installed al-Nasir II as king in Aleppo, she sent, in 1236, the *qadi* Zayn al-Din b. al-Ustadh and Badr al-Din as ambassadors to her brother al-Kamil, the sultan of Egypt and nominal chief of the Ayyubid realm. She wanted formal recognition from him of the new rule in Aleppo. Al-Kamil had other ideas; he wanted to install al-Salih, lord of 'Ain Tab, and son of the late al-Zahir, as king of Aleppo and regent for al-Nasir II. This was the only way that al-Kamil was going to recognise the rule in Aleppo. In addition, al-Kamil did not show the usual diplomatic respect and hospitality that was expected for the Aleppan envoy sent by Dayfa. He did not grant them the robes of honour of al-Nasir II, often granted by the sultan in such situations.

The two messengers returned to Dayfa and informed her of what had taken place in Cairo, and how al-Kamil was behaving in a hostile manner. After consulting her council, Dayfa declared her refusal to al-Kamil's demand.[39] Weeks later, al-Kamil attempted to increase the pressure on his sister; he dispatched to Aleppo the robes of honour to al-Nasir II, without sultanate boots (as a mark of derision). He also sent robes of honour to the leading commanders of Aleppo; he was trying to challenge Dayfa's authority over them. Al-Kamil dispatched a special separate envoy with robes of honour to his candidate, al-Salih b. al-Zahir. This move was designed to encourage him and other commanders in Aleppo to ally with him. As soon as Dayfa was informed of what had taken place, she ordered that only al-Nasir II should wear the robes, and not the Aleppan commanders, in order to assert her authority over them. She feared that such Egyptian robes sent by the sultan might encourage some of those commanders to rebel against her. Astonishingly, she ordered a force to intercept the sultanate envoy heading to al-Salih, and forced him to turn back to Egypt without meeting with al-Salih. Dayfa had decided to reject al-Kamil's authority.[40]

Dayfa's act reflects her full authority over the military and intelligence. Her deed could be interpreted as a counter-defensive measure against al-Kamil's intimidating behaviour and challenge to her authority. Dayfa saw al-Kamil's deed as a conspiracy against her interests by promoting his own candidate.

As a result of all that, Dayfa formed a political–military pact with her brother, al-Ashraf Musa, lord of Damascus and the Jazira. Al-Ashraf arrived in Aleppo in May 1137, and swore to Dayfa to join her alliance against al-Kamil. They also had on their side Prince Shirkuh, lord of Hims, and al-Muzaffar, Ayyubid lord of Hama.

Only al-Nasir Da'ud, lord of the strategic al-Karak, refused to join their pact and allied instead with al-Kamil.[41] For a woman, new in the field of political affairs, to initiate a military–political alliance of leading Ayyubid princes in the thirteenth century was definitely a rare achievement. Not only that, but she was also recognised as a leading partner among them.

Dayfa and al-Ashraf sent an envoy to the Seljuqid sultan, Kay Qabad, inviting him to join their alliance. Ibn al-'Adim was Aleppo's envoy for that mission. Upon his arrival he found that Kay Qabad had died in May 1237, but he met his successor Kay-Khusraw II; the latter welcomed the invitation and joined the Syrian alliance.[42]

Queen Dayfa's pact dispatched an ambassador to al-Kamil in Cairo. Their message to him was: 'We are all agreed and demand from you not to leave Egypt and enter Syrian dominions again.' Al-Kamil replied, sarcastically, to the envoy: 'My blessing that you all have agreed; do you want my oath? I demand that you, too, should swear to me that you will never attack my country or any of my dominions. Only then, will I meet your request.'[43]

It could be considered that it was pragmatism that united Dayfa, al-Ashraf and Kay-Khusraw II against al-Kamil. On Dayfa's side, she feared losing power to al-Salih, so she invited her powerful Seljuqid neighbours to help. As for the Seljuqs, they welcomed the pact to put an end to al-Kamil's ambitions in Syria and the Jazira, especially as in 1233 al-Kamil had tried to seize Akhlat from the Seljuqs, aided then by Aleppan forces.

Al-Ashraf was not happy with al-Kamil's policy, because he had been passive and did not support his brother against the Khwarazmian sacking of his Jazira dominions. That attack stripped al-Ashraf of vital cities in the Jazira. Al-Kamil partially rewarded him in 1230 with Damascus, but that was not enough for him, especially as al-Ashraf had to pay heavy taxes to al-Kamil and provide for his frequent long stays with his forces in Damascus, which was a financial burden for him[44]

Dayfa's Kurdish–Turkish pact held for only a few months before cracks started to appear. Al-Ashraf died on 28 August 1237, and was succeeded by his brother, 'Imad al-Din Isma'il, in Damascus. Isma'il sent a message to Dayfa requesting to join her alliance, to which she agreed.[45] However, al-Ashraf's departure meant the loss of a capable ally who might confront the mighty al-Kamil; Isma'il had to assert his authority first over the Jazira and Damascus, while confronting al-Kamil at the same time.

As a consequence of al-Ashraf's death, al-Muzaffar, lord of Hama, entered into a territorial dispute with Ayyubid Hims, and pulled out of the alliance until his territorial demands were resolved to his best interest. He wanted to take the town of Salamiyya and Shamaymash Castle to the south east of Hama from Hims.[46] Dayfa was fighting to hold the coalition together. She dispatched her trusted advisor, Ibn al-'Adim, as an ambassador to Shirkuh, lord of Hims, and also to meet al-Muzaffar of Hama in order to reach a reconciliation between the two members of her coalition. Her diplomatic efforts lasted for only three months. Shirkuh refused to hand over any of his dominions, while al-Muzaffar said to Ibn al-'Adim:

> If al-Malik al-Kamil is going to attack Hims, I will join him, but for Aleppo I sacrifice my soul and wealth to avoid any harm being done to one of the Aleppan villages. I will not go back on my oath which I gave to al-Satr al-'Ali (Queen Dayfa) and al-Malik al-Nasir.

Ibn al-'Adim replied to him:

> My lord knows the agreement between us in Aleppo and the lord of Hims. If someone attack Hims, we have to come to his rescue. What is my lord al-Muzaffar going to do if an Aleppan army arrives to aid Hims?

After some hesitation, al-Muzaffar replied: 'I will fight them. Whoever fights me, I will fight the aggressor back.' Ibn al-'Adim sent the result of his negotiation to his queen, and was ordered by her to end his mission in mid-December 1237 and return to Aleppo.[47]

Dayfa's interference in the Hims–Hama dispute aimed to save her alliance from collapsing, especially as she knew that Isma'il of Damascus was not capable militarily of defending the southern Syrian dominions from an attack by al-Kamil, not just because of al-Kamil's significant Egyptian resources and his military experience, but also because Isma'il had just taken over several dominions in the Jazira, including Sanjar and Nasibin, from al-Ashraf's deputies.[48] As a result, his priority was to organise the defences of these new territories with new commanders of his own.

During Ibn al-'Adim's final days in Hama in December 1237, al-Kamil arrived with a large Egyptian army and besieged Damascus, taking the opportunity of the disorder among the Ayyubids of Syria. In addition, al-Muzaffar was corresponding with him secretly, informing him of the military capability of Damascus and expressing his support for al-Kamil against Dayfa's coalition.[49]

Queen Dayfa swiftly sent a contingent from her realm to aid Isma'il in Damascus, together with a large force from Hims. It is rare to see a woman ordering troops to go on a military campaign, but to order them in the heart of winter was really an exceptional matter, as they could refuse to obey. Only very capable commanders such as Zengi, Nur al-Din and her hated brother, al-Kamil, would have such command.

Aleppo under Dayfa was fighting for its political survival, because al-Kamil, while besieging Damascus, dispatched his son, al-Salih Ayyub, to invade and seize the dominions of Isma'il in the Jazira. Thus, he was not just hitting Dayfa's ally, but was also closing in on her from the south and northeast.[50] On 7 January 1238 al-Kamil seized Damascus, the last city in the Syrian pact, after his brother Isma'il accepted his weakness and surrendered the city. In return, Isma'il received the city of Baalbek as an *iqta'* from al-Kamil. It is worth pointing out that al-Kamil treated the Aleppan troops taken captive in Damascus well, and sent them back to Dayfa. It was a different story, however, with the captive troops of Hims; al-Kamil ordered fifty of them to be hanged at once.[51] It is believed that al-Kamil's good gesture towards the Aleppan troops was aimed at improving the relationship with his sister, Dayfa.

As soon as the Aleppan contingent arrived back from Damascus, Dayfa started her military preparations against al-Kamil, believing that he would soon be marching to invade her realm. First, she had to secure the loyalty of the Ayyubid emirs and commanders to her and to al-Nasir II. So, she called on Prince Turan Shah, son of Saladin, who was the chief commander in Aleppo, in addition to all his brothers and relatives.[52] She also summoned all ranked emirs in the army and made them give the oath of allegiance to her as a queen-regent and to al-Nasir II.

Dayfa then summoned to the citadel the nobles of the city together with the *ra'is* (civil leader) of the locals and made them swear allegiance to her. Afterwards, she summoned the soldiers and the locals to do the same.[53] This action by her was a rare case of an Ayyubid woman taking the oath to herself by herself in public in the royal palace from all different strata in society, military and civilian; no one objected to the order, especially prestigious emirs like Turan Shah.

Queen Dayfa had sent pleading messages to the Seljuqid sultan Kay-Khusraw II, to whom she declared the *khutba* in her realm, urging him to send military help. He responded by dispatching a force of his finest elite troops to Aleppo. The sultan offered to send more reinforcements to Daya, if required, but she was content with what he had offered earlier. Kay-Khusraw II sent a message to al-Kamil in Damascus warning him not to attack Aleppo.[54] We could say that Kay-Khusraw II was following the policy of his father, which was to deter and refuse the sultan of Egypt from interfering in the affairs of northern Syria, which he considered to be a Seljuqid–Turkish strategic sphere of influence, especially as al-Kamil's son was expanding in the Jazira.[55]

Dayfa also took other urgent measures against al-Kamil. She ordered more food supplies and arms to be stored in Aleppo, anticipating a long siege by al-Kamil. In addition, she ordered stones for the mangonels to be carried to the city's gates. Dayfa had recruited several Khwarazmian Turkmen mercenaries who were in eastern Anatolia and the Jazira. She also welcomed defecting soldiers who had escaped from al-Kamil in Damascus. Dayfa employed realpolitik when she recruited a Turkmen nomadic chief named Qanghar, who had plundered her dominions the previous year; she made him commander to all the Turkmen nomads in the kingdom.[56] Dayfa wanted to use his horseback warriors in her anticipated confrontation with al-Kamil.

All these military measures demonstrate how queen–regent Dayfa was an extraordinary woman, capable of acting equal to men in a political–military crisis. She was capable of controlling the army, mobilising foreign troops and supervising military efforts. She was now the only Ayyubid left in Syria who could resist the authority of the sultan of Egypt, as Shirkuh of Hims had sent his son, al-Mansur, to Damascus to negotiate with al-Kamil; he offered an annual tribute of two million dirhams in return for forgiveness and keeping Hims – al-Kamil agreed.[57] As mentioned earlier, the lord of Hama had pulled out earlier and Damascus had surrendered.

While the sultan of Egypt was preparing for the final march on Aleppo in March 1238, fate intervened in the queen's favour – al-Kamil died.[58] This was very good news for Dayfa, who had not negotiated a deal, and did not fear the might of al-Kamil; she refused to submit to him. There was more good news in that a civil war was triggered as a result of al-Kamil's death, between his son al-'Adil II in Cairo, who immediately assumed the sultanate, and his other son, al-Salih Ayyub, in Sanjar in the Jazira. There were also other Ayyubid lords fighting to control other dominions, such as her brother Isma'il and her nephew Jawad Yunus, who fought over Damascus.[59]

Now Queen Dayfa was facing a new political situation, dealing with the Ayyubids of Hama, her nephews, the successors of al-Kamil, the Crusaders and the Seljuqs of Anatolia.

Queen Dayfa and her Retaliation against Ayyubid Hama

Queen Dayfa tried through diplomacy to keep her nephew, al-Muzaffar of Hama, in her coalition against al-Kamil, but he threatened to fight Aleppan forces who might support his foe, the lord of Hims. In addition, he had secretly allied with Dayfa's enemy, al-Kamil of Egypt.

As soon as Queen Dayfa learned of al-Kamil's death, she appointed Emir Turan Shah, son of Saladin, as commander of an army that would move immediately to invade the dominions of Hama. Her force would start with the town of Ma'arrat al-N'uman and its citadel; then, after seizing it, they would march southwards to besiege the city of Hama itself.[60] The Aleppan army besieged Ma'arrat al-Nu'man and erected mangonels at its citadel. Al-Muzaffar sent a messenger to Queen Dayfa asking for forgiveness. Dayfa refused to meet his envoy, who was completely ignored. After a brief period of resistance, the town and citadel were successfully seized. The Aleppan army proceeded with the march south and besieged Hama, with al-Muzaffar inside.[61]

Turan Shah, with his forces, started to plunder the countryside in an economic war against Hama. The siege of Hama lasted nearly six months to late autumn 1238. That was a very long siege by medieval standards, and maintaining control over the troops would not have been an easy task, but Dayfa's orders had to be implemented. During the siege the nephew of Dayfa, al-Salih Ayyub, had sent an ambassador to Dayfa to mediate and secure a pardon for al-Muzaffar. Queen Dayfa refused his request.[62] Strangely enough, Turan Shah and his army had strict orders from the queen to besiege and cut supplies in order to cause economic and social hardship; however, she prohibited the army from invading and seizing Hama. According to Ibn al-'Adim and Ibn Wasil, Dayfa did not wish to uproot her nephew's rule, but wanted to punish him for his stance with al-Kamil. Moreover, she wanted him to renounce Ma'arrat al-Nu'man. In late 1238 Queen Dayfa ordered her army to withdraw back to Aleppo.[63]

I believe that Queen Dayfa took the opportunity of the readiness of her army following her preparations to confront al-Kamil; she used her military power for a limited expansion into northern Syria, to show her strength in Aleppo and to punish al-Muzaffar in the absence of a clear successor to al-Kamil. In addition, she showed her support to her ally, Shirkuh of Hims. The outcome of her policy is that she won Ma'arrat al-Nu'man, and Shirkuh kept Salamiyya, which had been disputed with al-Muzaffar; the latter would not threaten Dayfa's interests again.

What is remarkable here is Dayfa's undisputed leadership. She gave precise targets to her army commander, who was appointed by her; she decided on the timing of the withdrawal after six months of siege, which could have resulted in a rebellion by commanders and troops in the campaign, who were waiting to enter the ailing Hama and take their booty after the siege; and she was the one who decided which envoys could be received and which should be refused during the crisis, which was administered from her palace in Aleppo's citadel (see Figure 12).

Queen Dayfa's Relations with al-Kamil's Successors

Al-'Adil II

Al-'Adil II succeeded his father al-Kamil as the sultan of Egypt, but he lacked his father's military and political experience to govern. In mid-1238 he sent a messenger to Dayfa asking her to declare the *khutba* for him and to put his name on Aleppan coins, as she had done with his father before the hostilities. Dayfa turned down that request.[64] At the same time, Dayfa turned down another request from al-Jawad Yunus b. Mawdud b. al-'Adil I to form a military pact against al-'Adil II. Al-Jawad had been in al-Kamil's company in Damascus, and had confiscated all of al-Kamil's treasures after his death.[65]

In addition, when al-Salih b. al-Kamil captured Damascus in February 1239 from al-Jawad, al-Salih sent an envoy to Dayfa seeking her military support to seize Egypt from his brother. Queen Dayfa declined his request, replying: 'I will not interfere between you and your brother. Both of you are my brother's sons.'[66]

Here we have three Ayyubid lords, one of them the sultan of Egypt, and the other the king of Damascus, seeking help from a woman; that showed how some of the Ayyubids had no problem dealing politically with women for political gain. It also clearly reflects how eminent and legitimate Dayfa had become.

Why did Dayfa turn down al-'Adil's request? I believe there were several reasons: (1) Dayfa wanted to remain out of the civil war as long as her kingdom was not directly under threat; (2) she found no financial or political benefits in giving the *khutba* to al-'Adil II; (3) she had already given the *khutba* to the Seljuqid sultan some months earlier[67] – he was a more powerful neighbour, and she could not afford a confrontation with him; and (4) she was aware of al-Salih's strength, especially after he recruited in his service approximately 12,000 Khwarazmian horsemen from his Jazira dominions in

1236, who had remained in his army to that date. If she took al-'Adil's side, she would expose her northern territories to a significant threat from al-Salih. She did not have sufficient military resources to confront such a large power, especially as the Aleppan army comprised about 2,000 soldiers.[68] In addition, Dayfa had to protect her western dominions from her immediate neighbours, the Crusaders of Antionch. However, she remained amicable in her relations with al-'Adil. She dispatched to him her trusted advisor Ibn al-'Adim in June 1240 to congratulate him on his victory over the Crusaders at Ascalon in November 1239. She also asked him to permit his aunts, the daughters of her father, to travel to Aleppo to visit her. The Aleppan envoy did not have the chance to meet al-'Adil II, as he was arrested and deposed by his brother, al-Salih Ayyub.[69]

Al-Salih, the New Sultan of Egypt

In 1238 al-Salih Ayyub sent an ambassador to his aunt, Queen Dayfa, requesting her to mediate between him and the Seljuqid sultan to improve the political relationship between the two. Dayfa agreed, but no tangible steps were taken.[70] Nevertheless, the fact that Dayfa's mediation was sought by an Ayyubid prince again shows her acceptance in the fabric of Ayyubid–Levantine politics.

It is understood that al-Salih wanted to ease the relationship with the Seljuqs while focusing on fighting his brother, al-'Adil. In the same year, Prince al-Mughith, son of al-Salih, took refuge in Aleppo's dominions after he was defeated by a group of Khwarazmian seasonal mercenaries first in Harran, and then in Ja'bar, on the Euphrates. He sought Dayfa's permission to remain in her territories for a short time. She sent a messenger to him saying: 'We fear that Kay-Khusraw will ask us to hand you over to him while you stay in our dominions. We will not turn down his request if that takes place.'[71]

We see that Dayfa wanted to keep herself out of any misunderstanding with her ally, the Seljuq sultan, who might question her loyalty. In addition, she wanted to avoid the threat of the undisciplined Khwarazmian mercenaries who were always plundering the vicinity. By giving al-Mughith a stay in her realm, that would bring them to her territories, which she wanted to avoid.

On the other hand, Dayfa did not want to upset al-Salih or take advantage of him while he was occupied with his war with al-'Adil. In mid-1238 the Seljuqid sultan had peacefully taken the city of Edessa and the town of Sarruj in eastern Anatolia from al-Salih. Kay-Khusraw II sent a sultanate messenger to Dayfa carrying a diploma allocating these dominions as an *iqta'* to Aleppo. Dayfa met the envoy, Qamar al-Din al-Khadim (a eunuch), and accepted the Seljuqid investiture, but did not put it into practice, for example, by appointing her own deputies there. When al-Salih learned of this gallant deed by the queen, he sent to her an envoy, saying: 'All the cities under my rule are subject to your rule. If you wish to send your deputy to take over these two cities and more, please do. I will execute whatever order you give me.' Dayfa wrote to him expressing her gratitude to such loyalty and submission. She reassured him that she would not harm his interests.[72]

As a result of this amicable relationship, al-Salih never interfered in Aleppo's affairs when he became sultan of Egypt. In August 1240 he met with Ibn al-'Adim in Cairo. Al-Salih warmly welcomed Dayfa's request to let her sisters leave Cairo to visit Aleppo. In addition, the sultan of Egypt gave her ambassador this significant massage:

> You kiss the ground before the queen, and tell her that al-Salih is her *mamluk*, and her status is like that of my late father, King al-Kamil. I offer myself fully to her service, and will follow her orders in any matter.

Ibn al-'Adim was asked to report the same message to al-Nasir.[73] Why did al-Salih behave in this way? We could say that al-Salih wanted to assure Dayfa that he would not interfere in Aleppan policy. That is because while al-Salih was held captive in Damascus in 1239 by al-Nasir Da'ud of Karak, al-Salih agreed under threat to invade Aleppo and hand it to al-Nasir, in return for financial agreements between the two men.[74] In addition, al-Salih wanted to secure Dayfa's neutrality in the Ayyubid civil war, which would benefit him by not adding new fronts to the conflict. That would keep his strategic Jazira dominions safe for the movement of his Turkmen troops and new recruits.

H. A. R. Gibb states that al-Salih was fully occupied with his domestic affairs in Egypt, re-organising his army after the Kurdish troops proved disloyal to him. In addition, he was facing the Crusaders led by Richard of

Cornwall, who was occupying Ascalon and would not enter into negotiations with him until December 1240.[75] Al-Salih was successful in his policy with Queen Dayfa, as she was very pleased with al-Salih's message to her, respecting her independence and recognising her as queen–regent. As a result, Dayfa refused to enter into an alliance with the Ayyubids of Damascus against Egypt. Ibn al-'Adim had met al-Salih Isma'il of Damascus while returning from his embassy to Cairo. The lord of Damascus sent a message to Dayfa, inviting her to form a pact against al-Salih Ayyub, but she refused.[76] From what is mentioned above, I cannot agree with Cahen's statement that 'a coalition of all the princes of upper Mesopotamia and Syria was formed against al-Salih Ayyub'.[77] Dayfa was clearly outside of such a pact. Indeed, as Humphreys states, Dayfa continued to give the *khutba* in her dominions to the Seljuqs and not to al-Salih. However, that did not affect her amicable relationship with the sultan of Egypt.[78]

The Crusaders

The queenship of Dayfa, or any female ruler who came to the throne of Muslim Aleppo, was a situation never experienced by the Crusaders of Antioch, the adjacent neighbours, since their arrival to the area in 1097. The relationship between Queen Dayfa and the Crusaders, especially in Antioch, was not one of serious hostility. Aleppo under her rule never initiated an attack on Crusader dominions with the aim of seizing them. The only confrontation between the two sides was in 1236, when the Templars at Baghras, north-west of Aleppo, took the opportunity of al-'Aziz's death, assuming that a vacuum of power would follow. They raided the countryside of Aleppo at a place called al-'Umq, seizing many livestock and other booty. Upon Dayfa's instruction, Turan Shah, the commander of the army, marched out of Aleppo with a force and besieged Crusader Baghras until it was exhausted and on the verge of surrendering. Prince Bohemond V, lord of Antioch (r. 1233–51), sent an ambassador to Dayfa seeking a truce. Following a discussion, Dayfa and her governing council agreed to Bohemond's request. The Aleppan force withdrew from Baghras after destroying the countryside.[79]

However, the Templars did not honour the truce and went on to attack the countryside of Darabsak, which was an Aleppan territory to the west of the city. The Templars were joined by a Crusading battalion from Jubayl.

Again, Dayfa dispatched Turan Shah, who managed to inflict a heavy defeat on the Crusaders. As a result, a peace was concluded between the two sides which held for many years.[80]

It could be said that Dayfa did not have the military resources nor the political will to open a western front with the Crusaders while fighting to assert her position inside Aleppo, and regionally. Moreover, the peace treaty reached during al-'Aziz's reign with Bohemond IV in 1225 was never broken by his successor, Bohemond V.[81]

As pointed out earlier, it was not just political necessity that brought Dayfa into politics. It was the influence of other surrounding cases from the Muslim sides, as already discussed, and also from the Armenian–Crusader sides in and around her vicinity, which had an accumulative effect. For instance, in 1112 the Armenian princess, widow of Vasil Dgha of parts of the Taurus mountains to the north of Aleppo, rebelled against the Franks. She contacted Aq Sunqur al-Bursuqi of Mosul to protect her from the Crusaders.[82] In 1130 Princess Alice of Antioch took the opportunity of her husband's death and assumed the rule herself as a regent for her young son. That was an act of rebellion against her father, King Baldwin II of Jerusalem, as an overlord. She sought protection from Zengi in Aleppo.[83]

The Seljuqs and the Khwarazmians
As already mentioned, Dayfa started her career by forming a political military pact with the Seljuqs of Rum in order to save her rule; that was successful. She consolidated the relationship by two political marriages: in 1237 she accepted the proposal of Kay-Khusraw II to marry her granddaughter, Ghaziya Khatun, and the following year Ibn al-'Adim was sent by her as her personal representative to conclude the marriage contract of al-Nasir II to a Seljuqid princess.[84]

In January 1238 Kay-Khusraw II dispatched a large force to Dayfa to fight al-Kamil; in return she gave the *khutba* to the Seljuqs in her dominions. She became a vassal to the Seljuqs, and received some *iqta'* from the sultan. Nevertheless, as a vassal to the Seljuqs, Dayfa, too, offered military assistance to the sultan. Ibn Bibi mentioned that in August 1240 the Mongols attacked eastern Anatolia. As a result, Dayfa dispatched an elite force to join the Seljuqid army to defend their dominions.[85]

The years 1240–2 were dominated by a chain of events: the Khwarazmian attacks on Aleppo. The Khwarazmians swept into the Jazira and eastern Anatolia in their thousands after their leader, Jalal al-Din, had been defeated and killed at the hands of the Mongols in 1230 at Amid in the northern Jazira. Many thousands of their horsemen warriors went into the service of Kay Qabad, the Seljuqid sultan. After he died in 1237, his successor Kay-Khusraw II imprisoned their leader Baraka Khan. As a result they escaped across the Euphrates with more than 12,000 knights and joined the service of al-Salih Ayyub, who allocated them several *iqta'* and managed to free their leader from captivity.[86]

These Khwarazmian troops were highly undisciplined, and followed different tribal chiefs; in short, they behaved like bandits. From 1238 to 1240 they were in control of most of the Jazira, then crossed the Euphrates and sacked the Syrian dominions down to Jerusalem.[87] Aleppo, under Dayfa, did not escape these destructive waves. In October 1240, in the region of 12,000 Khwarazmian horsemen under the leadership of Baraka Khan invaded Aleppo's countryside. In their company was the Ayyubid prince, al-Salih, son of Shirkuh, the former lord of Hims. Also with them was Prince al-Jawad, nephew of Dayfa. They were joined by several Arab tribes under the leadership of 'Ali b. Haditha of Aleppo.[88]

After they looted Minbaj and Buza'a to the east of Aleppo, they marched to al-Bira. There they went into battle with the Aleppan army led by Turan Shah and comprising about 1,500 knights. The rest of Aleppo's forces were dispatched to help the Seljuqs of Anatolia. The army of Aleppo suffered a humiliating defeat, while Turan Shah and leading commanders were taken captive.[89]

There are several reasons for the Khwarazmian attacks on Dayfa's realm: first, in September 1240 her brother al-Hafiz, lord of Ja'bar, feared that his son, al-Jawad, would surrender the town to the Khwarazmians; so al-Hafiz surrendered it to Dayfa in exchange for the town of A'zaz. In the same month, Dayfa sent her deputies to conclude the deal, while al-Jawad b. al-Hafiz went to ally with the Khwarazmians, encouraging them to invade Aleppo.[90] Second, the Arab chief in Aleppo, 'Ali b. Haditha, was angered when Dayfa marginalised him in favour of his rivals, the tribe of Ahlaf, for the leadership of the Arabs in the realm. So, he went to the Khwarazmians to ally with them against Dayfa. In addition, Prince al-Nasir Da'ud of Karak had also contacted the Khwarazmians while holding al-Salih Ayyub, asking them to invade Aleppo.[91] Third was Baraka Khan's probable knowledge about the state of the Aleppan army, from his Ayyubid and Arab allies.

The chronicler Ibn al-Fuwati wrote that Dayfa turned down a marriage proposal from Baraka and humiliated his messenger. As a result, he gathered his forces to avenge his pride, and gain by force part of what he had hoped to achieve through political marriage.[92] Queen Dayfa, who remained in Aleppo with a force of only 200 knights, while her countryside was sacked, feared her city would fall to Baraka's immense forces. She took some measures to save her kingdom. First, she summoned the remaining commanders, including Lu'Lu' and Ibn Mujalli, and asked them to guard the city walls and towers.[93] Then she sent an urgent message to her brother, Isma'il of Damascus, asking him to renew his oath of allegiance to her and al-Nasir II, and to swiftly dispatch a force to defend Aleppo; she asked the same of al-Mansur, Ayyubid lord of Hims. The latter arrived in person at the end of November 1240, leading a force of about 1,000 knights, some sent from Damascus to be in her service.[94]

Queen Dayfa also resorted to her Turkish ally, the Seljuqid sultan, for assistance. Kay-Khusraw II commissioned 3,000 elite knights to depart at once to defend Aleppo, under the authority of al-Mansur of Hims.[95]

On the domestic front, Dayfa released all the Templar Crusader knights who were held captive in Aleppo in order to avoid a threat from the west while she was preoccupied with the serious danger from the east.[96] In addition, she entered into a political marriage with a leading Arab chief, Tahir b. Ghannam, giving him one of her maids to marry, which was considered an honour. She appointed him as chief to all Arabs in the realm, following the defection of 'Ali b. Haditha. She also allocated Tahir a satisfactory *iqta*[97] to win him over to her camp, and to secure a pledge that the Arabs would resist the Khwarazmians as well.

All these measures to save Aleppo by Queen Dayfa reflects her political–diplomatic capability and the recognition of all the surrounding male rulers of her queenship. The Khwarazmian threat remained in Aleppo's dominions for five months until April 1241. During this time, they did not attack the city itself, but kept sacking its eastern and southern dominions, including al-Faya and Sarmin.[98]

It is believed that the Khwarazmians launched an economic war against Aleppo, but refrained from direct assault on the city after the reinforcements that arrived to support Dayfa. In addition, the nomadic culture of the Turkmen Khwarazmians saw them split into smaller undisciplined battalions satisfied with minor booty. Some of them actually crossed the Euphrates back to the Jazira. Ibn al-'Adim, who reported on their campaign in detail, presented them as hasty mercenaries who were not prepared for long siege warfare, but rather short gains.[99]

On 14 May 1241 the forces that were gathered to defend Aleppo, led by al-Mansur of Hims, managed to defeat the remaining Khwarazmian forces in a place between al-Bira and Harran, to the east of the Euphrates. The result of this victory was significant to Aleppo, not only as it reasserted Dayfa's authority over the western dominions of the Jazira,[100] but that it also reasserted Dayfa's position as a very capable female leader in dire situations.

By the end of the summer of 1241, the joint Aleppan–Seljuqid forces launched a sweeping campaign to finish off the Khwarazmian presence in the area and to restore cities like Edessa, Sarruj and Raqqa, among others, back to Dayfa's authority. In return, she paid the Seljuqs for their military expenses and surrendered the strategic city of Amid and some small towns. Turan Shah was set free.[101]

Due to this fruitful Aleppan–Seljuqid military–political cooperation, we see Dayfa in September 1241 refusing the request of her brother Ghazi, lord of Mayyafariqin, to join him in his fight against the Seljuqs. He was not the first Ayyubid lord to ask her for military assistance, which reflects her powerful status; she had also turned down al-'Adil II and al-Jawad Yunus in order to protect her own interests, as already examined.

Dayfa did not remain neutral regarding Ghazi's confrontation with the Seljuqs. When Ghazi and his force, joined by some Khwarazmian forces, attacked the Seljuqid city of Amid, Dayfa swiftly dispatched Turan Shah, leading an Aleppan army to join the Seljuqid forces on their attack on her brother in Mayyafariqin. The campaign was cancelled due to heavy rain, which affected the mobility of the attackers. However, the important matter here is that Dayfa again demonstrated her realpolitik ability, honouring her long-term pact and political marriages with the Seljuqid side. Another reason for abandoning the campaign was a message from the 'Abbasid caliph requesting the lifting of the siege.¹⁰² The 'Abbasid caliph here was no more than a political symbol, who could be disobeyed or totally ignored if the interests of the warring sides did not meet with his request. The same things had taken place previously under several Seljuqid lords, as discussed in Chapter Six.

At the age of fifty-nine, Queen Dayfa died on 8 November 1242.¹⁰³ In addition to her impact on political life, we see her giving special patronage to religious Sunni buildings, following the Seljuqid tradition. During her relatively short reign as queen–regent, she commissioned the marvellous complex of al-Firdaws (one of the names of paradise; this complex was totally demolished during the Syrian civil war, which started in Aleppo in 2013 – see Figure 13). The complex was a madrasa, a *ribat* (place for the Sufis/mystics to meet) and a tomb for Dayfa and her son. Robert Hillenbrand states that 'it was a time of lavish patronage of religious buildings, with new fashionable types'.¹⁰⁴

Dayfa's advisors, such as the eunuch Iqbal al-Khatuni and Ibn al-'Adim, each built a madrasa¹⁰⁵ as an act of piety, and also to elevate her status as a model to be followed. There was also a *khanqah* (place for Sufi gatherings) commissioned by her commander Iqbal al-Zahiri in 1242.¹⁰⁶ These institutions helped to root the Sunni faith in Aleppo, which until a century before had had a Shi'i majority and a substantial Christian population.¹⁰⁷

Like the several Seljuqid madrasas built before, the madrasas under the Ayyubids were for the education of male children. Females were considered children of a lesser God until the fifteenth/sixteenth centuries. That does not answer the vital question: where did all those women mentioned in the chronicles, such as in the writings of Ibn 'Asakir of twelfth-century Damascus, have their education? He mentioned, for instance, the female scholar of Hadith, Malaka bt. Da'ud, whom he called an *'alima* (savant). She studied in Egypt under male teachers, and went on to teach him. That was not all; he said that 'she gave me licence to teach all the Hadith she had taught me'.¹⁰⁸ The same could be said about Muslim Spain in the tenth–thirteenth centuries. The chroniclers Ibn 'Abd Rabbuh (d. 1070) and al-Maqarri (d. 1632), among others, made mention of tens of educated women in Spain, especially in religious and literature studies.¹⁰⁹

Queen–regent Dayfa was a landmark in medieval Islamic history. She was described by her contemporaries, like Ibn Wasil: 'She behaved like sultans do, al-Nasir II became a ruler, only after her death.' Ibn al-'Adim wrote that 'she was resolute in her kingdom', and 'Aleppo was in the hands of *khatun* the queen'.[110]

Dayfa was distinguished among other Ayyubid women of her age, for instance, Rabi'a Khatun (d. 1245), sister of Saladin, who lived in Damascus, and 'Aisha Khatun, the granddaughter of Dayfa and wife of al-Mansur of Hama in 1247,[111] or Dayfa's sister, Ghaziya Khatun, who was the first wife of al-Zahir. These women, among others mentioned by al-Hanbali, hardly influenced political life as Dayfa did.

If the Fatimid caliphate had recognised the queenship of Arwa in Yemen in the eleventh and twelfth centuries, we see the 'Abbasid caliphate showing no objection to Dayfa becoming a queen–regent for six years. What confirms this opinion is that the messenger of the 'Abbasid caliph to her and the Seljuqs to lift their siege on her brother Ghazi, lord of Mayyafariqin, as discussed.

Certainly, her rule influenced a similar experience in Ayyubid Hama in 1244 on a smaller scale, but no details have been provided by chroniclers. Dayfa did pave the way for another Ayyubid woman, Shajar al-Durr, only eight years later, to dominate the political affairs of Egypt.

Shajar al-Durr: from Concubine to the Sultana of All Muslims in Egypt for Eighty Days, 1250

> Women have lesser minds and faith
> We (men) have never seen a wise opinion from them
> Almighty God never chose a woman as a prophet.[112]

These lines of poetry were penned by an anonymous poet when Shajar al-Durr (lit. trees of pearls) declared herself '*sultanat al-Muslimin*' (female sultan of Muslims) on 2 May 1250 in Ayyubid Egypt.[113] Clearly, this misogynous poet was influenced by the Prophet's tradition discussed in the Introduction, but he is adding his own rationale – that even God had never selected a woman to be his messenger or prophet.

Shajar al-Durr, who reigned as sultana (feminine form of sultan, or supreme ruler) between 2 May and 30 July 1250, was a rare case in medieval Islamic history, despite her very short sultanate, for the following reasons:

- She succeeded in confronting the king of France, Louis IX, during the Seventh Crusade on Egypt, following the sudden death of her husband during the campaign.
- She was loyal to her deceased husband, al-Salih Ayyub (d. 1249), and installed his only son, Turan Shah, as sultan of Egypt.[114]
- Shajar al-Durr, with the help of her *mamluk* commanders, assassinated Turan and declared herself sultana of Egypt.
- Shajar al-Durr was the last Ayyubid ruler and the first Mamluk one, contributing to a new political paradigm in political Muslim rule in the Middle East.
- Her legacy was recorded in the folktales of the Egyptian literature as a warrior woman of Islam as R. Kruk calls her.[115]

King Louis IX of France (d. 1270) led the Seventh Crusade on Egypt; he managed to lead a huge army and fleet that landed on the north-eastern side of the Nile Delta and occupied the city of Damietta in June 1249. The Ayyubid forces in Egypt evacuated Damietta without a fight and established their camp at the city of Mansura some 50 km to the south of the Crusaders, where their ill sultan, al-Salih Ayyub, joined them from Damascus.[116] The two warring sides did not alter their positions until November of the same year, due to the indecision of the Crusaders as regards attacking Alexandria or Cairo first.

On Sunday 24 November 1249 the sultan, who led the resistance while suffering severe pain from fistula, in addition to tuberculosis, died in his camp in Mansura.[117] It is at this point that we see the appearance of Shajar al-Durr in politics. Shajar al-Durr was a concubine of Turkish or Armenian origin, bought by al-Salih in 1239. She was the only person to accompany him when they were jailed in Karak in 1239 upon the orders of al-Nasir Da'ud.[118] It was during this year of captivity in Karak that Shajar al-Durr gave birth to her only child by al-Salih – a boy named Khalil. He died a few weeks after birth.[119] Apart from these very short anecdotes in the chronicles, the rest of her early life is shrouded in mystery, including her real name.

When al-Salih became sultan of Egypt, he freed and married Shajar al-Durr, who was also known as Um Khalil, after her deceased son. However, we do not hear of any role played by her prior to al-Salih's death in Mansura, as he was a very dominant ruler.

The night that al-Salih died, Shajar al-Durr concealed the news as she feared that it would adversely affect the morale of the troops fighting the Crusaders just metres away. She invited the chief eunuch of al-Salih, Jamal al-Din Muhsin, to consult with her. He was the commander of large numbers of the Mamluks in Egypt. They agreed to invite Emir Fakhr al-Din Yusuf, as the only commander capable of leading the army in these critical conditions. They gave him the post of *atabeg al-'askar* (commander of the army). These events took place without the knowledge of the sultan's deputy, Husam al-Din b. Abi 'Ali, who was in Cairo.[120]

There are several versions of what took place during these hours. However, it is understood that the chief commanders were summoned by Shajar al-Durr and Fakhr al-Din, and were told that the sultan was gravely ill. They were shown a forged decree, written by a eunuch called al-Suhayli, in the same handwriting of the deceased sultan. Al-Suhayli was ordered by Shajar al-Durr to write: 'The sultan asks the commanders to renew the oath of allegiance to him and his son (Turan Shah) as his successor, and to Fakhr al-Din as *atabeg*.'[121]

The deputy sultan continued to receive letters from al-Suhayli, dictated by the three people, as if it was dictated by the sultan, and using his insignia. Ibn Wasil, who was an eyewitness in the camp to these events, wrote that he was informed by al-Salih's physician that the sultan was probably dead due to his fast-deteriorating health in the preceding few days.[122]

Shajar al-Durr was not ambitious to take power herself, especially in these circumstances. She dispatched an envoy to bring the only surviving son of al-Salih (by another woman), Turan Shah, who had been exiled by his father to Hisn Kayfa in the Jazira. Al-Salih did not think that his son had the mental capacity to succeed him.[123]

Until Turan Shah arrived in Egypt on 28 February 1250, Shajar al-Durr was 'the one who conducted all affairs, and concealed the death of the sultan until Turan arrived in Mansura'.[124] During these decisive three months, King Louis IX had become aware of the reports of al-Salih's death, which was a disaster for the Muslim side.[125] Looking at Shajar al-Durr's role with her men, without getting into the complicated military details reported by de Joinville and Ibn Wasil, who were both eyewitnesses to events, we can say that the Crusaders attacked Egyptian forces in December 1249, and by the end of the month, they had pushed their way across several canals and succeeded in camping opposite Mansura (which was five days' march from Cairo), where Shajar al-Durr and her commanders stood.[126] On 8 February 1250 the king's brother, Count Robert of Artois, together with the Templars, led a surprising and swift attack on the city of Mansura itself. Due to this unexpected attack, the head of the Egyptian army, Fakhr al-Din, was killed along with many others. The genius *mamluk* emir, Baybars (the future Mamluk sultan), led the resistance and trapped the Crusaders in the city with its narrow alleys before launching his own surprise attacks with the help of the local Egyptian peasants in the streets of the city.[127] This was a disaster for the elite force of the Crusaders, and many Templars and Count Robert were massacred. Negotiations started between the Ayyubids and the Crusaders as regards surrendering Damietta for Jerusalem. The Ayyubids also demanded the surrender of the French king in order to guarantee the conclusion of the agreement.[128]

In the absence of the sultan's deputy, and with the murder of Fakhr al-Din, it was down to Shajar al-Durr, the eunuch commander Muhsin, and Baybars to lead the diplomatic negotiations with King Louis IX. They also had to manage the morale of the troops in order to prevent potential rebellion. Negotiating the surrender of Jerusalem required great leadership and pragmatism, although it should be noted that Jerusalem had previously been offered to the Crusaders by al-Kamil during the Fifth Crusade (1218–21), when Damietta was under Crusader occupation.

On 28 February 1250 Turan Shah, stepson of Shajar al-Durr, arrived in Mansura and entered the palace of his father and Shajar al-Durr. In April 1250 Turan Shah, with the Mamluk emirs of his father, managed to achieve victory over the Crusaders in the Battle of Mansura; the king was captured by Muhsin on 6 April 1250, and was jailed in Mansura.[129]

Despite the good fortune of Turan Shah, he treated Shajar al-Durr and his father's commanders badly. He accused Shajar al-Durr of not giving him all his father's treasures, and he appointed some of his men from the Jazira to key positions, ignoring the commanders who had called him to Egypt and who had bravely confronted the Crusaders for months while he was away. His drunken bad behaviour, together with his declaration that he would kill his father's commanders (naming some of them publicly, including Shajar al-Durr), led to him being assassinated by Baybars on 2 May 1250, who was acting on behalf of the commanders. Ibn Aybak accused Shajar al-Durr directly of instigating the assassination of Turan.[130]

The Sultanate of Shajar al-Durr

On the same day of the dramatic assassination of Turan Shah, the *mamluk* emirs held a council at the entrance of the court in Mansura. They discussed whom should be *atabeg al-'askar*:

> That is after they had all agreed that Shajar al-Durr should become sultan, and run all affairs, and have her own royal insignia. They (the commanders) offered the atabegate of the army to the deputy of al-Salih, Husam al-Din. They told him that the sultan was counting on him. He declined. Husam al-Din suggested Emir Shihab al-Din Rashid as *atabeg*. They offered Rashid the office, but he also declined. They offered it to Emir Turk al-Kabir, and he also declined. They agreed to bring forward Emir 'Izz al-Din Aybak, who agreed. The council gave the oath to Shajar al-Durr as sultan, and Aybak as *atabeg al-'askar*.
>
> A messenger was dispatched to Cairo, and went up the citadel (place of government), and Queen Shajar al-Durr was informed. All affairs came under her control. She had her insignia on documents, and the *khutba* of her sultanate was declared in her name in all the mosques of Cairo and the entire Egyptian dominions.[131]

This very detailed narrative of Ibn Wasil reflects the following:

1. The political vacuum resulting from the murder of Sultan Turan Shah was filled on the same day by the *mamluk* commanders of the army.
2. The council divided the affairs of the state into two: military under the *atabeg*'s authority as a man, and political under Shajar al-Durr as sultan. At least with the title, Shajar al-Durr, with her insignia, had the upper and final word in the new realm.
3. It is far from clear why three leading commanders turned down the post of *atabeg*, even though they had achieved victory over the Crusaders and the Frankish king was in their jail. Was it the fear of the political conditions with no Ayyubid male in power? Or the refusal to submit to a

woman? Or the fear of the reaction of the rest of the Ayyubids in Syria and the Jazira?
4. The military commanders had no hesitation in naming a woman as the new ruler, and they considered her legitimate, as the widow of their deceased sultan.

Ibn Wasil was very well informed of the unfolding of events from different leading commanders. He described the appointment of Shajar al-Durr as follows: 'This is a new situation, unheard of in Islamic history; but the queen consort post has been witnessed before in the case of Dayfa, who conducted the rule and the affairs, but the *khutba* was given to her grandson.'[132] It should be noted that some of the *mamluk* commanders were contemporary to Dayfa Khatun. In addition to that, they were used to gendered politics, as Queen Margaret, wife of Louis IX, had negotiated the terms of her husband's release with the *mamluk* commanders, with full coordination with Shajar al-Durr.[133]

Four days after sitting as sultana of Egypt, Shajar al-Durr released the French king as part of a financial–political arrangement, and Damietta was surrendered to Shajar al-Durr's deputies. The new revolutionary rule in Egypt kept the brother of the king (Alfonso of Poitou) hostage, until the king could pay the rest of his huge ransom (400,000 dinars).[134] Indeed the negotiation was mainly conducted by the *mamluk* emirs, but with the knowledge of and coordination with the new sultana.

Shajar al-Durr's political involvement received different reactions from the various Muslim powers. She put her name on the dinar (Queen of Muslims, al-Musta'simiyya, al-Salihiyya, mother of King Khalil). She named herself as servant to the 'Abbasid caliph, al-Musta'sim, and belonged also to al-Salih, but she avoided including her own name. Her insignia was '*walidat Khalil*' (mother of Khalil), in memory of her son who had died weeks after birth in Karak, as mentioned above.

The *khutba* declared for her after the name of the 'Abbasid caliph al-Musta'sim stated: 'God may protect al-Salih's side, queen of Muslims, guardian of the secular and religious worlds. Mother of Khalil, al-Musta'simiyya, wife of al-Salih.'[135] It is clear from the *khutba* and the mint that Shajar al-Durr was too shy to include her own name, instead associating herself with three males: the 'Abbasid caliph, her deceased husband and their deceased son.

She probably thought that, in addition to being a woman, there had been too many changes in the political situation with the transitional period between Ayyubids and Ayyubid–Mamluk rule. This is despite her being a true heroine, who had led Egypt in her darkest moments, but society was not familiar with that, with precedents being limited to Arwa, Dayfa and Radiyya.

The reaction of the Egyptian locals and army *mamluk*s was very positive. There are no reports of any dismay or objection from prayers to have the *khutba* declared for a woman. Shajar al-Durr spent lavishly on the *mamluk* commanders, granting them lands and money to secure their loyalty, just as most male rulers had done before her.[136]

The local Egyptians even commemorated Shajar al-Durr in their folktales. She was also named Fatima in 'Sirat al-Malik al-Zahir Baybars' ('The Legend of King Baybars') (Baybars reigned from 1260 to 1277), and was considered mother of Baybars.[137] She was claimed to be a daughter of an assumed caliph named al-Muqtadir. When the sitting caliph objected to her rule due to her gender, she replied: 'Nothing in the Qur'an forbids women from ruling the Muslims.'[138]

In reality, Caliph al-Musta'sim sent a strong and sarcastic message to the commanders of Egypt, saying: 'If men who are capable of ruling have ceased to exist in Egypt, we will dispatch a capable male for that mission. Did not you hear of the Prophet's saying: "Failed are the people who appoint a female as their ruler?"'[139] The question here is: Why did the 'Abbasid caliph al-Mustansir (d. 1242) not object to Queen Dayfa's rule, but al-Musta'sim rejected Shajar al-Durr? Is it because Dayfa was a free woman and Shajar al-Durr was originally a slave concubine? Furthermore, there is no evidence that al-Mustansir objected to the rule of Queen Radiyya, who was a *mamluk* slave too, and gave the *khutba* in his name.

Shajar al-Durr did not resist the 'Abbasid pressure, although the caliph could not remove her by force due to the long decay of his institution, but his religious symbol was eminent.[140] The objection came from other fronts in addition to 'Abbasid Iraq. The Ayyubids of Syria rejected the sultanate of Shajar al-Durr, who had been ambitious enough to send to Damascus asking for the oath of allegiance to her. That move by the new queen followed a long-standing tradition of Ayyubid rulers before her in Egypt to extend their authority to Syria.

The queen's envoy, al-Khatib, was humiliated by the Qaymariyya *mamluk* commanders of Damascus. They swiftly dispatched a messenger to King al-Nasir II of Aleppo asking him to come and take Damascus.[141] Another misogynist reaction came from the Ayyubids of al-Karak in Jordan. King al-Mughith 'Umar b. al-'Adil II b. al-Kamil was released from prison and was declared king of Jordan, refusing the authority of a slave woman in Cairo.[142]

Despite these negative reactions to the sultanate of a slave woman, Shajar al-Durr, on 30 July 1250, abdicated and married 'Izz al-Din Aybak al-Turkomani, *atabeg* of the army (*al-'asakir*), and passing the sultanate to him, thus making him the first ruler of the Mamluk Sultanate. This event was attended by the military commanders and leading judges of Egypt.[143]

Aybak continued to declare the *khutba* to the 'Abbasid caliph, who did not object to a slave man becoming the sultan of the Muslims in Egypt. Clearly, it was the gender and not the social status that had aggravated the 'Abbasid caliphate.

Until her murder in 1257, Shajar al-Durr's appearance in the chronicles is limited; yet, the reports reflect a powerful persona, who remained in the political arena.

Three months into her marriage to Aybak, Shajar al-Durr completed the dome she had started as a burial place for her first lord and husband, al-Salih Ayyub. In October 1250 she moved the remains of al-Salih from Rawda Island in the Nile to his new mausoleum in Cairo. It was built next to his madrasa, and she ordered a museum containing his banners next to it (see Figure 14).[144]

She commissioned her own mausoleum, which was very rare in Muslim Egypt, with the mihrab decorated with mosaics in the shape of trees of pearls, symbolising her name (see Figure 15).[145] Why her dome was not built next to that of al-Salih is not known. It was built outside Cairo, next to the domes of several Fatimid women, descendants of the prophets, such as those of Nafisa and Ruqayya, built in the eleventh century, who are considered saints by Shi'i followers.

Inside her dome, Shajar al-Durr wrote: 'God glorify al-Satr al-Rafi' (queen) 'ismat al-Dunya wa al-Din (guardian of secular and religious world), mother of King Khalil, son of Sultan al-Salih Ayyub.'[146] I believe that she emphasised her political status, which was briefly mentioned on the mint and *khutba*, in her dome, which was completed after her abdication.

The most revealing information about Shajar al-Durr's role in politics comes from Ibn Taghri Bardi, who wrote: 'She dominated Aybak in all his affairs. He had no opinion with her.'[147] Although we cannot apply this opinion to the seven years of their marriage, if we include the opinion of Ibn Iyas who wrote: 'She was always reminding him of her favour to him by bringing him to power, after her abdication. Shajar al-Durr said to him: "Without me, you would have never made it to the sultanate"',[148] we could say that Shajar al-Durr interfered in the politics of Egypt while her husband was constantly occupied by warfare from 1254 to 1257 to protect his new rule from the Ayyubids of Syria. In addition to that, her relationship with the *mamluk* commanders of her deceased husband al-Salih probably was strong too. What supports this opinion is Shajar al-Durr's influential behaviour towards Aybak. When she knew that Aybak had engaged a Lu'Lu'id princess from Mosul in 1257 (although of *mamluk* origin too), she was greatly angered and felt humiliated. She wrote to King al-Nasir II of Aleppo, informing him that she would murder Aybak, and then she would propose to marry al-Nasir II and surrender Egypt to him,[149] which was his unaccomplished dream.

Shajar al-Durr's ambitious proposal and plan could not be pulled off unless she had enough supporters and loyal connections among the commanders. When al-Nasir II hesitated and did not answer her, she ordered her very loyal eunuch commander, Muhsin, who had previously arrested King Louis IX, to kill Sultan Aybak. He executed the order on 20 March 1257, when Aybak was in the citadel of Cairo.

Shajar al-Durr then summoned her advisor, Safi al-Din Ibrahim, who was also a close advisor to al-Ashraf b. al-'Adil II, to consult with him about the matter; he could not give an opinion, and warned her of the dire consequences.[150] Shajar al-Durr sent a message to Emir Jamal al-Din Aydaghli informing him of the situation. She sent with the message the insignia of Aybak and one of his fingers, and asked him to sit on the throne as sultan. He refused. The same thing was repeated with Emir Aybak al-Halabi.[151]

Why did Shajar al-Durr not take the throne herself, instead offering to marry al-Nasir II of Syria, or offering the sultanate to two *mamluk* commanders? Clearly, she feared the same anti-women reaction by the 'Abbasid caliph. In addition, al-Nasir II had previously attacked Egypt, but was defeated by Aybak. Since he was an Ayyubid king, he would use his legitimacy, in addition to her power, to rule Egypt.

The assassination of Sultan Aybak was followed by a few days of turbulent and fast-moving events. Some *mamluks* wanted to murder Shajar al-Durr, while others protected her. The commanders selected Emir 'Alam al-Din Sanjar al-Halabi as *atabeg* for the fifteen-year-old al-Mansur 'Ali b. Aybak. The latter briefly became ceremonial lord of Egypt, while his *atabeg* was the de facto one.[152]

Soon after, the commanders of Aybak, led by Emir Qutuz, arrested the *mamluk*s of Shajar al-Durr who had killed Aybak and crucified them on the wall of the citadel of Cairo. Afterwards, in April 1257, Emir Qutuz arrested Sanjar. Shajar al-Durr was mysteriously killed soon after in the same month. Chroniclers give different reports about who threw her naked corpse from the citadel walls: the commanders or the mother of 'Ali, Aybak's first wife.[153]

The model of Shajar al-Durr as sovereign queen, even for only eighty days, was not repeated in the Middle East until the late thirteenth century, when Queen Abish of the Salghurids ruled Shiraz as a girl of seven or eight years old under the Mongols, as mentioned.

Yet, we see the echo of Shajar al-Durr in Yemen. We see the Turkmen Rasulids who were *mamluks* of the Ayyubids and succeeded them in Yemen in 1228, producing another powerful woman: Queen al-Shamsiyya (d. 1295), daughter of the first Rasulid king, al-Mansur (d. 1250). She interfered in political matters when her father was killed, as her brother and the successor al-Muzaffar was away from Zabid; she took control of Zabid, and spent lavishly on the troops and the local militia. When al-Muzaffar arrived in Zabid he 'installed her as queen. Zabid was the first city to witness a queen'[154] (after Arwa). Al-Shamsiyya helped her brother to capture other key citadels during this difficult political transitional period.[155]

The Mamluks, who succeeded the Ayyubids in Egypt and then Syria, produced some influential women in politics. For example, in 1294, while al-Nasir Qalawun faced his first coup against him, his mother Khund Ashlun led a military resistance in Cairo citadel against his enemies.[156] Khund Baraka, mother of Sultan Sha'ban II (d. 1382), was always known as Um al-Sultan (mother of the sultan), a title never used by other mothers of Mamluk sultans. Al-Maqrizi wrote that when she married Emir al-Jay al-Yusufi, 'al-Yusufi became prominent and powerful by her influence'.[157] There was also Khund Zaynab, wife of Sultan Inal (r. 1453–61). Ibn Iyas wrote that she would conduct the affairs of the state with her husband, regarding appointing and dismissing: 'Her word and opinion were always implemented.'[158] Having said that, Muslim countries in the Middle East until the twenty-first century never witnessed a sovereign female ruler, unlike the Far East kingdom of Aceh in Indonesia in the second half of the sixteenth century, when three sisters succeeded one another as queens in northern Sumatra.

While women rulers came to power in the early twenty-first century in Muslim countries such as Indonesia, Pakistan and Bangladesh, maybe echoing Radiyya and Aceh's queens, we do not see that taking place in the foreseeable future in the Middle East due to the misogynist patriarchal interpretation of the Qur'an and shari'a, which has not changed for more than a millennium. One of my many reasons for saying that is that all the Muslim Middle Eastern and North African countries forbid women from even reciting the Qur'an on radio and television stations. Although, from the turn of the twentieth century until the Second World War Egyptian radio, both locally owned and state owned, used to broadcast female reciters of the Qur'an, such as the famous Karima al-'Adliyya; however, she was stopped as a result of a fatwa in 1940 that stated that the female voice was a disgrace (without providing any clear evidence from the Qur'an).[159] Also important to note is that women across the Muslim world have never been allowed to call for prayers like men do, although nothing in the Qur'an prevents them from doing so, but they are nevertheless seen as inferior.

The Ayyubid Eunuch–*Atabegs*

The office of the *atabeg* was introduced to Egypt and Yemen under the Ayyubids and maintained in Syria. Having said that, we see several important changes taking place under the Ayyubids: (1) the Turkish monopoly to the atabegate was broken and Rumi/Slavic *atabeg*s now held office in addition to the Turks; (2) for the first time the Ayyubids also installed a royal prince (a Kurd) to the post: al-Afdal, son of Saladin, was *atabeg* in 1199 for his nephew, al-Mansur;[160] (3) the Ayyubids introduced the new office of *atabeg al-'askar* in 1216 under al-Zahir, son of Saladin, in Aleppo. It was meant to be as a leader of the army, and survived through the Mamluk dynasty (most of the Mamluk sultans were originally *atabeg al-'askar*, like Aybak, whom Shajar al-Durr married);[161] and (4) the majority of the *atabeg*s who were at the top of the political military hierarchy in the realm were castrated commanders. Thus, we have the eunuch–*atabeg* phenomenon; not as a single case like that of Lu'Lu' in 1117 in Seljuqid Aleppo, but as dominating figures of the affairs of the state.

I propose to examine the examples outlined above, and explore their different roles and impacts, but I will consider the joint cases of the eunuch–*atabeg*s as one entity, since most of the cases are identical or connected.

Saladin had partially followed the Zengid–Seljuqid tradition of appointing *atabeg*s for some of his children. In 1183, after seizing Aleppo from the Zengids, he appointed the Turkmen emir Yazkuj as *atabeg* for his young son, al-Zahir, to run the city in his name.[162] The *atabeg* had no free hand in the presence of the formidable dominating persona of Saladin. Saladin did not appoint any other *atabeg*s for his sons or nephews, including his designated successor, al-Afdal. That shows that, as a Kurd, he was unconvinced about the Turkish institution of atabegate. However, in 1198, when King al-'Aziz of Egypt, the son of Saladin, was suffering his final illness, he appointed his long-serving eunuch commander and deputy of his father, Qaraqush, as *atabeg* for his ten-year-old son, al-Mansur (r. 1198–1200).[163]

That was the first time a eunuch and a non-Turkish emir had been appointed to the atabegate by the king himself. Qaraqush was a Rumi or of Byzantine/Balkan origin. Due to this strange and unprecedented development, the powerful commanders of the army found it hard to accept him as an *atabeg*, even though he was a deputy to Saladin, as will be explained. They deposed him after less than two months in office and, in January 1199, called on al-Afdal, son of Saladin, to be *atabeg* for al-Mansur, without the right to mention his name in the *khutba*.[164]

The devious al-'Adil, the long-serving assistant of his brother Saladin, seized the moment in coordination with several commanders in Egypt and installed himself as *atabeg* to al-Mansur in February 1200. Al-'Adil, having ousted his nephew al-Afdal, granted him some *iqta'* in the Jazira.¹⁶⁵ Al-'Adil agreed to the conditions put to him by the emirs of the army, namely to leave the atabegate when al-Mansur reached adulthood. After only a week in the atabegate, al-'Adil desired to seize the throne for himself, rather than ruling in the name of another. He gathered the leading commanders of the army in a council and said to them:

> It is repulsive that I should become *atabeg* to a boy at my age, and of my status. The kingship is not gained by inheritance, but seized by force.
>
> I should have been the sultan after my brother Saladin, but I renounce it in his honour. When the internal feud took place, I feared that the rule would be taken out of my hands and those of my nephews. When I came to Egypt, I pledged to serve as *atabeg* to this young boy until he grew up, but I saw the turmoil was not over. I fear the fate of al-Afdal, and a group of commanders could replace me with someone else. The young boy al-Mansur should receive an education, and I will appoint someone to nurture him until he reaches adulthood; then I will do what is best for him.¹⁶⁶

To secure himself against a hostile counter-movement from commanders who might object to his move and might use the physical presence of al-Mansur to their advantage, al-'Adil deported the boy to Syria in 1203.¹⁶⁷ Why did al-'Adil take such step or, in real terms, launch a coup? As he himself explained, he was aware of the weakness of the post of the atabegate and saw it as a bridge to the throne, especially as he considered himself as having not been sufficiently rewarded by his brother Saladin, who had allocated key and important cities and *iqta'* to his sons, neglecting al-'Adil.

From the cases discussed above, we see that the eunuch–*atabeg* Qaraqush, who enjoyed great respect during Saladin's lifetime, was deposed from this post due to his gender and old age. In addition, we see for the first time Kurdish royals becoming *atabeg*s for members of their own family, unlike the Seljuqs. Here the philosophy and aim of the Seljuqid *atabeg* would change. The Kurds were an organic ethnic group in the Middle East, living centuries before the arrival of the Turkmen Seljuqs in the eleventh century; so apart from the military and traditional religious teachings, the Kurdish *atabeg* theoretically had a different approach to that of the Turkmen equivalent. This is because the Kurdish persona existed in several Middle Eastern countries, while the Seljuqs needed to preserve their own tradition, under threat from being far away from their original home in Mongolia.

Moving to the case of *atabeg al-'askar*, for the first time since the introduction of the post of *atabeg* by the Seljuqs, we see in October 1216, during his final illness, al-Zahir, king of Aleppo, appointing Emir Tughril as *atabeg* to his two sons, al-'Aziz and his half-brother al-Salih. It was the first time that we see an *atabeg* for two kings at the same time. It may be that al-Zahir wanted to avoid any clash of authority if he had another *atabeg*. Al-Zahir empowered Tughril with controlling the treasury, supervising the harem, administering the treasury, commanding the formidable citadel and running all affairs of the realm in the name of the nascent king. At the same time, al-Zahir invented the post of *atabeg al-'askar* (lit. father of the army, and practically commander of the army). He appointed Sayf al-Din 'Ali to that post.[168] Now we have two *atabeg*s in the same realm: Tughril and 'Ali. As the Ayyubid Kurds always had fewer numbers than the Turkmen army, even during Saladin's reign, the post of *atabeg al-'askar* was an indication of the continuation of that status; the Turkish word even symbolises that.

Having said that, Tughril had absolute power in Aleppo, after al-Zahir, and was in full control of the *atabeg al-'askar*. A few weeks after the death of al-Zahir, he re-organised the entire administration of Aleppo according to his will and needs. Thus, he deposed the new *atabeg al-'askar*, and appointed the exiled former king of Egypt, al-Malik al-Mansur, as the new *atabeg al-'askar*.[169] Several commanders from the Ayyubid house rejected that appointment, in addition to the Seljuqs of Rum, who suggested a new *atabeg al-'askar*: the luckless al-Afdal, eldest son of Saladin, and his legitimate successor, lord of the insignificant Sumaysat in eastern Anatolia. Tughril and his allies in Aleppo rejected this idea and kept his candidate, al-Mansur, who was in charge of supervising the *iqta's* and their distribution to the emirs. Al-Mansur worked in full coordination with Tughril, as the political decision to use the army remained with Tughril.[170]

From the evidence in the sources, we do not see any details of the activities of the *atabeg al-'askar*. However, the presence of a Kurdish former Ayyubid king might have secured the loyalty of the army, especially that Tughril was a Rumi *mamluk*; and the failure of the Rumi atabegate of Qaraqush a few years earlier in Egypt was still in memory.

We have seen during the Seljuqid rule that many *atabeg*s were previously holders of the *isfahsalar* post (commander of the army). It may be that al-Zahir wanted to create a political balance for his son and successor, but the office of *atabeg al-'askar* did not flourish in the remaining three decades in Ayyubid Syria or Egypt. Having said that, the newly introduced Ayyubid post had an immense impact on the Mamluk dynasty, with both its lines, the Bahri and Burji (the latter was borne out of the Ayyubid state and ruled until 1517). It started with Aybak, who was chosen as *atabeg al-'askar*. Mamluk commanders agreed to install an Ayyubid boy king, al-Ashraf Musa III, who was only six years old and grandson of al-Kamil, to be the ceremonial king of Egypt, but Aybak would be the de facto ruler: 'By this step, they (the *mamluk*s and *atabeg*) would consume the rule and the world by it.' Aybak remained as *atabeg al-'askar* to the boy king until 1254.[171] To monitor the effect on the Mamluk administration without getting into details beyond the limits of this book, I can provide a few examples. We see that *atabeg al-'askar* developed into *al-'asakir* (plural), as written by al-Maqrizi and Ibn Taghri Bardi.

A great number of *atabeg al-'asakir* succeeded their sultans or deposed them by coup. In 1279 the *atabeg* Qalawun deposed Sultan Salamish and seized the sultanate.[172] The *atabeg* al-Zahir Barquq was controlling the army from 1380 to 1382 for Sultan al-Salih Hajji II, and then deposed and replaced him. The *atabeg* al-Mu'ayyad Shaykh became sultan in 1412.[173] And the *atabeg* Chaqmaq deposed Sultan Yusuf b. Barsbay in 1438 and seized the sultanate. In turn, the *atabeg* Inal deposed 'Uthman b. Chaqmaq in 1453 and became sultan.[174]

In addition to these ambitious *atabeg*s who used their command of the army to seize the throne, we see other *atabeg*s who were de facto rulers while their sultans had nominal authority, such as the *atabeg* Sanjar under Sultan al-Nasir Qalawun I during his first reign in 1293, and also the *atabeg* Asan Damur under Sultan al-Ashraf Sha'ban II in 1363.[175] In addition to the post of *atabeg al-'asakir* in Egypt, the *atabeg al-'askar* appeared in Mamluk Damascus and Aleppo in the late fourteenth century.[176]

Some *atabeg*s were installed by sultans as regent and tutor for their infant sons, like the case of Sultan Barsbay (d. 1438), who asked the *atabeg* Chaqmaq to raise his son Yusuf, and rule the realm in his name.[177] Clearly, the *atabeg* in this case was not just a commander of the army, but also conductor of the sultanate. David Ayalon argues that *atabeg al-ʿasakir* became the second most powerful office in the Mamluk realm, replacing the post of deputy sultan. The contemporary *mamluk* historian, Ibn Taghri Bardi (d. 1470), whose father was an elite emir, puts it at the top of the leading seventeen emirs in the army.[178]

It should be noted that while the Seljuq Turks were a family and tribal collective homogenous society who needed to preserve their traditions, the Mamluks were individual slaves, brought at a young age from slave markets to serve in the military. They came not only from Central Asia and the Caucasus, but also from the northern shores of the Black Sea area.[179] As a result, they had no specific common values to preserve, apart from the military traditions they inherited, mainly from the Ayyubids.

The Atabeg *Post in Ayyubid Yemen*

The Ayyubids were Turkicised by the Seljuq–Zengid tradition and administration, and passed it on in Egypt and Syria to the Mamluks after them. The Ayyubids who ruled Yemen from 1174 to 1229 introduced to their new territories in Yemen the Turkish administration they knew, including the post of *atabeg*, which was passed to their successors, the Rasulids, who were Turkmen Ghuzz and ruled until the mid-fifteenth century.

Before Saladin sent his brother Turan Shah to invade Yemen in 1174, aiming to use it as a refuge from his sultan Nur al-Din Mahmud, Yemen did not experience any Turkish or Kurdish influence, having been ruled since the rise of Islam by Arab elements.

During the first half of the short-lived Ayyubid period up to 1197, the two brothers of Saladin, Turan Shah and then Tughtekin, ruled Yemen without using *atabeg*s. Saladin, who died in 1193, was keen to give power to his own sons, no matter how inexperienced they were, and not to his brothers. The office of *atabeg* appeared in the chronicles as commander and deputy during the reign of al-Muʿizz b. Tughtekin's (r. 1197–1202) final year in power. The *atabeg* Sunqur did not have any teaching tasks, only military ones. When al-Muʿizz claimed the caliphate for himself, and murdered a large number of his commanders and those of his father, Sunqur, a Turkish *mamluk* of his father, interfered by advising him to reinstate the *khutba* to the 'Abbasids and win the rest of his commanders back.[180] Al-Mu'izz refused and tried to kill Sunqur, who won the support of most of the Ghuzz (Turks–Kurds) and murdered al-Mu'izz near Zabid. Sunqur managed to win the support of the Turko-Kurdish commanders in Yemen, and declared himself *atabeg* for the infant al-Nasir b. Tughtekin, who was in Ta'izz.[181] The supreme Ayyubid sultan, al-'Adil in Egypt, was supposed to interfere during this crisis, but he could not for several pressing reasons. He was establishing his new sultanate in Egypt, which was suffering from severe famine, in addition to a damaging earthquake that had devastated the Ayyubid defences in the Levant.[182] The limited financial–military resources of al-'Adil, who had learned about the Fourth Crusade in 1203, but not yet of its final goal,[183] led him to him neglect Yemen, thus giving Sunqur a free hand in these far and remote territories.

Sunqur, who became the de facto ruler of Ayyubid Yemen, married the mother of al-Nasir for more legitimacy, but without the official permission of an Ayyubid lord,[184] unlike the cases of Tughtekin in Seljuqid Damascus or Eldiguz in Azerbaijan, when they were permitted by their lords. One Yemeni chronicler wrote: 'The throne was secured for *atabeg*.'[185] Until his death in Ta'izz in 1211, Sunqur was heavily involved in domestic Yemeni tribal affairs, trying to balance his power between upper and lower Yemen, as the sources describe it. He entered different tribal pacts, including with Shi'i leaders, to keep his dominions.[186] However, without any sign of Ayyubid contact with him from Egypt, this indicated that the Ayyubid rule in Egypt was weak.

Sunqur had a son from his wife, the mother of al-Nasir.[187] That certainly consolidated his grip on power as father to a brother of the Ayyubid king of Yemen. Sunqur did exactly as Eldiguz had done in Azerbaijan, but he did not live long enough to see his son on the throne. Chroniclers observe that after Sunqur's death, al-Nasir, who was about thirteen/fourteen years old, gained independence. Yet, we see him install Ghazi b. Jibril as his new *atabeg* in the same year.[188]

Information is scarce and unclear, but it appears that the *atabeg* Ghazi remained as de facto ruler, and as commander of the realm until 1214 when he killed al-Nasir by poisoning him in Sana'a, before seizing the rule for himself. He even minted the dinar in his name. A few months later, some of al-Nasir's *mamluk*s, in coordination with the mother of the deceased king, managed to kill Ghazi in Ibb.[189]

The Ayyubid rule in Yemen fell into complete chaos. Al-Nasir's mother sent a message to Sultan al-'Adil in Egypt, urging him to send an Ayyubid prince to take over the rule, but he did not respond. She then took over Zabid herself and gathered in all treasures of that city. Ibn Wasil wrote: 'She waited for any Ayyubid prince to arrive so she could marry him and give him the rule.'[190]

Why did this royal mother did not follow Arwa's example and rule herself? The Ayyubid Kurds, with their Turkmen troops, were new to the complicated Yemeni society, and lacked large numbers for the military; on the other hand, Arwa was a Yemeni with a strong tribe to back her up, in addition to the political–religious support she always received from the Fatimid caliph. Why she did not install her son by Sunqur is not clear, but it seems to be concerned with financial difficulties; the troops would refuse anyone but a free Kurd in power.

During the pilgrimage season, al-Nasir's mother dispatched some of her *mamluk*s to Mecca to get news from Ayyubid Egypt. They found an Ayyubid prince dressed in Sufi garments; his name was Sulayman Shah, and he claimed to be the son of Taqi al-Din 'Umar, nephew of Saladin. They informed her by post, and she invited him to Zabid, married him and surrendered the rule to him.[191] This was a rule transferred to a man through the legitimacy and power of a woman who certainly had enough support among the commanders of her late husband and her son. However, Sulayman had no experience in ruling and marginalised the wife who had given him such power. She wrote again to al-'Adil in Egypt, asking for help.

Sultan al-'Adil finally decided to give some attention to Yemen. In 1215 he dispatched his grandson, King Mas'ud b. al-Kamil, as ruler of Yemen (at the age of thirteen/fourteen) with a massive army. Due to Mas'ud's young age, the *atabeg* Fulayt was sent with him as conductor of his realm.[192]

When he arrived in Yemen, Mas'ud arrested Sulayman. In addition, he married Jawzi, daughter of the former *atabeg* Sunqur, which reflects her power and the existing connection to her father's *mamluk*s.[193] It was rare for power to be given to a daughter of a former *atabeg* in the Ayyubid state. She continued to play a political role with her two sons under the Rasulid state until 1252, controlling key citadels in Yemen. (She was a contemporary of Shajar al-Durr.)[194]

For two years until his death in 1217, Fulayt was drowning in the ever-changing tribal politics of Yemen. Afterwards, King Mas'ud had a limited success in controlling parts of Yemen, especially in the north, but he did not install another *atabeg*, and neither did his father, now the sultan in Egypt. In 1229 Mas'ud died while on a visit to Egypt, and his deputy there, 'Umar b. Rasul, took power, establishing the Turkmen Rasulid state in Yemen, which lasted until the fifteenth century.[195]

The Ayyubid influence on Yemeni political–military administration was extended to their successors, the Rasulids, who were their *mamluks*, similar to the case of the Mamluks of Egypt and Syria after the Ayyubids. Al-Khazraji, among others, wrote about the increase of *mamluk*s in Yemeni society and compared their military skills with those in Egypt. The posts of *atabeg* and *atabeg al-'asakir* were used for a long time under the Rasulids, for example, under King al-Mu'ayyad (d. 1322) and King al-Mujahid (d. 1363). The post of *atabeg al-'asakir* came second in the hierarchy, after the king.[196]

Finally, after examining the non-Turkish *atabeg*s, royal Kurdish *atabeg*s and the *atabeg al-'askar*, I will examine the dual entity of the *eunuch–atabeg* under the Ayyubids and their impact.

The Case of Saladin and his Son

Saladin, the founder of the Ayyubid dynasty, started his career in Egypt by confronting a conspiracy from the chief eunuch of the Fatimid palace, Mu'taman al-Khilafa Jawhar. Jawhar contacted the Crusaders, seeking assistance to remove Saladin from office. In 1170 Saladin managed to defeat Jawhar and his large Sudanese support, uprooting their influence from the Egyptian military. Saladin installed his uncle's *mamluk*, a eunuch named Baha' al-Din Qaraqush, as the new chief of the Fatimid caliph's palace. He entrusted Qaraqush with observing the Fatimid caliph and all other Fatimid palaces occupied by the Fatimid royal family and their entourage; in addition, Qaraqush assumed control of the Fatimid treasures.[197]

Clearly, Saladin could not trust anyone else to safeguard the Fatimid wealth, which he needed for his own Kurdish rule, and to report any conspiracy from the palace during that decisive, transitional period. In addition to the post of *ustadh qasr* (palace chief), Saladin appointed Qaraqush as his *na'ib* (deputy) in Egypt while he was fighting in Syria. Ibn Khallikan wrote: 'He (Qaraqush) became his deputy in Egypt, empowering him with all state affairs, and depending on him for governance.'[198] So, we see Saladin replacing a Fatimid chief eunuch with another one, not only influenced by the Seljuq tradition, but by the Fatimid one as well.

During this time Qaraqush had the authority to implement his master's plan and control the country. In 1184, for instance, he dispatched an army to al-Sharqiyya in the eastern Delta to put down a rebellion there by the Ghudhami Arab tribe. At the same time, he secured the Ayyubid royals in Cairo by getting them to safety across to the western bank of the Nile.[199] Qaraqush managed to construct several military buildings in Egypt and Syria. In 1176 he started the massive project of the citadel in Cairo, which he supervised relentlessly for more than a decade while he was occupying the post of deputy. He also accomplished the bridges to the west of Cairo. He surrounded the citadel, Cairo and Fustat with one wall, which was an ambitious project, to protect the new rule. Due to the success he achieved and the trust he enjoyed from Saladin, he was commissioned to rebuild the fortification of Acre in Palestine in 1188, after it had been seized from the Crusaders.[200]

The third post Qaraqush occupied under Saladin was as a fighting emir during the long siege of Acre in the Third Crusade in 1190. Due to the unique importance of that eunuch to his master, Saladin paid the huge ransom of 10,000 dinars to free him from captivity. He was delighted when Qaraqush returned to his service.[201] This reflects the great weight or status Qaraqush represented in the Ayyubid state.

The influence of eunuchs was present in another area of the kingdom under Saladin. In an illuminating piece of information in Muslim and Latin sources alike, we see that Saladin's army depended heavily on eunuchs for many years. William of Tyre (d. 1186) mentioned in 1177 that Saladin's army contained 18,000 soldiers, and that '8,000 belonged to those splendid soldiers called in their own language "toassin-tawashi"'. Al-Maqrizi, in his account of 1181, wrote that Saladin's army 'consisted of nearly 11,000 soldiers, 111 emirs and 6,976 *tawashi*–eunuchs'.[202] We can see that in both reports almost half the army was composed of eunuchs, which reflects how the Ayyubid state needed and depended on their great skills. In addition, these eunuchs had political influence due to their large numbers and high status.

This large number of eunuchs leads us to disagree with David Ayalon, who denied the existence of eunuch units on the battlefield to that point.[203] As we have seen under the Fatimid eunuchs and also here, they even carried the name of their eunuch commanders during some events.

After Saladin the influence of eunuchs increased. We see how Qaraqush occupied different posts, civil and military alike. He was the deputy to al-ʿAziz b. Saladin throughout his rule, while the latter was fighting in Syria or engaged outside Cairo. Qaraqush played a vital role in protecting the throne of al-ʿAziz during a crucial period after Saladin's death. That is when Saladin's sons and their uncle al-ʿAdil I were engaged in a civil war. In 1193, when al-ʿAziz (who was not the official successor to Saladin, but his elder brother al-Afdal) departed from Egypt to Jubayl on the Syrian coast to fight the Crusaders, he entrusted the deputyship to Qaraqush. He knew that his brother, al-Afdal in Syria, was lurking to seize the rule in Cairo. Also in the same year, Qaraqush was left with half of the army and one third of the knights to guard Cairo, while al-ʿAziz was absent from the capital.[204]

In this critical period between the warring brothers, Qaraqush secured the throne for al-ʿAziz in 1194 after strife erupted between the different brigades of the army – some of them were supporting the legitimate candidate and successor, al-Afdal. The pro-al-Afdal Asadiyya planned a coup, aiming to desert their places as soon as al-ʿAziz left Syria for his return to Cairo, and to arrest him. The plot was underway, and al-Samin, the leader of the Asadiyya, deserted the army with his troops, weakening al-ʿAziz. However, since Qaraqush was an Asadi himself, and had his own supporters, he managed to counter the coup, allowing al-ʿAziz to enter Cairo safely. In addition to that, Qaraqush managed the financial difficulties facing the rule, and he protected Cairo when al-ʿAziz marched out to the eastern Delta to fight al-Afdal and al-ʿAdil in Belbays.[205]

Why did Qaraqush ally himself with one of Saladin's sons against the others? As a eunuch he should have been loyal to the will of Saladin as he had no family; but we could say that he felt that he would not enjoy the position he had held in Egypt if al-Afdal and al-ʿAdil were ruling the country.

Qaraqush also managed the *diwan* of finance during the severe famine that affected Egypt in 1195, after Khutlugh had failed in that post.[206]

The famine affected the emirs and commanders of the army, who did not receive their stipends for a year; however, no civil disorder or defection to al-Afdal's camp was allowed by Qaraqush. One of the most striking of Qaraqush's civil posts was his appointment by al-'Aziz to replace him at the *mazalim* in front of the palace in Cairo.[207] This was a rare case of a eunuch being assigned some jurisprudence power (the only other occasion was concerned with another eunuch, Kafur the Ikhshidid, also in Egypt, as well as the *qahramana* Thumal in ninth-century Baghdad, as previously mentioned).

The final post assigned to Qaraqush was also unique. Before al-'Aziz died in November 1198, he had appointed Qaraqush as *mudabbir* (marshal of the kingdom) and *atabeg* for his ten-year-old son, al-Mansur. This was the first time under the Ayyubids that a eunuch, and non-Turk, was given the atabegate. Qaraqush was deposed two months later by al-Afdal and the leaders of the army.[208] It was due to the old age of Qaraqush by that time that the commanders managed to depose him in coordination with al-Afdal. Qaraqush died two years later, but the important matter here is that, even as a eunuch, he was not considered lesser than a normal person and became *atabeg* for a boy king, a case that was taken as a model and repeated in Ayyubid Aleppo, as will be discussed shortly.

Despite the respect the eunuch Qaraqush enjoyed from his kings, we see sarcasm about his person and collegial jealousy coming from the chief of the army *diwan*, Ibn Mamati, who served under Saladin and al-'Aziz. Ibn Mamati wrote a book condemning and ridiculing Qaraqush. He called it *Al-Fashush fi Hukm Qaraqush* (*The Foolishness of Qaraqush's Rule*). The purpose of writing that book, says Ibn Mamati, was that after seeing the injustice of Qaraqush, he wrote his book for Saladin, hoping to spare the Muslims from Qaraqush.[209] This was the first piece of literature openly criticising a eunuch emir who was an elite government official. However, the criticism was not made public, but sent to Saladin. One of the stories ridiculing Qaraqush in the book was as follows:

> It is said that he raced a man with his horse, but the other person won. Qaraqush swore he would not feed the horse for three days. The winner said

to Qaraqush: 'My lord, the horse will perish.' Qaraqush replied: 'Swear to me that if I let you feed the horse, you will not tell the horse that I knew.'[210]

Naturally, Ibn Mamati was in a position to deliver this book to his sultan, but Saladin did not pay attention to such false accusations. Nevertheless, maybe the strict measures Qaraqush used in his administration opened the way for some criticism. It is mentioned that he spared no one, weak or poor, to work by force in building the new wall around Cairo. Also, during al-'Aziz's rule, Qaraqush would punish the emirs who refused to campaign with the sultan, putting them in shackles and forcing them to labour in the construction of the wall.[211]

Even now in Egypt there is a saying used by the public: '*hukm* Qaraqush' (the rule of Qaraqush), as a mark of hard tenacious opinion.

The eunuch–atabeg *in Ayyubid Aleppo*

In 1216, during his final illness, al-Zahir, the son of Saladin and king of Aleppo, appointed a Rumi eunuch, Shihab al-Din Tughril, as governor of Aleppo's citadel, which was the seat of government and where the royal palace was located. Tughril was also the head of the treasury, chief of the harem and *atabeg* to al-Zahir's two sons: his first successor al-'Aziz, by Dayfa Khatun, and his other son, al-Salih, by a concubine.[212]

This was clearly a high concentration of power in the hands of one eunuch, running the state's political, financial and security affairs. Tughril managed to resist the will of al-Zahir's brothers, some military commanders and the Seljuqid sultan of Rum, Kaykaus I (d. 1219), who refused the atabegate of a eunuch and wanted to replace him with al-Afdal, son of Saladin, as *atabeg* and regent of Aleppo. Tughril had achieved his position through skilful manoeuvring with two emirs in the army and the powerful *qadi* Ibn Shaddad, who together had formed a council that agreed to give the oath to al-'Aziz and Tughril together. Furthermore, they managed to depose the influential vizier Ibn Abi Ya'li and to change the new *atabeg al-'askar*, selected by the deceased al-Zahir:[213] 'Tughril became independent and free in running the realm, castles, *iqta'*s, and distributing money among commanders.'[214]

When the Seljuqs of Rum, together with al-Afdal, decided to invade Aleppo, Tughril asked for military help from al-Ashraf, al-Zahir's cousin and lord of the Jazira. Together they inflicted a defeat at Minbaj on the Seljuqid forces in 1218. The pact was keen to use the victory by advancing into Anatolia, but the death of the Ayyubid sultan al-ʿAdil and the arrival of the Fifth Crusade in Egypt halted this project.[215] Tughril had tried his entire career to extricate himself from the 'long cold war', as Stephen Humphreys calls it, between the sons of al-ʿAdil; yet we see him send a symbolic force to aid al-Kamil against the Fifth Crusade in Egypt in 1221.[216] In addition, al-Ashraf asked for his help in 1227 against his two brothers, al-Kamil of Egypt and al-Muʿazzam of Damascus. However, Tughril refused, preferring not to anger al-Kamil in Egypt, to whom he declared the *khutba* in Aleppo with al-ʿAziz.[217] Tughril also had a particular modus operandi with the Crusaders of Antioch: he never launched an attack against them aiming to seize their territories. However, Tughril succeeded in defending Aleppo's dominions twice against minor Crusader attacks in 1225 and he secured peace with Bohemond IV of Antioch. Again in 1231, when the Crusaders attacked the Aleppan dominion of Jabla, Tughril sent a force to attack the Crusader castles of al-Marqab and the town of Banyas. The result was another peace agreement.[218]

For fifteen years the eunuch–*atabeg* Tughril resided in Aleppo citadel and never left it. He felt that he was safer inside his power base, and was always in fear of coups being launched against him, especially by al-Afdal. However, eyewitness chroniclers reported how strange it was that Tughril was able to run all his affairs from his isolated position. In 1231, when al-ʿAziz turned eighteen, Tughril surrendered all powers to him, and left the citadel for his own home (outside the citadel) where he died peacefully.[219] Tughril was a rare case in the history of eunuchs and *atabeg*s, as he did not conspire against his very young king, although he could have seized the chance, like many other *atabeg*s, as we have seen. Not only that, but Tughril left his post voluntarily, showing a great deal of loyalty to his master.

Before moving to the final section on Ayyubid eunuchs under al-Salih Najm al-Din Ayyub, I should mention that in 1244 Ayyubid Hama experienced similar political conditions to those under Dayfa and the eunuchs around her. In that year, King al-Muzaffar II, the Ayyubid king of Hama, died. His chief commander in the realm for more than two decades had been the eunuch Shujaʿ al-Mansuri. Al-Muzaffar had installed the emir eunuch

Sayf al-Din Tughril, who was chief of his palace, as *atabeg* for his ten-year-old successor, al-Mansur.[220] To aid the *atabeg*, the eunuch al-Mansuri was appointed, referred to by Ibn Wasil as *mushir*, the chief adviser to the sultan. They ruled together with a council including the vizier, but 'they all refer to Princess Ghaziya Khatun, mother of the new king and daughter of al-Kamil, and wait for her orders'.[221] That resembles the experience of Dayfa in Aleppo, who had died two years earlier. Ghaziya managed to secure the approval of this arrangement from her brother and sultan of Egypt, al-Salih. Information about Ayyubid Hama at that time is scarce but we know that al-Mansuri was deputy to al-Mansur until the Mongols sacked Hama in 1260.[222]

The Influence of Eunuchs on Politics at the End of the Ayyubid Rule

The Case of al-Salih Ayyub

When Sultan al-Kamil died in 1238 he was succeeded in Egypt by his younger son al-'Adil II; however, a civil war started between al-'Adil II and his elder brother, al-Salih Ayyub, lord of the Jazira, over the sultanate of Egypt. In September 1239 al-Salih marched with his army to invade Damascus, which was under al-'Adil's rule. On his way, he learned that al-'Adil had arrived with a large army in Damascus, so al-Salih camped near Damascus, but many of his commanders deserted him.[223] Among them was the eunuch commander Shihab al-Din Fakhir, who looted many of al-Salih's arms and encouraged many *mamluk*s to desert him. This weakened al-Salih's military position tremendously; three weeks later, he was arrested and taken to al-Karak in Jordan; he was imprisoned there with his concubine Shajar al-Durr.[224]

Two other eunuchs reversed the fate of al-Salih. In April 1240 al-Salih was released and marched to invade Egypt. He failed at Belbays in the Nile Delta because al-'Adil II had a much larger force from Egypt, Damascus and Hims. As a result, al-Salih retreated to al-Karak.[225] While al-'Adil was still in his camp in the Delta, following the confrontation with his brother, two leading eunuch emirs of his father from the Egyptian army, the *tawashi*s Jawhar al-Nubi and Shams al-Khawwas, together with some other eunuchs, arrested al-'Adil, in collaboration with al-Salih, and also because they were dissatisfied with his conduct. As a result, al-Salih managed to enter Egypt and headed to Cairo citadel at once, without obstruction, and assumed the sultanate.[226] We can see here the vital role of these two eunuchs, tipping the balance of power to al-Salih despite the numerous armies of al-ʿAdil.

In addition to that, these eunuchs and other commanders of Turkish ethnicity resisted an attempt by the Kurdish troops to free and restore al-ʿAdil to power, and heavily defeated al-ʿAdil's supporters.[227]

It is my view that such a pragmatic act by these eunuchs, who had no biological future or families, could be looked at as an attempt to create better personal political positions for themselves. Also, they had their political opinion in matters in which they were involved, like others before them.

Al-Salih Ayyub used different eunuchs in key posts in his kingdom. For example, in 1245 when he was fighting his uncle, al-Salih Ismaʿil, for the domination of Damascus, and seizing Damascus for the second time, al-Salih Ayyub entrusted the eunuch emir Shihab al-Din Rashid al-Kabir as governor of the citadel there. Al-Salih appointed a normal emir as governor of the city, a post considered to be less important.[228] That eunuch managed to save Damascus for al-Salih Ayyub in the same year, at a time when plundering Khwarazmian troops in the area had sacked southern Syria down to Jerusalem, due to their dissatisfaction with al-Salih. They allied with al-Salih Ismaʿil, the foe of Ayyub, and besieged Damascus. Despite the small numbers of forces in Damascus, the lack of a significant commander of the forces and a famine that resulted from the siege, the eunuch Rashid al-Kabir and the governor Husam al-Din would meet daily to administer the crisis until the invading massive forces withdrew.[229] Due to such loyalty and bravery, Rashid al-Kabir was rewarded by having his office as governor of Damascus citadel renewed, while the governor of the city was changed.[230]

Rashid al-Kabir remained as governor of Damascus citadel until 1250, which is a considerably long time in an important post. He surrendered to al-Nasir II of Aleppo after the death of al-Salih Ayyub.

Among other posts occupied by eunuchs in the late Ayyubid period was that of the *hajib*. Al-Salih depended on them to the extent that chroniclers wrote that he declined to receive or meet any of his elite commanders in person, but rather expected them to follow up on his written orders that the commanders had received on signed papers from these eunuchs.[231] This reflects the trust these eunuchs enjoyed from al-Salih Ayyub in following and carrying out his instructions.

Al-Salih Ayyub had entrusted his close and loyal eunuch, Emir Jamal al-Din Muhsin, the task of killing his imprisoned brother al-'Adil II in February 1249 without leaving a trace, making it look as if it was a suicide. Muhsin carried out his sultan's order skilfully.[232] No other emir could have been entrusted with such a job, as another emir might free the former sultan, or use him in a plot to change the rule, especially as al-Salih was suffering from a terminal illness at that time. Another highly important military post was given to the eunuch commander Badr al-Sawabi in September 1249 during the occupation of Damietta under the Seventh Crusade; he was appointed as al-Salih's deputy in al-Karak citadel, a very strategic position in southern Syria. Al-Karak had been surrendered to al-Salih by Hasan b. al-Nasir Da'ud, while al-Nasir was away in Aleppo. Al-Sawabi must have been loyal and capable to prevent al-Karak from falling back into the hands of Da'ud, especially due to the significance of controlling al-Karak, it being the last place under al-Salih's authority in southern Syria.[233] In addition, al-Karak had always been used as a platform to launch a swift attack on Damascus, among other places, in southern Syria.

As mentioned under the section on Shajar al-Durr, the eunuch Muhsin played a pivotal role when al-Salih Ayyub died, collaborating in all matters with Shajar al-Durr during the Seventh Crusade.

Another eunuch who has had his name commemorated in the public mind until the present day was Subayh. When King Louis IX of France was captured in Egypt in April 1250, he was jailed in Mansura in a house of Ibn Luqman under the guardianship of the eunuch Subayh.[234] The poet Ibn Matruh wrote a poem commemorating the imprisonment and humiliation of the French king, and praising Subayh:

> Say to them, the French, if they intended to return
> For revenge or any other ugly deed
> The house of Ibn Luqman is still standing
> The shackle is waiting, as well as *tawashi* Subayh.[235]

This clearly shows the trust given to eunuchs under the Ayyubids in delicate situations. We can only imagine what could have happened if Subayh had collaborated with the French and released the king. Due to their success in carrying out their duties, eunuchs were proudly praised, including in Tunisia, where King Louis IX launched his final Crusade in 1270 and where he died. The Tunisian poet Ahmad b. Isma'il wrote:

> Oh French people, Tunisia is the sister of Egypt
> So be prepared for the bad fortune awaiting you
> In Egypt the house of Ibn Luqman was like a grave
> Here (Tunisia) your eunuchs are Munkar and Nakir.[236]

After the coming to power of Shajar al-Durr, as we have seen, her late husband's eunuchs played a significant role in resisting slaves taking control. We see the eunuch Badr al-Sawabi, who was appointed, as mentioned, by al-Salih as deputy of al-Karak, release Prince al-Mughith 'Umar, nephew of al-Salih, who had been imprisoned under his authority in al-Shawbak Castle. Al-Sawabi declared al-Mughith as the new Ayyubid king, taking the oath of allegiance from the locals there to the boy king. Al-Sawabi installed himself as his *atabeg* in June 1250.[237] The significance of that step is that it created an independent Ayyubid principality in Transjordan and southern Syria, challenging the new Mamluk authority and rule in Egypt. Al-Karak, with its mighty fortifications and strategic location, had always been a threat to commercial and military movements between Egypt and Syria. Three months later al-Sawabi allied with King al-Nasir II in Aleppo and became his vassal in Damascus and southern Syria.[238] In 1258 the chronicler al-Yunini mentioned that al-Sawabi and his boy king 'Umar tried to invade Egypt in May of that year, but were defeated and they retreated to Transjordan. Other eunuch commanders formed a pact with al-Sawabi and al-Nasir of Aleppo. The eunuch Rashid al-Kabir surrendered the strategic Damascus citadel to al-Nasir in 1250; together with the eunuch commander Rashid al-Saghir, he preceded an Aleppan army that invaded Egypt. They managed for a short time to declare the *khutba* in the eastern Delta to boy king 'Umar of al-Karak, in full collaboration with al-Sawabi.[239]

It was only in 1261 when the Mamluk sultan Baybars I managed to take over al-Shawbak and al-Karak from the deputies of King 'Umar.[240] That meant that al-Sawabi's actions created a political entity threatening and challenging the legitimacy of Mamluk Egypt for eleven years. In addition, it was the only Ayyubid entity to survive after the Mongols sacked Aleppo and Damascus in 1260.

We can see that al-Salih Ayyub's eunuchs in Syria posed an immense threat to the new Mamluks in Egypt. Ironically, being slaves themselves, they declined to support the Mamluk state, first by creating an Ayyubid principality, and second by aiding the Ayyubids in Aleppo. Were they supporting what they considered an Ayyubid legitimacy, or supporting their own fortunes?

The eunuchs under the Ayyubid dynasty developed differently than the Seljuqs, in that some of them were associated with the *atabeg* post.

Shaun Marmon, who has written on the role of eunuchs under the Mamluks, argues that either Nur al-Din b. Zengi or Saladin had introduced the service of eunuchs to the mosque of the Prophet, which continued until the second half of the twentieth century.[241] We have no concrete evidence on the Nurid side, but the Andalusian traveller Ibn Jubayr, who visited Medina in 1182, wrote that the Prophet's mosque 'had guards and servant eunuchs of Abyssinian and Saqlabi ethnicity'.[242] The Baghdadi traveller Ibn al-Najjar, who visited Medina in 1198, wrote about eunuchs serving the holy mosque in Medina.[243] It is not clear why those badly victimised third-gendered persons were introduced to the holy place. They were considered to be better servants, but they made a counter-argument about the cruelty of such a culture, to say the least. They continued to be used under the Mamluks, and sometimes their numbers reached forty eunuchs, such as in 1342.[244] It has been mentioned before that during the nineteenth and twentieth centuries, under the strict Saudi government, eunuchs were used to guard the women's entrance to the Prophet's mosque.

Eunuchs under the Maluks did not occupy high military posts, but they were involved in lower ranks in the army. However, the chief of the palace for the sultan was always a eunuch, according to Ibn Taghri Bardi.[245] In Rasulid Yemen, we see the influence of the Ayyubids; for example, al-Muzaffar (d. 1295), after almost half a century in power, had eunuchs as chief commanders to his armies.[246]

Notes

1. Ibn al-'Adim, *Zubdat*, Vol. 3, p. 247.
2. Al-Maqrizi, *Itti'az*, Vol. 3, p. 305; D. S. Richards, art.: 'Salah al-Din', *EI²*.
3. Hillenbrand, *The Crusades*, pp. 171–94; Yaacov Lev, art.: 'Saladin'. *The Crusades: An Encyclopedia*, ed. A. Murray, Santa Barbara, 2006, Vol. 4.

4. Kamal al-Din Ibn al-ʿAmid, *Akhbar al-Ayyubiyyin*, Cairo, n.d., p. 32.
5. Claude Cahen, art.: 'Ayyubids', *EI²*.
6. W. F. Spengler and W. G. Sayles, *Turkoman Figural Bronze Coins and Their Iconography, Vol. 1: The Artuqids*, Lodi, 1992, pp. 105–6. I am very grateful to my dear friend and mentor Professor Robert Hillenbrand, who supplied me with this important study. Stephen Album, *Marsden's Numismata Orientalia Illastrata*, New York, 1977, pp. 114–19.
7. Hillenbrand, *Islamic Art*, p. 133; Stephen Album, *Marsden's Numismata Orientalia Illustrata*, New York, 1977, pp. 114–19.
8. This study was presented to the Leeds Medieval Congress in July 1998, and published in *Annals of Japan Association for Middle East Studies*, 2000, Vol. 15, pp. 27–55.
9. Ibn Wasil, *Mufarrij*, Vol. 5, p. 312; Ahmad b. Ibrahim al-Hanbali, *Shifaʾ al-Qulub fi Manaqib Bani Ayyub*, ed. M. al-Sharqawi, Cairo, 1996, p. 283.
10. Al-ʿAmid, *Akhbar*, p. 32; al-Maqrizi, *Al-Suluk*, ed. M. Ziyada, Cairo, 1957, Vol. 1, p. 311.
11. Al-Hanbali, *Shifaʾ*, p. 283.
12. Ibid.
13. Abu al-Fidaʾ, *Al-Mukhtasar*, Vol. 3, p. 171.
14. Ibn al-Athir, *Al-Kamil*, Vol. 12, pp. 313–14.
15. Ibn Wasil, *Mufarrij*, Vol. 3, p. 241.
16. Ibn al-ʿAdim, *Zubdat*, Vol. 3, pp. 155, 169.
17. Ibn al-Athir, *Al-Kamil*, Vol. 12, p. 313.
18. Ibn Wasil, *Mufarrij*, Vol. 3, pp. 240–1.
19. Ibid., Vol. 3, p. 240.
20. Ibid., Vol. 5, p. 30
21. Ibn al-ʿAdim, *Zubdat*, Vol. 3, p. 221; al-Maqrizi, *Al-Suluk*, Vol. 1, p. 294.
22. Ibn Wasil, *Mufarrij*, Vol. 5, pp. 113–16.
23. Ibn al-ʿAdim, *Zubdat*, Vol. 3, p. 221.
24. Qutb al-Din al-Yunini, *Dhayl Mirʾat al-Zaman*, Hyderabad, 1954, Vol. 1, p. 461; Baybars al-Duwadar, *Zubdat al-Fikra*, ed. Z. Ata, Cairo, 1977, p. 71.
25. Ibn Wasil, *Mufarrij*, Vol. 5, p. 119; al-Duwadar, *Zubdat*, p. 71; al-ʿAmid, *Akhbar*, p. 21.
26. Ibn Wasil, *Mufarrij*, Vol. 5, p. 312.
27. Peter Jackson, 'Muslim India: The Delhi Sultanate', in *The New Cambridge History of Islam*, eds D. Morgan and A. Reid, Cambridge, 2011, Vol. 3, pp. 100–27, 102; C. E. Bosworth, *New Islamic Dynasties*, pp. 300–3.

28. Peter Jackson, 'Sultan Radiyya', p. 184.
29. Baldwin's Auction Catalogue, November 90, 2003, London, p. 26, Item no. D 101. Baldwin's is the world-leading expert in numismatics and coin auctioneer.
30. Jackson, 'Muslim India', p. 102.
31. Al-Maqrizi, *Al-Suluk*, Vol. 1, p. 280.
32. Ibn al-'Adim, *Zubdat*, Vol. 3, pp. 235–47; Ibn Wasil, *Mufarrij*, Vol. 5, p. 268; Ibn Bibi, *Ta'rikh Salajiqat al-Rum*, trans. M. Mansur, Cairo, 1994, p. 150; Ibn Shaddad, *Al-'Alaq*, Vol. 2, p. 95.
33. Ibn Wasil, *Mufarrij*, Vol. 5, p. 121.
34. Ibn al-'Adim, *Zubdat*, Vol. 3, pp. 233–4; Ibn Wasil, *Mufarrij*, Vol. 5, p. 253.
35. Al-Maqrizi, *Al-Suluk*, Vol. 1, p. 272; Ibn al-'Adim, *Zubdat*, Vol. 3, p. 239; Anne-Marie Eddé, *La Principaute Ayyoubide d'Alep (579/1183–658/1260)*, Stuttgart, 1999, pp. 481–2.
36. Ibn Wasil, *Mufarrij*, Vol. 5, pp. 190–1. Ibn Bibi, the Seljuqid contemporary historian, surprisingly ignored this story, and the political marriage between his sultan and the daughter of al-'Aziz of Aleppo.
37. Ibn Taghri Bardi, *Al-Nujum*, Vol. 6, p. 321; R. Stephen Humphrey, *From Saladin to the Mongols: The Ayyubids of Damascus, 1193–1260*, Albany, 1977, p. 272.
38. Claude Cahen, *Pre-Ottoman Turkey: A General Survey of the Material and Spiritual Culture and History, c. 1071–1330*, trans. J. Williams, London, 1968, p. 134. Cahen mentions that Dayfa was the mother of al-Nasir II, but in fact she was his grandmother.
39. Ibn Wasil, *Mufarrij*, Vol. 5, p. 120; Ibn al-'Adim, *Zubdat*, Vol. 3, p. 260; Humphreys, *From Saladin to the Mongols*, p. 236.
40. Al-Maqrizi, *Al-Suluk*, Vol. 1, p. 294; Ibn al-'Adim, *Zubdat*, Vol. 3, p. 226; Hans L. Gottschalk, *Al-Malik al-Kamil von Agypten*, Wiesbaden, 1958, p. 223.
41. Abu al-Fida', *Al-Mukhtasar*, Vol. 3, pp. 158–9; Ibn al-'Adim, *Zubdat*, Vol. 3, p. 227; Sibt Ibn al-Jawzi, *Mir'at*, Vol. 8, p. 700; Humphreys, *From Saladin to the Mongols*, p. 231.
42. Ibn Wasil, *Mufarrij*, Vol. 5, p. 124; al-Maqrizi, *Al-Suluk*, Vol. 1, p. 294; H. A. R. Gibb, 'The Ayyubids', in *A History of The Crusades*, ed. K. Setton, London, 1962, Vol. 2, pp. 693–714, 702.
43. Ibn al-'Adim, *Zubdat*, Vol. 3, p. 228; Eddé, *La Principaute*, p. 490.
44. Ibn al-'Adim, *Zubdat*, Vol. 3, p. 227; Cahen, *Pre-Ottoman Turkey*, p. 132; Taef el-Azhari, art.: 'Dayfa', *EI³*, online, Leiden, 2017.

45. Al-Maqrizi, *Al-Suluk*, Vol. 1, p. 297.
46. Ibn Wasil, *Mufarrij*, Vol. 5, p. 148; Gottschalk, *Al-Malik al-Ibn al-Athir*, pp. 228–9.
47. Ibn al-'Adim, *Zubdat*, Vol. 3, p. 233–5; Ibn Wasil, *Mufarrij*, Vol. 5, pp. 148–9.
48. Ibn Wasil, *Mufarrij*, Vol. 5, p. 153.
49. Ibn al-'Adim, *Zubdat*, Vol. 3, p. 235.
50. Ibn Wasil, *Mufarrij*, Vol. 5, p. 153.
51. Ibid., pp. 151–2; Humphreys, *From Saladin to the Mongols*, p. 237; Gottschalk, *Al-Malik al-Ibn al-Athir*, pp. 230–1.
52. Ibn Taghri Bardi, *Al-Manhal al-Wafi*, ed. M. Amin, Cairo, 1986, Vol. 4, p. 182; al-Duwadar, *Zubdat*, p. 66; al-Yunini, *Dhayl*, p. 429.
53. Ibn al-'Adim, *Zubdat*, Vol. 3, p. 235; Ibn Wasil, *Mufarrij*, Vol. 5, p. 186.
54. Ibn al-'Adim, *Zubdat*, Vol. 3, pp. 229–30; Ibn Wasil, *Mufarrij*, Vol. 5, p. 181.
55. The strained geopolitical Seljuqid–Ayyubid Egyptian relations extended to the Ottoman–Mamluk conflict in Egypt and Syria until the Ottomans defeated the Mamluks in 1517. Ironically, in 2018 the Turkish state is occupying by force large areas of northern Syria, west of Aleppo and on the Euphrates, to prevent Kurdish Syrian troops from expanding during the Syrian crisis.
56. Ibn Wasil, *Mufarrij*, Vol. 5, p. 180.
57. Al-Maqrizi, *Al-Suluk*, Vol. 1, p. 298.
58. Ibn al-'Adim, *Zubdat*, Vol. 3, p. 236.
59. Ibid., p. 240.
60. Ibn Wasil, *Mufarrij*, Vol. 5, p. 181; Ibn al-'Adim, *Zubdat*, Vol. 3, pp. 237–8.
61. Abu al-Fida', *Al-Mukhtasar*, Vol. 3, p. 163; Ibn al-'Adim, *Zubdat*, Vol. 3, pp. 237–8.
62. Ibn Wasil, *Mufarrij*, Vol. 5, pp. 179–82.
63. Ibid., p. 182; Ibn al-'Adim, *Zubdat*, Vol. 3, p. 244.
64. Al-Maqrizi, *Al-Suluk*, Vol. 1, p. 272; Ibn al-'Adim, *Zubdat*, Vol. 3, p. 239.
65. Ibn al-'Adim, *Zubdat*, Vol. 3, p. 244; Humphreys, *From Saladin to the Mongols*, p. 245; Gibb, 'Ayyubids', p. 705.
66. Ibn al-'Adim, *Zubdat*, Vol. 3, p. 245.
67. Ibn Wasil, *Mufarrij*, Vol. 5, p. 190.
68. Ibid., pp. 135–6, 282.
69. Ibn al-'Adim, *Zubdat*, Vol. 3, p. 247.
70. Ibn Wasil, *Mufarrij*, Vol. 5, p. 179.
71. Al-Maqrizi, *Al-Suluk*, Vol. 1, p. 271.
72. Ibn Wasil, *Mufarrij*, Vol. 5, pp. 185–6.

73. Ibn al-'Adim, *Zubdat*, Vol. 3, p. 247.
74. Sibt Ibn al-Jawzi, *Mir'at*, Vol. 8, p. 728.
75. Gibb, 'Ayyubids', pp. 707–8.
76. Ibn al-'Adim, *Zubdat*, Vol. 3, p. 248.
77. Cahen, *Pre-Ottoman Turkey*, p. 134.
78. Humphreys, *From Saladin to the Mongols*, p. 266.
79. Abu al-Fida', *Al-Mukhtasar*, Vol. 3, p. 159; Mary Nickerson Hardwicke, 'The Crusader States, 1192–1243', in *A History of the Crusades, Vol. 2*, ed. R. Lee Wolff, Philadelphia, 1962, pp. 522–56, 550; Claude Cahen, *La Syrie du Nord a l'Epoque des Croisades et la Principaute Franque d'Antioche*, Paris, 1940, p. 650.
80. Ibn al-'Adim, *Zubdat*, Vol. 3, pp. 230–2; Steven Runciman, *A History of The Crusades*, Cambridge, 1981, Vol. 3, p. 208.
81. Cahen, *La Syrie*, p. 645.
82. Ibn al-Athir, *Al-Kamil*, Vol. 10, p. 502.
83. Ibn al-'Adim, *Zubdat*, Vol. 2, p. 305; Steven Runciman, *The Crusades*, Cambridge, 1952, Vol. 2, pp. 183–4.
84. Al-Maqrizi, *Al-Suluk*, Vol. 1, p. 272; Ibn al-'Adim, *Zubdat*, Vol. 3, pp. 237–9.
85. Ibn Bibi, *Ta'rikh*, pp. 271–4; Ibn al-'Adim, *Zubdat*, Vol. 3, p. 249.
86. Ibn Wasil, *Mufarrij*, Vol. 5, pp. 320–1; Sawsan Nasr, 'Al-Khuwarazmiyya', *Journal of the Egyptian Historical Society*, Vols 30–1, 1983–4, pp. 61–98, 70–1.
87. Ibn Taghri Bardi, *Al-Nujum*, Vol. 6, p. 323; Ibn Wasil, *Mufarrij*, Vol. 5, p. 187.
88. Sibt Ibn al-Jawzi, *Mir'at*, Vol. 8, p. 735; Abu al-Fida', *Al-Mukhtasar*, Vol. 3, p. 167; Cahen, *La Syrie*, p. 648.
89. Ibn al-'Adim, *Zubdat*, Vol. 3, pp. 250–1; Ibn Wasil, *Mufarrij*, Vol. 5, pp. 282–3.
90. Sibt Ibn al-Jawzi, *Mir'at*, Vol. 8, p. 733.
91. Humphreys, *From Saladin to the Mongols*, p. 262.
92. Mahmud Takriti, *Al-Ayyubiyyun fi Shamal al-Sham wa al-Jazira*, Beirut, 1985, p. 223.
93. Ibn al-'Adim, *Zubdat*, Vol. 3, p. 286; Ibn Wasil, *Mufarrij*, Vol. 5, pp. 284–5.
94. Sibt Ibn al-Jawzi, *Mir'at*, Vol. 8, p. 735. Abu al-Fida', *Al-Mukhtasar*, Vol. 3, p. 168. Humphreys mentions that al-Mansur was on his way to fight the Crusader Lord Richard of Cornwall, but altered his plan as he realised that saving Aleppo was a priority, *From Saladin to the Mongols*, p. 269.
95. Ibn Bibi, *Ta'rikh*, p. 261.

96. Abu al-Fida', *Al-Mukhtasar*, Vol. 3, p. 168; Ibn al-'Adim, *Zubdat*, Vol. 3, pp. 253–4.
97. Ibn al-'Adim, *Zubdat*, Vol. 3, p. 254.
98. Ibn Wasil, *Mufarrij*, Vol. 3, pp. 289–90.
99. Ibn al-'Adim, *Zubdat*, Vol. 3, pp. 254–7.
100. Sibt Ibn al-Jawzi, *Mir'at*, Vol. 8, p. 734; Ibn Bibi, *Ta'rikh*, pp. 261–2; Ibn Aybak, *Kanz*, ed. S. Ashur, Cairo, 1972, p. 344
101. Ibn al-'Adim, *Zubdat*, Vol. 3, pp. 255–8; al-Yunini, *Dhayl*, p. 429; al-Duwadar, *Zubdat*, p. 66.
102. Ibn Bibi, *Ta'rikh*, pp. 268–9; Ibn Wasil, *Mufarrij*, Vol. 5, p. 305.
103. Abu al-Fida', *Al-Mukhtasar*, Vol. 3, p. 171; al-'Amid, *Akhbar*, p. 32; Ibn al-'Adim, *Zubdat*, Vol. 3, p. 266.
104. Ibn al-Shihna, *Al-Durr al-Muntakhab*, Damascus, 1988, p. 113; Robert Hillenbrand, *Islamic Art*, pp. 116–17.
105. Ibn Shaddad, *Al-'Alaq*, Vol. 1, pp. 109, 120–2; Ibn al-Shihna, *Al-Durr*, p. 122.
106. Ibn Shaddad, *Al-'Alaq*, Vol. 1, p. 94.
107. El-Azhari, *The Saljuqs*, pp. 322–9.
108. Ibn 'Asakir, *Tarajim*, p. 393.
109. Ibn 'Abd Rabbuh, *Bahgat al-Majalis*, Beirut, 2001, Vol. 3, pp. 173, 189; al-Maqarri, *Nafh al-Tib*, Vol. 6, pp. 245–60; James M. Nichols, 'Arabic Women Poets in al-Andalus', *Maghreb Review*, Vol. 4, December 1981, pp. 85–8.
110. Ibn Wasil, *Mufarrij*, Vol. 5, p. 313; Ibn al-'Adim, *Zubdat*, Vol. 3, p. 237.
111. Sibt Ibn al-Jawzi, *Mir'at*, Vol. 8, p. 756; al-Hanbali, *Shifa'*, p. 375.
112. Ibn Iyas, *Bada'i' al-Zuhur fi Waqa'i' al-Duhur*, Cairo, 1982, Vol. 1, p. 287.
113. Ibn Wasil, *Mufarrij al-Kurub fi Ta'rikh bani Ayyub*, ed. U. Tadmuri, Beirut, 2004, Vol. 6, p. 132.
114. Linda Goldsmith, art.: 'Crusade of Louis IX to the East', *The Crusades: An Encyclopaedia*, ed. A. Murray, Santa Barbara, 2006, Vol. 1.
115. Remke Kruk, *The Warrior Women of Islam: Female Empowerment in Arabic Popular Literature*, London, 2014, pp. 164, 167.
116. Al-Maqrizi, *Al-Suluk*, Vol. 1, pp. 437–41.
117. Ibn Wasil, *Mufarrij*, Vol. 6, pp. 80–1.
118. Ibn Taghri Bardi, *Al-Nujum*, Vol. 6, pp. 372–3; Götz Schregle, *Die Sultanin von Ägypten*, Wiesbaden, 1961, pp. 4–5.
119. Al-Maqrizi, *Al-Suluk*, Vol. 1, pp. 397–8.
120. Ibn Wasil, *Mufarrij*, Vol. 6, pp. 101–2.

121. Ibid., p. 102.
122. Ibid., p. 103.
123. Taef el-Azhari, art.: 'Turan Shah', *The Crusades: An Encyclopedia*, ed. Alan Murray, Santa Barbara, 2006, Vol. 4.
124. Ibn Taghri Bardi, *Al-Nujum*, Vol. 6, p. 364.
125. Ibn Wasil, *Mufarrij*, Vol. 6, p. 107; Runciman, *Crusades*, Vol. 3, p. 265.
126. Jean de Joinville and Geoffrey of Villehardouin, *Chronicles of The Crusades*, trans. B. Shaw, New York, 1985, pp. 214–17.
127. Ibid., pp. 222–7; Al-Maqrizi, *Al-Suluk*, Vol. 1, pp. 447–8; Joseph Strayer, 'The Crusades of Louis IX', in *A History of The Crusades*, ed. K. Setton, London, 1962, Vol. 2, pp. 487–521, 511.
128. Strayer, 'The Crusades', p. 512; Runciman, *Crusades*, Vol. 3, pp. 267–8.
129. Al-Maqrizi, *Al-Suluk*, Vol. 1, pp. 455–6; Jonathan Riley-Smith, *The Crusades*, New Haven, 1986, p. 201.
130. Ibn Taghri Bardi, *Al-Nujum*, Vol. 6, pp. 367–8; Ibn Wasil, *Mufarrij*, Vol. 5, pp. 128–9; Ibn Aybak, *Kanz*, Vol. 7, p. 382; Strayer, 'The Crusades', p. 712.
131. Ibn Wasil, *Mufarrij*, Vol. 6, pp. 132–3.
132. Ibid., p. 133.
133. Strayer, 'The Crusades', p. 741; Runciman, *Crusades*, Vol. 3, p. 275.
134. De Joinville, *Chronicles*, p. 220.
135. Al-Maqrizi, *Al-Suluk*, Vol. 1, p. 459; Ibn Taghri Bardi, *Al-Nujum*, Vol. 7, pp. 3–4.
136. Ibn Wasil, *Mufarrij*, Vol. 6, p. 136.
137. Kruk, *Warrior Women*, pp. 164, 167.
138. *Sirat al-Malik al-Zahir Baybars*, Cairo, 1983, pp. 43–6.
139. Ibn Iyas, *Al-Zuhur*, Vol. 1, p. 287.
140. Ibn Wasil, *Mufarrij*, Vol. 6, p. 140; Mernissi, *The Forgotten Queens*, p. 156.
141. Al-Maqrizi, *Al-Suluk*, Vol. 1, p. 460.
142. Ibid., p. 461.
143. Ibn Wasil, *Mufarrij*, Vol. 6, p. 140.
144. Al-Maqrizi, *Al-Khitat*, Vol. 2, p. 347; Ibn Wasil, *Mufarrij*, Vol. 6, p. 143.
145. Al-Maqrizi, *Al-Khitat*, Vol. 2, p. 374.
146. Hasan al-Basha, *Al-Qahira: Tarikhaha Fununuha wa Atharuha*, Cairo, 1970, p. 193.
147. Ibn Taghri Bardi, *Al-Nujum*, Vol. 6, p. 374.
148. Ibn Iyas, *Al-Zuhur*, Vol. 1, pp. 293–4.
149. Al-Maqrizi, *Al-Suluk*, Vol. 1, pp. 480–1.

150. Al-Yunini, *Dhayl*, Vol. 1, pp. 46–7.
151. Ibid., p. 50; al-Maqrizi, *Al-Suluk*, Vol. 1, p. 484; Ibn Wasil, *Mufarrij*, Vol. 6, pp. 194–6.
152. Ibn Wasil, *Mufarrij*, Vol. 6, pp. 196–8; al-Yunini, *Dhayl*, Vol. 1, pp. 47–8.
153. Abu al-Fida', *Al-Mukhtasar*, Vol. 3, p. 192; Ibn Wasil, *Mufarrij*, Vol. 6, p. 201.
154. Al-Yamani, *Bahjat*, pp. 163–4.
155. Al-Khazraji, *Al-'Uqud*, Vol. 1, pp. 244–6.
156. Al-Maqrizi, *Al-Suluk*, Vol. 2, p. 90.
157. Al-Maqrizi, *Al-Khitat*, Vol. 2, p. 399.
158. Ibn Iyas, *Al-Zuhur*, Vol. 5, p. 87.
159. Mahmud al-Sa'dani, *Alhan al-Sama'*, Cairo, 1959, pp. 35–9.
160. Ibn Wasil, *Mufarrij*, Vol. 3, p. 108.
161. Ibn al-'Adim, *Zubdat*, Vol. 3, pp. 170–5; David Ayalon, art.: 'Atabak al-Ibn 'Asakir', *EI*²; David Ayalon, 'Studies on the Structure of the Mamluk Army', *Bulletin of the School of Oriental and African Studies*, Vol. 16, 1954, pp. 57–90, 58.
162. Ibn al-Athir, *Al-Kamil*, Vol. 11, p. 501.
163. Ibn Wasil, *Mufarrij*, Vol. 3, pp. 87–8.
164. Ibn Taghri Bardi, *Al-Nujum*, Vol. 6, p. 150.
165. Ibn al-Athir, *Al-Kamil*, Vol. 12, p. 155.
166. Ibn Wasil, *Mufarrij*, Vol. 3, p. 111; Ibn al-Athir, *Al-Kamil*, Vol. 12, p. 155.
167. Ibn Wasil, *Mufarrij*, Vol. 3, p. 140.
168. Ibn al-'Adim, *Zubdat*, Vol. 3, p. 170; Ibn Bibi, *Ta'rikh*, p. 145.
169. Ibn Wasil, *Mufarrij*, Vol. 3, pp. 249–51.
170. Ibid.
171. Ibn Taghri Bardi, *Al-Nujum*, Vol. 7, p. 5.
172. Ibid., p. 286.
173. Ibn Taghri Bardi, *Al-Nujum*, Vol. 14, pp. 1–3.
174. Ibn Taghri Bardi, *Al-Nujum*, Vol. 15, pp. 223–56, Vol. 16, p. 57.
175. Ibn Taghri Bardi, *Al-Nujum*, Vol. 8, pp. 41–50, Vol. 11, pp. 46–9.
176. Ibn Taghri Bardi, *Al-Nujum*, Vol. 11, p. 359, Vol. 12, p. 48.
177. Ibn Taghri Bardi, *Al-Nujum*, Vol. 15, pp. 256–61.
178. Ibn Taghri Bardi, *Al-Nujum*, Vol. 12, p. 180; Ayalon. 'Atabak al-Ibn 'Asakir'.
179. P. M. Holt, art.: 'Mamluks', *EI*².
180. Al-Yamani, *Bahjat*, p. 155; 'Ali, *Ghayat*, Vol. 1, p. 356.

181. Badr al-Din al-Hamadani, *Al-Simt al-Ghali al-Thaman fi Akhbar al-Muluk min al-Ghuzz bi al-Yaman*, ed. G. Rex Smith, London, 1974, Vol. 1, pp. 120–9; al-Yamani, *Bahjat*, pp. 155–6.
182. Ibn al-Athir, *Al-Kamil*, Vol. 12, pp. 170–98; Ibn Aybak, *Kanz*, Vol. 7, p. 177.
183. Ibn Wasil, *Mufarrij*, Vol. 3, pp. 145–6.
184. Al-Hamadani, *Al-Simt*, Vol. 1, p. 134.
185. Al-Yamani, *Bahjat*, p. 155.
186. 'Ali, *Ghayat*, Vol. 1, pp. 357–95.
187. Ibn Wasil, *Mufarrij*, Vol. 3, p. 137.
188. Ibid., p. 138; 'Ali, *Ghayat*, Vol. 1, p. 398.
189. Al-Yamani, *Bahjat*, p. 156.
190. Ibn Wasil, *Mufarrij*, Vol. 3, p. 138; Ibn Aybak, *Kanz*, Vol. 7, pp. 177–8.
191. 'Ali, *Ghayat*, Vol. 1, pp. 401–2; Ibn Wasil, *Mufarrij*, Vol. 3, pp. 138–9.
192. Al-Yamani, *Bahjat*, p. 157; 'Ali, *Ghayat*, Vol. 1, pp. 402–3.
193. Al-Yamani, *Bahjat*, p. 157.
194. Ibid., p. 168.
195. Ibid., pp. 158–9; Bosworth, *New Islamic Dynasties*, pp. 108–9.
196. Al-Khazraji, *Al-'Uqud*, Vol. 1, pp. 268–91, Vol. 2, pp. 1–46.
197. Nasir al-Din Ibn al-Furat, *Ta'rikh*, ed. H. Shamma, Basra, 1967, Vol. 4, section 1, p. 131; al-Maqrizi, *Al-Khitat*, Vol. 2, pp. 2–3.
198. Ibn Khallikan, *Wafayat*, Vol. 3, p. 517.
199. Al-Maqrizi, *Al-Suluk*, Vol. 1, pp. 199–200.
200. Ibid., pp. 173, 204, 213; Ibn Khallikan, *Wafayat*, Vol. 3, p. 517; M. Sobernheim, art.: 'Karakush', *EI²*.
201. Ibn Taghri Bardi, *Al-Nujum*, Vol. 6, p. 178.
202. William of Tyre, *A History of Deeds*, Vol. 2, pp. 430–1; al-Maqrizi, *Al-Suluk*, Vol. 1, p. 187.
203. Ayalon, *Outsiders*, p. 73.
204. Al-Hanbali, *Shifa'*, p. 290; al-Maqrizi, *Al-Suluk*, Vol. 1, pp. 231–5.
205. Ibn Wasil, *Mufarrij*, Vol. 3, pp. 46–52.
206. Al-Maqrizi, *Al-Suluk*, Vol. 1, pp. 204–45.
207. Ibid., p. 248.
208. Ibid., pp. 258–9.
209. 'Abd Allatif Hamza, *Hukm Qaraqush*, Cairo, 1945, pp. 36–47.
210. Ibid., p. 50.
211. Al-Maqrizi, *Al-Suluk*, Vol. 1, pp. 204–5.
212. Ibn al-'Adim, *Zubdat*, Vol. 3, p. 170; Sibt Ibn al-Jawzi, *Mir'at*, Vol. 8, p. 703.

213. Ibid., pp. 176–8.
214. Ibn Wasil, *Mufarrij*, Vol. 3, pp. 249–51.
215. Ibn al-Athir, *Al-Kamil*, Vol. 12, pp. 348–50.
216. Ibn Wasil, *Mufarrij*, Vol. 3, p. 92; Humphreys, *From Saladin to the Mongols*, p. 170.
217. Ibn al-'Adim, *Zubdat*, Vol. 3, p. 200.
218. Ibn al-Athir, *Al-Kamil*, Vol. 12, p. 66; Ibn al-'Adim, *Zubdat*, Vol. 3, pp. 209–10.
219. Ibn al-Athir, *Al-Kamil*, Vol. 12, pp. 348–9; Ibn al-'Adim, *Zubdat*, Vol. 3, pp. 210–11; Ibn Wasil, *Mufarrij*, Vol. 3, pp. 209–10.
220. Al-Hanbali, *Shifa'*, p. 343; Badr al-Din al-'Ayni, *'Iqd al-Jaman*, ed. M. Amin, Cairo, 1987, Vol. 1, p. 231.
221. Ibn Wasil, *Mufarrij*, Vol. 5, p. 345.
222. Al-'Ayni, *Iqd al-Jaman*, Vol. 1, pp. 306–20.
223. Al-Maqrizi, *Al-Suluk*, Vol. 1, pp. 389–92.
224. Ibid., p. 397.
225. Humphreys, *From Saladin to the Mongols*, pp. 263–4.
226. Ibn Taghri Bardi, *Al-Nujum*, Vol. 6, p. 638; al-Maqrizi, *Al-Suluk*, Vol. 1, pp. 401–5.
227. Ibn Taghri Bardi, *Al-Nujum*, Vol. 6, p. 639.
228. Ibn Wasil, *Mufarrij*, Vol. 5, pp. 349–50; Humphreys, *From Saladin to the Mongols*, p. 284.
229. Ibn Wasil, *Mufarrij*, Vol. 5, pp. 349–50.
230. Ibid., p. 372; Ayalon, *Eunuchs*, p. 344.
231. Sibt Ibn al-Jawzi, *Mir'at*, Vol. 8, p. 771.
232. Ibid., p. 772.
233. Humphreys, *From Saladin to the Mongols*, p. 297.
234. Al-Maqrizi, *Al-Suluk*, Vol. 1, p. 455; Ayalon, *Eunuchs*, p. 185.
235. Ibn Taghri Bardi, *Al-Nujum*, Vol. 6, p. 370.
236. Al-Maqrizi, *Al-Suluk*, Vol. 2, p. 74. Munkar and Nakir are believed to be two angels who meet the deceased in the grave.
237. Al-'Ayni, *Iqd al-Jaman*, Vol. 1, p. 32; Humphreys, *From Saladin to the Mongols*, p. 305.
238. Humphreys, *From Saladin to the Mongols*, p. 305.
239. Al-'Ayni, *Iqd al-Jaman*, Vol. 1, p. 33–6.
240. Al-Yunini, *Dhayl*, Vol. 1, pp. 90, 439.
241. Marmon, *Eunuchs and Sacred Boundaries*, pp. 31–3.

242. Ibn Jubaiyr, *Rihla*, p. 153.
243. Marmon, *Eunuchs and Sacred Boundaries*, p. 33.
244. Al-Maqrizi, *Al-Suluk*, Vol. 3, p. 387.
245. Ibn Taghri Bardi, *Al-Nujum*, Vol. 15, p. 261.
246. Al-Khazraji, *Al-'Uqud*, Vol. 1, p. 97.

Appendix 1
The 'Abbasid Caliphs from 749 to the Coming of the Seljuqs in 1055

al-Saffah	749–54
al-Mansur	754–75
al-Mahdi	775–85
al-Hadi	785–6
al-Rashid	786–809
al-Amin	809–13
al-Ma'mun	813–33
al-Mu'tasim	833–42
al-Wathiq	842–7
al-Mutawakkil	847–61
al-Muntasir	861–2
al-Musta'in	862–6
al-Mu'tazz	866–9
al-Mutadi	869–70
al-Mu'tamid	870–92
al-Mu'tadid	892–902
al-Muktafi	902–8
al-Muqtadir	908 (first reign)
al-Murtada	908 (in Baghdad)
al-Muqtadir	908–29 (second reign)
al-Qahir	929 (first reign in Baghdad)
al-Muqtadir	929–32 (third reign)
al-Qahir	932–4 (second reign)
al-Radi	934–40
al-Muttaqi	940–4
al-Mustakfi	944–6
al-Muti'	946–74
al-Ta'i'	974–91
al-Qadir	991–1031
al-Qa'im	1031–75

Based on C. E. Bosworth, *The New Islamic Dynasties*, Edinburgh, 2004, p. 6.

Appendix 2
The Fatimid Caliphs, North Africa and Egypt

al-Mahdi	909–34
al-Qa'im	934–46
al-Mansur	946–53
al-Mu'izz	953–75
al-'Aziz	975–96
al-Hakim	996–1021
al-Zahir	1021–36
al-Mustansir	1036–94
al-Musta'li	1094–1101
al-Amir	1101–30
al-Hafiz	1130–1 (as a regent but not yet as a caliph)
al-Hafiz	1131–49
al-Zafir	1149–54
al-Fa'iz	1154–60
al-'Adid	1160–71

Based on C. E. Bosworth, *The New Islamic Dynasties*, Edinburgh, 2004, p. 63.

Appendix 3
Dynasties

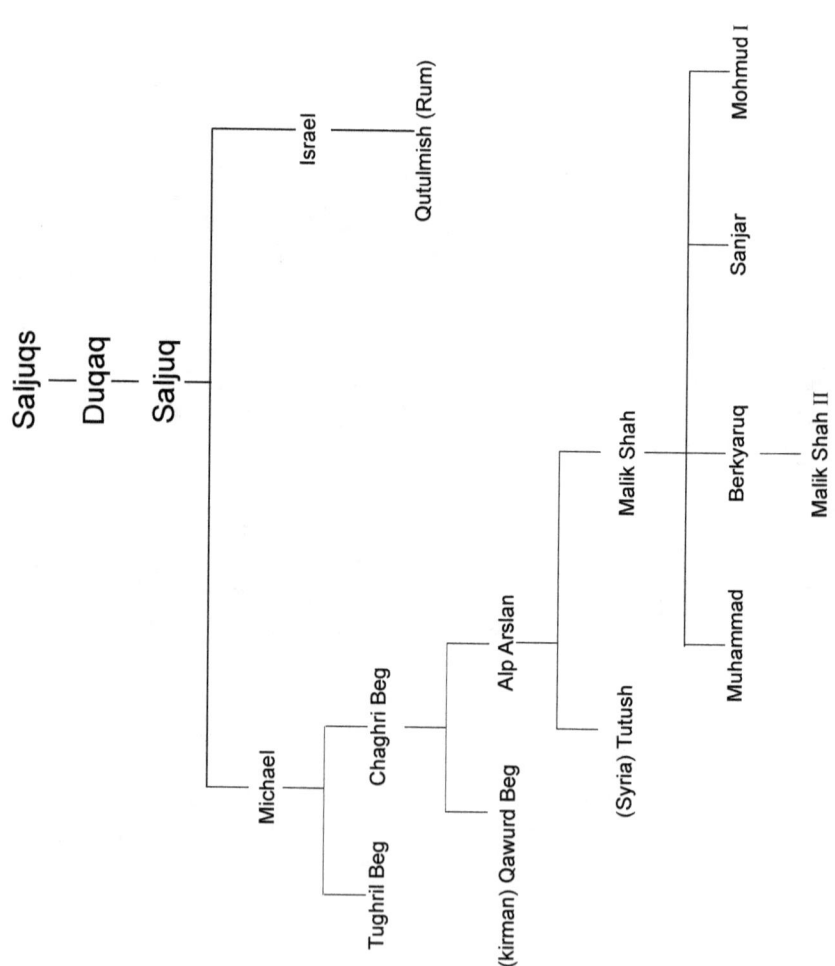

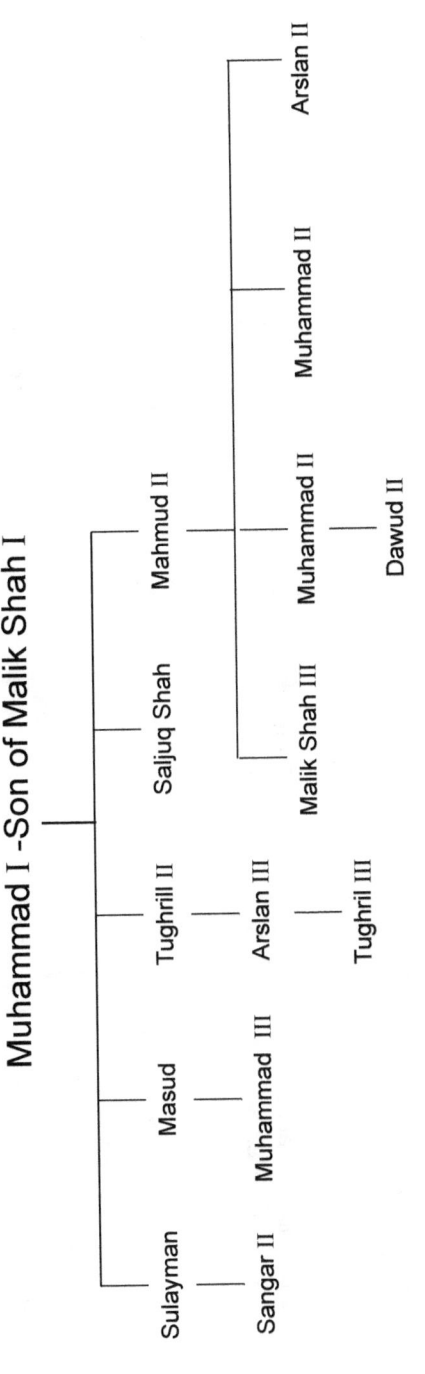

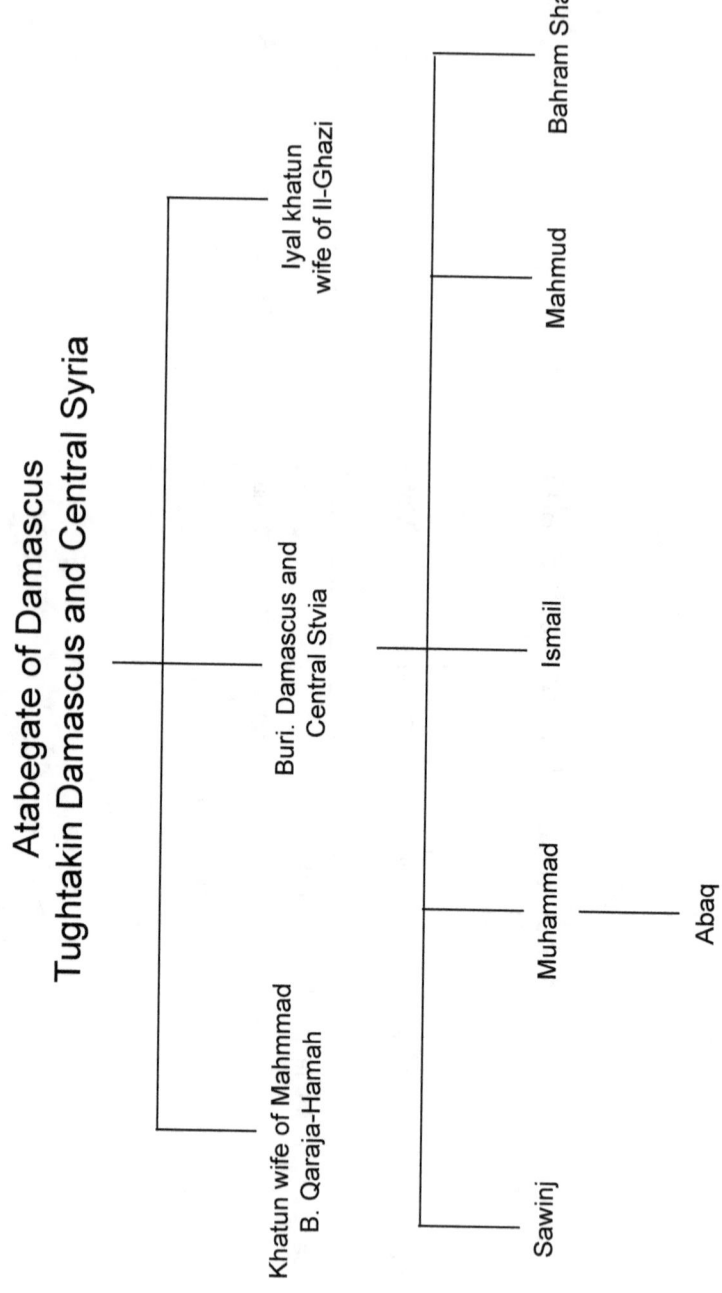

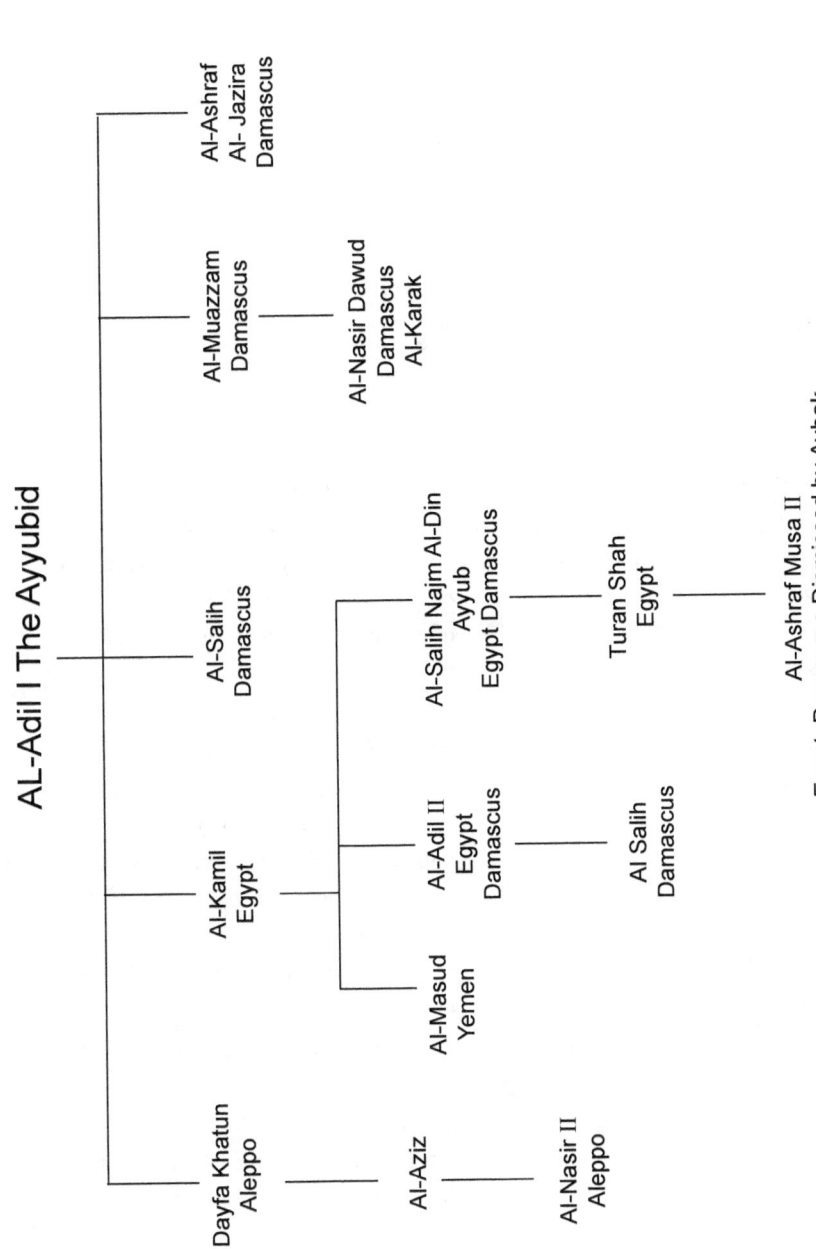

Glossary

agha	master
'alam	flag
'alama	insignia
'alima	savant
ama	female slave
amir al-umara'	chief commander
atabeg	tutor/regent for future ruler
atabeg al-'askar (pl. *atabeg al-'asakir*)	leader of the army (under the Ayyubids)
a'yan	elite personnel
barid	official post and intelligence service
bay'a	pledge of political loyalty
burqu'	veil, covering the face
da'i	political/religious propagandist
Dar al-Hikma	House of Wisdom (intellectual centre established by the 'Abbasids)
dargah	nomadic court, which travelled with the sultan or king
da'wa	movement
dhimmi	a non-Muslim living under Muslim rule
dibaj	silk
diwan	royal court/special office
emir	prince
fata	youth
fida'	annual exchange of prisoners of war
fiqh	understanding of religious texts
fitna	revolt
gharaniq	goddesses

ghazwa	invasion
ghulam (pl. *ghilman*)	servant used in civil services (lit. young boy)
ghulam amrad	pre-pubescent boy
ghulamiyya	lust
Ghulamiyyat	female regiment, officers dressed as eunuchs
Ghurabiyya	regiment (lit. crows)
Hadith	sayings of the Prophet Muhammad
hafiz	keeper/regent
hajib	chamberlain
hajj	pilgrimage
haram (pl. *hurum*)	sanctum
Hegira	start of Muslim era (check wording)
hijab	veil (lit. curtain/screen)
hisba	inspector of markets and adherence to Islamic law in public places
hujja	undisputed/absolute proof
hur	beautiful females
hurra (pl. *hara'ir*)	free woman
al-Hurra	the noble (title)
ijtihad	reaching a legal decision through independent interpretation
iqta'	feudal system
isfahsalar	chief or commander of the army
jahiliyya	the period before Islam
janaba (pl. *junub*)	someone who is unwashed after copulation
Jaradiyya	regiment (lit. locusts)
jariya (pl. *jawari*)	female slave (lit. runner for service)
Jeushiyya	regiment
jihad	holy war
jilbab	cloak
kafala	guardianship
Kafuriyya	regiment, established by Kafur al-Aswad
katib	secretary
khadim (pl. *khadam*)	male slave used in domestic service
khankah	gathering place for Sufis
khasis	close confidant
khasiyy (pl. *khisyan*)	eunuch (castrated)

khatun	queen
khawadja	teacher/lord
khodja	teacher
khumur	veils
khutba	sermon delivered at the Friday prayer, during which the official declaration of the ruler would have been made or renewed
mahziyya (pl. *hazaya* or *mahziyyat*)	concubine
majbub	eunuch (entire sexual organ removed)
malik/malika	king/queen
mamluk (pl. *mamalik*)	slave mainly used in military service
manshur	decree
mawali	non-Arab Muslim
mawla	male slave
mazalim	complaints court
mu'allim	instructor
mudabbir	marshal of the kingdom
muhannak	the highest rank of eunuch in the Fatimid court; they would wear a turban, part of which passed under the chin
muhtasib	market monitor
mukhannath	transsexual/epicene
Mu'nisiyya	regiment of eunuchs under al-Muqtadir
mushir	chief adviser
Muzaffariyya	regiment, named after the eunuch Muzaffar
na'ib	deputy
nass	declared religious–political will
qadi	judge
qahir	vanquisher
qahramana (pl. *qahramanat*)	stewardess
qa'id al-quwwad	chief commander
qina' (pl. *qiyan*)	female slave musician/singer
qina'	veil, covering head and face
ra'is	civic leader
ribat	place for Sufis/mystics to meet
Rihaniyya	regiment, named after 'Aziz al-Dawla Rihan
sabiyya (pl. *sabaya*)	female prisoner of war

Sa'diyya	regiment comprised of eunuchs
sa'ifa	summer raid
Saqlabi (pl. Saqaliba)	Slavic
sariyya	one who gives pleasure
sayyida	mistress
shaikh	teacher/chief
Shakiriyya	female regiment, officers dressed as eunuchs
shamma	garment, pulled over one shoulder
shari'a	Islamic law
shihna	police prefect
shurta	police
tafwid	delegated
tanabbat	prophetess
taqlid	diploma
tawashi	servant
tughra	insignia
um walad	slave who has had a child to her master (lit. mother of a son)
umma	community (of the Prophet Muhammad)
'umra	short pilgrimage
ustadh	ruler/teacher
ustadh qasr	palace chief
wakil	agent
wali	protector/helper, also used for 'provincial governor'
wali al-'ahd	heir apparent (for Muslims)
wasita	prime minister
Yanisiyya	regiment, named after the eunuch Yanis
zinatahunna	adornment

Bibliography

Anon., *Al-'Uyun wa al-Hada'iq fi Akhbar al-Haqa'iq*, Leiden, 1869.
Abadi, al-Fairuz, *Al-Qamus al-Muhit*, Cairo, 2003.
Abbott, Nabia, 'Pre-Islamic Arab Queens', *The American Journal of Semitic Languages and Literatures*, Vol. 58, No. 1, 1941, pp. 1–2.
Abbott, Nabia, 'Women and the State on the Eve of Islam', *The American Journal of Semitic Languages and Literatures*, Vol. 58, No. 3, July 1941, pp. 259–84.
Abbott, Nabia, *Aishah: The Beloved of Muhammad*, Chicago, 1942.
Abbott, Nabia, *Two Queens of Baghdad: Mother and Wife of Harun al-Rashid*, Chicago, 1946.
'Abd al-Hadi, Sha'ira M., *Sirat al-Ustadh Jawdhar*, Cairo, 1954.
al-Abshihi, *Al-Mustatraf fi kul fan mustazraf*, 2 vols, Beirut, 2016.
Abu Dawud, *Sunan*, Beirut, 1998.
Abu al-Fida', *Al-Mukhtasar*, 4 vols, Beirut, 1979.
Abu Shama, *Al-Rawdatayn fi Akhbar al-Dawlatayn*, 3 vols, Cairo, n.d.
Ahmad, Aziz, *A History of Islamic Sicily*, trans. A. Taibi, Tripoli, 1979.
Ahmed, Leila, *Women and Gender in Islam*, New Haven, 1992.
Album, Stephen, *Marsden's Numismata Orientalia Illustrata*, New York, 1977.
Alf Layla wa Layla [*The Arabian Nights*], 4 vols, Cairo, 2001 and 2006.
'Ali, Yahya b., *Ghayat al-Amani fi Akhbar al-Qutr al-Yamani*, 2 vols, ed. S. Ashur, Cairo, 1968.
Allen, William E. D., *A History of the Georgian People from the Beginning down to the Russian Conquest in the Nineteenth Century*, New York, 1971.
Anderson, Glaire D., 'Concubines, Eunuchs and Patronage in Early Islamic Cordoba', in *Reassessing the Role of Women as Makers of Medieval Art and Architecture*, Vol. 2, ed. T. Martin, Leiden, 2012, pp. 633–70.
Andreasen, Niels-Erik, 'The Role of the Queen Mother in Israelite Society', *The Catholic Biblical Quarterly*, Vol. 45, No. 2, April 1983, pp. 179–94.

Asbridge, Thomas, *The Crusades: The Authoritative History of the War for the Holy Land*, London, 2010.

Ashtor, Eliyahu, *A Social and Economic History of the Near East in the Middle Ages*, trans. A. Abla, Damascus, 1985.

al-'Askari, Murtada, *Ma'alim al-Madrasatine*, Beirut, 2010.

Ateyya, Ahmad, *Al-Qamus al-Islami*, Cairo, 1972.

Ayalon, David, 'Studies on the Structure of the Mamluk Army', *Bulletin of the School of Oriental and African Studies*, Vol. 16, 1954, pp. 57–90.

Ayalon, David, *Outsiders in the Land of Islam: Mamluks, Mongols and Eunuchs* (Variorum Reprints), London, 1988.

Ayalon, David, *Eunuchs, Caliphs and Sultans: A Study of Power Relationships*, Jerusalem, 1999.

Ayalon, David, art.: 'Atabek al-Ibn 'Asakir', *Encyclopaedia of Islam*, 2nd edition, Leiden, 2002.

al-'Ayni, Badr al-Din, *'Iqd al-Jaman*, 4 vols, ed. M. Amin, Cairo, 1987.

el-Azheri, Taef, *The Saljuqs of Syria during the Crusades, 463–549 AH, 1070–1154 AD*, Berlin, 1997.

el-Azhari, Taef, 'Dayfa Khatun, Ayubid Queen of Aleppo 634–640/1236–1242', *Annals of Japan Association for Middle East Studies*, Vol. 15, 2000, pp. 27–55.

el-Azhari, Taef, 'The Influence of the Ayyubid Eunuchs in the Ayyubid Kingdom', in *Orientalia Lovaniensia Analecta*, eds U. Vermeulen and J. Van Steenbergen, Vol. IV, 2005, pp. 127–42.

el-Azhari, Taef, 'The Role of Salguqid Women in Medieval Syria', in *Orientalia Lovaniensia Analecta*, eds U. Vermeulen and J. Van Steenbergen, Vol. IV, Leuven, 2005, pp. 111–26.

el-Azhari, Taef, art. 'Atabeg', *The Crusades: An Encyclopedia*, Vol. 1, ed. Alan Murray, Santa Barbara, 2006.

el-Azhari, Taef, art. 'Turan Shah', *The Crusades: An Encyclopedia*, Vol. 4, ed. Alan Murray, Santa Barbara, 2006.

el-Azhari, Taef, *Zengi and the Muslim Response to the Crusades*, London, 2016.

el-Azhari, Taef. art.: 'Dayfa', *Encyclopaedia of Islam*, online, 3rd edition, Leiden, 2017.

Bacharach, Jere, *Islamic History through Coins*, Cairo, 2006.

al-Baghdadi, al-Khatib, *Ta'rikh Baghdad*, 22 vols, Beirut, 1993.

al-Baladhuri, *Futuh al-Bildan*, Cairo, 1965.

Baldwin's Auction Catalogue, November 90, 2003, London, p. 26, Item no. D 101.

al-Ballawi, *Sirat Ahmad b. Tulun*, 2 vols, Cairo, 1999.

Barlas, Asma, *Believing Women in Islam: Unreading Patriarchal Interpretations of the Qur'an*, Austin, 2002.

Barthold, W., *Turkestan down to the Mongol Invasion*, trans. H. A. R. Gibb, London, 1958.

Barthold, W. and Dominique Sourdel, art.: 'Al-Baramika', *Encyclopaedia of Islam*, 2nd edition, Leiden, 2002.

al-Basha, Hasan, *Al-Qahira Tarikhaha Fununuha wa Atharuha*, Cairo, 1970.

Behnamfar, Mohammad, 'Feminist Criticism of the Story of Homay Cherhzad's Kingdom in Shahnameh', *Theory and Practice in Language Studies*, Vol. 2, No. 9, 2012, pp. 1,980–6.

van Berkel, Maaike, 'The Young Caliph and His Wicked Advisors: Women and Power Politics under Caliph al-Muqtadir (r. 295–320/908–932)', *Al-Masaq, Journal of the Medieval Mediterranean*, Vol. 19, No. 1, March 2007, pp. 3–15.

Bianquis, T., 'Autonomous Egypt from Ibn Tulun to Kafur, 868–969', in *The Cambridge History of Egypt*, ed. C. Petry, Cambridge, 2006, pp. 86–119.

Bierman, Irene, *Writing Signs: The Fatimid Public Text*, Oakland, 1998.

Bosworth, C. E., 'The Political and Dynastic History of the Iranian World (AD 1000–1217)', in *The Cambridge History of Iran*, 6 vols, Vol. 5, ed. J. Boyle, Cambridge, 1968, pp. 1–202.

Bosworth, C. E., *The Later Ghaznavids: Splendour and Decay, the Dynasty in Afghanistan and Northern India, 1040–1186*, New York, 1977.

Bosworth, C. E., *The Islamic Dynasties*, Edinburgh, 1980.

Bosworth, C. E., *The New Islamic Dynasties*, Edinburgh, 2004.

Bosworth, C. E. (ed.), *The History of the Seljuq Turks, from the Jami' al-Tawarikh: An Ilkhanid Adaptation of the Saljuq-nama of Zahir al Din Nishapuri*, trans. K. Luther, London, 2001.

Bosworth, C. E., art.: 'Eldiguzids', *Encyclopaedia of Islam*, 2nd edition, Leiden, 2002.

Bosworth, C. E., art.: 'Ikhshid', *Encyclopaedia of Islam*, 2nd edition, Leiden, 2002.

Bosworth, C. E., art.: 'Saldjukids', *Encyclopaedia of Islam*, 2nd edition, Leiden, 2002.

Bou Hdeiba, A., *Sex in Islam*, trans. H. Alouri, Beirut, 2001.

Bowen, H., art.: 'Mu'nis al-Muzaffar', *Encyclopaedia of Islam*, 2nd edition, Leiden, 2002.

Bray, Julia, 'Men, Women and Slaves in Abbasid Society', in *Gender in the Early Medieval World, East and West, 200–900*, ed. L. Brubaker, Cambridge, 2004, pp. 121–46.

Brooks, Beatrice, 'Some Observations Concerning Ancient Mesopotamian Women', *The American Journal of Semetic Languages*, Vol. 39, No. 3, 1923, pp. 187–94.

al-Bukhari, *Sahih al-Bukhari*, Beirut, 2015.

Cahen, Claude, *La Chronique Abregee d'al-'Azimi*, Paris, 1938.

Cahen, Claude, *La Syrie du Nord a l'Epoque des Croisades et la Principaute Franque d'Antioche*, Paris, 1940.

Cahen, Claude, *Pre-Ottoman Turkey: A General Survey of the Material and Spiritual Culture and History*, c. 1071–1330, trans. J. Williams, London, 1968.

Cahen, Claude, art.: 'Atabek', *Encyclopaedia of Islam*, 2nd edition, Leiden, 2002.

Cahen, Claude, art.: 'Ayyubids', *Encyclopaedia of Islam*, 2nd edition, Leiden, 2002.

C. Cahen, art.: 'Ghuzz', *Encyclopaedia of Islam*, 2nd edition, Leiden, 2002.

Cahen, Claude, art.: 'Lu'Lu', *Encyclopaedia of Islam*, 2nd edition, Leiden, 2002.

Canard, M., art.: 'Djawdhar', *Encyclopaedia of Islam*, 2nd edition, Leiden, 2002.

Canard, M., art.: 'Fatimids', *Encyclopaedia of Islam*, 2nd edition, Leiden, 2002.

Canard, M., art.: 'Al-Hakim', *Encyclopaedia of Islam*, 2nd edition, Leiden, 2002.

Canard, M., art.: 'Hamdanids', *Encyclopaedia of Islam*, 2nd edition, Leiden, 2002.

Caswell, Fuad, *The Slave Girls of Baghdad: The Qiyan in the Early Abbasid Era*, London, 2011.

Comnena, Anna, *The Alexiad*, London, 1985.

Cook, Michael, 'Did the Prophet Muhammad Keep Court?', in *Court Cultures in the Muslim World: Seventh to Nineteenth Centuries*, eds A. Fuess and J.-P. Hartung, New York, 2011, pp. 23–9.

Cortese, Delia and Simonetta Calderini, *Women and the Fatimids in the World of Islam*, Edinburgh, 2006.

Crawford, R. W., 'Ridwan the Maligned', in *World of Islam: Studies in Honour of Philip Hitti*, eds J. Kritzeck and R. B. Winder, London, 1959, pp. 135–44.

Dachroui, F., art.: 'Al-Sakaliba', *Encyclopaedia of Islam*, 2nd edition, Leiden, 2002.

Dadayan, S. art.: 'Badr al-Jamali', *Encyclopaedia of Islam*, online, 3rd edition, 2010.

Daftary, Farhad, *The Isma'ilis: Their History and Doctrines*, Cambridge, 1990.

Daftary, Farhad, 'Sayyida Hurra: The Ismaili Sulayhid Queen of Yemen', in *Women in the Medieval Islamic World*, ed. Gavin Hambly, London, 1999, pp. 117–30.

Daftary, Farhad, art.: 'Al-Tayyibiyya', *Encyclopaedia of Islam*, 2nd edition, Leiden, 2002.

Dalkesen, N., 'Gender Roles and Women's Status in Central Asia and Anatolia between the Thirteenth and Sixteenth Centuries', unpublished PhD thesis, Middle East Technical University, Istanbul, 2007.

Darley-Doran, R. E., 'Examples of Islamic Coinage from Yemen', in *Yemen: 3000 Years of Art and Civilization in Arabia Felix*, ed. W. Daum, Frankfurt, 1987, pp. 182–203.

Daum, Werner, 'From Aden to India and Cairo: Jewish World Trade in the 11th and 12th Centuries', in *Yemen: 3000 Years of Art and Civilization in Arabia Felix*, ed. W. Daum, Frankfurt, 1987, pp. 167–73.

al-Deresi, Wafa', *Al-Jawari wa al-Ghulman fi al-Thaqafa al-Islamiyya*, Rabat, 2016.

al-Dhahabi, *Al-I'bar fi Khabar Man Ghabar*, 4 vols, Vol. 4, Kuwait, 1961.

al-Dhahabi, *Ta'rikh al-Islam*, 17 vols, ed. A. Tadmuri, Beirut, 1991.

al-Din, Idris Imad, *'Uyun al-Akhbar*, ed. A. Sayyed, London, 2002.

al-Duri, 'Abd al-'Aziz, *Al-'Asr al-'Abbasi al-Awwal*, Beirut, 1998.

al-Duwadar, Baybars, *Zubdat al-Fikra*, ed. Z. Ata, Cairo, 1977.

Earenfight, Theresa, *Queenship in Medieval Europe*, London, 2013.

Eddé, Anne-Marie, 'Ridwan, Prince d'Alep de 1095 à 1113', *Revue des Études Islamiques*, Vol. 54, 1986, pp. 101–25.

Eddé, Anne-Marie, *La Principauté Ayyoubide d'Alep (579/1183–658/1260)*, Stuttgart, 1999.

Editor, art.: 'Al-Khayzuran', *Encyclopaedia of Islam*, 2nd edition, Leiden, 2002.

Editor, art.: 'Liwat', *Encyclopaedia of Islam*, 2nd edition, Leiden, 2002.

Ehlert, T., art.: 'Muhammad', *Encyclopaedia of Islam*, 2nd edition, Leiden, 2002.

Ehrenkreutz, A. S., art.: 'Kafur', *Encyclopaedia of Islam*, 2nd edition, Leiden, 2002.

El Cheikh, Nadia, 'The Qahramana in the 'Abbasid Court: Position and Functions', *Studia Islamica*, Vol. 97, 2003, pp. 41–55.

El Cheikh, Nadia, 'Servants at the Gate: Eunuchs at the Court of al-Muqtadir', *Journal of the Economic and Social History of the Orient*, Vol. 48, No. 2, 2005, pp. 234–52.

El Cheikh, Nadia, *Women, Islam, and Abbasids Identity*, Cambridge, MA, 2015.

Elias, Elias A., *Arabic–English Dictionary*, Cairo, 1994.

Encyclopaedia of Islam, 2nd edition, Leiden, 2002.

Fahmy, Aly Mohamed, *Muslim Sea-power in the Eastern Mediterranean from the Seventh to the Tenth Century* AD, Cairo, 1966.

Fathi, Leila, 'The Study of Statue of Women on Iranian Coins', *Journal of History and Art Research*, Vol. 5, No. 4, 2016, pp. 278–95.

Ferdowsi, *Shahnameh*, trans. al-Fath al-Bindari, ed. A. Azzam, Cairo, 1993.

Foucault, Michel, *The History of Sexuality*, 2 vols, trans. R. Hurley, New York, 1978.

Frye, Richard N., 'Women in Pre-Islamic Central Asia: The Khatun of Bukhara', in *Women in the Medieval Islamic World: Power, Patronage and Piety*, ed. G. Hambly, London, 1999, pp. 55–68.

Gabbay, Alyssa, 'In Reality a Man: Sultan Iltutmish, His Daughter Raziya and Gender Ambiguity in Thirteenth-century Northern India', *Journal of Persianate Studies*, Vol. 4, 2011, pp. 45–63.
al-Ghazali, Abu Hamid, *Ihya' 'Ulum al-Din*, 4 vols, Cairo, 1985.
al-Ghazali, Abu Hamid, *Al-Tibr al-Masbuk fi Nasihat al-Muluk*, Cairo, 2008.
Gibb, H. A. R., 'The Ayyubids', in *A History of the Crusades*, 6 vols, Vol. 2, ed. K. Setton, London, 1962, pp. 693–714.
Gibb, H. A. R., art.: 'Al-Mustansir', *Encyclopaedia of Islam*, 2nd edition, Leiden, 2002.
Goitein, Shelomo, 'New Lights on the Beginning of the Karim Merchants', *Journal of the Economic and Social History of the Orient*, Vol. 1, No. 2, 1958, pp. 175–84.
Goldsmith, Linda, art.: 'Crusade of Louis IX to the East', *The Crusades: An Encyclopaedia*, Vol. 1, ed. A. Murray, Santa Barbara, 2006.
Gottschalk, Hans L., *Al-Malik al-Kamil von Agypten*, Wiesbaden, 1958.
Guseynov, R., 'Institut Atabekov (The Institution of Atabeks)', *Palestinskii Sbornik*, Vol. 15, No. 78, 1966, pp. 181–96.
Halm, Heinz, *The Empire of the Mahdi: The Rise of the Fatimids*, trans. M. Bonner, Leiden, 1996.
Halm, Heinz, *The Fatimids and Their Traditions of Learning*, London, 1997, trans. S. Qusair, Damascus, 1999.
Halm, Heinz, art.: 'Sitt al-Mulk', *Encyclopaedia of Islam*, 2nd edition, Leiden, 2002.
al-Hamadani, Badr al-Din, *Al-Simt al-Ghali al-Thaman fi Akhbar al-Muluk min al-Ghuzz bi al-Yaman*, ed. G. Rex Smith, London, 1974.
al-Hamawi, Yaqut, *Mu'jam al-Buldan*, 5 vols, Beirut, 1989.
al-Hamdani, Husain b. Fayid, 'The Life and Times of Queen Saiyidah Arwa the Sulaihid of the Yemen', *Journal of the Royal Central Asian Society*, Vol. 18, No. 4, 1931, pp. 505–17.
al-Hamdani, Husain b. Fayid, *Al-Sulayhiyyun wa al-Haraka al-Fatimiyya fi al-Yaman*, Cairo, 1955.
Hamza, 'Abd Allatif, *Hukm Qaraqush*, Cairo, 1945.
Hanbal, Ahmad b., *Al-Musnad*, 50 vols, Cairo, 2002.
al-Hanbali, Ahmad b. Ibrahim, *Shifa' al-Qulub fi Manaqib Bani Ayyub*, ed. M. al-Sharqawi, Cairo, 1996.
Hanne, Eric, 'Women, Power, and the Eleventh and Twelfth-Century 'Abbasid Court', *Hawwa*, Vol. 3, 2005, pp. 80–110.
Hasan, Sulaf, *Dawr al-Jawari wa al-Qahramanat fi dar al-Khilafa al-'Abbasiyya*, Damascus, 2013.

Hasanain, 'Abd al Na'im, *Persian–Arabic Dictionary*, Cairo, 1982.

Hekmat, Anwar, *Women and the Koran: The Status of Women in Islam*, Amherst, 1997.

Hillenbrand, Carole, 'The Career of Najm al-Din Il-Ghazi', *Der Islam*, Vol. 58, No. 2, 1981, pp. 250–92.

Hillenbrand, Carole, 'Jihad Propaganda in Syria from the Time of the First Crusade until the Death of Zengi: The Evidence of Monumental Inscriptions', in *The Frankish Wars and Their Influence on Palestine*, eds K. Athamina and R. Heacock, Birzeit, 1994, pp. 60–9.

Hillenbrand, Carole, '1092: A Murderous Year', in *Proceedings of the 14th Congress of the Union Européene des Arabisants et Islamists*, Budapest, 1995, pp. 281–96.

Hillenbrand, Carole, *The Crusades: Islamic Perspectives*, Edinburgh, 1999.

Hillenbrand, Carole, 'Aspects of the Court of the Great Seljuqs', in *The Seljuqs: Politics, Society and Culture*, eds C. Lange and S. Meçit, Edinburgh, 2011, pp. 22–38.

Hillenbrand, Robert, *Islamic Art and Architecture*, London, 1999.

Hoffman, Eva, 'Between East and West: The Wall Paintings of Samarra and the Construction of Abbasid Princely Culture', *Muqarnas*, Vol. 25, 2008, pp. 107–32.

Holt, P. M , art.: 'Mamluks', *Encyclopaedia of Islam*, 2nd edition, Leiden, 2002.

Homerin, Th. Emil, 'Living Love: The Mystical Writings of 'A'ishah al-Ba'uniyah (d. 922/1516)', *Mamluk Studies Review*, Vol. 7, 2003, pp. 211–34.

Humphreys, R. Stephen, *From Saladin to the Mongols: The Ayyubids of Damascus, 1193–1260*, Albany, 1977.

al-Husayni, Sadr al-Din, *Zubdat al-Tawarikh, Akhbar al-Umara' wa al-Muluk al-Saljuqiyya*, ed. M. Nur al-Din, Beirut, 1985.

Ibn 'Abd al-Hakam, *Futuh Misr wa al-Maghrib*, 2 vols, Cairo, 1961.

Ibn 'Abd Rabbuh, *Bahgat al-Majalis*, Beirut, 2001.

Ibn Abi al-Rabi', *Siyasat al-Malik fi Tadbir al-Mamalik*, Cairo, 1930.

Ibn Abi Usabi'a, Muwaffaq al-Din, *Tabaqat al-Atibba'*, 3 vols, Beirut, 1987.

Ibn 'Adhara al-Marakishi, *Al-Bayan al-Mughrib*, 4 vols, ed. L. Provencal, Beirut, 2009.

Ibn al-'Adim, *Zubdat al-Halab fi Ta'rikh Halab*, 3 vols, ed. S. al-Dahhan, Damascus, 1959.

Ibn al-'Adim, *Bughyat al-Talab fi Ta'rikh Halab*, ed. A. Sevim, Ankara, 1976.

Ibn al-'Amid, Kamal al-Din, *Akhbar al-Ayyubiyyin*, Cairo, n.d.

Ibn Arnus, *Ta'rikh al-Qada'*, Cairo, 1972.

Ibn al-Athir, *Al-Ta'rikh al-Bahir fi'l-Dawla al-Atabekiyya*, ed. A. A. Tulaymat, Cairo, 1963.
Ibn al-Athir, *Al-Kamil fi al-Tarikh*, 13 vols, Beirut, 1982.
Ibn 'Asakir, *Tadhib Ta'rikh Dimashq al-Kabir*, 7 vols, ed. A. Badran, Beirut, 1979.
Ibn 'Asakir, *Ta'rikh Madinat Dimashq: Tarajim al-Nisa'*, ed. S. al-Shihabi, Damascus, 1981.
Ibn 'Asakir, *Wulat Dimashq*, ed. S. al-Munajjid, Damascus, 1985.
Ibn Aybak, *Al-Durra al-Mudi'a fi Akhbar al-Dawla al-Fatimiyya*, ed. S. al-Munajjid, Cairo, 1961.
Ibn Aybak, *Kanz al-Durar*, 7 vols, Cairo, 1965.
Ibn Aybak, *Kanz*, ed. S. Ashur, Cairo, 1972.
Ibn Aybak al-Safadi, *Tuhfat Dhawi al-Albab*, ed. I. Khulusi, Damascus, 1992.
Ibn 'Azara al-Marakishi, *Al-Bayan al-Mughrib*, Beirut, 2009.
Ibn al-Azraq al-Fariqi, *Ta'rikh al-Fariqi*, ed. B. Awwad, Cairo, 1959.
Ibn Bibi, *Ta'rikh Salajiqat al-Rum*, trans. M. Mansur, Cairo, 1994.
Ibn al-Furat, Nasir al-Din, *Ta'rikh*, 9 vols, ed. H. Shamma, Basra, 1967.
Ibn al-Fuwati, *Al-Hawadith al-Jami'a*, Baghdad, 1931.
Ibn Hawkal, *Surat al-Ard*, 2 vols, Leiden, 1890.
Ibn Hisham, *Al-Sira al-Nabawiyya*, 4 vols, Beirut, 2014.
Ibn Iyas, *Bada'i' al-Zuhur fi Waqa'i' al-Duhur*, 5 vols, Cairo, 1982.
Ibn al-Jawzi, *Al-Muntazam fi Ta'rikh al-Muluk wa al-Umam*, 20 vols, ed. M. Ata, Beirut, 2007.
Ibn Jubaiyr, *Rihla*, Beirut, 1986.
Ibn Kathir, *Tafsir al-Qur'an*, Beirut, 1984.
Ibn Khaldun, *Al-'Ibar*, Beirut, 1990, and Amman, 2003.
Ibn Khaldun, *Muqaddimah*, Beirut, 2008.
Ibn Khallikan, *Wafayat al-A'yan*, 6 vols, Beirut, 1985.
Ibn Muyassar, *Al-Muntaqa min Akhbar Misr*, ed. A. al-Sayyed, Cairo, 1981.
Ibn al-Nadim, *Kitab al-Fihrest*, 4 vols, ed. A. al-Sayyed, London, 2014.
Ibn al-Qalanisi, *Dhayl Ta'rikh Dimashq*, ed. S. Zakkar, Damascus, 1983.
Ibn Qayyim al-Jawziyya, *Akhbar al-Nisa'*, Beirut, 1998.
Ibn Ridwan al-Milqi, *Siyasat al-Nafi'a*, Beirut, 1976.
Ibn Sa'd, *Al-Tabaqat al-Kubra*, 10 vols, Beirut, 2004.
Ibn al-Sa'i, *Nisa' al-Khulafa'*, ed. M. Jawad, Beirut, 2011.
Ibn Sa'id, *Al-Maghribi fi Huliyy al-Maghrib*, 2 vols, ed. S. Daif, Cairo, 1955.
Ibn Sa'id al-Antaki, Yahya, *Ta'rikh*, ed. U. Tadmuri, Tripoli, 1990.
Ibn al-Sairafi, *Al-Isharah ila man nal al-Wizara*, ed. A. Mukhlis, Cairo, 1924.

Ibn Shaddad, 'Izz al-Din, *Al-Nawadir al-Sultaniyya*, ed. M. Subhi, Cairo, n.d.
Ibn Shaddad, 'Izz al-Din, *Al-'Alaq al-Khatira fi Dhikr Umara' al-Sham wa al-Jazira*, 3 vols, Vol. 2, ed. S. al-Dahhan, Damascus, 1956.
Ibn al-Shihna, *Al-Durr al-Muntakhab*, Damascus, 1988.
Ibn Taghri Bardi, *Al-Nujum al-Zahira fi Muluk Misr wa al-Qahira*, 16 vols, Cairo, 1963.
Ibn Taghri Bardi, *Al-Manhal al-Wafi*, 5 vols, ed. M. Amin, Cairo, 1986.
Ibn Taqataqa, *Al-Fakhri fi al-Adab al-Sultaniyya*, Beirut, 1986.
Ibn Wasil, *Mufarrij al-Kurub fi Ta'rikh bani Ayyub*, 6 vols, Vol. 1, ed. J. al-Shayyal, Cairo, 1953.
Ibn Wasil, *Mufarrij al-Kurub fi Ta'rikh bani Ayyub*, 6 vols, Vol. 6, ed. U. Tadmuri, Beirut, 2004.
Ibn Zafir al-Azdi, *Akhbar al-Duwal al-Munqati'a*, ed. F. Andrea, Cairo, 1972.
Ibn al-Zubayr, *Al-Dhakha'ir wa al-Tuhaf*, 2 vols, ed. M. Hamid, Kuwait, 1984.
Ilal, Rashid, *Sahih al-Bukhari: Nehayat Austora (Al-Bukhari, the End of a Myth)*, Rabat, 2017.
al-Isfahani, Abi al-Faraj, *Kitab al-Aghani*, 25 vols, ed. I. Abbas, Beirut, 2008.
al-Isfahani, 'Imad al-Din, *Ta'rikh Dawlat al-Saljuq*, Beirut, 1980.
al-Jabiri, Muhammad, *Ibn Rushd Sirah wa Fikr*, Beirut, 1998.
Jackson, Peter, 'Sultan Radiyya bint Iltutmish', in *Women in the Medieval Islamic World: Power, Patronage and Piety*, ed. Gavin Hambly, London, 1999, pp. 181–98.
Jackson, Peter, 'Muslim India: The Delhi Sultanate', in *The New Cambridge History of Islam*, Vol. 3, eds D. Morgan and A. Reid, Cambridge, 2011, pp. 100–27.
al-Jahiz, Abu 'Amr, *Al-Mahasin wa al-Addad*, Cairo, 1906.
al-Jahiz, Abu 'Amr, *Al-Taj fi akhbar al-Muluk*, ed. A. Zaki, Cairo, 1914.
al-Jahiz, Abu 'Amr, *Tahdhib al-Akhlaq*, Cairo, 1989.
al-Jahiz, Abu 'Amr, *Al-Hayawan*, 4 vols, Beirut, 1990.
al-Jahiz, Abu 'Amr, *Rasa'il*, Cairo, 1996.
al-Jashyari, Abu Abdulla Ibn Abdus, *Kitab al-Wuzara' wa al-Kuttub*, Cairo, 1980.
al-Jawdhari, Abi 'Ali, *Sirat al-Ustadh Jawdhar*, ed. M. Husain, Cairo, 1954.
Jeffery, Arthur, *The Foreign Vocabulary of the Qur'an*, Leiden, 2007.
Johnson, Janet, 'The Legal Status of Women in Ancient Egypt', in *Mistress of the House, Mistress of Heaven: Women in Ancient Egypt*, eds Betsy M. Bryan, Anne K. Capel and Glenn Markoe, New York, 1997, pp. 175–86.
De Joinville, Jean and Geoffrey of Villehardouin, *Chronicles of the Crusades*, trans. B. Shaw, New York, 1985.

Joseph, Suad, Sarah Gualtieri, Lyn Parker, Elora Shehabuddin and Zeina Zaatari (eds), *The Encyclopedia of Women and Islamic Cultures*, 5 vols, Leiden, 2007.

Kahala, 'Umar, *A'lam al-Nisa' fi 'Alami al-Arab wa al-Islam*, 5 vols, Damascus, 1959.

Kashghari, Mahmud, *Diwan Lughat al-Turk*, 3 vols, ed. Kilisli Rifat Bey, Istanbul, 1918.

al-Kashif, Sayyeda, *Misr fi Ahd al-Ikhshidiyyun*, Cairo, 1950.

Kennedy, Hugh, *The Prophet and the Age of the Caliphate*, London, 1986.

Kennedy, Hugh, *The Court of the Caliphs: The Rise and Fall of Islam's Greatest Dynasty*, London, 2004.

Kennedy, Hugh, 'Mu'nis al-Muzaffar: An Exceptional Eunuch', in *Celibate and Childless Men in Power: Ruling Eunuchs and Bishops in the Pre-modern World*, eds A. Höfert, M. Mesley and S. Tolino, London, 2018, pp. 79–91.

Kharbotly, 'Ali, *Al-Mahdi al-Abbasi*, Cairo, 1966.

al-Khazraji, 'Ali b. Hasan, *Al-'Uqud al-Lu'lu'iyya*, 2 vols, Vol. 1, Cairo, 1983.

al-Kindi, *Al-Wulat wa al-Quda*, Beirut, 1908.

Kira, Najwa, *Al-Jawari wa al-Ghulman fi Misr fi al-'Asrain, Alfatimi wa Alayyubi*, Cairo, 2007.

Kouymijan, D. K., 'A Numismatic History of Southeastern Caucasia and Adharbayjan', PhD thesis, Columbia University, New York, 1969.

Krachkovski, Ignati, *Istoria Arabskoi Geograficheskoi Literatury*, trans. S. Hashem, Cairo, 1963.

Kruk, Remke, *The Warrior Women of Islam: Female Empowerment in Arabic Popular Literature*, London, 2014.

al-Kurdi, Amal, *Dor al-Nisa' fi al-Khilafa al-'Abbasiyya*, Amman, 2014.

Lagrange, Frederic, art.: 'Sexuality and Queer Studies', *Encyclopedia of Women and Islamic Cultures*, Vol. 1, ed. S. Joseph, Leiden, 2003.

Lambton, A. K. S., 'Contributions to the Study of the Seljuq Institutions', PhD thesis, University of London, 1939.

Lambton, A. K. S., 'The Internal Structure of the Seljuqid Empire', in *The Cambrdige History of Iran*, Vol. 5, ed. J. Boyle, Cambridge, 1968, pp. 203–81.

Van Leeuwen, Richard, *The Thousand and One Nights: Space, Travel and Transformation*, London, 2007.

Lev, Yaacov, 'The Fatimid Princess Sitt al-Mulk', *Journal of Semitic Studies*, Vol. 32, 1987, pp. 319–28.

Lev, Yaacov, *State and Society in Fatimid Egypt*, Leiden, 1991.

Lev, Yaacov, art.: 'Saladin', *The Crusades: An Encyclopaedia*, Vol. 4, ed. A. Murray, Santa Barbara, 2006.

Lewis, Bernard, art.: "Abbasids', *Encyclopaedia of Islam*, 2nd edition, Leiden, 2002.
Lewis, Bernard, art.: 'Bardjawan', *Encyclopaedia of Islam*, 2nd edition, Leiden, 2002.
Lewis, Bernard, *The Crisis of Islam*, London, 2003.
Lewis, Bernard, *Race and Slavery in the Middle East: An Historical Enquiry*, Oxford, 2014.
Lewis, Geoffrey, 'Heroines and Others in the Heroic Age of the Turks', in *Women in the Medieval Islamic World*, ed. G. Hambly, London, 1999, pp. 147–60.
Luther, K. A., art.: 'Atabakan-e Maraga', *Encyclopaedia Iranica*, Vol. 2, London, 2011, pp. 898–900.
Luxenberg, Christoph, *The Syro-Aramaic Readings of the Koran: A Contribution to the Decoding of the Language of the Koran*, Berlin, 2007.
Lyons, Malcolm C. and D. E. P. Jackson, *Saladin: The Politics of the Holy War*, Cambridge, 1988.
Madelung, W., art.: 'Isma'iliyya', *Encyclopaedia of Islam*, 2nd edition, Leiden, 2002.
Majid, 'Abd al-Mun'im, *Al-Sijillat al-Mustansiriyya*, Cairo, 1954.
Majid, 'Abd al-Mun'im, *Al-Hakim bi Amr Allah*, Cairo, 1982.
Majid, 'Abd al-Mun'im, *Al-Imam al-Mustansir*, Cairo, 1982.
Majid, 'Abd al-Mun'im, *Nuzum al-Fatimiyyin wa Rusumihim fi Misr*, 2 vols, Cairo, 1985.
Makdisi, George, 'The Marriage of Tughril Beg', *International Journal of Middle East Studies*, Vol. 1, No. 3, 1970, pp. 259–75.
al-Manawi, Muhammad, *Al-Wizara wa al-Wuzara' fi al-'Asr al-Fatimi*, Cairo, 1970.
al-Maqarri, Ahmad, *Nafh al-Tib min Ghusn al-Andalus al-Ratib*, 8 vols, ed. I. 'Abbas, Beirut, 2008.
al-Maqrizi, *Al-Mawa'iz wa al-I'tibar bi Dhikr al-Khitat al-Athar*, 2 vols, Cairo, n.d.
al-Maqrizi, *Itti'az al-Hunafa' bi Akhbar al-A'imma al-Fatimiyyin al-Khulafa'*, 3 vols, ed. M. Hilmi, Cairo, 1971.
al-Maqrizi, *Al-Suluk le M'arifat Duwal al-Muluk*, 12 vols, ed. M. Ziyada, Cairo, 1957, and Beirut, 1997.
Marmon, Shaun, *Eunuchs and Sacred Boundaries in Islamic Society*, Oxford, 1995.
al-Mas'udi, *Al-Tanbih wa Ishraf*, Beirut, 2003.
al-Mas'udi, *Muruj al-Dhahab*, 4 vols, Beirut, 2005.
Mayer, Hans Eberhard, *The Crusades*, Oxford, 1978.
Melville, Charles, 'History: from the Saljuqs to the Aq Qoyunlu', *Journal of Iranian Studies*, Vol. 31, Nos 3–4, 1998, pp. 473–82.
Merçil, Erdoğan, *Fars Atabegleri Salgurlular*, Ankara, 1991.
Mernissi, Fatema, *The Forgotten Queens of Islam*, Minneapolis, 1993.

Meskawayh al-Razi, Abu 'Ali, *Tarajib al-Umam*, 8 vols, ed. Abu al-Qasim Imami, Tehran, 2001.
Metz, Adam, *The Renaissance of Islam*, trans. M. Abu Rida, Cairo, 2008.
Minorsky, V., art.: 'Ahmadilis', *Encyclopaedia of Islam*, 2nd edition, Leiden, 2002.
Moreno, Eduardo, 'The Iberian Peninsula and North Africa', in *The New Cambridge History of Islam*, Vol. 1, ed. C. Robinson, Cambridge, 2010, p. 581–622.
Morgan, David, *Medieval Persia*, London, 1988.
al-Mulk, Nizam, *Siyasat Nameh*, trans. H. Darke, London, 1978.
al-Munajjid, S., *Bayna al-Khulafa' wa al-Khula'a' fi al-'Asr al-'Abbasi*, Damasus, n.d.
Murray, A., art.: 'Al-Sinnabra Battle', *The Crusades: An Encyclopedia*, 4 vols, Vol. 4, ed. A. Murray, Santa Barbara, 2006.
al-Musabbihi, Muhammad b. 'Ubayd Allah, *Akhbar Misr*, ed. A. al-Sayyed, Cairo, 2001.
al-Mutannabi, *Diwan*, Cairo, 2005.
al-Naqib, Murtaza, 'The Political and Military Career of Mu'nis al-Muzafar at the 'Abbasid Court', unpublished master's dissertation, McGill University, Montreal, 1969.
Nasr, Sawsan, 'Al-Khuwarazmiyya', *Journal of the Egyptian Historical Society*, Vols 30–1, 1983–4, pp. 61–98.
Nejad, Mohammad Aziz and Ali Reza Karimi, 'Eldiguzid–Georgian Relations during the Rule of Attabak Abubakr Eldegizi', *Journal of the History of Foreign Relations*, Vol. 16, No. 63, 2015, pp. 70–95.
Nichols, James, M., 'Arabic Women Poets in al-Andalus', *Maghreb Review*, Vol. 4, December 1981, pp. 85–8.
Nickerson Hardwicke, Mary, 'The Crusader States, 1192–1243', in *A History of the Crusades, Vol. 2*, ed. R. Lee Wolff, Philadelphia, 1962, pp. 522–56.
de Nicola, Bruno, *Women in Mongol Iran: The Khatuns, 1206–1335*, Edinburgh, 2017.
Pearson, J. D., art.: 'Al-Kuran', *Encyclopaedia of Islam*, 2nd edition, Leiden, 2002.
Pellat, Ch., art.: 'Khasi', *Encyclopaedia of Islam*, 2nd edition, Leiden, 2002.
Phillips, Jonathan, *Holy Warriors: A Modern History of the Crusades*, New York, 2009.
Pierce, Leslie, 'Beyond Harem Walls: Ottoman Royal Women and the Exercise of Power', in *Servants of the Dynasty: Palace Women in World History*, ed. A. Wathhall, Oakland, 2008, pp. 81–95.
Prawer, Joshua, *The Latin Kingdom of Jerusalem: European Colonialism in the Middle Ages*, London, 1972.
al-Qalqashandi, *Subh al-'Asha*, 14 vols, Beirut, 1987.

al-Qurtubi, 'Arib, *Silat Ta'rikh al-Tabari*, Cairo, 1999.

al-Rawandi, Muhammad b. 'Ali, *Rahat al-Sudur wa Ayat al-Surur*, trans. A. Hasanain, Cairo, 1960.

al-Razi, Abu Bakr Muhammad, 'Al-Bah', in *Nisa'*, ed. H. Abd al-Aziz, Cairo, 1999, pp. 1–18.

Renate, J., art.: 'Zubayda bt. Dja'far', *Encyclopaedia of Islam*, 2nd edition, Leiden, 2002.

Richards, D. S., art.: 'Salah al-Din', *Encyclopaedia of Islam*, 2nd edition, Leiden, 2002.

Riley-Smith, Jonathan, *The Crusades*, New Haven, 1986.

Ringrose, Kathryn, *The Perfect Servant: Eunuchs and the Social Construction of Gender in Byzantium*, Chicago, 2003.

Robinson, Chase (ed.), *The New Cambridge History of Islam*, Vol. 1, Cambridge, 2010.

Rodinson, Maxime, *Muhammad*, London, 2002.

Roded, Ruth, *Women in Islam and the Middle East: A Reader*, London and New York, 1999.

Runciman, Steven, *A History of the Crusades*, 3 vols, Vol. 2, Cambridge, 1952.

Runciman, Steven, *A History of the Crusades*, 3 vols, Vol. 3, Cambridge, 1981.

al-Sabi', al-Hilal, *Tuhfat al-Umara' fi Ta'rikh al-Wuzara'*, Beirut, 2012.

al-Sa'dani, Mahmud, *Alhan al-Sama'*, Cairo, 1959.

al-Sajistani, *Kitab al-Masahif*, Beirut, 1988.

Saleh, Abd al-Aziz, *Misr wa al-Iraq* (*Egypt and Mesopotamia in the Ancient Near East*), Cairo, 1982.

Sanders, Paula, 'Gendering the Ungendered Body: Hermaphrodites in Medieval Islamic Law', in *Women in Middle Eastern History: Shifting Boundaries in Sex and Gender*, ed. N. Keddie, New Haven, 1991, pp. 74–95.

al-Sayyed, A., *Al-Dawla al-Fatimiyya fi Misr*, Cairo, 2000.

Schirrmacher, Christine, *Islam and Politics*, Bonn, 2008.

Schregle, Götz, *Die Sultanin von Ägypten*, Wiesbaden, 1961.

Shahrur, Muhammad, *Fiqh al-Mar'a*, Beirut, 2016.

al-Shayyal, Jamal al-Din, *Majmuat al-Watha'iq al-Fatimiyya*, Cairo, 2001.

Shehadeh, Lamia, *The Idea of Women in Fundamentalist Islam*, Gainsville, 2003.

Shuo Wang, 'Qing Imperial Women: Empresses, Concubines and Aisin Gioro Daughters', in *Servants of the Dynasty: Palace Women in World History*, ed. A. Wathhall, Oakland, 2008, pp. 137–58.

Sibt Ibn al-Jawzi, *Mir'at al-Zaman*, 8 vols, Hyderabad, 1951, and Damascus, 2013.

Sirat al-Malik al-Zahir Baybars, Cairo, 1983.

Smith, G. Rex, *The Ayyubids and Early Rasulids in the Yemen (567–694/1173–1295)*, Oxford, 1978.

Smith, G. Rex, 'The Political History of the Islamic Yemen down to the First Turkish Invasion (1–945/622–1538)', in *Yemen: 3000 Years of Art and Civilization in Arabia Felix*, ed. W. Daum, Frankfurt, 1987, pp. 129–40.

Smith, G. Rex, art.: 'Sulayhids', *Encyclopaedia of Islam*, 2nd edition, Leiden, 2002.

Smith, William, 'Eunuchs and Concubines in the History of Islamic South East Asia', *Journal of Humanities*, No. 14, 2007, pp. 8–19.

Sobernheim, M., art.: 'Karakush', *Encyclopaedia of Islam*, 2nd edition, Leiden, 2002.

Sonbol, Amira (ed.), *Beyond the Exotic: Women's Histories in Islamic Societies*, Cairo, 2006.

Sourdel, Dominique, *Le Vizirat 'Abbasid*, 2 vols, Vol. 2, Damascus, 1960.

Sourdel, Dominique, art.: 'Dar al-Hikma', *Encyclopaedia of Islam*, 2nd edition, Leiden, 2002.

Spellberg, Denise, 'Political Action and Public Example: 'Aisha and the Battle of the Camel', in *Women in Middle Eastern History*, ed. Nikki Keddie, New Haven, 1991, pp. 45–56.

Spengler, W. F. and W. G Sayles, *Turcoman Figural Bronze Coins and Their Iconography, Vol. 1: the Artuqids*, Lodi, 1992.

Stern, S. M., 'The Epistle of the Fatimid Caliph al-Amir (al-Hidaya al-Amiriyya): Its Date and Purpose', *Journal of the Royal Asiatic Society*, Vol. 1/2, 1950, pp. 20–31.

Stern, S. M., 'The Coins of Thamal and of Other Governors of Tarsus', *Journal of the American Oriental Society*, Vol. 80, No. 3, 1960, pp. 217–25.

Stillman, Yedida, *Arab Dress: A Short History: From the Dawn of Islam to Modern Times*, Leiden, 2003.

Strayer, Joseph, 'The Crusades of Louis IX', in *A History of the Crusades*, Vol. 2, ed. K. Setton, London, 1962, pp. 487–521.

al-Suyuti, *Akam al-'Iqyan fi Ahkam al-Khisyan*, Cairo, Dar al-Kutub, ms. no. 4991/82, n.d.

al-Suyuti, Jalal, *Ta'rikh al-Khulafa'*, Beirut, 1997.

al-Suyuti, Jalal, *Nawadir al-Iyk fi Ma'rifat al-Naik*, ed. T. Hasan, Damascus, 2004.

al-Suyuti, Jalal and Jalal al-Mahalli, *Tafsir al-Jalalayn*, Damascus, 1995.

al-Tabari, *Ta'rikh al-Umam wa al-Muluk*, Amman, 2000.

al-Tabari, *Jami' al-Bayan fi Tafsir al-Qur'an*, 26 vols, Beirut, 2002.

Taifur, Ahmad b., *Balaghat al-Nisa'*, Tehran, 1997.

Takriri, Mahmud, *Al-Ayyubiyyun fi Shamal al-Sham wa al-Jazira*, Beirut, 1985.

al-Tannukhi, Abu 'Ali, *Al-Faraj B'ad al-Shidda*, Beirut, 1987.

al-Tha'alibi, *Thimar al-Qulub*, Beirut, 1993.

Tillion, Germaine, *The Republic of Cousins*, trans. E. Khatabi, Beirut, 2000.

Tolino, Serena, 'Eunuchs in the Fatimid Empire: Ambiguities, Gender and Sacredness', in *Celibate and Childless Men in Power: Ruling Eunuchs and Bishops in the Pre-modern World*, eds A. Hofert, M. Mesley and S. Tolino, London, 2017, pp. 246–67.

Tougher, Shaun, *The Eunuch in Byzantine History and Society*, London, 2008.

Traboulsi, Samer, 'The Queen Was Actually a Man: Arwa Bint Ahmad and the Politics of Religion', in *Arabica*, T. 50, Fasc. 1, 2003, pp. 96–108.

Tucker, Judith, *In the House of Law: Gender and Islamic Law in Ottoman Syria and Palestine*, Cairo, 1998.

Tyldesley, Joyce, *Daughters of Isis: Women of Ancient Egypt*, London, 1995.

Usama Ibn Munqidh, *Al-I'tibar*, Beirut, 2003.

Wadud, Amina, *Qur'an and Woman*, Oxford, 1999.

Walker, Paul, *Exploring an Islamic Empire: Fatimid History and Its Sources*, London, 2002.

Watt, W. Montgomery, *Muhammad at Medina*, London, 1956.

Watt, W. Montgomery, *Muhammad at Mecca*, Oxford, 1991.

Whittow, Mark, 'The Late Roman/Early Byzantine Near East', in *The New Cambridge History of Islam*, Vol. 1, ed. Chase Robinson, Cambridge, 2010, pp. 72–97.

William of Tyre, *A History of Deeds Done Beyond the Sea*, Vols 1 and 2, trans. E. A. Babcock, New York, 1976.

al-Yamani, Taj al-Din, *Bahjat al-Zaman fi Ta'rikh al-Yaman*, ed. A. Habashi, Sana'a, 1988.

al-Yamani, 'Umara, *Ta'rikh al-Yaman*, Kay edition, Cairo, 1957.

al-Yamani, 'Umara, *Al-Nukat al-'Asriyya fi Akhbar al-Wazara al-Misriyya*, Cairo, 1991.

al-Ya'qubi, *Ta'rikh al-Ya'qubi*, Baghdad, 1989.

al-Yazdi, Muhammad Ibn al-Nizam, *Al-'Irada fi al-Hekaya al-Seljuqiyya*, trans. A. Hasanain, Baghdad, 1979.

al-Yunini, Qutb al-Din, *Dhayl Mir'at al-Zaman*, Hyderabad, 1954.

al-Zabidi, Abd al-Rahman, *Qurrat al-'Uyun bi Akhbar al-Yaman al-Maymun*, ed. M. al-Akwa, Sana'a, 1988.

Zahran, Yasmine, *Zenobia: Between Reality and Legend*, London, 2010.

Zankabadi, Jalal, *Diwan Omar al-Khayyam*, Baghdad, 2010.

Index

Aba al-'Abbas b. al-Muqtadir, 173, 175
Aba Raf'i, 30
'Abbas al-Sinhaji, 218–19
al-'Abbas b. al-Hasan, 104
'Abbasa, Princess, 79, 81, 82
'Abbasids, 3, 4–5, 8, 75–8, 100–1
    and caliphs, 411
    and concubines, 87–90
    and eunuchs, 142–3, 149–58, 159–62, 254, 338
    and Fatimids, 197
    and *qahramanat*, 126–30
    and royal women, 78–87
    and Seljuqs, 299–300
    and slaves, 61
Abbott, Nabia, 1, 47, 78, 80, 95, 97
    Aishah: The beloved of Muhammad, 4
    Two Queens of Baghdad: Mother and Wife of Harun al-Rashid, 4
'Abd al-Malik b. Marwan, 67, 70
'Abd al-Masih, 335
'Abd al-Mustansir, 232
'Abd al-Rahmin Ilyas, 201
'Abd al-Wahid b. al-Muqtadir, 176
'Abd Allah, 40, 200
'Abd Allah b. 'Ali, 76
'Abd Allah b. Ibrahim, 106
'Abd Allah b. Malik, 94–5
'Abd Allah, Prince, 104
Abi Taghlib, 86
Abish bint S'ad, Queen, 6, 330, 381
al-Abrash, 150
Abu al-'Anbar, 150
Abu al-Barakat b. Nasir al-Dawla, 86
Abu al-Hasan, 180
Abu al-Qasim, 268
Abu Bakr, 1, 20, 27, 37–9
Abu Bakr (Eldiguzid), 326, 327, 328
Abu Lahab, 11

Abu Nuwas, 88, 154
Abu Sufyan, 11, 26
Abu Talib, 11
al-'Adi I, 146
al-'Adid, 220
al-'Adil, 350, 351, 383–4, 388, 389, 396–7
al-'Adil II, 355, 361, 363–4
al-'Adliyya, Karima, 382
adultery, 44
al-Afdal, 215, 236, 383–4
Agha Muhammad, 2
al-Aghani, 88
Aghlabids, 161, 162, 267
al-Ahmad, King, 226, 227, 228, 231
Ahmad, Prince, 117
Ahmad b. 'Ali, 184, 185
Ahmad b. Taifur
    Eloquences of Women, 61
Ahmadili atabegate, 312–16, 323
Ahmed, Laila, 23, 31, 36, 47–8
'Aisha, 23, 24–5, 29, 36–7, 39–40
    and political-military ambitions, 40–2
    and Umayyads, 62–3
'Aisha Khatun, 372
'Ala' al-Din Korp Arslan, 315
'Alam, 242
'Alam (Husn), 127–8
Alexander the Great, 46
'Ali, 19, 26, 31, 37–8, 40, 41
'Ali al-Rida, 84
'Ali al-Sulayhi, 222
'Ali b. Abi Talib, 11
'Ali b. Haditha, 368–9
'Ali b. 'Isa, 151, 155, 164
'Ali b. Muhammad al-Ikhshid, 180, 182
'Ali b. al-Muqtadir, 106
'Ali, Sayf al-Din, 385
Alice of Antioch, Princess, 367
al-'Allaqa, 268–9

Almashi b. Yaltiwar, 166
Alp Arslan, 290, 301, 316–18, 333
Altunjan Khatun, 299
al-Amin, 80, 81, 82, 142, 148, 153–8
Amina Khatun, 294–5, 309
al-Amir, 238, 259–60, 261
Amir Amiran, 325, 327
Amir b. al-Musta'li (al-), 216–17
'Amir al-Zawahi, 229–30, 231–2
Andalusia, 70–1, 98, 198
Andreasen, Niels-Erik, 48
anti-women sentiment, 121–2, 124, 285, 289–90, 381
Aq Sunqur, 312–13
Aq Sunqur II, 313–14
Aq Sunqur II al-Ahmadil, 323
Arabian Nights, 76, 129, 310
Aristotle, 46
army, 163, 181–3, 336–7; see also *atabeg al-'askar*; *mamluks*; Mu'nis al-Khadim
Arslan III b. Tughril II, 323, 324–5
Arslan Shah I, 336
Artash, 294
Artuqids, 5, 351
Arwa, 2, 5, 80, 89–90, 196, 198, 221–5
  and early days, 225–7
  and empowerment, 227–31
  and influence, 237–43
  and queen regent, 231–4
  and Rasad, 211, 212–15
  and rule, 234–7
As'ad Abu al-Futuh, Prince, 236
al-Ashraf, 394–5
al-Ashraf b. al-'Adil II, 380
al-Ashraf Musa, 357, 358
al-Ashraf Musa III, 386
Ashtor, Eliyahu, 129
Asma', 91, 225, 226
Asma' bt. Abu Bakr, 39
atabeg al-'askar, 383, 385–90
atabegs, 5, 6, 60–1, 298–302
  and Ahmadili, 312–16
  and Ayyubids, 382–96
  and Eldiguzids, 322–31
  and eunuchs, 334–5
  and Seljuqs, 286, 294
  and women, 302–10
  and Zengids, 316–22
'Atika, 65–6
Ay Abah, 326
Ayalon, David, 70, 253, 387
  and eunuchs, 152, 153, 157, 262, 392
  Eunuchs, Caliphs and Sultans, 142

Aybak, 386
Aybak al-Turkomani, 'Izz al-Din, 379, 380, 381
Aydaghli, Jamal al-Din, 380
Aytakin, 303–4, 308
Ayyub, Najm al-Din, 349
Ayyubid Kurds, 3, 5, 7, 9, 349–51
  and *atabegs*, 382–96
  and eunuchs, 280, 281, 394–400
  see also Dayfa of Aleppo; Shajar al-Durr
Azarmedukht, Queen, 48
Azerbaijan, 312–16, 322–31
al-'Aziz, 2, 199, 352, 353
al-'Aziz b. Saladin, 392, 393

Badr, Battle of, 11
Badr al-Jamali, 210, 213, 230
Baghdad, 76, 78, 93–4
Baha' al-Dawla, King, 85
Bakhtiar, 85, 91
Bakkara al-Helaliyya, 41
al-Baladhuri, 64
Baldwin II, King, 297, 367
Baldwin III, King, 220
Baldwin IV, King, 320
Bangladesh, 122
al-Banna, Hasan, 34
Banu al-Mustaliq, 27
Banu Qurayza, 26–7
Baraka Khan, 368, 369
barid (intelligence service), 151, 153, 156, 157, 166, 171
Barjawan, 199, 200–1, 255–7, 258–9
  and Byzantines, 264
  and judiciary, 276
  and North Africa, 271
Barmakids, 81–2, 151–2
Bashshar b. Burd, 93
Basil II, Emperor, 205
Bathsheba, Queen, 48
al-Ba'uniyya, 'Aisha, 42
Baybars, 375, 376
Bazwaj, 308
Beirut, 273
Berbers, 62, 66, 198, 256
Berkyaruk, 289, 302
Bihruz, 337
Bishara, 271, 272, 273
Bishir, 338
Bishr, 171
Bohemond IV, 395
Bohemond V, 366, 367
Boko Haram, 28

Book of Songs, 61, 98, 129
Bosworth, C. E., 289
Bray, Julia, 124
al-Bukhari, 22, 23, 41–2
Buri, 307
Bushra, 174, 175, 177, 263
Buwayhids, 75, 84–5, 103, 126–30, 179
Byzantine Empire, 46–7, 71, 76, 160, 168, 178
   and eunuchs, 143, 145, 264
   and women, 209–10

Cahen, C., 285, 301, 303
Calderini, Simonetta, 184, 198, 201, 206, 213
   Women and the Fatimids in the World of Islam, 5
caliphs, 37–42, 57
   and 'Abbasids, 76, 411
   and Fatimids, 412
   and Umayyads, 62–4, 67–8
Camel, Battle of the, 40, 41–2
castration, 69–70, 71, 144–7, 170
   and Seljuqs, 332, 333–4
   see also eunuchs
Caswell, Fuad
   The Slave Girls of Baghdad, 4
Celibate and Childless Men in Power: Ruling Eunuchs and Bishops in the Pre-modern World (Höfert/Mesley/Tolino), 4
Christianity, 45, 46–7, 228–9
Cleopatra VII, Queen, 46
coins, 170–1, 186
   and Arwa, 243
   and Ayyubids, 350–1
   and Dayfa of Aleppo, 355–6
   and Eldiguz, 324
   and Radiyya, 354
   and Shajar al-Durr, 377–8
   and Tamar of Georgia, 328
   and women, 330–1
concubines, 3, 42, 44, 59, 129
   and 'Abbasids, 77, 87–90, 98–100
   and Fatimids, 199
   and Muhammad, 23, 28–9
   and Umayyads, 66–8
   see also Khayzuran; Qahiba; Rasad; Shaghab; Shajar al-Durr
Concubines and Courtesans: Women and Slavery in Islamic History (Gordon/Hain), 4
Constantine, Emperor, 178
Cook, Michael, 113

Cortese, Delia, 184, 198, 201, 206, 213
   Women and the Fatimids in the World of Islam, 5
Council of Nicaea, 143
Crusades, 58, 197
   and Ayyubids, 350, 395
   and Dayfa of Aleppo, 364, 366–7, 369
   and eunuchs, 265, 266
   and Fatimids, 219, 221, 236
   and Louis IX of France, 373, 374–5
   and Saladin, 391
   and Seljuqs, 234, 305–6, 309
Cyrus, 29

Daftary, Farhad, 5, 220, 239
al-Dallal, 71
Damascus, 58, 66, 271–2, 273
Dananir, 98
Dandaqan, battle of, 286
Dar al-Hikma (House of Wisdom), 76
al-Dar al-Shamsi, 242
dargah (nomadic court), 331–2
al-Dargazini, 313
Darius of Persia, King, 46
Dastanwayh, 123
Da'ud, King, 312, 313
Da'ud b. Mahmud II, 313–14
Dayfa Khatun, 319, 324
Dayfa of Aleppo, Queen, 2, 6, 78, 349, 351–5
   and Crusaders, 366–7
   and Hama, 361–3
   and al-Kamil, 356–61
   and al-Kamil successors, 363–6
   and Seljuqs, 367–72
   and titles, 355–6
Daylami, 103
Dede Korkut, 310
al-Deresi, Wafa', 130
al-Dhahabi, 173–4, 187
Dhu Jibla, 227–8
al-Dhu'ayb, 238, 239, 240, 241
Dihya, Queen, 62, 66
Dimna, 112, 123
divorce, 18, 44
domestic violence, 44
Duqaq, 293, 294, 302, 304, 305
Durant, Will, 43

Earenfight, Theresa, 46
education, 61, 239–40, 371

Egypt, 39
  and 'Abbasids, 76
  and al-Salih Ayyub, 396–400
  and Fatimid invasions, 168, 170
  and gender, 42–3, 46
  and judiciary, 122
  and Kafur al-Aswad, 181–7
  and marriage age, 25
  and prisoners of war, 28
  and Saladin, 390–5
  and Tulunids, 84, 85, 159–60
  and Zaynab, 64
  see also Ayyubid Kurds; Fatimids
El Cheikh, Nadia, 1, 36, 120, 192n144
  Women, Islam, and Abbasids Identity, 4–5
Eldiguz, Shams al-Din, 323–4
Eldiguzids, 314–15, 319, 322–31
Emir Qutuz, 381
Emma, Queen, 229
empresses, 46–7
Encyclopaedia of Islam, The, 7
Encyclopaedia of Women and Islamic Cultures, The, 7, 147
Eudoxia, Empress, 46
eunuchs, 2, 3, 5, 9
  and 'Abbasids, 77, 142–3, 149–58
  and *atabegs*, 383
  and Ayyubids, 391–400
  and category, 60
  and characteristics, 143–5
  and classification, 145–8
  and evolution, 159–62
  and Fatimids, 259–62
  and military system, 262–9
  and Muhammad, 29, 30–2
  and Persia, 46
  and police, 269–70
  and provincial governors, 270–5
  and Seljuqs, 308–9, 331–9
  and titles, 148–9, 275–81
  and Umayyads, 68–72
  see also Barjawan; Jawdhar; Kafur al-Aswad; Mu'nis al-Khadim
Europe, 228–9
Eustace, 178
Eve *see* Muslim Eve

al-Fadl, 155
al-Fadl b. Sahl, 82, 83
Fa'iq al-Hurami, 175
al-Fa'iz b. al-Zafir, 218–19, 220
Fakhita, 64, 68–9
Fakhr al-Din Yusuf, 374, 375

al-Falahi, 208
Faraj, 338
Fars, 106
Fath b. Muftah, 236
Fatima (daughter), 10, 24, 25, 26, 29
  and Fatimids, 196
  and marriage, 31–2
  and royal legitimacy, 37–40
Fatima (granddaughter), 63–4
Fatima, Qahramana, 114
Fatima al-Kurdiyya, 86
Fatima bt. Al-Fath, 102
Fatima the Sulayhid, 242–3
Fatimids, 2, 5, 7, 8–9, 196–9
  and Arwa, 230–1, 236, 238–9
  and caliphs, 412
  and education, 239–40
  and Egypt, 168, 170
  and eunuchs, 253–67, up to 281
  and Kafur al-Aswad, 183, 184
  and maritime activities, 267–9
  and Mu'nis al-Khadim, 178
  and rise, 162
  and Saladin, 390–1
  and Yemen, 222
  see also Rasad; Sitt al Mulk
Fayruz, 296, 297, 307
female circumcision, 33, 70
Ferdowsi
  Shahnameh, 326
fida' (exchange of prisoners of war), 160
fiqh (understanding of religious texts), 147–8
fitna (revolt), 39–40
Forak, 337
Foucault, Michel
  The History of Sexuality, 147
Fulayt, 389–90
Fulk, count of Anjou, 297–8

Gabbay, Alyssa, 6
Gabriel, 20, 21, 22
gender, 12–14, 33–4, 42–5, 113–25; *see also* women
Ghadi, 264
al-Ghallas, al-Bahari, 28
Gharib, 102, 110
Ghayn, 269–70, 275
al-Ghazali, Abu Hamid, 33–4, 288
  Advice to Kings (*Nasihat al-Muluk*), 331
Ghazi b. Jibril, 388–90
Ghazi I b. Zengi, 318
Ghazi II, 319, 321, 335, 336

Ghazi of Mayyafariqin, 370
Ghaziya Khatun, 350, 351, 367, 372
Ghaznavids, 286
Ghitrif, 91
ghulman (slave soldiers/beardless boys), 7, 9, 13, 60, 87–8, 148, 166
    and 'Abbasids, 104, 108, 128
    and Seljuqs 291–3
Gibb, H. A. R., 365
goddesses (*gharaniq*), 20–1
Greece, 46
Gujurat, 241
Gumushtegin, 307–8, 321, 335

Habashiyya, 101
Habbaba, 67–8
al-Hadi, 90, 92, 93, 94–6, 150
Hadith, 22–3, 32–5, 42
al-Hafiz, 217, 238–9, 262
al-Hafiz of Ja'bar, 368
Hafsa, 26, 29, 40
hajibs (chamberlains), 70, 102, 108, 143, 150, 163
    and Ayyubids, 397
    and Seljuqs, 332
hajj, 39
al-Hakim, 128, 264, 269–70
    and Barjawan, 255–7, 258–9
    and Sitt al-Mulk, 200–3, 205
al-Hallaj, 166
Halm, Heinz, 199, 239
Hama, 355, 357, 358–9, 361–3, 395–6
al-Hamdani, Husain, 226
Hamdanids, 85–7, 183–4
Hammawayh, 153
Hammurabi, King, 44
Hamza, 36
harems, 23–32, 44, 46
    and 'Abbasids, 76–7
    and Buwayhids, 126–7, 128–30
    and eunuchs, 143–4, 146–7
    and Fatimids, 198–9
    and Shaghab, 107, 108
    and Umayyads, 69
Harthama, 96
Harthama b. A'yan, 151, 152
Harun, 102, 110–11, 112, 171–3, 174
Harun al-Rashid, 4, 76
al-Hasan, 62, 82–3
Hasan b. Thabit, 29
Hatshepsut, Queen, 43
Hawwa' bt. Yazid, 34–5
Hekmat, Anwar, 30, 31

Helena, St, 46
hijab see veil
Hilal al-Sabi', 202
Hilana of al-Rashid, 98
Hillenbrand, Carole, 6, 287, 312
Hillenbrand, Robert, 68, 351, 371
Hims, 183, 273, 297, 358–60, 360
Hind bt. 'Utba, 35, 36
Hind bt. 'Uthata, 36
hisba (market inspector), 269–70, 276
Hisham, 71
Hisham II b. al-Mustansir, 209
homosexuality, 61, 122, 147–8, 153–4, 157, 291–2
    and Seljuqs, 332–4
hujja (absolute proof), 198, 232, 233, 234, 237, 238–42
al-Husain b. 'Ali, 63
al-Husayn b. Hamdan, 105, 119, 166
al-Husayni, Sadr al-Din, 311, 326
Husna, 93

Ibn 'Abd al-Hamid, 106
Ibn Abi Rabi', 121–2
Ibn al-'Adim, 296, 349, 370
    and Dayfa of Aleppo, 352, 353, 357, 358–9, 365, 372
Ibn 'Ammar, 256
Ibn 'Asakir, 61
Ibn al-Athir, 85, 86, 92, 127, 316
    and Barjawan, 256
    and eunuchs, 146, 149, 155–6
    and Fatimids, 221
    and Kafur al-Aswad, 187
    and Mu'nis al-Khadim, 174
    and al-Muqtadir, 105
Ibn Ayyub, Salah al-Din *see* Saladin
Ibn Baghl, 116
Ibn Baliq, 176, 177
Ibn Bassam, 122
Ibn Batlan, 166
Ibn Butlan, 88–9
Ibn Dawwas, 202–3, 204–5, 260–1, 267
Ibn al-Daya, Shams al-Din, 319–20, 321
Ibn al-Furat, 105, 106, 107, 109, 110
    and Mu'nis al-Khadim, 164, 166
    and Thumal, 123
    and Um Musa, 116, 117
    and Zaydan, 118–19
Ibn al-Fuwati, 369
Ibn Ghalbun, 181
Ibn Hanbal, 41
Ibn Hisham, 22

Ibn al-Jawzi, 123
Ibn Jubayr, 80, 400
Ibn Kathir
  Tafsir, 14
Ibn Khallikan, 186–7
Ibn Khaqan, 116
Ibn Killis, 199
Ibn Kindad, 255, 262, 263
Ibn Mamati, 393–4
Ibn Massal, 217–18
Ibn Mas'ud, 19
Ibn Mujalli, 'Umar, 353–4
Ibn al-Muqaddam, 320, 321
Ibn Muqla, 126
Ibn al-Nadim, 19, 113
Ibn al-Najjar, 400
Ibn al-Qalanisi, 200, 202
Ibn Qasim, 165
Ibn Qayyim al-Jawziyya
  Stories of Women, 62
Ibn Qutn, 70–1
Ibn Ridwan al-Milqi, 122
Ibn Rushd (Averroes), 331
Ibn Sa'd, 22, 29
Ibn Sa'id, 180
Ibn al-Sa'i, 102
  Women of the Caliphs, 62
Ibn al-Salar, 218
Ibn Taghri Bardi, 181, 184, 380, 387
Ibn Taqataqa, 80, 100
  Al-Fakhri fi al-Adab, 103
Ibn Tulun, 101, 159
Ibn Wasil, 352, 354, 371–2, 376–7
Ibn Yalbaq, 126
Ibrahim, 91
al-Ikhshid, Muhammad b. Tughj, 179, 180–1
Ikhshidids, 143, 159; *see also* Kafur al-Aswad
Ikhtyar, 126, 176
Ilal, Rashid, 23
Ilturinjan, 287–8
Ilyas, 205
'Imad al-Din Idris
  'Uyun al-Akhbar wa Funun al-Athar, 223
Inanj Khatun, 325, 326, 327, 338
insignia, 154–5
invasions (*ghazwa*), 26–7
Iqbal, 338
Iqbal al-Khatuni, 353–4, 356
iqta' (feudal system), 100
Iran, 39
  and 'Abbasids, 76, 103
  and *atabegs*, 311–16, 330
  and governors, 169–70
  and *khatuns*, 287–93
  and Tughtekin, 306–7
  and women, 48
Iraq, 39, 40
  and 'Abbasids, 75
  and gender, 43–5
  and *khatuns*, 293–8
  and Zengid atabegate, 316–22
  see also 'Abbasids; Baghdad
'Isa, 'Ali b., 119
'Isa b. Musa, 92
al-Isfahani, Abu al-Faraj, 65, 98, 279–80, 324–5
  Book of Songs, 61
Ishaq al-Mosuli, 67, 91
Isis, 43
Islam *see* Qur'an, the; Shi'i Islam; Sunni Islam
Islamic State of Iraq and Syria (IS), 28
Isma'il, 101
Isma'il b. Buri, 295–6
Isma'il b. Ja'far al-Sadiq, 197
Isma'il b. Yaquti b. Chaghri Beg, 289
Isma'il, 'Imad al-Din, 358, 359–60
Isma'ilis, 222–3
Israel, 48

Jackson, Peter, 6, 354–5
Ja'da bt. al-Ash'ath, 62
Ja'far, 79, 81, 82, 97, 152
jahiliyya (pre-Islamic period), 10, 31, 36, 40–1
al-Jahiz, 38, 67, 88, 124, 170, 333
  The Animal, 143, 146, 147
  The Crown in the Manners of Kings, 61
al-Jahshyari, 83
Jalal al-Din, 368
jariya (runner for service), 59
al-Jarjara'i, 'Ali, 207
al-Jawad b. al-Hafiz, 368
al-Jawad Yunus b. Mawdud b. al-'Adil, 363
jawari (female slaves), 7, 23, 87, 96, 129
  and eunuchs, 146
  and Fatimids, 199
Jawdhar, 178, 253–5, 257–8, 268, 270–1
  and roles, 275–6, 278
Jawhar, 266
Jawhar Khatun, 290
Jeffrey, Arthur, 19
jewellery, 120
Jordan, 39

judiciary, 120–2, 183, 276
Juwayriyya, 27

Kafur, 2, 143, 172
Kafur al-Aswad, 179–87
Kafur the Ikhshidid, 171
Kafuriyya battalion, 266–7
Kahala, 'Umar
    A'lam al-Nisa, 7
Kahina *see* Dihya
al-Kamil, 355, 356–61, 395
al-Kamil b. al-'Adil, 350
Karbala' massacre, 63
Kardabadhu, 337
Karima, 199
Kawthar, 142, 148, 154, 158
Kay-Khusraw II, 330–1, 356
    and Dayfa of Aleppo, 357, 358, 360, 365, 367, 369
Kay Qabad, 357, 368
Keddie, Nikki, 1
Kennedy, Hugh, 75, 128, 164, 175–6
    and 'Abbasids, 78, 80, 112
    The Court of the Caliphs, 5
Khadija, 10, 11, 17, 24, 36–7
al-Khadim, Qamar al-Din, 365
Khalid b. al-Walid, 38–9
al-Khaqani, 107, 110, 116, 123, 164
al-Khasibi, 106, 110, 119, 123
khasiyy see eunuchs
al-Khatib, 379
Khatif, 102, 109–10
al-Khattab b. al-Hasan, 240–1
khatuns (queen/lady), 286, 287–98
Khawala bt. Hakim, 30
Khayzuran, 4, 78, 79, 81, 90–8
Khint Kaws, Princess, 43
khisyan see eunuchs
Khomeni, Ayatollah, 34
Khumarawayh, 84, 146, 159–60
Khumartakin, 332
Khund Ashlun, 381–2
Khund Baraka, 382
Khund Zaynab, 382
Khurasan, 81, 82–3, 151
Khwarazmians, 367–72
al-Kindi, 187
Kira, Najwa
    Al-Jawari and Ghulman in Egypt under the Fatimids and Ayyubids, 7
Kohra'in, Sa'd al-Dawla, 336–7
Kruk, Remke, 1
al-Kuludhani, 165

al-Kunduri, 333
al-Kurdi, Amal
    The Role of Women under the 'Abbasid Caliphate, 7–8
Kurds *see* Ayyubid Kurds
Kuwait, 28

Lagrange, Frederic, 147
Lambton, A. K. S., 299
Al-Lat, 20–1
Leo II, Emperor, 46
Leo VI, Emperor, 178
Lev, Yaacov, 262, 270, 273
Lewis, Geoffrey, 310
literature, 87–8, 129
Louis IX of France, King, 373, 374–5, 377, 398–9
Lu'Lu', Shams al-Din, 353–4
Lu'Lu' al-Baba, 308–9, 334–5
Lu'Lu' b. 'Abdallah, 322
Luxenberg, Christoph, 21

Ma'arrat al-Nu'man, 362
Mabur, 29, 31, 143
madrasas, 61, 371
al-Mahdi, 77, 78, 90–3, 114
    and concubines, 134n95, 199
    and eunuchs, 150
    and marriage, 79–80
Mahmud II, Sultan, 291
Mahmud, lord of Tadmur, 296–7
Mahmud Qutlugh, 325
mahziyya see concubines
Makhariq, 100
Maknuna, 91–2
Malaka bt. Da'ud, 371
male slaves, 60–1
Malik Shah, 234, 287, 301–2
Malika al-Laythiyya, 27
Mamluks, 374, 381–2, 400
mamluks (troops), 296, 377, 378, 379, 381
al-Ma'mun, 98, 157, 259–60
    and al-Amin, 154, 155, 156
al-Ma'mun b. al-Rashid, 82–4
Manara, 150
Mankopars, 313
al-Mansur, 61, 76, 78, 98, 113–14
    and eunuchs, 149–50
    and Jawdhar, 253, 255, 257, 258
    and succession, 79
al-Mansur (Ayyubid), 383–4
al-Mansur 'Ali b. Aybak, 381
al-Mansur b. al-Qa'im, 199

al-Mansur of Hims, 361, 369, 370
al-Maqrizi, 201, 210, 221, 256, 277, 391
Margaret of France, Queen, 377
Mariyya bt. Sham'un, 29, 30–1
Marmon, Shaun, 400
  Eunuchs and Sacred Boundaries, 142
marriage, 16–18, 25, 26, 62–3, 298–302; see also polygamy
Marsden, W. F., 351
Marwan b. al-Hakam, 64
Marwan II, 71
Maryam, 18
Masrur, 151, 152–3, 157
Mas'ud, King, 313, 322, 323
Mas'ud (Seljuq), 336
Mas'ud b. al-Kamil, 389, 390
al-Mas'udi, 82, 145
mawali (non-Arab Muslims), 75
al-Mawdardi, 333, 338
Mawdud, 318–19
Mawiyya bt. 'Afzar, 41
Maymona bt. Sa'd, 30
Maymuna, Princess, 123
Maysara, 30
Maysun bt. Bahdal, 63
Maysur, 262–3
Mayyafariqin, 86
mazalim court, 120–2, 183
Mecca, 10, 11, 80, 170, 214
Medina, 11, 36, 71, 170
Mediterranean, 45–7
Melisende, Queen, 220, 297–8
Menat, 20–1
Merçil, Erdoğan, 6
Mernissi, Fatima, 92, 97, 129–30, 226
Meskawayh, 97, 104, 105, 114, 125, 165
  and *qahramanat*, 114, 127
Mesopotamia *see* Iraq
Mi'dad, 260–1, 264–5, 267
misogyny, 14, 31, 39, 201
money *see* wealth
Mongols, 315, 330, 367
monogamy, 44
Morsi, Muhammad, 25
Mosul, 85–6
Mu'awiya, 35, 41, 62–3, 68–9, 70
Mu'awiya II, 64
al-Mu'ayyad, 101
al-Mufaddal b. Abi al-Barakat, 235–6, 243
Muflih, 162, 166, 192n144
al-Mughith, 364

al-Mughith 'Umar b. al-'Adil II b. al-Kamil, 379
Muhammad, Prophet, 10–11, 15, 18, 34–6
  and eunuchs, 143, 144
  and female circumcision, 33
  and Hadith, 22–3
  and harem, 23–32
  and the Qur'an, 20, 21
Muhammad b. al-Qasim, 126, 176
Muhammad b. Mas'ud, 323
Muhammad b. Yaqut, 165, 166, 176
Muhammad II b. Mahmud, 318
Muhammad Tapar, 311–12
Muhayyat, 91
Muhsin, Jamal al-Din, 374, 375, 398
al-Muhtadi, 102
al-Mu'izz, 199, 263, 387–8
  and eunuchs, 270–1, 273
  and Jawdhar, 253, 255, 257, 258, 276
Mu'izz al-Dawla Ahmad, 127–8, 185
al-Muktafi, 103–4
Mu'mina Khatun, 323, 324
Munir, 272
Mu'nis al-Khadim, 5, 104, 105–6, 109, 110, 111, 112, 161–3
  and caliphs, 171–9
  and empire, 167–71
  and role, 163–7
  and Um Musa, 117
Mu'nis al-Khazin, 104, 105, 126
al-Muqtadi, 288, 300
al-Muqtadir, 77, 90, 102–13
  and gendered politics, 113–25
  and Mu'nis al-Khadim, 163, 164, 171–5
al-Muqtadir b. al-Mu'tadid, 162–3
al-Murtada, 163–4
al-Murtadi b. Allah, 104, 105
al-Musabbihi, 202
Muslim Brotherhood, 25, 34, 51n53
Muslim Eve, 12–13, 16, 18
al-Musta'in, 100, 158
al-Mustakfi, 127
al-Musta'li, 214, 215, 233
al-Mustansir, 206, 207, 209, 213, 215
  and Arwa, 227
  and eunuchs, 272
Mustansiriyya Crisis, 197, 198, 210
al-Mustarshid, 338
al-Musta'sim, 79, 378
al-Mu'tadid, 84, 85, 102, 113

al-Mutairi, Salwa, 28
al-Muʻtamid, 159, 161
al-Mutanabbi, 86–7, 186
al-Muʻtasim, 99
al-Muʻtasim b. al-Rashid, 158
al-Mutawakkil, 77, 98, 99–100, 117, 158
al-Muʻtazz, 100–2, 163
al-Mutiʻ, 128
al-Muttaqi b. al-Muqtadir, 127
al-Muwaffaq b. Najib al-Dawla, 236–7
al-Muzaffar, 242
al-Muzaffar II, 395–6
al-Muzaffar of Hama, 357, 358–9, 361–3

Nafidh, 270
Najahids, 225, 228, 229, 235
al-Nasaʼi, 22
Nasim, 267
al-Nasir, 326
Nasir al-Dawla, 86
al-Nasir b. Tughtekin, 388–9
al-Nasir Daʼud, 357, 365, 369
al-Nasir II Salah al-Din, 353, 356, 357, 380, 381
Nasr, 109, 110, 123
Nasr al-Thumali, 171
Nassim, 204–5, 260, 261
Nawfal, 157
Nawwar, 68
Nazar, 338
Nazm, 123
Nazuk, 111, 166, 172
Nicola, Bruno de 330
  Women in Mongol Iran: The Khatuns, 1206–1335, 6
Nihrir, 168
Nizam al-Mulk, 34, 122, 301–2, 331, 333
  Siyasat Nameh (*Rules for Kings*), 285, 289
Nizar, 215–17, 233, 259–60
nomadism, 331
North Africa, 2, 5, 76, 159, 270–2; *see also* Berbers
Nubians, 89, 179, 182–3, 184–5
Nujh al-Tulani, 166
al-Nuʻman, 200
Nur al-Din, 221, 280, 324, 349, 350
Nur al-Din b. Zengi, 335
Nur al-Din I, 318, 319–20
Nusayʼ, 264
Nusaybah bt. Kaʻb, 36
Nusayr, 273

Omar Khayyam, 331
  Rubaʻiyyat, 222
Ottoman Empire, 6–7, 403n55
Ozbeg b. Pahlawan, 328

Pahlawan Muhammad, 324–5
Pakistan, 58, 122, 242, 382
palaces, 44–5, 66–71, 77, 89, 90, 108
paradise, 13–14
Pearson, J. D., 19
Persia, 46
police, 94–5, 105, 110–11
  and eunuchs, 147, 152, 157, 162–3, 269–70
politics, 39–42, 85–7
  and ʻAbbasids, 79–85
  and Dayfa of Aleppo, 352–3
  and eunuchs, 276–8
  and Khayzuran, 94–7
  and marriage, 298–302
  and Shaghab, 113–25
  and Umayyads, 64–5, 67–8
polygamy, 14, 31–2
prayers, 39, 74n43
prisoners of war (*sabaya*), 23, 27, 160
property, 65–6, 107
Puran, Queen, 48, 83

Qabiha, 100–2
Qadi al-Yami, 222
al-Qadir, 85, 128
al-Qadir b. Allah, 124
al-Qahir, 102, 104, 111, 125, 126, 175–7
qahramanas (stewardesses), 3, 5, 59, 113–25, 199
  and ʻAbbasids, 87–9, 126–30
al-Qaʼim, 199, 253, 255, 262–3, 275–6
Qajars, 2
Qanghar, 361
Qara Sunqur, 313, 323
Qarakhanids, 286
Qaramita, 103, 107, 110, 166, 167–8
Qaraqush, 2, 266, 383, 384, 390–1, 392–4
Qatr al-Nada, 84
Qaymaz, Mujahid al-Din, 336, 338
al-Qifti, 353–4
Qinbaj al-Khadim, 106
qiyan see slave singers
Qizil Arslan, 324, 325–7
al-Qudaʻi, 202, 211
Queen of Sheba, 18, 40–1, 47
al-Qummi, 302

Qur'an, the, 10–21
   and devoted women, 29–30
   and eunuchs, 144
   and Khadija, 24
   and marriage, 25
   and Umayyads, 58
   see also Hadith
Quraysh tribe, 10, 35

al-Rabi', 150
al-Rabi' b. Yunus, 94
Rabi'a Khatun, 372
Radiyya, Queen, 6, 354–5
Raghib, 160
Ra'iq al-Kabir, 166
Raja', 151, 152, 153
Ramla bint Abi Sufyan, 26
Rasad, 206–15
al-Rashid, 77, 80, 81, 82, 90
   and concubines, 99
   and eunuchs, 145, 150, 151–3
   and Khayzuran, 93–4, 95, 96, 97
   and Zubayda, 91
Rashid al-Kabir, Shihab al-Din, 397, 399
Rasulids, 6, 381
Raydan, 200, 256–7, 258–9, 263, 268
   and Damascus, 271–2, 273
Rayta, Princess, 79–80, 90
al-Razi
   Al-Bah, 88
Renate, J., 80
Ridda Wars *see* Wars of Apostasy
Ridwan, 293, 304, 308
Rifq, 261, 265, 270, 272, 275
Rihan, 261
Rihana, 27, 28–9
Rihaniyya battalion, 267
riots, 108, 110, 165–6
Robert of Anjou, Count, 375
Roman Empire, 46, 76
Ruqaiyya, 10, 24, 26, 39, 92
Rus, 326
Rushd, 157

Saba' al-Sulayhi, 229, 231–2, 233
Sabiq al-Khuwarizmi, 149
Sa'd al-Dawla, 265
Sa'diyya battalion, 267
al-Saffah, 79, 80, 149
Safi al-Hurami, 163, 164, 192n144
Safiyya, 27
Safiyya the 'Uqaylid, 293
Safwat al-Mulk, 293–4, 302, 305

Sa'id al-Ahwal, 229
Sajah bint al-Harith, 1, 38, 41
al-Sajistani, 19
al-Sakran, 24
Saladin, 198, 262, 266, 335–6, 350
   and atabegate, 320–2, 383, 387, 390–4
   and eunuchs, 279, 280
Salaf, 199
Salghurids, 6, 330
al-Salih, 352, 353, 356–7
al-Salih Ayyub, 362, 363, 364–6, 396–400
   and Khwarazmians, 368, 369
   and Shajar al-Durr, 373–4, 379
al-Salih b. Ruzayq, 218–19, 220–1
Salih, Suad, 28
Salma, 30, 149
Salsal, 91
Samarra', 76, 99
Samona, 178
Sancha of Leon, Queen, 229
Sandal, 176, 280
Sanjar, Sultan, 290–2
Sanjar II b. Sulayman, 325
Sapur, 176
Saqaliba, 145, 254
Sasanids, 143
Saudi Arabia, 34, 54n134, 147
al-Sawabi, Badr, 398, 399
Sawda, 24–5
Sawsan, 162, 163, 166
Sawtakin, 332, 335
Sayf al-Dawla II, Prince, 86, 183–4
Seljuqs, 5, 9, 75, 285–6
   and *atabegs*, 302–10, 311–16
   and Ayyubids, 356, 364, 367–72
   and eunuchs, 331–9
   and Fatimids, 197
   and political marriage, 298–302
   and Yemen, 234
   see also khatuns
Semiramis, Queen, 45
Shafi' al-Lu'lu'i, 166
al-Shafi'i, 146
Shaghab, 90, 102–13, 162
   and Mu'nis al-Khadim, 163, 164, 167, 168–9, 171–3, 175–6
   and *qahramana*, 113–25
Shahrayar, King, 129
Shajar al-Durr, Queen, 6, 78–9, 372–82
Shakala, 91
Shakiriyya regiment, 156
Shams al-Nahar, 300

al-Shamsiyya, Queen, 381
Shi'i Islam, 2, 3, 17, 19, 34, 38, 83–4
    and 'Aisha, 40, 41
    and Qaramita, 103
    and Zaynab, 64
    see also Buwayhids; Fatimids
Shirkuh, 349, 357, 358
shrines, 64, 73n25
Sicily, 274–5
Sijillat, 224
al-Sindi, 152
Sirin, 29
Sitt al-Mulk, 200–6, 258–9, 261
Sitt al-Qusur, 221
slave singers (*qiyan*), 4, 59
slaves, 3, 12–13, 59–61
    and 'Abbasids, 87–8
    and the army, 181
    and ethnicity, 88–9
    and eunuchs, 144
    and Khayzuran, 98
    and Muhammad, 27–8, 30
    and Umayyads, 57, 58
    see also concubines
Smith, G. Rex
    The Ayyubids and Early Rasulidss in the Yemen, 6
Solomon, King, 48
Sonbol, Amira, 7
Spain, 2, 3, 76, 145
    and women, 209, 229, 371
    see also Andalusia; Umayyads
Spengler, W. G., 351
stewardesses see qahramanas
Stillman, Yedida, 15
Subayh, 398
Subh, 209
al-Subkuri, 177
al-Suhayli, 374
Sulafa, 36
Sulafa Khatun, 315
Sulayhids, 211, 213–14; see also Arwa the Sulayhid
Sulayman, 71, 165, 318
Sulayman (Seljuq), 337
Sulayman al-Zawahi, 230
Sulayman Shah, 389
Sunna, 13
Sunni Islam, 2, 3, 17, 19, 83–4
    and 'Aisha, 40, 41
    and al-Hakim, 201
    see also 'Abbasids; Seljuqs
Sunqur, 387–8

al-Suyuti, 108, 148
    The Distinct Book in the Science of Copulation, 89
    The Hills of Gold in the Rules of Eunuchs, 338–9
Syria, 39, 159, 180, 183–4, 205
    and *atabegs*, 302–10, 316–22
    and *khatuns*, 293–8
    and women, 47–8
    see also Ayyubid Kurds; Damascus

al-Tabari, 1, 14, 20–1, 22, 26–7
    and 'Aisha, 40
    and Khayzuran, 92, 96, 97
    and Umayyads, 61
Taghlib tribe, 85–6
Tahir b. Ghannam, 369
Tahrids, 83, 84
al-Ta'i', 85, 128
Taj al-Mulk al-Shirazi, 287, 288
Talha, 40, 41
Talha b. Tahir, 83
Taliban, 51n53
Tamar of Georgia, Queen, 315, 316, 327–8
al-Tannukhi, 115–16
Tarshak, 234
Tarsus, 159, 160, 168, 170
Tawaddud, 310
al-Tayyib, 238, 260
Tayyibis, 242
Templars see Crusades
Thabit, 151
Theodora, Empress, 210, 211
Thiqat al-Din, 334
third gender see eunuchs
Thousand and One Nights, 129
Thumal, 120–3, 168, 170–1, 173, 178
Tillion, Germaine, 45
Tolino, Serena, 253–4
Torah, 45
Traboulsi, Samer, 241
trade, 80
transsexuals (*mukannath*), 31, 71
Tripoli, 273
Tucker, Judith
    In the House of Law, 7
Tughj, 191n105
Tughril Beg, 211, 286, 287–8, 385
    and Dayfa of Aleppo, 352, 355
    and eunuchs, 332–3, 337
    and marriage, 299–300
Tughril II, Sultan, 313, 323, 337–8
Tughril III, Sultan, 325, 327

Tughril, Sayf al-Din, 396
Tughril, Shihab al-Din, 394–5
Tughtekin, 293–4, 303–7
Tulunids, 84, 85, 159–60, 161
Tunisia, 28, 161, 398–9
Turan Shah, 289
   and Dayfa of Aleppo, 360, 362, 366, 367
   and Khwarazmians, 368, 370
   and Shajar al-Durr, 373, 374, 375–6
Turkan Khatun, 287–90, 300–1
Turkey, 311–16
Turkish age, 100–1
Turkmen, 2, 5–6, 234, 349, 350; see also Seljuqs
al-Tustari, Abu Sa'd, 208
Tutush, 289, 293, 300–1, 302–4
Tutush II, 294
Tuzun, 127
Twelvers, 197
Tyre, 268–9

Ubayy b. K'ab, 19, 21
Uhud, Battle of, 35–7
'Ulayya, 92
Um 'Abd Allah, 92
um al-Banin (mother of sons), 65–6
Um al-Fadl, 84
Um al-Nasir, 242
Um Ayman, 30
Um 'Ayyash, 30
Um Eban bt. 'Utba, 39
Um Habiba, 39, 40, 84
Um Kulthum, 10, 24, 26, 63
Um Musa, 107, 114–18
Um Salama, 40, 80, 89
um walad (mother of a son), 59, 61
'Umar b. al-Khattab, 26, 37–8, 39
'Umar b. Mahran, 97
'Umar of al-Karak, 399
'Umara al-Yamani
   History of Yemen, 223
Umayya bt. Qays, 35
Umayyads, 3, 8, 57–8, 75
   and concubines, 66–8
   and eunuchs, 68–72, 143, 145
   and women, 61–6
Unar, 288, 289
Unujur b. al-Ikhshid, 179, 180, 181–2
Unur, 308
ustahun (chief eunuchs), 277
'Uthman, 20, 39, 40
'Uthman b. 'Affan, 26

'Uthman b. Maz'un, 30
al-'Uzza, 20–1

Van Berkel, Maaike, 124
veil, 14–16, 44–6
Verina, Empress, 46

Wadud, Amina
   Qur'an and Woman, 13
Wafyy Ishaq, 262
wali (provincial government), 169–70
al-Walid b. Yazid, 57, 68, 71
al-Waqidi, 92–3
Waraqa b. Nawfal, 24
Wars of Apostasy (Ridda Wars), 27, 38
Wasif al-Khadim, 161, 162, 168
wealth, 77, 94, 99–100, 102, 107–9, 117
Whittow, Mark, 47
William II of Sicily, King, 275
William of Tyre, 297, 391
women, 1–2, 3, 209–10
   and 'Abbasids, 77–87
   and *atabegs*, 302–10
   and Ayyubids, 350–1
   and Buwayhids, 128
   and caliphs, 37–42
   and coins, 330–1
   and education, 239–40
   and Egypt, 42–3
   and eunuchs, 161
   and Fatimids, 219–20
   and freedom, 34–5
   and Hadith, 32–4
   and Iraq, 43–5
   and law, 120–2
   and Mamluks, 381–2
   and the Mediterranean, 45–7
   and Ottoman caliphate, 6–7
   and politics, 40–2
   and the Qur'an, 10–18, 20–1
   and slave categories, 59
   and Syria, 47–8
   and Turkmen, 310
   and Uhud, 35–6
   and Umayyads, 61–6
   see also anti-women sentiment; concubines; harems; *khatuns*; misogyny

Yahya, 93, 94, 96, 97
Yahya al-Barmaki, 151–2
Yahya b. Aktham, 157
Yamani tribe, 63
Yamin al-Dawla, 232

Yannas al-Mu'nisi, 178
Ya'qub b. Dawud, 93
Yaruqtash, 295, 335
Yazid b. Mu'awiya, 62–4
Yazid II, 67–8
Yazkuj, 383
Yazman, 159–60
al-Yazuri, 208, 211
Yemen, 36, 211, 213–15; *see also* Arwa the Sulayhid; Ayyubids
Yunis al-Khadim, 191n105
Yusuf b. Abi al-Saj, 119

al-Zafir b. al-Hafiz, 217–18
al-Zahir, 201, 205, 350, 383, 385
   and Dayfa of Aleppo, 351, 352–3
   and eunuchs, 260
   and Rasad, 207
al-Zahir (Ayyubid), 394–5
Zahran, Yasmine, 47
Zarafa, 191n105
Zarinebaf-Shahr, Fariba, 7
al-Zarqa' bt. 'Udayy, 41
Zayd, 30

Zayd b. Haritha, 11, 17
Zayd b. Thabit, 20
Zaydan, Qahramana, 114, 115, 116–17, 118–20
Zaydis, 197
Zaynab (daughter), 10, 17, 24
Zaynab (granddaughter), 63–4
Zaynab bint Jahsh, 15–16
Zengi, 145, 148, 308, 314, 349
   and eunuchs, 333–4, 338
   and Zumurrud, 295–6, 297
Zengi, Imad al-Din, 316–18
Zengids, 5, 71, 316–22
Zenobia, Queen, 47, 48
Ziyadat Allah III, Prince, 161
Zoe, Empress, 209
Zubayda (daughter of Salsal), 91
Zubayda (queen mother), 78, 80–1
Zubayda (wife of al-Rashid), 4, 156
Zubayda Khatun, 288, 289–91
al-Zubayr, 40, 41
al-Zubayr b. al-'Awwam, 57
Zumurrud Khatun, 242, 295–7, 298, 307

EU representative:
Easy Access System Europe
Mustamäe tee 50, 10621 Tallinn, Estonia
Gpsr.requests@easproject.com

www.ingramcontent.com/pod-product-compliance
Lightning Source LLC
Chambersburg PA
CBHW052053300426
44117CB00013B/2108